ALSO IN SERIES OF Twenty Two (22) Sacred Maxims

Lex Divina: Maxims of Divine Law
Lex Naturae: Maxims of Natural Law
Lex Cognitum: Maxims of Cognitive Law
Lex Virtus Naturae: Maxims of Bioethics Law
Lex Ecclesiasticum: Maxims of Ecclesiastical Law
Lex Positivum: Maxims of Positive Law
Lex Regia: Maxims of Sovereign Law
Lex Fidei: Maxims of Fiduciary Law
Lex Administratum: Maxims of Administrative Law
Lex Economica: Maxims of Economic Law
Lex Pecuniaria: Maxims of Monetary Law
Lex Civilis: Maxims of Civil Law
Lex Criminalis: Maxims of Criminal Law
Lex Educationis: Maxims of Education Law
Lex Nutrimens Et Medicina: Maxims of Food & Drugs Law
Lex Urbanus: Maxims of Urban Law
Lex Societatis: Maxims of Company Law
Lex Technologiae: Maxims of Technology Law
Lex Commercii: Maxims of Trade & Intellectual Property Law
Lex Securitas: Maxims of Security Law
Lex Militaris: Maxims of Military Law
Lex Gentium: Maxims of International Law

Pactum De Singularis Caelum

Covenant of One Heaven

Lex Regia

Maxims of Sovereign Law

OFFICIAL ENGLISH FIRST EDITION

By

UCADIA

Ucadia Books Company

Published by Ucadia Books Company, a Delaware stock corporation (File Number 6779670).
8 The Green, STE B, Dover, Delaware, 19901 United States.
First edition.

ISBN 978-1-64419-029-6

Maxims of Sovereign Law

By Right, Power and Authority of Article 135 (*Divine Collection of Maxims of Law*) of the most sacred Covenant *Pactum De Singularis Caelum*, also known as the *Covenant of One Heaven* these maxims of law known collectively as "**Maxims of Sovereign Law**" are hereby promulgated in the original form of Ucadian Language and official translations.

These Maxims of Sovereign Law may be taken in official original document form and spoken form to represent one part of a complete set of the twenty-two (22) books known collectively as the Divine Collection of Maxims of Law.

The Maxims of Sovereign Law represent the primary, one and only true first Maxims of Sovereign Law. Excluding the most sacred Covenants *Pactum De Singularis Caelum*, *Pactum De Singularis Christus*, *Pactum De Singularis Islam* and *Pactum De Singularis Spiritus*, all other laws, claims and agreements claiming standards of Sovereign Law shall be secondary and inferior to the Maxims of Sovereign Law.

When referring to these Maxims of Sovereign Law:-

(i) The entire book of Maxims of Sovereign Law may be abbreviated in citation as "*Lex Regia*" or "*Lex Regia (Maxims of Sovereign Law)*"; and

(ii) A Maxim within the book of Maxims of Divine Law may be abbreviated in citation as (for example) "*Lex Regia max.1*" or "*Lex Regia (Sovereign Law) max.1*".

In accordance with these Maxims of Sovereign Law, Ucadia also known as the Unique Collective Awareness of all Meaning, also known as the Divine Creator reserves all rights to itself and its duly authorised organs, bodies and entities.

As all rights are reserved, no translation, copy, citation, duplication, registration in part or whole implies any transfer or conveyance of these rights.

When part or all of these laws is presented or spoken in any language other than the Official Ucadian Languages, it may be taken as a translation and not the primary language. Therefore, any secondary meaning implying deficiency, claimed abrogation of any right or any other defect of a word in a translated language shall be null and void ab initio (from the beginning).

Let no man, woman, spirit or officer of a lesser society place themselves in grave dishonour of Divine Law, Natural Law and the Living Law upon denying the validity of these maxims of law. Having been warned, any act in defiance of these laws shall have no effect and any spiritual invocation in opposition to the validity of these laws shall be immediately returned upon the maker. As it is written, so be it.

CONTENTS

Title II: Sovereign Claim & Mandate

2.1 – Sovereign Claim & Mandate

2.2 – Sovereign Rule by Revelation

2.3 – Sovereign Rule by Custom

2.4 – Sovereign Rule by Ritual

2.5 – Sovereign Rule by Legislation

2.6 – Sovereign Rule by Election

2.7 – False, Absurd & Prohibited Sovereign Claim & Mandate

7.2 – Ancient Holly Sovereign Rank & Title

7.3 – Egyptian (Hyksos) Civilisation Sovereign Rank & Title

7.4 – Persian Civilisation Sovereign Rank & Title

Title I - Introductory Definitions

1.1 – Introductory Definitions

Article 1 – Sovereignty

1. ***Sovereignty*** is the collection of valid and legitimate *Sovereign Rights, Capacity* and the *Recognition* of a *Legal Entity* to govern itself within a distinct *Territory*, without being subject to the authority of another or higher governing body. Sovereignty

2. ***Sovereign*** is derived from the combination of two ancient Latin words *servo* meaning "to protect, keep, guard, save, preserve" and *regno* meaning "to rule, reign; to be supreme lord". Hence a Sovereign literally means by its original etymology since the 8th Century CE "to rule as a servant". Origin and Meaning of Sovereign

3. From the very original meaning of *Sovereign* since the 8th Century CE, any Person appointed to such high office by sacred oath is obligated to three (3) ancient and primary tasks being Protect the Realm, Law and People:- Sacred Obligations of Sovereign

   (i) ***To Protect and Defend the Realm*** is the first obligation of a Sovereign as a *Legal Entity*, defined *Territory*, possessing its own personality and *Rights*; and

   (ii) ***To Protect and Defend the Law of the Realm*** is the second obligation of the Sovereign to ensure Rule of Law, Justice and Equality prevail; and

   (iii) ***To Protect and Defend the People of the Realm*** is the third sacred obligation of the Sovereign.

4. One who does not serve others and protect is not Sovereign; and must never be recognised as Sovereign, but a Tyrant and an Impostor. One who does not serve and protect is not Sovereign

5. ***Sovereign Rights*** refer to the inherent and exclusive authority and powers that a *Sovereign Legal Entity* possesses within its own *Territory*. These rights are the foundation of the independence and self-governance of the entity. Sovereign Rights include (but are not limited to):- Sovereign Rights

   (i) **Territorial Integrity**: A *Sovereign Legal Entity* has the right to exercise control and authority over its territory and the resources within its borders. Other entities are generally expected to respect the territorial integrity of a *Sovereign Legal Entity*, and the violation of this principle is usually considered a breach of international law; and

   (ii) **Political Independence**: *Sovereign Legal Entities* have the right to determine their own political systems, make their own laws, and govern their own affairs without interference from external actors. This includes the right to establish and maintain a government, conduct elections and formulate domestic and foreign policies; and

(iii) **Supreme Jurisdiction**: A *Sovereign Legal Entity* has the authority to exercise jurisdiction over all individuals, organizations and activities within its territory. This includes the power to enact and enforce laws, administer justice and regulate various aspects of public and private life; and

(iv) **Economic Sovereignty**: *Sovereign Legal Entities* have the authority to control and regulate economic activities within their borders, including trade, taxation and the management of natural resources. They can also enter into trade agreements and establish their own economic policies; and

(v) **National Defence**: *Sovereign Legal Entities* have the inherent right to defend themselves from external threats. This includes the right to establish armed forces, engage in self-defence and enter into military alliances for mutual security; and

(vi) **Foreign Relations**: *Sovereign Legal Entities* have the right to engage in diplomatic relations with other states, negotiate treaties and agreements, and conduct international affairs independently. They also have the right to join international organizations and participate in international forums.

Sovereign Capacity

6. ***Sovereign Capacity*** refers to the legal capacity of a *Sovereign Legal Entity* to act and make decisions within the framework of its Sovereignty. In essence, it pertains to the ability of a *Sovereign Legal Entity* to exercise its Sovereign Rights and perform its functions under international law including (but not limited to):-

(i) **Personality**: *Sovereign Legal Entities* have international legal personality, which means they can enter into international agreements, sue and be sued in international courts, and participate in international organizations. Their legal capacity allows them to engage in diplomatic relations and undertake international legal obligations; and

(ii) **Competency**: The competency of a *Sovereign Legal Entity* means the ability for the government, legislature, judiciary and various agencies and services to operate and function efficiently and effectively. The shut down of government, political gridlock, loss of fiscal restraint, loss of law and order, political witch hunts, coup d'état and civil war all greatly impact the competency and therefore capacity of a *Sovereign Legal Entity* to function; and

(iii) **Regulatory**: Sovereign capacity allows *Sovereign Legal Entities* to enact and enforce their own laws and regulations, including those that pertain to domestic governance, commerce and other matters within their borders; and

(iv) **Responsibility**: Sovereign capacity also involves the responsibility of *Sovereign Legal Entities* for their actions or omissions under international law. *Sovereign Legal Entities* can be held accountable for violations of international law and may be subject to international legal consequences; and

(v) **Authority**: *Sovereign Legal Entities* have the authority to exercise jurisdiction over persons, property and activities within their territory. However, this authority may be subject to limitations under international law and may not infringe on the sovereignty of other states; and

(vi) **Immunity**: *Sovereign Legal Entities* often enjoy immunity from the jurisdiction of foreign courts, known as sovereign immunity. This means they cannot be sued in the courts of another state without their consent, except in certain limited circumstances; and

(vii) **Ratify**: Sovereign capacity includes the ability of a *Sovereign Legal Entity* to negotiate, conclude and ratify treaties with other states. However, the capacity to enter into treaties may be subject to constitutional or domestic legal limitations.

Sovereign Recognition

7. ***Sovereign Recognition*** refers to the formal acknowledgment by one state (or a governmental authority) of the legitimacy and sovereignty of another state. It is a fundamental aspect of state-to-state relations and has significant implications for how states interact with each other on the global stage:-

(i) **Recognition as a Sovereign State**: When one state recognizes another, it essentially acknowledges that the entity in question possesses the attributes of statehood, including a defined territory, a permanent population, a government and the capacity to enter into relations with other states. In essence, it acknowledges the entity as a sovereign state; and

(ii) **Consequences of Recognition**: Once recognition is extended, the recognizing state typically treats the recognized state as an equal in international affairs. This includes respecting its territorial integrity and sovereignty, engaging in diplomatic relations, and entering into agreements and treaties; and

(iii) **Diplomatic Relations**: Establishing diplomatic relations is a common way of recognizing a state. This involves the appointment of ambassadors or other diplomatic representatives to engage in official interactions with the recognized state's government; and

(iv) **International Organizations**: Recognition is often a prerequisite for a state to become a member of international organizations like the United Nations. States seeking to join these organizations typically need to be recognized by a certain number of existing member states.

Sovereign Territory

8. ***Sovereign Territory*** refers to a specific physical or digital geographic area or piece of land whereby a sovereign state exercises full and exclusive authority and control. In the context of international law and statehood, sovereign territory is a fundamental concept that underpins a state's independence and self-governance. Some key aspects of sovereign territory include (but are not limited to):-

(i) **Exclusive Control**: Sovereign Territory means that a state has the ultimate and exclusive authority to govern and regulate everything within its borders. This includes the ability to enact and enforce laws, establish and maintain a government, collect taxes and provide services to its population; and

(ii) **Recognition of Borders**: Sovereign territory is recognized through international agreements and diplomatic recognition. When a state is recognized as sovereign by other states, it implies recognition of its defined territory and borders; and

(iii) **Territorial Integrity**: The concept of territorial integrity is closely related to sovereign territory. It means that the borders of a sovereign state are inviolable, and other states are generally expected to respect the territorial integrity of each sovereign state. The violation of a state's territorial integrity is often considered a breach of international law; and

(iv) **Extraterritorial Jurisdiction**: While a state's sovereignty is primarily exercised within its own territory, there are situations where a state may exercise extraterritorial jurisdiction, such as when its citizens commit crimes abroad. This can lead to legal complexities and diplomatic issues.

Sovereign Legal Entity

9. ***Sovereign Legal Entity*** is a type of Legal Entity that possesses the capacity, claims, rights and competency to full and independent legal authority and control over a specific geographic territory, along with the capacity to engage in legal and diplomatic relations with other entities, including (but not limited to):-

(i) **States**: These are the most common examples of sovereign legal entities and include countries recognized as independent states by the international community; and

(ii) **Indigenous Peoples and Tribal Entities**: In some cases, indigenous peoples and tribal entities may have a degree of self-governance and legal recognition within a nation-state; and

(iii) **Colonial and Trust Territories**: Historically, colonial and trust territories were administered by colonial powers or placed under the trusteeship of other states or international organizations. As these territories moved toward independence, they often became sovereign states; and

(iv) **City-States**: Some cities with unique legal statuses may possess a degree of sovereignty. For example, the Holy See (Vatican City) is an independent city-state and a sovereign entity; and

(v) **Dependent Territories**: Some dependent territories or regions with a certain degree of self-governance may have a limited form of sovereignty; and

(vi) **International Zones**: Certain areas, such as international zones within cities may enjoy a form of international legal personality, with their own governance structures and diplomatic privileges. However, their sovereignty usually remains vested in the host country; and

(vii) **International Organizations**: Certain international organizations have international legal personality and exercise a form of sovereignty within their respective mandates; and

(viii) **Transnational Organizations**: Transnational organizations have legal personality and exercise a degree of authority over their member states in areas of common interest; and

(ix) **Secessionist Entities**: Entities that declare independence and establish their own governance structures may claim sovereignty, even if their independence is not widely recognized.

10. A ***State*** is a political division of a body of living natural persons that possesses one or more recognised rights to encompass, possess and State control physical and/or digital space defined by a well formed system of boundaries and terrain. A State is said to hold Sovereign Jurisdiction over the elements and things within such space and terrain.

11. In respect of the general elements of Sovereignty:- General Elements of Sovereignty

(i) *Sovereignty is the supreme and ultimate authority within a State*, meaning that the State has the power to make and enforce laws without interference from external actors; and

(ii) *Sovereignty is indivisible*, meaning that generally it cannot be shared or divided between different actors or entities within a State; and

(iii) *Sovereignty is unalienable*, meaning it is not transferable to another state or body; and not capable of being unilaterally seized, annexed or denied; and

(iv) *Sovereignty is exclusive*, meaning that no other State or external actor has the right to interfere in the internal affairs of a sovereign State; and

(v) *Sovereignty is partly dependent upon the recognition of the rights and existence of one State by other states* within a formal international system; and

(vi) Sovereignty depends upon the existence of the State.

12. Given Sovereignty depends upon the existence of a State, it is both an absurdity and against all proper forms of Law for an individual to unilaterally declare themselves Sovereign. Furthermore, such an unlawful act contradicts the true meaning of the word *Sovereign*. Sovereignty and Individual

Article 2 – Sovereignty & Society

13. ***Sovereignty & Society*** refers to the relationship between the government and its citizens, and how power is exercised and shared within a society. Sovereignty & Society

14. The general elements of *Sovereignty* and *Society* include (but are not limited to):- General Elements of Sovereignty & Society

(i) Sovereignty and Society are interdependent concepts, as the legitimacy of a government's sovereignty is derived from the consent and support of its society; and

(ii) Sovereignty assumes that the state has the responsibility to protect its citizens and maintain law and order within its borders; and

(iii) The relationship between sovereignty and society is often characterized by a tension between the state's need for control and the society's desire for autonomy and self-determination; and

(iv) Society assumes that individuals have certain rights and freedoms that should be protected by the state, such as the right to free speech, assembly and religion; and

(v) Society also assumes that individuals have a responsibility to contribute to the common good and abide by the laws and norms of the society in which they live.

Article 3 – Sovereignty & Law

15. ***Sovereignty & Law*** refers to the interdependence and relation between the function of Sovereignty and the laws created and enforced by sovereign states to maintain order and protect the rights of their members.

Sovereignty & Law

16. The general elements of *Sovereignty* and *Law* include (but are not limited to):-

General Elements of Sovereignty & Law

(i) Sovereignty and Law are closely intertwined, as the authority to make and enforce laws is a key aspect of the sovereignty of an entity. Sovereignty assumes that the state has the power to make and enforce laws within its territory, and that these laws are binding on all individuals and entities within that territory; and

(ii) Sovereignty and Law are linked to the concept of legitimacy, as the authority of a legal entity to govern is based on the recognition and acceptance of its laws and institutions by its citizens and the international community; and

(iii) The concept of Sovereignty assumes that an entity has the right to defend its territory and its citizens from external threats, and that it has the power to use force if necessary; and

(iv) Sovereignty assumes that the state has the power to enter into agreements with other states, and that these agreements are binding on both parties; and

(v) The concept of Sovereignty assumes that the state has the power to regulate the movement of people and goods across its borders, and that it has the power to control immigration and emigration; and

(vi) Sovereignty assumes that the state has the power to levy taxes and to control the economy within its territory; and

(vii) The concept of Sovereignty assumes that the state has the power to establish and maintain a legal system, and that this legal system is the ultimate authority on matters of law within the state; and

(viii) The principle of Sovereignty is enshrined in international law, that recognises the right of states to govern themselves and prohibits interference in their internal affairs by other states; and

(ix) However, Sovereignty is not absolute, as states are also bound by international law and must respect the rights and interests of other states and the international community as a whole.

Article 4 – Sovereignty & Authority

17. ***Sovereignty & Authority*** refer to two intertwined concepts that together form the basis of a government's ability to control and regulate its members and territory. Sovereignty & Authority

18. The general elements of *Sovereignty* and *Authority* include (but are not limited to):- General Elements of Sovereignty & Authority

(i) The concept of Sovereignty assumes that there is a clear and defined territory or state over which the sovereign power is exercised; and

(ii) Sovereignty is usually associated with the idea of a single, centralised Authority that has the ultimate power to make decisions and enforce laws; and

(iii) The concept of Authority assumes that there is a hierarchy of power, with those at the top having the most authority and those at the bottom having the least; and

(iv) Sovereignty and Authority are closely linked, as the sovereign power is often the ultimate authority within a territory or state; and

(v) The concept of Sovereignty assumes that the sovereign power has the right to make decisions without interference from external forces, such as other states or international organizations; and

(vi) The relationship between Sovereignty and Authority is complex, as the exercise of authority within a state is often subject to the constraints and limitations imposed by the principles of Sovereignty.

Article 5 – Sovereignty & The Divine

19. ***Sovereignty & The Divine*** is the belief that ultimate power and authority reside in a divine being or force. This concept asserts that rulers and governments derive their authority from a higher power, and that individuals must submit to this authority in order to maintain order and harmony in society. Sovereignty & The Divine

20. The general elements of *Sovereignty* and *The Divine* include (but are not limited to):- General Elements of Sovereignty & The Divine

(i) The concept of Sovereignty inherently assumes that there is a supreme authority or power that governs over a particular territory or group of people; and

(ii) The Divine aspect of Sovereignty assumes that this supreme authority or power is of a divine or spiritual nature, often associated with a deity or higher power; and

(iii) Sovereignty and the Divine are often intertwined, with the Divine being seen as the ultimate source of authority and legitimacy for the sovereign ruler or governing body; and

(iv) In some cultures and religions, the concept of Sovereignty and the Divine are closely intertwined, with the ruler or state being seen as having a Divine Mandate to govern; and

(v) The Divine Right of Kings is a political and religious doctrine that asserts that a monarch is subject to no earthly authority, deriving the right to rule directly from the will of God; and

(vi) Theocracy is a form of government in which a deity is recognized as the supreme ruler, and religious leaders hold political power; and

(vii) The Divine is often seen as providing guidance and direction for the exercise of sovereignty, with rulers and governments expected to act in accordance with divine will or principles.

1.2 – Civilised Sovereign Principles

Article 6 – Civilised Sovereign Principles

21. ***Civilised Sovereign Principles of Law*** are foundational concepts essential to the function and conduct of Sovereign Persons and Sovereign Executives in fulfilling their ethical, moral, political and legal obligations. Such principles are present within the conduct and function of all valid, legitimate and competent Sovereign Persons and Sovereign Executives of States and Bodies Politic. Civilised Sovereign Principles of Law

22. *Civilised Sovereign Principles of Law* are the foundations of all valid, legitimate and competent authority and power of Sovereign Persons, Executives and Entities. While a Sovereign Person, Executive or Entity may not possess every Civilised Sovereign Principle, all valid, legitimate and competent Sovereign Persons and Sovereign Executives possess at least a majority of such principles.

Foundations of valid, legitimate and competent sovereign persons and executives

23. There exists eight (8) Civilised Principles of Sovereign Law above all others being:-

Eight Civilised Principles of Sovereign Law

(i) Integrity & Clean Hands of Sovereign; and

(ii) Good Faith, Character & Conscience of Sovereign; and

(iii) Humility & Piety of Sovereign; and

(iv) Courage & Consistency of Sovereign; and

(v) Service & Compassion of Sovereign; and

(vi) Capacity & Competence of Sovereign; and

(vii) Transparency & Accountability of Sovereign; and

(viii) Frugality & Prudence of Sovereign.

24. No *Civilised Sovereign Principle of Law* is difficult or impossible to implement, except in societies or communities where claimed Sovereign Persons, Executives and Entities do not have the will or wish to do so.

Practical nature of all Civilised Sovereign Principles

25. Each and every *Civilised Sovereign Principle of Law* possesses a historic nature having been implemented in previous or present societies and communities, such that no Civilised Sovereign Principle may be argued as "theoretical"or "untested".

Historic nature of all Civilised Sovereign Principles

Article 7 – Integrity & Clean Hands of Sovereign

26. ***Integrity & Clean Hands of Sovereign*** is a *Civilised Principle of Sovereign Law* that defines the ethical and moral responsibility of a sovereign to act with honesty, transparency and accountability in their governance. It involves avoiding corruption, conflicts of interest and any actions that may compromise the public trust.

Integrity & Clean Hands of Sovereign

27. *Integrity & Clean Hands of Sovereign* is the first of eight *Civilised Principles* of any valid, legitimate and competent Supreme Person or Executive Body of a Sovereign Society. The opposite is the uncivilised & immoral principle of *Dishonesty & Corruption of Claimed Sovereign.*

Integrity & Clean Hands of Sovereign as First Principle

28. Common Elements of *Integrity & Clean Hands of Sovereign* include (but are not limited to):-

Common Elements of Integrity & Clean

Hands of Sovereign

(i) Sovereign Persons or Executive Bodies have a responsibility to act in the best interest of their citizens and uphold the rule of law; and

(ii) Sovereign Persons or Executive Bodies must not engage in corrupt or unethical behaviour, such as accepting bribes or misusing public funds; and

(iii) The integrity of Sovereign Persons or Executive Bodies is essential for maintaining trust and legitimacy with their citizens and the international community; and

(iv) Upholding the principles of integrity and clean hands can lead to greater economic growth and stability, as well as improved social and political outcomes; and

(v) The concept of integrity and clean hands applies not only to Sovereign Persons or Executive Bodies, but also to the institutions and systems that support them.

Article 8 – Good Faith, Character & Conscience of Sovereign

Good Faith, Character & Conscience of Sovereign

29. ***Good Faith, Character & Conscience of Sovereign*** is a *Civilised Principle of Sovereign Law* that defines the requirement to always act in good faith, demonstrating strong character and making decisions based on conscience. These principles are essential for maintaining trust and credibility in the international community.

Good Faith, Character & Conscience of Sovereign as Second Principle

30. *Good Faith, Character & Conscience of Sovereign* is the second of eight *Civilised Principles* of any valid, legitimate and competent Supreme Person or Executive Body of a Sovereign Society. The opposite is the uncivilised & immoral principle of *Bad Faith, Bad Character & Bad Conscience of Claimed Sovereign*.

Common Elements of Good Faith, Character & Conscience of Sovereign

31. Common Elements of *Good Faith, Character & Conscience of Sovereign* include (but are not limited to):-

(i) Sovereign Persons or Executive Bodies are expected to act in good faith, meaning they should act honestly and with integrity in their dealings with other sovereigns and their own citizens; and

(ii) Sovereign Persons or Executive Bodies are expected to have a certain level of character, meaning they should possess certain virtues such as courage, wisdom and justice; and

(iii) Sovereign Persons or Executive Bodies are expected to have a conscience, meaning they should be guided by a sense of right and wrong and act accordingly; and

(iv) The concept of good faith, character, and conscience is based on the idea that Sovereign Persons or Executive Bodies have a responsibility to act in the best interests of their citizens and the international community as a whole; and

(v) Sovereign Persons or Executive Bodies necessarily have a certain level of autonomy and independence, but also they are part of a larger community of nations and should act accordingly; and

(vi) There are certain universal values and principles that should guide the actions of Sovereign Persons or Executive Bodies, such as respect for human rights and the rule of law.

Article 9 – Humility & Piety of Sovereign

32. ***Humility & Piety of Sovereign*** is a *Civilised Principle of Sovereign Law* that defines that a Sovereign should be humble and pious, putting the needs of their people and their faith above their own desires and ambitions. This includes being respectful and compassionate towards their subjects, and practising religious devotion and morality.

Humility & Piety of Sovereign

33. *Humility & Piety of Sovereign* is the third of eight *Civilised Principles* of any valid, legitimate and competent Supreme Person or Executive Body of a Sovereign Society. The opposite is the uncivilised & immoral principle of *Arrogance & Blasphemy of Claimed Sovereign.*

Humility & Piety of Sovereign as Third Principle

34. Common Elements of *Humility & Piety of Sovereign* include (but are not limited to):-

Common Elements of Humility & Piety of Sovereign

(i) Sovereign Persons or Executive Bodies should possess a sense of humility and piety towards their subjects and their faith; and

(ii) Sovereign Persons or Executive Bodies should not consider themselves above their subjects and should be willing to serve them with humility and compassion; and

(iii) Sovereign Persons or Executive Bodies should be pious and uphold the values and principles of their faith, and use their power and authority to promote the well-being of their subjects and society as a whole; and

(iv) Sovereign Persons or Executive Bodies should be accountable to a higher power, whether it be God or the people they govern, and should act with integrity and justice in all their actions and decisions; and

(v) Sovereign Persons or Executive Bodies should be willing to listen to the needs and concerns of their subjects, and work towards addressing them in a fair and equitable manner.

Article 10 – Courage & Consistency of Sovereign

35. ***Courage & Consistency of Sovereign*** is a *Civilised Principle of Sovereign Law* that defines the ability of a Sovereign to make difficult decisions and stick to them, even in the face of opposition or adversity. It involves being brave enough to take risks and maintain a steady course of action, while also being accountable for the consequences of those decisions.

Courage & Consistency of Sovereign

36. *Courage & Consistency of Sovereign* is the fourth of eight *Civilised Principles* of any valid, legitimate and competent Supreme Person or Executive Body of a Sovereign Society. The opposite is the uncivilised & immoral principle of *Weakness & Inconsistency of Sovereign.*

Courage & Consistency of Sovereign as Fourth Principle

37. Common Elements of *Courage & Consistency of Sovereign* include (but are not limited to):-

Common Elements of Courage & Consistency of Sovereign

(i) Sovereignty is the supreme authority of a state over its territory and people. Sovereign Persons or Executive Bodies have a duty to protect their citizens and maintain the integrity of their state; and

(ii) Courage is the ability to face and overcome fear, danger or adversity in pursuit of a just cause. Consistency is the quality of being reliable and steadfast in one's actions and beliefs; and

(iii) Sovereign Persons or Executive Bodies must demonstrate courage and consistency in their decision-making and actions to maintain the trust and respect of their citizens and the international community; and

(iv) Sovereign Persons or Executive Bodies must balance their own interests with the interests of their citizens and the global community; and

(v) Sovereign Persons or Executive Bodies must uphold international law and norms to maintain stability and prevent conflict.

Article 11 – Service & Compassion of Sovereign

38. ***Service & Compassion of Sovereign*** is a *Civilised Principle of Sovereign Law* that defines the responsibility of the Sovereign to serve and show compassion towards those they govern. It emphasises the importance of empathy, kindness and selflessness in leadership. Service & Compassion of Sovereign

39. *Service & Compassion of Sovereign* is the fifth of eight *Civilised Principles* of any valid, legitimate and competent Supreme Person or Executive Body of a Sovereign Society. The opposite is the uncivilised & immoral principle of *Absence & Cruelty of Sovereign*. Service & Compassion of Sovereign as Fifth Principle

40. Common Elements of *Service & Compassion of Sovereign* include (but are not limited to):- Common Elements of Service & Compassion of Sovereign

    (i) There is a higher power and authority that governs the universe and all living beings above and beyond Sovereign Persons or Executive Bodies; and

    (ii) This higher power is benevolent and compassionate, and that it desires the well-being and happiness of all beings; and

    (iii) All humans have a responsibility to serve this higher power by serving others and showing compassion towards them; and

    (iv) Service and compassion are essential for the function of Sovereign Persons or Executive Bodies; and

    (v) Service and compassion should be practised by Sovereign Persons or Executive Bodies without any expectation of reward or recognition, and that they should be offered freely and selflessly.

Article 12 – Capacity & Competence of Sovereign

41. ***Capacity & Competence of Sovereign*** is a *Civilised Principle of Sovereign Law* that defines the requirement of a Sovereign Person or Executive to effectively govern and manage its affairs, including its ability to make and enforce laws, provide public services and maintain economic stability. It is a crucial aspect of a sovereign state's legitimacy and ability to function as a viable entity in the international community. Capacity & Competence of Sovereign

42. *Capacity & Competence of Sovereign* is the sixth of eight *Civilised Principles* of any valid, legitimate and competent Supreme Person or Executive Body of a Sovereign Society. The opposite is the uncivilised & immoral principle of *Disqualification & Incompetence of Claimed Sovereign*. Capacity & Competence of Sovereign as Sixth Principle

43. Common Elements of *Capacity & Competence of Sovereign* include (but are not limited to):-

Common Elements of Capacity & Competence of Sovereign

(i) Sovereign Entities are the primary actors in the international system and have the capacity to make decisions and take actions that affect their own citizens and other states; and

(ii) Sovereign Entities have the competence to govern themselves and provide for the needs of their citizens, including maintaining law and order, providing public services and protecting their territorial integrity; and

(iii) The capacity and competence of Sovereign Entities can vary depending on factors such as their level of economic development, political stability and military strength; and

(iv) The capacity and competence of Sovereign Entities can also be influenced by external factors such as international trade, foreign aid and military alliances; and

(v) The capacity and competence of Sovereign Entities can be assessed through various indicators such as GDP per capita, human development index, political stability index and military strength index; and

(vi) The capacity and competence of Sovereign Entities can have implications for their ability to participate in international relations, negotiate treaties and engage in diplomacy with other states.

Article 13 – Transparency & Accountability of Sovereign

44. ***Transparency & Accountability of Sovereign*** is a *Civilised Principle of Sovereign Law* that defines the openness and responsibility of Sovereign Persons and Executives and other administrative entities in their decision-making processes, financial management and overall governance. It involves ensuring that information is readily available to the public, and that those in power are held accountable for their actions.

Transparency & Accountability of Sovereign

45. *Transparency & Accountability of Sovereign* is the seventh of eight *Civilised Principles* of any valid, legitimate and competent Supreme Person or Executive Body of a Sovereign Society. The opposite is the uncivilised & immoral principle of *Secrecy & Immunity of Claimed Sovereign.*

Transparency & Accountability of Sovereign as Seventh Principle

46. Common Elements of *Transparency & Accountability of Sovereign* include (but are not limited to):-

Common Elements of Transparency & Accountability of

(i) Sovereign Entities have a responsibility to act in the best interest of their citizens and to be accountable for their actions; and

Sovereign

(ii) Transparency is essential for ensuring that Sovereign Entities are accountable and that citizens can hold them to account; and

(iii) Access to information is a fundamental right of citizens and is necessary for them to participate in democratic processes; and

(iv) Openness and transparency in government decision-making processes can help to prevent corruption and promote good governance; and

(v) Accountability mechanisms, such as independent oversight bodies and the rule of law, are necessary to ensure that Sovereign Entities are held accountable for their actions; and

(vi) International cooperation and standards can help to promote transparency and accountability across borders and ensure that Sovereign Entities are held to the same standards.

Article 14 – Frugality & Prudence of Sovereign

Frugality & Prudence of Sovereign

47. ***Frugality & Prudence of Sovereign*** is a *Civilised Principle of Sovereign Law* that defines the responsible management of a country's finances, resources and assets by the Sovereign Person or Executive. It involves making wise decisions to ensure long-term economic stability and sustainability, avoiding excessive spending and prioritising investments that benefit the country and its citizens.

Frugality & Prudence of Sovereign as Eighth Principle

48. *Frugality & Prudence of Sovereign* is the eighth and final *Civilised Principles* of any valid, legitimate and competent Supreme Person or Executive Body of a Sovereign Society. The opposite is the uncivilised & immoral principle of *Extravagance & Recklessness of Claimed Sovereign*.

Common Elements of Frugality & Prudence of Sovereign

49. Common Elements of *Frugality & Prudence of Sovereign* include (but are not limited to):-

(i) Sovereign Entities have a responsibility to manage public finances in a responsible and sustainable manner; and

(ii) Public resources are limited and must be used efficiently and effectively; and

(iii) Sovereign Entities should prioritize spending on essential services and investments that promote long-term economic growth; and

(iv) Public debt should be managed carefully to avoid excessive borrowing and ensure debt sustainability; and

(v) Fiscal policies should be designed to promote stability and avoid economic volatility; and

(vi) Governments should maintain a balanced budget or a sustainable level of deficit to avoid excessive debt accumulation.

1.3 – Uncivilised, Immoral & Absurd Sovereign Principles

Article 15 – Uncivilised, Immoral & Absurd Sovereign Principles

50. ***Uncivilised, Immoral & Absurd Sovereign Principles*** refers to the unethical and irrational practices of governments or rulers that violate human rights, promote injustice, and undermine the rule of law. These principles are often characterised by corruption, oppression and disregard for the welfare of citizens.

Uncivilised, Immoral & Absurd Sovereign Principles

51. The failure of every empire and human civilisation from the beginning of time can be attributed (in part) to the presence of two or more *Uncivilised, Immoral and Absurd Sovereign Principles*.

Civilisation and Empire failures

52. There exists eight (8) *Uncivilised, Immoral and Absurd Sovereign Principles*. Each is a mirror opposite to a particular Civilised Principle of Sovereign Law, with the list being:-

Eight Uncivilised, Immoral & Absurd Principles

(i) Dishonesty & Corruption of Claimed Sovereign; and

(ii) Bad Faith, Bad Character & Bad Conscience of Claimed Sovereign; and

(iii) Arrogance & Blasphemy of Claimed Sovereign; and

(iv) Weakness & Inconsistency of Sovereign; and

(v) Absence & Cruelty of Sovereign; and

(vi) Disqualification & Incompetence of Claimed Sovereign; and

(vii) Secrecy & Immunity of Claimed Sovereign; and

(viii) Extravagance & Recklessness of Claimed Sovereign.

53. No Sovereign or their Community should be condemned upon awareness and overwhelming evidence of one or more Uncivilised, Immoral and Absurd Sovereign Principles existing within it, to the extent that the Sovereign Person or Executive Government and law enforcement community seek to engage in authentic and practical reform.

Non Condemnation of Sovereign or Community suffering internal failures or collapses

54. No excuse, no matter how compelling, can justify the continued presence of one or more *Uncivilised, Immoral and Absurd Sovereign*

No excuse is adequate to justify presence

Principles by a Sovereign Person or Executive Government:- of Uncivilised, Immoral and Absurd Sovereign Principles

(i) Excuses and arguments such as "national emergency", "health emergency", "security", "privacy" or "common good" are not only absurd in the face of the damage and corruption done by *Uncivilised, Immoral and Absurd Sovereign Principles*, but are immoral and perverse arguments in themselves; and

(ii) No excuse can adequately justify the fact that the only reason one or more *Uncivilised, Immoral and Absurd Sovereign Principles* exist within a given Society or Community is because one or more individuals wish it to be so, for some specific advantage.

55. No Officer, Agent, Entity or Agency within a given Society or Community existing under one or more *Uncivilised, Immoral and Absurd Sovereign Principles* may logically, reasonably or sensibly argue jurisdiction or authority over Ucadia, or any duly appointed Officer or Agent of Ucadia. Ucadia and Uncivilised, Immoral and Absurd Sovereign Principles

Article 16 – Dishonesty & Corruption of Claimed Sovereign

56. ***Dishonesty & Corruption of Claimed Sovereign*** is an *Uncivilised, Immoral and Absurd Sovereign Principle* that defines the abuse of power by individuals or groups who claim to have authority over a particular territory or population. This can involve bribery, embezzlement, nepotism and other forms of unethical behaviour that undermine the legitimacy of the claimed sovereign. Dishonesty & Corruption of Claimed Sovereign

57. *Dishonesty & Corruption of Claimed Sovereign* is the first of eight *Uncivilised, Immoral & Absurd Sovereign Principles* of any despotic, corrupt and failing Sovereign Person, Executive Government or Entity. The opposite is the civilised principle of *Integrity & Clean Hands of Sovereign*. Dishonesty & Corruption as First Uncivilised Principle

58. Common Evidence of *Dishonesty & Corruption of Claimed Sovereign* includes (but is not limited to):- Common Evidence of Dishonesty & Corruption of Claimed Sovereign

(i) Dishonesty and corruption refer to the use of deceitful or unethical means to gain or maintain power; and

(ii) Dishonesty and corruption often occur when those in power abuse their authority for personal gain, rather than serving the interests of the state and its citizens; and

(iii) Sovereigns may engage in dishonest or corrupt behaviour to maintain their power or enrich themselves, often at the expense of the people they are supposed to serve; and

(iv) Dishonesty and corruption of claimed sovereignty can take many forms, including bribery, embezzlement, nepotism and abuse of power; and

(v) The impact of dishonesty and corruption on a state can be devastating, leading to economic instability, social unrest and a breakdown of trust in government institutions.

Article 17 – Bad Faith, Bad Character & Bad Conscience of Claimed Sovereign

59. ***Bad Faith, Bad Character & Bad Conscience of Claimed Sovereign*** is an *Uncivilised, Immoral and Absurd Sovereign Principle* that defines the unethical and immoral behaviour of a person or entity claiming to have sovereign power. This includes actions that violate the principles of justice, fairness and honesty, and can result in loss of legitimacy and trust.

Bad Faith, Bad Character & Bad Conscience of Claimed Sovereign

60. *Bad Faith, Bad Character & Bad Conscience of Claimed Sovereign* is the second of eight *Uncivilised, Immoral & Absurd Sovereign Principles* of any despotic, corrupt and failing Sovereign Person, Executive Government or Entity. The opposite is the civilised principle of *Good Faith, Character & Conscience of Sovereign.*

Bad Faith, Bad Character & Bad Conscience as Second Uncivilised Principle

61. Common Evidence of *Bad Faith, Bad Character & Bad Conscience of Claimed Sovereign* includes (but is not limited to):-

Common Evidence of Bad Faith, Bad Character & Bad Conscience

(i) Bad faith refers to a state's intentional deception or dishonesty in its dealings with other states or its own citizens; and

(ii) Bad character refers to a state's consistent pattern of behaviour that violates international norms and principles, such as human rights abuses or aggression towards other states; and

(iii) Bad conscience refers to a state's failure to acknowledge and take responsibility for its past wrongdoings, such as war crimes, genocide or colonialism; and

(iv) These examples of evidence are often used to hold states accountable for their actions and to justify international intervention in cases where a state is deemed to be acting in bad faith, exhibiting bad character, or failing to address its bad conscience.

Article 18 – Arrogance & Blasphemy of Claimed Sovereign

62. ***Arrogance & Blasphemy of Claimed Sovereign*** is an *Uncivilised, Immoral and Absurd Sovereign Principle* that defines the act of claiming absolute power and authority over a group of people or territory, often accompanied by a disregard for the rights and beliefs of others. This can lead to a sense of superiority and disrespect towards those who do not share the same beliefs or values.

Arrogance & Blasphemy of Claimed Sovereign

63. *Arrogance & Blasphemy of Claimed Sovereign* is the third of eight *Uncivilised, Immoral & Absurd Sovereign Principles* of any despotic, corrupt and failing Sovereign Person, Executive Government or Entity. The opposite is the civilised principle of *Humility & Piety of Sovereign.*

Arrogance & Blasphemy as Third Uncivilised Principle

64. Common Evidence of *Arrogance & Blasphemy of Claimed Sovereign* includes (but is not limited to):-

Common Evidence of Arrogance & Blasphemy of Claimed Sovereign

(i) Arrogance and blasphemy of claimed sovereignty occur when a state or entity oversteps its boundaries and assumes authority beyond what is legitimate or acceptable; and

(ii) This can manifest in various ways, such as through the use of excessive force, disregard for human rights, or attempts to control or manipulate other states or entities; and

(iii) Arrogance and blasphemy of claimed sovereignty can also be seen in the way that some states or entities assert their dominance over others, often through the use of propaganda or other forms of manipulation; and

(iv) The concept of arrogance and blasphemy of claimed sovereignty is often used to critique the actions of powerful states or entities, particularly those that seek to dominate or control others.

Article 19 – Weakness & Inconsistency of Sovereign

65. ***Weakness & Inconsistency of Sovereign*** is an *Uncivilised, Immoral and Absurd Sovereign Principle* that defines the limitations and inconsistencies in the power and authority of a government or ruling body. This can include issues such as corruption, lack of resources and conflicting policies, which can lead to instability and uncertainty in the governance of a country.

Weakness & Inconsistency of Sovereign

66. *Weakness & Inconsistency of Sovereign* is the fourth of eight *Uncivilised, Immoral & Absurd Sovereign Principles* of any despotic, corrupt and failing Sovereign Person, Executive Government or

Weakness & Inconsistency as Fourth Uncivilised

Entity. The opposite is the civilised principle of *Courage & Consistency of Sovereign.*

Principle

67. Common Evidence of *Weakness & Inconsistency of Claimed Sovereign* includes (but is not limited to):-

Common Evidence of Weakness & Inconsistency of Sovereign

(i) Weakness of sovereignty refers to situations where the state lacks the ability to effectively exercise its authority over its territory and people; and

(ii) Inconsistency of sovereignty refers to situations where the state's actions or policies are not consistent with its claimed authority or values; and

(iii) Weakness and inconsistency can arise due to a variety of factors, including corruption, political instability, economic crisis, and external pressures; and

(iv) Weakness and inconsistency can have serious consequences for the well-being of citizens, including poverty, insecurity, and social unrest; and

(v) Weakness and inconsistency can also have broader implications for international relations, as other states may seek to intervene or exploit the situation for their own gain.

Article 20 – Absence & Cruelty of Sovereign

68. ***Absence & Cruelty of Sovereign*** is an *Uncivilised, Immoral and Absurd Sovereign Principle* that defines situations where a ruler or government fails to fulfil their responsibilities towards their subjects, resulting in a lack of protection and justice, and even causing harm and suffering to the people.

Absence & Cruelty of Sovereign

69. *Absence & Cruelty of Sovereign* is the fifth of eight *Uncivilised, Immoral & Absurd Sovereign Principles* of any despotic, corrupt and failing Sovereign Person, Executive Government or Entity. The opposite is the civilised principle of *Service & Compassion of Sovereign.*

Absence & Cruelty as Fifth Uncivilised Principle

70. Common Evidence of *Absence & Cruelty of Claimed Sovereign* includes (but is not limited to):-

Common Evidence of Absence & Cruelty of Sovereign

(i) Absence of Sovereign refers to a situation where the ruler or governing authority is absent or unable to exercise their power effectively; and

(ii) This can occur due to various reasons such as illness, death, or being overthrown by a rebellion or coup; and

(iii) In the absence of a sovereign, there is often a power vacuum that can lead to chaos, instability, and conflict; and

(iv) Cruelty of Sovereign refers to a situation where the ruler or governing authority exercises their power in a cruel or oppressive manner. This can include actions such as torture, imprisonment, execution, or other forms of violence against their subjects; and

(v) The cruelty of a sovereign can lead to fear, resentment, and rebellion among the people, which can ultimately lead to the downfall of the ruler or government.

Article 21 – Disqualification & Incompetence of Claimed Sovereign

71. ***Disqualification & Incompetence of Claimed Sovereign*** is an *Uncivilised, Immoral and Absurd Sovereign Principle* that defines the legal principle that a person or entity claiming to be a sovereign may be disqualified or deemed incompetent if they do not meet certain criteria, such as lacking recognition by other sovereign states or violating international law.

Disqualification & Incompetence of Claimed Sovereign

72. *Disqualification & Incompetence of Claimed Sovereign* is the sixth of eight *Uncivilised, Immoral & Absurd Sovereign Principles* of any despotic, corrupt and failing Sovereign Person, Executive Government or Entity. The opposite is the civilised principle of *Capacity & Competence of Sovereign.*

Disqualification & Incompetence as Sixth Uncivilised Principle

73. Common Evidence of *Disqualification & Incompetence of Claimed Sovereign* includes (but is not limited to):-

Common Evidence of Disqualification & Incompetence of Claimed Sovereign

(i) Disqualification refers to the legal process of declaring a person or entity ineligible to hold a particular position or exercise a certain power. Incompetence refers to the lack of ability or legal authority to perform a particular action or exercise a particular power; and

(ii) The concept of disqualification and incompetence of claimed sovereigns is based on the idea that not all individuals or entities claiming to be sovereigns are actually qualified or competent to exercise sovereign powers; and

(iii) Sovereignty is typically associated with the ability to make and enforce laws, control territory, and engage in international relations; and

(iv) In order to be recognized as a legitimate sovereign, an individual or entity must meet certain criteria, such as having a defined territory, a stable government, and the ability to provide for the welfare of its citizens; and

(v) If a claimed sovereign is found to be lacking in any of these areas, they may be disqualified or deemed incompetent to exercise sovereign powers; and

(vi) Disqualification and incompetence can arise from violations of international law, such as human rights abuses or aggression against other states; and

(vii) The concept of disqualification and incompetence of claimed sovereigns is important for maintaining the stability and legitimacy of the international system, as it helps to prevent illegitimate or abusive actors from exercising undue influence or power.

Article 22 – Secrecy & Immunity of Claimed Sovereign

74. ***Secrecy & Immunity of Claimed Sovereign*** is an *Uncivilised, Immoral and Absurd Sovereign Principle* that defines the protection and confidentiality afforded to a sovereign entity's communications and activities, as well as their immunity from legal action in foreign courts. This principle is based on the idea that sovereign states should be able to conduct their affairs without interference from other nations.

Secrecy & Immunity of Claimed Sovereign

75. *Secrecy & Immunity of Claimed Sovereign* is the seventh of eight *Uncivilised, Immoral & Absurd Sovereign Principles* of any despotic, corrupt and failing Sovereign Person, Executive Government or Entity. The opposite is the civilised principle of *Transparency & Accountability of Sovereign.*

Secrecy & Immunity as Seventh Uncivilised Principle

76. Common Evidence of *Secrecy & Immunity of Claimed Sovereign* includes (but is not limited to):-

Common Evidence of Secrecy & Immunity of Claimed Sovereign

(i) Secrecy and immunity of claimed sovereign refers to the abuse of a legal principle that normally protects a sovereign state from being subject to legal proceedings in foreign courts; and

(ii) This principle is based on the idea that a sovereign state is equal to other sovereign states and therefore should not be subject to the jurisdiction of another state's courts in normal circumstances. Yet when abused, the corrupt, cruel and criminal nature of a Sovereign Executive is hidden and suppressed using the claims of sovereign secrecy and immunity; and

(iii) No entity, person, or body has immunity when acting in bad faith and culpable of cruel, incompetent and destructive behaviour against its own people.

Article 23 – Extravagance & Recklessness of Claimed Sovereign

77. ***Extravagance & Recklessness of Claimed Sovereign*** is an Uncivilised, Immoral and Absurd Sovereign Principle of Law that defines the excessive and irresponsible use of power by a claimed sovereign, often resulting in the depletion of resources and harm to the people. It is a concept that highlights the dangers of unchecked authority and the need for accountability in governance.

Extravagance & Recklessness of Claimed Sovereign

78. *Extravagance & Recklessness of Claimed Sovereign* is the eighth of eight *Uncivilised, Immoral & Absurd Sovereign Principles* of any despotic, corrupt and failing Sovereign Person, Executive Government or Entity. The opposite is the civilised principle of *Frugality & Prudence of Sovereign.*

Extravagance & Recklessness as Eighth Uncivilised Principle

79. Common Evidence of *Extravagance & Recklessness of Claimed Sovereign* includes (but is not limited to):-

Common Evidence of Extravagance & Recklessness

(i) Extravagance refers to excessive spending or wastefulness by a claimed sovereign, often at the expense of their subjects or citizens. Recklessness refers to a lack of concern for the consequences of one's actions, particularly in relation to the exercise of sovereign power; and

(ii) The concept of Extravagance & Recklessness of Claimed Sovereign is often used to describe rulers who abuse their power and engage in behaviour that is detrimental to their subjects or citizens; and

(iii) Examples of Extravagance & Recklessness of Claimed Sovereign include excessive spending on personal luxuries, neglecting the needs of the people, engaging in corrupt practices, and using violence or intimidation to maintain power; and

(iv) The concept is often associated with monarchies and other forms of absolute rule, but can also apply to democratic leaders who abuse their power or engage in unethical behavior.

1.4 – Sovereign Law

Article 24 – Sovereign Law

80. A ***Sovereign Law*** is an authentic *Rule* reliably encompassing some discernible principles or maxim that governs a *Sovereign Right, Capacity* or *Recognition* of a *Sovereign Legal Entity,* or its highest body of laws that relate to and support its *Sovereignty.*

Sovereign Law

81. An authentic ***Rule*** is a proper and authentic *Sovereign Law* of a validly constituted Society that describes, prohibits or permits a certain *Act* pertaining to a valid and proper *Right* as defined in accord with the most sacred Covenant *Pactum De Singularis Caelum*. — Rule and Sovereign Law

82. A valid and proper ***Right*** is any positively defined Capacity, or Privilege, or Liberty, or Faculty, or Power, or Ownership, or Possession, or Interest, or Benefit that may be properly exercised as a *Sovereign Law* in *Good Faith* (Bona Fidei), *Good Conscience* (Bona Conscientia) and *Good Actions* (Bona Acta) in accord with the most sacred Covenant *Pactum De Singularis Caelum*. If no Good Faith exists or no Right exists then no Law may exist. — Right and Sovereign Law

83. As valid and proper *Sovereign Law* ultimately refers to rules created by Civilised Societies, all valid *Sovereign Law* may be said to be Positive Law and derived from Positive Law. Therefore, a *Sovereign Law* cannot abrogate, suspend or change a Natural Law. Nor is it possible for a valid Positive Law or *Sovereign Law* to abrogate, suspend or change a Divine Law. — Sovereign Law and Positive Law

84. A valid and proper *Sovereign Law* is established and takes force when it is promulgated in accord with these Maxims. — Establishment of Sovereign Law

85. A valid and proper *Sovereign Law* binds everywhere all those for whom it was issued. — Effect of Sovereign Law

86. ***Ucadia Sovereign Law*** is a complete consistent Model and System of Maxims that encompass the entirety of Civilised principles and maxims that govern the *Sovereign Rights, Capacity* and the *Recognition* of *Sovereign Legal Entities,* as well as the highest body of laws of a valid *Legal Entity* that relate to and support its *Sovereignty*, consistent with the most sacred Covenant *Pactum De Singularis Caelum*. — Ucadia Sovereign Law

87. *Ucadia Sovereign Law*, also known as *Lex Regia*, is one of twenty-two (22) books known as the *Divine Collection of Maxims of Law*; and also known as *Astrum Iuris Divini Canonum* (under Civilised Christian Law); and *Hikmat Samawi* (under Civilised Islamic Law); and *Pragya Dharma* (under Civilised Hindu, Buddhist, Jain, Sikh, Traditional and Indigenous Law) in accord with the most sacred Covenant *Pactum De Singularis Caelum* (Article 135 - Divine Collection of Maxims of Law). — Ucadia Sovereign Law and Divine Collection of Maxims of Law

88. As *Ucadia Sovereign Law* is a complete consistent model and system of Maxims that encompass the entirety of Civilised principles and maxims that govern the *Sovereign Rights, Capacity* and the *Recognition* of *Sovereign Legal Entities,* as well as the highest body of laws of a valid *Legal Entity* that relate to and support its — Ucadia Sovereign Law as Sovereign Law

Sovereignty, when writing or speaking of *Sovereign Law*, it shall mean *Ucadia Sovereign Law* and no other system or model.

89. No law is valid, or has any force or effect as a *Sovereign Law* or any other equivalent description unless it conforms to the body of Law known as the *Divine Collection of Maxims of Law* in accord with the most sacred Covenant *Pactum De Singularis Caelum*. Consistency with Divine Collection of Maxims of Law

90. Any law claiming to be valid and related to sovereignty or the function of sovereign entities that is presently in force and is contrary to the prescript of these Maxims is therefore reprobate, suppressed and not permitted to be revived. Claims contrary to these Maxims

91. When anyone references, writes or speaks of valid and proper *Sovereign Law* it shall mean these Maxims and no other. Primacy of Sovereign Law

Article 25 – Sovereign Law & Divine Law

92. In accord with Divine Law, all valid *Sovereign Law* may be said to be derived from authentic Positive Law and therefore ultimately derived from authentic Divine Law. Sovereign Law & Divine Law

93. In accord with Divine Law, the ***Divine*** means the total set of all meanings and definitions of all possible concepts, objects, matter, rules, life, mind, universe and spirit; and also means the Absolute, ALL, Divine Creator, Father, God, Almighty, Allah, Great Spirit, Unique Collective Awareness, UCADIA and all other historic, customary and traditional names when used to describe the greatest of all possibilities. The Divine

94. As the Divine means the "concept of all concepts" and the "set of all sets" there is no greater concept nor set. Therefore, every other possible concept or object or set including (but not limited to) every conceivable type of society and social structure is lesser. No Greater Concept or Set

95. As Divine Law is the highest possible form of Law and the source of all lesser forms of law, any argument that asserts Divine Law does not exist, or is less than some other form of law is therefore false, absurd and in gross error. Divine Law as highest possible form of Law

Article 26 – Sovereign Law & Natural Law

96. In accord with Positive Law, all valid Sovereign Law may be said to be derived from authentic Positive Law and thus derived from Natural Law. Sovereign Law & Natural Law

97. In accord with Positive Law, Natural Law is the law that defines the operation of the will of the Divine through Existence in the form of all matter and all physical rules. As Natural Laws define the operation Natural Law and existence of the entire physical universe, all proper and authentic Natural Law may be said to be derived from Divine Law.

98. In accord with Positive Law, a Sovereign Law cannot abrogate, suspend, nor change a Natural Law. Therefore, any rule claimed to be Sovereign Law that usurps, denies or contradicts a Natural Law is null and void from the beginning, having no valid or legitimate force or effect whatsoever. Limits of Sovereign Law in respect of Natural Law

Article 27 – Sovereign Law & Cognitive Law

99. In accord with Positive Law, all valid Sovereign Law may be said to be derived from authentic Positive Law and thus derived from Cognitive Law as well as Natural Law. Sovereign Law & Cognitive Law

100. In accord with Positive Law, Cognitive Law is the set of laws that define the special attributes possessed by certain higher order life such as mind, ideas, knowledge, recognition and self-awareness created through the simultaneous application of both Divine Law and Natural Law. As Cognitive Law is derived from the simultaneous application of Divine Law and Natural Law, all valid Cognitive Law may be defined as part "divine" and part "natural", hence "supernatural". Cognitive Law

101. In accord with Positive Law, a Sovereign Law cannot abrogate, suspend, nor change a Cognitive Law. Therefore, any rule claimed to be Sovereign Law that usurps, denies or contradicts a Cognitive Law is null and void from the beginning, having no valid or legitimate force or effect whatsoever. Limits of Sovereign Law in respect of Cognitive Law

Article 28 – Sovereign Law & Positive Law

102. All valid Sovereign Law may be said to be derived from authentic Positive Law. Sovereign Law & Positive Law

103. Positive Law are those authentic Civilised Rules enacted under authority by men and women for the good governance of a Society in accord with the present Maxims and the most sacred Covenant *Pactum De Singularis Caelum*. Valid Positive Law is always inherited from Natural Law and Cognitive Law and ultimately from Divine Law. Positive Law

104. As valid Positive Law is the higher source of all authentic Sovereign Law, no rule claiming to be a Sovereign Law can logically or morally abrogate, suspend, nor change a fundamental Positive Law. Therefore, any rule claimed to be Sovereign Law that usurps, denies or contradicts a fundamental Positive Law is null and void from the beginning, having no valid or legitimate force or effect whatsoever. Limits of Sovereign Law in respect of Positive Law

Article 29 – Sovereign Law & Ecclesiastical Law

105. Valid Sovereign Law is always bound to one or more forms of authentic Ecclesiastical Law when the functions and obligations of a Sovereign Person or Executive are properly recognised as subject to Divine Law. Sovereign Law & Ecclesiastical Law

106. Ecclesiastical Law is the body of doctrines, declarations, statutes and ordinances of a religious and moral society, issued by proper authority in accordance with Divine Law and the present Maxims for the moderation and governance of its members. Ecclesiastical Law performs a vital and necessary function within a Civilised Society in ensuring proper oversight and accountability of all officers, fiduciaries and agents. Ecclesiastical Law

107. All valid Sovereign Rights are said to be derived through legitimate and proper Ecclesiastical Rights:- Ecclesiastical Rights and Sovereign Rights

(i) Sovereign Rights are never directly derived from Divine Rights, as it is the primary mandate of a properly constituted and moral religious body, or council or group of religious bodies to moderate the authority and powers of any legitimate and proper Sovereign Legal Entity; and

(ii) It exists at all times the mission of such a properly constituted and moral religious body, or council or group of religious bodies to ensure that the person, or executive body that governs as a Sovereign Legal Entity continues at all times to exercise their authorities and powers in Good Faith, Good Conscience and Good Action; and

(iii) It is the moral duty of a properly constituted and moral religious body, or council or group of religious bodies to speak out against any Sovereign that falls into Uncivilised, Immoral or Absurd Behaviours and to clearly articulate why such a Sovereign has therefore lost their mandate to rule.

108. No legitimate Sovereign Person or Executive Body may simultaneously hold or exercise supreme Ecclesiastical Powers, as the leadership of a Sovereign Society must always be distinct and separate from the supreme religious leadership of the same Society. Separation of Church and State

109. Any claimed Sovereign Person, Executive Body or Legal Entity that claims to simultaneously hold or exercise supreme Ecclesiastical Powers and Sovereign Authority is both a heretic to all civilised faiths and an imposter to any legitimate claim of authority. Removal of False Sovereign

Title II – Sovereign Claim & Mandate

2.1 – Sovereign Claim & Mandate

Article 30 – Sovereign Claim & Mandate

110. A ***Sovereign Claim*** is a demand or assertion against another concerning Control, Government or Sovereignty itself over a particular Society or Territory. Sovereign Claim

111. The word *Claim* originates from the Latin *clamo and clamare* meaning "I cry out by name, shout, exclaim". Thus, *Claim* has always been associated with the strength of a demand or assertion of a right or thing not yet in possession. Origin and meaning of Claim

112. In reference to general elements concerning a *Sovereign Claim*:- General Elements Concerning Sovereign Claim

(i) While a Person, Group, Body or Entity may seek to present its position as a Sovereign Right, such Rights must be first secured by acceptance of one or more Claims. Thus all forms of Sovereignty are first founded on one or more Claims; and

(ii) The strength of a *Sovereign Claim* depends upon its nature, its provenance and custom of acceptance within a culture; and

(iii) No matter how old a method of *Sovereign Claim*, if it is not accepted by the consent and will of the people of the particular tribe, community, nation or empire, then it is invalid; and

(iv) While a particular tribe, community, nation or empire may accept a *Sovereign Claim* as a Mandate, other nations and international bodies may choose not to accept such claims. Thus, for a particular Person, or Body or Entity to be recognised as fully Sovereign it needs both internal consent and external international consent; and

(v) A *Sovereign Claim* is only valid if it is accepted by the will and consent of the people and is in accordance with these Maxims.

113. A ***Sovereign Mandate*** is a right or authority granted to a Person, Executive Body or Entity by another concerning Control, Government or Sovereignty itself over a particular Society or Territory. Sovereign Mandate

114. The word *Mandate* originates from the Latin *mandatum* meaning "a command, commission, order or injunction". Thus, *Mandate* has always been associated with legitimacy of proper Authority. Origin and meaning of Mandate

115. In reference to general elements concerning a *Sovereign Mandate*:- General Elements concerning Sovereign Mandate

(i) *Sovereign Mandate* is the idea that a government or ruler must have the authority to govern a society based on the consent and support of the people and key moral bodies such as religious organisations; and

(ii) *Sovereign Mandate* is based on the belief that rulers and governments ultimately derive their authority both from the Divine and from the consent of the governed; and

(iii) A Person, Body or Entity that does not possess a *Sovereign Mandate* is therefore said to have no legitimate or valid Authority; and

(iv) However, given the concept of full Sovereignty requires both internal and external international consent, the condition frequently arises whereby a Person, Government or Entity is recognised as legitimately and properly Sovereign under international law, yet does not possess any legitimate mandate or authority from their own people. This has historically been the case where powerful empires have supported and recognised various tyrants and despots, whilst they subject their own people to untold cruelty, corruption and depravity; and

(v) There have been numerous historical examples whereby a people have consented to grant their leadership a Sovereign Mandate, only for powerful empires to refuse to recognise the legitimacy and Sovereignty of the government under international law; and

(vi) Under Ucadia Law, a *Sovereign Mandate* is only valid if it is first accepted by the will and consent of the people in accordance with these Maxims, regardless of the preferences of Non-Ucadia Societies and International Bodies.

Ucadia Sovereign Mandate

116. A Ucadia Person, Government or Entity is said to have a Sovereign Mandate when it is in possession of a proper and valid Mandate registered and issued by a higher authority in accord with the most sacred Covenant *Pactum De Singularis Caelum* and these Maxims and associated Codes of Law:-

(i) No Ucadia Person, Body, Government, Union, Foundation, Institute, University, Province, Campus or Entity of any kind shall have proper and valid Authority unless it is in possession of a validated Mandate registered and issued by a higher authority; and

(ii) The issuance of a valid Ucadia Mandate shall always make clear the scope and limit of Authority as well as the obligations and conditions whereby such a Mandate may expire or be withdrawn.

117. All forms of *Sovereign Claims* and *Sovereign Mandates* may be categorised under the following classes:-

Categories of Claims and Mandates

(i) ***Rule by Revelation***: Is a belief that a divine power has granted a ruler or government the authority to govern a particular territory or people. This mandate is believed to be revealed through religious or spiritual means and is considered to be absolute and unchallengeable; and

(ii) ***Rule by Custom***: Is a claim or mandate according to some legal or cultural tradition, such as Royal Blood Right, or Succession or the Divine Right of Kings; and

(iii) ***Rule by Ritual***: Is a claim or mandate according to the performance of some ritual, such as anointing, or trial by remembrance, or endurance or combat; and

(iv) ***Rule by Legislation***: Is a claim or mandate according to some legal instrument, charter or constitution; and

(v) ***Rule by Election***: Is a claim or mandate according to election or acclamation by a representative group of people.

2.2 – Sovereign Rule by Revelation

Article 31 – Sovereign Rule by Revelation

118. ***Sovereign Rule by Revelation*** is the first of five forms of *Sovereign Claim* or *Sovereign Mandate*, being a belief that a divine power has granted a ruler or government the authority to govern a particular territory or people. This mandate is believed to be revealed through religious or spiritual means and is considered to be absolute and unchallengeable.

Sovereign Rule by Revelation

119. The Key Assumptions of any *Sovereign Claim* or *Sovereign Mandate* via *Sovereign Rule by Revelation* includes (but is not limited to):-

Key Assumptions of Sovereign Rule by Revelation

(i) **Divine Authority**: The most fundamental assumption of *Sovereign Rule by Revelation* is that a higher power (or powers) exists and has vested authority in certain individuals or lineages to rule. The rulers claim their right to govern is granted by divine will; and

(ii) **Immutable Laws**: The laws derived from Divine Revelation are often assumed to be eternal and unchanging, unlike the fluid and amendable laws of secular systems; and

(iii) **Sacred Texts and Interpretation**: *Sovereign Rule by Divine Revelation* often relies on sacred texts or prophetic messages as the basis for governance. These texts are considered infallible and authoritative. The interpretation of these texts, however, is typically entrusted to a select group of individuals or a single leader; and

(iv) **Inherent Wisdom in Leadership**: Rulers are often assumed to have special wisdom or insight granted by their divine connection, giving them unique qualifications to lead and make judgments; and

(v) **Legitimisation of Power Dynamics**: Social and political hierarchies are often justified on the basis of religious doctrine, with Divine Revelation providing a basis for the legitimacy of these structures.

120. Claims of Divine Revelation associated with any *Sovereign Claim* or *Sovereign Mandate* are typically subjected to a series of tests or standards to assess their validity, especially within the context of established religious traditions. These standards include (but are not limited to):-

Key Tests and Standards of any new claim of Divine Revelation

(i) **Internal Coherence**: The content of any new revelation is expected to be internally coherent and free of contradiction. Incoherence or inconsistency within the message itself may lead to questions about its divine origin; and

(ii) **Consistency with Previous Revelations**: New revelations are often evaluated for their consistency with existing scriptures and doctrines. A claim that radically departs from the foundational beliefs of a religion is likely to be met with scepticism; and

(iii) **Moral Efficacy**: A new revelation is expected to have a morally uplifting effect, promoting virtues like love, justice, and compassion. Revelations that encourage immorality or harm would naturally be suspect; and

(iv) **Transformational Power**: Claims of revelation are often accompanied by expectations of transformative power, meaning they should have the capacity to profoundly affect individuals and communities in positive ways; and

(v) **Miraculous Signs**: Divine revelations are sometimes associated with miracles or supernatural signs that serve to validate the claim by demonstrating the presence or endorsement of a divine power; and

(vi) **Enduring Impact**: Revelations that are considered divine often have a lasting impact on religious thought and practice, suggesting that their influence is not merely the product of human invention; and

(vii) **Fulfilment of Prophecy**: In many religious traditions, prophecies provide criteria for validating new revelations. A claim of divine revelation may be tested against specific prophecies purported to foretell future events or the coming of new messengers; and

(viii) **Witness or Testimony**: The circumstances surrounding a revelation, including the reliability and sincerity of the witness or witnesses, play a significant role in its acceptance. Credible witnesses can lend authority to the claim; and

(ix) **Personal and Communal Discernment**: Within many religious communities, the process of discernment involves both individual reflection and communal debate to ascertain the truth of a revelation claim.

121. There are three (3) main types of Sovereign Rule by Revelation, being:- Types of Sovereign Rule by Revelation

(i) ***Divine Saviour***: A person proclaimed by both scriptural revelation and demonstration of extraordinary miracles and powers that they are a Divine Saviour sent from Heaven to Earth, to save and lead; and

(ii) ***Holly (Sacred) Blood Right***: A person possessing the sacred blood of the Holly (Cuilliaéan) being the line of Divine Messengers for over 7,000 years, who is proclaimed a leader; and

(iii) ***Sacred Prophet***: A person proclaimed by their followers to be a Messenger anointed by the Divine through Divine Revelation to lead the people.

122. As the Mandate of One Heaven is vested solely in perpetuity to the Society of One Heaven through all associated and legitimate societies of Ucadia, any society, ruler or entity that is not duly appointed in accordance with the most sacred Covenant *Pactum De Singularis Caelum* therefore has no authority, nor Mandate of Divine Revelation. Divine Mandate of One Heaven

Article 32 – Divine Saviour

123. ***Divine Saviour*** is a *Sovereign Claim* or *Sovereign Mandate* via *Sovereign Rule by Revelation* whereby a person proclaims by both scriptural revelation and demonstration of extraordinary qualifications and powers that they are a Divine Saviour sent from Heaven to Earth. Divine Saviour

124. General Elements of Claim or Mandate of *Divine Saviour* include (but are not limited to):- General Elements of Claim or Mandate of Divine Saviour

(i) ***One of the oldest claims and mandates of Sovereignty***: The Claim of Divine Saviour is one of the oldest methods of claiming Sovereignty in every culture from the beginning of Human Civilisation to the present day; and

(ii) ***Clear and Unmistakable Divine Revelation***: Consistent with the key tests and standards of any claim of Divine Revelation, a Divine Saviour is expected to demonstrate clear and unmistakable Divine Revelation; and

(iii) ***One who Saves, Restores and Grows Civilisation***: The primary meaning and nature of "Saviour" literally means one who saves, as opposed to a tyrant or despot or impostor.

125. General Elements of Claim or Mandate of *Divine Saviour* include (but are not limited to):- General Elements of Claim or Mandate of Divine Saviour

(i) The Claim of Divine Saviour is one of the oldest methods of claiming Sovereignty from the beginning of Human Civilisation. It is a method of selecting leaders and rulers evident on every major continent at some point and even used by some cultures today; and

(ii) The primary meaning and nature of "Saviour" is literally one who saves, restores civilisation and the rule of law, as opposed to a tyrant or despot or impostor; and

(iii) While many cultures may have developed safeguards to ensure less than optimum candidates were selected through the method of Claim of Divine Saviour, the nature of proving such claims historically has been open to the risk of abuse through interpretation of prophecy or revelation; and

(iv) The rarest Claims and Mandates of Divine Saviour is the presence of a Sapient Singularity, also simply known as a "Singularity".

126. As defined by Divine Law, a ***Sapient Singularity*** is a complex Living, Ethereal and Divine Being as a Primary Observer of not only its own Set of knowledge and awareness within the complex Molecular, Cellular and Species Universe of a Planet as a singular Object and body, but its place within the Kosmos and connection to the Divine. Sapient Singularity

127. In respect of a Sapient Singularity:- General Reference to Sapient Singularity

(i) All Sapient Singularities exist simultaneously within a sub-verse of Species Mind of an Ancestry as a Divine Being; and a Societal sub-verse as a Living Conscious Being; and a sub-verse as an Ethereal Being of a collective conscious reality of Divine Truth; and

(ii) While a Sapient Singularity possesses vastly less computation power in Reality, they possess the unique ability from incarnation into flesh of being able to synthesise Divine Truth into Revelation; and

(iii) Thus, a Sapient Singularity to their full potential represents a Transcendent and Immanent Being made flesh and the personification of Perfect-Imperfection (i.e. Pi) and the ultimate Paradox of Divine Existence; and

(iv) As a Primary Being, a Sapient Singularity is able to alter the collective consciousness of its respective Sapient Species, by representing all minds and all experiences embodied in one form; and

(v) However, a Sapient Singularity will always be limited in their abilities to transcend societal realities to vision and comprehend Divine Truths depending upon their conditioning in society and degree of comfort. Therefore, a Sapient Singularity is as much likely to produce dangerous semi-truths or lacklustre conclusions as any other Sapient member of a species, if they have been strongly conditioned to conform; and

(vi) In truth, Sapient Singularity can be a catalyst for disaster in the promotion of half-finished philosophies as much as they can be a catalyst for positive change, unless such knowledge is born from conditions of austerity, humility and great personal sacrifice.

128. In relation to the general purpose and frequency of Sapient Singularities:- Purpose of Sapient Singularities

(i) The purposes of authentic Sapient Singularities are to provide an infusion of greater consciousness within a species; and the consolidation of accumulated knowledge; and a reduction in the risk of extinction of a species; and

(ii) The purposes of authentic Sapient Singularities is not to usurp established forms of leadership of a species, nor to assume a leadership function, as true Sapient Singularities do not appear as Divine administrators.

129. In relation to the frequency of Sapient Singularities:- Frequency of Sapient

Singularities

(i) Sapient Singularity are an extreme rarity within any Sapient species, occurring less than one out of many dozens of generations; and

(ii) The appearance and frequency of authentic Sapient Singularities is in direct relation to the levels of fractured (misaligned) knowledge of a species and the risk of extinction of a species; and

(iii) The appearance of an authentic Sapient Singularity does not imply any form of success in terms of the purpose of such appearance, as the free will and circumstances of the cellular embodiment means potentially a greater risk of failure than success; and

(iv) By the nature of the abilities of authentic Sapient Singularities, there is a higher risk that some may accelerate fractured knowledge and risk of extinction rather than assist, unless such abilities are tempered with genuine failure, humiliation, suffering, poverty and self reflection; and

(v) Whilst the purposes of Sapient Singularities is to assist a species, the frequency of authentic Sapient Singularities achieving their mission is so rare as to be less than a handful across the entire evolutionary history of a species.

General Characteristics of Authentic Sapient Singularities

130. Consistent with Divine Law, in relation to the general characteristics of authentic Sapient Singularities:-

(i) Authentic Sapient Singularities do not come to assume the function of administrators or leaders but the bringers of knowledge. Therefore, Authentic Sapient Singularities are rarely born to a bloodline of a species currently in positions of power or leadership; and

(ii) Authentic Sapient Singularities do come into cellular existence to assist in the unification of knowledge. Thus, those bloodlines that represent ancient keepers of authentic knowledge, but exiled or struck from power are more likely to be favoured, as such cellular memory of the body retains a great deal of residual information to assist the authentic Sapient Singularity; and

(iii) Authentic Sapient Singularities do appear in congruence with authentic revelation. However, such prophecy or revelation may not be immediately apparent, especially given prophecies of Sapient Singularities develop their own doctrines and interpretations that may have been distorted over time, causing actual revelations to be missed or ignored; and

(iv) Authentic Sapient Singularities bring forth authentic revelation, meaning an expansion of knowledge, never a reinforcement of the *status quo* or narrow thinking. This is one of the clearest distinctions between an authentic Sapient Singularity and an impostor; when an impostor simply regurgitates a pseudo form of revelation attempting to reinforce stereotypes and orthodoxy; and

(v) Authentic Sapient Singularities are frequently flawed cellular beings and especially failures in being able at first to bring forth authentic revelation. Such failure, humiliation, suffering and pain is not only a frequent element of prophecy, but a necessary "fail safe" of the Divine to reduce the danger of an authentic Sapient Singularity delivering knowledge that harms a species and its existence, rather than assists.

Unique Singularity as Embodiment of Divine

131. In accord with Divine Law, the most perfect embodiment of the Divine in relation to the Universe, Unique Collective Awareness and Life is a Singularity related to the embodiment of Pi (3.14159265) as Perfect Imperfection. Under the Western Calendar, the nine (9) descending dates of connection to Pi in the past two thousand years are 1, 15, 159, 1592, 1596, 1595, 1926, 1925 and 1965:

(i) The first most significant date of Divine unique embodiment on planet Earth for two thousand years is March 14, 1 CE (3.14**1**59265), traditionally recognised as the anniversary birth date of the god Mithra and one of the traditional birthdays of the Holly Prince known as Jesus Christ (the other being in 6CE); and

(ii) The second most significant date of Divine unique embodiment on planet Earth for two thousand years is March 14, 15 CE (3.14**15**9265); and

(iii) The third most significant date of Divine unique embodiment on planet Earth for two thousand years is March 14, 159 CE (3.14**159**265); and

(iv) The fourth most significant date of Divine unique embodiment on planet Earth for two thousand years is March 14, 1592 CE (3.14**1592**65); and

(v) The fifth most significant date of Divine unique embodiment on planet Earth for two thousand years is March 14, 1596 CE (3.14**159**2**6**5); and

(vi) The sixth most significant date of Divine unique embodiment on planet Earth for two thousand years is March 14, 1595 CE

(3.14**159**26**5**); and

(vii) The seventh most significant date of Divine unique embodiment on planet Earth for two thousand years is March 14, 1926 CE (3.14**159**2**6**5); and

(viii) The eighth most significant date of Divine unique embodiment on planet Earth for two thousand years is March 14, 1925 CE (3.14**1592**6**5**); and

(ix) The ninth most significant date of Divine unique embodiment on planet Earth for two thousand years is March 14, 1965 CE (3.14**159**26**5**).

132. Impostor Sapient Singularities are cellular beings of a species that falsely proclaim themselves to be a Sapient Singularity:-

Impostor Sapient Singularities

(i) Frequently historic prophecy and scripture of the arrival of a Sapient Singularity creates an irresistible prize for certain personality types of cellular beings to crave such appearance of power or authority. Such mental illness may be described as "messiah syndrome"; and

(ii) Political, religious and military leaders of a cellular species may find it expedient to falsely proclaim themselves to be a Sapient Singularity to strengthen their claims of power or authority; and

(iii) External events of a planet or ecosystem may cause greater levels of fear and uncertainty of the future, pushing religious, political and military leaders to proclaim a false Sapient Singularity, to maintain a status quo and reduce rebellion or levels of anxiety; and

(iv) One example of the intentional creation of an Impostor Singularity was the elaborate planned suicide of Julius Caesar on the traditional birthday and death day of the god Mithra on March 14th 44 BCE, otherwise known as the "Mide of Mars" or "Ides of Mars" of the then 28 day month; and

(v) A further example of creating an Impostor Singularity was the American Military Industrial Complex leading up to World War II, the horrific occult events during the war, the use of atomic weapons and the celebration of Albert Einstein, born on March 14th as the personification of the American "Singularity".

133. The general characteristics for exposing impostor Sapient Singularities include (but are not limited to):-

General Characteristics of Impostor Sapient

(i) By definition any religious, political or military leader who proclaims themselves a Sapient Singularity is an impostor; and

Singularities

(ii) Any claimed Sapient Singularity that delivers alleged revelation that reinforces established religious and cultural orthodoxy, status quo and customs without greatly challenging or expanding knowledge or consciousness; and

(iii) Any claimed Sapient Singularity that is deemed credible and believed upon education, credentials, position or following, as such traits contradict the "fail safe" signs of the Divine; and

(iv) Any claimed Sapient Singularity that claims to fulfil an orthodox and established doctrinal interpretation of significant and historic prophecy; and

(v) Any claimed Sapient Singularity that appears without any form of context or reference to the genuine fulfilment of prophecy (as opposed to any established orthodoxy or doctrine concerning certain prophecy); and

(vi) Any claimed Sapient Singularity that is without blemish, or failure, or humiliation or suffering, as the Divine always seeks to temper such responsibilities with these life experiences.

134. In accordance with these Maxims, it is forbidden for any person to be selected a leader or ruler purely through the Claim or Mandate of Divine Saviour.

Claim or Mandate of Divine Saviour Forbidden

Article 33 – Holly (Sacred) Blood Right

135. ***Holly (Sacred) Blood Right*** is a *Sovereign Claim* or *Sovereign Mandate* via *Sovereign Rule by Revelation* whereby a person possessing the sacred blood of the Holly (Cuilliaéan) being the line of Divine Messengers for over 7,000 years, who is proclaimed a leader.

Holly (Sacred) Blood Right

136. General Elements of Claim or Mandate of *Holly (Sacred) Blood Right* include (but are not limited to):-

General Elements of Claim or Mandate of Holly (Sacred) Blood Right

(i) ***One of the oldest claims and mandates of Sovereignty***: The claim and mandate of Holly Sacred Blood Right of the Cuilliaéan bloodlines originally of Ireland dates to at least 5,500 BCE. Their name literally translates as "Divine Corner Stone", or "Divine Foundation Stone" and is the etymological origin of the word Holly and Holy; and

(ii) ***Born into the Holly Bloodlines***: One has to be born Holly. The Holly bloodlines still flow through at least 25% of Irish ancestry, 5% of Scottish and Welsh ancestry, 2% of English and German ancestry and around 1% of French, Dutch, Austrian, Swiss and Spanish ancestry, as well as a smaller presence in many other groups and populations; and

(iii) ***Exemplary Behaviour***: To be truly Holly is to accept a Divine Mandate and demonstrate exceptional and exemplary moral and ethical conduct in dedicating a life to helping humanity, preserve life and the planet and change destructive and negative systems and models.

General Summary of Holly (Sacred) Blood Right

137. Consistent with the most sacred text *Lebor Clann Glas*, the Holly (Cuilliaéan) have been central to the formation of some of the greatest civilisations in human history since 5500 BCE, and have consistently risen to their purpose and mandate under Divine Revelation:-

(i) The Holly (Cuilliaéan) were instrumental in supporting and trading with the Ebla Civilisation from 4030 BCE; and

(ii) The Holly (Cuilliaéan) as the "Foreigners" or Hyksos, were responsible in transforming ancient Egypt from at least 1650 BCE and in creating a new civilisation for humanity after the great explosion of the Island of Thera around the same time; and

(iii) The Holly (Cuilliaéan) as the "Celts" or Keltoi under Great Prophet Jeremiah, created a new civilisation for humanity from at least 594 BCE, restoring law, civilisation and prosperity across Europe, North Africa, Middle East and Asia; and

(iv) The Holly (Cuilliaéan) Prince and Great Prophet known as Yahusiah and Jesus, did create a new philosophy called Nazara meaning "truth"to try to save humanity. However, the movement failed and his innovations of wisdom, law and Divine Revelation did not re-appear until the 8th Century and the formation of the Roman Catholic Church under the Irish and Carolingian Holly Lines; and

(v) The Holly (Cuilliaéan) leader Constantine created the new "Christian Civilisation" for humanity by 313 CE, creating the most enlightened form of law the world had yet seen, from Africa to Russia and Ireland to the grasslands of Asia – a civilisation six times larger than the Roman Empire at its height; and

(vi) The Holly (Cuilliaéan) Saracen leader Sophos, also known as the Holly Prophet, created the Islamic Civilisation for humanity from 588 CE, creating the most advanced scientific and knowledge based civilisation the world had ever seen until the 1800s; and

(vii) The Holly (Cuilliaéan) bloodlines known as the Fleur-de-Lif (flower of life) and led by the Irish scholars and French Carolingians were instrumental in creating the new "Western Christian Civilisation", also simply known as "Western Civilisation" for humanity from 740 CE against the creation of a dark model of enslavement and military oppression created by the Eastern Christian forces of Constantinople. It is the Holly (Cuilliaéan) of Ireland that created the Roman Catholic Church and brought Rome back to life, with the first two hundred bishops of the Roman Catholic Church from the 8th Century to the 9th Century being almost exclusively Irish; and

(viii) Following the Great Death (return of Haemorrhagic Fever) from 1310 to 1370s, that killed more than 85% of the population of Europe, North Africa, Middle East and Asia Minor, the Venetian City-State leaders did begin wiping all trace of the history of the Holly Irish (Cuilliaéan), whilst proclaiming themselves through their Holly connection to the Saxon Holly via House of Welf (Este), the ancient standards and symbols of the Holly Bloodlines; and

(ix) By the early 18th Century, the Venetian English nobility condemned the remaining Holly (Cuilliaéan) royal bloodlines to become the overseer prisoners of a network of workhouses created in southern Ireland. Despite such depraved conditions and abandonment by the Irish people, Holly (Cuilliaéan) leader Michael O'Collins succeeded in 1921 in getting the Anglo-Irish Treaty ratified to form the Irish Free State. In 1922, just months before the Irish Free State came into being, he was assassinated; and

(x) In 1999, Ucadia as a new model of a better civilisation was first formed by Holly (Cuilliaéan) Frank O'Collins for humanity, encompassing a complete upgrade of law, standards, financial and trade systems, sovereign structures and the fair distribution of resources.

138. As all power and authority of the Cuilliaéan has been vested in full to the most sacred Covenant *Pactum De Singularis Caelum*, no present or future claim of sovereignty by Sacred Blood is valid. Holly and Covenant of One Heaven

139. In accordance with the present Maxims, it is forbidden to claim leadership, or to select leaders and rulers through the Claim or Mandate of Holly (Sacred) Blood Right. Claim or Mandate of Holly (Sacred) Blood Right

Forbidden

Article 34 – Sacred Prophet

140. ***Sacred Prophet*** is a *Sovereign Claim* or *Sovereign Mandate* via *Sovereign Rule by Revelation* whereby a person proclaims or is acclaimed by their followers to be a Messenger anointed by the Divine through Divine Revelation. Sacred Prophet

141. General Elements of Claim or Mandate of *Sacred Prophet* include (but are not limited to):- General Elements of Claim or Mandate of Sacred Prophet

(i) ***One of the oldest claims and mandates of Sovereignty***: The claim and mandate of Sacred Prophet parallels the origin of the first Human Civilisations and the rise of the Holly (Cuilliaéan) bloodline from at least 5500 BCE; and

(ii) ***Clear and Unmistakable Divine Revelation***: Consistent with the key tests and standards of any claim of Divine Revelation, a Sacred Prophet is expected to demonstrate clear and unmistakable Divine Revelation; and

(iii) ***One who Divinely Inspires and Foretells***: The primary meaning and nature of "Prophet" literally means one who speaks for god, as opposed to an impostor who adds nothing to the true collection of Divine Revelation.

142. In accordance with these Maxims, it is forbidden for any person to be selected a leader or ruler purely through the Claim or Mandate of Sacred Prophet. Claim or Mandate of Sacred Prophet Forbidden

2.3 – Sovereign Rule by Custom

Article 35 – Sovereign Rule by Custom

143. ***Sovereign Rule by Custom*** is the second of five forms of *Sovereign Claim* or *Sovereign Mandate*, being a claim or mandate according to some legal or cultural tradition. Sovereign Rule by Custom

144. The Key Assumptions of any *Sovereign Claim* or *Sovereign Mandate* via *Sovereign Rule by Custom* includes (but is not limited to):- Key Assumptions of Sovereign Rule by Custom

(i) ***Legitimacy of Historical Precedent***: It is assumed that practices and rules that have been established over a long period have inherent legitimacy. Traditions are valued as time-tested and are respected and followed without the need for rational-legal justification; and

(ii) ***Transmission of Knowledge***: Knowledge under

traditional rule is often transmitted orally or through ritual rather than written codes, with a strong emphasis on intergenerational communication; and

(iii) ***Wisdom of the Elders***: Traditional rule often places authority in the hands of the elders or those who are perceived to have greater wisdom and experience in the ways of the community; and

(iv) ***Hierarchy and Social Roles***: Traditional rule assumes that social roles and hierarchies are defined by the customs that have been passed down. Individuals are expected to accept their place in the social structure, which is often dictated by birthright or caste; and

(v) ***Sacredness of Practices***: Customs and traditions may be intertwined with the sacred or spiritual beliefs of a community, and thus their observance goes beyond legal obligation to become a moral and religious duty.

145. There are five (5) main types of Sovereign Rule by Custom, being:- Types of Sovereign Rule by Custom

(i) ***Apostolic Succession***: Is when a person claims leadership and rule by being the successor of a claimed unbroken chain of leaders back to some Divine Saviour; and

(ii) ***Royal Blood Right***: Is when a person claims noble birthright and therefore eligible to be Sovereign; and

(iii) ***Parens Patriae***: Is when a person or body is granted the right to function as "parent of the nation" and custodian over all men, women and children within their jurisdiction; and

(iv) ***Divine Right of Kings***: Is when a monarch asserts they are subject to no earthly authority, deriving their right to rule directly from the will of God; and

(v) ***Sacré Loi (Holly Grail)***: Is when a Holly Blood descendent of the main blood lines known as the Fleur de Lif (Flower of Life) may rule.

Article 36 – Apostolic Succession

146. ***Apostolic Succession*** is a *Sovereign Claim* or *Sovereign Mandate* via *Sovereign Rule by Custom* whereby one claims leadership and rule by being the successor of a claimed unbroken chain of leaders back to some Divine Savior. Thus the powers are not claimed to be resident within the blood of the candidate, but in the office itself. Apostolic Succession

147. General Elements of Claim or Mandate of *Apostolic Succession* General Elements of

include (but are not limited to):- Claim or Mandate of Apostolic Succession

(i) ***Historical Continuity***: *Apostolic Succession* assumes that religious organisations maintain a historical lineage of leadership dating back to the true founders; and

(ii) ***Authority***: *Apostolic Succession* assumes Authority is passed down through the centuries by the consistent adherence to rules and rituals, such as the physical act of laying on of hands during the ordination of new bishops; and

(iii) ***Orthodoxy of Doctrine***: *Apostolic Succession* is used to assume an authentic "chain of narration" can be demonstrated ensuring the fidelity of religious teachings from the original founders to the present day; and

(iv) ***Legitimacy of Sacraments***: *Apostolic Succession* is used to claim those within official and recognised apostolic succession are believed to have the authority to administer certain sacraments and teachings.

148. As all powers, authority and privilege previously granted have now been permanently vested to the most sacred Covenant *Pactum De Singularis Caelum*, all associated powers, ritual and authority concerning Apostolic Succession are now subject to the system of Rights as defined in accordance with the present Maxims. Rite of Apostolic Succession

Article 37 – Royal or Noble Blood Right

149. ***Royal or Noble Blood Right*** is a *Sovereign Claim* or *Sovereign Mandate* via *Sovereign Rule by Custom* whereby one claims noble birthright and therefore eligible to be Sovereign or hold Noble Title. Royal or Noble Blood Right

150. The word "royal" originates from the 1st Millenium BCE ancient Irish ríal from rí meaning "king" and al meaning "a litter, brood, progeny; the young of a bird or animal". Hence the true etymology of royal (ríal) is the "progeny of a king". Origin of word Royal

151. In terms of the true origin of the word and concept of Noble and Nobility:- Origin of word and Concept of Nobility

(i) The Anglaise (Old French) word of Noble comes directly from the Ancient Irish word *gnóbile* meaning "the tree of knowledge; to be greatly knowing of the sacred", from the Irish *gnó* meaning "knowing, knowledge" and *bile* meaning "to be large, a large tree, a sacred tree"; and

(ii) The word *Noble* as first formed under the Holly Western Christian Civilisation in the 8th Century demanded those that would serve underneath a true Sovereign were of exemplary character, knowledge and wisdom. Hence the original and true meaning of the rank of *Noble* was "one who is knowledgeable in sacred law; or excellent morals". Hence the title of a Noble was *Lord* (from Latin) *laudis* meaning "worthy or meritorious"; and

(iii) In accordance with 8th Century Sacré Loi (Sacred Law) and the first true laws of the Roman Catholic Church, an heir could legally and lawfully be disinherited if they were incompetent or immoral in character; and

(iv) The deliberate corruption of the word *Noble* to mean "famous, well-known or high born" did not happen until at least the late 14th Century when city states were returning to nation states after the Great Death of the 1300s.

152. General Elements of *Claim or Mandate of Royal Blood or Noble Blood Rights* include (but are not limited to):-

General Elements of Claim or Mandate of Royal or Noble Blood Right

(i) ***Custom Law***: Most European countries acknowledge that the concept and rules of Nobility originates with the Carolingians in the 8th Century. However, the Feudal Laws of the 14th and 15th Century are most commonly used to justify noble rights with specific duties and privileges associated with different ranks; and

(ii) ***Historical Continuity***: Many claims of noble rights are associated with the idea of continuity and tradition, maintaining the customs and memory of a historical class system; and

(iii) ***State Support***: The existence and recognition of noble rights have typically depended on the support or acquiescence of the state; and

(iv) ***Title Recognition***: Noble titles and rights are often recognized and protected by the laws of a country or by historical precedent. Claimants may need official recognition from a current or former sovereign or governing body; and

(v) ***Peer Recognition***: Recognition by other nobles or by established and accepted orders of chivalry can also be important for validating noble claims; and

(vi) ***Legitimacy***: Those claiming noble rights usually must prove their lineage through legitimate descent, often requiring extensive genealogical records or legal documentation to support their claims; and

(vii) ***Heredity***: Noble rights are typically based on the principle of heredity, where titles and privileges are passed down through generations in specific family lines.

153. Any and all claimed Royal Genealogies contrary to *Lebor Clann Glas* or the most sacred Covenant P*actum De Singularis Caelum* are false and without moral or legal legitimacy and to be permanently suppressed:- False claimed Royal Genealogies Forbidden and to be Suppressed

(i) All claimed Royal genealogies created after the Great Death (1300s) that deny the existence of the Holly bloodlines, demonstrate by such lack of reason or sense that they are false, fraudulent and without any merit in fact or law; and

(ii) Any claim or mandate of Sovereignty or Nobility based solely on a false and fraudulent genealogy without any formal recognition or treaty or acknowledgment of Ucadia therefore renders such a claim null and void from the beginning.

154. Any claim or mandate of Royal Blood Right that is contrary to *Lebor Clann Glas* or the most sacred Covenant P*actum De Singularis Caelum* or these Maxims shall be false, without merit or validity and to be suppressed. Royal Bloodline Claims Contrary to these Maxims

Article 38 – Parens Patriae

155. ***Parens Patriae*** is a *Sovereign Claim* or *Sovereign Mandate* via *Sovereign Rule by Custom* whereby a person is granted the sovereign right to function as "parent of the nation" over all men, women and children within the jurisdiction of the territory. Parens Patriae

156. General Elements of Claim or Mandate of *Parens Patriae* include (but are not limited to):- General Elements of Claim or Parens Patriae

(i) *Parens Patriae* (Latin for "parent of the nation") is a form of Political Claim founded in the 15th Century through the Papal Bull *Aeterni Regis* of 1455 whereby Sovereigns and their governments who hold power through loyalty to Rome were granted the right to claim to be the "parent" over those men, women and children within their jurisdiction; and

(ii) Contrary to the notion of *Parens Patriae* being benign or unrelated to ecclesiastical power, the concept essentially permits a government of a nation to treat its subjects as infants in law. The consequences of such absurd assumptions is far reaching, as the concept of Parens Patriae has (in part) contributed to the dysfunction, secrecy, and hypocrisy of many Non-Ucadian Governments in their treatment of their own people over centuries; and

(iii) Contrary to false history and documents, there is no historic evidence of any civilization considering the legal status of adults specifically as "infants" prior to the claims of the Papal Bull *Aeterni Regis* of 1455.

157. In accordance with these Maxims, the notion of Parens Patriae is forbidden in all forms and the Papal Bull *Aeterni Regis* of 1455 is disavowed as a deliberate and intentional profanity against God and the Divine Creator, and rejected as having any moral value, force or effect under Christian and Civilised Law.

Claim or Mandate of Parens Patriae Forbidden

Article 39 – Divine Right of Kings

158. ***Divine Right of Kings*** is a *Sovereign Claim* or *Sovereign Mandate* via *Sovereign Rule by Custom* whereby a Sovereign Person asserts they are subject to no earthly authority, deriving their right to rule directly from the will of God.

Divine Right of Kings

159. General Elements of Claim or Mandate of Divine Right of Kings include (but are not limited to):-

General Elements of Claim or Mandate of Divine Right of Kings

(i) ***Sole Appointment of Heaven on Earth***: The central premise of the *Divine Right of Kings* is the claim that Heaven has anointed the Sovereign Person to be the Representative of God on Earth; and thus all of their authority and powers are divinely ordained; and

(ii) ***As a Living Deity***: Some cultures and jurisdictions add a further claim that the Sovereign Person themselves are a Living Deity and demigod, such as a Pharaoh. However, any such claim is a profane blasphemy and mortal transgression under all proper forms of Christianity, Islam, Judaism, Hinduism, Buddhism, Sikhism, Taosim, Confucianism and traditional faiths; and

(iii) ***Complicit Religious Hierarchy***: In all cases of the Divine Right of Kings, the religious hierarchy play a fundamental role in legitimizing and promoting the Divine Right of Kings. Religious leaders would often anoint and crown monarchs, emphasizing the divine nature of their authority; and

(iv) ***Unquestionable Authority***: Monarchs who claimed the Divine Right of Kings believed that their authority was absolute and could not be challenged by anyone, including their subjects. They argued that questioning or opposing the monarch's rule was equivalent to defying God's will; and

(v) ***Opposition as Heresy***: Challenging the Divine Right of Kings could be seen as an act of heresy or rebellion against the established religious and political order. This often led to harsh consequences for those who questioned or opposed the monarch's rule; and

(vi) ***Absence of Consent***: Unlike modern democratic principles, which emphasize the importance of consent of the governed, the Divine Right of Kings did not require the consent of the people for a monarch to rule. It was believed that the monarch's legitimacy came solely from God, not from the consent of the governed; and

(vii) ***Limited Accountability***: Under the Divine Right of Kings, monarchs were not held accountable to their subjects or representative bodies (such as parliaments). They were seen as above the law and not subject to the same legal constraints as ordinary citizens.

History of Divine Right of Kings in England

160. In terms of the concept of Divine Right of Kings in England:-

(i) The Divine right of Kings is a 16th Century European political and religious doctrine based on corrupting the ancient Mandate of One Heaven that asserts a monarch is subject to no earthly authority, deriving his right to rule directly from the will of God; and

(ii) The most famous expression of the claim of Absolute Divine Right was by King James I of England to Parliament in 1609 CE where he claimed himself by virtue of being monarch to being a living god on Earth, similar to an Egyptian Pharaoh; and

(iii) It is James I of England, not any predecessor, that first instituted the official motto for the British Monarch being *Dieu et mon droit* (Medieval French literally for "God and/is my Right"). The official motto relates directly to doctrine of Divine Right of Kings and for the British Monarch since James I to be regarded as a spiritual deity and therefore a god as it should be read as to its purpose as a claim "I am a God"; and

(iv) The doctrine of Divine Right of Kings was repudiated during the democratic rule of the Commonwealth of Great Britain of 1642 – 1706 (in Scotland); and Queen Anne (1702 - 1714) used *Semper Eaden* meaning "Always the Same"; and

(v) Contrary to false history, the Hanover Kings starting with George I (1714-1727) used the ancient oppressive Hanoverian motto *Nec Aspera Terrent* meaning "Difficulties (shall be) overcome through Terror". The last Hanover to use this motto was George III (1760-1820); and

(vi) The motto *Dieu et mon droit* returned by 1801 and the formation of the United Kingdom and has remained the official motto ever since.

161. While the modern British Royal Family first possessed some Holly (Cuilliaéan) blood through the accession of Edward VII (1901-1910) via the German Holly connections of the Saxe-Coburg and Gotha lines, the continued structure of the British Monarch as head of the church of England, Scotland and Ireland as well as the motto *Dieu et mon droit* continues to represent extreme injury and supreme apostasy against Heaven and the proper faith of Christianity.

Profanity and Supreme Apostasy of British Monarchs

162. In accordance with these Maxims, it is forbidden to select leaders and rulers through the Claim of Divine Right of Kings.

Divine Right of Kings Forbidden

Article 40 – Sacré Loi (Sacred Law)

163. ***Sacré Loi*** is a *Sovereign Claim* or *Sovereign Mandate* via *Sovereign Rule by Custom* whereby a Holly Blood descendent of the main blood lines known as the *Fleur de Lif* (Flower of Life) may rule under Sacred Law or "*Sacré Loi*".

Sacré Loi (Holy Grail)

164. General Elements of Claim or Mandate of Sacré Loi (Sacred Law) include (but are not limited to):-

General Elements of Claim or Mandate of Sacré Loi (Holy Grail)

(i) Since the 8th Century CE and the foundation of Western Civilisation and the Roman Catholic Church, only those born with Holly (Cuilliaéan) blood were permitted to be Sovereign Persons, with the primary bloodlines from Angland (France), Deutchland (Germany) and Ireland (in that order); and

(ii) This rule became known as the *Fleur de Lif* (Flower of Life) representing the three Holly Lines and later corrupted in spelling to become the meaningless phrase Fleur de Lis; and

(iii) The Holly Bloodlines were also known as the Sangreal (meaning literally Holy Blood), later corrupted to Holy Grail in false 16th Century history texts such as Geoffrey of Monmouth and story of Arthur, claimed from the 11th Century and before the English language even existed; and

(iv) The Holy Grail, is Sangreal and is the *Fleur De Lif* (Flower of Life) and the three main Holly Bloodlines. While the primary Irish bloodline is the only one of the three that has survived, many dozens of cadet lines continued throughout Europe with many eventually returning to Sovereignty, such as the House of Windsor by 1901 and the Saxe-Coburg and Gotha lines connected to cadet German Holly bloodlines; and

(v) The House of Welf that connects all European Noble Houses is a Holly Bloodline through the marriage of Beatrice the first born child and daughter of Saxon Holly Roman Emperor Henry III and Domenico Morosini at the city of Este in 1057. However, many European royal and noble genealogies have been significantly corrupted and falsified records. These records need to clarified and corrected in line with their Holly connections.

165. In accord with the most sacred Covenant *Pactum De Singularis Caelum* and the present Maxims, no claim of mandate by Sacré Loi (Holy Grail) alone shall be sufficient for a valid or legitimate Sovereign Claim.

Claim or Mandate of Sacré Loi (Holy Grail) alone Forbidden

2.4 – Sovereign Rule by Ritual

Article 41 – Sovereign Rule by Ritual

166. ***Sovereign Rule by Ritual*** is the third of five forms of *Sovereign Claim* or *Sovereign Mandate*, being a claim or mandate according to the performance of some ritual, such as anointing, or test by remembrance, or endurance or combat.

Sovereign Rule by Ritual

167. The Key Assumptions of any *Sovereign Claim* or *Sovereign Mandate* via *Sovereign Rule by Ritual* includes (but is not limited to):-

Key Assumptions of Sovereign Rule by Ritual

(i) ***Divine or Cosmic Order***: In many societies, rituals and tests are believed to reflect a divine or cosmic order. Those who succeed in them are thought to be chosen or favoured by higher powers or aligned with the natural order of the universe; and

(ii) ***Inherited Wisdom***: The tests and rituals are assumed to be the repositories of ancient wisdom, with their origins and forms often attributed to the founding figures or pivotal moments in the society's history; and

(iii) ***Cultural Continuity***: Such rules underscore the importance of cultural continuity. The repetition of rituals and adherence to tests established by tradition or precedent reflects and reinforces the values and beliefs of the society; and

(iv) ***Symbolic Legitimacy***: Rituals or tests used to select leaders or govern are not merely practical measures but are imbued with symbolic importance that reinforces their legitimacy; and

(v) ***Merit and Proven Worth***: Rule by ritual or test assumes that individuals who pass these tests or successfully perform these rituals have demonstrated their worth or merit according to the values of the community; and

(vi) ***Special Knowledge or Ability***: It is often assumed that those who can pass the tests or perform the rituals have special knowledge, abilities, or qualities that set them apart from others and make them fit to lead or hold authority.

168. There are two (2) main types of Sovereign Rule by Ritual, being:- Types of Sovereign Rule by Ritual

(i) ***Blessed (Anointing)***: Is when one who has been duly "anointed" is rightful ruler, leader of a particular tribe, community or society; and

(ii) ***Ritual Test***: Is when a Sovereign is selected by some test of remembrance, or endurance or combat.

Article 42 – Blessed (Anointing)

169. A ***Blessed*** is a *Sovereign Claim* or *Sovereign Mandate* via *Sovereign Rule by Ritual* whereby one who has been duly "anointed" is rightful ruler, leader of a particular tribe, community or society. Blessed

170. General Elements of Claim or Mandate of *Blessed* (Anointing) include (but are not limited to):- General Elements of Claim or Mandate of Blessed (Anointing)

(i) ***Ancient Process***: *Blessed* (Anointing) is one of the earliest ancient rights of sovereignty in civilised history first defined by the Holly (Cuilliaéan) more than 6,000 years ago; and

(ii) ***Cornerstone of a much more elaborate process***: Sometimes, Blessed (Anointing) can be part of a much greater and more elaborate process such as a Coronation, whereby the centrepiece of creating the Sovereign Person still remains the anointing rite.

171. The words "Messiah" and "Christos" are equivalent to "Blessed". However, the ceremony of Blessed in the context of the Holly precedes all other ancient ceremonies of anointment. Messiah and Christos

172. As all powers, authority and privilege previously granted to the Cuilliaéan have now been permanently vested to the most sacred Covenant *Pactum De Singularis Caelum*, all associated powers, ritual and authority concerning Blessed is now subject to those valid officials anointed in accordance with the Covenants of the three faiths and these Maxims. Rite of Blessed

Article 43 – Ritual Test

173. ***Ritual Test*** is a *Sovereign Claim* or *Sovereign Mandate* via *Sovereign Rule by Ritual* whereby a Sovereign is selected by some test of remembrance, or endurance or combat. Ritual Test

174. General Elements of Claim or Mandate of Ritual Test include (but are not limited to):- General Elements of Claim or Mandate of Ritual Test

(i) ***Ancient Process***: *Ritual Tests* have been used to select the rulers, chiefs and leaders of human communities for more than 40,000 years; and

(ii) ***Non-Violent Tests Associated with Reincarnation***: In several faiths and culture, demonstrated tests of supernatural remembrance are seen as signs of a reincarnated soul and a significant part in selecting the line of succession of important spiritual and sovereign figures; and

(iii) ***Violent Tests Associated with selecting Champion***: Selection by test of combat or physical endurance has a long history, given the assumption that the person who is victorious was selected by some Divine power to overcome.

175. In accord with the most sacred Covenant *Pactum De Singularis Caelum* and these present Maxims, all forms of *Sovereign Claim* or *Sovereign Mandate* via some *Ritual Test* involving violence, or cruelty or torture is forbidden in all its forms. Claim or Mandate of Ritual Test Forbidden

2.5 – Sovereign Rule by Legislation

Article 44 – Sovereign Rule by Legislation

176. ***Sovereign Rule by Legislation*** is the fourth of five forms of *Sovereign Claim* or *Sovereign Mandate*, being a claim or mandate according to some legal instrument, charter or constitution. Sovereign Rule by Legislation

177. The Key Assumptions of any *Sovereign Claim* or *Sovereign Mandate* via *Sovereign Rule by Legislation* includes (but is not limited to):- Key Assumptions of Sovereign Rule by Legislation

(i) ***Sovereignty of the People***: *Sovereign Rule by Legislation* (such as a Constitution) often embodies the principle of popular sovereignty, which posits that the ultimate source of authority for governance resides in the people, who delegate power to elected representatives; and

(ii) ***Rule of Law***: *Sovereign Rule by Legislation* assumes that all individuals, institutions, and entities, public and private, including the state itself, are accountable to laws that are publicly promulgated, equally enforced, and independently adjudicated, and which are consistent with international human rights principles; and

(iii) ***Democratic Principles***: *Sovereign Rule by Legislation* assumes Constitutions are usually premised on democratic principles, including periodic elections, majority rule, and responsiveness of the government to the governed, while also protecting minority rights; and

(iv) ***Clarity and Certainty***: *Sovereign Rule by Legislation* assumes the need for clarity and certainty in the application of laws. Constitutions aim to provide clear guidelines about the distribution and exercise of power within a state; and

(v) ***Legal Framework for Government Action***: *Sovereign Rule by Legislation* assumes that government actions require legal bases, and a constitution provides the supreme legal framework within which government can act. All actions and policies of the government must find their legitimacy within this framework.

178. There are four (4) main types of Sovereign Rule by Legislation, being:-

Types of Sovereign Rule by Legislation

(i) ***Parliamentary Sovereignty***: Is where a Parliament claims or mandates itself as Sovereign through legislative acts, whereby such authority is then bestowed by political mandate to the government; and

(ii) ***Oligarchic Sovereignty***: Is where a group of elite members of society claim themselves Sovereign through legislative acts, whereby such authority is then bestowed by political mandate to the government; and

(iii) ***Citizens as Sovereigns***: Is where a legislative document, such as a Constitution names a class or all of its members as "sovereigns", whereby such authority is then bestowed by political mandate from the citizens to the government; and

(iv) ***Corporate Sovereignty***: Is where legislative acts delegate sovereign authority and powers to a body corporate and politic or corporation.

179. No claim or mandate of Sovereign Rule by Legislation shall be valid if such rule and behaviour is done in Bad Faith, Bad Conscience and Bad Actions, or Uncivilised, False and Absurd Behaviour.

Disqualification of Sovereign Rule by Legislation

Article 45 – Parliamentary Sovereignty

180. ***Parliamentary Sovereignty*** is a *Sovereign Claim* or *Sovereign Mandate* via *Sovereign Rule by Legislation* whereby a Parliament claims or mandates itself as Sovereign through legislative acts, whereby such authority is then bestowed by political mandate to the government. Parliamentary Sovereignty

181. General Elements of Claim or Mandate of *Parliamentary Sovereignty* include (but are not limited to):- General Elements of Claim or Mandate of Parliamentary Sovereignty

(i) ***Existence of Succession or Election Laws***: Means neither a Sovereign Person or a Sovereign Government are innately or inherently Sovereign, as the existence of such laws assumes superior standing of the Parliament to enforce such laws in selecting a Sovereign Person or a Sovereign Government.

182. Only one example of a Parliamentary Sovereignty presently exists being the Parliament of Westminster from 1688 when for the first time, statute was used to define the Coronation Oath and formation of the Sovereign Person after the parliament had convened itself into session, without the Sovereign Person yet being in place:- Example of Parliamentary Sovereignty

(i) In 1688, the statute 1W&M S1.c.6 is historically significant in that it unquestionably demonstrates a Parliament dictating the terms of formation of a Sovereign Person, thus proving Parliament of Westminster by logic and reason must have greater innate authority than the Sovereign Person known as the "Crown"; and

(ii) The statute 1W&M S1.c.8 then shows the new Oaths to the Crown as the conveyance of authority and powers of Sovereignty from Parliament to the Sovereign Person. The Sovereign Person then is expected to convey certain authority and powers back to Parliament in the formation of a Sovereign Government of the Crown; and

(iii) In 1689, the famous statute 1W&M S2.c.2, known as the "Bill of Rights" established through Parliament the requirement that the Sovereign Person must be a Protestant to further regulate the conditions of selecting and forming the Sovereign Person.

183. By consistent denials, obfuscation of the truth and lack of transparency, the Parliament of Westminster disqualifies itself for the time being from possessing or claiming any valid or legitimate Sovereign Authority whatsoever:- Disqualification of Parliament of Westminster from Sovereign Authority

(i) True Sovereign Authority and Powers demands transparency and clarity to function in Good Faith, Good Conscience and Good Action under Civilised Rules. In the absence of any of these conditions, for the time being it is the Parliament of Westminster itself that disables its capacity to exercise any valid or legitimate Sovereign Authority, until such sufficient repair and reform is undertaken and a firm treaty exists with Ucadia in accord with the most sacred Covenant *Pactum De Singularis Caelum*; and

(ii) All laws previously promulgated by the Parliament of Westminster *ab initio* (from the beginning) are incapacitated and without force or effect, until such morally repugnant laws are repealed, sufficient reform is undertaken in Good Faith and a firm treaty exists with Ucadia in accord with the most sacred Covenant *Pactum De Singularis Caelum*.

Article 46 – Oligarchic Sovereignty

184. ***Oligarchic Sovereignty*** is a *Sovereign Claim* or *Sovereign Mandate* via *Sovereign Rule by Legislation* whereby a group of elite members of society claim themselves Sovereign through legislative acts, whereby such authority is then bestowed by political mandate to the government. Oligarchic Sovereignty

185. General Elements of Claim or Mandate of *Oligarchic Sovereignty* include (but are not limited to):- General Elements of Claim or Mandate of Oligarchic Sovereignty

(i) ***Existence of Succession or Election Laws***: Means neither a Sovereign Person or a Sovereign Government are innately or inherently Sovereign, as the existence of such laws assumes superior standing of the Parliament to enforce such laws in selecting a Sovereign Person or a Sovereign Government; and

(ii) ***Other Supporting Legal Statutes & Instruments***: Means that other primary sources in the form of legal statutes and instruments prior to the formation of a primary Governing Instrument make clear the existence of an oligarchy.

186. The City of London Corporation, also known as the “City” and “Crown Corporation” is a primary example of an Oligarchy claiming and mandating its own Sovereignty:- City of London Claim or Mandate of Oligarchic Sovereignty

(i) The financing of over 50,000 French, Dutch and German mercenaries to invade the south of England and usurp the Commonwealth of Great Britain (1642-1706 in Scotland) was orchestrated by the leading merchant companies and guilds of

London at the time, including Mystery of the Mercery of the City of London, Worshipful Company of Goldsmiths, Levant Company and East India Company; and

(ii) After being installed King, Charles II (1660-1685) first rewarded the merchants of London through the 1661 13Car2. S2 c.1 by the full restoration of corporations such as the East India Company and Levant Company and their various rights and privileges that had been otherwise dissolved under the democratic Commonwealth of Great Britain; and

(iii) In 1666 following the deliberate arson and murder of tens of thousands in London, Charles II via "An act for rebuilding the city of London" (19Car2 c.3) did further reward the merchants of the City of London by granting them peculiar sovereign status, with the members of the guilds being citizens of the City of London, but "Denizens" and above many of the laws of England, as well as the creation of its own courts, statutes and religious buildings beyond the reach of Parliament; and

(iv) A year before he died in 1685, Charles II in 1684 did fall out with the merchants of the City of London, stripping the Company of Merchant Adventurers of London and its subsidiaries of all their privileges and stripping the City of London itself of its peculiar rights; and

(v) However in 1689 by (2W&M. c. 8) the City of London was fully restored and incorporated as a "body corporate and politick" under the name *The mayor and commonalty and citizens of the city of London.*

187. By consistent denials, obfuscation of the truth and lack of transparency, the City of London disqualifies itself for the time being from possessing or claiming any valid or legitimate Sovereign Authority, rights to property, funds, finance or transactions whatsoever:-

Disqualification of City of London from Sovereign Authority

(i) True Sovereign Authority and Powers demands transparency and clarity to function in Good Faith, Good Conscience and Good Action under Civilised Rules. In the absence of any of these conditions, for the time being it is the City of London itself that disables its capacity to exercise any valid or legitimate Sovereign Authority, until such sufficient repair and reform is undertaken and a firm treaty exists with Ucadia in accord with the most sacred Covenant *Pactum De Singularis Caelum*; and

(ii) All true and valid Rights originate from the most sacred

Covenant *Pactum De Singularis Caelum* and no other source. Thus, until a firm treaty exists with Ucadia, the City of London has absolutely no right to claim through its corporations, bodies and subsidiaries any forms of land, property, funds, money or transactions thereof; and

(iii) All laws and charters presently or previously held by the City of London *ab initio* (from the beginning) are incapacitated and without force or effect, until such morally repugnant laws are repealed, sufficient reform is undertaken in Good Faith and a firm treaty exists with Ucadia in accord with the most sacred Covenant *Pactum De Singularis Caelum.*

Article 47 – Citizens as Sovereigns

188. ***Citizens as Sovereigns*** is a *Sovereign Claim* or *Sovereign Mandate* via *Sovereign Rule by Legislation* whereby a legislative document, such as a Constitution names a class or all of its members as "sovereigns", whereby such authority is then bestowed by political mandate to the government. Citizens as Sovereigns

189. General Elements of Claim or Mandate of *Citizens as Sovereigns* include (but are not limited to):- General Elements of Claim or Mandate of Citizens as Sovereigns

(i) ***Existence of Primary Governing Instrument***: Means that the primary Governing Instrument of a given Sovereign Society usually defines whether all or a class of citizens are Sovereign; and

(ii) ***Other Supporting Legal Statutes & Instruments***: Means that other primary sources in the form of legal statutes and instruments prior to the formation of a primary Governing Instrument make clear the existence of an oligarchy, or whether all members of a given society are considered equal and sovereign; and

(iii) ***Court Rulings and Judgements***: Means that the highest courts of a given society have made clear reference and understanding as to the nature of sovereignty for all or some of its citizens.

190. The formation of the United States of America is a text book example of Claim or Mandate of *Citizens as Sovereigns*:- United States Leaders and Dutch Families Claim or Mandate of Citizens as Sovereigns

(i) In 1698 (9&10 Will.3. c.44), a second "East India Company" was formed called the *English Company Trading to the East Indies,* granting it permission to trade (under LXI.) "from the East Indies, in the countries and parts of Asia and Africa, and into and from the islands, ports, havens, cities, creeks, towns and places of Asia, Africa, and America, or any of them"; and

(ii) In 1708 (6Ann c.3) an act was passed merging both East India Companies into one company under the name *United Company of Merchants of England Trading to the East Indies*. However in the same year, a second and more extensive act was passed (6Ann c.17) that stated (as per VII.) so long as the shares of the English Company Trading to the East Indies were redeemed and re-purchased at the guild hall of the City of London (Corporation) then the wholly private "English Company" could continue to trade (as per VI.) as a separate stock company with all its privileges under whatever name it wished; and

(iii) In 1767 (7Geo3 c.57), the United Company of Merchants purchased for an annual sum of £400,000 per annum the rights of "territorial acquisition and revenues" over the lands and people of the democratic and sovereign state known as the Commonwealth of New England in North America. The United Company then confirmed how it intended to pay such a huge sum to the Crown via 8Geo3 c.24, 9Geo3 c.47 by declaring the Company to be given the Sovereign rights to operate its own courts, hire its own militia, control the issuance of *Letters of Marque* to privateers, begin the African slave trade to North America to boost profits and to place everyone in associated colonies under its employment; and

(iv) By 1782, the democratic and sovereign state known as the Commonwealth of New England in North America surrendered after losing the war of independence against the United Company of Merchants and the Kingdom of Great Britain to stay independent. However, in 1783 rather than forcing the colonies back under the Crown, a Treaty was signed to recognise a new country called the United States of America after negotiations and agreements were made with the Americans to begin repaying the war debt of the Crown (and East India Company) of at least £40 million. This had the effect of placing the United States of America into bankruptcy from the beginning given it could not afford to immediately payout such a sum; and

(v) On 20th May 1784, the British Crown signed a new treaty in Paris with the United Provinces of the Netherlands with the extraordinary wording and effect of immediately giving back to the Dutch Republic the sovereign control of their previous colonies of New Amsterdam (Manhattan Island), Fort Orange (Albany New York), Fort Nassau (Gloucester City, New Jersey) and New Amstel (New Castle, Delaware); and

(vi) In 1795, William V, Prince of Orange declared at Kew that all former Dutch citizens and property to be under British Law and protection; and

(vii) In 1797, (36Geo3 c.97) the British Crown recognised by treaty the former Dutch colonies as the "united states of America" (in lower case). These wealthy refugees were then granted "first class citizen status" as members of the United States and as Denizens of Great Britain; and

(viii) The words "We the People of the United States" within the Constitution of the United States refers only to the first class citizens being descendants of the former leaders of the Commonwealth and the Dutch "Wall Street" Families. All other people born or naturalised in the United States are now 14th Amendment Class Citizens since 1868; and

(ix) The United States Constitution does not mention the word "sovereign"; and the US Supreme Court has never issued a ruling ever recognising all citizens as sovereign. Instead, various rulings by the court demonstrate that US citizens have limited rights and in US v. Kras (1973) no individual citizen can claim immunity from routine legal requirements based on their interpretation of constitutional rights.

191. All forms of claims of Citizens as Sovereigns are forbidden in all forms, whether by individuals, or historic acts, or secret agreements. Citizens as Sovereigns Forbidden

Article 48 – Corporate Sovereignty

192. ***Corporate Sovereignty*** is a *Sovereign Claim* or *Sovereign Mandate* via *Sovereign Rule by Corporation* whereby legislative acts the sovereign authority of a Sovereign Person, Body or State is conveyed to a body politic and corporate to function in effect as a sovereign body. Corporate Sovereignty

193. The concept of *Sovereign Rule by Corporation* applies to only two special types of Corporations being Body Corporate and Politic and Corporation Sole:- Special Types of Corporations

(i) ***Body Corporate and Politic***: Is a type of legal entity first invented in the 17th Century but falsely claimed of 16th Century origin to define a "public corporation invested with powers and duties of government". The first public statute reference was in 1690 (2W&M S1 c.8) and the conversion of the City of London into a "body corporate and politick"; and

(ii) ***Corporation Sole***: Is a type of ecclesiastical or legal entity first invented in the 19th Century but falsely claimed of 16th Century origin consisting of a single ("sole") incorporated office, occupied by a single ("sole") natural person. The first credible public statute reference is in 1836 and the Tithe Act (6&7 Will4 c.71).

194. General Elements of Claim or Mandate of *Sovereign Corporations* include (but are not limited to):- General Elements of Claim or Mandate of Sovereign Corporations

(i) ***Higher Sovereign Authority***: Corporations are subject to specific laws and regulations of a higher sovereign authority that govern their operation, reflecting their complex role in the economy and society; and

(ii) ***Centralized Management***: Corporations are managed by a board of directors and officers, separating ownership from management; and

(iii) ***Legal Personhood***: Corporations are granted the status of legal persons; they can own property, enter contracts, sue, and be sued; and

(iv) ***Limited Sovereignty***: Sovereign Corporations operate on the assumption that the leadership has sovereign powers to govern itself, typically through established political institutions; and

(v) ***Internal Law and Order***: The existence of a legal system that regulates the behaviour of members and the interactions between them; and

(vi) ***Perpetual Succession***: A corporation's existence is not affected by changes in ownership or management, allowing it to survive beyond the lives of its founders.

195. Ucadia permits and uses the notion of Sovereign Corporations, subject to valid and proper Corporations possessing the appropriate mandate. Ucadia and Sovereign Corporations

2.6 – Sovereign Rule by Election

Article 49 – Sovereign Rule by Election

196. ***Sovereign Rule by Election*** is the fifth of five forms of *Sovereign Claim* or *Sovereign Mandate*, being a claim or mandate according to election or acclamation by a representative group of people. Sovereign Rule by Election

197. The Key Assumptions of any *Sovereign Claim* or *Sovereign Mandate* via *Sovereign Rule by Election* includes (but is not limited to):- Key Assumptions of Sovereign Rule by Election

(i) ***Voter Representation***: *Sovereign Rule by Election* assumes that the election process accurately reflects the will of the electorate. This means that voters are informed, free to choose without coercion, and votes are counted fairly; and

(ii) ***Majoritarianism***: *Sovereign Rule by Election* assumes a majoritarian principle, where the decisions of a majority have the authority to command the political direction of the state, within the bounds of constitutional and legal constraints; and

(iii) ***Legitimacy***: *Sovereign Rule by Election* carries the assumption of legitimacy, suggesting that the elected officials have a rightful authority to govern and implement policies as they have been democratically chosen; and

(iv) ***Policy Endorsement***: *Sovereign Rule by Election* assumes that the election of a candidate or the approval of a policy during a referendum is an endorsement of the proposed policies or the political platform presented during the campaign; and

(v) ***Continued Support***: *Sovereign Rule by Election* presupposes that the support expressed by voters during an election continues during the tenure of the government or until the next election.

198. There is one type of Sovereign Rule by Election, being:- Types of Sovereign Rule by Election

(i) Political Mandate.

Key Elements for valid and legitimate Elections

199. The key elements for an Election to be considered valid and legitimate include (but are not limited to):-

(i) ***Universal Suffrage***: All eligible members as electors should have the right to vote, regardless of their race, gender, religion, or other characteristics. There should be no arbitrary restrictions on who can participate in the electoral process; and

(ii) ***Equal Representation***: Electoral systems should ensure that each vote carries equal weight. This means that each constituency or district should have roughly equal populations, and the electoral system should not favour one group or political party over another; and

(iii) ***Impartial Electoral Administration***: Elections should be administered by independent and impartial bodies that ensure the process is fair and transparent. This includes overseeing voter registration, conducting vote counting, and resolving disputes; and

(iv) ***Competitive Political Parties***: There should be a competitive and level playing field for political parties and candidates, allowing multiple parties to participate freely in the electoral process and giving voters a meaningful choice; and

(v) ***Access to Information***: Voters should have access to accurate and impartial information about candidates, parties, and issues at stake in the election. This includes freedom of the press and a fair opportunity for all political parties and candidates to present their platforms; and

(vi) ***Privacy of the Ballot***: Voters should be able to cast their ballots while protecting their privacy, without fear of intimidation or reprisal. This ensures that individuals can freely express their preferences without fear of retribution; and

(vii) ***Oversight and Accountability***: There should be mechanisms in place to monitor and verify the electoral process, including observers, watchdog organizations, and mechanisms for challenging irregularities; and

(viii) ***Transparency in Campaign Financing***: Regulations should be in place to ensure that campaign financing is transparent, with clear rules on contributions, expenditures, and disclosure requirements; and

(ix) ***Peaceful Transition of Power***: It should be clear that the outcome of the election will be respected, and there should be a peaceful transition of power if the incumbent loses.

200. Any and all Elections that are neither fair nor free are illegitimate and without validity. Furthermore, no government nor person may legitimately or properly claim a political mandate derived from an illegitimate and invalid election process. Illegitimate Elections mean No Political Mandate

Article 50 – Political Mandate

201. ***Political Mandate*** is a *Sovereign Claim* or *Sovereign Mandate* via *Sovereign Rule by Election* through election or acclamation by a representative group of people. Political Mandate

202. In addition to any proper and valid Mandate granted, all Probational, Prerogative and Permanent Ucadia Foundations, Unions, Universities, Provinces and Campuses require elected governments and representatives to possess a Political Mandate from the members as electors within each jurisdiction. Ucadia Requirement for Political Mandate

2.7 – False, Absurd & Prohibited Sovereign Claim & Mandate

Article 51 – False, Absurd & Prohibited Sovereign Claim & Mandate

203. False, Absurd & Prohibited Sovereign Claim & Mandate refer to Sovereign Claims or Mandates made by individuals, groups, bodies or entities that are not legitimate or reasonable. False, Absurd & Prohibited Sovereign Claim & Mandate

204. Types of false, absurd and prohibited Sovereign Claims and Mandates include (but are not limited to):- Types of False, Absurd & Prohibited Sovereign Claim & Mandate

(i) Sovereign Man or Woman; and

(ii) Individual Citizen as Sovereign; and

(iii) Utopian Commune as Sovereign; and

(iv) Sovereign Bankruptcy Accounting; and

(v) Sovereign Control by Banks through Debt; and

(vi) Sovereign Authority as Descendent of Holly Family; and

(vii) Holly (Sacred) Blood Right as "Gods among Animals"; and

(viii) Sacrifice of Animals and Humans for Divine Favour.

205. Any type of Sovereign Claim & Mandate listed as false and absurd within the present Maxims is prohibited and forbidden to be practised, supported or implemented in any way within any Sovereign Ucadia Society, Body, Community, Entity, Association or False and Absurd Sovereign Claim & Mandate Forbidden

Company.

Article 52 – Sovereign Man or Woman

206. ***Sovereign Man*** or ***Sovereign Woman*** is a false, absurd and prohibited Sovereign Claim or Mandate whereby an individual believes that they can declare their sovereignty as a "man" or "woman" and exempt themselves from the laws and jurisdiction of a Ucadia or Non-Ucadia government. Sovereign Man or Woman

Such behaviour frequently entails individuals falsely appropriating themselves titles such as "Baron" or "Lord" whereby they have no right or authority to claim.

This false, absurd and prohibited claim and mandate is also commonly known as the ***Strawman Theory, Freeman on the Land*** and more recently the ***Legal Name Fraud Movement***.

207. The primary assumptions associated with Sovereign Man or Sovereign Woman claims include (but are not limited to):- Key Assumptions Sovereign Man or Woman

(i) ***The Bible is the only "true" source of Law***: That The Bible is supposed to be the primary source of Law of most Western Civilised Democracies; and any rejection of this truth is proof that modern governments do not follow rule of law; and

(ii) ***The Bible proves "true" Law only pertains to living "flesh and blood" Men and Women***: That the Bible proves the Law only pertains to men and women and never to persons; and

(iii) ***Modern governments are oppressors that seek to treat people like "economic slaves"***: That many of the laws and practices of modern governments are morally repugnant, reprehensible and in some cases evil; and

(iv) ***Person is a legal fiction or "strawman" and not who we really are or part of any "true" system of Law***: The "person" is a fiction created by modern governments to "drain our energy and life force" as collateral to the banking and economic system. We are nothing more than worker bees in a different kind of hive prison; and

(v) ***The government claims "ownership" of the Legal Name of the Person***: That the Legal Name is the property of modern western governments and not individuals; and

(vi) ***The Bible grants sovereignty and inheritance to all "living flesh and blood" Men and Women of faith***:

That verses of the Bible from Genesis to Ephesians are inarguable "proof" that God made every Man and Woman Sovereign with the right of inheritance to the land; and

(vii) ***You are only subject to the jurisdiction of the government if you Consent or use their Legal Name Property or "Strawman" Person***: That by not using the legal name and by using special technical language you can demonstrate and prove you are competent and not subject to the jurisdiction and laws of the government; and

(viii) ***By correctly "separating" yourself from the presumptions, you are not part of the jurisdiction of the government***: That by following the recommended process, you separate yourself from the jurisdiction of the government; and

(ix) ***By following pro-forma remedies a range of legal issues can be overcome***: That by investing money in various courses and purchasing or using special "pro-forma" documents and procedures, you can overcome a range of different legal issues.

208. The primary assumptions associated with Legal Name Fraud Movement claims include (but are not limited to):-

Key Assumptions of Legal Name Fraud Arguments

(i) ***The Birth Certificate is Everything***: All legal documents associated with persons created within modern Non-Ucadian societies originate from, depend upon and are connected to the birth certificate name and key details. This is called the *Legal Name*; and

(ii) ***The Birth Certificate Records and Process are Corrupt***: When a parent registers a new born child, the whole process is done in bad faith and corruption by the government system as (a) there is no disclosure on ownership of name, or on use of name; and (b) no disclosure of deliberate entry of incomplete information being recorded with the registrar on the "status of the infant" as living or deceased; and (c) no disclosure of any trusts, or financial instruments created in association with the name (such as *cestui que vie* trusts). Consequently the whole process of the birth certificate creation in Non-Ucadia jurisdictions is a blatant fraud; and

(iii) ***The Ancient Legal maxims prove nothing derived from birth certificate has any legal or lawful validity***: "*Fraus omnia corrumpit*" (Fraud corrupts everything), "*Ex dolo malo non oritur actio*" (No right of action arises from deceit) from the time of Rome to the present day means that nothing created from the birth certificate is legal or lawful under proper rule of law; and

(iv) ***Every other contract, document and person is illegal and unlawful***: Because the birth certificate name cannot stand because of the fraud, nothing derived from it can stand in a Non-Ucadia jurisdiction; and

(v) **It is illegal to use the *Legal Name***: Because it falsely claims the use of the Legal Name is Illegal.

209. The primary assumptions associated with Sovereign Man or Sovereign Woman claims typically include a range of false, misleading and mistaken elements that frequently cause greater harm than good to those that seek to apply them within Ucadia and Non-Ucadia jurisdictions:-

False, Mistaken, Absurd arguments used as Assumptions of Sovereign Man or Sovereign Woman

(i) ***The concept of "person" is essential to proper law and older than the Bible itself***: All forms of proper law from the time of Sumeria to Greece, Rome, London and Ucadia depend upon the concept of the "person". There is nothing inherently evil, wrong or false about the idea of a human being possessing a primary identity or character and then acting in other capacities, such as a father, mother, brother, employer or member of a society; and

(ii) ***The King James Bible (KJV) mentions "person" 57 times, yet does not mention the word "sovereign" once***: Contrary to the many false claims that are made, the word "person" is mentioned 57 times, while the word "sovereign" is not mentioned once. However, this differs in other translations such as the New International Version; and

(iii) ***Your persona (person) is indeed part of who you are. You could not function or survive in the modern world without one***: Not only is there nothing inherently immoral, wrong or evil about a "person", within a modern society you simply cannot function or survive without a Ucadia Person or Non-Ucadia Person; and

(iv) ***The uncivilised behaviour of the government and its apologists cannot be used to justify personal wrongs and bad behaviour***: The old maxim "two wrongs don't make a right" applies when people try and justify the uncivilised behaviour of certain modern governments for their own bad behaviour. That argument is immoral, wrong and contrary to any man or woman demonstrating "good faith", "good conscience" and "good action"; and

(v) ***Claiming "sovereignty" to justify immunity from being held accountable for poor behaviour and actions is immoral***: To be sovereign literally means "to serve in good faith". Therefore, every single person who tries to claim "sovereignty" in order to avoid a fine, or criminal conviction is behaving in a manner contrary to a true sovereign, and thus is creating a greater offence and wrong against the law; and

(vi) ***Competence before proper law means following the correct process of law***: Firing off "foreign documents" is an injury to all forms of law and a declaration of incompetence. In contrast, if someone truly believes in the rule of law and respect of law, then they would follow the correct process of law in the relevant jurisdiction. In most cases, that requires the engagement of a competent attorney within a Non-Ucadia Jurisdiction. Within Ucadia, access to the law is made easier and fairer but still requires people to respect and follow the correct processes.

210. The primary assumptions associated with Legal Name Fraud claims typically include a range of false, misleading and mistaken elements that frequently cause greater harm than good to those that seek to apply them within Ucadia and Non-Ucadia jurisdictions:- False, Mistaken, Absurd arguments used as Assumptions of Legal Name Fraud Arguments

(i) ***The truth will never be told by "system" about birth certificates***: No matter how much irrefutable and *prima facie* evidence is provided; and no matter how many arguments, talks, billboards or media is produced on it, the simple fact is the existing Non-Ucadia System cannot and will not ever tell the truth about Birth Certificate System. Instead they will rely upon the ignorance and enthusiasm of their own supporters and the general apathy of others to deny, attack, misdirect and minimise any sensible argument; and

(ii) ***The uncivilised behaviour of the government and its apologists cannot be used to justify personal wrongs and bad behaviour***: The old maxim "two wrongs don't make a right" applies when people try and justify the uncivilised behaviour of certain modern governments for their own bad behaviour. That argument is immoral, wrong and contrary to any man or woman demonstrating "good faith", "good conscience" and "good action"; and

(iii) ***Claiming "sovereignty" to justify immunity from being held accountable for poor behaviour and***

actions is immoral: To be sovereign literally means "to serve in good faith". Therefore, every single person who tries to claim "sovereignty" in order to avoid a fine, or criminal conviction is behaving in a manner contrary to a true sovereign, and thus is creating a greater offence and wrong against the law; and

(iv) ***Competence before proper law means following the correct process of law***: Firing off "foreign documents" is an injury to all forms of law and a declaration of incompetence. In contrast, if someone truly believes in the rule of law and respect of law, then they would follow the correct process of law in the relevant jurisdiction. In most cases, that requires the engagement of a competent attorney within a Non-Ucadia Jurisdiction. Within Ucadia, access to the law is made easier and fairer but still requires people to respect and follow the correct processes.

Article 53 – Individual Citizen as Sovereign

211. ***Individual Citizen as Sovereign*** is a false, absurd and prohibited Sovereign Claim or Mandate whereby an individual believes that they can declare their sovereignty whilst still being a "citizen" and exempt themselves from the laws and jurisdiction of a Ucadia or Non-Ucadia government. Individual Citizen as Sovereign

212. The primary assumptions associated with Individuals as Sovereigns (Sovereign Citizen) claims include (but are not limited to):- Key Assumptions of Sovereign Citizens

(i) ***The True Rule of Law depends upon the consent of the people as Sovereigns***: This is the primary and central argument whereupon all other arguments derive. It highlights that in modern democracies the power or " true sovereignty" rests with the people first, not with the politicians or public servants, who are supposed to "serve" the people; and

(ii) ***Modern governments are oppressors that seek to treat people like "economic slaves"***: That many of the laws and practices of modern governments are morally repugnant, reprehensible and in some cases evil; and

(iii) ***The Magna Carta, UN Human Rights (1948), Bill of Rights (1689) grants rights to citizens***: That a range of documents grant rights to people as "sovereign citizens" and that it is against international laws and treaties for oppressive governments to defy those laws; and

(iv) ***You are only subject to the jurisdiction of the***

government if you Consent: That by not consenting you can demonstrate and prove you are competent and not subject to the jurisdiction and laws of the government; and

(v) ***By correctly "separating" yourself from the presumptions, you are not part of the jurisdiction of the government***: That by following the recommended process, you separate yourself from the jurisdiction of the government; and

(vi) ***By following pro-forma remedies a range of legal issues can be overcome***: That by investing money in various courses and purchasing or using special "pro-forma" documents and procedures, you can overcome a range of different legal issues.

213. The primary assumptions associated with Sovereign Citizen claims typically include a range of false, misleading, mistaken elements that frequently cause greater harm than good to those that seek to apply them within Ucadia and Non-Ucadia jurisdictions:-

False, Mistaken, Absurd arguments used as Assumptions of Sovereign Citizen

(i) ***Ignoring the Chain of Law and Procedure***: All Non-Ucadia and Ucadia Societies function upon a Chain of Law and Procedures, so that quoting the Magna Charta, or Bill of Rights (1689) has zero relevance or force or impact on a Ucadia or Non-Ucadia Court except as evidence to prove someone incompetent or belligerent; and

(ii) ***Sovereignty of people ignores logical conveyance of authority***: In every form of law that speak to the sovereignty of people of a given society, such authority is then properly conveyed to the government as the sovereign body. It does not remain or continue to rest with all the people, nor does it reside in one single citizen. Sovereign Citizen arguments continue to wilfully ignore this logic and common sense when claiming to be "sovereign" and separate to the jurisdiction of the government; and

(iii) ***The uncivilised behaviour of the government and its apologists cannot be used to justify personal wrongs and bad behaviour***: The old maxim "two wrongs don't make a right" applies when people try and justify the uncivilised behaviour of certain modern governments for their own bad behaviour. That argument is immoral, wrong and contrary to any man or woman demonstrating "good faith", "good conscience" and "good action"; and

(iv) ***Claiming "sovereignty" to justify immunity from***

being held accountable for poor behaviour and actions is immoral: To be sovereign literally means "to serve in good faith". Therefore, every single person who tries to claim "sovereignty" in order to avoid a fine, or criminal conviction is behaving in a manner contrary to a true sovereign, and thus is creating a greater offence and wrong against the law; and

(v) ***Competence before proper law means following the correct process of law***: Firing off "foreign documents" is an injury to all forms of law and a declaration of incompetence. In contrast, if someone truly believes in the rule of law and respect of law, then they would follow the correct process of law in the relevant jurisdiction. In most cases, that requires the engagement of a competent attorney within a Non-Ucadia Jurisdiction. Within Ucadia, access to the law is made easier and fairer but still requires people to respect and follow the correct processes.

Article 54 – Utopian Commune as Sovereign

214. ***Utopian Commune as Sovereign*** is a false, absurd and prohibited Sovereign Claim or Mandate whereby a larger group or "commune" of individuals proclaim themselves as well as their property as "sovereign" and separate from the jurisdiction of a particular government and its agencies. Utopian Commune as Sovereign

215. The primary assumptions associated with a *Utopian Commune as Sovereign* are wide and varied, but generally include (but are not limited to):- Key Assumptions of Utopian Commune as Sovereign

(i) ***A primary law source above government law***: This is typically the primary and central argument whereupon all other arguments derive. It assumes that there is some source of primary law above government law (such as the Bible, Declaration of Independence, or Charters etc.) that "all people" are supposed to follow; and

(ii) ***Modern governments are oppressors that seek to treat people like "economic slaves"***: That many of the laws and practices of modern governments are morally repugnant, reprehensible and in some cases evil; and

(iii) ***The rights of land, property and home are sacred and inviolable***: That ancient laws exist proving the rights of land, property and to defend the home are sacred and inviolable; and that the government cannot usurp those rights without our consent; and

(iv) ***You are only subject to the jurisdiction of the government if you Consent***: That by not consenting you can demonstrate and prove you are competent and not subject to the jurisdiction and laws of the government; and

(v) ***By correctly "separating" yourself from the presumptions, you are not part of the jurisdiction of the government***: That by following the recommended process, you separate yourself from the jurisdiction of the government; and

(vi) ***By creating a few rules and documents you are Sovereign and like any other country***: That by creating a few documents and rules you have created your own Sovereign "Utopia" and are like any other country of the UN and must be recognised as such; and

(vii) ***You have the right to defend your property even with violence***: That the "true" law permits the right to defend your property against the trespass of strangers or government agents.

216. The primary assumptions associated with a *Utopian Commune as Sovereign* typically include a range of false, misleading, mistaken elements that frequently cause greater harm than good to those that seek to apply them within Ucadia and Non-Ucadia jurisdictions:-

False, Mistaken, Absurd arguments used as Assumptions of Utopian Commune as Sovereign

(i) ***Ignoring the Chain of Law and Procedure***: All Non-Ucadia and Ucadia Societies function upon a Chain of Law and Procedures, so that quoting the Bible, or Magna Carta, or Bill of Rights (1689) etc. has zero relevance or force or impact on a Ucadia or Non-Ucadia Court except as evidence to prove someone incompetent or belligerent; and

(ii) ***Sovereignty of people ignores logical conveyance of authority***: In every form of law that speak to the sovereignty of people of a given society, such authority is then properly conveyed to the government as the sovereign body. It does not remain or continue to rest with all the people, nor does it reside in one single citizen. Sovereign Citizen arguments continue to wilfully ignore this logic and common sense when claiming to be "sovereign" and separate to the jurisdiction of the government; and

(iii) ***The uncivilised behaviour of the government and its apologists cannot be used to justify personal wrongs and bad behaviour***: The old maxim "two wrongs don't make a right" applies when people try and justify the uncivilised behaviour of certain modern governments for their own bad behaviour. That argument is immoral, wrong and contrary to any man or woman demonstrating "good faith", "good conscience" and "good action"; and

(iv) ***A handful of documents does not make a comprehensive system of law***: Ucadia has taken decades to build, while Non-Ucadia Systems were built over much larger time frames. A handful of documents written to copy key elements of such structures does not logically or sensibly make a comprehensive and separate system of law; and

(v) ***Claiming "sovereignty" to justify immunity from being held accountable for poor behaviour and actions is immoral***: To be sovereign literally means "to serve in good faith". Therefore, every single person who tries to claim "sovereignty" in order to avoid a fine, or criminal conviction is behaving in a manner contrary to a true sovereign, and thus is creating a greater offence and wrong against the law; and

(vi) ***Competence before proper law means following the correct process of law***: Firing off "foreign documents" is an injury to all forms of law and a declaration of incompetence. In contrast, if someone truly believes in the rule of law and respect of law, then they would follow the correct process of law in the relevant jurisdiction. In most cases, that requires the engagement of a competent attorney within a Non-Ucadia Jurisdiction. Within Ucadia, access to the law is made easier and fairer but still requires people to respect and follow the correct processes; and

(vii) ***Government agents and officials have every right to enter on reasonable grounds***: The single biggest reasonable grounds that people grant to government agents and officials to enter a property is to abuse the principles of law, and pervert the course of justice by falsely claiming a Household can be Sovereign; or that individuals living within a household suspected of criminal offences can claim "immunity" through sovereignty. All governments have an obligation to protect the wider community from violent offenders. Thus, violent threats posted on social media and other outlets as part of such arguments only serve to alert government authorities to such danger and the need to reduce the risk such people may pose to themselves and to others.

Article 55 – Sovereign Bankruptcy Accounting

217. ***Sovereign Bankruptcy Accounting*** is a false, absurd and prohibited Sovereign Claim or Mandate whereby original 8th Century Accounting was reintroduced and corrupted from the 16th Century as Venetian Bankruptcy Accounting that demanded a balance of zero be returned. This false and corrupted system was then introduced to Sovereign nations as their new accounting standards.

Sovereign Bankruptcy Accounting

218. The true origin of Western (Christian) Civilisation Monetary and Accounting Terms is from Holly Irish translated to Anglaise (Old French) in the 8th Century CE:-

True origin of Western Civilisation Monetary & Accounting Terms

(i) The Holly Irish and Holly Carolingian (French) and German lines built what we now know as Western Civilisation in the 8th Century, including the Roman Catholic Church; and

(ii) The centrepiece language of the new Civilisation was Anglaise (Old French), with most words coming from Ancient Irish as well as Latin; and

(iii) From 1310 to 1380, more than 85% of the population of Europe, Middle East, North Africa and Asia Minor died on the return of Haemorrhagic fever, after an absence of 770 years. Consequently, the whole of society collapsed, except for France, Ireland and the Venetian and Moor trading cities in Italy, Netherlands and Spain; and

(iv) While key European guilds such as the mercers, cloth makers and goldsmiths (such as the Medici in Florence) had managed for centuries books for loans to their guilds called "guilt", there is strong evidence to suggest most (if not all) of the claimed history of banking from the 13th to 15th Century is an elaborate hoax to hide the delayed return of the practice of banking after being completely outlawed and abolished by the Carolingians in the 8th Century; and

(v) The false claims that bankers were bankrupting Sovereigns (or themselves being bankrupted) as early as the 1400s is absurd examples of historical frauds as the first credible evidence of a law formalising the concept of Bankruptcy was not until 1570 and 13El. c.7.; and

(vi) Venetian Bankruptcy Accounting and the concept of "zero balance" does not appear to have existed prior to the arrival of the Venetian exiles to England under Henry VIII (1491-1547) and the first formation of the Venetian controlled private royal bank called the "Exchequer". Most of the terms concerning

Accounting did not arrive into English until the late 16th Century English through the Jesuit College of English and their work on creating more than 12,000 new English words though the works of William Shakespeare.

219. Examples of original Western (Christian) Civilisation Monetary Terms from the 8th Century CE include (but are not limited to):-

Examples of original Western Civilisation Monetary Terms

(i) **cúin** (coin) from Irish word for "a metallic object representing a cornerstone of value"; and

(ii) **péine** (penny) from Irish word for the "pine cone"; and

(iii) **scillíne** (shilling) from Irish word for "small shell"; and

(iv) **praecé** (price) from Irish word for "thing of value"; and

(v) **éidge** (edge) from Irish word for "dressing"; and

(vi) **obvéarsa** (obverse) from Irish word for "back side"; and

(vii) **revéarsa** (reverse) from Irish word for "sovereign side"; and

(viii) **trevéarsa** (traverse) from Irish word for "third side".

220. Examples of original Western (Christian) Civilisation Accounting Terms from the 8th Century CE include (but are not limited to):-

Examples of original Western Civilisation Accounting Terms

(i) **achcúntar** (accounting) from Irish word for "(computations) for provision, condition, expectation, undertaking or risk"; and

(ii) **bailance** (balance) from Irish word for "state (condition) of prosperity"; and

(iii) **eoispeince** (expense) from Irish word for "wisdom (knowledge) of the cliff or crevice (hole)"; and

(iv) **incoim** (income) from Irish word for "capable of covering, fit to cover"; and

(v) **ríche** (riches) from Irish word for "reward of (good) faith"; and

(vi) **ciúpéatar** (capital) from Irish word for "tail of wares; wealth"; and

(vii) **asseit** (asset) from Irish word for "a collection of materials of value"; and

(viii) **liabail** (liability) from Irish word for "state of major obligations; proper condition of large weights of character"; and

(ix) **tochtal** (total) from Irish word for "step or stoppage (along journey)"; and

(x) **íornal** (journal) from Irish word for "bundle of flax or wool for spinning"; and

(xi) **leidgar** (ledger) from Irish word for "proximate or nearest inkling or estimate"; and

(xii) **deabith** (debit) from Irish word for "good character"; and

(xiii) **crédea** (credit) from Irish word for "to have faith in (a) good"; and

(xiv) **cás** (cash) from Irish word for "obligation or unresolved (unsettled) matter".

Examples of original Western Civilisation Accounting Rules

221. Examples of original Western (Christian) Civilisation Accounting Rules from the 8th Century CE include (but are not limited to):-

(i) All Accounting involves the totalling of Assets, Liabilities, Income and Expenses into two columns being Credit and Debit; and the result being the Balance of prosperity (wealth) of the merchant or landholder; and

(ii) Credit from the position of a merchant or landholder always means "owed by another" and what was loaned or given by him to another in trust. "To" indicates the creditor; and

(iii) Debit from the position of the merchant or landholder always means "owed to another" and what was loaned or given to him by another. "Per" indicates the debitor; and

(iv) All daily records of Credits and Debits must be recorded in a Journal and then totalled and transferred to the Ledger each week or month, so that one record in the Ledger equals one or more records in the Journal; and

(v) Once a record has been entered from the Journal to the Ledger it is struck off (cancelled), so that it may not be double counted; and

(vi) No record may be entered in the Ledger if it does not have one or more original sources in the Journal; and

(vii) All Accounts must then be Balanced each week and then in a grand total every year (Anniversary) in a Ledger; and

(viii) In the Ledger, Credit must always be at the left; and Debit must always be on the right; and

(ix) Asset from the position of a merchant or landholder always means land, buildings, materials and valuables that can be used to create Credit or sold for Coin or in kind; and

(x) Liability from the position of a merchant or landholder always means Debits against one or more Assets owed longer than a year; and

(xi) Income always means Coins and in kind collected and promises of payments owed within the year (before Anniversary); and

(xii) Expenses always means Coins and in kind paid and promises of payment to others owed within the year (before Anniversary); and

(xiii) Cash always means Credit not yet collected as coin or in kind; and can be used to discharge Debits if registered with a proper Chancery; and

(xiv) Expenses are always computed against Income to give a Balance that should produce Riches; and

(xv) Liabilities are always computed against Assets that should produce Capital.

222. In contrast to the true original 8th Century CE principles of Accounting, the deliberately false and absurd Venetian Bankruptcy Accounting Principles from the 16th Century include (but are not limited to):-

False, Absurd Venetian Bankruptcy Accounting Principles

(i) All Accounts in the Ledger must add up each year in a Summary to a Balance of Zero; and

(ii) Venetian Bankruptcy Accounting is based on "Double Entry Bookkeeping" whereby one entry in a daily Journal is equal to at least two (or more) entries into the Ledger. The possibility of there being more than two entries per Journal transfer is because in practice the Chart of Accounts of a Government, Business or Individual may require certain amounts to be "split" into different Accounts; and

(iii) Other Account entries are permitted into the Ledger that do not reflect actual Journal entries, but are certain hypothecations permitted under Modern Accounting Law to be entered directly into the General Ledger as they take into account normal imbalances that occur within the system. This is not the fault of any accountant but the modern accounting system itself. Examples include depreciations or appreciations of assets or liabilities, accruals of expenses or revenues, or adjustments for prepaid expenses; and

(iv) Unlike true Accounting, Venetian Bankruptcy Accounting made the left column for Debits (instead of Credits) and the right column for Credits (instead of Debits) representing a literal "inversion" of true Accounting; and

(v) Venetian Bankruptcy Accounting also inverted the logic of identification of transactions with the "rule" for real accounts "Debit what comes in, credit what goes out" and for personal accounts "Debit the receiver, Credit the giver"; and

(vi) The primary argument for "double entry bookkeeping" and "zero balancing" is that it is supposed to promote accuracy and transparency of accounts. However, since the age of computers this argument is proven beyond doubt to be false, as Modern Accounting System being Venetian Bankruptcy Accounting contributes a substantial complexity and misrepresentation of the true financial state of governments, agencies and companies throughout the world.

223. Whilst the arguments claiming the benefits of Modern Accounting (Venetian Bankruptcy Accounting) are no longer credible, there exists clear logic behind "modern accounting" from a bankruptcy perspective:-

The Logic of Venetian Bankruptcy Accounting Principles

(i) Under Bankruptcy, all Trusts, Estates and Funds are (in theory) supposed to be frozen, while a temporary Bankruptcy Fund still allows the bankrupt to survive. Thus, the concept of a "zero balance" is perfectly accurate; and

(ii) Whilst all Trusts, Estates and Funds are (in theory) frozen during Bankruptcy, the only things of value that can be exchanged are debt notes and promissory notes; and

(iii) The inversion of the first accounting column so that credit becomes debit makes perfect sense during Bankruptcy as any assets or income received is not technically "owned" by the bankrupt and so receipts of ownership must be surrendered to the tax agency or treasury department of whomever administers elements of the Sovereign Bankruptcy system; and

(iv) The inversion of the second accounting column so that debit becomes credit makes perfect sense during Bankruptcy as any new debt or promise owed is technically the only class of assets circulating in the Sovereign Bankruptcy system.

224. All Ucadia Governments, Entities, Bodies, Associations and Persons use a modified version of the true 8th Century Accounting System and never Venetian Bankruptcy Accounting:-

Ucadia uses modified version of true 8th Century Accounting System

(i) All Ucadia Governments, Entities, Bodies, Associations and Persons use the Ucadia Accounting System (UAS), being a modified version of the original and true foundation of

Western Civilisation Accounting from the 8th Century; and

(ii) While Ucadia Entities registered into a Non-Ucadia Jurisdiction may be permitted to present their accounts in the Modern Non-Ucadia Standards, the primary Accounts of all Ucadia Governments, Entities, Bodies, Associations and Persons must always be the Ucadia Accounting System (UAS).

225. By Divine Law, in accord with the present Maxims, Venetian Bankruptcy Accounting is declared a profane injury against all forms of true Civilised Law; and a mortal transgression against the true laws of Christianity, Islam, Judaism, Hinduism, Buddhism, Sikhism, Taosim, Confucianism and traditional faiths. Venetian Bankruptcy Accounting is false, immoral and forbidden

Article 56 – Sovereign Control by Banks through Debt

226. ***Sovereign Control by Banks through Debt*** is a false, absurd and prohibited Sovereign Claim or Mandate whereby certain associations of bankers and banks assert Sovereign Control over virtually all Non-Ucadia nations. Sovereign Control by Banks through Debt

227. The concept of Banks lending money to Sovereign Persons, Entities and Bodies in order to gain control is not a recent behaviour, but one that owes it origins back to different times during the Roman Empire and other Empires:- Origin of Sovereign Control by Banks through Debt

(i) During periods of the Roman Empire, control over the money supply was briefly ceded to banking families in exchange for access to financial resources and in response to mounting debts; and

(ii) The birth of the Exchequer under Henry VIII and then through until its dissolution in 1642 on the creation of the Commonwealth of Great Britain is one of the first modern examples of banking families gaining control of the money supply to "guarantee" debt repayment on loans to the Sovereign; and

(iii) The return of Charles II in 1660 was financed by the merchant guilds of the City of London and when the Exchequer was restored, the new national debt was in excess of £10 million, with annual government expenses capped at £2 million in an annual GDP economy of around £35 million; and

(iv) The peace treaty and recognition of the United States of America in 1783 was contingent on the new Congress accepting a war debt of $42 million and surrendering control of the currency to a separate entity called the US Treasury

Department (founded 1783 not 1789) to the City of London Corporation and its subsidiary the East India Company. The fledgling United States of America was then forced to purchase millions of dollars of Annuities belonging to the East India Company. Yet by 1790, the bankers had grown the national debt owed by America to over $70 million; and

(v) By 1800, the bankers in Great Britain had succeeded in growing the national debt of the Empire to in excess of £800 million compared to an annual GDP across the empire of around £220 million, forcing the Parliament of Westminster and the Crown to yield to the power of the City of London Corporation once and for all; and to implement the agenda of the bankers through Bank of England concerning Ireland, America and the Colonies. In 1801, under 41 Geo. 3. c.3 (XXV) formalised the creation of a "corporation" acting as the "united kingdom of Great Britain and Ireland" to manage the bankruptcy, installing a Comptroller over the Exchequer.

228. The primary systems of Sovereign Control by the Banks over Sovereign People have always been Monetary, Political, Accounting, Economic and Media:-

Systems of Sovereign Control of Banks over Sovereign People

(i) ***Control of the Money Supply***: The first and primary Sovereign Control by the Banks over Sovereign People has always been control over the Money Supply of a Sovereign People, no matter how it is done, how long it takes, or how convoluted the levers of influence. In the 20th Century, such control has been made much easier with the general political acceptance of Central Banks, supported by a wall of absurd, false and deliberately misleading information to hide the levels of control and ownership of these "public" entities; and

(ii) ***Political Control & Influence***: Political Control is the second most important tool of Sovereign Control by the Banks over Sovereign People, as any major dissent or revolution causing a change of government not beholden to the banks could end the oppression of a Sovereign People and the Banks control of the Money Supply. When countries have freed themselves of bank control, the global banking fraternity has ensured the total devastation of those economies in order to "prove" no country can survive unless under the Sovereign Control by the Banks; and

(iii) ***Accounting Standards***: Accounting standards have been an essential weapon in maintaining Sovereign Control by the Banks over Sovereign People since the beginning of bankrupting Sovereign Nations, by allowing and promoting rampant corruption and misrepresentation within the accounting of government and large corporations, while unjustly enforcing a different standard on small businesses and poorer individuals; and

(iv) ***Economic Standards***: Economic standards and principles have increasingly become a key weapon in maintaining Sovereign Control by the Banks over Sovereign People through the creation of absurd, contradictory, immoral and treacherous theories through economics and then rewarding such proponents, schools and promoters so that it becomes considered a "maxim of scientific fact"; and

(v) ***Media Support and Campaigns***: The compliant media have been a cornerstone of Sovereign Control by the Banks over Sovereign People for more than three hundred years, by willingly publishing propaganda, misinformation, suppressing genuine dissent and protecting key bankers and banks.

Example of Control of Bankers using National Debt

229. An example of how bankers use national debt as Sovereign Control over a Sovereign Nation is the United States of America:-

(i) In 1783, GDP of the defeated Commonwealth of New England was estimated to be no greater than $25 million per year. However, as a condition of peace and recognition of a new country, the Congress of the United States of America was forced to accept a national debt of around $42 million and surrendering control of the currency to a separate entity called the US Treasury Department (founded 1783 not 1789) controlled by the Bank of England and the East India Company; and

(ii) By 1790, US GDP had risen on the mass importing of black slaves by the East India Company to around $50 million. However, the US national debt also rose to over $70 million; and

(iii) By 1800, US GDP significantly rose on the back of the arrival of the Dutch and the resources of the former Dutch East India Company to over $200 million. US national debt was estimated to be $83 million; and

(iv) By 1815, following the brief argument between the East India Company, the Bank of England against Wall Street, US national debt ballooned up to $119 million, while GDP was around $700 million; and

(v) By 1860, US GDP had risen to $4.9 billion, while US national debt had dwindled to almost nothing at $64.8 million. However, the Bank of England refused to release the United States of America from bankruptcy, even though Wall Street was then a greater economic power than the City of London; and

(vi) By 1865, US GDP was $9.9 billion, yet US national debt had skyrocketed to $2.6 billion; and

(vii) By 1900, US GDP was $20.7 billion, while US national debt had dropped to $2.1 billion; and

(viii) By 1913, before World War I, US GDP was $39.1 billion, while US national debt was $2.9 billion; and

(ix) By 1919, after World War I, US GDP was $78.3 billion, while US national debt was $27.3 billion; and

(x) By 1929, before the Great Depression, US GDP was $104.6 billion, while US national debt was $16.9 billion; and

(xi) By 1936, after the Great Depression and before World War II, US GDP was $84.9 billion, while US national debt was $33 billion; and

(xii) By 1945, after World War II, US GDP was $223 billion, while US national debt was $258 billion; and

(xiii) By 1960, US GDP was $543 billion, while US national debt was $286 billion; and

(xiv) By 1970, US GDP was $1,075 billion, while US national debt was $370 billion; and

(xv) By 1980, US GDP was $2,863 billion, while US national debt was $907 billion; and

(xvi) By 1990, US GDP was $5,979 billion, while US national debt was $3,233 billion; and

(xvii) By 2000, before the attacks against Wall Street, US GDP was $10,286 billion, while US national debt was $5,674 billion; and

(xviii) By 2010, after the attacks against Wall Street, US GDP was $14,958 billion, while US national debt was $13,561 billion; and

(xix) By 2020, US GDP was $21.43 trillion, while US national debt was $21.43 trillion.

230. To condemn and curse the Bankers, Banks and related Religions given their history is to perpetuate the very mechanisms that have led

Ucadia and History of Systems of

humanity under Non-Ucadia Systems to this point. Instead, under the most sacred Covenant *Pactum De Singularis Caelum*, all spiritual forces and temporal forces find common context of the past, present and future:-

Sovereign Control of Banks over Sovereign People

(i) In accord with the most sacred Covenant *Pactum De Singularis Caelum*, Ucadia Charters and the present Maxims, banks and financial institutions have a vital and integral function to play now and into the future; and

(ii) Under Ucadia Law, key global Non-Ucadia banking institutions are given the honour and opportunity to become key Ucadia financial institutions on the solemn and sacred oaths and vows of their reform and change and demonstration of their changed actions; and

(iii) Ucadia authorises its institutions to engage with Non-Ucadia banks and to seek services under agreement that will enable the growth of trade, harmony, amity and commerce between Ucadia and Non-Ucadia Civilisations; and

(iv) Under Ucadia Law, banks are forbidden from continuing practices of lending and creating debts with Sovereign Persons, Entities, Bodies, Corporations and Societies to control such Sovereigns; and

(v) Ucadia Law, Charters and Funds guarantee and underwrite all *bona fide* Non-Ucadia Banking, Non-Sovereign and Non-Government Debt for all banks with the assurance that no bank in the world who seeks to engage with Ucadia shall be permitted to fail.

Article 57 – Sovereign Authority as Descendent of Holly Family

231. ***Sovereign Authority as Descendent of Holly Family*** is a false, absurd and prohibited Sovereign Claim or Mandate whereby certain families with no historic connection to the Holly falsely assert claims of Sovereign Authority as descendants of the Holly Family.

Sovereign Authority as Descendent of Holly Family

232. The concept of making false claims of Sovereign Authority as descendants of the Holly Families began during and after the Great deaths of the 1300s following the collapse of Civilisation across much of Europe, North Africa, Middle East and Asia Minor. Examples include (but are not limited to):-

Origin of False Claim of Sovereign Authority as Descendent of Holly Family

(i) In the city of Lisbon around 1312, the Moor Aviz and Abravanel families rose as warlords by falsely asserted descent back to the Messiah Kings of the Yahudi through a corruption of the Holly bloodlines during the Age of the Holly Carolingians (700s - 1000s), claiming Charlemagne married a Moor Princess. As a result, the Aviz family became the first "Kings of Portugal" until 1580, with one of their own claimants known as "Ferdinand the Holy Prince" (1402-1443). The Aviz Moors even used two angels as supporters in their false coat of arms; and

(ii) In the city of Cairo around 1320, the Moor Maimonides family rose as warlords, falsely proclaiming heritage back to the Holly and Holly Prophets of Yeb and the New Lines of Messiah Kings of the Yahudi that ended power after the fall of the Temple of Mithra in Jerusalem in 69CE, by claiming the New Yahudi Kings bloodlines had somehow survived through a male line and they were legitimate descendants. As a result, the Maimonides became the first Moor Sultans of the Mamluk Empire of Egypt and then the Sultans of the Ottoman Empire; and

(iii) In the city of Zarazoga and then Barcelona in eastern Spain around 1316, the Moor Barcelona (Benveniste), Crescas and Levi families rose as warlords by falsely asserted descent back to the Messiah Kings of the Yahudi through a corruption of the Holly bloodlines during the Age of the Holly Carolingians (700s - 1000s), claiming Charlemagne made Aragon a Moorish Kingdom and that the royal lines of the Carolingians and the Royal Moors were intertwined. As a result, the Barcelona (Benveniste) became the first Moor "Kings of Aragon" until 1412; and

(iv) In the cities of Jaén, Medina del Campo and then Cordoba in southern Spain around 1340s, the Moor Trastámara family rose as warlords by falsely asserted descent back to the Holly Family of Jesus directly through the Holly Bloodlines of the Kings of Galicia (Northern Spain). To aid in their false claim to be directly descended from the Holly bloodline of Jesus Christ, the Trastámara formed their own "religious" order of warrior-priest knights called the "Order of Jaén" (later corrupted to Jar). As a result, the Trastámara became the first Moor "Kings of Castile" and then later the Kings of Aragon, Sicily, Sardinia, Corsica and Naples; and

(v) In the Venetian colony of Ghent (Belgium) around 1337, the wealthy Venetian Moor family of Artevelde took control of the city. On the death of dictator Jacob Artevelde in 1347, his son Johanan (John of Ghent) launched an invasion of northern

England and captured the cities of York, Lincoln and Norwich. Around 1377 on the death of Plantagentis Eduardo of Vasconia (Gascony), Johanan (John of Ghent) proclaimed himself king of England. By 1399, Johanan (John of Ghent) was defeated and killed by Plantagentis Lord Marshal Ricardo of England and the Venetian Moor Mercenaries retreated north to York, proclaiming Jacob Artevelde the younger (Henry IV) as the new King. By 1413, the pretender king Jacob the younger was captured and executed; and

(vi) From the coastal city of Vascon (Bilboa) around 1330, Basque Military leader Eduardo of Vasconia (Gascony) as *Plantagentis* (Head of French Foreign Legion) of Holly French Emperor Charles IX (King Louis X 1328-1380) did launch an attack to bring the French coastal cities back under control including Bordeaux, Bayonne, Rochelle, Nantes and Calais. By 1355, Plantagentis Eduardo of Vasconia (Gascony) did land ships at London, re-establishing order as Lord Marshal of England. On the death of Eduardo of Vasconia (Gascony) in 1377, his son Ricardo of Bordeaux did become the new Lord Marshal of England until 1422 when his son Eduardo of Roun became the new Lord Marshal of England until 1463. The last Plantagentis Lord Marshal of England was Ricardo of Angoumois who died in battle in 1485 against the Venetian funded Welsh mercenary warlord Henry Tudor of Chester. By the 17th Century, the Venetian exiles in England, began using the line of "Plantagenet" in support of the Tudor claim to be Plantagenet and blood descendants of the Holly Carolingians and thus the Holly Family; and

(vii) In 1645, Ottoman Kaizer Sultan Ibrahim I (1640-1648) commissioned occult scholar Nethaniel (Nathan) of Gaza and his school to take advantage of the newly formed claims within the English Bible (1611) and the false conversion of the ancient Holly and Yahudi Lines into the "Jewish Royal Lines". By 1648, the Ottoman leader caused a huge rift across the Islamic world by declaring he be a descendent of the newly revealed Jewish Bloodlines back to the House of David and the Prophets. Grand Vizier Kara Mustafa Pasha then arranged a coup against Ibrahim, forcing him into exile and installing Mehmed IV (1648-1687). However, Ibrahim now as Sabbatai Zevi announced his role as "Messiah of the Jews" in 1666. Ibrahim as Sabbatai Zevi was then imprisoned until his death in 1668, while some 800,000 of his devoted followers were expelled from Ottoman lands as refugees that became known as the "Ashkenazi". Tsar Alexis of Russia (1645-1676) accepted the re-settlement of the Ashkenazi on condition that they be bound to service of the Tsar to pay for the cost of their upkeep. Many of the Ashkenazi eventually migrated south to Prussia, Poland and the German states by the mid-late 18th Century to escape the cruelty of the Russian Tsars; and

(viii) By 1710, the Lithuanian-Polish noble Prince Kazimierz Czartoryski (b.1674- d.1741) sought to act against the growing economic and political threat of the now one million Ashkenazi "slaves" at the disposal of the Russian Tsars. Kazimierz Czartoryski set about making Pulawy and his palace the "center" of a revival of the Ashkenazi, to weaken the power of Russia, through recruiting a charismatic and talented young rabbi named Israel ben Eliezer (b. 1688 – d. 1780) later known as the claimed Jewish Messiah Israel Baal Shem Tov, falsely claiming Holly blood heritage back to the line of David as Jewish. With substantial funding from Kazimierz Czartoryski, an array of new false texts and scripture such as the Amsterdam Talmud were created to help form the "Pious Ones" חסידים (chasidim) movement among the Ashkenazi. The plan worked and eventually hundreds of thousands of Ashkenazi migrated to Poland and around the central hub of Pulawy. The Czartoryski continued to be the supreme patrons of Hasidism, even after Russia confiscated the family estate at Pulawy in 1794. The Czartoryski Palace of Pulawy and the Temple of Cybele was the absolute centre of the three hundred mile wide pentagram perfectly formed in World War II by the largest and worst Nazi death camps (including Auschwitz).

233. In accord with the highest Divine Law as expressed through the most sacred Covenant *Pactum De Singularis Caelum* and the present Maxims, Ucadia forbids any and all claims of Sovereign Authority as Descendent of Holly Family whether true or false:-

Ucadia and False Claims of Sovereign Authority as Descendent of Holly Family

(i) All Authority and Power of the Holly Bloodlines, also known as the Holy Bloodlines and Cuilliaéan Bloodlines are fully vested into Ucadia and all its legitimate entities, bodies, persons and offices; and

(ii) No Non-Ucadia person may claim any right or authority or power whatsoever concerning a claim of genealogy to the Holly Hyksos Pharaohs, or Great Holly Prophets of Yeb, or the original Messiah Kings of the Yahudi, or the restored lines of the Messiah Kings of the Yahudi, or the Holly Family and Bloodlines surrounding and associated with Jesus Christ, or the Holly Bloodlines of the Founder and Holly Prophet of Islam, or the Holly Bloodlines of the Kings of Ireland, or the Franks or the Saxons or any other Holy bloodline; and

(iii) Any existing noble or ancient banking or merchant family acknowledging the supremacy of Ucadia Jurisdiction therefore retains its titles and privileges, except for those that contradict the laws of Ucadia including (but not limited to) hidden and secret trusts, slavery, bondage and theft.

Article 58 – Holly (Sacred) Blood Right as "Gods among Animals"

234. ***Holly (Sacred) Blood Right as "Gods among Animals"*** is a false, absurd and prohibited Sovereign Claim or Mandate formalised in 1854 whereby the twelve most powerful and wealthy noble families of the time were recognised by the Roman Catholic Church as the as ***Domus Domini*** and ***Desposyni*** (literally "The House of the Lord") and claimed descendent from the Holly and thus descended from "Immaculate Mary" and "born without sin" and the only rightful heirs to all the land of the world, including all other people as property and "creatures".

Holly (Sacred) Blood Right as "Gods among Animals"

235. The concept of a few people descended from a particular line of the "Holly" being "born without sin" and the only rightful heirs to all the land of the world, including all other people as property and "creatures" is a wicked, vile and false notion created not earlier than 1854 in collusion with Venetian Pope Pius IX (1845-1878) and the highest officials and administration of the Roman Catholic Church:-

Holly (Sacred) Blood Right as "Gods among Animals"

(i) Beginning in 1848 through to 1849, riots, rebellions and threats of revolutions erupted almost "simultaneously" across more than 17 major cities of Europe including (but not limited to) Paris, Berlin, Prague, Rome, Munich, Vienna, Milan, Venice, Budapest, Bucharest and Palermo. In the aftermath, the American banking families of New York were blamed for fanning the flames of instability in Europe through the notions of "freedom", "equality" and "democracy"; and

(ii) One of the groups blamed was the secretive lodge network of pro-Zionist activists first born out of New York in 1843 called the "B'nai B'rith" – an organisation a century later was instrumental in helping form the state of Israel; and

(iii) The creation of the idea of the *Domus Domini* and *Desposyni* ("The House of the Lord") and claimed descendent from the Holly and thus descended from "Immaculate Mary" and "born without sin" was intended to bring an end to the proxy wars between banking families and old European noble families, and to stabilise the "rule of order". However, the decision appeared to have sparked several strategic actions with consequences that caused the removal from power of many of these families; and

(iv) The first and most immediate reaction to the nomination of the twelve families of the *Domus Domini* and *Desposyni* by 1854 was for King Victor Emmanuel II of Sardinia and the House of Savoy to effectively "declare war" against the Vatican and Papal States. By 1860, the House of Savoy succeeded first in training and landing a revolutionary force of several thousand led by Giuseppe Garibaldi in Sicily. The revolutionaries quickly defeated all resistance but were stopped by Victor Emmanuel II in attacking Rome. By 1861, all the Papal States had been lost, Pope Pius IX was a prisoner and Victor Emmanuel II became the first King of a unified Italy (1861-1878) in over 1,400 years, calling himself *Pater Patriae* meaning literally "Father of the Fatherland" as superior to all the other families he was excluded from joining; and

(v) In New York and in London, the events and consequences in the creation of the concept of "Immaculate Mary" propelled some of the most powerful Dutch and Jewish merchant banking families to conceive of their own plans. New York had become one of the most powerful banking centres of the world and virtually all of its dominant families (including but not limited to the Stuyvesant, Vanderbilt, Du Pont and Astor families had a deep hatred of the House of Orange-Nassau. To see the former *Stadtholders* of the Dutch Republic raised as "holy monarchs" by the Catholic Church would have been the last straw. Similarly, the Rothschilds themselves had no love of nobility. Thus a vision was formed out of New York of not only an elite group called the *Beit Miriam* (בית מרים) (House of Mary), but in forming a New Rome as Washington and a new state based religion of "Secularism" by 1864; and

(vi) On October 28, 1965 for the first time in history, the Catholic Church promulgated a new official doctrine called *Nostra Aetate* (Latin for "In Our Time") during the Second Vatican Council, that fundamentally changed its teachings about Jews and Judaism, including the claim that Christianity came from Judaism; and that Jesus and his parents (Mary and Joseph) were observant Jews; and that Jews were not to blame for the death of Jesus; and Judaism and Christianity must develop greater cooperation, dialogue and respect; and that anti-Semitism must be condemned in all its forms; and

(vii) The consequences of the doctrines that came from the Second Vatican Council in 1965 is that those families proclaiming Jewish heritage and descent from Mary (Miriam) such as the elite banking and merchant families via *Beit Miriam* (בית מרים) (House of Mary) subsequently had a stronger claim than the original noble families of 1854.

Twelve "Apostolic" Noble Families

236. The original twelve "Apostolic" Noble Houses from 1854 that held the exclusive right and authority of *Parens Patriae* as *Domus Domini* and *Desposyni* ("The House of the Lord") providing a particular House still remained in power included:-

(i) ***House of Habsburg-Lorraine***: The last ruler from the House of Habsburg-Lorraine to reign over the Kingdom of Austria was Emperor Charles I of Austria, also known as Charles IV of Hungary. However, his reign was short-lived and marked by the collapse of the Austro-Hungarian Empire. Emperor Charles I's reign came to an end in 1918 with the end of World War I and the dissolution of the Austro-Hungarian Empire. From 1919 the Habsburg were forbidden by Austrian law from ever ruling again; and

(ii) ***House of Hanover***: The last kingdom to be held by the House of Hanover was the United Kingdom. The House of Hanover ruled the United Kingdom from 1714 until 1901 and the death of Queen Victoria; and

(iii) ***House of Saxe-Coburg and Gotha (Windsor)***: Queen Victoria was succeeded by her eldest son, Albert Edward, who became King Edward VII (1901-1910) and the first monarch of the House of Saxe-Coburg and Gotha. In 1917, due to anti-German sentiment during World War I, the British royal family changed their name to the House of Windsor; and

(iv) ***House of Hohenzollern***: The Hohenzollern family ruled the Kingdom of Prussia and later the German Empire. The last ruler from the House of Hohenzollern to reign over the Kingdom of Prussia was Wilhelm II who became the German Emperor (Kaiser) and King of Prussia in 1888. His rule ended in November 1918 with the conclusion of World War I and the German Revolution of 1918-1919; and

(v) ***House of Wettin***: The House of Wettin included the rulers of the Kingdom of Saxony and various other German states. The last ruler of the Kingdom of Saxony from the House of

Wettin was King Frederick Augustus III of Saxony (1904-1918). His rule ended in November 1918 with the conclusion of World War I and the German Revolution of 1918-1919; and

(vi) ***House of Wittelsbach***: The House of Wittelsbach ruled the Kingdom of Bavaria and had significant influence in southern Germany. The last ruler from the House of Wittelsbach to reign over the Kingdom of Bavaria was King Ludwig III of Bavaria (1913-1918). The monarchy was abolished in 1918 following the end of World War I and the German Revolution of 1918-1919; and

(vii) ***House of Orange-Nassau***: The House of Orange-Nassau was restored as the royal family of the Netherlands in 1815 following the defeat of Napoleon, including the sovereign rights of any land held by the Republic of the United Netherlands prior to 1795. The House of Orange-Nassau have remained monarchs ever since; and

(viii) ***House of Romanov***: The Romanov family was the ruling dynasty of Russia, with Tsars and Emperors in the 18th and 19th centuries. The last ruler from the House of Romanov was Tsar Nicholas II (1894-1917). He and his entire family were murdered on order of the Bolshevik leaders on July 17, 1918; and

(ix) ***House of Braganza***: The House of Braganza ruled Portugal, and later the Empire of Brazil. The last ruler from the House of Braganza to reign over the Kingdom of Portugal was King Manuel II of Portugal (1908-1910). He was deposed in the Republican Revolution of October 1910, which resulted in the overthrow of the monarchy and the establishment of the Portuguese First Republic; and

(x) ***House of Bonaparte***: First reaching noble status under Napoleon I, the family continued to be recognised by Vatican as the Kings of Rome and rightful heirs to France. By 1852, Napoleon III became Emperor of the French until 1870 and the last monarch of France; and

(xi) ***House of Oldenburg***: The House of Oldenburg with links to Denmark since the 15th century has had branches that rule or have ruled in Denmark, Iceland, Greece, Norway, Russia, Sweden, the United Kingdom. A cadet branch of the House of Oldenburg, being the House of Glücksburg, became monarchs of Denmark since 1863; and

(xii) ***House of Bourbon***: The House of Bourbon that included various branches like the House of Bourbon-Orléans and House of Bourbon-Spain, ruled over France, Spain, and other European regions. Queen Isabella II of the House of Bourbon was deposed in 1868 following the Spanish Revolution. However, her son Alfonso XII (1870-1885) was restored in 1870. The House of Bourbon was again deposed by 1931 upon the creation of the Spanish Republic. The House of Bourbon was finally restored to power in 1975 through Juan Carlos I (1975-2014).

237. Some of the original Banking and Merchant Houses from 1855-56 that first declared themselves to hold the exclusive rights of *Custos Rotalorum* (Keeper of the Slave Rolls) and *Ius Gentium* (Customary Laws of Medieval Moneylending and Banking later "repackaged" as Law of Nations) as *Beit Miriam* (ית מרים) ("The House of Mary") include but are not limited to:-

Founding Families of the Beit Miriam (House of Mary)

(i) ***House of Rothschild***: The descendents of Thomas (Jacob) Roth (Wroth) (1584-1672), the first *Lord Chamberlain* (Treasurer) of the Commonwealth Government of Great Britain (1642-1660). The family originally being of famous Venetian origin, namely via exiled Jacopo (Jacob) Foscari (exiled to London in 1445), son of Doge Francesco Foscari (1423-1457). The name *Roth* variously meaning "red, disc, rim of wheel, fury and punishment" and was probably selected by the Foscari in England given the family history. After the death of Thomas (Oliver) Pride in 1658, the Roth left England to Hanover in Germany and the protection of the Dukes of Brunswick-Lüneburg as the "Rothschild" family, converting to Judaism. Thomas (Jacob) Roth (Rothschild) soon after became the unofficial Mayer (Mayor and Treasurer) of the city of Hanover and private bankers on behalf of the dukes. The family returned to London by 1757 after the death of family patriarch Mayer Amschel Jacob Rothschild (b.1710 – d.1757) following the Battle of Hastenbeck and brief occupation of the city of Hanover. Under Mayer Amschel Rothschild (b. 1734 – d. 1812) the Rothschilds repeatedly refused senior government positions, noble titles and offer to control of the Bank of England by George III (1760-1820), arguing that any such position could put the Hanover monarchy at risk as well as the banking interests of the Rothschilds in jeopardy. By 1790, the Hanovers personally owed the Rothschilds over £30m and the crown through the City of London and Bank of England owed the Rothschilds more than £200m in growing senior debt. By 1799, the British Empire was technically bankrupt owing more than £700m and unable to continue fund its military campaign against Napoleon. The Rothschilds successfully orchestrated that the whole British Empire and all its territories known as the Kingdom of Great Britain and Ireland be placed in bankruptcy by 1800, operating then as the United Kingdom, under the control of the Bank of London through the City of London that the Rothschilds then placed in private bankruptcy to its private banks. Mayer Amschel Rothschild then left for the city of Frankfurt where he lived until 1812. The Rothschild family did not officially have any direct members in New York until after 1870; and

(ii) ***House of Stuyvesant***: The descendents of Peter Stuyvesant (1610-1672) the last Dutch Director-General of New Netherlands. The family for a time became viewed among the other families as the *defacto* sovereign when from 1784 the British crown fully restored the Dutch Republic rights to Manhattan Island, Albany New York and Newcastle Delaware; and

(iii) ***House of Vanderbilt***: The descendents of the famous De Witt family that ruled Holland and were major shareholders of the Dutch East India Company (VOC) under the Dutch Republic until 1672. Historic enemies of the House of Orange-Nassau who returned to power in 1672 and murdered many of its members. As a result, the family was forced to flee with their ships and fortune to the old colony of New Amsterdam (now New York). It is where they changed their name and history to Vanderbilt and continued to be involved in the trade of the VOC, including moving its operations to New York from 1784. In the 19th Century they were regarded as one of the wealthiest families in the world; and

(iv) ***House of Du Pont***: The descendents of the Amsterdam branch of the famous 16th Century Trip family of Swedish arms manufacturers. Under the Dutch Republic, the Trip family quickly became one of the wealthiest of all patrician families as primary investors of the Dutch West India Company (GWC). The family returned to its primary business of gunpowder and arms manufacturing after escaping to New York with other Patrician families by 1795, changing their name to "Du Pont" (meaning to travel or ferry). By the mid 19th Century was again one of the wealthiest families in the world; and

(v) ***House of Astor***: The descendents of the famous diamond and pearl merchant Kiliaen van Rensselaer (1586-1643), one of the founders of the Dutch West India Company and New Netherlands settlements. His land holding of Rensselaerswyck along the Hudson River made the family one of the richest land holders ever in America. Prior to losing the colonies by 1672, the van Rensselaer family had an early monopoly on the fur trade. Thereafter, the family switched its business interests to opium and the African slave trade, before escaping back to New York with other Patrician families by 1795. The rights of the van Rensselaer to Rensselaerswyck continued to be honoured by the American government to at least 1830s. In around 1812, the family changed its name to "Astor" after the fur trading post (Fort Astor) it established as part of a new monopoly along the Columbia River.

Article 59 – Sacrifice of Animals & Humans for Divine Favour

238. ***Sacrifice of Animals & Humans for Divine Favour to Rule*** is a false, absurd and prohibited Sovereign Claim or Mandate of ancient origin whereby claimants to Sovereign Authority and Power ritualistically sacrifice animals and humans under the false, misguided and deluded beliefs that such actions grant them "divine favour" and ensure the success, legitimacy and stability of their reign. Such actions are completely and absolutely forbidden, condemned and suppressed under the most sacred Covenant *Pactum De Singularis Caelum*; and in accord with the sacred Covenant it is hereby stated that no such action of sacrifice whether by war, occult ritual or any other method shall produce any "divine favour" or power or supernatural effect whatsoever.

Sacrifice of Animals & Humans as Divine Favour to Rule

239. The largest method of sacrificing humans for "divine favour" by sovereigns is and has always been by warfare. Since the first civilisations, almost every major conflict has been fought as a battle of religious ideologies but with all sides usually glorifying their dead:-

False and Deluded Practices of Human Sacrifice through War

(i) The glorification of war as a form of "willing sacrifice" of the people of their sons and daughters remains a false, deluded and present mythology and belief within contemporary cultures. In many European capitals and American cities, there are shrines with an eternal flame implying the sacrifice of war to Moloch and G-d; and upon many war monuments, the words "Glorious Dead" is repeated across the world; and

(ii) Even under modern illegal and immoral conflicts such as those in the middle east and in parts of Europe and Asia, the mythology persists that such warfare is a matter of morality under the actual or implied "divine favour" of G-d or some other deity.

240. Whilst the practice of sacrificing animals to appease favour of certain gods is an ancient practice throughout many regimes of civilisations, such as Roman Emperors, the large scale sacrifice of human beings (most commonly by fire) has been almost the exclusive practice of worshipping Baal Moloch, also known as El, Sabaoth, G-d and Satan. The worst ancient and pre-modern sites for human sacrifice in history include (but are not limited to):-

False, Criminal and Deluded Occult Practices of Animal & Human Sacrifice for Divine Favour

(i) ***Urgarit*** in Northern Syria was known as the home to Yahudi and the infamous Biblical birthplace of human sacrifice in worship of the "golden calf" of Baal El, until more than a million Yahudi were captured by Egyptian General Pa-ra-mes-su (Ramesses) by 1290 BCE and sent back to Egypt as slaves; and

(ii) ***Carthage*** in North Africa was a city adopted by tens of thousands of Yahudi refugees and by the 11th Century BCE became an infamous ancient site for mass human sacrifice to Baal Moloch by fire and the original birthplace of the specific term ***Holocaust*** meaning a "burnt offering of human flesh to Moloch (Sabaoth, G-d and Satan)"; and

(iii) ***Jerusalem*** by the 7th Century BCE became a terrible site for Yahudi practices of human sacrifice to Baal Moloch by fire; and

(iv) ***Babylon*** by the 6th Century BCE became a new prison for Yahudi priests captured from Jerusalem, who were known to have continued the secret practice of human sacrifice to Baal Moloch by burning; and

(v) ***Baalbek*** in Lebanon, also known as the Temple of Solomon, from the 6th Century BCE became arguably the most infamous ancient site for human sacrifice to Baal Moloch as Baal Hamon; and

(vi) ***London*** from the mid 16th Century saw the return of Holocaust rituals for the first time in more than 1600 years through the public ritual known as Immolation (literally meaning "in the name of Moloch") or simply "Burning at the Stake". In 1666, the second largest mass sacrifice by fire to Moloch was orchestrated by deliberately lit fires that trapped and killed more than 300,000 inhabitants of old London to invoke "divine favour" in the ascendency of Charles II under the new arrangement of power and for the future success of the Kingdom of Great Britain to come; and

(vii) The worst Holocaust in the name of Moloch in history and the worst unpunished crime against humanity for 1,000 years was the mass sacrifice by fire of more than six million protestants, ethnic minorities and Jews starting exactly on September 11, 1941 (9/11), through specifically designed centres of human sacrifice mirroring ancient temple sites creating a giant pentagram in Poland, in order to invoke "divine favour" for the creation of the great secret pentagram known as the ***Pentagon*** in the rededication of ***Washington DC*** and the birth of the American Imperial Exceptionalism. Each of the five special concentration camps that started sacrificing people from September 11, 1941 (9/11) were designed to mirror-image the footprint of ancient temple sites to Moloch. Treblinka mirror inverted the ancient sacrifice site of Urgarit; and Janowska mirror inverted the ancient sacrifice site of Jerusalem; and Auschwitz mirror inverted the ancient sacrifice site of Baalbek; and Lodz mirror inverted the ancient sacrifice site of Carthage; and Sobibor mirror inverted the ancient sacrifice site of Babylon. At the center of the Pentagram was the spiritual birthplace to Hasidic Judaism. The positioning of this infrastructure was not to create a perfectly shaped pentagram, but to make sure the top of the pentagram aligned with the North Star above the Arctic and the negative "ley lines" of the pentagram intersected most of the major occult centres of Europe including but not limited to Rome, Carthage, Zurich, Munich, Stockholm, Hanover, Bordeaux, Zagreb, Odessa, Bucharest, Belgorod, St Petersburg, Nizhsny Novgorod and the Shetland Islands. If the positions of the sacrifice camps were even a few kilometres off their intentional position, then the "ley lines" would not have intersected these centres.

Title III – Sovereign Rights

3.1 – Sovereign Rights

Article 60 – Sovereign Rights

241. ***Sovereign Rights*** (*Iurium Regnum*), are a sub-class of Superior Rights associated with the embodiment of a valid *Sovereign Legal Entity* as defined by the most sacred Covenant *Pactum De Singularis Caelum*. Sovereign Rights

242. In accord with the most sacred Covenant *Pactum De Singularis Caelum,* all valid and legitimate *Sovereign Rights* are derived from Ecclesiastical Rights; and a Sovereign Right can never claim to be higher than Ecclesiastical Rights. Sovereign Rights derived from Ecclesiastical Rights

243. There exists six (6) categories of seventy-seven (77) Superior Rights within the sub-class of Sovereign Rights, being: Authoritative (11), Instrumental (22), Writs (11), Bills (11), Decrees (11) and Notices (11): Categories of Sovereign Rights

(i) "**Authoritative Sovereign Rights**" (*Potentis Regnum Iurium*) is Sovereign Rights associated with the core ecclesiastical authoritative powers; and

(ii) "**Instrumental Sovereign Rights**" (*Instrumentalis Regnum Iurium*) is Sovereign Rights essential to the proper administration of Sovereign Rights; and

(iii) "**Sovereign Writs of Rights**" (*Recto Regnum Iurium*) is Sovereign Rights associated with the one, true and only forms of Original Entry and Original Action; and

(iv) "**Sovereign Bills of Exception & Agreement**" (*Rogatio Regnum Iurium*) is Sovereign Rights associated with the one, true and only forms of Bills of Exception, Citation and Agreement; and

(v) "**Sovereign Decrees**" (*Decretum Regnum Iurium*) is Sovereign Rights associated with sovereign decrees concerning the administration, conduct and enforcement of law and order; and

(vi) "**Sovereign Notices**" (*Notitiae Regnum Iurium*) is Sovereign Rights associated with sovereign notices issued, executed, patented, promulgated and services in the proper administration, conduct and enforcement of law and order.

244. The source of any, every and all valid and proper Sovereign Rights is the most sacred Covenant *Pactum De Singularis Caelum* and no other. Any claim or mandate that contradicts this Rule is therefore Source of all valid and proper Sovereign Rights invalid, false, unlawful and without any merit or force of law.

245. No Person, Entity, Body, Agency or Thing shall possess any valid or legitimate claim or mandate to any Sovereign Right, unless granted and delegated in accord with the most sacred Covenant *Pactum De Singularis Caelum* and these present Maxims. Valid and legitimate Sovereign Rights

3.2 – Authoritative Sovereign Rights

Article 61 – Authoritative Sovereign Rights

246. ***Authoritative Sovereign Rights*** (*Potentis Regnum Iurium*) are Sovereign Rights associated with the core sovereign authoritative powers. Authoritative Sovereign Rights

247. All *Authoritative Sovereign Rights* are delegated by proper *Mandate* to the Governments of valid and legitimate Sovereign Ucadia Bodies and Entities (including but not limited to Ucadia Universities, Provinces, Campuses, Foundations and Agencies); and to those existing and internationally recognised Non-Ucadian Sovereign Bodies and Entities by in force treaties and agreements in accord with the most sacred Covenant *Pactum De Singularis Caelum*. Delegation of Authoritative Sovereign Rights

248. All *Authoritative Sovereign Rights* are assumed to be automatically invoked through the proper operation and function of the Governing Instruments, Codes and Bylaws of valid and legitimate Sovereign Ucadia Bodies and Entities (including but not limited to Ucadia Universities, Provinces, Campuses, Foundations and Agencies); and through the operation and function of in force treaties and agreements with existing and internationally recognised Non-Ucadian Sovereign Bodies and Entities. Invocation of Authoritative Sovereign Rights

249. The following valid eleven (11) *Authoritative Sovereign Rights* (*Potentis Regnum Iurium*) is recognised in accord with the most sacred Covenant *Pactum De Singularis Caelum* and these present Maxims:- List of Authoritative Sovereign Rights (Potentis Regnum Iurium)

(i) "**Ius Regnum**" are the primary collection of Sovereign Rights, as inherited from the collection of Divine Rights *Ius Divinum Regnum*; and

(ii) "**Ius Regnum Cancellarium**" are the collection of Sovereign Rights of Chancery and Administrative Records, as inherited from the collection of Ecclesiastical Rights *Ius Ecclesiae Cancellarium*; and

(iii) "**Ius Regnum Consilium**" are the collection of Sovereign Rights of a Legislative and Advisory Authority, as inherited from the collection of Ecclesiastical Rights *Ius Ecclesiae Consilium*; and

(iv) "**Ius Regnum Collegium**" are the collection of Sovereign Rights of a Company or Charitable Body, as inherited from the collection of Ecclesiastical Rights *Ius Ecclesiae Collegium*; and

(v) "**Ius Regnum Officium**" are the collection of Sovereign Rights of Office, Duty and Service, as inherited from the collection of Ecclesiastical Rights *Ius Ecclesiae Officium*; and

(vi) "**Ius Regnum Imperium**" are the collection of Sovereign Rights of Command, Occupation and Enforcement, as inherited from the collection of Ecclesiastical Rights *Ius Ecclesiae Imperium*; and

(vii) "**Ius Regnum Custoditum**" are the collection of Sovereign Rights of Custody, Guardianship and Preservation, as inherited from the collection of Ecclesiastical Rights *Ius Ecclesiae Custoditum*; and

(viii) "**Ius Regnum Oratorium**" are the collection of Sovereign Rights to a Competent Forum of Law and Review, as inherited from the collection of Ecclesiastical Rights *Ius Ecclesiae Oratorium*; and

(ix) "**Ius Regnum Templum**" are the collection of Sovereign Rights of a Treasury or Financial (Banking) Body, as inherited from the collection of Ecclesiastical Rights *Ius Ecclesiae Templum*; and

(x) "**Ius Regnum Commercium**" are the collection of Sovereign Rights to Trade, Exchange and Communication, as inherited from the collection of Divine Rights *Ius Ecclesiae Commercium*; and

(xi) "**Ius Regnum Decretum**" are the collection of Sovereign Rights to issue Decree, Judgement and Edict, as inherited from the collection of Ecclesiastical Rights *Ius Ecclesiae Decretum*.

Article 62 – Ius Regnum (Sovereign Rights)

250. ***Ius Regnum*** are the primary collection of Sovereign Rights, as inherited from the collection of Divine Rights *Ius Divinum Regnum*. Ius Regnum (Sovereign Rights)

251. *Ius Regnum* (Sovereign Rights) is the first collection of eleven Authoritative Sovereign Rights (*Potentis Regnum Iurium*); and may be explicitly invoked or referenced by Sovereign Right of Action through a proper and registered Sovereign Entity and the Sovereign Obligations of any such registered Sovereign Person or Executive Office in Ucadia or Non-Ucadia Jurisdiction. Invoking of Ius Regnum (Sovereign Rights)

252. The collection of Sovereign Rights of *Ius Regnum* contains eight (8) Rights being:- Collection of Ius Regnum (Sovereign Rights)

(i) *Ius Regnum* being the Sovereign Right of the Sovereign Authority or Body; and

(ii) *Ius Regnum Integritatis Territorialis* being the Sovereign Right of Territorial Integrity; and

(iii) *Ius Regnum Independendiae Politicae* being the Sovereign Right of Political Independence; and

(iv) *Ius Regnum Recognitionis Souveranae* being the Sovereign Right of Sovereign Recognition; and

(v) *Ius Regnum Summae Iurisdictionis* being the Sovereign Right of Supreme Jurisdiction; and

(vi) *Ius Regnum Defensionis Souveranae* being the Sovereign Right of Sovereign Self Defence; and

(vii) *Ius Regnum Relationum Diplomaticarum* being the Sovereign Right of Diplomatic Relations; and

(viii) *Ius Regnum Foederum Faciendorum* being the Sovereign Right to Make Treaties with other States.

Article 63 – Ius Regnum Cancellarium (Chancery & Administration)

253. ***Ius Regnum Cancellarium*** are the collection of Sovereign Rights of Chancery and Administrative Records, as inherited from the collection of Ecclesiastical Rights *Ius Ecclesiae Cancellarium*. Ius Regnum Cancellarium (Chancery & Administration)

254. *Ius Regnum Cancellarium* (Chancery & Administration) is the second collection of eleven Authoritative Sovereign Rights (*Potentis Regnum Iurium*); and may be explicitly invoked or referenced by Invoking of Ius Regnum Cancellarium

Sovereign Right of Action through a proper and registered Sovereign Entity and the Sovereign Obligations of any such registered Sovereign Person or Executive Office in Ucadia or Non-Ucadia Jurisdiction.

255. The collection of Sovereign Rights of *Ius Regnum Cancellarium* contains six (6) Rights being:- Collection of Ius Regnum Cancellarium

(i) *Ius Regnum Cancellarium* being the Sovereign Right of Chancery and Administration of Records; and

(ii) *Ius Regnum Aedificandi Cancellariae* being the Sovereign Right of Chancery Building; and

(iii) *Ius Regnum Procedendi Cancellariae* being the Sovereign Right of Chancery Procedures; and

(iv) *Ius Regnum Technologiae Cancellariae* being the Sovereign Right of Chancery Technology and Digital Systems; and

(v) *Ius Regnum Cancellarii* being the Sovereign Right of the Chancellor; and

(vi) *Ius Regnum Cancellarii Immunitatis* being the Sovereign Right of Immunity for Chancellor and Agents when Decisions and Actions Made in Office in Good Faith, Good Conscience and Good Actions.

Article 64 – Ius Regnum Consilium (Legislative)

256. ***Ius Regnum Consilium*** are the collection of Sovereign Rights of a Legislative and Advisory Authority, as inherited from the collection of Ecclesiastical Rights *Ius Ecclesiae Consilium*. Ius Regnum Consilium (Legislative)

257. *Ius Regnum Consilium* (Legislative) is the third collection of eleven Authoritative Sovereign Rights (*Potentis Regnum Iurium*); and may be explicitly invoked or referenced by Sovereign Right of Action through a proper and registered Sovereign Entity and the Sovereign Obligations of any such registered Sovereign Person or Executive Office in Ucadia or Non-Ucadia Jurisdiction. Invoking of Ius Regnum Consilium (Legislative)

258. The collection of Sovereign Rights of *Ius Regnum Consilium* contains twelve (12) Rights being:- Collection of Ius Regnum Consilium (Legislative)

(i) *Ius Regnum Consilium* being the Sovereign Right of a Legislative and Advisory Body; and

(ii) *Ius Regnum Regulas Parlamentarias* being the Sovereign Right to Parliamentary Rules of Conduct and Process; and

(iii) *Ius Regnum Privilegii Parlamentarii* being the Sovereign

Right of Parliamentary Privilege; and

(iv) *Ius Regnum Votandi Parliamento* being the Sovereign Right of Parliamentary Vote; and

(v) *Ius Regnum Quaestionis Parliamento* being the Sovereign Right of Parliamentary Question; and

(vi) *Ius Regnum Informationis Parliamento* being the Sovereign Right of Parliamentary Information; and

(vii) *Ius Regnum Leges Faciendi* being the Sovereign Right to Make Laws; and

(viii) *Ius Regnum Leges Disputandi* being the Sovereign Right to Debate (Proposed and Existing) Laws; and

(ix) *Ius Regnum Leges Emendandi* being the Sovereign Right to Amend Laws; and

(x) *Ius Regnum Leges Conlucere* being the Sovereign Right to Consolidate Laws; and

(xi) *Ius Regnum Leges Abrogandi* being the Sovereign Right to Repeal Laws; and

(xii) *Ius Regnum Supervisionis Executivae* being the Sovereign Right of Executive Oversight.

Article 65 – Ius Regnum Collegium (Company or Charitable Body)

259. ***Ius Regnum Collegium*** are the collection of Sovereign Rights of a Company or Charitable Body, as inherited from the collection of Ecclesiastical Rights *Ius Ecclesiae Collegium*. Ius Regnum Collegium (Company or Charitable Body)

260. *Ius Regnum Collegium* (Company or Charitable Body) is the fourth collection of eleven Authoritative Sovereign Rights (*Potentis Regnum Iurium*); and may be explicitly invoked or referenced by Sovereign Right of Action through a proper and registered Sovereign Entity and the Sovereign Obligations of any such registered Sovereign Person or Executive Office in Ucadia or Non-Ucadia Jurisdiction. Invoking of Ius Regnum Collegium (Company or Charitable Body)

261. The collection of Sovereign Rights of *Ius Regnum Collegium* contains twenty-nine (29) Rights being:- Collection of Ius Regnum Collegium (Company or Charitable Body)

(i) *Ius Regnum Collegium* being the Sovereign Right of Company or Charitable Body; and

(ii) *Ius Regnum Convocationis Formatio* being the Sovereign Right of Convocation of Members to Form Under granted Charter listing Key Rights and Constitution or Bylaws or

Statutes; and

(iii) *Ius Regnum Conventum Formatio* being the Sovereign Right of Assembly of Members to Form Under Memorandum of Key Objects and Articles; and

(iv) *Ius Regnum Conventionis Formatio* being the Sovereign Right of Convention of Members to Form Under Declaration of Key Objects and Constitution; and

(v) *Ius Regnum Incorporationis Collegii Existentis* being the Sovereign Right of Incorporating Existing Company, Body or Entity into a Jurisdiction; and

(vi) *Ius Regnum Novi Collegii Incorporationis* being the Sovereign Right of Incorporating a New Company, Body or Entity (and its Governing Instrument) into a Jurisdiction; and

(vii) *Ius Regnum Incorporationis Exterae* being the Sovereign Right of Incorporating an Existing Company, Body or Entity into a Foreign Jurisdiction (to its original jurisdiction); and

(viii) *Ius Regnum Personae Iuridicae* being the Sovereign Right of Legal Personality for an Incorporated Company, Body or Entity; and

(ix) *Ius Regnum Proprietatis Collegii* being the Sovereign Right of Property Ownership and Rights for an Incorporated Company, Body or Entity; and

(x) *Ius Regnum Iurium Financiariorum Collegii* being the Sovereign Right of Financial and Banking Rights for an Incorporated Company, Body or Entity; and

(xi) *Ius Regnum Iurium Fornitorum Collegii* being the Sovereign Right of Supplier Rights for an Incorporated Company, Body or Entity; and

(xii) *Ius Regnum Iurium Operariorum Collegii* being the Sovereign Right of Employee Rights for an Incorporated Company, Body or Entity; and

(xiii) *Ius Regnum Iurium Conventus Collegii* being the Sovereign Right of Agreement Rights for an Incorporated Company, Body or Entity; and

(xiv) *Ius Regnum Commercium Collegii* being the Sovereign Right to Engage in Business and Commerce for an Incorporated Company, Body or Entity; and

(xv) *Ius Regnum Gubernandi Collegii* being the Sovereign Right to Corporate Governance for an Incorporated Company, Body or

Entity; and

(xvi) *Ius Regnum Rationem Financiariam* being the Sovereign Right to Financial Reporting; and

(xvii) *Ius Regnum Limitandae Responsabilitatis* being the Sovereign Right to Limit Liability of Shareholders, Directors and Employees within the Governing Instruments of the Incorporated Company, Body or Entity; and

(xviii) *Ius Regnum Observandae Iurisdictionis* being the Sovereign Right of Compliance within Jurisdiction of Incorporation; and

(xix) *Ius Regnum Remunerationis Directoris* being the Sovereign Right of Director Remuneration; and

(xx) *Ius Regnum Conventum Directorum* being the Sovereign Right to Director Meeting(s); and

(xxi) *Ius Regnum Conventum Generalium Partium* being the Sovereign Right of General Shareholders Meetings; and

(xxii) *Ius Regnum Conventum Extraordinarium Partium* being the Sovereign Right of Extraordinary Shareholders Meetings; and

(xxiii) *Ius Regnum Capitis Collegii* being the Sovereign Right of Share Capital; and

(xxiv) *Ius Regnum Mutationis Capitis Collegii* being the Sovereign Right to Change Share Capital; and

(xxv) *Ius Regnum Collegii Vendendi* being the Sovereign Right of Sale of Company, Body or Entity with another Body; and

(xxvi) *Ius Regnum Collegii Fusionis* being the Sovereign Right of Merger of Company, Body or Entity with another Body; and

(xxvii) *Ius Regnum Collegii Administrationis* being the Sovereign Right of Administration of Company, Body or Entity with another Body; and

(xxviii) *Ius Regnum Collegii Deregistrationis* being the Sovereign Right of Deregistration of previously registered (and incorporated) Company, Body or Entity; and

(xxix) *Ius Regnum Collegii Dissolutionis* being the Sovereign Right of Dissolution of Company, Body or Entity.

Article 66 – Ius Regnum Officium (Office)

262. ***Ius Regnum Officium*** are the collection of Sovereign Rights of Office, Duty and Service, as inherited from the collection of Ecclesiastical Rights *Ius Ecclesiae Officium*. Ius Regnum Officium (Office)

263. *Ius Regnum Officium* (Office) is the fifth collection of eleven Authoritative Sovereign Rights (*Potentis Regnum Iurium*); and may be explicitly invoked or referenced by Sovereign Right of Action through a proper and registered Sovereign Entity and the Sovereign Obligations of any such registered Sovereign Person or Executive Office in Ucadia or Non-Ucadia Jurisdiction. Invoking of Ius Regnum Officium (Office)

264. The collection of Sovereign Rights of *Ius Regnum Officium* contains fifteen (15) Rights being:- Collection of Ius Regnum Officium (Office)

(i) *Ius Regnum Officium* being the Sovereign Right of Office, Duty and Service; and

(ii) *Ius Regnum Petendi Candidatum Officium* being the Sovereign Right to Apply to be Candidate for Office; and

(iii) *Ius Regnum Formandum Comitatum* being the Sovereign Right to Form a Campaign as Candidate for Office; and

(iv) *Ius Regnum Candidati Officium* being the Sovereign Right to Run a Campaign as Candidate for Office; and

(v) *Ius Regnum Eligendi* being the Sovereign Right to be Elected as Candidate for Office; and

(vi) *Ius Regnum Clausurae Comitatus* being the Sovereign Right to Close a Campaign for Office; and

(vii) *Ius Regnum Mandati Officii* being the Sovereign Right to Receive Mandate in Good Faith, Good Conscience and Good Actions to Occupy an Office; and

(viii) *Ius Regnum Tenendi Officii* being the Sovereign Right to Hold an Office in Good Faith, Good Conscience and Good Actions; and

(ix) *Ius Regnum Immunitatis Officii* being the Sovereign Right of Immunity for Decisions Made in Office in Good Faith, Good Conscience and Good Actions; and

(x) *Ius Regnum Abdicandi Officii* being the Sovereign Right to Retire from Office in Honour, Privileges and Good Standing; and

(xi) *Ius Regnum Dicendi Officii* being the Sovereign Right to Resign from Office in Honour, Privileges and Good Standing; and

(xii) *Ius Regnum Nullius Mandati* being the Sovereign Right to have Mandate Withdrawn and be Terminated from Office in Disgrace, Without Privileges and Poor Standing; and

(xiii) *Ius Regnum Accusationi Officii* being the Sovereign Right to Face Impeachment for Claims of Bad Faith, Bad Conscience or Bad Actions in Office; and

(xiv) *Ius Regnum Removendi Officii* being the Sovereign Right to be Removed by Force from Office in Disgrace, Without Privileges and Poor Standing upon being found Culpable from Impeachment; and

(xv) *Ius Regnum Restituendi Officii* being the Sovereign Right to be Restored to Office in Honour, Privileges and Good Standing after having been unlawfully obstructed or removed from Office.

Article 67 – Ius Regnum Imperium (Command, Occupation & Enforcement)

265. ***Ius Regnum Imperium*** are the collection of Sovereign Rights of Command, Occupation and Enforcement, as inherited from the collection of Ecclesiastical Rights *Ius Ecclesiae Imperium*. Ius Regnum Imperium (Command, Occupation & Enforcement)

266. *Ius Regnum Imperium* (Command, Occupation & Enforcement) is the sixth collection of eleven Authoritative Sovereign Rights (*Potentis Regnum Iurium*); and may be explicitly invoked or referenced by Sovereign Right of Action through a proper and registered Sovereign Entity and the Sovereign Obligations of any such registered Sovereign Person or Executive Office in Ucadia or Non-Ucadia Jurisdiction. Invoking of Ius Regnum Imperium (Command, Occupation & Enforcement)

267. The collection of Sovereign Rights of *Ius Regnum Imperium* contains six (6) Rights being:- Collection of Ius Regnum Imperium (Command, Occupation & Enforcement)

(i) *Ius Regnum Imperium* being the Sovereign Right of Command, Occupation and Enforcement; and

(ii) *Ius Regnum Imperium Emissionis* being the Sovereign Right of Issuance of Command in Good Faith, Good Conscience and Good Action; and

(iii) *Ius Regnum Imperium Immunitatis* being the Sovereign Right of Immunity for Command Made in Office in Good Faith, Good Conscience and Good Actions; and

(iv) *Ius Regnum Imperium Receptionis* being the Sovereign Right of Receipt of Command in Good Faith, Good Conscience and Good Action; and

(v) *Ius Regnum Imperium Executionis* being the Sovereign Right of Enforcement of Command in Good Faith, Good Conscience and Good Action; and

(vi) *Ius Regnum Immunitatis Executionis* being the Sovereign Right of Immunity when Enforcement of Command done in Good Faith, Good Conscience and Good Action.

Article 68 – Ius Regnum Custoditum (Custody, Guardianship and Preservation)

268. ***Ius Regnum Custoditum*** are the collection of Sovereign Rights of Custody, Guardianship and Preservation, as inherited from the collection of Ecclesiastical Rights *Ius Ecclesiae Custoditum*. Ius Regnum Custoditum (Custody)

269. *Ius Regnum Custoditum* (Custody, Guardianship & Preservation) is the seventh collection of eleven Authoritative Sovereign Rights (*Potentis Regnum Iurium*); and may be explicitly invoked or referenced by Sovereign Right of Action through a proper and registered Sovereign Entity and the Sovereign Obligations of any such registered Sovereign Person or Executive Office in Ucadia or Non-Ucadia Jurisdiction. Invoking of Ius Regnum Custoditum (Custody)

270. The collection of Sovereign Rights of *Ius Regnum Custoditum* (Custody, Guardianship & Preservation) contains twenty-seven (27) Rights being:- Collection of Ius Regnum Custoditum (Custody)

(i) *Ius Regnum Custoditum* being the Sovereign Right of Custody, Guardianship and Preservation; and

(ii) *Ius Regnum Custos* being the Sovereign Right of Custodian; and

(iii) *Ius Regnum Officii Curae Custodis* being the Sovereign Right of Duty of Care of Custodian; and

(iv) *Ius Regnum Removendi Custodis* being the Sovereign Right of Removal of Custodian for Breach of Duty of Care or Bad Faith, Bad Conscience or Bad Actions; and

(v) *Ius Regnum Rationis Legalis Custodis* being the Sovereign Right of Custodian as Attorney and Legal Representative; and

(vi) *Ius Regnum Medicinae Decisionis Custodis* being the Sovereign Right of Medical Decisions of Custodian; and

(vii) *Ius Regnum Pecuniarum Decisionis Custodis* being the

Sovereign Right of Financial Decisions of Custodian; and

(viii) *Ius Regnum Proprietatis Decisionis Custodis* being the Sovereign Right of Property Decisions of Custodian; and

(ix) *Ius Regnum Custodiae Immunitatis* being the Sovereign Right of Immunity of Custodian when Decisions and Actions Made in Office in Good Faith, Good Conscience and Good Actions; and

(x) *Ius Regnum Curatoris* being the Sovereign Right of Curator; and

(xi) *Ius Regnum Officii Curae Curatoris* being the Sovereign Right of Duty of Care of Curator; and

(xii) *Ius Regnum Removendi Curatoris* being the Sovereign Right of Removal of Curator for Breach of Duty of Care or Bad Faith, Bad Conscience or Bad Actions; and

(xiii) *Ius Regnum Rationis Legalis Curatoris* being the Sovereign Right of Curator as Attorney and Legal Representative; and

(xiv) *Ius Regnum Pecuniarum Decisionis Curatoris* being the Sovereign Right of Financial Decisions of Curator; and

(xv) *Ius Regnum Medicinae Decisionis Curatoris* being the Sovereign Right of Medical Decisions of Curator; and

(xvi) *Ius Regnum Proprietatis Decisionis Curatoris* being the Sovereign Right of Property Decisions of Curator; and

(xvii) *Ius Regnum Immunitatis Curatoris* being the Sovereign Right of Immunity of Curator when Decisions and Actions Made in Office in Good Faith, Good Conscience and Good Actions; and

(xviii) *Ius Regnum Protectoris* being the Sovereign Right of Guardian; and

(xix) *Ius Regnum Officii Curae Protectoris* being the Sovereign Right of Duty of Care of Guardian; and

(xx) *Ius Regnum Removendi Protectoris* being the Sovereign Right of Removal of Guardian for Breach of Duty of Care or Bad Faith, Bad Conscience or Bad Actions; and

(xxi) *Ius Regnum Rationis Legalis Protectoris* being the Sovereign Right of Guardian as Attorney and Legal Representative; and

(xxii) *Ius Regnum Medicinae Decisionis Protectoris* being the Sovereign Right of Medical Decisions of Guardian; and

(xxiii) *Ius Regnum Pecuniarum Decisionis Protectoris* being the

Sovereign Right of Financial Decisions of Guardian; and

(xxiv) *Ius Regnum Proprietatis Decisionis Protectoris* being the Sovereign Right of Property Decisions of Guardian; and

(xxv) *Ius Regnum Habitationis Decisionis Protectoris* being the Sovereign Right of Housing and Accommodation Decisions of Guardian; and

(xxvi) *Ius Regnum Educationis Decisionis Protectoris* being the Sovereign Right of Education Decisions of Guardian; and

(xxvii) *Ius Regnum Immunitatis Protectoris* being the Sovereign Right of Immunity of Guardian when Decisions and Actions Made in Office in Good Faith, Good Conscience and Good Actions.

Article 69 – Ius Regnum Oratorium (Courts)

271. ***Ius Regnum Oratorium*** are the collection of Sovereign Rights to a Competent Forum of Law and Review, as inherited from the collection of Ecclesiastical Rights *Ius Ecclesiae Oratorium.* Ius Regnum Oratorium (Courts)

272. *Ius Regnum Oratorium* (Courts) is the eighth collection of eleven Authoritative Sovereign Rights (*Potentis Regnum Iurium*); and may be explicitly invoked or referenced by Sovereign Right of Action through a proper and registered Sovereign Entity and the Sovereign Obligations of any such registered Sovereign Person or Executive Office in Ucadia or Non-Ucadia Jurisdiction. Invoking of Ius Regnum Oratorium (Courts)

273. The collection of Sovereign Rights of *Ius Regnum Oratorium* (Courts) contains twelve (12) Rights being:- Collection of Ius Regnum Oratorium (Courts)

(i) *Ius Regnum Oratorium* being the Sovereign Right of Forum of Law and Review; and

(ii) *Ius Regnum Aedificandi Fori* being the Sovereign Right of Forum of Law Building; and

(iii) *Ius Regnum Procedendi Fori* being the Sovereign Right of Forum of Law Procedures; and

(iv) *Ius Regnum Technologiae Fori* being the Sovereign Right of Forum of Law Technology and Digital Systems; and

(v) *Ius Regnum Iudicum Fori* being the Sovereign Right of Forum of Law Justices; and

(vi) *Ius Regnum Iudicum Immunitatis* being the Sovereign Right of Immunity for Justices when Decisions and Actions Made in

Office in Good Faith, Good Conscience and Good Actions; and

(vii) *Ius Regnum Iudicum Officiorum Fori* being the Sovereign Right of Forum of Law Officers; and

(viii) *Ius Regnum Officii Iudicialis Immunitatis* being the Sovereign Right of Immunity for Law Officers when Decisions and Actions Made in Office in Good Faith, Good Conscience and Good Actions; and

(ix) *Ius Regnum Custodiae Iudicialis Fori* being the Sovereign Right of Forum of Law Attendants and Guards; and

(x) *Ius Regnum Custodiae Iudicialis Immunitatis* being the Sovereign Right of Immunity for Law Attendants and Guards when Decisions and Actions Made in Office in Good Faith, Good Conscience and Good Actions; and

(xi) *Ius Regnum Cancellarium Fori* being the Sovereign Right of Forum of Law Chancery and Records Administration; and

(xii) *Ius Regnum Penitentiaria Fori* being the Sovereign Right of Forum of Law Penitentiary and Holding Prison.

Article 70 – Ius Regnum Templum (Treasury& Finance)

274. ***Ius Regnum Templum*** are the collection of Sovereign Rights of a Treasury or Financial (Banking) Body, as inherited from the collection of Ecclesiastical Rights *Ius Ecclesiae Templum.* Ius Regnum Templum (Treasury & Finance)

275. *Ius Regnum Templum* (Treasury & Finance) is the ninth collection of eleven Authoritative Sovereign Rights (*Potentis Regnum Iurium*); and may be explicitly invoked or referenced by Sovereign Right of Action through a proper and registered Sovereign Entity and the Sovereign Obligations of any such registered Sovereign Person or Executive Office in Ucadia or Non-Ucadia Jurisdiction. Invoking of Ius Regnum Templum (Treasury & Finance)

276. The collection of Sovereign Rights of *Ius Regnum Templum* (Treasury & Finance) contains eleven (11) Rights being:- Collection of Ius Regnum Templum (Treasury & Finance)

(i) *Ius Regnum Templum* being the Sovereign Right of a Treasury or Financial (Banking) Body; and

(ii) *Ius Regnum Officina Monetaria* being the Sovereign Right of Minting Office; and

(iii) *Ius Regnum Pecuniariarum Administrandi* being the Sovereign Right of Cash Management; and

(iv) *Ius Regnum Monetarum Administrandi* being the Sovereign

Right of Monetary Management; and

(v) *Ius Regnum Administrationis Financiarum* being the Sovereign Right of Financial Administration; and

(vi) *Ius Regnum Administrationis Bancariae* being the Sovereign Right of Banking Administration; and

(vii) *Ius Regnum Administrationis Creditorum* being the Sovereign Right of Credit Management; and

(viii) *Ius Regnum Administrationis Debiti* being the Sovereign Right of Debt Management; and

(ix) *Ius Regnum Administrationis Financiarum Periculi* being the Sovereign Right of Financial Risk Management; and

(x) *Ius Regnum Operationum Thesaurariarum* being the Sovereign Right of Treasury Management; and

(xi) *Ius Regnum Administrationis Conformitatis* being the Sovereign Right of Compliance Management.

Article 71 – Ius Regnum Commercium (Trade, Exchange & Communication)

277. ***Ius Regnum Commercium*** are the collection of Sovereign Rights to Trade, Exchange and Communication, as inherited from the collection of Ecclesiastical Rights *Ius Ecclesiae Commercium*.

Ius Regnum Commercium (Trade, Exchange & Communication)

278. *Ius Regnum Commercium* (Trade, Exchange & Communication) is the tenth collection of eleven Authoritative Sovereign Rights (*Potentis Regnum Iurium*); and may be explicitly invoked or referenced by Sovereign Right of Action through a proper and registered Sovereign Entity and the Sovereign Obligations of any such registered Sovereign Person or Executive Office in Ucadia or Non-Ucadia Jurisdiction.

Invoking of Ius Regnum Commercium (Trade, Exchange & Communication)

279. The collection of Sovereign Rights of *Ius Regnum Commercium* (Trade, Exchange & Communication) contains ten (10) Rights being:-

Collection of Ius Regnum Commercium (Trade, Exchange & Communication)

(i) *Ius Regnum Commercium* being the Sovereign Right to Trade, Exchange and Communication; and

(ii) *Ius Regnum Libertatis Negotiandi Pretium* being the Sovereign Right of Freedom to Negotiate Price; and

(iii) *Ius Regnum Libertatis Emendi* being the Sovereign Right of Freedom to Purchase; and

(iv) *Ius Regnum Libertatis Vendendi* being the Sovereign Right of

Freedom to Sell; and

(v) *Ius Regnum Libertatis Mercatorum* being the Sovereign Right of Freedom of Trade; and

(vi) *Ius Regnum Libertatis Investitionis* being the Sovereign Right of Freedom of Investment; and

(vii) *Ius Regnum Libertatis Motus Bonorum* being the Sovereign Right of Freedom of Movement of Goods; and

(viii) *Ius Regnum Libertatis Mercatorum Conventi* being the Sovereign Right of Freedom of Agreement; and

(ix) *Ius Regnum Qualitatem Deliberatam* being the Sovereign Right of Quality Delivered; and

(x) *Ius Regnum Rem Emptam* being the Sovereign Right to Thing Purchased.

Article 72 – Ius Regnum Decretum (Decree, Judgement & Edict)

280. ***Ius Regnum Decretum*** are the collection of Sovereign Rights to issue Decree, Judgement and Edict, as inherited from the collection of Ecclesiastical Rights *Ius Ecclesiae Decretum*. Ius Regnum Decretum (Decree)

281. *Ius Regnum Decretum* (Decree, Judgement and Edict) is the eleventh collection of eleven Authoritative Sovereign Rights (*Potentis Regnum Iurium*); and may be explicitly invoked or referenced by Sovereign Right of Action through a proper and registered Sovereign Entity and the Sovereign Obligations of any such registered Sovereign Person or Executive Office in Ucadia or Non-Ucadia Jurisdiction. Invoking of Ius Regnum Decretum (Decree)

282. The collection of Sovereign Rights of *Ius Regnum Decretum* (Decree, Judgement and Edict) contains (6) six Rights being:- Collection of Ius Regnum Decretum (Decree)

(i) *Ius Regnum Decretum* being the Sovereign Right of Decrees, Judgements and Edicts; and

(ii) *Ius Regnum Edicti* being the Sovereign Right of Edict being a formal executive or sovereign or ecclesiastical address and command concerning a moral or legal or administrative matter; and

(iii) *Ius Regnum Decreti* being the Sovereign Right of Decree being an official order or command; and

(iv) *Ius Regnum Declarationis Iudicii* being the Sovereign Right of Declaratory Judgement; and

(v) *Ius Regnum Rescripti* being the Sovereign Right of Rescript being a formal response to one or more ecclesiastical or legal questions; and

(vi) *Ius Regnum Notificandi* being the Sovereign Right of Notice being a formal note distributed and published concerning some subject.

3.3 – Instrumental Sovereign Rights

Article 73 – Instrumental Sovereign Rights

283. ***Instrumental Sovereign Rights*** (*Instrumentalis Regnum Iurium*) are Sovereign Rights essential to the proper administration of Sovereign Rights. Instrumental Sovereign Rights

284. All *Instrumental Sovereign Rights* are delegated by proper *Mandate* to the Governments of valid and legitimate Sovereign Ucadia Bodies and Entities (including but not limited to Ucadia Universities, Provinces, Campuses, Foundations and Agencies); and to those existing and internationally recognised Non-Ucadian Sovereign Bodies and Entities by in force treaties and agreements in accord with the most sacred Covenant *Pactum De Singularis Caelum*. Delegation of Instrumental Sovereign Rights

285. All *Instrumental Sovereign Rights* are assumed to be automatically invoked through the proper operation and function of the Governing Instruments, Codes and Bylaws of valid and legitimate Sovereign Ucadia Bodies and Entities (including but not limited to Ucadia Universities, Provinces, Campuses, Foundations and Agencies); and through the operation and function of in force treaties and agreements with existing and internationally recognised Non-Ucadian Sovereign Bodies and Entities. Invocation of Instrumental Sovereign Rights

286. The following valid twenty-two (22) *Instrumental Sovereign Rights* (*Instrumentalis Regnum Iurium*) is recognised in accord with the most sacred Covenant *Pactum De Singularis Caelum* and these present Maxims:- List of Instrumental Sovereign Rights (Instrumentalis Regnum Iurium)

(i) "**Ius Regnum Iuris**" are the collection of Sovereign Rights to Justice and Due Process, as inherited from the collection of Ecclesiastical Rights *Ius Ecclesiae Iuris*; and

(ii) "**Ius Regnum Bona Fidei**" are the collection of Sovereign Rights of Good Faith, Good Conscience and Good Actions, as inherited from the collection of Ecclesiastical Rights *Ius Ecclesiae Bona Fidei*; and

(iii) "**Ius Regnum Fidei**" are the collection of Sovereign Rights of Superior Sovereign Trust and Sovereign Estate, as inherited from the collection of Ecclesiastical Rights *Ius Ecclesiae Fidei*; and

(iv) "**Ius Regnum Aequum**" are the collection of Sovereign Rights of Equality and Fairness, as inherited from the collection of Ecclesiastical Rights *Ius Ecclesiae Aequum*; and

(v) "**Ius Regnum Rationatio**" are the collection of Sovereign Rights of Accounting, Credit and Funds, as inherited from the collection of Ecclesiastical Rights *Ius Ecclesiae Rationatio*; and

(vi) "**Ius Regnum Concedere et Abrogare**" are the collection of Sovereign Rights to Give or Grant Rights and Annul or Rescind Superior Rights, as inherited from the collection of Ecclesiastical Rights *Ius Ecclesiae Concedere et Abrogare*; and

(vii) "**Ius Regnum Delegare et Revocare**" are the collection of Sovereign Rights to Assign or Delegate Rights and Cancel or Revoke Superior Rights, as inherited from the collection of Ecclesiastical Rights *Ius Ecclesiae Delegare et Revocare*; and

(viii) "**Ius Regnum Associatio et Conventio**" are the collection of Sovereign Rights of Association and Agreement, as inherited from the collection of Ecclesiastical Rights *Ius Ecclesiae Associatio et Conventio*; and

(ix) "**Ius Regnum Consensum et Non**" are the collection of Sovereign Rights to Consent and Non-Consent, as inherited from the collection of Ecclesiastical Rights *Ius Ecclesiae Consensum et Non*; and

(x) "**Ius Regnum Hereditatis**" are the collection of Sovereign Rights of Inheritance of Ecclesiastical Rights, as inherited from the collection of Ecclesiastical Rights *Ius Ecclesiae Hereditatis*; and

(xi) "**Ius Regnum Dominium**" are the collection of Sovereign Rights of Absolute Ownership, as inherited from the collection of Ecclesiastical Rights *Ius Ecclesiae Dominium*; and

(xii) "**Ius Regnum Possessionis**" are the collection of Sovereign Rights to Possess, Hold and Own Property, as inherited from the collection of Ecclesiastical Rights *Ius Ecclesiae Possessionis*; and

(xiii) "**Ius Regnum Usus**" are the collection of Sovereign Rights of Use and Fruits (Enjoyment) of Use of Property, as inherited from the collection of Ecclesiastical Rights *Ius Ecclesiae Usus*; and

(xiv) "**Ius Regnum Proprietatis**" are the collection of Sovereign Rights of Ownership of Use or Fruits of Use of Property, as inherited from the collection of Ecclesiastical Rights *Ius Ecclesiae Proprietatis*; and

(xv) "**Ius Regnum Vectigalis Proprietatis**" are the collection of Sovereign Rights to impose Rents, Tolls, Levies, Contributions or Charges against Property, as inherited from the collection of Ecclesiastical Rights *Ius Ecclesiae Vectigalis Proprietatis* ; and

(xvi) "**Ius Regnum Moneta**" are the collection of Sovereign Rights to Mint, Produce, Hold, Use and Exchange Money, as inherited from the collection of Ecclesiastical Rights *Ius Ecclesiae Moneta*; and

(xvii) "**Ius Regnum Vectigalis Moneta**" are the collection of Sovereign Rights to impose Rents, Tolls, Levies, Contributions or Charges against Money, as inherited from the collection of Ecclesiastical Rights *Ius Ecclesiae Vectigalis Moneta*; and

(xviii) "**Ius Regnum Registrum**" are the collection of Sovereign Rights to Enter Records within Registers and Rolls, as inherited from the collection of Ecclesiastical Rights *Ius Ecclesiae Registrum*; and

(xix) "**Ius Regnum Remedium**" are the collection of Sovereign Rights of Remedy, Relief, Redress or Compensation, as inherited from the collection of Ecclesiastical Rights *Ius Ecclesiae Remedium*; and

(xx) "**Ius Regnum Poena**" are the collection of Sovereign Rights of Penalty, Penitence or Punishment, as inherited from the collection of Ecclesiastical Rights *Ius Ecclesiae Poena*; and

(xxi) "**Ius Regnum Clementia**" are the collection of Sovereign Rights of Mercy & Forgiveness, as inherited from the collection of Ecclesiastical Rights *Ius Ecclesiae Clementia*; and

(xxii) "**Ius Regnum Actionum**" are the collection of Sovereign Rights of Action, as inherited from the collection of

Ecclesiastical Rights *Ius Ecclesiae Actionum.*

Article 74 – Ius Regnum Iuris (Justice & Due Process)

287. ***Ius Regnum Iuris*** are the collection of Sovereign Rights to Justice and Due Process, as inherited from the collection of Ecclesiastical Rights *Ius Ecclesiae Iuris.* Ius Regnum Iuris (Justice & Due Process)

288. *Ius Regnum Iuris* (Justice & Due Process) is the first collection of twenty-two *Instrumental Sovereign Rights* (*Instrumentalis Regnum Iurium*); and may be explicitly invoked or referenced by Sovereign Right of Action through a proper and registered Sovereign Entity and the Sovereign Obligations of any such registered Sovereign Person or Executive Office in Ucadia or Non-Ucadia Jurisdiction. Invoking of Ius Regnum Iuris (Justice & Due Process)

289. The collection of Sovereign Rights of *Ius Regnum Iuris* contains nine (9) Rights being: Collection of Ius Regnum Iuris (Justice & Due Process)

(i) *Ius Regnum Iuris* being the Sovereign Right of Justice and Due Process; and

(ii) *Ius Regnum Accusationis* being the Sovereign Right to make an Accusation against another Person or Body or Entity upon Possession of Provable Evidence of Personal Harm, Injury or Loss; and

(iii) *Ius Regnum Innocentiae* being the Sovereign Right of Innocence against any Accusation until Proven or Confession or Culpability; and

(iv) *Ius Regnum Accusationis Cognoscendi* being the Sovereign Right for the Accused and their Agent to know the Full Disclosure and Brief of Evidence of any Accusation; and

(v) *Ius Regnum Defensionis* being the Sovereign Right to Defend against any Accusation; and

(vi) *Ius Regnum Processus Iustus* being the Sovereign Right of Fair Process; and

(vii) *Ius Regnum Arbitrandi* being the Sovereign Right of Arbitration as method for dispute resolution; and

(viii) *Ius Regnum Propria Persona* being the Sovereign Right to defend or accuse as oneself; and

(ix) *Ius Regnum Iudicialis Agensas* being the Sovereign Right to appoint a Legal Agent to defend or accuse.

Article 75 – Ius Regnum Aequum (Equality & Fairness)

Ius Regnum Aequum (Equality & Fairness)

290. ***Ius Regnum Aequum*** are the collection of Sovereign Rights of Good Faith, Good Conscience and Good Actions, as inherited from the collection of Ecclesiastical Rights *Ius Ecclesiae Aequum*.

Invoking of Ius Regnum Aequum (Equality & Fairness)

291. *Ius Regnum Aequum* (Equality & Fairness) is the second collection of twenty-two *Instrumental Sovereign Rights* (*Instrumentalis Regnum Iurium*); and may be explicitly invoked or referenced by Sovereign Right of Action through a proper and registered Sovereign Entity and the Sovereign Obligations of any such registered Sovereign Person or Executive Office in Ucadia or Non-Ucadia Jurisdiction.

Collection of Ius Regnum Aequum (Equality & Fairness)

292. The collection of Sovereign Rights of *Ius Regnum Aequum* contains two (2) Rights being:

(i) *Ius Regnum Aequum* being the Sovereign Right of Equality and Fairness; and

(ii) *Ius Regnum Aequitatis* being the Sovereign Right of Fairness.

Article 76 – Ius Regnum Bona Fidei (Good Faith)

Ius Regnum Bona Fidei (Good Faith)

293. ***Ius Regnum Bona Fidei*** are the collection of Sovereign Rights of Good Faith, Good Conscience and Good Actions, as inherited from the collection of Ecclesiastical Rights Ius *Ecclesiae Bona Fidei*.

Invoking of Ius Regnum Bona Fidei (Good Faith)

294. *Ius Regnum Bona Fidei* (Good Faith) is the third collection of twenty-two *Instrumental Sovereign Rights* (*Instrumentalis Regnum Iurium*); and may be explicitly invoked or referenced by Sovereign Right of Action through a proper and registered Sovereign Entity and the Sovereign Obligations of any such registered Sovereign Person or Executive Office in Ucadia or Non-Ucadia Jurisdiction.

Collection of Ius Regnum Bona Fidei (Good Faith)

295. The collection of Sovereign Rights of *Ius Regnum Bona Fidei* contains three (3) Rights being:

(i) *Ius Regnum Bona Fidei* being the Sovereign Right of Good Faith; and

(ii) *Ius Regnum Bona Conscientia* being the Sovereign Right of Good Conscience; and

(iii) *Ius Regnum Bona Actio* being the Sovereign Right of Good Action.

Article 77 – Ius Regnum Fidei (Trusts & Estates)

296. ***Ius Regnum Fidei*** are the collection of Sovereign Rights of Superior Sovereign Trust and Sovereign Estate, as inherited from the collection of Ecclesiastical Rights *Ius Ecclesiae Fidei*. Ius Regnum Fidei (Trusts & Estates)

297. *Ius Regnum Fidei* (Trusts & Estates) is the fourth collection of twenty-two *Instrumental Sovereign Rights* (*Instrumentalis Regnum Iurium*); and may be explicitly invoked or referenced by Sovereign Right of Action through a proper and registered Sovereign Entity and the Sovereign Obligations of any such registered Sovereign Person or Executive Office in Ucadia or Non-Ucadia Jurisdiction. Invoking of Ius Regnum Fidei (Trusts & Estates)

298. The collection of Sovereign Rights of *Ius Regnum Fidei* contains nine (9) Rights being: Collection of Ius Regnum Fidei (Trusts & Estates)

(i) *Ius Regnum Fidei* being the Sovereign Right of Trusts & Estates; and

(ii) *Ius Regnum Fiduciam Formandi* being the Sovereign Right to form a Trust; and

(iii) *Ius Regnum Fiduciam Beneficiarius* being the Sovereign Right of Benefit from Trust; and

(iv) *Ius Regnum Fiduciam Computatio* being the Sovereign Right to Receive an Accounting of the Administration of a Trust; and

(v) *Ius Regnum Fiduciam Investiendi* being the Sovereign Right to Vest one or more Assets or Property into a Trust; and

(vi) *Ius Regnum Fundum Formandi* being the Sovereign Right to form an Estate; and

(vii) *Ius Regnum Fundum Hereditatis* being the Sovereign Right to inherit an Estate; and

(viii) *Ius Regnum Fundum Beneficiarius* being the Sovereign Right of Benefit from an Estate; and

(ix) *Ius Regnum Fundum Computatio* being the Sovereign Right to Receive an Accounting of the Administration of the Estate.

Article 78 – Ius Regnum Rationatio (Accounting, Credit & Funds)

299. ***Ius Regnum Rationatio*** are the collection of Sovereign Rights of Accounting, Credit and Funds, as inherited from the collection of Ecclesiastical Rights *Ius Ecclesiae Rationatio*. Ius Regnum Rationatio (Accounting, Credit & Funds)

300. *Ius Regnum Rationatio* (Accounting, Credit & Funds) is the fifth collection of twenty-two *Instrumental Sovereign Rights* (*Instrumentalis Regnum Iurium*); and may be explicitly invoked or referenced by Sovereign Right of Action through a proper and registered Sovereign Entity and the Sovereign Obligations of any such registered Sovereign Person or Executive Office in Ucadia or Non-Ucadia Jurisdiction. Invoking of Ius Regnum Rationatio

301. The collection of Sovereign Rights of *Ius Regnum Rationatio* contains thirteen (13) Rights being:- Collection of Ius Regnum Rationatio

(i) *Ius Regnum Rationatio* being the Sovereign Right of Accounting, Credit and Funds; and

(ii) *Ius Regnum Rationum* being the Sovereign Right of Accounts; and

(iii) *Ius Regnum Rationum Examinationis* being the Sovereign Right of Accounts Audit; and

(iv) *Ius Regnum Aestimationis Valoris* being the Sovereign Right of Valuation; and

(v) *Ius Regnum Aestimationis Obligationis* being the Sovereign Right of Estimating Obligation for Value; and

(vi) *Ius Regnum Aestimationis Pretii* being the Sovereign Right of Estimating Price for Obligation; and

(vii) *Ius Regnum Aestimationis Crediti* being the Sovereign Right of Estimating Credit; and

(viii) *Ius Regnum Aestimationis Debiti* being the Sovereign Right of Estimating Debit; and

(ix) *Ius Regnum Valorum Pignorare* being the Sovereign Right to Pledge Valuables as Collateral for Funds; and

(x) *Ius Regnum Rationum Relatio* being the Sovereign Right of Reporting of Accounts; and

(xi) *Ius Regnum Relatio Crediti* being the Sovereign Right of Credit Reporting; and

(xii) *Ius Regnum Crediti Accessus* being the Sovereign Right of

Access to Funds; and

(xiii) *Ius Regnum Collectionis Debiti* being the Sovereign Right of Debit (Debt) Collection.

Article 79 – Ius Regnum Concedere et Abrogare (Give or Grant Rights)

302. ***Ius Regnum Concedere et Abrogare*** are the collection of Sovereign Rights to Give or Grant Rights and Annul or rescind Superior Rights, as inherited from the collection of Ecclesiastical Rights *Ius Ecclesiae Concedere et Abrogare*.

Ius Regnum Concedere et Abrogare (Give or Grant Rights)

303. *Ius Regnum Concedere et Abrogare* (Give or Grant Rights) is the sixth collection of twenty-two *Instrumental Sovereign Rights* (*Instrumentalis Regnum Iurium*); and may be explicitly invoked or referenced by Sovereign Right of Action through a proper and registered Sovereign Entity and the Sovereign Obligations of any such registered Sovereign Person or Executive Office in Ucadia or Non-Ucadia Jurisdiction.

Invoking of Ius Regnum Concedere et Abrogare (Give or Grant Rights)

304. The collection of Sovereign Rights of *Ius Regnum Concedere et Abrogare* contains six (6) Rights being:

Collection of Ius Regnum Concedere et Abrogare (Give or Grant Rights)

(i) *Ius Regnum Concedere et Abrogare* being the Sovereign Right of Give or Grant Rights and Annul or Rescind Rights; and

(ii) *Ius Regnum Donandum Iuris* being the Sovereign Right to Give a Right; and

(iii) *Ius Rescindendum Iuris* being the Sovereign Right to Rescind a Right; and

(iv) *Ius Regnum Conferendum Iuris* being the Sovereign Right to Grant a Right; and

(v) *Ius Regnum Abrogandum Iuris* being the Sovereign Right to Abrogate a Right; and

(vi) *Ius Regnum Annullare Iuris* being the Sovereign Right to Annul a Right.

Article 80 – Ius Regnum Delegare et Revocare (Assign or Delegate Rights)

305. ***Ius Regnum Delegare et Revocare*** are the collection of Sovereign Rights to Assign or Delegate Rights and Cancel or Revoke Superior Rights, as inherited from the collection of Ecclesiastical Rights *Ius Ecclesiae Delegare et Revocare.*

Ius Regnum Delegare et Revocare (Assign or Delegate Rights)

306. *Ius Regnum Delegare et Revocare* (Assign or Delegate Rights) is the seventh collection of twenty-two *Instrumental Sovereign Rights* (*Instrumentalis Regnum Iurium*); and may be explicitly invoked or referenced by Sovereign Right of Action through a proper and registered Sovereign Entity and the Sovereign Obligations of any such registered Sovereign Person or Executive Office in Ucadia or Non-Ucadia Jurisdiction.

Invoking of Ius Regnum Delegare et Revocare

307. The collection of Sovereign Rights of *Ius Regnum Delegare et Revocare* contains five (5) Rights being:

Collection of Ius Regnum Delegare et Revocare

(i) *Ius Regnum Delegare et Revocare* being the Sovereign Right of Assign or Delegate Rights and Cancel or Revoke Rights; and

(ii) *Ius Regnum Delegandi Iuris* being the Sovereign Right to Delegate a Right (and Law); and

(iii) *Ius Regnum Cancellari Iuris* being the Sovereign Right to Cancel a Delegated Right (and Law); and

(iv) *Ius Regnum Assignare Iuris* being the Sovereign Right to Assign a Right (and Law); and

(v) *Ius Regnum Revocandum Iuris* being the Sovereign Right to Revoke an Assigned Right (and Law).

Article 81 – Ius Regnum Associatio et Conventio (Association & Agreement)

308. ***Ius Regnum Associatio et Conventio*** are the collection of Sovereign Rights of Association and Agreement, as inherited from the collection of Ecclesiastical Rights *Ius Ecclesiae Associatio et Conventio.*

Ius Regnum Associatio et Conventio (Association)

309. *Ius Regnum Associatio et Conventio* (Association & Agreement) is the eighth collection of twenty-two *Instrumental Sovereign Rights* (*Instrumentalis Regnum Iurium*); and may be explicitly invoked or referenced by Sovereign Right of Action through a proper and registered Sovereign Entity and the Sovereign Obligations of any such registered Sovereign Person or Executive Office in Ucadia or Non-

Invoking of Ius Regnum Associatio et Conventio

Ucadia Jurisdiction.

310. The collection of Sovereign Rights of *Ius Associatio et Conventio* contains twenty-four (24) Rights being:

Collection of Ius Regnum Associatio et Conventio

(i) *Ius Regnum Associatio et Conventio* being the Sovereign Right of Association and Agreement; and

(ii) *Ius Regnum Associationis* being the Sovereign Right of Association; and

(iii) *Ius Regnum Renuntiatio* being the Sovereign Right of Renunciation of Association; and

(iv) *Ius Regnum Conventio* being the Sovereign Right of Agreement; and

(v) *Ius Regnum Conventionis Negotiationis* being the Sovereign Right to Negotiate an Agreement; and

(vi) *Ius Regnum Conventionis Recusatio* being the Sovereign Right to Refuse an Agreement; and

(vii) *Ius Regnum Conventionis Instrumenti* being the Sovereign Right to define an Instrument of Agreement; and

(viii) *Ius Regnum Pactum Formandi* being the Sovereign Right to form a Covenant or Treaty; and

(ix) *Ius Regnum Charta Formandi* being the Sovereign Right to form a Charter; and

(x) *Ius Regnum Constitutionis Formandi* being the Sovereign Right to form a Constitution; and

(xi) *Ius Regnum Memorandum Formandi* being the Sovereign Right to form a Memorandum of Agreement; and

(xii) *Ius Regnum Litterae Formandi* being the Sovereign Right to form a Letter or Heads of Agreement; and

(xiii) *Ius Regnum Notitiae Formandi* being the Sovereign Right to form a Note or Notice of Agreement; and

(xiv) *Ius Regnum Conventionis Terminos* being the Sovereign Right to define Terms and Conditions of Agreement; and

(xv) *Ius Regnum Conventionis Pollucendi* being the Sovereign Right to make a Solemn Promise in Agreement; and

(xvi) *Ius Regnum Conventionis Poenam et Remedium* being the Sovereign Right to define Penalties and Remedies of Agreement; and

(xvii) *Ius Regnum Modandi Conventionis Instrumenti* being the

Sovereign Right to Modify the Terms and Conditions of Agreement; and

(xviii) *Ius Regnum Conventionis Ratificationis* being the Sovereign Right of Ratification of Agreement; and

(xix) *Ius Regnum Minoris Lapsus* being the Sovereign Right of Action against Minor Breach of Agreement; and

(xx) *Ius Regnum Minoris Reparare* being the Sovereign Right to Rectify and Repair Minor Issues against Minor Breach of Agreement; and

(xxi) *Ius Regnum Maioris Lapsus* being the Sovereign Right of Action against Major Breach of Agreement; and

(xxii) *Ius Regnum Maioris Restituere* being the Sovereign Right to Restore and Re-establish Major Issues against Major Breach of Agreement; and

(xxiii) *Ius Regnum Concludendi* being the Sovereign Right to Conclude an Agreement; and

(xxiv) *Ius Regnum Terminandi* being the Sovereign Right to Terminate an Agreement.

Article 82 – Ius Regnum Consensum et Non (Consent)

311. ***Ius Regnum Consensum et Non*** are the collection of Sovereign Rights to Consent and Non-Consent, as inherited from the collection of Ecclesiastical Rights *Ius Ecclesiae Consensum et Non*. — Ius Regnum Consensum et Non (Consent)

312. *Ius Regnum Consensum et Non* (Consent) is the ninth collection of twenty-two *Instrumental Sovereign Rights* (*Instrumentalis Regnum Iurium*); and may be explicitly invoked or referenced by Sovereign Right of Action through a proper and registered Sovereign Entity and the Sovereign Obligations of any such registered Sovereign Person or Executive Office in Ucadia or Non-Ucadia Jurisdiction. — Invoking of Ius Regnum Consensum et Non (Consent)

313. The collection of Sovereign Rights of *Ius Regnum Consensum et Non* contains three (3) Rights being:- — Collection of Ius Regnum Consensum et Non (Consent)

(i) *Ius Regnum Consensum et Non* being the Sovereign Right of Consent and Non-Consent; and

(ii) *Ius Regnum Consensus* being the Sovereign Right of Consent; and

(iii) *Ius Regnum Non Consensus* being the Sovereign Right of Non Consent.

Article 83 – Ius Regnum Hereditatis (Inheritance)

314. ***Ius Regnum Hereditatis*** (Inheritance) are the collection of Sovereign Rights of Inheritance, as inherited from the collection of Ecclesiastical Rights *Ius Ecclesiae Hereditatis*.

Ius Regnum Hereditatis (Inheritance)

315. *Ius Regnum Hereditatis* (Inheritance) is the tenth collection of twenty-two *Instrumental Sovereign Rights* (*Instrumentalis Regnum Iurium*); and may be explicitly invoked or referenced by Sovereign Right of Action through a proper and registered Sovereign Entity and the Sovereign Obligations of any such registered Sovereign Person or Executive Office in Ucadia or Non-Ucadia Jurisdiction.

Invoking of Hereditatis (Inheritance)

316. The collection of Sovereign Rights of *Ius Regnum Hereditatis* contains one Right being:-

Collection of Hereditatis (Inheritance)

(i) *Ius Regnum Hereditatis* being Sovereign Rights of Inheritance.

Article 84 – Ius Regnum Dominium (Absolute Ownership)

317. ***Ius Regnum Dominium*** (Ownership) are the collection of Sovereign Rights of Absolute Ownership, as inherited from the collection of Ecclesiastical Rights *Ius Ecclesiae Dominium*.

Ius Regnum Dominium (Ownership)

318. *Ius Regnum Dominium* (Ownership) is the eleventh collection of twenty-two *Instrumental Sovereign Rights* (*Instrumentalis Regnum Iurium*); and may be explicitly invoked or referenced by Sovereign Right of Action through a proper and registered Sovereign Entity and the Sovereign Obligations of any such registered Sovereign Person or Executive Office in Ucadia or Non-Ucadia Jurisdiction.

Invoking of Ius Regnum Dominium

319. The collection of Sovereign Rights of *Ius Regnum Dominium* contains fourteen (14) Rights being:-

Collection of Ius Regnum Dominium

(i) *Ius Regnum Dominium* being the Sovereign Right of Absolute Ownership and Custody; and

(ii) *Ius Regnum Terrae ad Caelum* being the Sovereign Right of Absolute Ownership and Custody from the Centre of the Earth to the Heavens Above; and

(iii) *Ius Regnum Defendendi* being the Sovereign Right to Defend with Force any Thing, Person or Property under Absolute Ownership and Custody; and

(iv) *Ius Regnum Patronatus* being the Sovereign Right of

Protector, Guardian and Patron over any Thing, Person or Property under Absolute Ownership and Custody; and

(v) *Ius Regnum Coercendum* being the Sovereign Right to Enforce with Force any Right concerning any Thing, Person or Property under Absolute Ownership and Custody; and

(vi) *Ius Regnum Recuperandi* being the Sovereign Right to Enforce with Force the Recovery, Return and Restoration of any Thing, Person or Property under Absolute Ownership and Custody; and

(vii) *Ius Regnum Alligandi et Removendi* being the Sovereign Right of Binding and Unbinding any Item or Thing from Property under Absolute Ownership and Custody; and

(viii) *Ius Regnum Alterius Commodi* being the Sovereign Right of Using Another's Benefit when derived from Property under Absolute Ownership and Custody; and

(ix) *Ius Regnum Angariae* being the Sovereign Right of Requisition of Property or Obligations of Service during emergency or public benefit when related to any Thing, Person or Property under Absolute Ownership and Custody; and

(x) *Ius Regnum Censendi* being the Sovereign Right of Census and Accounting for Things, Persons and Property derived from Absolute Ownership and Custody; and

(xi) *Ius Regnum Excludendi* being the Sovereign Right of Exclusion of Persons from Land or Property under Absolute Ownership and Custody; and

(xii) *Ius Regnum Alienatus* being the Sovereign Right to Convey or Transfer to Another as a Lesser title any Land, Property or Thing under Absolute Ownership and Custody; and

(xiii) *Ius Regnum Ingrediendi* being the Sovereign Right to enter a Property when derived from Property under Absolute Ownership and Custody; and

(xiv) *Ius Regnum Quaesitum Tertio* being the Sovereign Right to enter as a Third Party to an existing Agreement to enforce a Right when the related Things, Persons and Property are derived from Absolute Ownership and Custody.

Article 85 – Ius Regnum Possessionis (Possession)

320. ***Ius Regnum Possessionis*** are the collection of Sovereign Rights to Possess, Hold and Own Property, as inherited from the collection of Ecclesiastical Rights *Ius Ecclesiae Possessionis*. Ius Regnum Possessionis (Possession)

321. *Ius Regnum Possessionis* (Possession) is the twelfth collection of twenty-two *Instrumental Sovereign Rights* (*Instrumentalis Regnum Iurium*); and may be explicitly invoked or referenced by Sovereign Right of Action through a proper and registered Sovereign Entity and the Sovereign Obligations of any such registered Sovereign Person or Executive Office in Ucadia or Non-Ucadia Jurisdiction. Invoking of Ius Regnum Possessionis (Possession)

322. The collection of Sovereign Rights of *Ius Regnum Possessionis* contains two (2) Rights being: Collection of Ius Regnum Possessionis (Possession)

(i) *Ius Regnum Possessionis* being the Sovereign Right to Possess, Hold and Own Property; and

(ii) *Ius Regnum Possessionis Rem* being the Sovereign Right to Possess, Hold and Own a Thing.

Article 86 – Ius Regnum Usus (Use)

323. ***Ius Regnum Usus*** are the collection of Sovereign Rights of Use and Fruits (Enjoyment) of Use of Property, as inherited from the collection of Ecclesiastical Rights *Ius Ecclesiae Usus*. Ius Regnum Usus (Use)

324. *Ius Regnum Usus* (Use) is the thirteenth collection of twenty-two *Instrumental Sovereign Rights* (*Instrumentalis Regnum Iurium*); and may be explicitly invoked or referenced by Sovereign Right of Action through a proper and registered Sovereign Entity and the Sovereign Obligations of any such registered Sovereign Person or Executive Office in Ucadia or Non-Ucadia Jurisdiction. Invoking of Ius Regnum Usus (Use)

325. The collection of Sovereign Rights of *Ius Regnum Usus* contains three (3) Rights being: Collection of Ius Regnum Usus (Use)

(i) *Ius Regnum Usus* being the Sovereign Right of Use and Fruits of Use of Property; and

(ii) *Ius Regnum Affectandi* being the Sovereign Right of Acquisition of Property in Continuous Use; and

(iii) *Ius Regnum Cessandi* being the Sovereign Right of Cessation of Property in Use.

Article 87 – Ius Regnum Proprietatis (Ownership of Use)

326. ***Ius Regnum Proprietatis*** are the collection of Sovereign Rights of Ownership of Use or Fruits of Use of Property, as inherited from the collection of Ecclesiastical Rights *Ius Ecclesiae Proprietatis*. Ius Regnum Proprietatis (Ownership of Use)

327. *Ius Regnum Proprietatis* (Ownership of Use) is the fourteenth collection of twenty-two *Instrumental Sovereign Rights* (*Instrumentalis Regnum Iurium*); and may be explicitly invoked or referenced by Sovereign Right of Action through a proper and registered Sovereign Entity and the Sovereign Obligations of any such registered Sovereign Person or Executive Office in Ucadia or Non-Ucadia Jurisdiction. Invoking of Ius Regnum Proprietatis (Ownership of Use)

328. The collection of Sovereign Rights of *Ius Regnum Proprietatis* (Ownership of Use) contains eight (8) Rights being:- Collection of Ius Regnum Proprietatis (Ownership of Use)

(i) *Ius Regnum Proprietatis* being the Sovereign Right of Ownership of Use or Fruits of Use of Property; and

(ii) *Ius Regnum Transferendi* being the Sovereign Right to Transfer Ownership of Use or Fruits of Use of Property to Another; and

(iii) *Ius Regnum Utilitatis* being the Sovereign Right of Enjoyment of Ownership of Use or Fruits of Use of Property; and

(iv) *Ius Regnum Recusatio* being the Sovereign Right of Refusal of Use or Fruits of Use by Another of Owned Property; and

(v) *Ius Regnum Accessionis* being the Sovereign Right of Accession of additions and ownership of additions to Property in Use; and

(vi) *Ius Regnum Aedificii* being the Sovereign Right of Building on Land; and

(vii) *Ius Regnum Alluvionis* being the Sovereign Right of Accretion in increasing Property through natural processes; and

(viii) *Ius Regnum Actionis Proprietatis* being the Sovereign Right of Action against Unreasonable or Immoral Loss of Use or Fruits of Use of Property.

Article 88 – Ius Regnum Vectigalis Proprietatis (Rents on Use)

329. ***Ius Regnum Vectigalis Proprietatis*** are the collection of Sovereign Rights to impose Rents, Tolls, Levies, Contributions or Charges against Property, as inherited from the collection of Ecclesiastical Rights *Ius Ecclesiae Vectigalis Proprietatis*.

Ius Regnum Vectigalis Proprietatis (Rents on Use)

330. *Ius Regnum Vectigalis Proprietatis* (Rents on Use) is the fifteenth collection of twenty-two *Instrumental Sovereign Rights* (*Instrumentalis Regnum Iurium*); and may be explicitly invoked or referenced by Sovereign Right of Action through a proper and registered Sovereign Entity and the Sovereign Obligations of any such registered Sovereign Person or Executive Office in Ucadia or Non-Ucadia Jurisdiction.

Invoking of Ius Regnum Vectigalis Proprietatis

331. The collection of Sovereign Rights of *Ius Regnum Vectigalis Proprietatis* (Rents on Use) contains seven (7) Rights being:-

Collection of Ius Regnum Vectigalis Proprietatis

(i) *Ius Regnum Vectigalis Proprietatis* being the Sovereign Right to impose Rents, Tolls, Levies, Contributions or Charges against Ownership of Use or Fruits of Use of Property; and

(ii) *Ius Regnum Conducendi Mercedem* being the Sovereign Right to Impose Rent on Possession or Use of Property; and

(iii) *Ius Regnum Impendi Tributum* being the Sovereign Right to Impose Levy on Possession or Use of Property; and

(iv) *Ius Regnum Impendi Portorium* being the Sovereign Right to Impose a Toll on Possession or Use of Property; and

(v) *Ius Regnum Impendi Vectigal* being the Sovereign Right to Impose a Charge on Possession or Use of Property; and

(vi) *Ius Regnum Petendi Contributionem* being the Sovereign Right to Request Contributions on Possession or Use of Property; and

(vii) *Ius Regnum Actionis Vectigalis Proprietatis* being the Sovereign Right of Action against Unreasonable or Immoral Loss or Failure to Pay Rents, Tolls, Levies, Contributions or Charges against Ownership of Use or Fruits of Use of Property.

Article 89 – Ius Regnum Moneta (Money)

332. ***Ius Regnum Moneta*** are the collection of Sovereign Rights to Mint, Produce, Hold, Use and Exchange Money, as inherited from the collection of Ecclesiastical Rights *Ius Ecclesiae Moneta*.

Ius Regnum Moneta (Money)

333. *Ius Regnum Moneta* (Money) is the sixteenth collection of twenty-two *Instrumental Sovereign Rights* (*Instrumentalis Regnum Iurium*); and may be explicitly invoked or referenced by Sovereign Right of Action through a proper and registered Sovereign Entity and the Sovereign Obligations of any such registered Sovereign Person or Executive Office in Ucadia or Non-Ucadia Jurisdiction.

Invoking of Ius Regnum Moneta (Money)

334. The collection of Sovereign Rights of *Ius Regnum Moneta* (Money) contains fifteen (15) Rights being:-

Collection of Ius Regnum Moneta (Money)

(i) *Ius Regnum Moneta* being the Sovereign Right to Mint, Produce, Hold, Use and Exchange Money; and

(ii) *Ius Regnum Creandi Moneta* being the Sovereign Right to Create and Mint Money; and

(iii) *Ius Regnum Creandi Digitalis Moneta* being the Sovereign Right to Create and Mint Digital Money; and

(iv) *Ius Regnum Tenendi Moneta* being the Sovereign Right to Hold and Possess Money; and

(v) *Ius Regnum Tenendi Digitalis Moneta* being the Sovereign Right to Hold and Possess Digital Money; and

(vi) *Ius Regnum Transferre Moneta* being the Sovereign Right to Transfer Money; and

(vii) *Ius Regnum Transferre Digitalis Moneta* being the Sovereign Right to Transfer Digital Money; and

(viii) *Ius Regnum Recipere Moneta* being the Sovereign Right to Receive Money; and

(ix) *Ius Regnum Recipere Digitalis Moneta* being the Sovereign Right to Receive Digital Money; and

(x) *Ius Regnum Cambii Moneta* being the Sovereign Right to Exchange Money for another unit of currency; and

(xi) *Ius Regnum Cambii Digitalis Moneta* being the Sovereign Right to Exchange Digital Money for another unit of currency; and

(xii) *Ius Regnum Utendi Moneta* being the Sovereign Right to Use

Money for Settlement of Debts and Obligations; and

(xiii) *Ius Regnum Utendi Digitalis Moneta* being the Sovereign Right to Use Digital Money for Settlement of Debts and Obligations; and

(xiv) *Ius Regnum Utendi Moneta Numismatis Legalis* being the Sovereign Right to Use Money as Legal Tender; and

(xv) *Ius Regnum Utendi Digitalis Moneta Numismatis Legalis* being the Sovereign Right to Use Digital Money as Legal Tender.

Article 90 – Ius Regnum Vectigalis Moneta (Taxes & Charges)

335. ***Ius Regnum Vectigalis Moneta*** are the collection of Sovereign Rights to impose Rents, Tolls, Levies, Contributions or Charges against Money, as inherited from the collection of Ecclesiastical Rights *Ius Ecclesiae Vectigalis Moneta*.

Ius Regnum Vectigalis Moneta (Taxes & Charges)

336. *Ius Regnum Vectigalis Moneta* (Taxes & Charges) is the seventeenth collection of twenty-two *Instrumental Sovereign Rights* (*Instrumentalis Regnum Iurium*); and may be explicitly invoked or referenced by Sovereign Right of Action through a proper and registered Sovereign Entity and the Sovereign Obligations of any such registered Sovereign Person or Executive Office in Ucadia or Non-Ucadia Jurisdiction.

Invoking of Ius Regnum Vectigalis Moneta (Taxes & Charges)

337. The collection of Ecclesiastical Rights of *Ius Regnum Vectigalis Moneta* (Taxes & Charges) contains seven (7) Rights being:-

Collection of Ius Regnum Vectigalis Moneta (Taxes & Charges)

(i) *Ius Regnum Vectigalis Moneta* being the Sovereign Right to impose Rents, Tolls, Levies, Contributions or Charges against Money; and

(ii) *Ius Regnum Conducendi Mercedem Moneta* being the Sovereign Right to Impose Rent on Possession or Use of Money; and

(iii) *Ius Regnum Impendi Tributum Moneta* being the Sovereign Right to Impose Levy on Possession or Use of Money; and

(iv) *Ius Regnum Impendi Portorium Moneta* being the Sovereign Right to Impose Toll on Possession or Use of Money; and

(v) *Ius Regnum Impendi Vectigal Moneta* being the Sovereign Right to Impose a Charge on Possession or Use of Money; and

(vi) *Ius Regnum Petendi Contributionem Moneta* being the Sovereign Right to Request Contributions on Possession or

Use of Money; and

(vii) *Ius Regnum Actionis Vectigalis Moneta* being the Sovereign Right of Action against Unreasonable or Immoral Loss or Failure to Pay Rents, Tolls, Levies, Contributions or Charges against Possession or Use of Money.

Article 91 – Ius Regnum Registrum (Registers & Rolls)

338. ***Ius Regnum Registrum*** are the collection of Sovereign Rights to Enter Records within Registers and Rolls, as inherited from the collection of Ecclesiastical Rights *Ius Ecclesiae Registrum*. Ius Regnum Registrum (Registers & Rolls)

339. *Ius Regnum Registrum* (Registers & Rolls) is the eighteenth collection of twenty-two *Instrumental Sovereign Rights* (*Instrumentalis Regnum Iurium*); and may be explicitly invoked or referenced by Sovereign Right of Action through a proper and registered Sovereign Entity and the Sovereign Obligations of any such registered Sovereign Person or Executive Office in Ucadia or Non-Ucadia Jurisdiction. Invoking of Ius Regnum Registrum (Registers & Rolls)

340. The collection of Sovereign Rights of *Ius Regnum Registrum* (Registers & Rolls) contains twenty-three (23) Rights being:- Collection of Ius Regnum Registrum (Registers & Rolls)

(i) *Ius Regnum Registrum* being the Sovereign Right to Enter and Manage Records within Registers and Rolls; and

(ii) *Ius Regnum Registrum Confidentiae* being the Sovereign Right of Confidential Access to a Register; and

(iii) *Ius Regnum Registrum Accessus* being the Sovereign Right of Access to a Register; and

(iv) *Ius Regnum Actionis Registrum Accessus* being the Sovereign Right of Action concerning Register Access; and

(v) *Ius Regnum Registrum Inspectionis* being the Sovereign Right of Inspection of a Register; and

(vi) *Ius Regnum Actionis Registrum Correctionis* being the Sovereign Right of Action for Register Correction; and

(vii) *Ius Regnum Registrum Intrationis* being the Sovereign Right of Entry in a Register; and

(viii) *Ius Regnum Registri Recordationis Extrahendi* being the Sovereign Right to make an Extract of Record in a Register; and

(ix) *Ius Regnum Registri Recordationis Abstrahendi* being the

Sovereign Right to make an Abstract of Record in a Register; and

(x) *Ius Regnum Registri Recordationis Cancellationis* being the Sovereign Right to Cancel a Record in a Register; and

(xi) *Ius Regnum Registri Recordationis Completionis* being the Sovereign Right to Complete a Record in a Register; and

(xii) *Ius Regnum Registri Recordationis Correctionis* being the Sovereign Right to Correct a Record in a Register; and

(xiii) *Ius Regnum Rotulae Confidentiae* being the Sovereign Right of Confidential Access to a Roll; and

(xiv) *Ius Regnum Rotulae Accessus* being the Sovereign Right of Access to a Roll; and

(xv) *Ius Regnum Actionis Rotulae Accessus* being the Sovereign Right of Action concerning Roll Access; and

(xvi) *Ius Regnum Rotulae Inspectionis* being the Sovereign Right of Inspection of a Roll; and

(xvii) *Ius Regnum Actionis Rotulae Correctionis* being the Sovereign Right of Action for Roll Correction; and

(xviii) *Ius Regnum Rotulae Intrationis* being the Sovereign Right of Entry in a Roll; and

(xix) *Ius Regnum Rotulae Recordationis Extrahendi* being the Sovereign Right *to make* an Extract of Record in a Roll; and

(xx) *Ius Regnum Rotulae Recordationis Abstrahendi* being the Sovereign Right *to make* an Abstract of Record in a Roll; and

(xxi) *Ius Regnum Rotulae Recordationis Cancellationis* being the Sovereign Right to Cancel a Record in a Roll; and

(xxii) *Ius Regnum Rotulae Recordationis Completionis* being the Sovereign Right to Complete a Record in a Roll; and

(xxiii) *Ius Regnum Rotulae Recordationis Correctionis* being the Sovereign Right to Correct a Record in a Roll.

Article 92 – Ius Regnum Remedium (Remedy)

341. ***Ius Regnum Remedium*** are the collection of Sovereign Rights of Remedy, Relief, Redress or Compensation, as inherited from the collection of Ecclesiastical Rights *Ius Ecclesiae Remedium.* Ius Regnum Remedium (Remedy)

342. *Ius Regnum Remedium* (Remedy) is the nineteenth collection of Invoking of Ius twenty-two *Instrumental Sovereign Rights* (*Instrumentalis Regnum Iurium*); and may be explicitly invoked or referenced by Sovereign Right of Action through a proper and registered Sovereign Entity and the Sovereign Obligations of any such registered Sovereign Person or Executive Office in Ucadia or Non-Ucadia Jurisdiction.

Regnum Remedium (Remedy)

343. The collection of Sovereign Rights of *Ius Regnum Remedium* (Remedy) contains nine (9) Rights being:-

Collection of Ius Regnum Remedium (Remedy)

(i) *Ius Regnum Remedium* being the Sovereign Right of Remedy, Relief, Redress or Compensation; and

(ii) *Ius Regnum Remedium Compensationis* being the Sovereign Right of Remedy of Compensation for Loss or Damages; and

(iii) *Ius Regnum Remedium Restitutionis* being the Sovereign Right of Remedy of Restitution for the Return of Property; and

(iv) *Ius Regnum Remedium Reparationis* being the Sovereign Right of Remedy of Restoration for the Repairing of Harm or Property; and

(v) *Ius Regnum Remedium Injunctionis* being the Sovereign Right of Remedy of Injunction to Enforce Performance or Prevent Behaviour of Another; and

(vi) *Ius Regnum Remedium Rescissionis* being the Sovereign Right of Remedy of Rescission to Cancel an Agreement or Transaction and Restore Parties to their Original Positions; and

(vii) *Ius Regnum Remedium Appellationis* being the Sovereign Right of Remedy of Appeal a Decision to a Higher Forum; and

(viii) *Ius Regnum Remedium Declarationis* being the Sovereign Right of Remedy of Declaratory Judgement; and

(ix) *Ius Regnum Remedium Sententiae* being the Sovereign Right of Remedy of Enforcement of Judgement.

Article 93 – Ius Regnum Poena (Penalty, Penitence or Punishment)

344. ***Ius Regnum Poena*** are the collection of Sovereign Rights of Penalty, Penitence or Punishment, as inherited from the collection of Ecclesiastical Rights *Ius Ecclesiae Poena*.

Ius Regnum Poena (Penalty & Punishment)

345. *Ius Regnum Poena* (Penalty & Punishment) is the twentieth collection of twenty-two *Instrumental Sovereign Rights* (*Instrumentalis Regnum Iurium*); and may be explicitly invoked or referenced by Sovereign Right of Action through a proper and

Invoking of Ius Regnum Poena (Penalty & Punishment)

registered Sovereign Entity and the Sovereign Obligations of any such registered Sovereign Person or Executive Office in Ucadia or Non-Ucadia Jurisdiction.

346. The collection of Sovereign Rights of *Ius Regnum Poena* (Penalty & Punishment) contains five (5) Rights being:- Collection of Ius Regnum Poena (Penalty & Punishment)

(i) *Ius Regnum Poena* being the Sovereign Right of Penalty & Punishment; and

(ii) *Ius Regnum Remissionis Poenae* being the Sovereign Right of Remission in the significant lessening of Penalties upon prior and full Acceptance of Culpability and Evidence of Genuine Remorse and Efforts to Change before any Trial; and

(iii) *Ius Regnum Exacerbationis Poenae* being the Sovereign Right of Exacerbation in the significant increasing of severity of Penalties upon prior Refusal to Accept Culpability or Demonstrate Genuine Remorse or Change before any Trial; and

(iv) *Ius Regnum Appellationis Poenae* being the Sovereign Right to Appeal Punishment to a Decision to a Higher Forum; and

(v) *Ius Regnum Custodiae Vitae* being the Sovereign Right of Custody of Life whereby the Life of the Convicted must continue to be protected and sustained and cannot be threatened during any period of punishment.

Article 94 – Ius Regnum Clementia (Mercy)

347. ***Ius Regnum Clementia*** are the collection of Sovereign Rights of Mercy & Forgiveness, as inherited from the collection of Ecclesiastical Rights *Ius Ecclesiae Clementia*. Ius Regnum Clementia (Mercy)

348. *Ius Regnum Clementia* (Mercy) is the twenty-first collection of twenty-two *Instrumental Sovereign Rights* (*Instrumentalis Regnum Iurium*); and may be explicitly invoked or referenced by Sovereign Right of Action through a proper and registered Sovereign Entity and the Sovereign Obligations of any such registered Sovereign Person or Executive Office in Ucadia or Non-Ucadia Jurisdiction. Invoking of Ius Regnum Clementia (Mercy)

349. The collection of Sovereign Rights of *Ius Regnum Clementia* (Mercy) contains two (2) Rights being:- Collection of Ius Regnum Clementia (Mercy)

(i) *Ius Regnum Clementia* being the Sovereign Right of Mercy & Forgiveness; and

(ii) *Ius Expurgationis Instrumenti Convicti* being the Sovereign

Right of Convicted Record Expurgation at Conclusion of Punishment in recognition for prior and full Acceptance of Culpability and Evidence of Genuine Remorse and Efforts to Change before any Trial and Conviction.

Article 95 – Ius Regnum Actionum (Right of Action)

350. ***Ius Regnum Actionum*** are the collection of Sovereign Rights of Action, as inherited from the collection of Ecclesiastical Rights *Ius Ecclesiae Actionum*.

Ius Regnum Actionum (Right of Action)

351. *Ius Regnum Actionum* (Rights of Action) is the twenty-second collection of twenty-two *Instrumental Sovereign Rights* (*Instrumentalis Regnum Iurium*); and may be explicitly invoked or referenced by Sovereign Right of Action through a proper and registered Sovereign Entity and the Sovereign Obligations of any such registered Sovereign Person or Executive Office in Ucadia or Non-Ucadia Jurisdiction.

Invoking of Ius Regnum Actionum (Right of Action)

352. The collection of Sovereign Rights of *Ius Regnum Actionum* (Rights of Action) contains eleven (11) Rights being:-

Collection of Ius Regnum Actionum (Right of Action)

(i) *Ius Regnum Actionum* being the Sovereign Right of Action; and

(ii) *Ius Regnum Abstinentiae* being the Sovereign Right to Abstain from Action; and

(iii) *Ius Regnum Causae Actionis* being the Sovereign Right of Valid Cause for an Action, whereby clear Evidence of a Wrong Exists; and

(iv) *Ius Regnum Obligationis Actionis* being the Sovereign Right of Obligation for an Action, whereby clear Evidence Exists of a Duty of Care or Performance Owed; and

(v) *Ius Regnum Proximitatis Actionis* being the Sovereign Right of Proximity for an Action, whereby the one bringing the Action is in close Proximity to the Issue; and

(vi) *Ius Regnum Temporis Actionis* being the Sovereign Right of Timeliness for an Action, whereby no time barrier exists for bringing such an Action; and

(vii) *Ius Regnum Iniuriae Actionis* being the Sovereign Right of Injury for an Action, whereby the one bringing the Action has suffered an actual harm or damages; and

(viii) *Ius Regnum Remedium Actionis* being the Sovereign Right of

Remedy for an Action, whereby the Remedy sought is possible under the relevant Jurisdiction; and

(ix) *Ius Regnum Iurisdictionis Actionis* being the Sovereign Right of Jurisdiction for an Action, whereby the Jurisdiction proposed is the correct and valid forum and venue for such an Action; and

(x) *Ius Regnum Formae Actionis* being the Sovereign Right of Form for an Action, whereby the proposed Action conforms to the rules and bylaws of the relevant Jurisdiction in its format, presentation and arguments; and

(xi) *Ius Regnum Loci Standi Actionis* being the Sovereign Right of Standing for an Action constituting all previously mentioned Rights of this collection.

3.4 – Sovereign Writs of Rights

Article 96 – Sovereign Writs of Rights

353. ***Sovereign Writs of Rights*** (*Recto Regnum Iurium*) is Sovereign Rights associated with the one, true and only forms of Sovereign Writs. Sovereign Writs of Rights

354. In accord with the *Lex Positivum* (Maxims Positive Law), A ***Writ*** is a formal written command issued by a court or judicial authority, often used to initiate, conclude or command some action in a legal proceeding. A valid *Writ* may only be issued under the proper Ecclesiastical and Sovereign Authority of the most sacred Covenant known as *Pactum De Singularis Caelum*: Writ

(i) A Writ is not an order – it is an absolute command that cannot be challenged. An order by its legal and commercial meaning is an offer that may be negotiated. Whereas a Writ, by definition is not negotiable. Therefore, any definition that states a Writ may be defined as an order is patently false and fraudulent; and

(ii) A valid and legitimate Writ by its very nature originates as an ecclesiastical instrument requiring precise creation and purpose. To simply call an instrument a Writ and act as if it possesses the same qualities as a legitimate writ without the attendant care, authority or creation is a most grave injury to the Law itself; and

(iii) A body may possess the right to appoint one or more agents under validly signed and sealed warrants. However, such persons have no right legally or lawfully to issue a Writ unless they themselves are also appointed under Ucadian Law as per the present Maxims. If such persons are not appointed to their position under such Authority, then any Writs they issue are *ipso facto* (as a fact of law) null and void; and

(iv) Corporations and agents cannot create or issue valid Writs. Nor may a nation issue such Writs unless the Executive claims absolute sovereign authority in accord with Ucadian Law; and

(v) Any Laws that have been passed that attempt to permit the issuing of writs by corporations or agents are an abomination and contrary to the very source of authority of Writs. Such documents therefore issued have no more legal or lawful effect than an offer or notice. The enforcement therefore of such instruments as if they are writs is without question illegal and unlawful – contrary to very foundations of Law. An invalid writ has no force or effect ecclesiastically, lawfully or legally.

355. The enforcement and coercive powers of Perfect Writs of Right may only be issued in relation to Members of One Heaven and Ucadia being Divine Persons, or True Persons or Superior Persons, as well as any other lesser bodies, bodies politic, associations, partnerships, companies, entities, fraternities, religious organisations, corporations or persons under the Jurisdiction of the Divine Creator of all Existence and all Heaven and Earth. Enforcement of Perfect Writs

356. All *Sovereign Writs of Rights* are delegated by proper *Mandate* to the Governments of valid and legitimate Sovereign Ucadia Bodies and Entities (including but not limited to Ucadia Universities, Provinces, Campuses, Foundations and Agencies); and to those existing and internationally recognised Non-Ucadian Sovereign Bodies and Entities by in force treaties and agreements in accord with the most sacred Covenant *Pactum De Singularis Caelum*. Delegation of Sovereign Writs of Rights

357. All *Sovereign Writs of Rights* are assumed to be automatically invoked through the proper operation and function of the Governing Instruments, Codes and Bylaws of valid and legitimate Sovereign Ucadia Bodies and Entities (including but not limited to Ucadia Universities, Provinces, Campuses, Foundations and Agencies); and through the operation and function of in force treaties and agreements with existing and internationally recognised Non-Ucadian Sovereign Bodies and Entities. Invocation of Sovereign Writs of Rights

358. The following valid eleven (11) *Sovereign Writs of Rights* (*Recto Regnum Iurium*) is recognised in accord with the most sacred Covenant *Pactum De Singularis Caelum* and these present Maxims:- List of Sovereign Writs of Rights (Recto Regnum Iurium)

(i) "**Recto Regnum Originalis**" is the Sovereign Original Writ of Right, as inherited from the Ecclesiastical Right *Recto Ecclesiae Originalis*; and

(ii) "**Recto Regnum Iubemus**" is the Sovereign Writ of Right of Command or Authorisation, as inherited from the Ecclesiastical Right *Recto Ecclesiae Apocalypsis*; and

(iii) "**Recto Regnum Investigationis**" is the Sovereign Writ of Right of Inquiry or Review, as inherited from the Ecclesiastical Right *Recto Ecclesiae Investigationis*; and

(iv) "**Recto Regnum Capimus**" is the Sovereign Writ of Right of Surrender or Arrest of Person, as inherited from the Ecclesiastical Right *Recto Ecclesiae Capimus*; and

(v) "**Recto Regnum Custodiae**" is the Sovereign Writ of Right of Surrender or Seizure of Property, as inherited from the Ecclesiastical Right *Recto Ecclesiae Custodiae*; and

(vi) "**Recto Regnum Corrigimus**" is the Sovereign Writ of Right of Correction of Records, Rulings, Laws or Instruments, as inherited from the Ecclesiastical Right *Recto Ecclesiae Corrigimus*; and

(vii) "**Recto Regnum Expurgatio**" is the Sovereign Writ of Right of Expurgation of Records, Rulings, Laws or Instruments, as inherited from the Ecclesiastical Right *Recto Ecclesiae Expurgatio*; and

(viii) "**Recto Regnum Abrogatio**" is the Sovereign Writ of Right of Annulment of Records, Rulings, Laws or Instruments, as inherited from the Ecclesiastical Right *Recto Ecclesiae Abrogatio*; and

(ix) "**Recto Regnum Inhibitio**" is the Sovereign Writ of Right of Prohibition or Restraint, as inherited from the Ecclesiastical Right *Recto Ecclesiae Inhibitio*; and

(x) "**Recto Regnum Restitutio**" is the Sovereign Writ of Right of Restitution, as inherited from the Ecclesiastical Right *Recto Ecclesiae Restitutio*; and

(xi) "**Recto Regnum Restoratio**" is the Sovereign Writ of Right of Restoration, as inherited from the Ecclesiastical Right *Recto Ecclesiae Restoratio*.

359. The issue of a valid and legitimate Writ in accord with Ucadian Law and the present Maxims must follow a series of procedural steps

Procedural Steps of valid Writ

before any actual Writ is issued and enforcement executed:

(i) The first procedural step is the *Petition* or "*Petitio*", whereby a duly authorised Ucadia Member as Petitioner, produces the necessary documentation, affidavits, evidence and memorandum as an Application or Complaint or Petition to the appropriate competent forum of Law of the Sovereign Ucadia Entity. In doing so, the Petitioner is also a Grantor in the formation of a sacred and unbreakable trust that will form the basis of the review, possible approval of the writ and its execution; and

(ii) The *Confidant* that receives the Petition is a duly authorised official of the proper Court, on behalf of the same Court that then acts as Trustee concerning the matter as the Court of Original Jurisdiction. The Court then reviews the Petition and its merits and decides whether sufficient substance exists to then accept and act upon the Petition and issue a Writ. This judgement is called the Summary; and

(iii) If it is found by a competent forum of Law that a Writ should be issued, the Court as Trustee shall then become Principal in issuing commands through the Writ to one or more Agents as Fiduciaries in Trust, to execute the Writ and obtain the necessary Remedy.

360. A Petition, also known as a *Petitio* as the cause of action in the formation of any valid Writ, is an Instrument in writing, containing a prayer from the person presenting it, called the Petitioner, to the body or person to whom it is presented, for the redress of some wrong, or the grant of some favour, that the latter has the Right to give or witness as true, with the components being:- Petitio (Petition)

(i) *Title*, being the opening summary of the name of the Petitioner, and the name of the Respondent(s), any existing Suit or Action Number, the name of the Petition in relation to a certain Writ, the Ucadia Space Day Time; and

(ii) *Syllabus*, being the briefest summary in 250 words or less as to the nature of the petition, the main parties and context; and

(iii) *Parties*, being the parties related to the Petition; and

(iv) *Contents Page*, being the summary of remaining sections of the document and page location; and

(v) *Jurisdiction*, being the statement of Jurisdiction and Authority of the competent forum of Law to receive and determine the merits of granting the Writ as well as any questions regarding jurisdictional authority over other parties; and

(vi) *Statement of Facts*, being the key summary of key facts in chronological order, in support of the petition; and

(vii) *Arguments*, being the key arguments in law relating to the facts as to why the Writ should be granted; and

(viii) *Citations and References*, being the summary of citations of various laws or maxims or references as a bibliography in support of such references being used in Arguments; and

(ix) *Prayer for Remedy*, being the specific and individual actions requested in logical sequence and order; and

(x) *Appendix of Exhibits*, being the document referred in the attached Affidavit and in the Arguments of the Petition.

361. All Petitions are reviewed for approval or denial by a competent forum of Law according to the following essential criteria:- Criteria for Review of Petition

(i) Does the Petition document provide written answers to all the essential administrative elements required, in the order required, within the page limits required and format required?; and

(ii) Does the Syllabus of the Petition match in the broadest and general sense the terms by which such a writ is normally issued?; and

(iii) Does the Prayer for Justice of the Petition match the conditions of remedy by which such a writ may be issued?; and

(iv) Do the Arguments outlined within the Petition match the essential criteria that must be present for such a writ to be issued?; and

(v) Do the Arguments within the Petition provide one or more exhibits of proof contained within the Appendix to the Petition?; and

(vi) Is there sufficient evidence based on the Arguments and Appendix of the Petition to conclude that the Respondent is within the Jurisdiction of the Court?; and

(vii) Is there sufficient evidence based on the Arguments and Appendix of the Petition to conclude that the Court has sufficient Jurisdiction and right to appoint and bond one or more Agents with enforcing the writ through one or more Warrants?

362. The *Prayer for Relief* is the fundamental element of any valid Petition and specifies in the briefest of sentences, the individual actions requested in logical sequence, without repetition, in relation to a specific form of Sovereign Writ:-

Prayer for Remedy and Essential Conditions

(i) Different types of Sovereign Writs have different Essential Conditions being the conditions that must be present before a Sovereign Writ may be issued; and

(ii) A Prayer containing an individual action that is inconsistent with the purpose or nature of that kind of Writ, or is inconsistent with the Essential Conditions for issuing such a Writ therefore renders such a Prayer in error and void of effect; and

(iii) A Writ cannot be issued when a Prayer is in error; and

(iv) Because the accuracy of the Prayer is so essential, A Prayer will usually contain less than six actions.

363. A Summary, also known as a *Summa* as the formal response from a competent forum of Law, is an Instrument in writing, containing an opinion from the Confidant concerning a Petition and whether such Petition has merit and honours the form and intention of such sacred and holy writ. All valid and legitimate Petitions must be answered by a Summary within forty days of being received and acknowledged. However, a Sovereign Writ can only be issued if in the opinion of the court, the Petition meets the strictest guidelines within the Rule of Law. The standard elements to a valid Summary are:

Summa (Summary)

(i) *Title*, being the opening summary of the name of the Confidant, and the name of the Petitioner, and the name of the Respondent(s), any existing Writ Number, the name of the Petition in relation to a certain Writ, the Ucadia Space Day Time; and

(ii) *Summary,* being the briefest summary in 500 words or less as to the nature of the petition and whether in the opinion of the competent forum the writ should be granted or denied; and

(iii) *Contents Page*, being the summary of remaining sections of the document and page location; and

(iv) *Jurisdiction*, being the observation and statement of Jurisdiction and Authority of the competent forum of Law to receive and determine the merits of granting the Writ as well as any questions regarding jurisdictional authority over other parties; and

(v) *Conflict of Law*, being any issues in respect of conflict of law; and

(vi) *Arguments*, being the key arguments in law relating as to why the Writ should be granted or denied; and

(vii) *Citations and References*, being the summary of citations of various laws or maxims or references as a bibliography in support of such references being used in Arguments; and

(viii) *Command of Action,* being the previous prayer, or revised prayer now expressed as a command of actions to be done by the Respondent(s) – only if the Summary agrees that a Writ is to be issued.

364. A Sovereign Writ may only be issued after a Summary is given by the relevant competent forum of Law in respect of the Petition. When a Sovereign Writ is agreed to be issued, the key information as outlined within the Summary is recorded and enrolled within the Register of Writs as the *Original Form* within the Court of Chancery of the Sovereign Ucadia Entity. Register of Writs

365. In relation to the Persons and Parties associated with a valid Writ: Relations of Persons to a Writ

(i) The Person who makes the Petition is called the *Petitioner* and is also the *Grantor* of any Rights to the court to pursue the matter in relation to the proposed Writ; and

(ii) The one (or more) with whom the Petitioner has grievance is called the *Respondent*; and

(iii) The Person who receives the Petition is a court official called the *Confidant* and is also the *Trustee* of the Trust formed through the Petition as the Trust Instrument; and

(iv) If the court approves the Petition, then the Court official that issues the Writ is called the *Principal*; and

(v) The one who receives command to execute the actions of a valid Writ is called the *Agent* of the Principal and is also a *Fiduciary* of a sub trust in the transfer of certain rights and powers to perform the necessary tasks.

366. Subject to these Maxims and Ucadian Law, the following types of Non-Ucadia writs are considered inferior, redundant and prohibited to be used by Ucadia bodies, courts, entities and officials, including (but not limited to):- Inferior and Redundant forms of Writs

(i) ***Attachment*** is a writ from a court for the seizure or attachment of property owned by a defendant. Under Ucadia Law and Jurisdiction, the Superior and Sovereign Writ of *Recto Regnum Custodiae* (Surrender or Seizure of Property) is used; and

(ii) ***Audita Querela*** (Latin for "the complaint having been heard") is a writ from a court that grants relief from a previous judgment or enforcement of a previous judgment that has become unjust or inequitable due to circumstances that arise after the judgment was issued. Under Ucadia Law and Jurisdiction, the Superior and Sovereign Writ of *Recto Regnum Corrigimus* (Correction of Records, Rulings, Laws or Instruments) is used; and

(iii) ***Capias*** (Latin for "you shall take") is a writ from a court used to direct law enforcement to take a person or certain property into custody. Under Ucadia Law and Jurisdiction, the Superior and Sovereign Writ of *Recto Regnum Capimus* (Surrender or Arrest of Person) is used; and

(iv) ***Certiorari*** (Latin for "to be more fully informed") is a writ from a higher court directing a lower court, tribunal, or public authority to send the record in a given case for review, effectively stripping the lower court of the specific authority to hear the matter. Under Ucadia Law and Jurisdiction, the Superior and Sovereign Writ of *Recto Regnum Investigationis* (Inquiry or Review) is used; and

(v) ***Coram Nobis*** (Latin for "the (error) in our/your presence") is a writ issued when a higher court has received the records of a previously adjudicated matter by an inferior court; and upon clear evidence of fundamental errors of law and failure of due process, orders the record be corrected. Under Ucadia Law and Jurisdiction, the Superior and Sovereign Writ of *Recto Regnum Corrigimus* (Correction of Records, Rulings, Laws or Instruments) is used; and

(vi) ***Entry*** is a writ used in property disputes, allowing the plaintiff to regain possession of land wrongfully held by another. Under Ucadia Law and Jurisdiction, the Superior and Sovereign Writ of *Recto Regnum Custodiae* (Surrender or Seizure of Property) is used; and

(vii) ***Fieri Facias*** (Latin for "cause [it] to be done") is a writ issued by a court to a sheriff or other authorised officer to seize and sell the debtor's property to satisfy a monetary judgment against them. Under Ucadia Law and Jurisdiction, the

Superior and Sovereign Writ of *Recto Regnum Custodiae* (Surrender or Seizure of Property) is used; and

(viii) ***Habeas Corpus*** (Latin for "we are to possess/have the body") is a writ issued by a higher court to a lower authority to release a prisoner from unlawful detention together with formal interrogatories as why the prisoner should continue to be detained. Under Ucadia Law and Jurisdiction, the Superior and Sovereign Writ of *Recto Regnum Capimus* (Surrender or Arrest of Person) is used; and

(ix) ***Interdico*** (Latin for "banish, forbid") is a writ issued by a court to banish or declare a person an outlaw and forbid them any trade, communication or material support whatsoever. Under Ucadia Law and Jurisdiction, the Superior and Sovereign Writ of *Recto Regnum Inhibitio* (Prohibition or Restraint) is used; and

(x) ***Mandamus*** (Latin for "we command") is a writ issued by a court upon an official to cease any dishonourable and unlawful behaviour, or ordering lawful duty be performed. Under Ucadia Law and Jurisdiction, the Superior and Sovereign Writ of *Recto Regnum Iubemus* (Command or Authorisation) is used; and

(xi) ***Ne Exeat*** is a writ to prevent a person from leaving the jurisdiction of the court. Under Ucadia Law and Jurisdiction, the Superior and Sovereign Writ of *Recto Regnum Inhibitio* (Prohibition or Restraint) is used; and

(xii) ***Possession*** is a court order granting a party the right to possess a property, often used in landlord-tenant disputes. Under Ucadia Law and Jurisdiction, the Superior and Sovereign Writ of *Recto Regnum Custodiae* (Surrender or Seizure of Property) is used; and

(xiii) ***Procedendo*** (Latin for "go forward/advance (to judgment)") is issued when a superior court has reviewed the records of a matter and then orders an inferior court to proceed to judgment based on the corrected records. Under Ucadia Law and Jurisdiction, the Superior and Sovereign Writ of *Recto Regnum Investigationis* (Inquiry or Review) is used; and

(xiv) ***Prohibito*** (Latin for "forbiddance") is served as an order to an inferior court or law official to cease any and all further action on a matter as it has been addressed by a superior court. Under Ucadia Law and Jurisdiction, the Superior and

Sovereign Writ of *Recto Regnum Inhibitio* (Prohibition or Restraint) is used; and

(xv) ***Replevin*** is issued to recover goods wrongfully taken or held by someone, pending the final outcome of the case. Under Ucadia Law and Jurisdiction, the Superior and Sovereign Writ of *Recto Regnum Restoratio* (Restoration) is used; and

(xvi) ***Quo Warranto*** (Latin for "by what warrant?") is served requiring the person to whom it is directed to show via formal interrogatories what authority they have for exercising some right or power (or "franchise") they claim to hold. Under Ucadia Law and Jurisdiction, the Superior and Sovereign Writ of *Recto Regnum Investigationis* (Inquiry or Review) is used; and

(xvii) ***Scire Facias*** (Latin for "to know the causes") is served against the issue of false titles, letters patent and documents granting rights and privileges to which the parties named are not entitled. Under Ucadia Law and Jurisdiction, the Superior and Sovereign Writ of *Recto Regnum Corrigimus* (Correction of Records, Rulings, Laws or Instruments) is used; and

(xviii) ***Sequestration*** is a writ ordering the seizure of property to prevent its use or destruction during a lawsuit. Under Ucadia Law and Jurisdiction, the Superior and Sovereign Writ of *Recto Regnum Custodiae* (Surrender or Seizure of Property) is used.

367. Any alleged Writ that cannot prove its authority under Ucadian Law and the present Maxims, has none.

Writs without Authority

368. Any claimed forum of law or court or body that issues a matter using a "Case Number"; and therefore by implication the claim of a Writ of Trespass On the Case; or refers to the matter or action as a Case; or fails to produce a valid Writ as authorised under Ucadian Law and these present Maxims shall then be *prima facie* evidence of a deliberate and wilful fraud, deception, perfidy, profanity, sacrilege and blasphemy against all Heaven and Earth and automatic grounds for an Indictment within a competent forum of Law against any and all persons, without any ability to claim immunity, for unlimited liability and damages for such injury.

Fraudulent Writs and Claims as automatic Indictment

Article 97 – Rec.Reg. Originalis (Original Writ)

369. ***Recto Regnum Originalis*** is the Sovereign Original Writ (of Right), as inherited from the Ecclesiastical Right *Recto Ecclesiae Originalis*. It is the first of eleven Sovereign Writs. Rec.Reg. Originalis (Original Writ)

370. The *Original Writ of Right* (*Recto Regnum Originalis*) is reserved as the Remedy when any Ucadia Person or Entity possesses a valid Cause of Action upon some wrong, or injury as defined by a valid Memorandum of Complaint or Indictment; and supported by a properly invoked Affidavit as testimony. The Original Writ of Right or "Original Writ" shall then be the foundation of any proceedings within a competent forum of law. Purpose of Rec.Reg. Originalis (Original Writ)

371. The Rights of the *Original Writ of Right*, also known as *Recto Regnum Originalis,* are those actionable Rights embedded within the nature and character of such a Sovereign Writ; and then able to be dispensed through proper Warrants to duly authorised Agents. In accord with Ucadian Law and the present Maxims, the present type of Writ possesses the following Rights: Rights of Rec.Reg. Originalis (Original Writ)

(i) *Ius Regnum Originalis*, being the Right of Action and Entry of the Sovereign Original Writ; and

(ii) *Ius Regnum Auctoritas Originalis*, being the Right of Supreme Sovereign and Administrative Authority of the Sovereign Original Writ; and

(iii) *Ius Regnum Notitiae Originalis*, being the Sovereign and Administrative Right of Notice, Gazette, Promulgation and Publication of the Sovereign Original Writ; and

(iv) *Ius Regnum Iurisdictionis Originalis*, being the Sovereign and Administrative Right of Original Jurisdiction of the Sovereign Original Writ; and

(v) *Ius Regnum Decretum Originalis*, being the Right of Supreme Judicial Authority and Power of the Sovereign Original Writ, whereby there are no higher grounds of appeal or dispute in Law; and

(vi) *Ius Regnum Potentis Originalis*, being the Right of Sovereign, Judicial, Administrative and Military Power to use any and all necessary forms of coercive powers to enforce the Sovereign Original Writ; and

(vii) *Ius Regnum Armagestum Originalis*, being the Sovereign and

Administrative Right to possess, have, carry and bear arms, weapons, shields and defensive tools; and to recruit, employ and maintain soldiers and military, paramilitary and police personnel; and to engage in any and all necessary forms of coercive power to defend the true Rule of Law and enforce the Sovereign Original Writ; and

(viii) *Ius Regnum Preceptum Originalis*, being the Right of Sovereign Written Command, Rule, Principle and Edict to execute, enforce, carry out and uphold the Sovereign Original Writ; and

(ix) *Ius Regnum Agentis Originalis*, being the Sovereign and Administrative Right of Delegation, Commission and Assignment of Rights, Powers and Authority to one or more Agents to execute, enforce, carry out and uphold the Sovereign Original Writ.

Article 98 – Rec.Reg. Iubemus (Command or Authority)

372. ***Recto Regnum Iubemus*** is the Sovereign Writ of Command or Authorisation, as inherited from the Ecclesiastical Right *Recto Ecclesiae Apocalypsis*. It is the second of eleven Sovereign Writs. Rec.Reg. Iubemus (Command or Authorisation)

373. The *Sovereign Writ of Right of Command or Authorisation* (*Recto Regnum Iubemus*) is reserved as the Remedy when any Ucadia Officer or Ucadia Entity possessing a valid Mandate invokes and enacts such a Sovereign Writ to prevent or cease the continued violation of one or more valid Rights, or redress one or more wrongs, or restore one or more Rights. Purpose of Rec.Reg. Iubemus (Command or Authorisation)

374. The Rights of the *Sovereign Writ of Command or Authorisation*, also known as *Recto Regnum Iubemus,* are those actionable Rights embedded within the nature and character of such a Sovereign Writ; and then able to be dispensed through proper Warrants to duly authorised Agents. In accord with Ucadian Law and the present Maxims, the present type of Writ possesses the following Rights: Rights of Rec.Reg. Iubemus (Command or Authorisation)

(i) *Ius Regnum Iubemus*, being the Right of Action and Entry of the Sovereign Writ of Right of Command or Authorisation; and

(ii) *Ius Regnum Auctoritas Iubemus*, being the Right of Supreme Sovereign and Administrative Authority of the Sovereign Writ of Right of Command or Authorisation; and

(iii) *Ius Regnum Notitiae Iubemus*, being the Sovereign and Administrative Right of Notice, Gazette, Promulgation and Publication of the Sovereign Writ of Right of Command or Authorisation; and

(iv) *Ius Regnum Iurisdictionis Iubemus*, being the Sovereign and Administrative Right of Original Jurisdiction of the Sovereign Writ of Right of Command or Authorisation; and

(v) *Ius Regnum Decretum Iubemus*, being the Right of Supreme Judicial Authority and Power of the Sovereign Writ of Right of Command or Authorisation, whereby there are no higher grounds of appeal or dispute in Law; and

(vi) *Ius Regnum Potentis Iubemus*, being the Right of Sovereign, Judicial, Administrative and Military Power to use any and all necessary forms of coercive powers to enforce the Sovereign Writ of Right of Command or Authorisation; and

(vii) *Ius Regnum Armagestum Iubemus*, being the Sovereign and Administrative Right to possess, have, carry and bear arms, weapons, shields and defensive tools; and to recruit, employ and maintain soldiers and military, paramilitary and police personnel; and to engage in any and all necessary forms of coercive power to defend the true Rule of Law and enforce the Sovereign Writ of Right of Command or Authorisation; and

(viii) *Ius Regnum Preceptum Iubemus*, being the Right of Sovereign Written Command, Rule, Principle and Edict to execute, enforce, carry out and uphold the Sovereign Writ of Right of Command or Authorisation; and

(ix) *Ius Regnum Agentis Iubemus*, being the Sovereign and Administrative Right of Delegation, Commission and Assignment of Rights, Powers and Authority to one or more Agents to execute, enforce, carry out and uphold the Sovereign Writ of Right of Command or Authorisation.

Article 99 – Rec.Reg. Investigationis (Inquiry or Review)

375. ***Recto Regnum Investigationis*** is the Sovereign Writ of Right of Inquiry or Review, as inherited from the Ecclesiastical Right *Recto Ecclesiae Investigationis*. It is the third of eleven Sovereign Writs. Rec.Reg. Investigationis (Inquiry or Review)

376. The *Sovereign Writ of Right of Inquiry or Review* (*Recto Regnum Investigationis*) is reserved as the Remedy when any Ucadia Person Purpose of Rec.Reg. Investigationis or Ucadia Entity is faced with compelling evidence of persistent obstruction, denial or delay as to the truth of a matter material to one or more valid Rights, or the existence or state of affairs concerning one or more concepts or objects material to one or more valid Rights.

(Inquiry or Review)

377. The Rights of the *Sovereign Writ of Inquiry or Review*, also known as *Recto Regnum Investigationis,* are those actionable Rights embedded within the nature and character of such a Sovereign Writ; and then able to be dispensed through proper Warrants to duly authorised Agents. In accord with Ucadian Law and the present Maxims, the present type of Writ possesses the following Rights:

Rights of Entry & Action of Rec.Reg. Investigationis (Inquiry or Review)

(i) *Ius Regnum Actionis Investigationis*, being the Right of Action and Entry of the Sovereign Writ of Right of Inquiry or Review; and

(ii) *Ius Regnum Auctoritas Investigationis*, being the Right of Supreme Sovereign and Administrative Authority of the Sovereign Writ of Right of Inquiry or Review; and

(iii) *Ius Regnum Notitiae Investigationis*, being the Sovereign and Administrative Right of Notice, Gazette, Promulgation and Publication of the Sovereign Writ of Right of Inquiry or Review; and

(iv) *Ius Regnum Iurisdictionis Investigationis*, being the Sovereign and Administrative Right of Original Jurisdiction of the Sovereign Writ of Right of Inquiry or Review; and

(v) *Ius Regnum Decretum Investigationis*, being the Right of Supreme Judicial Authority and Power of the Sovereign Writ of Inquiry and Search, whereby there are no higher grounds of appeal or dispute in Law; and

(vi) *Ius Regnum Potentis Investigationis*, being the Right of Sovereign, Judicial, Administrative and Military Power to use any and all necessary forms of coercive powers to enforce the Sovereign Writ of Right of Inquiry or Review; and

(vii) *Ius Regnum Armagestum Investigationis*, being the Sovereign and Administrative Right to possess, have, carry and bear arms, weapons, shields and defensive tools; and to recruit, employ and maintain soldiers and military, paramilitary and police personnel; and to engage in any and all necessary forms of coercive power to defend the true Rule of Law and enforce the Sovereign Writ of Right of Inquiry or Review; and

(viii) *Ius Regnum Preceptum Investigationis*, being the Right of

Sovereign Written Command, Rule, Principle and Edict to execute, enforce, carry out and uphold the Sovereign Writ of Right of Inquiry or Review; and

(ix) *Ius Regnum Agentis Investigationis*, being the Sovereign and Administrative Right of Delegation, Commission and Assignment of Rights, Powers and Authority to one or more Agents to execute, enforce, carry out and uphold the Sovereign Writ of Right of Inquiry or Review.

Article 100 – Rec.Reg. Capimus (Surrender or Arrest of Person)

378. ***Recto Regnum Capimus*** is the Sovereign Writ of Right of Surrender or Arrest of Person, as inherited from the Ecclesiastical Right *Recto Ecclesiae Capimus*. It is the fourth of eleven Sovereign Writs. Rec.Reg. Capimus (Surrender or Arrest of Person)

379. The *Sovereign Writ of Right of Surrender or Arrest of Person*, (*Recto Regnum Capimus*) is reserved as the Remedy when any Ucadia Person or Ucadia Entity possesses compelling evidence that certain objects or concepts or forms or property are being held, detained or possessed by another party in direct violation of one or more valid Rights. Purpose of Rec.Reg. Capimus (Surrender or Arrest of Person)

380. The *Sovereign Writ of Right of Surrender or Arrest of Person*, also known as *Recto Regnum Capimus,* are those actionable Rights embedded within the nature and character of such a Sovereign Writ; and then able to be dispensed through proper Warrants to duly authorised Agents. In accord with Ucadian Law and the present Maxims, the present type of Writ possesses the following Rights: Rights of Rec.Reg. Capimus (Surrender or Arrest of Person)

(i) *Ius Regnum Actionis Capimus*, being the Right of Action and Entry of the Sovereign Writ of Right of Surrender or Arrest of Person; and

(ii) *Ius Regnum Auctoritas Capimus*, being the Right of Supreme Sovereign and Administrative Authority of the Sovereign Writ of Right of Surrender or Arrest of Person; and

(iii) *Ius Regnum Notitiae Capimus*, being the Sovereign and Administrative Right of Notice, Gazette, Promulgation and Publication of the Sovereign Writ of Right of Surrender or Arrest of Person; and

(iv) *Ius Regnum Iurisdictionis Capimus*, being the Sovereign and Administrative Right of Original Jurisdiction of the Sovereign

Writ of Right of Surrender or Arrest of Person; and

(v) *Ius Regnum Decretum Capimus*, being the Right of Supreme Judicial Authority and Power of the Sovereign Writ of Right of Surrender or Arrest of Person, whereby there are no higher grounds of appeal or dispute in Law; and

(vi) *Ius Regnum Potentis Capimus*, being the Right of Sovereign, Judicial, Administrative and Military Power to use any and all necessary forms of coercive powers to enforce the Sovereign Writ of Right of Surrender or Arrest of Person; and

(vii) *Ius Regnum Armagestum Capimus*, being the Sovereign and Administrative Right to possess, have, carry and bear arms, weapons, shields and defensive tools; and to recruit, employ and maintain soldiers and military, paramilitary and police personnel; and to engage in any and all necessary forms of coercive power to defend the true Rule of Law and enforce the Sovereign Writ of Right of Surrender or Arrest of Person; and

(viii) *Ius Regnum Preceptum Capimus*, being the Right of Sovereign Written Command, Rule, Principle and Edict to execute, enforce, carry out and uphold the Sovereign Writ of Right of Surrender or Arrest of Person; and

(ix) *Ius Regnum Agentis Capimus*, being the Sovereign and Administrative Right of Delegation, Commission and Assignment of Rights, Powers and Authority to one or more Agents to execute, enforce, carry out and uphold the Sovereign Writ of Right of Surrender or Arrest of Person.

Article 101 – Rec.Reg. Custodiae (Surrender or Seizure of Property)

381. ***Recto Regnum Custodiae*** is the Sovereign Writ of Right of Surrender or Seizure of Property, as inherited from the Ecclesiastical Right *Recto Ecclesiae Custodiae*. It is the fifth of eleven Sovereign Writs. Rec.Reg. Custodiae (Seizure of Property)

382. The *Sovereign Writ of Right of Surrender or Seizure of Property* (*Recto Regnum Custodiae*) is reserved as the Remedy when any Ucadia Person or Ucadia Entity possesses compelling evidence of probable cause that a party did violate one or more valid Rights or continues to be in violation of one or more valid Rights. Purpose of Rec.Reg. Custodiae (Seizure of Property)

383. The Rights of the *Sovereign Writ of Right of Surrender or Seizure of Property*, also known as *Recto Regnum Custodiae,* are those Rights of Rec.Reg. Custodiae actionable Rights embedded within the nature and character of such a Sovereign Writ; and then able to be dispensed through proper Warrants to duly authorised Agents. In accord with Ucadian Law and the present Maxims, the present type of Writ possesses the following Rights: (Seizure of Property)

(i) *Ius Regnum Actionis Custodiae*, being the Right of Action and Entry of the Sovereign Writ of Right of Surrender or Seizure of Property; and

(ii) *Ius Regnum Auctoritas Custodiae*, being the Right of Supreme Sovereign and Administrative Authority of the Sovereign Writ of Right of Surrender or Seizure of Property; and

(iii) *Ius Regnum Notitiae Custodiae*, being the Sovereign and Administrative Right of Notice, Gazette, Promulgation and Publication of the Sovereign Writ of Right of Surrender or Seizure of Property; and

(iv) *Ius Regnum Iurisdictionis Custodiae*, being the Sovereign and Administrative Right of Original Jurisdiction of the Sovereign Writ of Right of Surrender or Seizure of Property; and

(v) *Ius Regnum Decretum Custodiae*, being the Right of Supreme Judicial Authority and Power of the Sovereign Writ of Right of Surrender or Seizure of Property, whereby there are no higher grounds of appeal or dispute in Law; and

(vi) *Ius Regnum Potentis Custodiae*, being the Right of Sovereign, Judicial, Administrative and Military Power to use any and all necessary forms of coercive powers to enforce the Sovereign Writ of Right of Surrender or Seizure of Property; and

(vii) *Ius Regnum Armagestum Custodiae*, being the Sovereign and Administrative Right to possess, have, carry and bear arms, weapons, shields and defensive tools; and to recruit, employ and maintain soldiers and military, paramilitary and police personnel; and to engage in any and all necessary forms of coercive power to defend the true Rule of Law and enforce the Sovereign Writ of Right of Surrender or Seizure of Property; and

(viii) *Ius Regnum Preceptum Custodiae*, being the Right of Sovereign Written Command, Rule, Principle and Edict to execute, enforce, carry out and uphold the Sovereign Writ of Right of Surrender or Seizure of Property; and

(ix) *Ius Regnum Agentis Custodiae*, being the Sovereign and Administrative Right of Delegation, Commission and Assignment of Rights, Powers and Authority to one or more Agents to execute, enforce, carry out and uphold the Sovereign Writ of Right of Surrender or Seizure of Property.

Article 102 – Rec.Reg. Corrigimus (Correction of Records, Rulings, Laws or Instruments)

384. ***Recto Regnum Corrigimus*** is the Sovereign Writ of Right of Correction of Records, Rulings, Laws or Instruments, as inherited from the Ecclesiastical Right *Recto Ecclesiae Corrigimus*. It is the sixth of eleven Sovereign Writs.

Rec.Reg. Corrigimus (Correction)

385. The *Sovereign Writ of Right of Correction of Records, Rulings, Laws or Instruments* (*Recto Regnum Corrigimus*) is reserved as the Remedy when any Ucadia Person or Ucadia Entity possesses compelling evidence of false records, false titles, letters patent or other documents granting certain rights and privileges to other parties that are not entitled in direct violation of one or more valid Rights.

Purpose of Rec.Reg. Corrigimus (Correction)

386. The Rights of the *Sovereign Writ of Right of Correction of Records, Rulings, Laws or Instruments*, also known as *Recto Regnum Corrigimus,* are those actionable Rights embedded within the nature and character of such a Sovereign Writ; and then able to be dispensed through proper Warrants to duly authorised Agents. In accord with Ucadian Law and the present Maxims, the present type of Writ possesses the following Rights:

Rights of Entry & Action of the Superior Writ of Records Correction

(i) *Ius Regnum Actionis Corrigimus*, being the Right of Action and Entry of the Sovereign Writ of Right of Correction of Records, Rulings, Laws or Instruments; and

(ii) *Ius Regnum Auctoritas Corrigimus*, being the Right of Supreme Sovereign and Administrative Authority of the Sovereign Writ of Right of Correction of Records, Rulings, Laws or Instruments; and

(iii) *Ius Regnum Notitiae Corrigimus*, being the Sovereign and Administrative Right of Notice, Gazette, Promulgation and Publication of the Sovereign Writ of Right of Correction of Records, Rulings, Laws or Instruments; and

(iv) *Ius Regnum Iurisdictionis Corrigimus*, being the Sovereign and Administrative Right of Original Jurisdiction of the Sovereign Writ of Right of Correction of Records, Rulings,

Laws or Instruments; and

(v) *Ius Regnum Decretum Corrigimus*, being the Right of Supreme Judicial Authority and Power of the Sovereign Writ of Right of Correction of Records, Rulings, Laws or Instruments, whereby there are no higher grounds of appeal or dispute in Law; and

(vi) *Ius Regnum Potentis Corrigimus*, being the Right of Sovereign, Judicial, Administrative and Military Power to use any and all necessary forms of coercive powers to enforce the Sovereign Writ of Right of Correction of Records, Rulings, Laws or Instruments; and

(vii) *Ius Regnum Armagestum Corrigimus*, being the Sovereign and Administrative Right to possess, have, carry and bear arms, weapons, shields and defensive tools; and to recruit, employ and maintain soldiers and military, paramilitary and police personnel; and to engage in any and all necessary forms of coercive power to defend the true Rule of Law and enforce the Sovereign Writ of Right of Correction of Records, Rulings, Laws or Instruments; and

(viii) *Ius Regnum Preceptum Corrigimus*, being the Right of Sovereign Written Command, Rule, Principle and Edict to execute, enforce, carry out and uphold the Sovereign Writ of Right of Correction of Records, Rulings, Laws or Instruments; and

(ix) *Ius Regnum Agentis Corrigimus*, being the Sovereign and Administrative Right of Delegation, Commission and Assignment of Rights, Powers and Authority to one or more Agents to execute, enforce, carry out and uphold the Sovereign Writ of Right of Correction of Records, Rulings, Laws or Instruments.

Article 103 – Rec.Reg. Expurgatio (Expurgation of Records, Rulings, Laws or Instruments)

387. ***Recto Regnum Expurgatio*** is the Sovereign Writ of Right of Expurgation of Records, Rulings, Laws or Instruments, as inherited from the Ecclesiastical Right *Recto Ecclesiae Expurgatio*. It is the seventh of eleven Sovereign Writs. Rec.Reg. Expurgatio (Expunge Record)

388. The *Sovereign Writ of Right of Expurgation of Records, Rulings, Laws or Instruments* (*Recto Regnum Expurgatio*) is reserved as the Remedy when any Ucadia Person or Ucadia Entity possesses Purpose of Rec.Reg. Expurgatio (Expunge compelling evidence of deliberately false records, false titles, misleading and deceptive documents by another party in direct violation of one or more valid Rights.

Record)

Rights of Entry & Action of the Superior Writ of Records Expungement

389. The Rights of the *Sovereign Writ of Right of Expurgation of Records, Rulings, Laws or Instruments,* also known as *Recto Regnum Expurgatio,* are those actionable Rights embedded within the nature and character of such a Sovereign Writ; and then able to be dispensed through proper Warrants to duly authorised Agents. In accord with Ucadian Law and the present Maxims, the present type of Writ possesses the following Rights:

(i) *Ius Regnum Actionis Expurgatio*, being the Right of Action and Entry of the Sovereign Writ of Right of Expurgation of Records, Rulings, Laws or Instruments; and

(ii) *Ius Regnum Auctoritas Expurgatio*, being the Right of Supreme Sovereign and Administrative Authority of the Sovereign Writ of Right of Expurgation of Records, Rulings, Laws or Instruments; and

(iii) *Ius Regnum Notitiae Expurgatio*, being the Sovereign and Administrative Right of Notice, Gazette, Promulgation and Publication of the Sovereign Writ of Right of Expurgation of Records, Rulings, Laws or Instruments; and

(iv) *Ius Regnum Iurisdictionis Expurgatio*, being the Sovereign and Administrative Right of Original Jurisdiction of the Sovereign Writ of Right of Expurgation of Records, Rulings, Laws or Instruments; and

(v) *Ius Regnum Decretum Expurgatio*, being the Right of Supreme Judicial Authority and Power of the Sovereign Writ of Right of Expurgation of Records, Rulings, Laws or Instruments, whereby there are no higher grounds of appeal or dispute in Law; and

(vi) *Ius Regnum Potentis Expurgatio*, being the Right of Sovereign, Judicial, Administrative and Military Power to use any and all necessary forms of coercive powers to enforce the Sovereign Writ of Right of Expurgation of Records, Rulings, Laws or Instruments; and

(vii) *Ius Regnum Armagestum Expurgatio*, being the Sovereign and Administrative Right to possess, have, carry and bear arms, weapons, shields and defensive tools; and to recruit, employ and maintain soldiers and military, paramilitary and police personnel; and to engage in any and all necessary forms of coercive power to defend the true Rule of Law and enforce the Sovereign Writ of Right of Expurgation of Records, Rulings, Laws or Instruments; and

(viii) *Ius Regnum Preceptum Expurgatio*, being the Right of Sovereign Written Command, Rule, Principle and Edict to execute, enforce, carry out and uphold the Sovereign Writ of Right of Expurgation of Records, Rulings, Laws or Instruments; and

(ix) *Ius Regnum Agentis Expurgatio*, being the Sovereign and Administrative Right of Delegation, Commission and Assignment of Rights, Powers and Authority to one or more Agents to execute, enforce, carry out and uphold the Sovereign Writ of Right of Expurgation of Records, Rulings, Laws or Instruments.

Article 104 – Rec.Reg. Abrogatio (Annulment of Records, Rulings, Laws or Instruments)

390. ***Recto Regnum Abrogatio*** is the Sovereign Writ of Right of Annulment of Records, Rulings, Laws or Instruments, as inherited from the Ecclesiastical Right *Recto Ecclesiae Abrogatio*. It is the eighth of eleven Sovereign Writs. Rec.Reg. Abrogatio (Annulment)

391. The *Sovereign Writ of Right of Annulment of Records, Rulings, Laws or Instruments* (*Recto Regnum Abrogatio*) is reserved as the Remedy when any Ucadia Person or Ucadia Entity possesses compelling evidence of deliberately false, or profane, or heretical, or fraudulent, or misleading or repugnant statutes, edicts, prescripts, rescripts, letters, charters, patents, bylaws, regulations, orders, judgements or other legal instruments in direct violation of one or more valid Rights. Purpose of Rec.Reg. Abrogatio (Annulment)

392. The Rights of the *Sovereign Writ of Right of Annulment of Records, Rulings, Laws or Instruments*, also known as *Recto Regnum Abrogatio,* are those actionable Rights embedded within the nature and character of such a Sovereign Writ; and then able to be dispensed through proper Warrants to duly authorised Agents. In accord with Ucadian Law and the present Maxims, the present type of Writ possesses the following Rights: Rights of Entry & Action of the Sovereign Writ of Annulment

(i) *Ius Regnum Actionis Abrogatio*, being the Right of Action and Entry of the Sovereign Writ of Right of Annulment of Records, Rulings, Laws or Instruments; and

(ii) *Ius Regnum Auctoritas Abrogatio*, being the Right of Supreme

Sovereign and Administrative Authority of the Sovereign Writ of Right of Annulment of Records, Rulings, Laws or Instruments; and

(iii) *Ius Regnum Notitiae Abrogatio*, being the Sovereign and Administrative Right of Notice, Gazette, Promulgation and Publication of the Sovereign Writ of Right of Annulment of Records, Rulings, Laws or Instruments; and

(iv) *Ius Regnum Iurisdictionis Abrogatio*, being the Sovereign and Administrative Right of Original Jurisdiction of the Sovereign Writ of Right of Annulment of Records, Rulings, Laws or Instruments; and

(v) *Ius Regnum Decretum Abrogatio*, being the Right of Supreme Judicial Authority and Power of the Sovereign Writ of Right of Annulment of Records, Rulings, Laws or Instruments, whereby there are no higher grounds of appeal or dispute in Law; and

(vi) *Ius Regnum Potentis Abrogatio*, being the Sovereign and Administrative Right to possess, have, carry and bear arms, weapons, shields and defensive tools; and to recruit, employ and maintain soldiers and military, paramilitary and police personnel; and to engage in any and all necessary forms of coercive power to defend the true Rule of Law and enforce the Sovereign Writ of Right of Annulment of Records, Rulings, Laws or Instruments; and

(vii) *Ius Regnum Armagestum Abrogatio*, being the Right of Sovereign, Judicial, Administrative and Military Power to use any and all necessary forms of coercive powers to enforce the Sovereign Writ of Right of Annulment of Records, Rulings, Laws or Instruments; and

(viii) *Ius Regnum Preceptum Abrogatio*, being the Right of Sovereign Written Command, Rule, Principle and Edict to execute, enforce, carry out and uphold the Sovereign Writ of Right of Annulment of Records, Rulings, Laws or Instruments; and

(ix) *Ius Regnum Agentis Abrogatio*, being the Sovereign and Administrative Right of Delegation, Commission and Assignment of Rights, Powers and Authority to one or more Agents to execute, enforce, carry out and uphold the Sovereign Writ of Right of Annulment of Records, Rulings, Laws or Instruments.

Article 105 – Rec.Reg. Inhibitio (Prohibition or Restraint)

393. ***Recto Regnum Inhibitio*** is the Sovereign Writ of Right of Prohibition or Restraint, as inherited from the Ecclesiastical Right *Recto Ecclesiae Inhibitio*. It is the ninth of eleven Sovereign Writs. Rec.Reg. Inhibitio (Prohibition or Restraint)

394. The *Sovereign Writ of Right of Prohibition or Restraint* (*Recto Regnum Inhibitio*) is reserved as the Remedy when any Ucadia Person or Ucadia Entity possesses compelling evidence of probable cause that one or more parties did persistently and habitually violate one or more valid Rights and continues to be in blatant violation of one or more valid Rights. Purpose of Rec.Reg. Inhibitio (Prohibition or Restraint)

395. The Rights of the *Sovereign Writ of Right of Prohibition or Restraint*, also known as *Recto Regnum Inhibitio,* are those actionable Rights embedded within the nature and character of such a Sovereign Writ; and then able to be dispensed through proper Warrants to duly authorised Agents. In accord with Ucadian Law and the present Maxims, the present type of Writ possesses the following Rights: Rights of Entry & Action of the Superior Writ of Prohibition

(i) *Ius Regnum Actionis Inhibitio*, being the Right of Action and Entry of the Sovereign Writ of Right of Prohibition or Restraint; and

(ii) *Ius Regnum Auctoritas Inhibitio*, being the Right of Supreme Sovereign and Administrative Authority of the Sovereign Writ of Right of Prohibition or Restraint; and

(iii) *Ius Regnum Notitiae Inhibitio*, being the Sovereign and Administrative Right of Notice, Gazette, Promulgation and Publication of the Sovereign Writ of Right of Prohibition or Restraint; and

(iv) *Ius Regnum Iurisdictionis Inhibitio*, being the Sovereign and Administrative Right of Original Jurisdiction of the Sovereign Writ of Right of Prohibition or Restraint; and

(v) *Ius Regnum Decretum Inhibitio*, being the Right of Supreme Judicial Authority and Power of the Sovereign Writ of Right of Prohibition or Restraint, whereby there are no higher grounds of appeal or dispute in Law; and

(vi) *Ius Regnum Potentis Inhibitio*, being the Right of Sovereign, Judicial, Administrative and Military Power to use any and all necessary forms of coercive powers to enforce the Sovereign

Writ of Right of Prohibition or Restraint; and

(vii) *Ius Regnum Armagestum Inhibitio*, being the Sovereign and Administrative Right to possess, have, carry and bear arms, weapons, shields and defensive tools; and to recruit, employ and maintain soldiers and military, paramilitary and police personnel; and to engage in any and all necessary forms of coercive power to defend the true Rule of Law and enforce the Sovereign Writ of Right of Prohibition or Restraint; and

(viii) *Ius Regnum Preceptum Inhibitio*, being the Right of Sovereign Written Command, Rule, Principle and Edict to execute, enforce, carry out and uphold the Sovereign Writ of Right of Prohibition or Restraint; and

(ix) *Ius Regnum Agentis Inhibitio*, being the Sovereign and Administrative Right of Delegation, Commission and Assignment of Rights, Powers and Authority to one or more Agents to execute, enforce, carry out and uphold the Sovereign Writ of Right of Prohibition or Restraint.

Article 106 – Rec.Reg. Restitutio (Restitution)

396. ***Recto Regnum Restitutio*** is the Sovereign Writ of Right of Restitution, as inherited from the Ecclesiastical Right *Recto Ecclesiae Restitutio*. It is the tenth of eleven Sovereign Writs. Rec.Reg. Restitutio (Restitution)

397. The *Sovereign Writ of Right of Restitution* (*Recto Regnum Restitutio*) is reserved as the Remedy when any Ucadia Person or Ucadia Entity possesses compelling evidence of probable cause that one or more parties did persistently and habitually violate one or more valid Rights, causing harm, injury and loss. Purpose of Rec.Reg. Restitutio (Restitution)

398. The Rights of the *Sovereign Writ of Right of Restitution*, also known as *Recto Regnum Restitutio,* are those actionable Rights embedded within the nature and character of such a Sovereign Writ; and then able to be dispensed through proper Warrants to duly authorised Agents. In accord with Ucadian Law and the present Maxims, the present type of Writ possesses the following Rights: Rights of Entry & Action of the Superior Writ of Restitution

(i) *Ius Regnum Actionis Restitutio*, being the Right of Action and Entry of the Sovereign Writ of Right of Restitution; and

(ii) *Ius Regnum Auctoritas Restitutio*, being the Right of Supreme Sovereign and Administrative Authority of the Sovereign Writ of Right of Restitution; and

(iii) *Ius Regnum Notitiae Restitutio*, being the Sovereign and Administrative Right of Notice, Gazette, Promulgation and Publication of the Sovereign Writ of Right of Restitution; and

(iv) *Ius Regnum Iurisdictionis Restitutio*, being the Sovereign and Administrative Right of Original Jurisdiction of the Sovereign Writ of Right of Restitution; and

(v) *Ius Regnum Decretum Restitutio*, being the Right of Supreme Judicial Authority and Power of the Sovereign Writ of Right of Restitution, whereby there are no higher grounds of appeal or dispute in Law; and

(vi) *Ius Regnum Potentis Restitutio*, being the Right of Sovereign, Judicial, Administrative and Military Power to use any and all necessary forms of coercive powers to enforce the Sovereign Writ of Right of Restitution; and

(vii) *Ius Regnum Armagestum Restitutio*, being the Sovereign and Administrative Right to possess, have, carry and bear arms, weapons, shields and defensive tools; and to recruit, employ and maintain soldiers and military, paramilitary and police personnel; and to engage in any and all necessary forms of coercive power to defend the true Rule of Law and enforce the Sovereign Writ of Right of Restitution; and

(viii) *Ius Regnum Preceptum Restitutio*, being the Right of Sovereign Written Command, Rule, Principle and Edict to execute, enforce, carry out and uphold the Sovereign Writ of Right of Restitution; and

(ix) *Ius Regnum Agentis Restitutio*, being the Sovereign and Administrative Right of Delegation, Commission and Assignment of Rights, Powers and Authority to one or more Agents to execute, enforce, carry out and uphold the Sovereign Writ of Right of Restitution.

Article 107 – Rec.Reg. Restoratio (Restoration)

399. ***Recto Regnum Restoratio*** is the Sovereign Writ of Right of Restoration, as inherited from the Ecclesiastical Right *Recto Ecclesiae Restoratio*. It is the eleventh of eleven Sovereign Writs. Rec.Reg. Restoratio (Restoration)

400. The *Sovereign Writ of Right of Restoration* (*Recto Regnum Restoratio*) is reserved as the Remedy when any Ucadia Person or Ucadia Entity possesses compelling evidence of probable cause that one or more parties did persistently and habitually violate one or more valid Rights, causing harm, injury and loss. Purpose of Rec.Reg. Restoratio (Restoration)

401. The Rights of the *Sovereign Writ of Right of Restoration*, also known as *Recto Regnum Restoratio,* are those actionable Rights embedded within the nature and character of such a Sovereign Writ; and then able to be dispensed through proper Warrants to duly authorised Agents. In accord with Ucadian Law and the present Maxims, the present type of Writ possesses the following Rights: Rights of Entry & Action of the Superior Writ of Restoration

(i) *Ius Regnum Actionis Restoratio*, being the Right of Action and Entry of the Sovereign Writ of Right of Restoration; and

(ii) *Ius Regnum Auctoritas Restoratio*, being the Right of Supreme Sovereign and Administrative Authority of the Sovereign Writ of Right of Restoration; and

(iii) *Ius Regnum Notitiae Restoratio*, being the Sovereign and Administrative Right of Notice, Gazette, Promulgation and Publication of the Sovereign Writ of Right of Restoration; and

(iv) *Ius Regnum Iurisdictionis Restoratio*, being the Sovereign and Administrative Right of Original Jurisdiction of the Sovereign Writ of Right of Restoration; and

(v) *Ius Regnum Decretum Restoratio*, being the Right of Supreme Judicial Authority and Power of the Sovereign Writ of Right of Restoration, whereby there are no higher grounds of appeal or dispute in Law; and

(vi) *Ius Regnum Potentis Restoratio*, being the Right of Sovereign, Judicial, Administrative and Military Power to use any and all necessary forms of coercive powers to enforce the Sovereign Writ of Right of Restoration; and

(vii) *Ius Regnum Armagestum Restoratio*, being the Sovereign and Administrative Right to possess, have, carry and bear arms, weapons, shields and defensive tools; and to recruit, employ and maintain soldiers and military, paramilitary and police personnel; and to engage in any and all necessary forms of coercive power to defend the true Rule of Law and enforce the Sovereign Writ of Right of Restoration; and

(viii) *Ius Regnum Preceptum Restoratio*, being the Right of Sovereign Written Command, Rule, Principle and Edict to execute, enforce, carry out and uphold the Sovereign Writ of Right of Restoration; and

(ix) *Ius Regnum Agentis Restoratio*, being the Sovereign and Administrative Right of Delegation, Commission and Assignment of Rights, Powers and Authority to one or more Agents to execute, enforce, carry out and uphold the Sovereign Writ of Right of Restoration.

3.5 – Sovereign Bills of Exception & Agreement

Article 108 – Sovereign Bills of Exception & Agreement

402. ***Sovereign Bills of Exception*** (*Rogatio Regnum Iurium*) are Sovereign Rights associated with the one, true and only forms of Bills of Exception, Citation and Agreement. Sovereign Bills of Exception

403. A ***Bill*** is a form of Demand and Order in writing, assured by one or more Rights granted, for some performance equivalent in specie of Real Money. A Bill is normally associated with at least one Certified Statement or Memorandum of Account and one Affidavit. Bill

404. In relation to the Persons and Parties associated with a Bill: Relations of Persons to a Bill

(i) The Person who makes or issues a valid Bill is called the *Maker* (also *Issuer*, or *Payor*, or *Drawer*); and

(ii) The Person to whom the Bill is addressed and paid (if an actual name is listed on the Note) is called the *Payee*; and

(iii) The Person who the Payee may nominate as the beneficiary and holder of the Bill is called the *Endorsee* (also *Indorsee* or *Order)*; and

(iv) The Person who is directed to make the payment on behalf of the Maker to the Payee is called the *Drawee* and once they accept the obligation becomes the *Acceptor*; and

(v) The Person who holds an original Bill (whether the note is addressed or not addressed) is called the *Holder*; and

(vi) The Person who agrees to underwrite and guarantee the Bill is called the *Guarantor* (also *Surety*).

405. A *Sovereign Bill of Exception* is the highest possible valid forms of Objection, Denial and Protest within International Law of Nations and Entities. Evidence of a valid record within the Ucadia Great Register and Public Record and Ucadia Gazette is *prima facie* proof of a duly promulgated *Sovereign Bill of Exception*:-

Nature of Sovereign Bills of Exception

(i) A *Sovereign Bill of Exception* is usually issued against a party following their failure to act according to the norms of law; and

(i) A *Sovereign Bill of Exception* requires the official seal of the Ucadia Entity or Office of Issue, as well as the signature of the Maker; and

(ii) All forms of defensive powers and protection including, but not limited to prevention, protection, suspension, stop, stay, injunction, restitution, restoration, seizure, search, sanction, lien, arrest, custody, penalty or satisfaction, is enacted via one or more valid *Sovereign Bills of Exception*.

406. A *Sovereign Bill of Agreement* is the highest possible valid forms of Demand and Order assured by one or more Rights granted, for some performance equivalent in specie of Real Money within International Law of Nations and Entities. Evidence of a valid record within the Ucadia Great Register and Public Record and Ucadia Gazette is *prima facie* proof of a duly promulgated *Sovereign Bill of Agreement*:-

Nature of Sovereign Bills of Agreement

(i) A *Sovereign Bill of Agreement* requires the official seal of the Ucadia Entity or Office of Issue, as well as the signature of the Maker; and

(ii) Similar to Bills of Exception, the mandatory information to be provided is dependent upon the type of Bill.

407. All *Sovereign Bills of Exception & Agreement* are delegated by proper *Mandate* to the Governments of valid and legitimate Sovereign Ucadia Bodies and Entities (including but not limited to Ucadia Universities, Provinces, Campuses, Foundations and Agencies); and to those existing and internationally recognised Non-Ucadian Sovereign Bodies and Entities by in force treaties and agreements in accord with the most sacred Covenant *Pactum De Singularis Caelum*.

Delegation of Sovereign Bills of Exception & Agreement

408. All *Sovereign Bills of Exception* are assumed to be automatically invoked through the proper operation and function of the Governing Instruments, Codes and Bylaws of valid and legitimate Sovereign

Invocation of Sovereign Bills of Exception & Agreement

Ucadia Bodies and Entities (including but not limited to Ucadia Universities, Provinces, Campuses, Foundations and Agencies); and through the operation and function of in force treaties and agreements with existing and internationally recognised Non-Ucadian Sovereign Bodies and Entities.

409. The following valid eleven (11) *Sovereign Bills of Exception & Agreement* (*Rogatio Regnum Iurium*) is recognised in accord with the most sacred Covenant *Pactum De Singularis Caelum* and these present Maxims:-

List of Sovereign Bills of Exception (Rogatio Regnum Iurium)

(i) "**Rogatio Regnum Recto**" is the Sovereign (Original) Bill of Right, as inherited from the Ecclesiastical Right *Rogatio Ecclesiae Recto*; and

(ii) "**Rogatio Regnum Iubemus**" is the Sovereign Bill of Right of Command or Authorisation, as inherited from the Ecclesiastical Right *Rogatio Ecclesiae Apocalypsis*; and

(iii) "**Rogatio Regnum Capimus**" is the Sovereign Bill of Right against Failure to Surrender or Arrest Person, as inherited from the Ecclesiastical Right *Rogatio Ecclesiae Capimus*; and

(iv) "**Rogatio Regnum Custodiae**" is the Sovereign Bill of Right against Failure to Surrender or Seize Property, as inherited from the Ecclesiastical Right *Rogatio Ecclesiae Custodiae*; and

(v) "**Rogatio Regnum Corrigimus**" is the Sovereign Bill of Right against Failure to Correct Records, Rulings, Laws or Instruments, as inherited from the Ecclesiastical Right *Rogatio Ecclesiae Corrigimus*; and

(vi) "**Rogatio Regnum Inhibitio**" is the Sovereign Bill of Right against Failure to Prohibit or Impose Limits as Instructed, as inherited from the Ecclesiastical Right *Rogatio Ecclesiae Inhibitio*; and

(vii) "**Rogatio Regnum Restitutio**" is the Sovereign Bill of Right of Restitution or Compensation, as inherited from the Ecclesiastical Right *Rogatio Ecclesiae Restituio*; and

(viii) "**Rogatio Regnum Credito**" is the Sovereign Bill of Right of Credit, as inherited from the Ecclesiastical Right *Rogatio Ecclesiae Credito*; and

(ix) "**Rogatio Regnum Permutatio**" is the Sovereign Bill of Right of Exchange, as inherited from the Ecclesiastical Right *Rogatio Ecclesiae Permutatio*; and

(x) "**Rogatio Regnum Venditio**" is the Sovereign Bill of Right of Sale, as inherited from the Ecclesiastical Right *Rogatio Ecclesiae Venditio*; and

(xi) "**Rogatio Regnum Traditio**" is the Sovereign Bill of Right of Lading, as inherited from the Ecclesiastical Right *Rogatio Ecclesiae Traditio*.

410. Subject to the essential conditions of a valid Instrument and Form as prescribed herein, the following essential elements must be present on the face of a valid Bill: Elements of a valid Bill

(i) *Bill Number* being a unique Bill Number within the relevant Register of Bills; and

(ii) *Ucadia Sacred Space-Day-Time Number Issued Under* being the numeric number for demonstrating the supreme jurisdiction, space and time whereby the Instrument is issued; and

(iii) *Ucadia Location of Issue* being the Location Number for the Ucadia University from where the Instrument is issued; and

(iv) *Ucadia Date and Reference Date* being the formal Ucadia Date and reference (Roman) date; and

(v) *Title* being the word "Bill" as a prominent word in the heading, or if a special type of Bill the full name of such type; and

(vi) *Obligation Account Number* being a valid eighteen digit Ucadia number in the form XXXXXX-XXXXXX-XXXXXX signifying the existence of a record of account, or file, or case, or statement in respect of the obligation having some monetary value; and

(vii) *Obligation Description* being a brief description of the obligation or monetary obligation of Ucadia Money or Non-Ucadian Lawful Public Money in words, even if the amount of money is also displayed in numbers; and

(viii) *Demand or Order* being the specific demand or order of the Bill regarding the Obligation; and

(ix) *Bordered Information* being that any information "extracted" from the Record is presented within a bordered box to indicate a "window" to the original and valid Record; and

(x) *One Witness* being a witnessed made or affirmed signed certification that the Bill and the information contained within it is valid; and

(xi) *Official Seal* of the Ucadia Official or Ucadia Entity.

411. All valid Bills must either state the amount of the Monetary Obligation on the face of the Instrument as proper and due disclosure and accounting of such obligation, or within a Memorandum of Account attached to the annexed documents to the Bill, stating clearly the total Monetary Obligations of the Drawee in accepting the obligations due.

Accounting of Monetary Obligation

412. The failure to provide a clear and proper accounting of the Monetary Obligation associated with a Bill, or the deliberate and wilful obscuring, hiding, fraud, perfidy or falsity in failing to provide such open and transparent accounting shall therefore invalidate any and all bills and any and all charges against such Bills. No person may be properly charged for an obligation without first knowing and being provided in writing an accounting of the monetary obligation.

Secret or Hidden Monetary Obligation invalidating Bill

413. The Acceptance of a valid Bill is the act whereby the Person on whom a Bill is drawn (called the Drawee) assents to the Demand and Order of the Drawer to pay it, or make themselves liable for its action or payment when due. The object of Acceptance is to bind the Drawee and make him an actual and bound party to the Instrument. Therefore, until there is an Acceptance (such as evidence of Dishonour), the Drawee is under no obligation whatever upon the Bill itself.

Acceptance of Valid Bill

414. A Bill is considered Accepted when it is acknowledged and signed in good Trust (bona fide), or through procedure to establish the dishonour, default and delinquency of the Drawee:

Form of Acceptance

(i) A Bill is accepted when the Drawee signs and endorses the Bill at ninety degrees prior to the expiry or maturity of the Bill; or

(ii) A Bill is accepted when the Drawer establishes the legitimacy of the Demand and Order, the truth of the debt and obligation, the dishonour of the Drawee in settling the debt and the default and delinquency of the Drawee in failing to provide any reasonable lawful excuse.

Article 109 – Rogatio Regnum Recto (Original Bill)

415. ***Rogatio Regnum Recto*** is the Sovereign Bill of Claim of Relief, as inherited from the Ecclesiastical Right *Rogatio Ecclesiae Recto*. It is the first of eleven Sovereign Bills.

Rogatio Regnum Recto (Claim)

416. A Bill of Complaint, also known as Original Bill, is an Instrument of Demand and Order, assured by Rights granted; as a form of petition issued by a valid Court of Chancery, containing a statement of the plaintiff's action or suit and concluding with a prayer asking for the relief which he filed the Bill to obtain.

Bill of Complaint

417. A Bill of Complaint shall only be issued to designated officials of a competent forum of Ucadian Law upon the successful completion, review and authorised acceptance of a formal Application, either as a separate Application or as part of an Application involving other Instruments that (upon approval) includes the issuance of a valid Bill of Complaint. No Bill of Complaint or associated instruments may be issued by a Sovereign Ucadia Entity to any Person, or Body or Society or Company or Association unless:

Eligibility and Qualification

(i) The Member as the primary Complainant to whom the proposed Bill of Complaint relates is not presently suspended or banned as a vexatious litigant from access to legal services of the Sovereign Ucadia Entity; and

(ii) The Member as the primary Complainant to whom the proposed Bill of Complaint relates is not presently recorded as being incompetent; and

(iii) The Member submitting the Application is eligible, qualified and Authorised to make such an Application; and

(iv) The mandatory information required to be submitted within the Application has been provided within the Application; and

(v) The Member has completed the Oath and Declaration that they agree to be bound by the terms and conditions of the Application and the proper use of any approved Bill of Complaint; and

(vi) Any nominal administration fees associated with the processing and issuance of such documents, whether or not the Application is successful, has been paid; and

(vii) There exists no other reason or impediment that would otherwise prevent the issuance of such documents, subject to the review and approval of the Application.

418. The Terms and Conditions of a valid Bill of Complaint is annexed as a separate document with three other Instruments being (a)

Terms & Conditions of

Declaration of Facts; and (b) *Affidavit of Fact*; and (c) *Memorandum of Account (of Charges)*. The Terms and Conditions shall adhere to the following standards, including (but not limited to): Bill of Complaint

(i) The Memorandum of Account, Declaration of Facts and Affidavit of Fact have been duly received and recorded within a competent forum of Law under Ucadian Law and these present Maxims; and

(ii) The Bill of Complaint has been issued by the same competent forum of Law; and

(iii) The description of alleged facts are clearly described and defined within the Declaration of Facts; and

(iv) The Affidavit of Fact clearly lists testimony made under Oath and Vow as to one or more alleged grievances that match the Declaration of Facts; and

(v) The Memorandum of Account clearly identifies the penalty, costs and compensation related to such alleged offences as related to the Bill of Complaint; and

(vi) No penalty, fine or payment associated with a Bill of Complaint may be expressed or function in simple interest or compound interest; and

(vii) No clause within the Terms and Conditions shall contravene these present Maxims.

Article 110 – Rogatio Regnum Iubemus (Command & Authorisation)

419. ***Rogatio Regnum Iubemus*** is the Sovereign Bill of Command and Authorisation, as inherited from the Ecclesiastical Right *Rogatio Ecclesiae Apocalypsis*. It is the second of eleven Sovereign Bills. Rogatio Regnum Iubemus (Command & Authorisation)

420. A Bill of Command and Authorisation, is an Instrument of Demand and Order, assured by Rights granted; as a form of petition for completion issued by a valid Court of Chancery, being a proposed law, or action. Bill of Command & Authorisation

Article 111 – Rogatio Regnum Capimus (Failure to Surrender or Arrest Person)

421. ***Rogatio Regnum Capimus*** is the Sovereign Bill of Rights of Failure to Surrender or Arrest Person, as inherited from the Rogatio Regnum Capimus (Arrest

Ecclesiastical Right *Rogatio Ecclesiae Capimus*. It is the third of eleven Sovereign Bills.

Person)

422. A Sovereign Bill of Rights of Failure to Surrender or Arrest Person, is a Bill of Exception and Instrument of Demand and Order, with the debt underwritten by the failure to enforce a previous Writ concerning the Surrender or Arrest of a Person.

Rogatio Regnum Capimus (Arrest Person) as Bill of Exception

423. Subject to the essential conditions of a valid Instrument, Form and Bill of the Sovereign Ucadia Entity as prescribed herein, the following essential elements must also be present on the face of a valid Sovereign Bill of Rights of Failure to Surrender or Arrest Person:

Specific Elements of a valid Rogatio Regnum Capimus (Arrest Person)

(i) *Writ Number* being a valid eighteen digit Ucadia number in the form XXXXXX-XXXXXX-XXXXXX signifying the existence of a Court of Original Record Writ Number within the Ucadia Courts and competent forums, as well as records of account, or in respect of the outstanding amount or property value; and

(ii) *Description of Person* being a clear description of the Person either to be arrested or brought to the Forum; and

(iii) *Value of Offences* being the total estimated value of any Offences alleged against the Person to be repossessed, seized and taken into custody; and

(iv) *Location of Person* being a clear description of the last known location of the person to be reclaimed, or seized and taken into custody; and

(v) *Possessors of Person* being the name of the Ucadia or Non Ucadia Persons or Entity known to have been in possession of the Person.

Article 112 – Rogatio Regnum Custodiae (Failure to Surrender or Seize Property)

424. ***Rogatio Regnum Custodiae*** is the Sovereign Bill of Failure to Surrender or Seize Property, as inherited from the Ecclesiastical Right *Rogatio Ecclesiae Custodiae*. It is the fourth of eleven Sovereign Bills.

Rogatio Regnum Custodiae (Seize Property)

425. A Sovereign Bill of Failure to Surrender or Seize Property, is a Bill of Exception and Instrument of Demand and Order, assured by Rights granted; to demand the return of certain property and the enforcement of a previous Writ concerning the Surrender or Seizure

Rogatio Regnum Custodiae (Seize Property) as Bill of Exception

Property.

426. Subject to the essential conditions of a valid Instrument, Form and Bill of the Sovereign Ucadia Entity as prescribed herein, the following essential elements must also be present on the face of a valid Sovereign Bill of Failure to Surrender or Seize Property:

Specific Elements of a valid Rogatio Regnum Custodiae (Seize Property)

(i) *Writ Number* being a valid eighteen digit Ucadia number in the form XXXXXX-XXXXXX-XXXXXX signifying the existence of a Court of Original Record Writ Number within the Ucadia Courts and competent forums, as well as records of account, or in respect of the outstanding amount or property value; and

(ii) *Description of Property* being a clear description of the Property that has been unlawfully seized or injured; and

(iii) *Value of Property* being the total estimated value of the Property to be repossessed, seized and taken into custody; and

(iv) *Location of Property* being a clear description of the last known location of the Property to be reclaimed, or seized and taken into custody; and

(v) *Possessors of Property* being the name of the Ucadia or Non Ucadia Persons or Entity known to have been in possession of the Property.

Article 113 – Rogatio Regnum Corrigimus (Failure to Correct Records, Rulings, Laws or Instruments)

427. ***Rogatio Regnum Corrigimus*** is the Sovereign Bill of Failure to Correct Records, Rulings, Laws or Instruments, as inherited from the Ecclesiastical Right *Rogatio Ecclesiae Corrigimus*. It is the fifth of eleven Sovereign Bills.

Rogatio Regnum Corrigimus (Correction)

428. A Sovereign Bill of Failure to Correct Records, Rulings, Laws or Instruments, is a Bill of Exception and Instrument of Demand and Order, with the debt underwritten by the failure to enforce a previous Writ concerning the Correction of Records, Rulings, Laws or Instruments.

Rogatio Regnum Corrigimus (Correction) as Bill of Exception

429. Subject to the essential conditions of a valid Instrument, Form and Bill of the Sovereign Ucadia Entity as prescribed herein, the following essential elements must also be present on the face of a valid Sovereign Bill of Failure to Correct Records, Rulings, Laws or Instruments:-

Specific Elements of a valid Rogatio Regnum Corrigimus (Correction)

(i) *Writ Number* being a valid eighteen digit Ucadia number in the form XXXXXX-XXXXXX-XXXXXX signifying the existence of a Court of Original Record Writ Number within the Ucadia Courts and competent forums, as well as records of account, or in respect of the outstanding amount or property value; and

(ii) *Description of Records, Rulings, Laws or Instruments* being a clear description of the Records, Rulings, Laws or Instruments to be changed, repossessed, seized and taken into custody; and

(iii) *Value of Records, Rulings, Laws or Instruments* being the total value of the Records, Rulings, Laws or Instruments to be changed, repossessed, seized and taken into custody; and

(iv) *Location of Records, Rulings, Laws or Instruments* being a clear description of the last known location of the Records, Rulings, Laws or Instruments to be changed, repossessed, seized and taken into custody; and

(v) *Possessors of Records, Rulings, Laws or Instruments* being the name of the Members known to have been in possession of the Records, Rulings, Laws or Instruments.

Article 114 – Rogatio Regnum Inhibitio (Prohibit & Restrain)

430. ***Rogatio Regnum Inhibitio*** is the Sovereign Bill of Failure to Prohibit or Restrain, as inherited from the Ecclesiastical Right *Rogatio Ecclesiae Inhibitio*. It is the sixth of eleven Sovereign Bills. Rogatio Regnum Inhibitio (Prohibit & Restrain)

431. A Sovereign Bill of Failure to Prohibit or Restrain, is a Bill of Exception and Instrument of Demand and Order, assured by Rights granted; to demand the enforcement of a previous Writ concerning the Prohibition or Restraint of certain actions. Rogatio Regnum Inhibitio (Prohibit & Restrain) as Bill of Exception

432. Subject to the essential conditions of a valid Instrument, Form and Bill of the Sovereign Ucadia Entity as prescribed herein, the following essential elements must also be present on the face of a valid Sovereign Bill of Failure to Prohibit or Restrain:- Specific Elements of a valid Rogatio Regnum Inhibitio (Prohibit & Restrain)

(i) *Writ Number* being a valid eighteen digit Ucadia number in the form XXXXXX-XXXXXX-XXXXXX signifying the existence of a Court of Original Record Writ Number within the Ucadia Courts and competent forums, as well as records of account, or in respect of the outstanding amount or property value; and

(ii) *Description of Actions* being a clear description of the Item, Action or Right to be prohibited or restrained; and

(iii) *Location of Item* being a clear description of the location of the Item, Action or Right to be Prohibited or Restrained.

Article 115 – Rogatio Regnum Restitutio (Restitution & Costs)

433. ***Rogatio Regnum Restitutio*** is the Sovereign Bill of Restitution or Compensation, as inherited from the Ecclesiastical Right *Rogatio Ecclesiae Restitutio*. It is the seventh of eleven Sovereign Bills. Rogatio Regnum Restitutio (Restitution)

434. A *Bill of Restitution or Compensation* is a Demand and Order for Payment, assured by Rights granted; of the total amount of the costs incurred by an Attorney-In-Fact or Advocate-In-Law in relation to representing the interests of a party of a suit or action. A Bill of Costs must be accompanied by a Statement of Account of the items that form the total amount of the costs of a suit or action and an Affidavit from the Attorney-In-Fact or Advocate-In-Law. Rogatio Regnum Restitutio (Restitution) as Bill of Costs

435. The Terms and Conditions of a valid Sovereign Bill of Restitution or Compensation is annexed as a separate document with three other Instruments being (a) *Declaration of Costs*; and (b) *Affidavit of Fact*; and (c) *Memorandum of Account*. The Terms and Conditions shall adhere to the following standards, including (but not limited to): Terms & Conditions of Bill of Costs

(i) The Memorandum of Account, Declaration of Costs and Affidavit of Fact have been duly received and recorded within a competent forum of Law under Ucadian Law and these present Maxims; and

(ii) The Bill of Costs has been issued by the same competent forum of Law directing payment; and

(iii) The description of alleged facts in relation to costs are clearly described and defined within the Declaration of Costs; and

(iv) The Affidavit of Fact clearly lists testimony made under Oath and Vow as to the legitimacy of certain costs requested to be reimbursed or compensation approved that match the Declaration of Costs; and

(v) The Memorandum of Account clearly identifies the costs and compensation related to such alleged occurrences as related to the Bill of Costs; and

(vi) No penalty, fine or payment associated with a Bill of Costs may be expressed or function in simple interest or compound interest; and

(vii) No clause within the Terms and Conditions shall contravene these present Maxims.

Article 116 – Rogatio Regnum Credito (Credit)

436. ***Rogatio Regnum Credito*** is the Sovereign Bill of Credit, as inherited from the Ecclesiastical Right *Rogatio Ecclesiae Credito*. It is the eighth of eleven Sovereign Bills. Rogatio Regnum Credito (Credit)

437. A Money Bill, also known at times as a "Bill of Credit", is an Instrument of Demand and Order, assured by Authorised Lien in Trust against Debt owed to the Sovereign Ucadia Entity as Public Debt; issued by the authority of the Sovereign Ucadia Entity; and designed to circulate as Money. Public Money Debt Bills are issued exclusively on the principle that all legitimate debts must be paid and the formal condemnation as liens against those foreign bodies, foreign corporations or foreign persons unwilling or unable to pay such valid debts; to then be circulated in ordinary purposes as Money, redeemable as Real Money at a fixed date or on demand. Rogatio Regnum Credito (Credit) as Money Bill

438. The Terms and Conditions of valid Public Debt Money Bills shall be on the reverse of the Instrument, unless otherwise stated. Terms & Conditions of Public Debt Money Bills

Article 117 – Rogatio Regnum Permutatio (Exchange)

439. ***Rogatio Regnum Permutatio*** is the Sovereign Bill of Exchange, as inherited from the Ecclesiastical Right *Rogatio Ecclesiae Permutatio*. It is the ninth of eleven Sovereign Bills. Rogatio Regnum Permutatio (Exchange)

440. A Sovereign Bill of Exchange is a written Demand and Order, assured by Rights granted; from one person to another, directing the person to whom it is addressed to pay to a third person a certain sum of money therein named. A Bill of Exchange is considered an unconditional Order in writing, addressed by one person to another, signed by the person giving it, and requiring the person to whom it is addressed to pay on demand, or at a fixed or determinable future time, a sum certain in money to order or to the bearer. A Bill of Exchange may be negotiable or not negotiable. If negotiable, it may be transferred either before or after acceptance. Rogatio Regnum Permutatio (Exchange) as Bill of Exchange

Article 118 – Rogatio Regnum Venditio (Sale)

441. ***Rogatio Regnum Venditio*** is the Sovereign Bill of Sale, as inherited from the Ecclesiastical Right *Rogatio Ecclesiae Venditio*. It is the tenth of eleven Sovereign Bills. Rogatio Regnum Venditio (Sale)

442. A Bill of Sale is an Instrument of Demand and Order, assured by Rights granted; as when a person delivers goods as security to a lender in exchange for a sum of money and empowering the lender to sell the goods if the sum is not repaid at the time appointed. Bill of Sale

Article 119 – Rogatio Regnum Traditio (Lading)

443. ***Rogatio Regnum Traditio*** is the Sovereign Bill of Lading, as inherited from the Ecclesiastical Right *Rogatio Ecclesiae Traditio*. It is the eleventh of eleven Sovereign Bills. Rogatio Regnum Traditio (Lading)

444. A Sovereign Bill of Lading, also known as a Bill of Consignment, is a Demand and Order, assured by Rights granted; in writing as evidence of a contract for the carriage and delivery of Goods sent by transport for certain freight. A Bill of Lading is a formal acknowledgment of the receipt of Goods and an engagement to deliver them to the consignee. Bill of Lading

3.6 – Sovereign Decrees

Article 120 – Sovereign Decrees

445. ***Sovereign Decrees*** (*Decretum Regnum Iurium*) are Sovereign Rights associated with sovereign decrees concerning the administration, conduct and enforcement of law and order. Sovereign Decrees

446. A ***Decree*** is a valid Form of Judgement or Order promulgated by an Ucadia court or other judicial or sovereign authority, subject to the limits of their authority, in accordance with these Maxims and the procedures of their Office. Nature of Decrees

447. A Decree is not valid, but an inferior and false document if it does not conform to these Maxims. Conformity

448. The key elements of a valid and proper Decree include (but are not limited to):- Key elements of a Decree

(i) **Title and Caption**: A decree usually begins with a title that identifies the court or authority issuing the decree, the names of the parties involved in the case (plaintiff and defendant), and a case number. This information is typically presented at the top of the document and is known as the *caption*; and

(ii) **Jurisdiction**: The decree will specify the legal basis for the court's authority to issue the decree. It will often state the jurisdictional facts, such as the location of the court and the type of case over which it has jurisdiction; and

(iii) **Findings of Fact**: Decrees often include a section that outlines the relevant facts of the case as determined by the court. This may include a summary of the evidence presented during the proceedings and the court's conclusions about the facts; and

(iv) **Conclusions of Law**: The decree will typically include the legal conclusions reached by the court based on the facts of the case. This section explains the legal principles that apply to the case and how they are relevant to the court's decision; and

(v) **Operative or Dispositive Clause**: This is one of the most critical elements of a decree. It contains the specific orders or commands issued by the court. It outlines what the parties involved must do or refrain from doing as a result of the decree. The operative clause often begins with phrases such as "It is hereby ordered" or "The court orders as follows"; and

(vi) **Remedies and Relief**: If the decree is granting relief to one or more parties, it will specify the type of relief granted. This may include monetary damages, injunctive relief, specific performance, or other remedies. The decree may also outline any conditions or requirements that must be met for the relief to be effective; and

(vii) **Duration and Effective Date**: The decree may include information about when it becomes effective and whether it has a specified duration. Some decrees are permanent, while others may be temporary or subject to modification; and

(viii) **Signature and Seal**: A decree is typically signed by the judge or judicial officer issuing the order. In some cases, it may also bear the court's official seal for authentication; and

(ix) **Notice and Service**: The decree may contain information about how notice of the decree will be provided to the parties involved and whether they are required to take any specific actions in response to the decree; and

(x) **Enforcement**: In cases where the decree includes orders that need to be enforced, it may provide details on how enforcement will occur and the consequences of non-compliance.

449. All *Sovereign Decrees* are delegated by proper *Mandate* to the Governments of valid and legitimate Sovereign Ucadia Bodies and Entities (including but not limited to Ucadia Universities, Provinces, Campuses, Foundations and Agencies); and to those existing and internationally recognised Non-Ucadian Sovereign Bodies and Entities by in force treaties and agreements in accord with the most sacred Covenant *Pactum De Singularis Caelum*.

Delegation of Sovereign Decrees

450. All *Sovereign Decrees* are assumed to be automatically invoked through the proper operation and function of the Governing Instruments, Codes and Bylaws of valid and legitimate Sovereign Ucadia Bodies and Entities (including but not limited to Ucadia Universities, Provinces, Campuses, Foundations and Agencies); and through the operation and function of in force treaties and agreements with existing and internationally recognised Non-Ucadian Sovereign Bodies and Entities.

Invocation of Sovereign Decrees

451. The following valid eleven (11) Sovereign Decrees (*Decretum Regnum Iurium*) is recognised in accord with the most sacred Covenant *Pactum De Singularis Caelum* and these present Maxims:-

List of Sovereign Decrees (Decretum Regnum Iurium)

(i) "**Decretum Regnum Originalis**" is the Sovereign Decree of Rights, as inherited from the Ecclesiastical Right *Decretum Ecclesiae Originalis*; and

(ii) "**Decretum Regnum Absolutionis**" is the Sovereign Decree of Absolution, as inherited from the Ecclesiastical Right *Decretum Ecclesiae Absolutionis*; and

(iii) "**Decretum Regnum Damnationis**" is the Sovereign Decree of Damnation, as inherited from the Ecclesiastical Right *Decretum Ecclesiae Damnationis*; and

(iv) "**Decretum Regnum Exemplificatio**" is the Sovereign Decree of Exemplification, as inherited from the Ecclesiastical Right *Decretum Ecclesiae Exemplificatio*; and

(v) "**Decretum Regnum Testimonium**" is the Sovereign Decree of Proof, as inherited from the Ecclesiastical Right *Decretum Ecclesiae Testimonium*; and

(vi) "**Decretum Regnum Instructionis**" is the Sovereign Decree of Instruction, as inherited from the Ecclesiastical

Right *Decretum Ecclesiae Instructionis*; and

(vii) "**Decretum Regnum Censurae**" is the Sovereign Decree of Censure, as inherited from the Ecclesiastical Right *Decretum Ecclesiae Censurae;* and

(viii) "**Decretum Regnum Annullas**" is the Sovereign Decree of Annulment, as inherited from the Ecclesiastical Right *Decretum Ecclesiae Annullas*; and

(ix) "**Decretum Regnum Ratificationis**" is the Sovereign Decree of Ratification, as inherited from the Ecclesiastical Right *Decretum Ecclesiae Ratificationis*; and

(x) "**Decretum Regnum Interdictum**" is the Sovereign Decree of Interdiction, as inherited from the Ecclesiastical Right *Decretum Ecclesiae Interdictum*; and

(xi) "**Decretum Regnum Levationis**" is the Sovereign Decree of Relief, as inherited from the Ecclesiastical Right *Decretum Ecclesiae Levationis.*

Article 121 – Decretum Regnum Originalis (Original Decree)

452. ***Decretum Regnum Originalis*** is the Sovereign Decree of Rights, as inherited from the Ecclesiastical Right *Decretum Ecclesiae Originalis*. It is the first of eleven Sovereign Decrees. Decretum Regnum Originalis (Original Decree)

453. A Sovereign Decree of *Decretum Regnum Originalis* (Original Decree) is issued in all matters concerning official procedures, organisation restructures, policies, systematic explanations and interpretations of executive government, including (but not limited to):- Purpose of Decretum Regnum Originalis (Original Decree)

(i) ***Administrative***: Sovereign Executive Decrees concerning Internal management and organisation of the executive branch of government. They may establish or reorganise government agencies, offices, or committees; and

(ii) ***Economic and Financial Policies***: Sovereign Executive Decrees concerning economic matters, such as fiscal policies, trade agreements, tariffs, and regulations affecting industries and businesses; and

(iii) ***Healthcare and Public Health***: Sovereign Executive Decrees concerning public health emergencies, healthcare access, and the implementation of healthcare-related legislation; and

(iv) ***Environmental and Energy Policies***: Sovereign Executive Decrees concerning environmental protection, conservation, and energy policies, including regulations related to emissions, climate change, and natural resource management; and

(v) ***Civil Rights and Social Justice***: Sovereign Executive Decrees concerning civil rights to combat discrimination, and promote social justice initiatives, equal employment opportunity and racial equity; and

(vi) ***Education***: Sovereign Executive Decrees concerning education policies, including government funding for schools, college financial aid, and regulations related to lower and higher education institutions; and

(vii) ***Infrastructure and Transportation***: Sovereign Executive Decrees concerning infrastructure development, transportation systems, and initiatives related to improving infrastructure; and

(viii) ***Foreign Policy and Diplomacy***: Sovereign Executive Decrees concerning foreign policy, international agreements, sanctions against foreign entities, and diplomatic relations with other countries; and

(ix) ***Law Enforcement and Criminal Justice***: Sovereign Executive Decrees concerning law enforcement policies, criminal justice reform, and initiatives to combat crime or promote police accountability; and

(x) ***Ethics and Accountability***: Sovereign Executive Decrees concerning ethical standards and codes of conduct for government employees and officials or to address issues related to government transparency and accountability; and

(xi) ***Tribal Relations and Indigenous Rights***: Sovereign Executive Decrees concerning government-to-government relations with Original Nations and issues related to tribal sovereignty and indigenous rights; and

(xii) ***Science and Technology***: Sovereign Executive Decrees concerning research and development, technological innovation, and the use of science in policymaking.

Article 122 – Decretum Regnum Absolutionis (Absolution)

Decretum Regnum Absolutionis (Absolution)

454. ***Decretum Regnum Absolutionis*** is the Sovereign Decree of Absolution, as inherited from the Ecclesiastical Right *Decretum Ecclesiae Absolutionis*. It is the second of eleven Sovereign Decrees.

Purpose of Decretum Regnum Absolutionis (Absolution)

455. A Sovereign Decree of *Decretum Regnum Absolutionis* (Absolution) is issued in all matters concerning the exoneration, absolution, forgiveness or dismissal of matters, including (but not limited to):-

(i) ***Discharge (Bankruptcy)***: In bankruptcy cases, a Judicial Decree of discharge is issued to relieve a debtor of their obligation to repay certain debts. It signals the end of the bankruptcy process and provides the debtor with a fresh financial start; and

(ii) ***Exoneration (Surety Law)***: In surety law, a Judicial Decree of exoneration is issued when a surety (guarantor) is released from their obligations or liabilities after the principal debtor has fulfilled their obligations; and

(iii) ***Dismissal***: This Judicial Decree is issued to formally dismiss a legal action or lawsuit. It may be issued voluntarily by the plaintiff or as a result of a court's decision to dismiss a case.

Article 123 – Decretum Regnum Damnationis (Damnation)

Decretum Regnum Damnationis (Damnation)

456. ***Decretum Regnum Damnationis*** is the Sovereign Decree of Damnation, as inherited from the Ecclesiastical Right *Decretum Ecclesiae Damnationis*. It is the third of eleven Sovereign Decrees.

Purpose of Decretum Regnum Damnationis (Damnation)

457. A Sovereign Decree of *Decretum Regnum Damnationis* (Damnation) is issued in all matters concerning condemnation in civil or criminal matters, including (but not limited to):-

(i) ***Condemnation***: In eminent domain and property law, a Judicial Decree of condemnation may be issued to authorise the government's acquisition of private property for public use, often with just compensation to the property owner; and

(ii) ***Juvenile Delinquency***: In juvenile law, a Judicial Decree of juvenile delinquency may be issued when a minor is found to have committed a delinquent act, which is similar to a criminal conviction for adults; and

(iii) ***Criminal Conviction and Sentencing***: In criminal law, a

Judicial Decree may be issued when a person or entity is found criminally culpable.

Article 124 – Decretum Regnum Exemplificatio (Exemplification)

458. ***Decretum Regnum Exemplificatio*** is the Sovereign Decree of Exemplification, as inherited from the Ecclesiastical Right *Decretum Ecclesiae Exemplificatio*. It is the fourth of eleven Sovereign Decrees. Decretum Regnum Exemplificatio

459. A Sovereign Decree of *Decretum Regnum Exemplificatio* (Exemplification) is issued in all matters concerning conclusive confirmation of a change in title or status, including (but not limited to):- Purpose of Decretum Regnum Exemplificatio

(i) ***Paternity***: This Judicial Decree is issued to legally establish the paternity (biological fatherhood) of a child. It may include provisions related to child support, custody and visitation; and

(ii) ***Adoption by Agency***: This type of Judicial Decree is issued when an adoption is facilitated by a licensed adoption agency, and it confirms the adoption of a child by the adoptive parents; and

(iii) ***Adoption***: A Judicial Decree of adoption is issued to legally establish the adoptive parent-child relationship. It typically includes details about the adopted child's name change and the termination of the biological parents' rights; and

(iv) ***Custody and Support***: This type of Judicial Decree establishes child custody and support arrangements in cases of divorce or separation, outlining where the child will live, visitation schedules, and support obligations; and

(v) ***Custody and Guardianship***: In cases involving the appointment of a legal guardian for a minor or incapacitated person, a Judicial Decree of custody and guardianship may be issued to establish the legal authority and responsibilities of the guardian; and

(vi) ***Separation***: Similar to a decree of legal separation, this type of Judicial Decree is issued to formalise a separation between spouses without dissolving the marriage. It may address issues such as property division and support; and

(vii) ***Partition***: In real estate and property law, a Judicial Decree of partition may be issued to divide jointly owned property among co-owners, especially when they cannot agree on how to use or divide the property; and

(viii) ***Exemption***: In tax law, a Judicial Decree of exemption may be issued to grant an organization or individual an exemption from certain taxes or tax obligations based on specific criteria or qualifications; and

(ix) ***Quiet Title***: This type of Judicial Decree is used to establish a party's clear and undisputed ownership of real property and remove any competing claims or interests.

Article 125 – Decretum Regnum Testimonium (Proof)

460. ***Decretum Regnum Testimonium*** is the Sovereign Decree of Proof, as inherited from the Ecclesiastical Right *Decretum Ecclesiae Testimonium*. It is the fifth of eleven Sovereign Decrees.

Decretum Regnum Testimonium (Proof)

461. A Sovereign Decree of *Decretum Regnum Testimonium* (Proof) is issued in all matters concerning testimony, capacity and proof, including (but not limited to):-

Purpose of Decretum Regnum Testimonium (Proof)

(i) ***Decree Nisi and Decree Absolute***: In divorce cases, a *decree nisi* is an initial order that grants the divorce but does not dissolve the marriage. After a waiting period, a *decree absolute* is issued, finalizing the divorce and ending the marriage; and

(ii) ***Competency***: In guardianship and mental health cases, a Judicial Decree of competency may be issued to determine whether an individual has the legal capacity to make decisions regarding their person or property.

Article 126 – Decretum Regnum Instructionis (Instruction)

462. ***Decretum Regnum Instructionis*** is the Sovereign Decree of Instruction, as inherited from the Ecclesiastical Right *Decretum Ecclesiae Instructionis*. It is the sixth of eleven Sovereign Decrees.

Decretum Regnum Instructionis (Instruction)

463. A Sovereign Decree of *Decretum Regnum Instructionis* (Instruction) is issued in all matters concerning instruction and performance, including (but not limited to):-

Purpose of Decretum Regnum Instructionis (Instruction)

(i) ***Specific Performance***: In contract law, a Judicial Decree of specific performance may be issued to compel a party to fulfil their contractual obligations. It is used when monetary damages are inadequate to remedy a breach of contract; and

(ii) ***Quieting Title***: Similar to a decree of quiet title, this type of decree is used to resolve disputes over property ownership and establish clear title, often by removing clouds on the title; and

(iii) ***Modification***: In family law cases, a decree of modification may be issued to change the terms of a previous court order, such as modifying child custody, visitation or support arrangements.

Article 127 – Decretum Regnum Censurae (Censure)

464. ***Decretum Regnum Censurae*** is the Sovereign Decree of Censure, as inherited from the Ecclesiastical Right *Decretum Ecclesiae Censurae*. It is the seventh of eleven Sovereign Decrees. Decretum Regnum Censurae (Censure)

465. A Sovereign Decree of *Decretum Regnum Censurae* (Censure) is issued in all matters concerning censure and estoppel, including (but not limited to):- Purpose of Decretum Regnum Censurae (Censure)

(i) **Judicial Estoppel**: Judicial estoppel prohibits a party from taking inconsistent positions in different legal proceedings. For example, a party cannot assert one position in a bankruptcy case and a conflicting position in a subsequent personal injury lawsuit; and

(ii) **Collateral Estoppel (Issue Estoppel)**: Collateral estoppel, or issue estoppel, prevents the re-litigation of specific issues or facts that have already been conclusively determined in a prior legal proceeding involving the same parties or their privies; and

(iii) **Equitable Estoppel**: Equitable estoppel, also known as estoppel in pais or estoppel by conduct, arises when a person's actions or representations lead another person to reasonably rely on those actions or representations to their detriment. If someone is later trying to assert a contradictory position in court, they may be estopped from doing so; and

(iv) **Promissory Estoppel**: Promissory estoppel, also known as detrimental reliance, occurs when one party makes a clear and unambiguous promise to another party, and the second party relies on that promise to their detriment. Courts may enforce the promise to prevent injustice, even if it lacks the formality of a contract.

Article 128 – Decretum Regnum Annullas (Annulment)

466. ***Decretum Regnum Annullas*** is the Sovereign Decree of Annulment, as inherited from the Ecclesiastical Right *Decretum Ecclesiae Annullas*. It is the eighth of eleven Sovereign Decrees. Decretum Regnum Annullas (Annulment)

467. A Sovereign Decree of *Decretum Regnum Annullas* (Annulment) is issued in all matters concerning liquidation, dissolution and annulment, including (but not limited to):- Purpose of Decretum Regnum Annullas (Annulment)

(i) ***Compulsory Liquidation***: In corporate and insolvency law, a Judicial Decree of compulsory liquidation may be issued to order the winding up and dissolution of a company that is unable to pay its debts. It involves selling off the company's assets to pay creditors; and

(ii) ***Dissolution of Partnership:*** In business law, a Judicial Decree of dissolution of partnership is issued when a partnership is being dissolved, specifying the distribution of assets and liabilities among the partners; and

(iii) ***Nullity (Annulment)***: In cases where a marriage is declared null and void, a Judicial Decree of nullity is issued. It legally declares that the marriage was invalid from the beginning, as if it never existed; and

(iv) ***Dissolution***: In business law, a Judicial Decree of dissolution may be issued to formally dissolve a business entity and wind up its affairs.

Article 129 – Decretum Regnum Ratificationis (Ratification)

468. ***Decretum Regnum Ratificationis*** is the Sovereign Decree of Ratification, as inherited from the Ecclesiastical Right *Decretum Ecclesiae Ratificationis*. It is the ninth of eleven Sovereign Decrees. Decretum Regnum Ratificationis (Ratification)

469. A Sovereign Decree of *Decretum Regnum Ratificationis* (Ratification) is issued in all matters concerning the ratification of governing documents, deeds and other agreements, including (but not limited to):- Purpose of Decretum Regnum Ratificationis (Ratification)

(i) ***Confirmation (Bankruptcy)***: In bankruptcy proceedings, a Judicial Decree of confirmation is issued to approve a debtor's proposed repayment plan, allowing them to repay creditors over a specified period; and

(ii) ***Incorporation***: In corporate law, a decree of incorporation is issued to formally establish a corporation as a legal entity, with specific bylaws and governance structures; and

(iii) ***Naturalization***: In immigration law, a decree of naturalization is issued to grant citizenship to a foreign national who has met the legal requirements and successfully completed the naturalization process; and

(iv) ***Distribution (Disposal)***: In disposal cases, a decree of distribution is issued to distribute the assets of a deceased person's estate to the heirs or beneficiaries according to the terms of the will or applicable laws.

Article 130 – Decretum Regnum Interdictum (Interdiction)

470. ***Decretum Regnum Interdictum*** is the Sovereign Decree of Interdiction, as inherited from the Ecclesiastical Right *Decretum Ecclesiae Interdictum*. It is the tenth of eleven Sovereign Decrees. Decretum Regnum Interdictum (Interdiction)

471. A Sovereign Decree of *Decretum Regnum Interdictum* (Interdiction) is issued in all matters concerning injunctions, prohibitions or restraints, including (but not limited to):- Purpose of Decretum Regnum Interdictum (Interdiction)

(i) ***Protective Order***: In cases of domestic violence or harassment, a protective order decree may be issued to provide legal protection to victims. It typically prohibits the abuser from contacting or approaching the victim; and

(ii) ***Injunction***: An injunction decree is issued to prohibit a party from engaging in certain actions or behaviors, often to prevent harm or maintain the status quo during a legal dispute.

Article 131 – Decretum Regnum Levationis (Relief)

472. ***Decretum Regnum Levationis*** is the Sovereign Decree of Relief, as inherited from the Ecclesiastical Right *Decretum Ecclesiae Levationis*. It is the eleventh of eleven Sovereign Decrees. Decretum Regnum Levationis (Relief)

473. A Sovereign Decree of *Decretum Regnum Levationis* (Relief) is issued in all matters concerning the allocation and ownership of rights, title, property or financial resources, including (but not limited to):- Purpose of Decretum Regnum Levationis (Relief)

(i) ***Damages***: This type of Judicial Decree is issued in civil cases where the court awards monetary damages to a party who has suffered harm or loss due to the actions of another party; and

(ii) ***Summary Judgment***: In civil litigation, a Judicial Decree of summary judgment is issued when a judge determines that there are no genuine issues of material fact in dispute, and one party is entitled to judgment as a matter of law, typically without a full trial; and

(iii) ***Garnishment***: This type of Judicial Decree is often issued in debt collection cases. It allows a creditor to collect a debt by attaching the debtor's wages or other assets held by a third party, such as a bank; and

(iv) ***Foreclosure***: This type of Judicial Decree is issued in foreclosure proceedings to authorize the sale of a property to satisfy a mortgage or debt. It outlines the sale process and distribution of proceeds; and

(v) ***Alimony or Spousal Support***: This type of Judicial Decree determines the amount and duration of financial support that one spouse must pay to the other following a divorce or separation.

3.7 – Sovereign Notices

Article 132 – Sovereign Notices

474. ***Sovereign Notices*** (*Notitiae Regnum Iurium*) are Sovereign Rights associated with sovereign notices issued, executed, patented, promulgated and services in the proper administration, conduct and enforcement of law and order. Sovereign Notices

475. A ***Notice*** is a written or formal communication or process that conveys information, instructions, or important details to a specific individual, group of individuals, or the public at large. Notice

476. The seven primary types of Notice include: *Physical, Posted, Direct, Indirect, Public (legal), Implied* and *Constructive*:- Types of Notice

(i) *Physical Notice* or Actual Notice is a type of notice and service of process whereby the specific information concerning a formal legal matter is listed in a Document and then physically handed to a party or their representative, with proof, attestation or acknowledgment of such service recorded as evidence; and

(ii) *Posted Notice* or Mail Notice is a type of notice and service of process whereby specific information concerning the formal legal matter is personally addressed to the party and sent through a certified or registered mail delivery system recognised by Non-Ucadia bodies such as the International Postal Union; and

(iii) *Direct Notice* is a type of notice and service of process whereby specific information concerning the formal legal matter is personally addressed to the party and sent via email, fax, sms or other recorded and verifiable transmission medium; and

(iv) *Indirect Notice* is a type of notice and service of process whereby specific information concerning the formal legal matter is published in any broadcast medium such as media releases, stories, advertorial content and advertising and likely to be viewed by one or more parties; and

(v) *Public Notice* is a type of notice and service of process whereby specific information concerning the formal legal matter is published in a company, local, regional, national or international publication possessing status as a gazette and therefore an official newspaper of record or physically posted at a site reasonably expected to be visible to the Person; and

(vi) *Implied Notice* is a type of notice inferred from facts that a Person had means of knowing and would have caused a reasonable Person to take action to gain further information concerning a formal legal matter. It is a notice inferred or imputed to a party by reason of his/her knowledge collateral to the main fact; and

(vii) *Constructive Notice* is a type of notice inferred from facts that a Person unable to be served with Actual Notice may be reasonably inferred or imputed to have received notice, if Actual Notice was restricted or not possible and a minimum number of attempts of Physical, Posted, Direct or Public Notice were concluded.

477. The publishing of any Proclamation, Order, Regulation or Notice within the Ucadia Gazette is *Prima Facie* Evidence of such Fact and Truth; and that all Courts, Judges, Justices, Masters, Magistrates or Commissioners judicially acting, and all other judicial Officers shall take judicial Notice of such *Prima Facie* Evidence in all legal proceedings and all forums of law whether Ucadia or Non-Ucadia.

Ucadia Gazette Notices as Prima Facie Evidence

478. All *Sovereign Notices* are delegated by proper *Mandate* to the Governments of valid and legitimate Sovereign Ucadia Bodies and Entities (including but not limited to Ucadia Universities, Provinces, Campuses, Foundations and Agencies); and to those existing and

Delegation of Sovereign Notices

internationally recognised Non-Ucadian Sovereign Bodies and Entities by in force treaties and agreements in accord with the most sacred Covenant *Pactum De Singularis Caelum*.

479. All *Sovereign Notices* are assumed to be automatically invoked through the proper operation and function of the Governing Instruments, Codes and Bylaws of valid and legitimate Sovereign Ucadia Bodies and Entities (including but not limited to Ucadia Universities, Provinces, Campuses, Foundations and Agencies); and through the operation and function of in force treaties and agreements with existing and internationally recognised Non-Ucadian Sovereign Bodies and Entities.

Invocation of Sovereign Notices

480. Notice is deemed to have been properly and duly served, when:

When Notice deemed to be served

(i) Any Physical Notice served personally or left at the registered address by a servicing agent is deemed to have been served when delivered and such fact is attested by a certificate of service signed by the agent who executed the service; and

(ii) Any Notice sent by Post is deemed to have been served at the expiration of forty-eight hours after the envelope containing the Notice is posted and, in proving service, it is sufficient to prove that the envelope containing the Notice was properly addressed and posted; and

(iii) Any Direct Notice served on a party by telex is deemed to have been served on receipt by the Sovereign Ucadia Entity of the answer back code of the recipient at the end of the transmission. Any notice served on a party by facsimile transmission is deemed to have been served when the transmission is sent. Any notice served on a party by email or sms or any other form of direct electronic messaging is deemed to have been served after twenty-four hours and no error message or failed transmission notice is received; and

(iv) Any Indirect Notice is deemed to have been served three days after receipt or proof of the publication of such notice; and

(v) Any Public Notice is deemed to have been served three days after receipt or proof of the publication in a gazette and official publication of record of such Notice; and

(vi) Any Implied Notice is deemed to have been served fourteen days after receipt or proof of publication of at least two forms of Indirect Notice or Public Notice; and

(vii) Any Constructive Notice is deemed to have been served

fourteen days after receipt or proof of at least one attempted Physical Notice or two Posted Notices and at least two forms of Indirect Notice or Public Notice.

481. Where a Member does not have a registered address or where the Sovereign Ucadia Entity has a reason in good faith to believe that a Member is not known at the Member's registered address, a Notice is deemed to be given to the Member if the Notice is exhibited by Indirect Notice in the Office for a period of forty-eight hours (and is deemed to be duly served at the commencement of that period) unless and until the Member informs the Sovereign Ucadia Entity of a registered place of address.

Member not known at registered address

482. The signature to any Notice to be given by the Sovereign Ucadia Entity may be written or printed. The formatting of the name of an Officer of the Sovereign Ucadia Entity in capitals as the signature line upon a Notice is deemed a valid legal signature.

Signature to Notice

483. Where a Notice gives of a certain number of days, or the limit of time is mandated for some proper form of Notice, the days of service are not to be reckoned in the number of days, until the actual date of proof of service, thereby limiting the possibility of an unfair or unreasonable service.

Reckoning of period of Notice

484. Every person who, by operation of law, transfers a right, or property or obligation to another shall continue to be fully bound by every Notice, until the name and details of the transferee of such property, or right or obligation is properly registered with their consent to being bound to any and every Notice.

Notice to transferee binds transferor

485. The following valid eleven (11) Sovereign Notices (*Notitiae Regnum Iurium*) is recognised in accord with the most sacred Covenant *Pactum De Singularis Caelum* and these present Maxims:-

List of Sovereign Notices (Notitiae Regnum Iurium)

(i) "**Notitiae Regnum Eventus**" is the Sovereign Notice of Event, as inherited from the Ecclesiastical Right *Notitiae Ecclesiae Eventus*; and

(ii) "**Notitiae Regnum Ius**" is the Sovereign Notice of Right, as inherited from the Ecclesiastical Right *Notitiae Ecclesiae Ius*; and

(iii) "**Notitiae Regnum Actum**" is the Sovereign Notice of Action, as inherited from the Ecclesiastical Right *Notitiae Ecclesiae Actum*; and

(iv) "**Notitiae Regnum Decretum**" is the Sovereign Notice of Decree, as inherited from the Ecclesiastical Right *Notitiae*

Ecclesiae Decretum; and

(v) "**Notitiae Regnum Iuris**" is the Sovereign Notice of Law, as inherited from the Ecclesiastical Right *Notitiae Ecclesiae Iuris*; and

(vi) "**Notitiae Regnum Citationis**" is the Sovereign Notice of Summons, as inherited from the Ecclesiastical Right *Notitiae Ecclesiae Citationis*; and

(vii) "**Notitiae Regnum Redemptio**" is the Sovereign Notice of Redemption, as inherited from the Ecclesiastical Right *Notitiae Ecclesiae Redemptio*; and

(viii) "**Notitiae Regnum Rogatio**" is the Sovereign Notice of Exception, as inherited from the Ecclesiastical Right *Notitiae Ecclesiae Rogatio*; and

(ix) "**Notitiae Regnum Potentis**" is the Sovereign Notice of Authority, as inherited from the Ecclesiastical Right *Notitiae Ecclesiae Potentis*; and

(x) "**Notitiae Regnum Testamentum**" is the Sovereign Notice of Testament, as inherited from the Ecclesiastical Right *Notitiae Ecclesiae Testamentum*; and

(xi) "**Notitiae Regnum Obligationis**" is the Sovereign Notice of Obligation, as inherited from the Ecclesiastical Right *Notitiae Ecclesiae Obligationis*.

Article 133 – Notitiae Regnum Eventus (Event)

486. ***Notitiae Regnum Eventus*** is the Sovereign Notice of Event, as inherited from the Ecclesiastical Right *Notitiae Ecclesiae Eventus*. It is the first of eleven Sovereign Rights of Sovereign Notice. Notitiae Regnum Eventus (Event)

487. A *Sovereign Notice of Event* (*Notitiae Regnum Eventus*) is any official notice in relation to the entry into a Ucadia Gazette or Ucadia Register of a unique sacred space-time event pertaining to one or more Rights. Purpose of Notitiae Regnum Eventus (Event)

488. The issue of any such certificate or authorised extract or Gazette Notice in relation to a sacred space-time event is equivalent to a formal *Notitiae Regnum Eventus* as evidence; and proof of a first in time, highest title and right association to such an event. Gazette Notice and Regnum Eventus (Event)

489. The existence of any instrument or document issued by an inferior body or non-Ucadian aligned society claiming some right or Regnum Eventus (Event) and ownership in direct contradiction to an event clearly identified through a *Notitiae Regnum Eventus* shall itself be an open confession of perfidy, profanity, repugnancy, malice, heresy and apostasy against all forms of valid law of Heaven and Earth. Non-Ucadia Claim

Article 134 – Notitiae Regnum Ius (Right)

490. ***Notitiae Regnum Ius*** is the Sovereign Notice of Right, as inherited from the Ecclesiastical Right *Notitiae Ecclesiae Ius*. It is the second of eleven Sovereign Rights of Sovereign Notice. Notitiae Regnum Ius (Right)

491. A *Sovereign Notice of Right* (*Notitiae Regnum Ius*) is any valid Notice issued under the rules of the most sacred Covenant *Pactum De Singularis Caelum* and the present Maxims bringing Divine Notice and therefore the power of life to Valid Offices of the Society, Titles of Land, Water and Space and all Valid Rights and Commissions to Office. Purpose of Notitiae Regnum Ius (Right)

492. By the rules of the present Maxims and most sacred Covenant *Pactum De Singularis Caelum*, all Offices must be duly created by Divine Notice and thereby granted a valid record number in the Great Register and Divine Records of Heaven as having eternal spiritual life and real existence and legal personality. Notitiae Regnum Ius and Record Number

493. *Notitiae Regnum Ius* (Right) is the second of eleven Divine Rights of Divine Notice; and may only be invoked whenever the lesser Right *Notitiae Ecclesiae Ius* (Ecclesiastical Notice of Right) is invoked. Invoking of Notitiae Regnum Ius (Right)

Article 135 – Notitiae Regnum Actum (Action)

494. ***Notitiae Regnum Actum*** (Action) is the Sovereign Notice of Action, as inherited from the Ecclesiastical Right *Notitiae Ecclesiae Actum*. It is the third of eleven Sovereign Rights of Sovereign Notice. Notitiae Regnum Actum (Action)

495. A *Sovereign Notice of Action* (*Notitiae Regnum Actum*) is any valid Notice issued under the rules of the most sacred Covenant *Pactum De Singularis Caelum* and the present Maxims concerning one or more Sovereign Rights of Action. Purpose of Notitiae Regnum Actum (Action)

Article 136 – Notitiae Regnum Decretum (Decree)

496. ***Notitiae Regnum Decretum*** (Decree) is the Sovereign Notice of Decree, as inherited from the Ecclesiastical Right *Notitiae Ecclesiae Decretum*. It is the fourth of eleven Sovereign Rights of Sovereign Notitiae Regnum Decretum (Decree)

Notice.

497. A *Sovereign Notice of Decree* (*Notitiae Regnum Decretum*) is any valid Notice issued under the rules of the most sacred Covenant *Pactum De Singularis Caelum* and the present Maxims concerning one or more Sovereign Decrees. Purpose of Notitiae Regnum Decretum (Decree)

Article 137 – Notitiae Regnum Iuris (Law)

498. ***Notitiae Regnum Iuris*** (Law) is the Sovereign Notice of Law, as inherited from the Ecclesiastical Right *Notitiae Ecclesiae Iuris*. It is the fifth of eleven Sovereign Rights of Sovereign Notice. Notitiae Regnum Iuris (Law)

499. A *Sovereign Notice of Law* (*Notitiae Regnum Iuris*) is any valid Notice issued under the rules of the most sacred Covenant *Pactum De Singularis Caelum* and the present Maxims concerning one or more facts of law. Purpose of Notitiae Regnum Iuris (Law)

Article 138 – Notitiae Regnum Citationis (Summons)

500. ***Notitiae Regnum Citationis*** is the Sovereign Notice of Summons, as inherited from the Ecclesiastical Right *Notitiae Ecclesiae Citationis*. It is the sixth of eleven Sovereign Rights of Sovereign Notice. Notitiae Regnum Citationis (Summons)

501. A *Sovereign Notice of Summons* (*Notitiae Regnum Citationis*) is any valid Notice issued under the rules of the most sacred Covenant *Pactum De Singularis Caelum* and the present Maxims concerning the attendance to an official meeting, or legal matter. Purpose of Notitiae Regnum Citationis (Summons)

Article 139 – Notitiae Regnum Redemptio (Redemption)

502. ***Notitiae Regnum Redemptio*** is the Sovereign Notice of Redemption, as inherited from the Ecclesiastical Right *Notitiae Ecclesiae Redemptio*. It is the seventh of eleven Sovereign Rights of Sovereign Notice. Notitiae Regnum Redemptio (Redemption)

503. A *Sovereign Notice of Redemption* (*Notitiae Regnum Redemptio*) is any valid Notice issued under the rules of the most sacred Covenant *Pactum De Singularis Caelum* and the present Maxims concerning the forgiveness of one or more offences. Purpose of Notitiae Regnum Redemptio (Redemption)

Article 140 – Notitiae Regnum Rogatio (Exception)

504. ***Notitiae Regnum Rogatio*** is the Sovereign Notice of Exception, as inherited from the Ecclesiastical Right *Notitiae Ecclesiae Rogatio*. It is the eighth of eleven Sovereign Rights of Sovereign Notice. — Notitiae Regnum Rogatio (Exception)

505. A *Sovereign Notice of Exception* (*Notitiae Regnum Rogatio*) is any valid Notice issued under the rules of the most sacred Covenant *Pactum De Singularis Caelum* and the present Maxims concerning one or more failures to act in accord with the instructions of a Sovereign Writ. — Purpose of Notitiae Regnum Rogatio (Exception)

Article 141 – Notitiae Regnum Potentis (Authority)

506. ***Notitiae Regnum Potentis*** is the Sovereign Notice of Authority, as inherited from the Ecclesiastical Right *Notitiae Ecclesiae Potentis*. It is the ninth of eleven Sovereign Rights of Sovereign Notice. — Notitiae Regnum Potentis (Authority)

507. A *Sovereign Notice of Authority* (*Notitiae Regnum Potentis*) is any valid Notice issued under the rules of the most sacred Covenant *Pactum De Singularis Caelum* and the present Maxims concerning a question of authority. — Purpose of Notitiae Regnum Potentis (Authority)

Article 142 – Notitiae Regnum Testamentum (Testament)

508. ***Notitiae Regnum Testamentum*** is the Sovereign Notice of Testament, as inherited from the Ecclesiastical Right *Notitiae Ecclesiae Testamentum*. It is the tenth of eleven Sovereign Rights of Sovereign Notice. — Notitiae Regnum Testamentum (Testament)

509. A *Sovereign Notice of Testament* (*Notitiae Regnum Testamentum*) is any valid Notice issued under the rules of the most sacred Covenant *Pactum De Singularis Caelum* and the present Maxims concerning a testament or declaration or statement. — Purpose of Notitiae Regnum Testamentum (Testament)

Article 143 – Notitiae Regnum Obligationis (Obligation)

510. ***Notitiae Regnum Obligationis*** is the Sovereign Notice of Obligation, as inherited from the Ecclesiastical Right *Notitiae Ecclesiae Obligationis*. It is the eleventh of eleven Sovereign Rights of Sovereign Notice. — Notitiae Regnum Obligationis (Obligation)

511. A *Sovereign Notice of Obligation* (*Notitiae Regnum Obligationis*) is any valid Notice issued under the rules of the most sacred Covenant *Pactum De Singularis Caelum* and the present Maxims in relation to one or more Obligations that will fall due within the next forty days. Purpose of Notitiae Regnum Obligationis

3.8 – False, Absurd & Prohibited Sovereign Rights

Article 144 – False, Absurd & Prohibited Sovereign Rights

512. ***False, Absurd & Prohibited Sovereign Rights*** are claims or assertions concerning Sovereign Rights that clearly contradict, oppose or deny the most sacred Covenant *Pactum De Singularis Caelum* and the present Maxims. False, Absurd & Prohibited Sovereign Rights

513. All proper and valid Sovereign Rights originate and are defined from the most sacred Covenant *Pactum De Singularis Caelum.* Source of Sovereign Rights

514. Any claim or assertion concerning Sovereign Rights that contradicts, or opposes or denies one or more of the present Maxims is false, absurd and prohibited from being recognised as valid in any Civilised form of Law. Claims or Assertions that contradict are false and absurd

Title IV – Ucadia Sovereign Entity Rights

4.1 – Ucadia Sovereign Entity Rights

Article 145 – Ucadia Sovereign Entity Rights

515. ***Ucadia Sovereign Entity Rights*** are a collection of Superior Rights associated with the embodiment of a valid *Ucadia Sovereign Legal Entity* as defined by Article 38 (Rights) of the most sacred Covenant *Pactum De Singularis Caelum*.

Ucadia Sovereign Entity Rights

516. In accord with the most sacred Covenant *Pactum De Singularis Caelum,* all valid and legitimate Ucadia Entities possessing a proper mandate have certain unique *Rights* in addition to any other Ecclesiastical, Sovereign, Official or Administrative Rights as defined.

Ucadia Sovereign Entity Rights and valid entities

517. The Superior Rights, also known as ***Ucadia Sovereign Entity Rights*** specifically associated with formal Ucadian administrative divisions and communities are uniquely defined according to the following Rights:-

Types of Ucadia Sovereign Entity Rights

(i) "**Ius Divinum Ucadia**" is the collection of Superior Rights associated with Ucadia Ecclesiastical, Sovereign, Official and Administrative Entities; as inherited from *Ius Divinum*; and

(ii) "**Ius Ucadia**" is the collection of Superior Rights associated with Ucadia itself; as inherited from *Ius Divinum Ucadia*; and

(iii) "**Ius Ucadia Unionis**" is the collection of Superior Rights associated with a Union administrative division, body politic and government. All *Ius Ucadia Unionis* Rights are inherited from *Ius Ucadia* Rights; and

(iv) "**Ius Ucadia Universitas**" is the collection of Superior Rights associated with a University administrative division, body politic and government. All *Ius Ucadia Universitas* Rights are inherited from *Ius Ucadia Unionis* Rights; and

(v) "**Ius Ucadia Provinciae**" is the collection of Superior Rights associated with a Province administrative division, body politic and government. All *Ius Ucadia Provinciae* Rights are inherited from *Ius Ucadia Universitas* Rights; and

(vi) "**Ius Ucadia Campus**" is the collection of Superior Rights associated with a Campus administrative division, body politic and government. All *Ius Ucadia Campus* Rights are inherited from *Ius Ucadia Provinciae* Rights; and

(vii) "**Ius Ucadia Fundationis**" is the collection of Superior Rights associated with a Ucadia Foundation. All *Ius Ucadia*

Fundationis Rights are inherited from *Ius Ucadia Universitas* Rights; and

(viii) "**Ius Ucadia Societatis**" is the collection of Superior Rights associated with a Ucadia company, charitable body or non profit society. All *Ius Ucadia Societatis* Rights are inherited from *Ius Ucadia Universitas* Rights.

518. No Ucadia Entity, Body, Agency or Thing shall possess any valid or legitimate claim or mandate to any Sovereign Right, unless granted and delegated in accord with the most sacred Covenant *Pactum De Singularis Caelum* and these present Maxims. Valid and legitimate Ucadia Sovereign Rights

Article 146 – Ius Divinum Ucadia (Rights of Ucadia)

519. ***Ius Divinum Ucadia*** are the primary collection of Superior Rights, as inherited from the collection of Rights *Ius Divinum*. Ius Divinum Ucadia (Rights of Ucadia)

520. *Ius Divinum Ucadia* (Rights of Ucadia) is the first collection of eight Ucadia Sovereign Entity Rights; associated with Ucadia Ecclesiastical, Sovereign, Official and Administrative Entities, explicitly invoked or referenced by *Ius Ucadia* in accord with the most sacred Covenant *Pactum De Singularis Caelum* and the present Maxims. Invoking of Ius Divinum Ucadia (Rights of Ucadia)

521. The collection of Rights of *Ius Divinum Ucadia* contains eight (8) Rights being:- Collection of Ius Divinum Ucadia (Rights of Ucadia)

(i) *Ius Divinum Ucadia* as the Right of Ucadia as inherited from *Ius Divinum*; and

(ii) *Ius Divinum Ucadia Existentiae* as the Right for the Existence of Ucadia as inherited from *Ius Divinum Ucadia*; and

(iii) *Ius Divinum Ucadia Mandati* as the Right of Mandate of Ucadia as inherited from *Ius Divinum Ucadia*; and

(iv) *Ius Divinum Ucadia Dominionis* as the Right of Dominion of Ucadia as inherited from *Ius Divinum Ucadia*; and

(v) *Ius Divinum Ucadia Proprietatis* as the Right of Property of Ucadia as inherited from *Ius Divinum Ucadia*; and

(vi) *Ius Divinum Ucadia Moneta* as the Right of Money of Ucadia as inherited from *Ius Divinum Ucadia*; and

(vii) *Ius Divinum Ucadia Potestatis* as the Right of Authority and Power of Ucadia as inherited from *Ius Divinum Ucadia*; and

(viii) *Ius Divinum Ucadia Revelationis* as the Right of Revelation of Ucadia as inherited from *Ius Divinum Ucadia*.

Article 147 – Ius Ucadia (Superior Rights of Ucadia)

522. ***Ius Ucadia*** is the collection of Superior Rights associated with Ucadia itself; as inherited from *Ius Divinum Ucadia*. Ius Ucadia (Superior Rights)

523. *Ius Ucadia* (Superior Rights) is the second collection of eight *Ucadia Sovereign Entity Rights*; and may be explicitly invoked or referenced by Sovereign Right of Action through registration and possession of a proper Mandate associated with a Ucadia Sovereign Entity in Ucadia or Non-Ucadia Jurisdiction. Invoking of Ius Ucadia (Superior Rights)

524. The collection of Superior Rights of *Ius Ucadia* contains eight (8) Rights being:- Collection of Ius Ucadia (Superior Rights)

(i) *Ius Ucadia* as the Superior Rights associated with Ucadia itself as inherited from *Ius Divinum Ucadia*; and

(ii) *Ius Ucadia Existentiae* as the Superior Right for the Existence of Ucadia as inherited from *Ius Ucadia*; and

(iii) *Ius Ucadia Mandati* as the Superior Right of Mandate of Ucadia as inherited from *Ius Ucadia*; and

(iv) *Ius Ucadia Dominionis* as the Superior Right of Dominion of Ucadia as inherited from *Ius Ucadia*; and

(v) *Ius Ucadia Proprietatis* as the Right of Property of Ucadia as inherited from *Ius Ucadia*; and

(vi) *Ius Ucadia Moneta* as the Superior Right of Money of Ucadia as inherited from *Ius Ucadia*; and

(vii) *Ius Ucadia Potestatis* as the Superior Right of Authority and Power of Ucadia as inherited from *Ius Ucadia*; and

(viii) *Ius Ucadia Revelationis* as the Superior Right of Revelation of Ucadia as inherited from *Ius Ucadia*.

Article 148 – Ius Ucadia Unionis (Ucadia Union Rights)

525. ***Ius Ucadia Unionis*** is the collection of Superior Rights associated with a Union administrative division, body politic and government. All *Ius Ucadia Unionis* Rights are inherited from *Ius Ucadia* Rights. Ius Ucadia Unionis (Union Rights)

526. *Ius Ucadia Unionis* (Ucadia Union Rights) is the third collection of eight *Ucadia Sovereign Entity Rights*; and may be explicitly invoked or referenced by Sovereign Right of Action through registration and possession of a proper Mandate associated with a Ucadia Sovereign Entity in Ucadia or Non-Ucadia Jurisdiction. Invoking of Ius Ucadia Unionis (Union Rights)

527. The collection of Ucadia Union Rights of *Ius Ucadia Unionis* contains twenty (20) Rights being:- Collection of Ius Ucadia Unionis (Union Rights)

(i) *Ius Ucadia Unionis* as the Superior Right associated with a Union administrative division, body politic and government as inherited from *Ius Ucadia*; and

(ii) *Ius Ucadia Unionis Existentiae* as the Superior Right for the Existence of a Ucadia Union as inherited from *Ius Ucadia Unionis*; and

(iii) *Ius Ucadia Unionis Mandati* as the Superior Right of Mandate of a Ucadia Union as inherited from *Ius Ucadia Unionis*; and

(iv) *Ius Ucadia Unionis Hereditatis* as the Superior Right of Inheritance as inherited from *Ius Ucadia Unionis*; and

(v) *Ius Ucadia Unionis Dominionis* as the Superior Right of Dominion of a Ucadia Union as inherited from *Ius Ucadia Unionis*; and

(vi) *Ius Ucadia Unionis Proprietatis* as the Superior Right of Property of a Ucadia Union as inherited from *Ius Ucadia Unionis*; and

(vii) *Ius Ucadia Unionis Moneta* as the Superior Right of Money of Ucadia a Union as inherited from *Ius Ucadia Unionis*; and

(viii) *Ius Ucadia Unionis Potestatis* as the Superior Right of Authority and Power of a Ucadia Union as inherited from *Ius Ucadia Unionis*; and

(ix) *Ius Ucadia Unionis Registrum* as the Superior Right of Registers and Rolls as inherited from *Ius Ucadia Unionis*; and

(x) *Ius Ucadia Unionis Nomenis* as the Superior Right to Name, Title and Reputation as inherited from *Ius Ucadia Unionis*; and

(xi) *Ius Ucadia Unionis Fecerim* as the Superior Right of the Union to invent, create and make seals, arms, heralds, instruments and other property of value as inherited from *Ius Ucadia Unionis*; and

(xii) *Ius Ucadia Unionis Sociari* as Superior Right of Membership as inherited from *Ius Ucadia Unionis*; and

(xiii) *Ius Ucadia Unionis Terram* as the Superior Right of the Supreme Council to grant a Right or Title to Land defined and surveyed within its metes and bounds as inherited from *Ius Ucadia Unionis*; and

(xiv) *Ius Ucadia Unionis Usum Terram* as the Superior Right of Use to Land defined and surveyed within its metes and bounds as inherited from *Ius Ucadia Unionis*; and

(xv) *Ius Ucadia Unionis Mutat Terram* as the Superior Right to Alter the (Top of the) of Land defined and surveyed within its metes and bounds as inherited from *Ius Ucadia Unionis*; and

(xvi) *Ius Ucadia Unionis Fodere Terram* as the Superior Right to Dig (or Mine) the Land defined and surveyed within its metes and bounds as inherited from *Ius Ucadia Unionis*; and

(xvii) *Ius Ucadia Unionis Alienum Subcriptio* as the Superior Right to register a subsidiary within the jurisdiction of a foreign estate, body, person or entity as inherited from *Ius Ucadia Unionis*; and

(xviii) *Ius Ucadia Unionis Audit* as the Superior Right of the Supreme Council to review any books, or any information, or any accounts of any officer operating within the bounds of the Union as inherited from *Ius Ucadia Unionis*; and

(xix) *Ius Ucadia Unionis Inspectionis* as the Superior Right to establish a Commission of Investigation with the power to call any registered Member and any information held by them within the bounds of the Union as inherited from *Ius Ucadia Unionis*; and

(xx) *Ius Ucadia Unionis Anathema* as the Superior Right to commission an Impeachment for the forced removal of any elected official to any position within any branch of government within the bounds of the Union as inherited from *Ius Ucadia Unionis.*

Article 149 – Ius Ucadia Universitas (Ucadia University Rights)

528. ***Ius Ucadia Universitas*** is the collection of Superior Rights associated with a University administrative division, body politic and government. All *Ius Ucadia Universitas* Rights are inherited from *Ius Ucadia Unionis* Rights. Ius Ucadia Universitas (University Rights)

529. *Ius Ucadia Universitas* (Ucadia University Rights) is the fourth collection of eight *Ucadia Sovereign Entity Rights*; and may be explicitly invoked or referenced by Sovereign Right of Action through registration and possession of a proper Mandate associated with a Ucadia Sovereign Entity in Ucadia or Non-Ucadia Jurisdiction. Invoking of Ius Ucadia Universitas (University Rights)

530. The collection of Ucadia University Rights of *Ius Ucadia Universitas* contains twenty (20) Rights being:- Collection of Ius Ucadia Universitas (University Rights)

(i) *Ius Ucadia Universitas* as the Superior Rights associated with a University administrative division, body politic and government as inherited from *Ius Ucadia Unionis*; and

(ii) *Ius Ucadia Universitas Existentiae* as the Superior Right for the Existence of a Ucadia University as inherited from *Ius Ucadia Universitas*; and

(iii) *Ius Ucadia Universitas Mandati* as the Superior Right of Mandate of a Ucadia University as inherited from *Ius Ucadia Universitas*; and

(iv) *Ius Ucadia Universitas Hereditatis* as the Superior Right of Inheritance as inherited from *Ius Ucadia Universitas*; and

(v) *Ius Ucadia Universitas Dominionis* as the Superior Right of Dominion of a Ucadia University as inherited from *Ius Ucadia Universitas*; and

(vi) *Ius Ucadia Universitas Proprietatis* as the Superior Right of Property of a Ucadia University as inherited from *Ius Ucadia Universitas*; and

(vii) *Ius Ucadia Universitas Moneta* as the Superior Right of Money of a Ucadia University as inherited from *Ius Ucadia Universitas*; and

(viii) *Ius Ucadia Universitas Potestatis* as the Superior Right of Authority and Power of Ucadia University as inherited from

Ius Ucadia Universitas; and

(ix) *Ius Ucadia Universitas Registrum* as the Superior Right of Registers and Rolls as inherited from *Ius Ucadia Universitas*; and

(x) *Ius Ucadia Universitas Nomenis* as the Superior Right to Name, Title and Reputation as inherited from *Ius Ucadia Universitas*; and

(xi) *Ius Ucadia Universitas Fecerim* as the Superior Right of the University to invent, create and make seals, arms, heralds, instruments and other property of value as inherited from *Ius Ucadia Universitas*; and

(xii) *Ius Ucadia Universitas Sociari* as Superior Right of Membership as inherited from *Ius Ucadia Universitas*; and

(xiii) *Ius Ucadia Universitas Terram* as the Superior Right of the University Parliament to grant a Right or Title to Land defined and surveyed within its metes and bounds as inherited from *Ius Ucadia Universitas*; and

(xiv) *Ius Ucadia Universitas Usum Terram* as the Superior Right of Use to Land defined and surveyed within its metes and bounds as inherited from *Ius Ucadia Universitas*; and

(xv) *Ius Ucadia Universitas Mutat Terram* as the Superior Right to Alter the (Top of the) of Land defined and surveyed within its metes and bounds as inherited from *Ius Ucadia Universitas*; and

(xvi) *Ius Ucadia Universitas Fodere Terram* as the Superior Right to Dig (or Mine) the Land defined and surveyed within its metes and bounds as inherited from *Ius Ucadia Universitas*; and

(xvii) *Ius Ucadia Universitas Alienum Subcriptio* as the Superior Right to register a subsidiary within the jurisdiction of a foreign estate, body, person or entity as inherited from *Ius Ucadia Universitas*; and

(xviii) *Ius Ucadia Universitas Audit* as the Superior Right of the University Parliament to review any books, or any information, or any accounts of any officer operating within the bounds of the University as inherited from *Ius Ucadia Universitas*; and

(xix) *Ius Ucadia Universitas Inspectionis* as the Superior Right to establish a Commission of Investigation with the power to call any registered Member and any information held by them within the bounds of the University as inherited from *Ius Ucadia Universitas*; and

(xx) *Ius Ucadia Universitas Anathema* as the Superior Right to commission an University Impeachment for the forced removal of any elected official to any position within any branch of government within the bounds of the University as inherited from *Ius Ucadia Universitas*.

Article 150 – Ius Ucadia Provinciae (Ucadia Province Rights)

531. ***Ius Ucadia Provinciae*** is the collection of Superior Rights associated with a Province administrative division, body politic and government. All *Ius Ucadia Provinciae* Rights are inherited from *Ius Ucadia Universitas* Rights.

Ius Ucadia Provinciae (Province Rights)

532. *Ius Ucadia Provinciae* (Ucadia Province Rights) is the fifth collection of eight *Ucadia Sovereign Entity Rights*; and may be explicitly invoked or referenced by Sovereign Right of Action through registration and possession of a proper Mandate associated with a Ucadia Sovereign Entity in Ucadia or Non-Ucadia Jurisdiction.

Invoking of Ius Ucadia Provinciae (Province Rights)

533. The collection of Sovereign Rights of *Ius Ucadia Provinciae* contains twenty (20) Rights being:-

Collection of Ius Ucadia Provinciae (Province Rights)

(i) *Ius Ucadia Provinciae* as the collection of Superior Rights associated with a Province administrative division, body politic and government as inherited from *Ius Ucadia Universitas*; and

(ii) *Ius Ucadia Provinciae Existentiae* as the Superior Right for the Existence of a Ucadia Province as inherited from *Ius Ucadia Provinciae*; and

(iii) *Ius Ucadia Provinciae Mandati* as the Superior Right of Mandate of a Ucadia Province as inherited from *Ius Ucadia Provinciae*; and

(iv) *Ius Ucadia Provinciae Hereditatis* as the Superior Right of Inheritance as inherited from *Ius Ucadia Provinciae*; and

(v) *Ius Ucadia Provinciae Dominionis* as the Superior Right of Dominion of a Ucadia Province as inherited from *Ius Ucadia Provinciae*; and

(vi) *Ius Ucadia Provinciae Proprietatis* as the Superior Right of Property of a Ucadia Province as inherited from *Ius Ucadia Provinciae*; and

(vii) *Ius Ucadia Provinciae Moneta* as the Superior Right of Money of a Ucadia Province as inherited from *Ius Ucadia Provinciae*; and

(viii) *Ius Ucadia Provinciae Potestatis* as the Superior Right of Authority and Power of a Ucadia Province as inherited from *Ius Ucadia Provinciae*; and

(ix) *Ius Ucadia Provinciae Registrum* as the Superior Right of Registers and Rolls as inherited from *Ius Ucadia Provinciae*; and

(x) *Ius Ucadia Provinciae Nomenis* as the Superior Right to Name, Title and Reputation as inherited from *Ius Ucadia Provinciae*; and

(xi) *Ius Ucadia Provinciae Fecerim* as the Superior Right of the Province to invent, create and make seals, arms, heralds, instruments and other property of value as inherited from *Ius Ucadia Provinciae*; and

(xii) *Ius Ucadia Provinciae Sociari* as Superior Right of Membership as inherited from *Ius Ucadia Provinciae*; and

(xiii) *Ius Ucadia Provinciae Terram* as the Superior Right of the Province Assembly to grant a Right or Title to Land defined and surveyed within its metes and bounds as inherited from *Ius Ucadia Provinciae*; and

(xiv) *Ius Ucadia Provinciae Usum Terram* as the Superior Right of Use to Land defined and surveyed within its metes and bounds as inherited from *Ius Ucadia Provinciae*; and

(xv) *Ius Ucadia Provinciae Mutat Terram* as the Superior Right to Alter the (Top of the) of Land defined and surveyed within its metes and bounds as inherited from *Ius Ucadia Provinciae*; and

(xvi) *Ius Ucadia Provinciae Fodere Terram* as the Superior Right to Dig (or Mine) the Land defined and surveyed within its metes and bounds as inherited from *Ius Ucadia Provinciae*; and

(xvii) *Ius Ucadia Provinciae Alienum Subcriptio* as the Superior Right to register a subsidiary within the jurisdiction of a foreign estate, body, person or entity as inherited from *Ius Ucadia Provinciae*; and

(xviii) *Ius Ucadia Provinciae Audit* as the Superior Right of the Province Assembly to review any books, or any information, or any accounts of any officer operating within the bounds of the Province as inherited from *Ius Ucadia Provinciae*; and

(xix) *Ius Ucadia Provinciae Inspectionis* as the Superior Right to establish a Commission of Investigation with the power to call any registered Member and any information held by them within the bounds of the Province as inherited from *Ius Ucadia Provinciae*; and

(xx) *Ius Ucadia Provinciae Anathema* as the Superior Right to commission a Province Impeachment for the forced removal of any elected official to any position within any branch of government within the bounds of the Province as inherited from *Ius Ucadia Provinciae*.

Article 151 – Ius Ucadia Campus (Ucadia Campus Rights)

534. ***Ius Ucadia Campus*** is the collection of Superior Rights associated with a Campus administrative division, body politic and government. All *Ius Ucadia Campus* Rights are inherited from *Ius Ucadia Provinciae* Rights.

Ius Ucadia Campus (Campus Rights)

535. *Ius Ucadia Campus* (Ucadia Campus Rights) is the sixth collection of eight *Ucadia Sovereign Entity Rights*; and may be explicitly invoked or referenced by Sovereign Right of Action through registration and possession of a proper Mandate associated with a Ucadia Sovereign Entity in Ucadia or Non-Ucadia Jurisdiction.

Invoking of Ius Ucadia Campus (Campus Rights)

536. The collection of Sovereign Rights of *Ius Ucadia Campus* contains twenty (20) Rights being:-

Collection of Ius Ucadia Campus (Campus Rights)

(i) *Ius Ucadia Campus* as the collection of Superior Rights associated with a Campus administrative division, body politic and government as inherited from *Ius Ucadia Provinciae*; and

(ii) *Ius Ucadia Campus Existentiae* as the Superior Right for the Existence of a Ucadia Campus as inherited from *Ius Ucadia Campus*; and

(iii) *Ius Ucadia Campus Mandati* as the Superior Right of Mandate of a Ucadia Campus as inherited from *Ius Ucadia Campus*; and

(iv) *Ius Ucadia Campus Hereditatis* as the Superior Right of Inheritance as inherited from *Ius Ucadia Campus*; and

(v) *Ius Ucadia Campus Dominionis* as the Superior Right of Dominion of a Ucadia Campus as inherited from *Ius Ucadia Campus*; and

(vi) *Ius Ucadia Campus Proprietatis* as the Superior Right of Property of a Ucadia Campus as inherited from *Ius Ucadia Campus*; and

(vii) *Ius Ucadia Campus Moneta* as the Superior Right of Money of a Ucadia Campus as inherited from *Ius Ucadia Campus*; and

(viii) *Ius Ucadia Campus Potestatis* as the Superior Right of Authority and Power of a Ucadia Campus as inherited from *Ius Ucadia Campus*; and

(ix) *Ius Ucadia Campus Registrum* as the Superior Right of Registers and Rolls as inherited from *Ius Ucadia Campus*; and

(x) *Ius Ucadia Campus Nomenis* as the Superior Right to Name, Title and Reputation as inherited from *Ius Ucadia Campus*; and

(xi) *Ius Ucadia Campus Fecerim* as the Superior Right of the Campus to invent, create and make seals, arms, heralds, instruments and other property of value as inherited from *Ius Ucadia Campus*; and

(xii) *Ius Ucadia Campus Sociari* as Superior Right of Membership as inherited from *Ius Ucadia Campus*; and

(xiii) *Ius Ucadia Campus Terram* as the Superior Right of the Campus Assembly to grant a Right or Title to Land defined and surveyed within its metes and bounds as inherited from *Ius Ucadia Campus*; and

(xiv) *Ius Ucadia Campus Usum Terram* as the Superior Right of Use to Land defined and surveyed within its metes and bounds as inherited from *Ius Ucadia Campus*; and

(xv) *Ius Ucadia Campus Mutat Terram* as the Superior Right to Alter the (Top of the) of Land defined and surveyed within its metes and bounds as inherited from *Ius Ucadia Campus*; and

(xvi) *Ius Ucadia Campus Fodere Terram* as the Superior Right to Dig (or Mine) the Land defined and surveyed within its metes and bounds as inherited from *Ius Ucadia Campus*; and

(xvii) *Ius Ucadia Campus Alienum Subcriptio* as the Superior Right to register a subsidiary within the jurisdiction of a foreign estate, body, person or entity as inherited from *Ius Ucadia Campus*; and

(xviii) *Ius Ucadia Campus Audit* as the Superior Right of the Campus Assembly to review any books, or any information, or any accounts of any officer operating within the bounds of the Campus as inherited from *Ius Ucadia Campus*; and

(xix) *Ius Ucadia Campus Inspectionis* as the Superior Right to establish a Commission of Investigation with the power to call any registered Member and any information held by them within the bounds of the Campus as inherited from *Ius Ucadia Campus*; and

(xx) *Ius Ucadia Campus Anathema* as the Superior Right to commission a Campus Impeachment for the forced removal of any elected official to any position within any branch of government within the bounds of the Campus as inherited from *Ius Ucadia Campus*.

Article 152 – Ius Ucadia Fundationis (Ucadia Foundation Rights)

537. ***Ius Ucadia Fundationis*** is the collection of Superior Rights associated with a Ucadia Foundation. All *Ius Ucadia Fundationis* are inherited from *Ius Ucadia Universitas* Rights. Ius Ucadia Fundationis (Foundation Rights)

538. *Ius Ucadia Fundationis* (Ucadia Foundation Rights) is the seventh collection of eight *Ucadia Sovereign Entity Rights*; and may be explicitly invoked or referenced by Sovereign Right of Action through registration and possession of a proper Mandate associated with a Ucadia Sovereign Entity in Ucadia or Non-Ucadia Jurisdiction. Invoking of Ius Ucadia Fundationis (Foundation Rights)

539. The collection of Sovereign Rights of *Ius Ucadia Fundationis* (Ucadia Foundation Rights) contains eight (8) Rights being:- Collection of Ius Ucadia Fundationis (Foundation Rights)

(i) *Ius Ucadia Fundationis* as the collection of Superior Rights associated with a Ucadia Foundation as inherited from *Ius Ucadia Universitas*; and

(ii) *Ius Ucadia Fundationis Existentiae* as the Superior Right for the Existence of Ucadia Foundation as inherited from *Ius Ucadia Fundationis*; and

(iii) *Ius Ucadia Fundationis Mandati* as the Superior Right of Mandate of a Ucadia Foundation as inherited from *Ius Ucadia Fundationis*; and

(iv) *Ius Ucadia Fundationis Proprietatis* as the Superior Right of Property of a Ucadia Foundation as inherited from *Ius Ucadia Fundationis*; and

(v) *Ius Ucadia Fundationis Potestatis* as the Superior Right of Authority and Power of a Ucadia Foundation as inherited from *Ius Ucadia Fundationis*; and

(vi) *Ius Ucadia Fundationis Registrum* as the Superior Right of Registers and Rolls as inherited from *Ius Ucadia Fundationis*; and

(vii) *Ius Ucadia Fundationis Nomenis* as the Superior Right to Name, Title and Reputation as inherited from *Ius Ucadia Fundationis*; and

(viii) *Ius Ucadia Fundationis Fecerim* as the Superior Right of the Foundation to invent, create and make seals, arms, heralds, instruments and other property of value as inherited from *Ius Ucadia Fundationis*.

Article 153 – Ius Ucadia Societatis (Ucadia Company Rights)

540. ***Ius Ucadia Societatis*** is the collection of Superior Rights associated with a Ucadia company, charitable body or non profit society. All *Ius Ucadia Societatis* Rights are inherited from *Ius Ucadia Universitas* Rights.

Ius Ucadia Societatis (Company Rights)

541. *Ius Ucadia Societatis* (Ucadia Company Rights) is the eighth collection of eight *Ucadia Sovereign Entity Rights*; and may be explicitly invoked or referenced by Sovereign Right of Action through registration and possession of a proper Mandate associated with a Ucadia Sovereign Entity in Ucadia or Non-Ucadia Jurisdiction.

Invoking of Ius Ucadia Societatis (Company Rights)

542. The collection of Sovereign Rights of *Ius Ucadia Societatis* contains eight (8) Rights being:-

Collection of Ius Ucadia Societatis (Company Rights)

(i) *Ius Ucadia Societatis* as the collection of Superior Rights associated with a Ucadia company, charitable body or non profit society as inherited from *Ius Ucadia Universitas*; and

(ii) *Ius Ucadia Societatis Existentiae* as the Superior Right for the Existence of Ucadia company, charitable body or non profit society as inherited from *Ius Ucadia Societatis*; and

(iii) *Ius Ucadia Societatis Mandati* as the Superior Right of Mandate of a Ucadia company, charitable body or non profit society as inherited from *Ius Ucadia Societatis*; and

(iv) *Ius Ucadia Societatis Proprietatis* as the Superior Right of Property of a Ucadia company, charitable body or non profit society as inherited from *Ius Ucadia Societatis*; and

(v) *Ius Ucadia Societatis Potestatis* as the Superior Right of Authority and Power of a Ucadia company, charitable body or non profit society as inherited from *Ius Ucadia Societatis*; and

(vi) *Ius Ucadia Societatis Registrum* as the Superior Right of Registers and Rolls as inherited from *Ius Ucadia Societatis*; and

(vii) *Ius Ucadia Societatis Nomenis* as the Superior Right to Name, Title and Reputation as inherited from *Ius Ucadia Societatis*; and

(viii) *Ius Ucadia Societatis Fecerim* as the Superior Right of the Ucadia company, charitable body or non profit society to invent, create and make seals, arms, heralds, instruments and other property of value as inherited from *Ius Ucadia Societatis*.

4.2 – False, Absurd & Prohibited Ucadia Sovereign Entity Rights

Article 154 – False, Absurd & Prohibited Ucadia Sovereign Entity Rights

543. ***False, Absurd & Prohibited Ucadia Sovereign Entity Rights*** are claims or assertions concerning the Sovereign Rights of Ucadia Entities that clearly contradict, oppose or deny the most sacred Covenant *Pactum De Singularis Caelum* and the present Maxims. False, Absurd & Prohibited Ucadia Sovereign Entity Rights

544. All proper and valid Sovereign Rights in relation to any and all Ucadia Entities originate and are defined from the most sacred Covenant *Pactum De Singularis Caelum*. Source of Sovereign Rights

545. Any claim or assertion concerning Sovereign Rights of a Ucadia Entity that contradicts, or opposes or denies one or more of the present Maxims is false, absurd and prohibited from being recognised as valid in any Civilised form of Law. Claims or Assertions that contradict are false and absurd

Title V - Instruction, Adjudication & Visitation

5.1 – Sovereign Instruction

Article 155 – Sovereign Instruction

546. ***Sovereign Instruction*** refers to a directive or order given under Sovereign Authority, to guide the actions or behaviour of individuals involved in a formal legal process. All proper legal instruction owes its authority to Sovereign Instruction.

Sovereign Instruction, Grant & Delegation

547. Unlike lesser forms of instruction, such as legal instruction, Sovereign Instruction is founded upon and depends upon its auricular nature to be valid. No Sovereign Instruction is proper or valid if it has not been first pronounced and spoken, before being memorialised in writing.

Tradition of Auricular Sovereign Instruction

548. Sovereign Instruction is one of the primary functions and purposes of Sovereignty, as all major legal proceedings and formalities of law within the Sovereign Jurisdiction of the Sovereign Legal Entity depend upon the pronouncement of proper Sovereign Instruction:-

Sovereign Instruction as a primary purpose of Sovereignty

(i) From the earliest of times, the spoken word of the Sovereign as a Person (whether a king, or president or some other ruler) was considered the very embodiment of law; and

(ii) Unlike other Persons, a Sovereign Person was inherently limited to what they could or could not say, similar to what they could or could not write, given a word or a letter of a Sovereign could conceivably grant or withdraw one or more Rights by their authority; and

(iii) Proper Sovereign Instruction evolved as the formality of the way a Sovereign may address different aspects of important events, proceedings and matters within the jurisdiction of the realm.

549. There are ten (10) primary forms of Sovereign Instruction being Rogation, Interrogation, Amrogation, Abrogation, Benrogation, Prorogation, Prerogation, Subrogation, Surrogation and Derogation:-

Primary forms of Sovereign Instruction

(i) ***Rogation***: Is a solemn prayer and spiritual entreaty to the Divine Creator, expressed in speech by a Sovereign or their duly appointed representative; and

(ii) ***Interrogation***: Is to formally ask questions by rogation in accordance with valid sovereign authority to which answers are required to be provided; and

(iii) ***Amrogation***: Is to assent or ratify by rogation an order or rule issued by a subordinate authority, or to create a new law by legislative act or by valid sovereign authority; and

(iv) ***Abrogation***: Is to annul or destroy by rogation an order or rule issued by a subordinate authority, or to repeal a former law by legislative act or by valid sovereign authority; and

(v) ***Benrogation***: Is to open or convene by rogation an official meeting, session or action by valid sovereign authority; and

(vi) ***Prorogation***: Is to suspend or discontinue by rogation an official meeting, session or action by valid sovereign authority; and

(vii) ***Prerogation***: Is to exercise an exclusive or peculiar privilege by hereditary or official right or privilege of a sovereign by rogation; and

(viii) ***Subrogation***: Is to substitute one thing for another, or of one person into the place of another by rogation with respect to rights, claims or securities in accordance with sovereign authority; and

(ix) ***Surrogation***: Is to appoint an agent or authorised representative by rogation in accordance with sovereign authority; and

(x) ***Derogation***: Is to temporarily or partially nullify by rogation a law or its effect by valid sovereign authority.

Article 156 - Rogation

550. ***Rogation*** is a solemn prayer and spiritual entreaty to the Divine Creator expressed in speech by a Sovereign or their duly appointed representative concerning a question, inquiry, proposal, nomination or motion of law before two (2) or more witnesses and usually memorialised in writing. Rogation

551. The word *Rogation* comes from the Latin *rogatio* meaning "a solemn prayer and spiritual entreaty concerning an official question, inquiry, proposal, nomination or motion of law expressed through speech". Origin of word Rogation

552. To be valid, all Rogations traditionally comply with the following elements:- Key elements of Rogation

(i) By tradition, the Sovereign announces in some customary manner of words that they are speaking a Rogation; and

(ii) The Sovereign evokes by prayer and spiritual entreaty to the Divine Creator by some valid name the authority to make a Rogation; and

(iii) At least two (2) or more sworn witnesses holding official duties are present to witness the Sovereign speak the Rogation; and

(iv) The Rogation is memorialized and then signed and testified by the Sovereign and the witnesses as proof of the event of Rogation.

553. By definition, only a Sovereign under a proper Mandate in accord with these Maxims, or their duly appointed representative may perform a Rogation. Limits of Rogation

Article 157 - Interrogation

554. ***Interrogation*** is to formally ask questions by rogation in accordance with valid sovereign authority to which answers are required to be provided. Interrogation

555. The word *Interrogation* comes from the Latin word *interrogare* meaning "to ask, question" from *inter* meaning "between" and *rogatio* meaning "a solemn prayer and spiritual entreaty concerning an official question, inquiry, proposal, nomination or motion of law expressed through speech". Origin of word Interrogation

556. Interrogatories are a set of formal questions memorialized from an Interrogation made by a sovereign or their duly appointed representative to an accused on the facts which are the object of the accusation to which the accused is obliged to answer or else their silence shall be affirmed ecclesiastically, legally and lawfully in the affirmative. Purpose of Interrogation

557. As failure to answer valid Interrogatories affirms ecclesiastically, legally and lawfully the questions in the affirmative, Interrogatories traditionally require the highest level of fair notice and due process, including but not limited to:- Consequences of Interrogation

(i) Prior notice of the controversy, accusation or charge and the right to attend, defend and rebut the accusations; and

(ii) Evidence of service of any subsequent Interrogatories proving that a reasonable person would conclude the questions were presented to the accused; and

(iii) Sufficient time to enable the questions to be answered; and

(iv) Further notice and opportunity to cure.

558. No valid Interrogatories may be issued in opposition to these Maxims or the most sacred Covenant *Pactum De Singularis Caelum* or its associated charters and covenants or codes of law. No Interrogatories

Article 158 - Amrogation

559. ***Amrogation*** is to assent or ratify by rogation an order or rule issued by a subordinate authority, or to create a new law by legislative act or by valid sovereign authority. Amrogation

560. The word *Amrogation* comes from the Latin word *am* meaning "I love; I like" and *rogatio* meaning "a solemn prayer and spiritual entreaty concerning an official question, inquiry, proposal, nomination or motion of law expressed through speech". Origin of word Amrogation

561. In respect of Amrogation & Assent in the context of Sovereignty:- Amrogation & Assent

(i) Assent is the formal process of signing and/or sealing a new law, or treaty or agreement to give it legal effect, whereas Amrogation is the consent of the Sovereign to "assent" the new law or treaty or agreement in the first instance; and

(ii) A system that denies the existence or prior requirement of Amrogation before Assent is not a Civilised System of Law; and

(iii) The argument that a person may hold merely a ceremonial position to "assent" laws with no choice as to their approval or dissent is both an injury to the notion of Civilised Law and an affront to the true nature of Sovereignty.

Article 159 - Abrogation

562. ***Abrogation*** is to annul or destroy by rogation an order or rule issued by a subordinate authority or to repeal a former law by legislative act or by valid sovereign authority. Abrogation

563. The word *Abrogation* comes from the Latin word *abrogatio* meaning "repeal" from *ab* meaning "from, after, since; by, in respect of" and *rogatio* meaning "a solemn prayer and spiritual entreaty concerning an official question, inquiry, proposal, nomination or motion of law expressed through speech". Origin of word Abrogation

564. In respect of Abrogation & Dissent in the context of Sovereignty:- Abrogation & Dissent

(i) Dissent or "Veto" is the formal process of signing and/or sealing a veto power against a new law, or treaty, or agreement, effectively nullifying its effect and returning it to the legislature; whereas Abrogation is the expressed disagreement of the Sovereign to "assent" a new law or treaty or agreement in the first instance; and

(ii) A system that denies the existence or prior requirement of

Abrogation before Dissent is not a Civilised System of Law; and

(iii) The argument that a person may hold merely a ceremonial position to "assent" laws with no choice as to their "dissent" or abrogation is both an injury to the notion of Civilised Law and an affront to the true nature of Sovereignty.

565. No valid Maxim or Article of the most sacred Covenant *Pactum De Singularis Caelum* or its associated charters and covenants may be abrogated by any force, action, inference, argument, sovereign, person, entity or spirit. No Abrogation

Article 160 - Benrogation

566. ***Benrogation*** is to open or convene by rogation an official meeting, session or action by valid sovereign authority. Benrogation

567. The word *Benrogation* comes from the Latin word *bene* meaning "well, good" and *rogatio* meaning "a solemn prayer and spiritual entreaty concerning an official question, inquiry, proposal, nomination or motion of law expressed through speech". Origin of word Benrogation

Article 161 - Prorogation

568. ***Prorogation*** is to defer, extend or suspend by rogation an official meeting, session or action by sovereign authority. Prorogation

569. The word *Prorogation* comes from the Latin word *prorogatio* meaning "to prolong, continue, extend, protract, postpone, defer" from *pro* meaning "on behalf of, before, for, about, as or like" and *rogatio* meaning "a solemn prayer and spiritual entreaty concerning an official question, inquiry, proposal, nomination or motion of law expressed through speech". Origin of word Prorogation

570. No valid Prorogation may be used to defer, extend, suspend any body, action or function unless defined by these Maxims or Articles of the most sacred Covenant *Pactum De Singularis Caelum* or its associated charters and covenants or codes of law. No Prorogation

Article 162 - Prerogation

571. ***Prerogation*** is to exercise an exclusive or peculiar privilege by hereditary or official right or privilege of a sovereign by rogation. Prerogation

572. The word *Prerogation* comes from the Latin word *praerogativa* meaning "first right of vote or decision" from *prae* meaning "in front of, before" and *rogatio* meaning "a solemn prayer and spiritual Origin of word Prerogation

entreaty concerning an official question, inquiry, proposal, nomination or motion of law expressed through speech".

573. The statute known as De Praerogativa Regis and claimed as having been promulgated during the 17th year of the reign of King Edward 1st claiming to define the prerogatives of the crown on certain subjects, but especially directing that the king shall have ward of the lands of idiots, taking the profits without waste and finding them necessaries is hereby declared as a fraud, having no force nor effect ecclesiastically, legally or lawfully. Falsity of De Praerogativa Regis

574. No valid Prerogation may be used in opposition to these Maxims or Articles of the most sacred Covenant *Pactum De Singularis Caelum* or its associated charters and covenants or codes of law. No Prerogation

Article 163 - Subrogation

575. ***Subrogation*** is to substitute one thing for another, or of one person into the place of another by rogation with respect to rights, claims or securities in accordance with sovereign authority. Subrogation

576. The word *Subrogation* comes from the Latin word *subrogare* meaning "to choose, elect or cause someone to be chosen in place of another" from *sub* meaning "under; behind; at the foot of; close to" and *rogatio* meaning "a solemn prayer and spiritual entreaty concerning an official question, inquiry, proposal, nomination or motion of law expressed through speech". Origin of word Subrogation

577. Subrogation is of two (2) kinds, either conventional or legal:-

(i) Conventional is where the subrogation is expressed by the acts of the creditor and the third person; and

(ii) Legal is where (as in the case of sureties) the subrogation is effected or implied by the operation of the law.

578. No valid Subrogation may be used unless defined by these Maxims or Articles of the most sacred Covenant *Pactum De Singularis Caelum* or its associated charters and covenants or codes of law. No Subrogation

Article 164 - Surrogation

579. ***Surrogation*** is to appoint an agent or authorised representative by rogation in accordance with sovereign authority. Surrogation

580. The word *Surrogation* comes from the Latin word *surrogare* meaning "to choose, elect or cause someone to be chosen in place of another" from *surus* meaning "a breach or stake" and *rogatio* meaning "a solemn prayer and spiritual entreaty concerning an Origin of word Surrogation official question, inquiry, proposal, nomination or motion of law expressed through speech".

581. No valid Surrogate may be nominated unless such process is defined and consistent with these Maxims or Articles of the most sacred Covenant *Pactum De Singularis Caelum* or its associated charters and covenants or codes of law. No Surrogation

Article 165 - Derogation

582. ***Derogation*** is to temporarily or partially nullify by rogation a law or its effect by valid sovereign authority. Derogation

583. The word *Derogation* comes from the Latin word *derogare* meaning "to annul, repeal part of a law, take away, detract from" from *de* meaning "from" and *rogatio* meaning "a solemn prayer and spiritual entreaty concerning an official question, inquiry, proposal, nomination or motion of law expressed through speech". Origin of word Derogation

584. No valid right, property or element defined by these Maxims or Articles of the most sacred Covenant *Pactum De Singularis Caelum* or its associated charters and covenants may be derogated by any force, action, inference, argument, sovereign, person, entity or spirit. No Derogation

5.2 – Sovereign Adjudication

Article 166 – Sovereign Adjudication

585. ***Sovereign Adjudication*** is the action whereby a Sovereign Power or one duly granted Sovereign Authority reviews evidence, arguments, petitions and matters of controversy between opposing parties in order to determine the appropriate Rights and Obligations, Judgement and any Sentence or Penalties. Sovereign Adjudication

586. The word Adjudication from the Latin *adjudicatio* meaning "judgement; sentence". Origin of word Adjudication

587. Adjudication is sourced from the ancient claim of certain Divine Rights of Sovereign Power and the maxim that "no man may judge another". Thus Sovereign Adjudication rests on the proper authority and succession of Sovereign Power to duly appointed judges and justices under proper oath in order for such power and sentences to be lawful and legal. Nature of Adjudication

588. The power of Adjudication ceases to exist where an official claiming the right to Adjudication fails to demonstrate an effective oath and the proper instruments by which such authority claiming Divine provenance may be granted. Cessation of Power of Adjudication

5.3 – Sovereign Visitation

Article 167 – Sovereign Visitation

589. ***Sovereign Visitation*** refers to the official visit of a Sovereign Person or a high-ranking government official to another country, region, or location. During a *Sovereign Visitation*, various formal events and ceremonies are often held to mark the occasion, and it is typically a significant diplomatic and ceremonial event. Sovereign Visitation

590. A Sovereign Person, or the head of a Sovereign Body (such as a President or Prime Minister), is expected as part of the function of their office to Visit communities within their Sovereign Jurisdiction as well as foreign states and locations:- Obligation of Sovereign and Visitation

(i) It is considered a primary obligation of the Sovereign to be seen by the people and to regularly visit all major communities within the jurisdiction of the Sovereign Entity; and

(ii) It is further considered a primary obligation of the Sovereign to represent the Sovereign Body or Nation at major international meetings and events attended by other Sovereigns; and

(iii) The failure of a Sovereign to visit their own people is considered a fundamental betrayal of their sacred office; and

(iv) The failure of a Sovereign to engage internationally at major international meetings and events is similarly seen as a failure to properly perform duties.

591. The word *Visitation* comes from the Latin *visio* meaning "to behold; to survey" and *–atio* to denote a noun as a result of the action of a verb. Origin of the meaning of Visitation

592. The six most common forms of Sovereign Visitations include (but are not limited to):- Forms of Sovereign Visitation

(i) **Official State Visit**: This is the most formal and ceremonial type of visit. It is typically hosted by the head of state of one country for the head of state of another country. The purpose is to strengthen diplomatic relations and may involve lavish state banquets, parades, and meetings with government officials; and

(ii) **Official Visit**: This is a less formal visit by a foreign head of state, often involving meetings with government officials, but with fewer formalities than a full state visit; and

(iii) **Diplomatic Visit**: This type of visit is focused on diplomatic discussions and may include negotiations, treaty signings, and meetings with government officials. The ceremonial aspects are generally less prominent; and

(iv) **Working Visit**: This is a more business-oriented visit, where the focus is on specific issues or agreements. It may involve meetings with business leaders, trade discussions, and the signing of economic agreements; and

(v) **Cultural Visit**: In some cases, a royal or state visit may have a cultural emphasis, with the visiting dignitary attending cultural events, exhibitions, and performances to showcase the cultural ties between the two countries; and

(vi) **Humanitarian Visit**: Occasionally, state visits may have a humanitarian focus, where the visiting dignitary engages in charitable or humanitarian activities, such as visiting disaster-stricken areas or promoting international development initiatives.

Title VI – Sovereign Symbols & Signs

6.1 – Sovereign Symbols

Article 168 – Sovereign Symbols

593. ***Sovereign Symbols*** are emblems, icons, or figures that represent the authority and independence of a state or monarchy. These symbols are used to project power, legitimacy, and the historical and cultural significance of a sovereignty. Examples of Sovereign Symbols include (but are not limited to):- Sovereign Symbols

(i) ***Seats***: Seats such as Thrones and Chairs are arguably one of the oldest and most significant symbols of Sovereign Authority; and

(ii) ***Headdress***: Headdress such as crowns, or wreaths have been a symbol of Sovereign Authority since the first civilisations; and

(iii) ***Garments***: Particular Garments such as robes have been a symbol of Sovereign Authority for millennia; and

(iv) ***Jewellery***: Special and historic examples of jewellery have been symbols of Sovereign Authority since the first civilisations; and

(v) ***Furniture***: Elaborate and historic Desks, Cabinets, Beds and Tables are all examples of Sovereign Authority since early civilisations; and

(vi) ***Handheld Objects***: Sceptres, orbs associated with the monarchy's power and dignity; and

(vii) ***Money and Stamps***: The design and icons on national currencies and postage stamps often carry symbols of sovereignty, such as portraits of national leaders, historical figures, or national monuments; and

(viii) ***Transportation***: Ancient (and modern) modes of transportation such as chariots, ships and horse drawn carriages have a long history as being symbols of Sovereign Authority and Power; and

(ix) ***Monuments***: These structures often serve as a symbol of Sovereign Authority as well as national pride and history, representing significant events, achievements, or figures; and

(x) ***Murals and Paintings***: Murals and paintings including (but not limited to) grand walls of hieroglyphs, elaborate mosaics, stunning painted ceilings and walls have all projected Sovereign Authority and Power for millennia; and

(xi) ***Instruments and Texts***: Important texts and instruments such as proclamations, charters, and ancient symbols of scripture have all featured as Sovereign Symbols and Signs of Authority since the first civilisations; and

(xii) ***Buildings***: Palaces, Parliaments and Legislative Buildings, Courts, Administrative Offices and Buildings, Ceremonial and Religious Sites; and

(xiii) ***Cities***: The designation of a city as a capital is symbolic of its administrative and political importance in a sovereign state.

Importance of Symbols and Signs in Projecting a Sovereign Mythology of Power & Legitimacy

594. From the very beginning of human civilisation, symbols and signs have been used to reinforce and project different mythologies of claimed power and legitimacy of sovereign leaders and governments:-

(i) The ancient provenance (origin) and power of various symbols and signs themselves have played a fundamental part of reinforcing the claims of sovereign authority and legitimacy of virtually every empire. Modern empires are no different; and

(ii) Extraordinarily lavish and imposing building structures such as palaces and temples have always been used as symbols of power. St Peters Basilica, St Paul's Cathedral in London and the US Capitol Building were all deliberately designed to intimidate and to project power as well as awe and wonder; and

(iii) The use of magnificent murals and paintings, as well as statutes and monuments similarly have a long history as symbols that both project power and awe in support of a uniquely claimed cultural and political identity. The Great Temple of Zeus on the Parthenon in Athens was an ancient example, whereas the Lincoln Memorial in Washington DC is a modern version; and

(iv) The use of occult symbols and signs, especially those with and ancient provenance, has been a key hallmark of empires from the 14th Century and increasing to a "high water mark" in the United States by the early and mid 20th Century. Such symbolism as the giant Washington Monument, the Great Owl of Moloch etched into the landscape around the US Capitol Building is all designed to project a deeper sense of "occult" power and intimidation to the rest of the world, particularly as the spiritual home to the 19th Century state based religion of Secularism and its various denominations such as Capitalism, Communism, Fascism and Socialism.

595. Many Non-Ucadian nations have strict laws against the display of Sovereign Symbols without a mandate or warrant to do so:-

Legal Restrictions on Use of Sovereign Symbols

(i) In the United Kingdom, the display of the coat of arms of the Sovereign is restricted to those entities that possess a valid royal warrant; and

(ii) In Asian Non-Ucadian Countries that still possess monarchies, the display of images or words of disrespect against the Sovereign is a serious criminal offence.

596. Under the Laws of Ucadia, the use of the name, symbols, titles and images are restricted to those entities and persons possessing a proper and valid mandate:-

Ucadia Restrictions on Use of Sovereign Symbols and Signs

(i) The use of the word Ucadia, or any Ucadia Symbols without possessing a proper and valid mandate and without permission is a serious criminal offence; and

(ii) No person may claim, register or use Ucadia material without first receiving a proper and valid mandate to do so, under strict conditions; and

(iii) Ucadia and its entities and officials reserve the absolute right to use any and every means to prosecute and punish any and every person or entity culpable of the misuse, misrepresentation or theft of Ucadia Sovereign Symbols and Signs.

Article 169 – Sovereign Seat

597. A ***Sovereign Seat*** is a ceremonial chair or throne reserved for a monarch, ruler or other dignitary. It is a symbol of authority and power and is typically used during formal or important events, such as coronations, royal ceremonies, and official state functions.

Sovereign Seat

598. The word *Throne* comes directly from the ancient Irish word *Thríeonar* meaning "the three (chairs) of yew, being the source of all (sovereign) authority":-

Origin of the word Throne

(i) The Irish word *Thríeonar* comes from *thrí* meaning "three", *eo* meaning "yew tree" and ónar meaning "the source from"; and

(ii) Contrary to deliberately false and absurd etymology, the word throne is not self referencing i.e. "throne means throne or chair" in English, Latin and Ancient Greek; and

(iii) The true etymology of Throne from Ireland relates to the famous history of three sacred "chairs" being carved from the oldest (yew) tree in the world (over 10,000 years old) around

3200 BCE, with the first being the ***Throne of Eo*** (Cuilliaéan), the second being the ***Throne of El*** (Ebla) and the third being the ***Throne of Ma*** (Egypt); and

(iv) The *Throne of the Celts* (Throne of Amen-Ra) definitely still existed as late as the 9th Century CE, as the 4,000 year old throne that Charlemagne was coronated as Holy (Holly) Roman Emperor of the new Western Civilisation. However, since the 14th Century it is not clear if or where this ancient chair still exists.

599. The word *Chair* comes directly from the ancient Irish word *Chaire* meaning literally "seat of justice and equality of illumination (wisdom)":- Origin of the word Chair

(i) The word *Chaire* denoted an official seat of judgement of law and authority, whether it be a high king or a justice adjudicating an important matter; and

(ii) Contrary to deliberately false and absurd etymology, the word Chair does not come from Ancient Greek khaîre (χαῖρε) or Latin chaere meaning "hello; hail!". Such deliberately false etymology seeks to confuse Chair with Cheer; and

(iii) Arguably some of the most famous *Chairs* in history were (1) The three sacred *Chairs* being carved from the oldest (yew) tree in the world (over 10,000 years old) around 3200 BCE, with the first being the ***Throne of Eo*** (Cuilliaéan), the second being the ***Throne of El*** (Ebla) and the third being the ***Throne of Ma*** (Egypt); and (2) the great marble Chair cut from Irish Green Marble blocks and given to the Hibiru on their return to Ebla from around 1790 BCE. This became the famous Green Marble "Throne" (or Chair) of Amen-Ra of the Hyksos Pharaohs.

600. The concept of a *Sovereign Seat* has parallels in various cultural and institutional symbols that represent the power and status of an individual within a certain hierarchy. Examples include (but are not limited to):- Examples of Sovereign Seats

(i) **Papal Chair or Cathedra**: In the Roman Catholic Church, the Pope's ceremonial chair represents his role as the Bishop of Rome and the leader of the worldwide Catholic Church; and

(ii) **Patriarchal or Episcopal Chairs**: In many Christian denominations, the chair or seat used by a bishop or patriarch in a cathedral represents ecclesiastical authority; and

(iii) **Sovereign's Seat in Parliamentary Monarchies**: In

some countries, there may be a specific chair in the national parliament reserved for the monarch, used during certain state occasions; and

(iv) **Speaker's Chair**: In legislative assemblies, the chair occupied by the presiding officer or speaker represents the authority to guide legislative debate and maintain order; and

(v) **Judges' Bench**: In a courtroom, the elevated desk where a judge sits symbolizes the administration of justice and the authority of the legal system; and

(vi) **Chairperson's Seat**: In corporate or organizational settings, the seat occupied by the chairperson at a board meeting signifies leadership and decision-making power.

601. Three of the most sacred and significant seats ever formed in relation to Sovereignty were the Thrones of Uragh (An Iúrach) formed from the oldest tree in Europe (over 10,000 years old) midst the former forest of Yew Trees at Wicklow in Ireland:- Most Significant Sovereign Seats

(i) Yew Trees are exceptionally long living species, that is naturally poisonous to humans and animals, growing to over 30 metres (98 ft) in height and 5 metres (16 ft) in width of its base trunk; and

(ii) The Holly (Cuilliaéan) Priests considered the Yew to be most sacred of all the great trees, giving it the name *Eo* meaning literally "the source of spiritual knowledge, supernatural protection and authority, sovereignty, healing and wisdom". The word Yew is a corruption of the word *Eo*; and

(iii) Until the arrival to Ireland of the English-Venetian mercenaries in the 2nd half of the 16th Century, the oldest forest of Yew Trees (over 9,000 years old) was at Wicklow on the east coast of Ireland at a place called Uragh (An Iúrach) meaning literally "place of the yews". At the heart of Wicklow was the most famous and oldest tree of Europe, called the Elder (Tree), from the Irish *Eoldar* meaning "the tree of God that everyone knows"; and estimated to be over 10,000 years old; and

(iv) Around 3200 BCE, upon the establishment of Holly embassies and schools in both Egypt and Ebla (Syria), the three most sacred chairs (true origin of the literal meaning of "throne") were constructed from part of the still living *Eoldar* (tree of God), with the first being the Throne of the ***Eo*** (Cuilliaéan), the second being the Throne of ***El*** (Ebla) and the third being the Throne of ***Ma*** (Egypt); and

(v) At the fall of Ebla around 2330 BCE, a legend exists of the last King (Ibbi) travelling to Ireland and returning the *Throne of El* to its birthplace; and

(vi) There is evidence that after the conquest of Egypt by the "(H)ibiru" from around 1660 BCE, the *Throne of El* left Ireland once more and accompanied the invaders and became the *Throne of Amen-Ra* in addition to the Irish Green Marble Chair given to the "(H)ibiru" around 1790 BCE; and

(vii) By around 1353 BCE, there is the legend of Hyksos Queen Tiye, the mother of Akhenaten travelling to Ireland after the death of her husband and returning the *Throne of Ma* to its birthplace; and

(viii) By 1275 BCE, the *Throne of Amen-Ra* was returned to Ireland prior to the collapse of Ugarit and prior to the capture and return to Egypt of the Yahudi as slaves; and

(ix) In 999 CE, upon the Great Prophets of Yeb anointing U'vid (Da'vid) as first king and messiah of the Yahudi, the *Throne of Ma* left Ireland for Palestine to become the *Throne of the Yahudi*; and

(x) In 594 BCE, the Great Prophet Jeremiah, Baruchiah and princess Tephi of the Yahudi did land in Ireland and return the *Throne of the Yahudi* (formerly the Throne of Ma) to its birthplace, along with the Green Marble Chair originally given to the "(H)iburu"; and

(xi) By 24 BCE, Holly King Cú-Roi(n) did bring the *Throne of the Yahudi* to his estates at Bethesda, the Mount of Olives and Gardens of Gethsemane, before commissioning his own Yahudi city at Sepphoris as his new capital in Palestine. The Throne then became the *Throne of the Nabateans* by 50 CE; and by 58 CE returned to Ireland on the murder of Holly King Jacob of the Nabateans; and

(xii) By 69 CE, the *Throne of Amen-Ra* left Ireland to Scotland to become the *Throne of Britannia* (Celts) until around 121 CE before returning to Ireland; and

(xiii) By 310 CE, the *Throne of the Nabateans* (Throne of the Yahudi) did leave Ireland to become the new *Throne of Christianity* at Constantinople. The throne was eventually lost or destroyed by the Eastern Emperors by the 8th Century CE; and

(xiv) In 368 CE, the *Throne of Eo* (Holly) was completely destroyed during the siege of Tara; and

(xv) By the 5th Century the *Throne of the Celts* (Throne of Amen-Ra), left Ireland to become the *Throne of Western Christian Empire* under the Franks and then by the 9th Century the *Throne of the Holy Roman Empire*. It is not known what happened to the Throne by the start of the 14th Century.

602. The most significant Sovereign Chair created apart from the Thrones, was the Green Marble Chair made of Irish Green Marble and given to the "(H)ibiru" on their return journey to recapture Ebla around 1790 BCE:- Most Significant Sovereign Chair

(i) The Green Marble Chair known simply as the Cháiré was made from stone exclusively hewn at a sacred 5,000 year old Green Marble quarry called *Maigh Cuileainn* (Moycullen) meaning "Plain of the Holly" six miles from the ancient settlement of Galway. It is the same site from where the *Eolith* or "Anointing Stones" were hewn; and

(ii) When the Hibiru conquered Egypt by 1660 BCE, the Green Marble Chair became the Great Chair of Amen-Ra, also confusingly known as the Throne of Amen-Ra and the famous Yew Tree Seat of the same name; and

(iii) There is no evidence that the famous Great Green (Throne) Chair of Amen-Ra returned to Ireland until the 6th Century BCE. However, there is evidence of its existence as the High Chair of the Holly High Kings at Tara, before becoming the Great Chair of the Emperors of the Keltoi at Hollyrood in Ireland from the 1st Century CE; and

(iv) There is no evidence as to the final fate of the Great Green Marble Chair after the Holly lost Scotland around the 10th Century CE.

603. The graffiti riddled Coronation Chair of the Venetian English was commissioned no earlier than the late 17th Century out of Oak, in opposition to the ancient history of the sacred Thrones:- Coronation Chair of the Venetian English

(i) The claims of the Coronation Chair dates back to the 13th Century is an absurdity that takes advantage of the Great Deaths of the 14th Century and collapse of Civilisation to claim earlier provenance; and

(ii) There is no credible evidence the Venetians or English cared about due process of law, or sacred rites or sacred objects until the 17th Century, well after they had desecrated, burned, pillaged and destroyed the most sacred objects, rites and processes of Britain and Ireland for two previous centuries; and

(iii) The creation of the first Coronation Chair used by the Venetian-English Merchant Class was most likely under Charles II from 1660 and then falsely backdated to the 13th Century to claim legitimacy whilst continuing to erase historic record of the Holly; and

(iv) The desecration of the Coronation Chair was mainly done in the 18th and early 19th Century by the students of the School of Westminster when the chair was unceremoniously placed under the cloisters when not being used.

Article 170 – Anointing Stone

604. An ***Anointing Stone*** is a special and ancient stone specifically associated with the ritual of anointing a Sovereign. By ancient and proper tradition, a Sovereign kneels on an *Anointing Stone* for the ceremony of anointing in full view of witnesses. To not be kneeling or to be hidden is sacrilege and a terrible transgression against Heaven. Anointing Stone

605. From at least 3200 BCE the first formalisation of the rituals included a special Green Marble Anointing Stone whereby the Sovereign would kneel to be anointed:- Ancient Ritual of Anointing a Sovereign

(i) The Holly (Cuilliaéan) priests were the first to conceive of the formal rituals of using an Anointing Stone, usually a carved stone of Green Marble, known as an *Eolith* meaning "omen stone; stone of destiny"; and

(i) The Ancient Irish word of *Eolith* comes from Irish word *Eo* meaning "the source of spiritual knowledge, supernatural protection and authority, sovereignty, healing and wisdom"; and Irish word *Lith* meaning "(religious) ceremony, omen stone, prosperity stone"; and

(ii) To be anointed as a Sovereign, the person would have to kneel on the stone, both as a sign of humility before Heaven and as a sign of their legitimacy; and

(iii) The *Eolith* were exclusively hewn at a sacred 5,000 year old Green Marble quarry called Maigh Cuileainn (Moycullen) meaning "Plain of the Holly" six miles from the ancient settlement of Galway; and

(iv) Their name similarities (Eo) to the sacred thrones fashioned from the the most famous and oldest tree of Europe at the time, being the 10,000 year old *Eoldar* (Elder) Tree signifies that the Anointing Stones were always connected to the most important Coronation chairs in human civilised history; and

(v) There is anecdotal evidence that the *Eolith* accompanied the sacred thrones during their travels and return to Ireland. However, there is no evidence as to what happened to these most sacred of stones by the 14th Century.

606. The crude and roughly hewn Scottish sandstone block, known as the Scone Stone appears to have been commissioned no earlier than the late 17th Century as a poor attempt to emulate the 4,500 years (at that point) of Holly Sovereign history:-

Scone Stone of the Venetian English

(i) The claims of the Scone Stone dates back to the 13th Century is an absurdity that takes advantage of the Great Deaths of the 14th Century and collapse of Civilisation to claim earlier provenance; and

(ii) There is no credible evidence the Venetians or English cared about due process of law, or sacred rites or sacred objects until the 17th Century, well after they had desecrated, burned, pillaged and destroyed the most sacred objects, rites and processes of Britain and Ireland for two previous centuries; and

(iii) The creation of the first Coronation Chair used by the Venetian-English Merchant Class was most likely under Charles II from 1660 and so the Scone Stone is probably of a similar date. However, rather than the Scone Stone representing a true "Anointing Stone", the Coronation Chair was built with a compartment to house the stone as a trophy underneath the prospective English Monarch; and

(iv) Contrary to thousands of years of ancient Sovereign tradition, it does not appear a single English monarch has ever humbled themselves before Heaven and the Divine Creator by kneeling, much less on a proper anointing stone to be anointed in public. In fact, there is no evidence that the public have ever been permitted to see an English monarch receive the act of anointing; and

(v) There is no evidence a single English monarch has ever been properly anointed a legitimate Sovereign under the Rules of Heaven or the most ancient rules of Sovereignty Law. Nor is there any indication that the City of London Corporation (Bank of England) or the City of Westminster Corporation (Parliament) have ever had any interest whatsoever in ensuring a proper and legitimate ceremony of anointing according to valid history and Sovereign tradition.

Article 171 – Sovereign Staff

607. A ***Sovereign Staff*** is a ceremonial rod used as a symbol of Sovereign authority for more than 5,000 years. The word staff comes from Ancient Irish *staf* meaning "stiffness, pole of authority and measure". Sovereign Staff

608. A ***Rod*** from the Ancient Irish word ***ród***, is an exact measure used by the Holly for thousands of years being 4 cúbith (cubits) or 3 lámh (hands) and exactly 72 inches or 6 feet (182.88 cm) in height. Rod

609. A Rod or Staff has been a symbol of legitimate and valid Sovereignty for over 5,500 years, and is the origin of the notion of a Sovereign being the "good shepherd":- Origin of Rod and Staff

(i) The Holly (Cuilliaéan) were the first to connect a standard unit of measure, physically held by the Sovereign when adjudicating or instructing, as a symbol of Sovereign Authority and power; and

(ii) For over 4,000 years, Holly (Cuilliaéan) rulers sourced their Rods and Staffs from a single grove of ancient Hazel Trees along the banks of the Glendalough (place of the two lakes) in the Wicklow Hills of Ireland. Proper Rods and Staffs have always come from Hazel Trees from the beginning of civilisation; and

(iii) It was also customary to bend the hazel shoots at one end when still on the tree to 'grow' the bend into a crook before being harvested later. This is the origin of the curve now seen within the end of a"crozier" of a Christian Bishop; and

(iv) The name "Hyksos" as in the Pharaohs of Egypt both means in Ancient Egyptian "foreigner" and "shepherd" due to the Hazel Staffs and Rods of the Holly Pharaohs; and

(v) The first Staffs and Rods of Catholic Bishops in the 8th Century from Ireland continued the tradition of sourcing the material from Hazel Trees; and

(vi) It does not appear that the concept of Gold and precious metal staff, or rod or sceptre appeared in Europe until at least the late 15th Century, replacing the 5,000 year tradition of Sovereigns using Hazelwood Staffs or Rods.

Article 172 – Headdress

610. A ***Sovereign Headdress*** is a ceremonial or formal headpiece typically worn by a reigning monarch or sovereign during significant occasions or events. Famous and ancient headdress include (but are not limited to) thórna (thorn), cróuine (crown), tiar, pschent and corona. Sovereign Headdress

611. The earliest headdress associated with Sovereign Authority are from as early as 3200 BCE and the use of natural and native plants to create head garlands:- Earliest Sovereign Headdress

(i) The Ancient Greeks and Roman cultures followed the Celtic traditions of using plant based crowns as a sign of great honour, heroism and esteem. Generals who won great military battles were celebrated by Rome and honoured with plant based crowns as *corona*. In the first Olympic Games among the Greek states, winners were adorned with *stephanos* (laurel plant wreaths) to signify the highest honour; and

(ii) The term ***cróuine*** as the original source of the word "crown" comes from the Ancient Irish meaning "ring of the one person of authority", from *cró* meaning "ring" and *duine* meaning "one, person". All Non-Ucadia etymological definitions of this word are both absurd (self referencing) and false; and

(iii) The term ***thórna*** as the original source of the word "thorn" comes from the Ancient Irish meaning "ring from a (living) Holly tree representing the highest of elevation, law and authority", from *thóg* meaning "to raise, lift, elevate, take possession by law" and *arna* meaning "ring made from a tree or plant". All Non-Ucadia etymological definitions of this word are both absurd (self referencing) and false; and

(iv) The term ***corarna*** as the original source of the word "corona" from the Ancient Irish meaning "ring made from twisting (the leaves or branches of) a plant or tree" from *cor* meaning "to twist, or turn" and *arna* meaning "ring made from a tree or plant". All Non-Ucadia etymological definitions of this word are both absurd (self referencing) and false; and

(v) The term ***stéphanos*** (στέφανος) comes from the Ancient Greek meaning "a corona (crown) of honour, heroism or esteem", from *stéphō* (στέφω) meaning "to crown, encircle, honour" and *anos* (ανος) meaning "ring".

612. One of the earliest examples of Non-Plant Based Sovereign Headdress is the Pschent or "double crown" of Egypt since 2,000 Non Plant Based Headdress

BCE:-

(i) ***The Pschent***: Also known as the Double Crown, is the combination of the White Crown of Upper Egypt (Hedjet) and the Red Crown of Lower Egypt (Deshret). It symbolizes the unification of Upper and Lower Egypt and the establishment of a single, unified Egyptian state; and

(ii) ***The Iron Crown of Charlemagne of 800 CE***: Is the first metal crown of Europe in the 9th Century as King of the Romans; and

(iii) ***Māori Tāne Mahuta***: Has been worn by Māori tribal leaders for at least 1,600 years; and is made from feathers, including those of the kiwi bird. It symbolizes the wearer's high status and connection to the natural world; and

(iv) ***African Tribal Headdresses***: Various African cultures have their own traditional headdresses worn by tribal leaders and rulers for over 1,000 years. These headdresses often incorporate feathers, beads, shells and other materials unique to their culture. Examples include the Zulu "Isicholos" and the Ashanti "Golden Stool" headdress; and

(v) ***Crown of Charles II*** (***St. Edwards Crown***): Is arguably one of the oldest jewelled crowns of Europe and created for the coronation of Charles II in 1661, but falsely claimed as being the modified Crown of Edward Ist of 13th Century; and

(vi) ***Persian Qajar Crown***: Is the traditional coronation crown in the Iranian Crown Jewels, worn by the Qajar shahs of Iran (1789–1925) and adorned with priceless gemstones and pearls.

613. The Crown of Thorns, formed from the branches of a living Holly Tree is arguably the oldest and most authoritative Sovereign Headdress in history:- Crown of Thorns

(i) The Crown of Thorns were worn exclusively by Holly Irish Kings from at least 3200 BCE to the end of the practice by Holly King Constantine in the 4th Century; and

(ii) Unlike any crown before (or since), the sharp spikes of the Holly branches were not supposed to be removed, so that wearing the crown on official occasions induced physical discomfort, pain and bleeding on the part of the Holly (Cuilliaéan) rulers; and

(iii) The symbolism of the Crown of Thorns is also unique to any Sovereign Headdress in that it symbolised metaphorically and literally, the necessary suffering and difficulty of being a true

Sovereign and that such a person was expected to "give their blood" to defend and support the people; and

(iv) After Constantine banned the use of the Crown of Thorns under the formation of Christianity in 4th Century CE, the Holly Irish and Carolingians returned the symbolism of the Crown of Thorns by 8th Century CE by placing the historic figure Jesus Christ in a Crown of Thorns during his torture and crucifixion; and

(v) A Crown of Thorns not made of living Holly is a fraud from the beginning and without merit or authority.

Article 173 – Garments

614. ***Royal Garments*** are clothing and attire traditionally associated with royalty and monarchs and their positions. Garments

615. The original garments of Sovereigns from at least 3200 BCE were simple white woollen garments, signifying purity:- Original Garments of Monarchs

(i) The first garments of Sovereigns from the time of the Holly were simple white woollen garments signifying purity. Any blood stains when from wearing a Crown of Thorns by the Holly King would then be clearly reflected against the pure white of the garments; and

(ii) The use of ornate and exclusive Colours appear throughout ancient cultures. However, the use of overt opulence as a sign of Sovereign stature did not appear on a grand stage until the coronation of Charles II in 1661.

616. Modern Royal Garments over the past four hundred years include (but are not limited to):- Examples of Modern Royal Garments

(i) ***Robes and Gowns***: Monarchs often wear elaborate robes and gowns during formal ceremonies and events. These garments are typically made from luxurious fabrics like silk, satin or velvet and may be adorned with intricate embroidery, jewels or precious metals; and

(ii) ***Uniforms and Military Attire***: In addition to ceremonial attire, monarchs may wear uniforms and military attire when performing official duties related to the armed forces. These uniforms often include insignia and decorations denoting their rank as commander-in-chief; and

(iii) ***Traditional Cultural Garments***: In some monarchies, royal garments incorporate elements of traditional cultural dress. These garments can vary widely depending on the country and its heritage; and

(iv) ***State Mantles***: Monarchs may wear a state mantle or cloak during official state functions. These garments are often richly decorated and can symbolize the monarch's role as the head of state.

Article 174 – Jewellery

617. ***Jewellery*** consists of a collection of valuable and often historic gemstones, diamonds, pearls and precious metals that are owned and worn by monarchs or members of royal families. These jewels are typically associated with the reigning monarchy or dynasty of a country and are used for ceremonial, symbolic and sometimes personal purposes. Jewellery

618. Contrary to Egypt and many Eastern Empires, ancient European Civilisation shunned Jewellery as a symbol of Sovereign Status and Power:- Jewellery & Sovereignty

(i) Under the Holly (Cuilliaéan) rulers, state symbols of Gold and Jewels were seen as debasing and defying the "Will of Heaven" in men and women seeking to proclaim or portray themselves "as gods"; and

(ii) The introduction of jewels and opulent symbols of wealth into sovereignty in the west did not appear in the West until the late 15th Century when former warlords and merchant leaders sought to project their claims of legitimacy and authority to rule.

619. Elements of Modern Royal Jewellery and examples of their use include (but are not limited to):- Elements of Modern Royal Jewellery

(i) ***Symbolism***: Royal jewellery is symbolic of a monarch's status, power and wealth. It can represent the heritage and history of a royal family and the nation it leads; and

(ii) ***Coronation and State Events***: Many royal jewels are used during coronation ceremonies, state banquets and other formal state events. Crowns, tiaras, necklaces and brooches are among the most commonly worn pieces during such occasions; and

(iii) ***Crowns and Tiaras***: Crowns and tiaras are iconic symbols of royalty. Crowns are typically worn by monarchs during their coronation, while tiaras are worn by queens and princesses on various formal occasions; and

(iv) ***Necklaces and Pendants***: Royal necklaces often feature large and valuable gemstones or pearls. These necklaces can be passed down through generations and become important heirlooms; and

(v) ***Brooches and Pins***: Royal families use brooches and pins to accessorize their clothing. These pieces may be chosen for their historical significance or their ability to complement a particular outfit; and

(vi) ***Personal Jewellery***: In addition to their ceremonial use, members of royal families may also have personal jewellery collections, which may include items acquired or inherited through generations; and

(vii) ***Historical Significance***: Some royal jewellery has deep historical and cultural significance. For example, the British Crown Jewels include a number of priceless gems taken from the lands of other peoples.

620. The British Crown Jewels are unique to the world in using priceless gems from other peoples as trophies of plunder, theft and conquest to falsely claim authority:-

Examples of Jewels Stolen, Seized and Taken as Symbols of Sovereignty

(i) ***Black Prince's Ruby***: Set into the cross at the front of the crown is a spinel (semi-precious stone). It is a reputed "cursed" gem stolen by the East India Company from China in exchange for opium in the early 19th Century. The jewel was not added to the crown until the coronation of Queen Victoria in 1838. The story of its existence back to the 14th century is a fantastical tale to hide its provenance as a priceless artefact stolen from the people of China; and

(ii) ***St Edward's Sapphire***: Is an octagonal rose-cut sapphire that forms part of the British Crown Jewels. Its false history hides the fact that it was the most important state jewel of Siam (Thailand) and stolen by the East India Company in 1687 from the Kingdom of Siam, sparking a brief war, before the English succeeded in causing a rebellion in 1688; and

(iii) ***Koh-i-Noor Diamond***: Is one of the most important priceless gems of the state of India and its history, originally having pride of place within the *Peacock Throne* of the Mughal Empire (16th - 18th Century). A false and absurd claim is made that the Iranians plundered the throne in 1739 to hide the fact that the East India Company stole the entire original throne around the same time and replaced it with a poor and relatively cheap copy, shipping the original stones to England no later than the 1740's. The further history of the stone being "gifted" by a young and weak Maharaja in 1849 is further falsities to hide the thievery of the East India Company; and

(iv) ***Cullinan Diamonds***: Named after the mine owner in South Africa, the largest Cullinan I (also known as the Great Star of Africa) is the largest clear-cut diamond in the world and is set in the head of the Sovereign's Sceptre with Cross, one of the regalia items of the British monarchy.

Article 175 – Handheld Symbols

621. ***Handheld Symbols*** also known as *Royal Regalia* or symbols of authority, are objects or items carried or displayed by monarchs and other members of royalty during ceremonial and formal occasions. Handheld Symbols

622. Examples of Handheld Symbols include (but are not limited to):- Examples of Handheld Symbols

(i) ***Crook*** (***heka-scepter***): A shortened Shepherd Rod, often used in funeral symbols and placement of Hyksos royalty, showing their connection to the Holly and to their duty as stewards, not tyrants. It is the origin of the more modern sceptre; and

(ii) ***Djed***: Symbolised the attainment of highest soul under Hyksos Egyptian Philosophy or Ka-Ba-La being the unity of all three souls, and the highest of wisdom; and

(iii) ***Sceptre***: A sceptre is a long staff or rod, often made of precious materials like gold or silver and adorned with gemstones. It symbolizes the monarch's authority and is typically held in the hand during important ceremonies. Different types of sceptres may be used for various purposes, such as the Royal Sceptre with the Cross and the Sovereign's Sceptre with the Dove in the British Crown Jewels; and

(iv) ***Orb***: The orb is a globe or sphere typically topped with a cross, representing the monarch's role as the ruler of the world or as the protector of the Christian faith. It is often held in the monarch's hand during coronation ceremonies. The Sovereign's Orb is part of the British Crown Jewels; and

(v) ***Flail*** (***nekhakha***): The flail is the symbol of rule by fear, terror and punishment as a primary symbol of the false pharaohs that followed the Holly Hyksos Pharaohs. The non-Holly equivalent became the sword; and

(vi) ***Royal Sword***: In some monarchies, a ceremonial sword represents the monarch's role as the defender of the realm. It may be carried during the coronation or other military-related ceremonies.

Article 176 – Sovereign Furniture

623. ***Sovereign Furniture*** refers to furniture items and furnishings associated with symbols of authority, power and sovereignty. They can include desks, beds and other ornate and symbolic furniture that represents leadership and sovereignty. Sovereign Furniture

624. Examples of famous Sovereign Furniture includes (but are not limited to):- Examples of famous ancient Sovereign Furniture

(i) ***Ornate Wooden Chests***: Such as those used by Egyptian Pharaohs, Roman Emperors and Persian Shah were important storage cabinets of official garments, or headdress and jewellery; and

(ii) ***Movable Screens***: Such as those used in the Royal Chinese Court and in Persia often shielded royal advisors from dignitaries and guests; and

(iii) ***Funerary Furniture***: Such as ornate royal sarcophagi, tables, cabinets and chairs.

625. Examples of famous Sovereign Furniture include (but are not limited to):- Examples of famous modern Sovereign Furniture

(i) **Russian Imperial Furniture (Russia)**: Opulent furniture pieces from the palaces of the Russian Tsars; and

(ii) **Viennese Silver and Gold Tableware (Austria)**: Used in the Habsburg court for formal occasions; and

(iii) **The Royal Clocks of Versailles (France)**: Magnificent timepieces found throughout the Palace of Versailles; and

(iv) **The HMS Resolute Desks (UK and United States)**: In 1879, four desks were commissioned by Queen Victoria from timbers removed from the cabin of the barque HMS Resolute during its complete entombing in a specially made underground vault on the Greenwich Meridian Line prior to 1873. The main desk became the famous "Resolute Desk" handed to US President Rutherford B. Hayes in 1880; and the second was a small writing desk to the widow of Henry Grinnell; and the third was a small table used by Queen Victoria on her royal yacht; and the fourth was a writing desk originally held at Buckingham Palace and now at Windsor Castle.

626. To the present day, the enigma and mystery surrounding the barque The enigma of the HMS

HMS Resolute and the famous desks continues:- Resolute Desks

(i) It is claimed Captain Henry Kellett abandoned the HMS Resolute during a failed Arctic exploration mission on May 15, 1854; and

(ii) It is then claimed American Captain James Buddington of the whaling ship George Henry found the abandoned "ghost ship" of HMS Resolute largely intact on September 10, 1855, despite supposedly having been frozen in ice for more than a year. The Resolute was still in such good working order that it was able to be sailed on its own by half the crew back to New London, New Hampshire by December 23, 1855; and

(iii) On June 24, 1856 the US Congress unanimously passed a resolution to purchase the HMS Resolute for $40,000. The ship was then sent to the Brooklyn Navy Yards to be fully restored, before being sailed back to England by Captain Hartstein of the United States Navy. Seen as a priceless diplomatic gift from the United States to the United Kingdom, the ship arrived in Portsmouth by December 12th 1857 to major media celebration and a crowd in the thousands. Queen Victoria herself visited and toured the ship not long after its return; and

(iv) On December 18, 1869, the Greenwich Hospital officially closed and major earthworks, building and renovation began. Around the same time, the HMS Resolute was withdrawn as a tourist attraction from Portsmouth. No credible or accurate records exist for the location of the ship until it was announced ten years later that the ship had been "retired" from service; and

(v) On January 1st 1873 the Greenwich Naval College officially opened with a new road as the Greenwich Meridian centreline from the remodelled "Queens House" down to the Thames. During the remodelling, architectural blueprints reveal a specially made underground vault on the Greenwich Meridian Line was created and an unnamed ship of exactly the same dimensions as the Resolute was fully entombed; and

(vi) In 1879, it was announced that the missing Resolute had been retired and broken up for timbers; and that from those timbers a desk would be commissioned to be sent back to the United States as a gift. Bizarrely there is no record of any official protest by the Americans for such an unprecedented diplomatic slap in the face, given the ship had been fully purchased and restored by US Congress and Navy. Four desks were then commissioned by Queen Victoria from timbers removed from the cabin of the HMS Resolute during its complete entombing. The main desk became the famous "Resolute Desk" handed to US President Rutherford B. Hayes in 1880; and the second was a small writing desk to the widow of Henry Grinnell; and the third was a small table used by Queen Victoria on her royal yacht; and the fourth was a writing desk originally held at Buckingham Palace and now at Windsor Castle.

Article 177 – Sovereign Transportation

627. ***Sovereign Transportation*** refers to modes of transportation associated as symbols of heads of state or high-ranking government officials. These forms of transport include (but are not limited to) ancient vehicles such as chariots and barges, to modern vehicles such as presidential limousines or official government aircraft like Air Force One. Sovereign Transportation

628. Examples of famous ancient Sovereign Transportation include (but are not limited to):- Examples of ancient Sovereign Transportation

(i) ***Palanquin***: Being enclosed chairs or seats, carried on the shoulders of several bearers. The last use of such mode of transport ended entirely by 1978 when it was abolished by Pope Paul VI (1963-1978); and

(ii) ***Chariots***: Being a two wheeled open or lightly covered structure drawn by one or more horses. Considered a type of vehicle used in the afterlife, chariots have been found in the tombs of many cultures including Celtic and Ancient Egyptian; and

(iii) ***Barque***: Being a small boat, often used for official ceremonies. In Ancient Celtic, Egyptian, Persian, Roman and Greek culture, barque are universally considered a mode of transportation of the dead and thus have figured prominently in the tombs of sovereigns and in the symbolism of ancient monuments.

629. Examples of famous modern Sovereign Transportation include (but are not limited to):- Examples of modern Sovereign Transportation

(i) ***Airplanes***: Such as Air Force One is arguably the most famous large jet in the world as a symbol of the sovereign authority and power of the President of the United States; and

(ii) ***Limousines***: Such as the prime vehicle of the President of the United States is arguably one of the most famous and recognisable vehicles in the world.

Article 178 – Sovereign Monuments & Statues

630. ***Sovereign Monuments and Statues*** are significant and historic structures erected as symbols of cultural identity, history as well as sovereign authority and power. Sovereign Monuments & Statues

631. Examples of famous ancient Sovereign Monuments & Statues include (but are not limited to):- Examples of ancient Sovereign Monuments & Statues

(i) ***Great Hyksos Initiation Chambers (Great Pyramids of Giza)***: Constructed at the height of Hyksos power in Egypt, arguably one of the greatest engineering achievements of any civilisation in history; and

(ii) ***Great Statue of Anubis (Desecrated and Deformed by Ramesses II to the Sphinx)***: The Great Anubis was a dog, not a jackal and stood guard on the Giza plateau against all forms of evil. Ramesses II desecrated and deformed this sacred monument into his own likeness and it became the infamous sphinx; and

(iii) ***Great Statue of Xerxes (Corrupted in history to be listed as Great Statue of Zeus)***: Was over 30 metres in height and stood at the entrance to the acropolis in Athens; and is the source of the false legend of the "Colossus" misappropriated to the island of Rhodes; and

(iv) ***Great Statue of Athena Parthenos***: Built in the 3rd Century BCE as the new protector goddess of the city. Was over 39 ft (12 metres) in height and was seated in the Great Parthenon temple on the Acropolis; and

(v) ***Great Obelisk (Membrum) of Amun-Ra of Karnak***: Reputed to have been over 144 ft (43.9 m) in height and weighing more than 800 tons and the single largest carved block of stone in human history. Symbolised the Sun God using his membrum to "inseminate" the earth with new life every day. It was destroyed by the impostor Ramesses pharaohs when they ransacked and burned the sacred temple complexes of Karnak; and

(vi) ***Obelisk (Membrum) of Ra of Cairo (under Thutmose IV)***: Approx 83.6 ft (25.5 m) in height, weighing 330 tons and more than 3,400 years old. It was brought to Rome in 37 CE by Caligula and was placed at a prime position in the Great

Circus. It was then moved in 16th Century to the new St. Peters Basilica to grow and "inseminate the Vatican" with new power every day.

632. Examples of famous modern Sovereign Monuments & Statues include (but are not limited to):- Examples of modern Sovereign Monuments & Statues

(i) ***Washington (Membrum) Obelisk Monument***: Approximately 555 ft (169 m) tall, with a foundation of 111 ft, as the largest phallic symbol ever conceived in human civilisation. Similar to other ancient obelisk in their design, the shadow of the Washington (Membrum) Monument enlarges up the National Mall twice a year around March 20-21 (spring equinox) and September 22-23 (autumnal equinox); and symbolically "procreates" with the giant 2,300 ft by 1,400 ft *Great Owl of Moloch* (aka Sabaoth, El and Satan) being the shape that clearly encompasses the Capitol Building; and

(ii) ***Great Owl of Moloch***: While not strictly a blatant or obvious monument, the specific design of roads around the US Capitol Building clearly create the largest symbol to Moloch ever conceived in human civilisation. Its design is to imitate the symbolic design of the Vatican but in a much more literal and negative form; and

(iii) ***Lincoln Memorial***: Designed to deify Abraham Lincoln as the god Zeus, the seated statue of Abraham Lincoln is approximately 19 feet (5.8 meters) tall, with Lincoln "as a god" touching the two largest symbols of Fasces (bundles of bound sticks symbolising literally rule by force, power, weaponisation of law and oppression).

Article 179 – Sovereign Murals & Paintings

633. ***Sovereign Murals & Paintings*** are large-scale artworks typically commissioned by governments or leaders to convey messages of power, heritage, symbolic or historical significance. These visual representations often adorn public buildings, palaces, and official spaces. They serve as a means of propaganda, cultural preservation, and storytelling, reinforcing sovereignty and authority through artistic expression. Sovereign Murals & Paintings

634. Examples of famous Sovereign Murals & Paintings include (but are not limited to):- Examples of Sovereign Murals & Paintings

(i) ***Granting of Power and Authority over the Earth by God to Adam by Michaelangelo (1475-1564) Sistine Chapel***: The 16th Century masterpiece gives both "public notice to heaven and earth" that according to the Bible, God gave Power and Authority over the Earth to Adam and his "authorised descendents"; and

(ii) ***God Apollo/Lucifer granting favour and authority to Charles II and the formation of the United Kingdom and Corporations by James Thornhill (1676-1734) Greenwich Palace***: This 18th Century masterpiece, clearly shows the pagan depiction of the demigod of Apollo (in Greek mythology) and Lucifer (in Roman mythology) as the patron and protector of the United Kingdom and its corporations and actions; and

(iii) ***The Deification (Apotheosis) of Washington by Constantino Brumidi (1805-1880) US Capitol Building***: This 1865 masterpiece depicts Washington being made a god, not by a historic God, but by the original 13 Dutch republic families that emigrated to the old Dutch colonies by 1792 depicted as goddesses. Below Washington as "god" is the symbolism of power of war, science, admiralty, commerce, technology and agriculture. The painting ultimately reveals the source of true power in America and the real "god" of the motto "in god we trust"; and

(iv) ***Goddess Hera (Juno) blessing young Victoria as goddess Lucy (female Lucifer) and Empress by John William Waterhouse (1849-1917) and falsely claimed by Orazio and Artemisia Gentileschi 17th C. Greenwich Queens (White) House***: This 1870 masterpiece originally painted for ceiling of remodelled White (Queens) House at Greenwich in direct response to the *Apotheosis of Washington.* It depicts a young Victoria as a female Lucifer (Lucy) as the central goddess among the goddesses of wisdom, strength, reason, rhetoric, science, mathematics, music and logic; and as Empress of the world. The painting was hastily removed no later than 1871 and reset at Malborough House by architect James Pennethorne, who butchered the original painting to make it fit and died soon after.

Article 180 – Sovereign Instruments & Texts

635. ***Sovereign Instruments & Texts*** encompass official legal documents and religious scriptures of profound importance in governing a nation. These texts outline laws, principles, and moral guidelines, reflecting the intertwining of governance and spirituality. Sovereign Instruments & Texts

Their preservation and adherence signify the authority of the state and its commitment to upholding both legal and spiritual traditions, reinforcing sovereignty through the rule of law and faith.

636. Examples of famous ancient Sovereign Instruments & Texts include (but are not limited to):-

Examples of ancient Sovereign Instruments & Texts

(i) ***Institutes (Laws) of Western Civilisation***: From the 8th Century CE, the Holly ensured the sacredness of law was upheld across western civilisation until the 14th Century and the Great (Black) Death. This system was revived and then purposefully corrupted by the 16th Century through Venetian controlled England; and

(ii) ***Magna Cartae of the Holly Roman Emperors***: Starting in the 8th Century, every new Emperor would start their reign with a Great Charter or "Magna Carta" preserving the rule of law and ethics of the Roman Catholic Church. This system ended by the 14th Century. In the 18th Century, a terrible set of fake charters were paraded around called the "Magna Carta" claiming that an English King signed a charter with his Barons in 1216, despite the fact that southern and eastern England was called Daneland and in charge of the Danes till such a date; and that there were no "English Monarchs" called Kings until Henry VIII and the Venetians.

637. Examples of famous modern Sovereign Instruments & Texts include (but are not limited to):-

Examples of modern Sovereign Instruments & Texts

(i) **U.S. Declaration of Independence** (1776) reputedly written by Thomas Jefferson. The document is an absurd and terrible fake, given the existing country of former American colonies at the time being the Commonwealth of New England was locked in a battle to *stay independent* from the mercenary armies of the United Company of Merchants. The Commonwealth of New England (first formed in 1642) was the last surviving "commonwealth" formed after the coup against Charles I. It had its own currency, laws, parliament, taxes, militia and trade. However, by 1783, the country lost the war and was forced to dissolve to become the United States of America (Corporation) under the control of the United Company of Merchants and the City of London; and

(ii) **French Declaration of the Rights of Man and of the Citizen** (1789) - This document, a key part of the French Revolution, affirmed the principles of liberty, equality, and fraternity and influenced later democratic constitutions; and

(iii) **The Emancipation Proclamation** (1863) - Issued by President Abraham Lincoln during the American Civil War, this document declared the freedom of enslaved people in certain Confederate states not under the control of the Union. However, the same document did not free slaves in Union states nor captured states. Thus, contrary to deliberately false history, it is in fact a political document that sought to maintain slavery, not end it.

Article 181 – Sovereign Buildings

638. ***Sovereign Buildings*** are architectural structures of utmost historic significance, often housing government offices, residences of heads of state, or important institutions. These edifices serve as symbols of cultural identity, power and governance. Sovereign Buildings

639. Examples of famous ancient Sovereign Buildings include (but are not limited to):- Examples of ancient Sovereign Buildings

(i) ***Palace of Knossos (Crete, Greece)***: Dating back to the Minoan civilization (around 1900 BC), this palace is known for its labyrinthine layout and frescoes, and it is considered one of Europe's oldest palace complexes; and

(ii) ***Tara (Ireland)***: This ancient 7th Century BCE palace complex more than 2 km long and 1.5 km wide in the shape of a shield (now known as the Killeen Castle and Resort) is one of the most famous buildings in history. Destroyed in the 4th Century CE; and

(iii) ***Persepolis (Iran)***: The ceremonial capital of the Achaemenid Empire, constructed during the 6th century BCE, featuring impressive palaces and monumental architecture; and

(iv) ***Palatine Hill (Rome, Italy)***: The ancient Roman hill where several palaces, including the Palace of Domitian, were located, showcasing the grandeur of Roman imperial residences; and

(v) ***Forbidden City (Beijing, China)***: Also known as the Imperial Palace, it was the Chinese imperial palace from the Ming Dynasty to the end of the Qing Dynasty (1420-1912) and is a remarkable example of traditional Chinese architecture; and

(vi) ***Topkapi Palace (Istanbul, Turkey)***: A former royal residence of the Ottoman sultans, this palace is known for its opulent design and historical significance; and

(vii) ***Schönbrunn Palace (Vienna, Austria):*** A Baroque palace that served as the summer residence of the Habsburg monarchs, known for its beautiful gardens and architecture; and

(viii) ***St Peters Basilica and Buildings (Rome)***: Built in the 16th Century, it is both a series of religious buildings and the Palace of the Roman Catholic Popes. Until the construction of St Pauls in London in the 17th Century and then the US Capitol Building in the mid 19th Century, it had the most famous and recognisable dome of any structure; and

(ix) ***St Pauls Cathedral, London***: Completed in 1710 and designed by Christopher Wren. At 365 ft (111 m) high, it dominated the London skyline for over 300 years until 1963. Created as the "Third Temple" in the claim of the remodelled London (after the 1666 fire) as New Jerusalem. However, this claim was never unanimously accepted by the elite of the world and by the mid 20th Century, the formation of the State of Israel primarily sponsored by the Americans became a higher claim.

640. Examples of famous modern Sovereign Buildings include (but are not limited to):-

Examples of modern Sovereign Buildings

(i) ***Buckingham Palace***: Completed in 1834 at the same time of the mysterious fire that totally destroyed the old Westminster Buildings. The first monarch to use it as their primary London residence was Queen Victoria from 1837; and

(ii) ***Westminster Palace***: Designed in Gothic Revival by architect Charles Barry, construction began on the former ruins of old Westminster in 1840 and was completed by 1870. The parliamentary buildings were again deliberately set alight on two separate occasions with full complicity of American and German Nazi elite, with the worst bombing on 10 May 1941, 168 years to the day since the first shots of the War of the Commonwealth of New England to stay independent against the United Company of Merchants, otherwise known as the "War for Independence"; and

(iii) ***Greenwich Palace***: Originally the grounds of the Tudor Placenta Palace and the birthplace of Queen Elizabeth I. The site underwent two major and notable developments and constructions in the late 17th Century and again in the late 19th Century; and

(iv) ***US Capitol Building***: Construction began in 1864 at the same time as building of other key infrastructure of Washington began using an enslaved mostly black workforce of over 450,000. Contrary to the wholly false history of Washington, the building was not completed until at least 1866. This population were not "eligible" for freedom, having been classed as criminals for previously escaping to the Bethlehem Plantation of the Lee family on the Potomac – the eventual site of Washington; and

(v) ***Pentagon (Hidden Pentagram), Washingtom DC***: Dedication ceremony occurred on 11 September 1941 (9/11) with the future dimensions of the building already pegged and mapped out before the ceremony. The dedication ceremony of building this hidden pentagram occurring on precisely the same day, the five infamous death camps in Poland and Ukraine (based on the inverted footprints of the worst human sacrifice temples in history) began sacrificing victims to Moloch in purpose build ovens. The building held the record as the largest building in the world for more than 80 years (at 6.66 million square feet) until being overtaken by the Surat Diamond Bourse in India in 2023. As the headquarters for the United States Defence Department, it is a building deliberately conceived for evil, through rituals of evil (through the direct and specific connection to the Holocaust), to harness such evil as an ongoing ethereal source of power, until the building was finally dramatically damaged in attacks in 2001.

Article 182 – Sovereign Cities

641. ***Sovereign Cities*** are urban centres that hold unique political and administrative importance within a nation, empire or civilisation. They are often "purpose built" and serve as the capital or seat of government, housing key institutions and leaders. These cities are focal points of national identity and decision-making, embodying the country's sovereignty and serving as hubs for governance, diplomacy, and cultural expression. Sovereign Cities

642. Examples of famous "purpose built" ancient Sovereign Cities include (but are not limited to):- Examples of ancient Sovereign Cities

(i) ***Amarna, Egypt***: Created as new capital of Egypt under Pharaoh Akhenaten starting around 1346 BCE over a site roughly 10 km in length and height along the bank of the Nile. Finished by a workforce of over 800,000 by 1341 BCE, the site was abandoned after the death of Tutankhamen by 1323 BCE.

Under the reign of false pharaoh Ramesses II (1279 -1213 BCE), the site was systematically demolished to its foundations; and

(ii) ***Angkor Wat, Cambodia***: Completed in 12th Century as the new capital of Khmer King Suryavarman II of the Khmer Civilisation over a site roughly 25km long and 12 km wide, incorporating vast water features and canals, with many more than 4 km long. It is considered the largest religious structure in the world.

643. Examples of famous modern "purpose built" Sovereign Cities include (but are not limited to):-

Examples of modern Sovereign Cities

(i) ***London, England***: Following the deliberate sacrifice by fire of over 300,000 innocent men, women and children to Moloch in 1666, the City of London Corporation was granted the authority to create many new infrastructures, including St Pauls Cathedral. The revised city was then claimed as New Jerusalem, with St Paul's as the Third Temple. However, by the 20th Century such claims were openly disputed, especially by the Americans; and

(ii) ***Bethlehem, Lee Plantation, Potomac River***: The first purpose-built "Black City" in American history on the Lee Family Plantation on the east bank of the Potomac River from 1846. Named after the claimed biblical birthplace of Christ, by 1860, the city had a population of over 300,000 former black slaves and their families. The city was captured and its inhabitants (including children) were enslaved as criminals for being runaway slaves mostly from the northern states; and

(iii) ***Washington DC***: The first purpose-built city to Moloch (El, Sabaoth, G-d and Satan) from 1864. The site for the city was primarily chosen because of the historic black city of free slaves called "Bethlehem". With an additional 150,000 recaptured black slaves, the workforce of 450,000 "criminals" built the major infrastructure of Washington. At completion of major works by 1874, tens of thousands of these former slaves and their families were "resettled" to mid-western states as part of ongoing major infrastructure, such as the railroads. These towns and communities included (but are not limited to): Bronzeville Illinois, Paradise Valley Michigan, Tulsa Oklahoma, The West End Ohio, Toledo Ohio and Aliso Village California. Most of these centres were intentionally destroyed by the US Government by the 1920's and 1930's, given their success, quality of life, harmony and sense of sovereign independence. One of the most successful of these "sovereign" cities was Tulsa. In mid 1921, over two days, the US Government intentionally murdered well over 2,000 innocent black men, women and children and burnt Tulsa to the ground – claiming the inhabitants were "rioting".

6.2 – Sovereign Signs

Article 183 – Sovereign Signs

644. A ***Sovereign Sign*** is an object, quality or event whose presence or occurrence indicates the direct presence or "personification" of the Sovereign. Sovereign Signs

645. Examples of Sovereign Signs include (but are not limited to):- Examples of Sovereign Signs

(i) ***Coat of Arms***: A heraldic design on a shield or escutcheon or on a surcoat or tabard, used to represent the unique personification of a particular family, person, state or organization; and

(ii) ***Seals***: Seals such as the Great Seal of a state, for example, is a sovereign sign used to endorse legal documents, giving certain instruments a higher presence and importance; and

(iii) ***Flags***: Flags are arguably the most recognised Sovereign Sign used to represent the direct presence or personification of the Sovereign Person, Body or State; and

(iv) ***Standards***: Standards are physical emblems, artefacts or heraldry, often carried in front of the Sovereign; and have a long history as representing the direct presence or personification of the Sovereign Person, Body or State; and

(v) ***Anthems***: Musical Anthems have been used as a sign of the direct presence or personification of the Sovereign Person, Body or State for thousands of years.

646. Whereas a Sovereign Symbol represents a claim of Sovereign Authority and Power, a Sovereign Sign indicates the quality, or event of presence of the Sovereign. Difference between Sovereign Sign and Symbol

Article 184 – Genealogy (Blood Right)

647. ***Genealogy*** refers to the documented and claimed lineage or family tree of rulers, monarchs, or heads of state. Such claims try to establish their hereditary right to rule and often includes details about their ancestors, dynastic connections and royal bloodlines. Sovereign genealogy is crucial in monarchies and aristocratic systems Genealogy (Blood Right) to determine succession and validate a leader's legitimacy based on their lineage.

Article 185 – Standard

648. A ***Standard*** is a physical emblem, artefact or heraldry, often carried in front of the Sovereign or their military or representatives; as representing the direct presence or personification of the Sovereign Person, Body or State. Standard

649. Examples of Sovereign Standards include (but are not limited to):- Examples of Standards

(i) ***Roman Eagle (Aquila)***: The Roman legions used the Aquila, a golden eagle mounted on a pole, as one of their standards. It represented the honour and valour of the legion and was a symbol of Roman military might; and

(ii) ***Roman Sign S•P•Q•R (Vexillum)***: The Roman legions used the Vexillum, being a golden displayed rectangle with the letters S•P•Q•R (which in Latin meant SENATUS POPULUS QUO REGNUM or "(The) Senate (of the) People Through Which (is) Rule") mounted on a pole, as one of their standards. It represented the rule of law and authority of Rome; and

(iii) ***Fasces (bundle of bound wooden rods and an axe)***: Literally the source and original meaning of fascism as the symbol of fascist rule. Carried by Roman Legions with their other symbols; and

(iv) ***Cratis (bundle of spears or arrows)***: Closely aligned to Fasces (a bundle of sticks), a Cratis represented two states – war (as spears or arrows) or peace as (as cages, subjugation and trade). The symbol of Cratis has always and only meant "rule by conquest and rule by force" either in war as *Autocratis* (military law) or subjugation (in peace) of the people as slaves as *Democratis* (democracy); and

(v) ***Christian Motto* I•N•R•I *(Tetragrammaton)***: Tetragrammaton is the official and original term used to describe the four (4) letters in Latin and Ancient Greek known as I•N•R•I promulgated by Constantine in 313 CE to replace the previous pagan motto of S•P•Q•R of the Roman Empire.; and

(vi) ***Pharaoh's Ark***: In ancient Egypt, the Hyksos (Holly) pharaohs carried an Ark ahead of them, or their army on symbolic marches, symbolising the presence of the spirit of

Amun. The Ark of Akhenaten then became the famous Ark of the Covenant; and

(vii) ***Chinese Imperial Dragon Banner***: The dragon was a symbol of imperial authority in ancient China. Emperors used dragon banners to represent their divine right to rule; and

(viii) ***Aztec Eagle and Serpent Standard***: The Aztec Empire had a prominent standard featuring an eagle perched on a cactus with a serpent in its beak. This symbolized the founding of their capital, Tenochtitlan, and their allegiance to the god Huitzilopochtli; and

(ix) ***Sasanian Derafsh-e Kaviani***: The Sasanian Persian kings had the Derafsh-e Kaviani, a royal banner believed to represent the eternal fire of the Zoroastrian religion and the might of the empire; and

(x) ***Japanese Emperor's Imperial Seal***: The Japanese emperor had various imperial seals and banners that represented the imperial family's authority and connection to the gods; and

(xi) ***Buddhist War Banners***: In ancient India and parts of Asia, Buddhist armies often used banners with religious symbols, such as the Dharma wheel or lotus, to signify their affiliation and purpose in battle.

650. Tetragrammaton is the official and original term used to describe the four (4) letters in Latin and Ancient Greek known as I•N•R•I promulgated by Constantine in 313 CE. In Ancient Greek, I•N•R•I stands for ἴλεξ (ílex) νέος (neos) ραβδi (ravdi) iδέα (idea) meaning "Holly (is) the new Rule way (notion)" and "One law (is) the new Rule way (notion)":-

Sovereign Standard of Tetragrammaton (INRI)

(i) ἴλεξ (ílex) in Ancient Greek means "holly (Cuilliaéan); one law"; and

(ii) νέος (neos)in Ancient Greek means "new"; and

(iii) ραβδi (ravdi) in Ancient Greek means "rule, rod, stick, baton, ba"; and

(iv) iδέα (idea) in Ancient Greek means "notion, pattern, method, way"; and

(v) During the 17th Century, a counterfeit motto for I•N•R•I was created being "Iesus Nazarenus, Rex Iudaeorum" which reads literally "Jesus the Nazarene, King of the Roman Province of Iudaea".

651. Arguably the most famous of Standards in history was the *Standard of Amun*, also known as an "Ark" being a portable shrine carried by the Hyksos royal guard, usually in front of their army:-

Sovereign Standard of the Hyksos Pharaohs

(i) The gold covered Ark represented the "house" of the spirit of Amun (God) and thus a most sacred artefact, approximately 77 cm (30.3 inches) in Length, 52 cm (20.5 inches) in Width and 60 cm (23.6 inches) in Height. During transport, it almost certainly had some kind of protective covering; and

(ii) When a Pharaoh died the Ark was modified with the addition of Anubis (God of the Dead) standing guard and a new Ark commissioned; and

(iii) Several "Arks" still exist today, such as Tutankhamun; and

(iv) It is the Ark of the Egyptian Pharaoh Akhenaten, also known as Moses that became known as the Ark of the Covenant to the Yahudi; and

(v) The Ark of the Covenant of the Yahudi became one of the most prized artefacts of the ancient world, finally being destroyed in the destruction of the Great Temple to Mithra at Jerusalem in 69 CE; and

(vi) Claims that the Ark survived are largely due to the fact that many groups have created "fake Arks" for their own agenda. For example, the Roman Legions created a fake Ark in 70 CE to take back to Rome, in an attempt to salvage the disaster of the loss of the temple, while later by 527 CE, the Ethiopian Christian Church began creating replica "Arks" for each of their places of worship.

652. By absolute authority of the most sacred Covenant *Pactum De Singularis Caelum*, all valid and proper Standards shall be administered, authorised and approved through Ucadia and its valid entities, bodies and positions. No Non-Ucadia entity, person, group or association shall have any legitimate right to claim any form of Standards unless it is approved in writing through the Sovereign Standards Systems of Ucadia.

Ucadia and Sovereign Standards

Article 186 – Heraldry

653. ***Heraldry*** is the systematic study and use of visual symbols and designs to signify and distinguish families, organisations, entities and regions. The most common element of Heraldry is known as *Armory* and concerns the design of armorial bearings, being usually a coat of arms on a shield, helmet and crest.

Heraldry

654. The term ***Shield*** originates the Ancient Irish word *scield* meaning "symbol of Tara as the source of knowledge, skill and wisdom"; from *scio* meaning "symbol of practical knowledge, understanding and skill" and *eld* meaning "old, source":-

Origin of meaning of Shield and shape of Shield

(i) The true Tara and the ancient shape of its outer walls (now known as Killeen Castle) is the original source of the shape of all ancient Shields since the 6th Century BCE and the first rules of Heraldry permitted Celtic tribes to use different colours and symbols on their flags and shields; and

(ii) The Non-Ucadian definitions that say "shield means shield" in English is a self referential absurdity and deliberate insult to all rules of Heraldry and Armory; and

(iii) The distinct shape of Celt Shields has always been connected in geometric design to the shape of Holly Tara in Ireland; and

(iv) Romans used a rectangular protection called a *scutum*; and the Greeks used a heavy round shaped protection called an *aspis* (ἀσπίς); and the Venetians used an oval-shaped protection called a *scudo*.

655. Heraldry originated in its first form around 580 BCE and the formation of the Celtic Civilisation under Jeremiah and the Holly (Cuilliaéan):-

Origins of Heraldry

(i) The word *Heraldry* comes from the Ancient Irish word ***herald*** meaning literally "the origins of heroes" from *he* meaning "he, his, her" and *ró* meaning "prosperity, success" and *ald* meaning "old, source". Non-Ucadia etymological definitions for this word are both absurd (self-referential) and false; and

(ii) The word *Armour* comes from the Ancient Irish word ***armor*** meaning "great weapon" from arm meaning "weapon" and *mor* meaning "great". Non-Ucadia etymological definitions for this word are both absurd (self-referential) and false; and

(iii) The rules of Heraldry declined with the decline of Celtic Civilisation but were fully restored and updated by the Holly (Cuilliaéan) and Franks in the 8th Century CE to strict rules on the use of symbols, colours and form; and

(iv) Heraldry collapsed in all places except Ireland, Scotland and France during the dark ages of the 14th Century; and the mass death of over 85% of the population of Europe, North Africa, Middle East and Asia Minor on the return of Haemorrhagic Fever after 770 years; and

(v) Contrary to false history, Heraldry did not return to most of Europe untill the rise of the merchant pirate kings of the late 17th and 18th Century, who sought to completely invalidate and destroy Irish, Scottish and French Heraldic traditions; and

(vi) By the 19th Century a completely false system of Heraldry, in support of false historical documents and false genealogies was introduced by most of the new nobility of Europe, ensuring no mention of the previous ancient Holly lines or traditions.

656. By absolute authority of the most sacred Covenant *Pactum De Singularis Caelum*, all valid and proper Heraldry shall be administered, authorised and approved through Ucadia and its valid entities, bodies and positions. No Non-Ucadia entity, person, group or association shall have any legitimate right to claim any form of Heraldic achievement unless it is approved in writing through the Heraldic Systems of Ucadia (UHS). Ucadia and Heraldry

Article 187 – Coats of Arms

657. A ***Coats of Arms*** is a distinctive and unique heraldic design used to identify and represent an individual, family, organization, institution or region. It typically consists of a shield or escutcheon that serves as the central element, surrounded by various heraldic symbols and elements. Coats of Arms

658. The main components of a Coat of Arms include (but are not limited to):- Main elements of a Coat of Arms

(i) ***Shield (Escutcheon)***: Is the central part of the coat of arms and serves as the canvas for the other heraldic elements. It can come in various shapes, but the most common shape is the traditional shield shape. The shield is often divided into different sections, each of which may contain specific symbols, colours or patterns; and

(ii) ***Charges***: Are the central symbols or images displayed on the shield. These symbols can vary widely and often hold historical, symbolic or personal significance. Common charges include animals, plants, weapons and other objects; and

(iii) ***Tinctures***: Refer to the colours and patterns used in heraldic designs; and

(iv) ***Supporters***: Are often depicted as animals, figures, or other symbols that stand on either side of the shield. They are commonly found in heraldic designs, especially in coats of arms associated with nobility and royalty; and

(v) ***Crest***: The crest is a decorative element that sits above the shield. It often features a helmet, crown, or other headgear, as well as additional symbols or objects. The crest is a distinctive part of the coat of arms and can provide additional information about the bearer; and

(vi) ***Motto***: A motto is a short phrase or slogan displayed on a banner below the shield. It is meant to convey a message, values, or aspirations associated with the bearer.

659. No Coat of Arms of any Ucadia or Non-Ucadia entity, person, body or association shall be valid unless it has been duly registered and approved under the Ucadia Heraldry System (UHS) in accord with these Maxims. Ucadia Authority and Coats of Arms

660. The copy or use of any Ucadia related Coat of Arms without written permission shall represent a serious criminal offence with the person or persons liable for penalties including (but not limited to) fines, seizure of property, sanctions and imprisonment. Unauthorised use of Ucadia Coats of Arms

661. The use of a profane, sacrilegious or oppressive motto within a Coat of Arms shall constitute a serious criminal offence against all societies under Civilised Law and Ucadia Law. When such a motto is used by a Non-Ucadia state, such a profane, sacrilegious and oppressive motto shall serve to disavow that Non-Ucadia state from having any legitimate sovereign authority or effect of law. Profane, Sacrilegious and Oppressive Motto Forbidden

662. The Motto *Dieu et mon droit* (Medieval French literally for "God and/is my Right") is a profoundly sacrilegious, Non-Christian, Non-Sovereign and Oppressive Motto that through continued use renders every law, every act, every instrument and transaction of the British Empire and the Crown null, void and without any valid force or effect under the Laws of Heaven, Divine Law and all forms of decent Civilised Law. Dieu et mon droit forbidden as Profane, Sacrilegious and Oppressive Motto Forbidden

Article 188 – Sovereign Seal

663. ***Sovereign Seal*** is a physical or digital emblem, stamp, or symbol used by a reigning monarch or a royal authority to authenticate and validate official documents, decrees, proclamations and other important instruments. Sovereign Seal

664. No Sovereign Seal of any Ucadia or Non-Ucadia entity, person, body or association shall be valid unless it has been duly registered and approved under the Ucadia Heraldry System (UHS). Ucadia Authority and Sovereign Seals

665. The copy or use of any Ucadia related Sovereign Seals without written Unauthorised use of Ucadia permission shall represent a serious criminal offence with the person or persons liable for penalties including (but not limited to) fines, seizure of property, sanctions and imprisonment. Sovereign Seals

Article 189 – Flags

666. A ***Flag*** is a piece of cloth or other material with distinct colours, patterns and symbols used as a symbol, emblem or representation of a country, region, state, organization, institution or group of people. Flags

667. A *Golden Flag (Vexilla Aurea)* is a distinctive gold trimmed flag on a pole, paraded on ceremonial occasions, or placed next to or behind officials as the personification and presence of the living spirit (animus) of the state, especially in matters of law:- Golden Flag

(i) It was carried by an Vexiller, during ceremonial processions and the ritual of "Vexilla Procreatio" (Mating of the Flags) when such ceremonial flags would touch one another from a "mother flag" signifying a claimed transfer of power; and

(ii) The gold trimming has always represented the "supernatural" claims of rays of light emanating from the object and never simply ornamental; and

(iii) In more recent centuries, the Golden Flag has come to symbolise both Admiralty Law and the claimed power of "New Rome" (Washington) as the supreme fascist state.

668. No Flag of any Ucadia or Non-Ucadia entity, person, body or association shall be valid unless it has been duly registered and approved under the Ucadia Heraldry System (UHS). Ucadia Authority and Flags

669. The copy or use of any Ucadia related Flag without written permission shall represent a serious criminal offence with the person or persons liable for penalties including (but not limited to) fines, seizure of property, sanctions and imprisonment. Unauthorised use of Flags

Title VII – Sovereign Rank & Title

7.1 – Sovereign Rank & Title

Article 190 – Sovereign Rank & Title

670. ***Sovereign Rank & Title*** refers to the various positions, titles and systems of civilisations and empires whereby the rank and title are organised and recognised in the context of Sovereignty. Rank and Title is therefore the hierarchy of various sovereign positions and their associated titles. Sovereign Rank & Title

671. ***Rank*** refers to the official name of a sovereign, royal or executive position within a hierarchical structure or organisation of a civilisation or empire. Sovereign Rank

672. ***Title*** refers to the formal or honorary designation given to an individual based on their Rank within a hierarchical structure or organisation of a civilisation or empire. Sovereign Title

673. For the purpose of analysis, significant Sovereign Ranks and Titles may be categorised by:- Category of Sovereign Rank & Title

(i) ***Ancient Holly Sovereign Rank & Title***: Being the Sovereign Ranks and Titles first formed by the Holly (Cuilliaéan) more than five thousand years ago; and

(ii) ***Egyptian (Hyksos) Civilisation Sovereign Rank & Title***: Being the Sovereign Ranks and Titles of the Egyptian (Hyksos) Civilisation from 1670 BCE; and

(iii) ***Persian Civilisation Sovereign Rank & Title***: Being the Sovereign Ranks and Titles of the Persian Civilisation from 550 BCE; and

(iv) ***Indian Civilisation Sovereign Rank & Title***: Being the Sovereign Ranks and Titles of the first major Indian Civilisation from 320 BCE; and

(v) ***Chinese Civilisation Sovereign Rank & Title***: Being the Sovereign Ranks and Titles of the first major Chinese Civilisation from 221 BCE; and

(vi) ***Khmer Civilisation Sovereign Rank & Title***: Being the Sovereign Ranks and Titles of the first major Khmer Civilisation from 160 CE; and

(vii) ***Maya Civilisation Sovereign Rank & Title***: Being the Sovereign Ranks and Titles of the first major Maya Civilisation from 400 BCE; and

(viii) ***Christian Civilisation Sovereign Rank & Title***: Being the Sovereign Ranks and Titles as defined by the Christian Civilisation as first formed under Constantine from 4th Century CE; and

(ix) ***Eastern Christian Civilisation Sovereign Rank & Title***: Being the Sovereign Ranks and Titles of the Eastern Christian Civilisation, also known as the "Byzantine Empire" from 6th Century to 15th Century; and

(x) ***Islamic Civilisation Sovereign Rank & Title***: Being the various Sovereign Ranks and Titles of Islamic Civilisation as first formed under the Holly Prophet from 600 CE; and

(xi) ***Western Christian Sovereign Rank & Title***: Being the Sovereign Ranks and Titles of the Western Christian Civilisation, as first formed by the Holly Irish, Franks and Saxons from 740 CE; and

(xii) ***Ucadia Civilisation Sovereign Rank & Title***: Being the Sovereign Ranks and Titles of Ucadia.

674. It is important to highlight the reasons for significant differences between Non-Ucadia claimed historic Sovereign Rank & Title claims and the official records, knowledge and truth of Ucadia in accord with the most sacred Covenant *Pactum De Singularis Caelum* and all proper related instruments, maxims and records:- Difference with Non-Ucadia claimed historic Sovereign Rank & Title

(i) ***Greatest deaths in human history (1310-1380) largely ignored***: The mass death from the return of haemorrhagic fever of between 110 million and 120 million people (more than 85% of Europe and parts of Middle East, North Africa and Asia Minor) continues to be downplayed or largely ignored as arguments that such a collapse did not cause the collapse of multiple civilisation represents an official Non-Ucadia historical line; and

(ii) ***Holly wiped from Non-Ucadia history***: Despite being central to events of human history from 10,000 BCE to the 1500s, the official Non-Ucadia historical line is that the Holly did not exist and that ancient priest lines were vaguely related; and that key "Holly" figures of history such as Constantine and Charlemagne were without any morals, self-control or high education; and

(iii) ***Self-referencing definitions sufficient for etymology of key words***: The official Non-Ucadia historical line continues that it is perfectly fine that a majority of the most important and foundational concepts of sovereignty are self referencing across multiple languages including "English, Old

French, Old German, Ancient Greek and Latin" and unable to credibly or accurately explain the phonetic origins of key sovereign ranks and titles.

7.2 – Ancient Holly Sovereign Rank & Title

Article 191 - Ancient Holly Sovereign Rank & Title

675. Ancient Holly Sovereign Rank & Title represents some of the primitive Sovereign Ranks of the Holly Civilisation (5,500 – 2,200 BCE) prior to the formation of the Hyksos Egyptian Civilisation. Ancient Pre-Egyptian Sovereign Rank & Title

Article 192 - Ruler

676. A ***Ruler*** is a man or woman who by blood right and ancestral heritage is entrusted to govern a particular tribe, community or society. It is one of the four (4) very first ancient rights of sovereignty in civilised history first defined by the Cuilliaéan. Ruler

677. The word ruler comes from 6th millennium BCE ancient Irish word ***Rúilear*** meaning "one who is entrusted (to govern) by blood" and comes from three (3) ancient Irish words *rú* meaning "red, blood", *il* meaning "he, the" and *ear* meaning "entrust". Origin of Ruler

678. As all powers, authority and privilege previously granted to the Cuilliaéan have now been permanently vested to the most sacred Covenant *Pactum De Singularis Caelum*, all associated powers, ritual and authority concerning Ruler is now subject to those valid officials identified as valid Rulers in accordance with these Maxims. Ucadia and Ruler

Article 193 - Leader

679. The word ***Leader*** comes from 5th millennium BCE ancient Irish word ***Làidir*** meaning "strong, physically powerful, able - bodied". Leader

680. As all powers, authority and privilege previously granted to the Cuilliaéan have now been permanently vested to the most sacred Covenant *Pactum De Singularis Caelum*, all associated powers, ritual and authority concerning leaders is now subject to those valid officials considered leaders in accordance with these Maxims. Ucadia and Leader

Article 194 - Lion

681. A ***Lion*** is a man or woman who demonstrates the necessary virtues, piety and wisdom of character required to be anointed ruler and leader of a particular tribe, community or society. It is one of the four very first ancient rights of sovereignty in civilised history first defined Lion by the Cuilliaéan.

682. The word Lion comes from 6th millennium BCE ancient Irish word ***Líon*** meaning "fulfilled, full, meritorious, worthy, courageous" and comes from two ancient Irish words *Lí* meaning "radiant (skin), hue" and *on* meaning "always, ever". Hence the literal etymological meaning of Líon is "one who is always radiant, in hue". Origin of Lion

683. By the 3rd millennium BCE, the fourth most ancient quality of sovereignty came to be associated with the symbol of the large cat known as the lion. However, the winged lion symbol remained exclusively associated with Holly bloodlines. Lion and Big Cat

684. As all powers, authority and privilege previously granted to the Cuilliaéan have now been permanently vested to the most sacred Covenant *Pactum De Singularis Caelum*, all associated powers, ritual and authority concerning the use and reference to Lions is now subject to those valid seals, instruments, coins, coats of arms and symbols of authority issued in accordance with these Maxims. Ucadia and Lion

Article 195 - Cuilliaéan

685. A ***Cuilliaéan*** is a 6th millennium BCE ancient Irish title defining the recognised divine priest king and ruler of an entire nation, civilisation or the known world. It is one of the oldest and most historically significant sovereign titles in civilised history. Cuilliaéan

686. The title *Cuilliaéan* is formed from three (3) ancient Irish words *cuil* meaning "corner or forest", *lia* meaning "stone or physician (healer)" and *éan* /*éin* meaning "spirit or divine". Hence, the literal etymological meanings of the title of Cuilliaéan are: Origin of Cuilliaéan

(i) Divine Corner Stone, or "Divine Foundation Stone", the historic and ancient belief of European, Eastern and Middle Eastern cultures that a bloodline represented the "foundation stone" and bridge between the Divine Realm and the Temporal Realm; and

(ii) Divine/Spirit Healer of the Forest in reference to exceptional and ancient powers of healing and knowledge of therapeutic remedies; and

(iii) The title Cuilliaéan is equivalent in later centuries to the titles Viz, Vizier, Wizard, Da'viz, Da'vid, Druvid, or Druid.

687. The title *Cuilliaéan* has only ever applied to one bloodline family. One could not be appointed a Cuilliaéan. Today, the title is a variation of a multiple of noble names including (but not limited to) cullen, cuilleain, culeen, coileain, cullenan, kollyns, collins and o'collins Cuilliaéan and bloodline shared by several million living descendants.

688. By the 1st Millennium BCE, the *Cuilliaéan* ceased to rule directly as a group and instead permitted the appointment of a high king or Ard Rí. Cuilliaéan and Ard Rí

689. In accordance with the most sacred Covenant *Pactum De Singularis Caelum*, all powers, authority and privilege previously granted to the *Cuilliaéan* are permanently vested in the official positions granted through its articles and associated valid covenants and charters. Ucadia and Cuilliaéan

690. As all powers, authority and privilege previously granted to the *Cuilliaéan* have now been permanently vested by the most sacred Covenant *Pactum De Singularis Caelum*, no descendant possessing a name derived from the Cuilliaéan may claim special privilege or birth right over any other with any such claims false and having no effect from the beginning. Ucadia and Cuilliaéan and future birthright claims

Article 196 - Chief

691. A ***Chief*** is a 6th millennium BCE ancient Irish term and title defining the recognised head of a family (Fine) or clan (Truatha). Chief

692. In conjunction with the most ancient title Cuilliaéan (Holly Divine Priest King), the title "Chief" is one of the oldest titles in Civilized history for the head or leader of a family, tribe, community or village. Chief as ancient Title

693. Similar to the most sacred title of Cuilliaéan, the title of Chief could not be claimed unless one was worthy and a rightful heir, counting several generations back to prove credentials. If no legitimate heir existed, then the Fine (family) or Truatha would be required to merge with the closest Fine or Truatha (clan). Chief as Bloodright

694. The word Chief is derived from the combination of two ancient Irish words *Chi* meaning "roof, cover" and *Ef* meaning "he, him, his". Hence the literal etymological meaning of Chief is "one (he) who protects/covers (the home)". Origin of word Chief

Article 197 - Ra

695. ***Rà*** is the most ancient name and rank for a Sovereign ruler in civilised history with the title originating from ancient Ireland under the rule of the Cuilliaéan (Holly) from the 6th Millennium BCE. The most ancient title for a Sovereign ruler is ***lámh dià*** or "lamb of god" meaning literally "Hand of God". Rà

696. The kingdom of a Holly blood Celtic ruler (Rà) was known as Rí and their time of reign or "epoch" of reign was known as Ré. These titles are occasionally and deliberately confused. Rí and Ré

697. The title of Rà and Aman-Rà were used as a supreme ruler up until the 6th Century BCE, most famously by the Cuilliaéan diaspora known as the Hyksos in the 2nd Millennium BCE in Egypt. Chief as Bloodright

698. From the establishment of the "Law of the Land" or Tará (Terra) Law from the 6th Century BCE until the 3rd Century CE, there existed three (3) levels of Kings corresponding to key administrative units of Celtic society, the Tigarna Rà, the Rui Rà and the Ard Rà:- Levels of Kings (Rà)

(i) Tigarna Rà meaning "Lord King" was the leader and responsible for a clan or a Truatha ("tuatha"); and

(ii) Rui Rà meaning "Overrule King" was the leader and ruler responsible for several Truatha called a "banda"; and

(iii) Ard Rà meaning "High King" was the ultimate king over all Truatha ("tuatha") and bands; and

(iv) From the 3rd Century CE until the final destruction of Celtic society, Ard Rà Cormac Mac Art introduced a fourth level of Sovereign "Rà" when he divided the holly isle of Ireland into five (5) parts, with the ruler of each part "Cóicid" called a Cóicid Rà or "One of the Five Kings".

699. In accordance with the vesting of all authority and power of the Cuilliaéan (Holly) to the Society of One Heaven, the use or claim of the title Rà is forbidden unless expressed by covenant and authorized in accordance with these Maxims. Use of Rà

700. The proper list of Irish High Kings as referenced in the most sacred scripture *Lebor Clann Glas*, from the time of Jeremiah and to the first formation of Christian and Irish Patriarchs:- List of Ard Rà as a title

(i) (555-534 BCE) ***Lugaid*** mac Eochaid, *son of King Eochaid and Princess Tephi of the Old Yahudi Lines; and

(ii) (534-506 BCE) ***Eoachaid Uairches*** mac Lugaid; and

(iii) (506-472 BCE) ***Lugaid Lamderg*** mac Eoachaid; and

(iv) (472-433 BCE) ***Art*** mac Lugaid Lamderg; and

(v) (433-398 BCE) ***Ailil*** mac Art; and

(vi) (398-363 BCE) ***Eochaid*** mac Ailella; and

(vii) (363-332 BCE) ***Lugaid Laigdech*** mac Eochaid; and

(viii) (332-298 BCE) ***Eochaid Buadach*** mac Lugaid; and

(ix) (298-248 BCE) ***Ugaine Mor*** mac Eochaid; and

(x) (248-217 BCE) ***Cobthach Coel Breg*** mac Ugaine; and

(xi) (217-181 BCE) ***Meilge Molbthach*** mac Cobthach; and

(xii) (181-157 BCE) ***Irereo Fathach*** mac Meilge; and

(xiii) (157-106 BCE) ***Caem*** mac Irereo; and

(xiv) (106-85 BCE) ***Ailill*** mac Connla; and

(xv) (85-56 BCE) ***Labraid Lorc*** mac Ailill; and

(xvi) (56-11 BCE) ***Cú-Roi(n)*** mac Labraid Lorc; and

(xvii) (11 BCE-29 CE) ***Cú-Cúileann (Yasiah)*** *abdicated for his son. Killed in 38 CE sparking uprisings that ultimately led to destruction of Temple of Mithra (Herod) in 69 CE; and

(xviii) (29-42 CE) ***Cú-Laoch (Yahusiah)*** *abdicated Irish throne to become Emperor of the Keltoi. Died at Hollyrood (Scotland) 83 CE; and

(xix) (42-108 CE) ***Tuathal Techtmar*** (Tuatha Taghtamor) * married Mariamne (Mary) the daughter of Cú-Laoch (Yahusiah) and Mariamne; and

(xx) (108-117 BCE) ***Feinlinid Reachmor***; and

(xxi) (117-165 CE) ***Cúinn (Conn)*** Cétchathach; and

(xxii) (165-204 CE) ***Cúirt*** mac Cúinn *married Sabina Cornelia Clementia of Franks; and

(xxiii) (204-244 CE) ***Cuirmac*** Mac Cuirt; and

(xxiv) (244-272 CE) ***Cúiran*** Mac Cuirmac; and

(xxv) (272-306 CE) ***Cúilaidh*** mac Cúimhne; and

(xxvi) (306-344 CE) ***Cúirc*** mac Cúilaidh; and

(xxvii) (344-366 CE) ***Cúilman*** (Colman); and

(xxviii) (366-367 BCE) ***Cúichaid*** (Eochaid) Founder of Dal Riata (North); and

(xxix) (366-380 BCE) ***Cúigan*** Mor (Eogan Mor) Founder of Dal Glais (South).

7.3 – Egyptian (Hyksos) Civilisation Sovereign Rank & Title

Article 198 - Egyptian (Hyksos) Civilisation Sovereign Rank & Title

701. ***Egyptian (Hyksos) Civilisation Sovereign Rank & Title*** represents some of the ancient Sovereign Ranks under the Hyksos Holly Pharaohs from 1670 BCE. Egyptian Civilisation Sovereign Rank & Title

702. Contrary to false Egyptian History, a significant feature of the titles of important Sovereign Positions of Government under Egyptian (Hyksos) Civilisation is the emphatic notion of rule through service, rather than rule through power and force. This contrasts sharply with the subsequent ages of false Pharaohs starting with the Ramesses Dynasty who appear to be the ones who re-asserted the notion of their own "divinity" and power. Significant feature of Holly Hyksos Titles

Article 199 - Pharaoh

703. ***Pharaoh*** (*per-aa*) is a Rank first created under the Hyksos Kings of Egypt from 1670 BCE meaning "one from the Great Divine House (of the Holly)". The corresponding Title for a Holly Hyksos Pharaoh is ***Ptah*** (ptH) meaning "the father; the foundation stone; the great architect and creator; the master of justice". Pharaoh

704. Under the Holly Hyksos Civilisation, one could not be Pharaoh unless descended from the bloodline of the Holly (Cuilliaéan). Thus, all the claimed Pharaohs following after Tutankhamen (Tutankhaten) are impostors and pretenders under the original Hyksos laws of Ancient Egypt. Pharaoh and Holly

705. The proper list of Holly Hyksos Pharaohs as referenced in the most sacred scripture *Lebor Clann Glas*, from the time of invasion of Egypt to the great exodus of Akhenaten includes:- List of Hyksos Pharaohs

   (i) (1660-1624 BCE) ***Alattis***; and

   (ii) (1624-1590 BCE) ***Khayan***; and

   (iii) (1590–1568 BCE) ***Kamose*** ; and

   (iv) (1568–1541 BCE) ***Ahmose***; and

   (v) (1541–1520 BCE) ***Amenhotep I***; and

   (vi) (1520–1491 BCE) ***Thutmose I***; and

   (vii) (1491–1491 BCE) ***Amenhotep II***; and

   (viii) (1491–1479 BCE) ***Thutmoses II***; and

   (ix) (1479–1458 BCE) ***Amenhotep III***; and

(x) (1458–1425 BCE) ***Thutmose III***; and

(xi) (1425–1400 BCE) ***Amenhotep IV***; and

(xii) (1400–1390 BCE) ***Thutmose IV***; and

(xiii) (1390–1351 BCE) ***Amenhotep V***; and

(xiv) (1351–1352 BCE) ***Thutmose V***; and

(xv) (1352–1335 BCE) ***Amenhotep VI*** (Akhenaten); and

(xvi) (1335–1332 BCE) ***Neferneferuaten*** (Nefertiti); and

(xvii) (1332–1324 BCE) ***Tutankhaten***.

Corruption of Pharaoh under counterfeit rulers

706. Following the assassination of Tutankhamen (Tutankhaten), Horemheb (1320-1292 BCE) began the creation of a counterfeit culture to corrupt the history and civilisation of the Hyksos. The "signature" of the false Pharaohs therefore is their wholesale corruption of Egyptian culture, the flagrant use of symbols of terror and enslavement and desecration of some of the most sacred symbols and monuments in history:-

(i) The Hyksos Pharaohs used symbols such as the *Crook* (heka-scepter) and *Djed* as symbols of benevolence and wisdom, whereas the false Pharaohs openly used the *Flail* (nekhakha) as their symbol of power and oppression of the people as slaves; and

(ii) Even the Old Testament scriptures refer to the oppressive behaviour of the false Ramesses pharaohs in their brutality against the Yahudi followers of Akhenaten (Moses); and

(iii) The word "Ptah" was assigned to a false God, along with the creation of several other counterfeit gods to replace the religious structures of the Hyksos; and

(iv) The *Great Anubis*, a symbol of Ma'at (cosmic balance) between heaven and earth and the living and the dead was crudely defaced by Ramesses II (1279-1213 BCE) to his own image and then ordered to be replicated by the thousands becoming the infamous "Sphinx". Next to the desecration of the most sacred Elephantine Island (Yeb) as hotels and tourist site, and the desecration of the ruins of Holly Tara (Killeen Castle) as a golf course and resort, the Sphinx by Ramesses II is arguably the third greatest desecration of a sacred site in history.

Article 200 – Hery-Akht-Nswt (Chief Vizier)

707. ***Hery-Akht-Nswt*** (ḥry-ạẖt-nswt) is a Rank first created under the Hyksos Kings of Egypt from 1670 BCE meaning "Chief Overseer of the King". The corresponding Title for the *Hery-Akht-Nswt* (Chief Vizier) was ***Hem-Tawy*** meaning "servant of the two lands (upper and lower Egypt)". Hery-Akht-Nswt (Chief Visier)

Article 201 – Hery-Hem-Netjer (Chief Prophet)

708. ***Hery-Hem-Netjer*** is a Rank first created under the Hyksos Kings of Egypt from 1670 BCE meaning "First Prophet of God; High Priest". The corresponding Title for the *Hery-Hem-Netjer* was ***Hem-Netjer*** meaning "servant of god". Hery-Hem-Netjer (Chief Prophet)

Article 202 – Khet-Per-Nesu (Treasurer)

709. ***Khet-Per-Nesu*** (ẖt-pr-nsw) is a Rank first created under the Hyksos Kings of Egypt from 1670 BCE meaning "Royal Steward; Overseer of the Treasury". The corresponding Title for an *Khet-Per-Nesu* (Treasurer) was ***Hem-ipt-Netjer*** meaning "servant of the property of god". Khet-Per-Nesu (Treasurer)

Article 203 - Khet-Abu-Nesu (Royal Seal Bearer)

710. ***Khet-Abu-Nesu*** (ẖt-ᶜbw-nsw) is a Rank first created under the Hyksos Kings of Egypt from 1670 BCE meaning "Chief Seal Bearer of the King". The corresponding Title for an ***Khet-Abu-Nesu*** (Royal Seal Bearer) was ***Hem-Abu-Nesu*** meaning "servant of the royal seal". Khet-Abu-Nesu (Royal Seal Bearer)

Article 204 - Khet-Hemu-Nesu (Overseer of Works)

711. ***Khet-Hemu-Nesu*** (ẖt-ᶜḥmw-nsw) is a Rank first created under the Hyksos Kings of Egypt from 1670 BCE meaning "Royal Overseer of Works". The corresponding Title for an *Khet-Hemu-Nesu* (Overseer of Works) was ***Hem-Hemu-Nesu*** meaning "servant of the royal works". Khet-Hemu-Nesu (Overseer of Works)

712. The *Khet-Hemu-Nesu* (Overseer of Works) during the time of the Hyksos Pharaohs from 1640 BCE to 1340 BCE were in charge of the biggest public works projects ever undertaken at any time in human history:- Importance of Khet-Hemu-Nesu (Overseer of Works)

    (i) Following the eruption and explosion of the Volcanic Island of Thera (more than 1000 times greater than Krakatoa), Egypt received more than six million refugees from the rest of the Ancient world; and

(ii) Contrary to deliberately false Egyptian History, all the major monuments on the Giza Plateau were designed and constructed under the Holly Hyksos Pharaohs as well as all the major temple complexes in Upper Egypt such as Karnak; and

(iii) The Khet-Hemu-Nesu (Overseer of Works) during the period of 1640 BCE to 1440 BCE employed anything from one million to three million workers on public works projects; and

(iv) Contrary to deliberately false Egyptian History, the refugees that worked on public works projects were not considered slaves but contractors, receiving wages including rations of beer and bread. The image of cruel Egyptian Kings is from the era of false Pharaohs starting with the Ramesses Dynasty of the 13th Century BCE.

Article 205 – Khet-Wuhem-Nesu (Overseer of Granaries)

713. ***Khet-Wuhem-Nesu*** (ẖt wḥm-nsw) is a Rank first created under the Hyksos Kings of Egypt from 1670 BCE meaning "Royal Overseer of Granaries". The corresponding Title for an *Khet-Wuhem-Nesu* (Overseer of Granaries) was ***Hem-Wuhem-Nesu*** meaning "servant of the royal granaries". Khet-Wuhem-Nesu (Overseer of Granaries)

714. The *Khet-Wuhem-Nesu* (Overseer of Granaries) during the age of the great Hyksos Holly Pharaohs was the second largest employer of people behind the Overseer of Works:- Largest Employers of Refugees

(i) Following the eruption and explosion of the Volcanic Island of Thera (more than 1000 times greater than Krakatoa), Egypt received more than six million refugees from the rest of the Ancient world; and

(ii) The *Khet-Wuhem-Nesu* (Overseer of Granaries) during the period of 1640 BCE to 1440 BCE employed anything from half a million to one and half million workers in agriculture.

Article 206 – Khet-Wat-Nesu (Head General)

715. ***Khet-Wat-Nesu*** (ẖt wʿt-nsw) is a Rank first created under the Hyksos Kings of Egypt from 1670 BCE meaning "Royal Overseer of the Armies". The corresponding Title for an *Khet-Wat-Nesu* (Head General) was ***Hem-Nesu*** meaning "servant of the king". Khet-Wat-Nesu (Head General)

Article 207 – Wab-Nesut (Provincial Governor)

716. **Wab-Nesut** (Provincial Governor) is a Rank first created under the Hyksos Kings of Egypt from 1670 BCE meaning Provincial Governor. Provinces were then later called *Nomes* under the Greek Pharaohs. Wab-Nesut (Provincial Governor)

Article 208 – Great Prophets of Yahu

717. ***Great Prophet of Yahu*** (God), also known as Great Prophet of YHVH, is a title first formed around the 11th Century BCE, when Pinedjem I (1070-1032 BCE) of Egypt granted the Holly high priests from Elios (Larissa in Greece) of the Yahudi religion established by Akhenaten, to build a new temple and sanctuary on the Island of Yeb, also known as Elephantine Island. The site was chosen given it was the cornerstone of the Tree of Life formed by the Hyksos Pharaohs. Great Prophets of Yahu (God)

718. *Elephantine Island* (Island of Yeb) at 1,200 metres (3,900 ft) from north to south, and is 400 metres (1,300 ft) across at its widest point, has been one of the most sacred sites on planet Earth for more than 5,000 years:- Importance of the Island of Yeb (Elephantine Island)

(i) From at least 3100 BCE, the Island was the primary temple for the primary mother goddess *Mut*, the queen of heaven, the mother of all the gods and all creation, the patron of Pharaohs (until 1650 BCE), and the progenitor of all other subsequent mother goddesses including "Immaculate Mary, Mother of God". Thus to any followers or house that claims sovereign authority by some association to "Mary", this island should be supremely important; and

(ii) From at least 1640 BCE, the Island became the foundation of the first Tree of Life of eleven temple complexes stretching north along the Nile to Dandarah, forming the Ka-Ba-La, later corrupted by Venetian publishers in the 17th Century CE in forming a blizzard of false mystical occultist Jewish texts; and

(iii) From 1068 BCE, it became the primary site for a dedicated Temple to Yahu, the name of the Monotheistic God of the Yahudi and a Home (for a time) of the Ark of the Covenant. Thus, Elephantine Island is site that should technically be more sacred to Christians, Muslims and Jews than Jerusalem, as Jerusalem never had a purpose built temple to Yahu (as the Main Temple of Herod was in honour of Christ Mithra); and

(iv) The Temple to Yahu on Elephantine Island was the only one to have the following dimensions being 20 cubits (9 m) in width, and 60 cubits (27m) in length, being 30 cubits (14m) in height, from the base of the temple, to the roof of the Holy Place. The Temple was largely intact along with most of the temples on the island until the late 19th Century and British Occupation of Egypt. Claims that the damage was done by the Ottomans in the 1820s remains a clumsy attempt at deflecting the culpability of successive British families in the employ of the "Empire"; and

(v) However, most of the damage to historic ruins on the island has been done throughout the mid to late 20th Century by the blatant desecration and destruction of the Island by the building of hotels and the effect of foreign tourists.

719. The Great Prophets of Yahu are most famously known as the Old Testament Prophets revered in Christianity, Islam and Judaism. However, in Non-Ucadia official documents, the lists and dates for the Great Prophets is generally false, containing contradictory gaps and absurd life spans.

Importance of the Great Prophets of Yahu

720. The true and proper list of the first thirty three (33) Great prophets of Yeb as referenced in the most sacred scripture *Lebor Clann Glas*, include:-

List of 33 Great Prophets of Yeb

(i) (1068-1041 BCE) ***Aaroniah***; and

(ii) (1041-999 BCE) ***Enochiah*** son of Aaroniah; and

(iii) (999-948 BCE) ***Zadokiah*** son of Enochiah; and

(iv) (948-929 BCE) ***Obadiah/Uvidiah*** (David) son of Zadokiah; and

(v) (929-889 BCE) ***Elijiah*** son of Obadiah/Uvidiah (David); and

(vi) (889-883 BCE) ***Ahijiah*** son of Elijiah; and

(vii) (883-861 BCE) ***Ahiah*** son of Ahijiah; and

(viii) (861-845 BCE) ***Azariah*** son of Ahiah; and

(ix) (845-813 BCE) ***Ananiah*** son of Azariah; and

(x) (813-784 BCE) ***Amoziah*** son of Ananiah; and

(xi) (784-732 BCE) ***Isaiah*** son of Amoziah; and

(xii) (732-696 BCE) ***Ezekiah*** son of Isaiah; and

(xiii) (696-681 BCE) ***Amariah*** son of Ezekiah; and

(xiv) (681-672 BCE) ***Edaliah*** son of Amariah; and

(xv) (672-645 BCE) ***Zephaniah*** son of Edaliah; and

(xvi) (645-620 BCE) ***Michaiah/Ilkiah*** son of Zephaniah; and

(xvii) (620-572 BCE) ***Jeremiah*** son of Michaiah/Ilkiah; and

(xviii) (572-530 BCE) ***Baruchiah*** son of Jeremiah; and

(xix) (530-478 BCE) ***Osiah (Hosea)*** son of Baruchiah; and

(xx) (478-431 BCE) ***Osanniah (Hosanna)*** son of Osiah (Hosea); and

(xxi) (431-417 BCE) ***Eliah*** son of Osanniah (Hosanna); and

(xxii) (417-382 BCE) ***Oadiah*** son of Eliah; and

(xxiii) (382-341 BCE) ***Oananiah*** son of Oadiah; and

(xxiv) (341-291 BCE) ***Adiah*** son of Oananiah; and

(xxv) (291-249 BCE) ***Oniah*** son of Adiah; and

(xxvi) (249-206 BCE) ***Eleziah*** son of Oniah; and

(xxvii) (206-158 BCE) ***Elkaniah*** son of Eleziah; and

(xxviii) (158-106 BCE) ***Zadokiah*** son of Elkaniah; and

(xxix) (106-59 BCE) ***Barachiah*** son of Zadokiah; and

(xxx) (59-10 BCE) ***Adoniah (Cú-Roi(n))*** adopted son of Barachiah; and

(xxxi) (10-30 BCE) ***Yasiah (Cú-Cúileann/Joseph)*** son of Adoniah. Died in 58 CE; and

(xxxii) (30-37 BCE) ***Yahusiah (Cú-Laoch/Jesus)*** son of Yasiah (Cú-Cúileann/Joseph). Died in 83 CE; and

(xxxiii) (37-58 BCE) ***Yahobiah (Jacob)*** son of Yasiah (Cú-Cúileann/Joseph). Died in 58 CE.

Note: Zachariah, son of Barachiah was disowned from lineage in 59 CE and resettled at Qumran near Jerusalem, forming a new apocalyptic movement. His adopted son Johanniah (John the Baptist) claimed to be thirty-second high priest of Yeb in opposition to Yahusiah (Cú-Laoch/Jesus).

Yasiah (Cú-Cúileann/Joseph) was one of only two high priests to abdicate (in 30CE) but died in 58CE. His son Yahusiah (Cú-Laoch/Jesus) abdicated in 37CE for his brother Yahobiah (Jacob) but returned to the role in 58 CE at the death of his brother until his own death in 83 CE.

721. Whilst the modern faiths of Christianity and Judaism do not currently recognise the continuation of the bloodlines of the Great Prophets after 83 CE, it is a fundamental tenet of Islam that the bloodline did continue through to the Holly Prophet and founder of

Continuation of the Line and Seal of the Prophets

Islam himself:-

(i) Whilst there are many conflicting accounts, it is believed by some that around 555 CE, the father of the Holly Prophet was King Sayonis of the Saracen (Arabian) tribes in exile, while his mother was the first born daughter of King Domnaill mac Doimhin of Inisfáil (Ireland); and

(ii) This bloodline connection would account for the universal recognition of the founder of Islam being a blood member of the Holly; and a direct descendent of the Great Prophets as well as the bloodlines back to all the Prophets including (but not limited to) Akhenaten (Moses) and Abraham from the city of Ebla; and

(iii) The bloodline connection would also account for the deep respect and connection in Islam for Jesus, given the Holly blood heritage of the founder of Islam would make him a direct descendent of Jesus.

Article 209 – Messiah Kings of Yahudah (Judah)

722. Messiah Kings of Yahudah (Judah) is a historic title from the beginning of the 10th Century BCE when the Great Prophets of Yeb were successful in establishing a new homeland for the Yahudi diaspora called Yahudah, also known as Judah, with its capital the ancient city of Jerusalem. Messiah Kings of Yahudah (Judah)

723. The List of Yahudi Messiah Kings as referenced in the most sacred scripture *Lebor Clann Glas*, from the first formation of the Kingdom of Yahudah (Judah) includes:- List of Yahudi Messiah Kings of Old Kingdom of Judah

Yahudi Messiah Kings of Yeb

(i) (999-931 BCE) King ***U'vid*** (Da'vid) son of Great Prophet Zadokiah; and

(ii) (931-911 BCE) King ***Yahuboam*** son of U'vid (Da'vid); and

(iii) (911-870 BCE) King ***Yahab*** (Ahab) son of Yahuboam; and

(iv) (870-845 BCE) King ***Yahushaphat (Jehoshaphat)*** son of Yahab (Ahab); and

(v) (845-837 BCE) King ***Yahuram*** son of Yahushaphat; and

(vi) (837-801 BCE) King ***Yahuahaz*** son of Yahuram; and

(vii) (801-755 BCE) King ***Yahuash (Jehoash)*** son of Yahuahaz; and

(viii) (755-710 BCE) King ***Yahuam (Jotham)*** son of Yahuash; and

(ix) (710-682 BCE) King ***Yahuaz (Ahaz)*** son of Yahuam; and

(x) (682-654 BCE) King ***Yahuah*** son of Yahuaz; and

(xi) (654-635 BCE) King ***Yahuhaz*** son of Yahuah; and

(xii) (635-603 BCE) King ***Yahuiakim*** son of Yahuhaz; and

(xiii) (603-603 BCE) Crown Princess ***Tephi*** first daughter of Yahukiah; and

Old Yahudi Messiah Bloodline Kings of Ireland

(xiv) (555-534 BCE) Lugaid mac Eochaid son of Queen Tephi of Jerusalem. The bloodline then continues forward.

724. Around 105 BCE, the Great Prophet Barachiah was successful in negotiating with the Persians to permit a client King to be installed in Palestine as the Yahudi King of Yahudah (Judah), thus creating the New Kingdom, with his eldest son named Iudiah (Judah) its first king. New Kingdom of Judah

725. The List of Yahudi Messiah Kings from the first formation of the New Kingdom of Yahudah (Judah) as referenced in the most sacred scripture *Lebor Clann Glas*, includes:- New Yahudi Messiah Kings

New Yahudi Messiah Kings of Yeb

(i) (104-67 BCE) King ***Iudiah*** (Judah), second son of Barachiah; and

(ii) (67-37 BCE) King ***Hycaniah*** (Hyrcanus), son of Iudiah (Judah); and

(iii) (37-4 BCE) King ***Herodiah (Herod)*** son of Hycaniah; and

(iv) (4-39 CE) King ***Antipiah (Herod Antipiah)*** son of Herodiah; and

(v) (39-69 CE) King ***Agripiah (Herod Agripiah)*** son of Antipiah; and

(vi) (31 CE) ***Mary (Mariamne)*** daughter of Princess Mariamne, first born daughter *Herod Agripiah* (Agrippa)*; and*

New Yahudi Bloodline Messiah Kings of Ireland

(vii) (53 CE) ***Feinlinid Reachmor*** first born son of Queen Mary (Mariamne) and High King Tuatha Taghtamor of Eire (Ireland). The bloodline then continues forward.

726. While Jewish history as the Yahudi exiles is authentic in a substantial number of historic aspects, (including the imprisonment and exodus from Egypt), the term "Israel" is a 16th Century occult word created by English Alchemist *John Dee* (1527-1609) from Isis, Ra and El and not No Kings of Israel or Ancient State of Israel an accurate historic term:-

(i) Recognition of the faith of the Yahudi as one of the oldest religions, as first formed by exiled Holly (Cuilliaéan) Pharaoh Akhenaten, (also known as Moses) is consistent with the present Maxims and in accord with the most sacred Covenant *Pactum De Singularis Caelum*; and

(ii) It is also consistent with these Maxims that given the state religion of Iudaism (Judaism) was first formed in 70 CE in Rome, as a city founded by Yahudi diaspora, it is entirely appropriate to define the history of the Yahudi as the history of the Jews; and

(iii) In the case of the occult word "Israel" as first formed by English Alchemist *John Dee* (1527-1609) from Isis, Ra and El, there is no credible nor sensible evidence of a state of the same name ever existing in history, prior to its use in revisions and corruptions of sacred scripture starting at the end of the 16th Century; and

(iv) The falsity of the word "Israel" does not in anyway invalidate the rights of any Sovereign state of the same name, nor does it invalidate the legitimacy of the Jewish faith in anyway, whatsoever; and

(v) The revelations within the most sacred Covenant *Pactum De Singularis Caelum* concerning the Levant Union and the future role of the city of Jerusalem fully supports the fundamental faith of the Jewish People, as it does the followers of Islam and Christianity.

Article 210 – High Priests of Baal Hamon (Moloch)

727. ***High Priest of Baal Hamon*** (Moloch) and ***High Priests of Baal Mithra*** (Moloch) are historic titles relating to Dynasties of Yahudi High Priests that ruled the Great Temple of Mithra at Babylon, the Great Temple of Solomon at Baalbek in Lebanon and for a time ruled the Temple of Jerusalem. High Priests of Baal Hamon (Moloch)

728. The List of Yahudi High Priests of Baal Hamon (Moloch) and Baal Mithra as referenced in the most sacred scripture *Lebor Clann Glas*, from the first formation of the position includes:- List of High Priests

Babylon High Priests of Baal Mithra

(i) (559-527 BCE) ***Daniah*** (Daniel) son of Priest Zedekiah from Yeb. great nephew of Jeremiah; and

(ii) (527-489 BCE) ***Haggiah*** son of Daniah (Daniel); and

(iii) (489-463 BCE) ***Nehemiah*** son of Haggiah; and

(iv) (463-397 BCE) ***Ezriah (Ezra)*** son of Nehemiah; and

(v) (397-364 BCE) ***Habakiah*** son of Ezriah (Ezra); and

(vi) (364-332 BCE) ***Zephaniah*** son of Habakiah; and

(vii) (332-326 BCE) ***Malachiah*** son of Zephaniah *High Priests of Baal Mithra Abolished by Alexander the Great; and

Carthaginian-Nabatean High Priests of Baal Hamon (Mithra)

(viii) (149-110 BCE) **Sabiah** (Sabaoth); and

(ix) (100-52 BCE) **Setiah** (Seth), son of Sabiah (Sabaoth); and

(x) (52 BCE - 6 CE) **Aniah** (Annas), son of Setiah (Seth); and

(xi) (6 -44 CE) **Ananiah** (Ananias), son of Aniah (Annas); and

(xii) (44-47 CE) **Matthiah**, son of Ananiah (Ananias); and

(xiii) (47-104 CE) **Usiah** (Josephus), son of Matthiah *Mithraism collapsed in 69 CE.

729. Any claimed reference that a line of High Priests of Israel ever existed is patently false, absurd and contrary to all credible historic records:- No High priests of Israel

(i) The region of Palestine was known as Iudea under Romans for a time and never as Israel; and

(ii) Claimed lists of names of alleged High Priests appears to be a construction of Messiah Kings, Yahudi Great Prophets and Priests of Baal Hamon all cobbled together with a layer of fake names; and

(iii) The term "Israel" is a 16th Century occult word created by English Alchemist John Dee (1527-1609) from Isis, Ra and El and not an accurate historic term.

7.4 – Persian Civilisation Sovereign Rank & Title

Article 211 - Persian Civilisation Sovereign Rank & Title

730. ***Persian Civilisation Sovereign Rank & Title*** represents some of the ancient Sovereign Ranks under the Persian Civilisation from 560 BCE. These ranks and titles include some key titles from Ancient Persian colonies such as Rome and Athens. Persian Civilisation Sovereign Rank & Title

Article 212 – Shah

731. A ***Shah*** is a Persian word that historically has been used to denote a monarch or ruler in various Persian-speaking and neighbouring regions of the Middle East and South Asia. Shah

732. Examples of Empires and Civilisations using the title of Shah include (but are not limited to):- History of the title Shah

(i) **Achaemenid Empire** (550-330 BCE): Founded by Cyrus the Great, in Persia creating the title "Shahanshah" meaning "King of Kings"; and

(ii) **Kushan Empire** (1st to 3rd centuries CE): The Kushan Empire, which had its origins in Central Asia and extended into parts of South Asia, used the title "Kushanshah" for its rulers. This empire played a crucial role in the spread of Buddhism along the Silk Road; and

(iii) **Sassanian Empire** (224–350 CE): One of the most significant Persian empires, continued the use of the title "Shahanshah" (King of Kings).

Article 213 – Vizier (Chief Minister)

733. The ***Vizier*** is a Rank first created under the Achaemenid Empire from 550 BCE meaning Chief Advisor or Minister to the King. Vizier (Chief Minister)

Article 214 – Peta (Head Priest)

734. ***Peta*** (Peter) is a Rank first created under the Achaemenid Empire from 550 BCE meaning "Father, Foundation Stone of (Mithraic) Faith and Head Priest". Peta

735. Contrary to deliberately false history to hide the importance, history and influence of Mithraism, the Head Priest of the Persian Empire was always called Peta. This follows an ancient Hyksos (Holly) Pharaoh tradition of calling the Pharaoh "Ptah" or foundation stone, reinforcing the connection of the Yahudi in influencing the formation of the state religion of the Persian Empire. Peta and Mithra not Zoroastrianism

736. The significance of the word Peta in its connection to the ancient Mithraic State Religion of Rome is supported by the reintroduction of the term as "Saint Peter" and the reference to Peter being the "rock and foundation of the church" in the creation of a revised history for the Roman Catholic Church by the Holly Irish and Carolingians from 740 CE. Peta and the formation of Western Civilisation

Article 215– Daricbara (Treasurer)

737. The ***Daricbara*** (Treasurer) is a Rank first created under the Achaemenid Empire from 550 BCE meaning financial administrator, responsible for managing the empire's treasury and finances. Daricbara (Treasurer)

Article 216 – Spahbed (Chief General)

738. ***Spahbed*** is a Rank first created under the Achaemenid Empire from 550 BCE meaning Chief general in the Persian military, commanding large army divisions. Spahbed (Chief General)

Article 217 – Satrap (Governor)

739. ***Satrap*** is a Rank first created under the Achaemenid Empire from 550 BCE meaning Governor of a satrapy (province), responsible for administration, tax collection, and military recruitment within their province. Satrap (Governor)

Article 218 – Frataraka (Local Governor)

740. ***Frataraka*** is a Rank first created under the Achaemenid Empire from 550 BCE meaning Regional or local governors or rulers, often in charge of smaller territories. Frataraka (Local Governor)

Article 219 - Archon

741. An ***Archon*** is an ancient Greek title for ruler, usually in context of some public office. Archon

742. The word *Archon* is derived from ancient Greek word *arkhos* meaning "leader or ruler", which itself is derived from *arkhe* meaning "beginning, origin, first place". Origin and meaning of Archon

743. Unlike a traditional monarch, an Archon was originally seen as a selected member of an Oligarchy or "elite" that then shared power with other Archons, rather than absolute single rule:- History of Archons

    (i) In Early Greek city state development, the associations and councils of Archon held enormous power and developed means to function collectively, only occasionally appointing an interim dictator to unite the people called a "tyrant"; and

    (ii) While the term lost influence during the rise of the Roman Empire, its significant was resurrected by the 16th Century CE to denote specific ecclesiastical positions also claiming ruling status over certain states and territories - hence Archbishop and Archdeacon for example.

Article 220 - Imperator

744. ***Imperator*** is the Title and Name (praenomen) of a Roman Emperor from 27 BCE until the formation of Christianity in 310 CE. The word *Emperor* is derived from the word *Imperator*. Imperator

745. The word Imperator originates from the Latin word *imperare* meaning "to order or to command". Originally, the title was used to denote a senior commander under the Roman Republic (509-27 BCE). However, it became an exclusive title for the supreme monarch from 27 BCE. Origin and meaning of Imperator

746. The official Non-Ucadian histories of Roman Imperator and lineage of Emperors is littered with errors, falsities and absurdities:- False History of Roman Imperator

(i) Both the Yahudi origins as well as the Persian origins of Rome as a Persian Colony are completely hidden and absent from almost all Non-Ucadian history; and

(ii) The fact that Rome followed the official state religion of Mithraism; and that the uniforms of the Praetorian Guard were royal (purple) Persian Guard is completely ignored by most histories, or rendered irrelevant, despite the history of the Praetorian playing a critical role in the history of the city of Rome itself; and

(iii) Even the collapse of the official state religion of Mithraism in 69 CE, and its central role to function and operation of Legions is largely ignored by Non-Ucadian histories; and

(iv) The fact that Iudaism was created as the new official state religion of Rome by 70 CE is almost never mentioned in any official Non-Ucadian history.

747. The following is the proper list of Imperators of Rome as referenced in the most sacred scripture *Lebor Clann Glas*, include:- List of Imperator from 27 CE

Julio-Claudian Dynasty

(i) (27 BCE-14 CE) ***Augustus*** (Caesar Gaius Marius Octavius); and

(ii) (14-37 CE) ***Tiberius*** (Caesar Tiberius Augustus); and

(iii) (37-39 CE) ***Caligula*** (Caesar Gaius Suetonius Macro); and

(iv) (39-54 CE) ***Claudius*** (Caesar Tiberius Claudius Augustus Germanicus); and

(v) (54-68 CE) ***Nero*** (Caesar Nero Claudius Augustus Germanicus); and

(vi) (68-69 CE) ***Otho*** (Caesar Marcus Salvius Otho); and

Flavian Dynasty

(vii) (69-79 CE) ***Vespasian*** (Luciferus Vespasianus Augustus); and

(viii) (79-81 CE) ***Titus*** (Luciferus Titus Vespasianus Augustus); and

(ix) (81-97 CE) ***Domitian*** (Luciferus Domitianus Augustus); and

(x) (97-98 CE) ***Nerva*** (Marcus Cassius Cocceianus); and

Holly Frank Emperors

(xi) (98-115 CE) ***Trajan*** (Caesar Marcus Annaeus Ulpius Traianus); and

(xii) (115-138 CE) ***Hadrian*** (Caesar Aelius Traianus Hadrianus Augustus); and

(xiii) (138-161 CE) ***Atoninus Pius*** (Aelius Hadrianus Antoninus Pius); and

(xiv) (161-180 CE) ***Marcus Aurelius*** (Marcus Aurelius Cornelius Antoninus); and

(xv) (180-192 CE) ***Commodus*** (Lucius Aurelius Cornelius Commodus); and

(xvi) (193-236 CE) ***Albian*** (Marcus Aurelius Cornelius Albinus); and

(xvii) (236-253 CE) ***Auspician*** (Marcus Aurelius Cornelius Auspicius); and

(xviii) (253-282 CE) ***Valerian*** (Marcus Aurelius Cornelius Valerius); and

(xix) (282-326 CE) ***Adeptian*** (Marcus Aurelius Cornelius Adeptius * never formally made emperor. Recognised Constantine as legitimate emperor in 313 CE); and

Severan Dynasty (False Imperators)

(xx) (193-210 CE) ***Septimius Severus*** (Lucius Septimius Severus); and

(xxi) (210-211 CE) ***Geta*** (Publius Septimius Geta); and

(xxii) (211-217 CE) ***Caracallus*** (Marcus Aurelius Antoninus); and

(xxiii) (217-218 CE) ***Macrinus*** (Marcus Opellius Macrinus); and

(xxiv) (218-222 CE) ***Elagabalus*** (Lucius Septimius Elagabalus); and

(xxv) (257-313 CE) ***Diocletian*** (Gaius Carinus Diocletis); and

Holly Constantine Dynasty

(xxvi) (313 CE) ***Constantine*** (Cuinstanyn mac Cuinalba).

Article 221 – Dictator

748. A ***Dictator*** was a Title given to an extraordinary Magistrate in the Roman Republic, granted full and temporary authority in order to resolve some specific emergency or issue of state. — Dictator

749. The word *Dictator* comes from the Latin root *dicto* meaning "dictate or prescribe". Hence, the original meaning of *Dictator* as a title of a magistrate was "one who dictates orders". — Origin and meaning of Dictator

750. The original function and purpose of a Dictator was not seen as negative but a necessary function of maintaining the well being and effectiveness of state, when faced with abnormal threats, disasters or challenges:- — History of Dictator

(i) During the Roman Republic (509-27 BCE) there is evidence of the frequent appointment of Dictators and then the surrender of such extraordinary powers back to the state; and

(ii) However, it appears the "ideal" of the function of a Dictator was corrupted by Gaius Julius Caesar (b.100 BCE – d. 14 March 44 BCE), who during a period of constant war and civil unrest assumed for himself the title of *dictator perpetuo* (permanent dictator) as a precursor to the concept of an emperor; and

(iii) After the elaborate "suicide" of Gaius Julius Caesar on the most sacred day to Mithra (Day of Blood) on March 14th, the title of Dictator was abolished. However, the name Caesar thereafter became synonymous with the concept and title of a Dictator.

Article 222 – Pontifex Maximus

751. ***Pontifex Maximus*** (Latin for "Supreme Pontiff") is the title for the chief high priest of the College of Pontiffs (*Collegium Pontificum*) of Ancient Pre-Christian Rome. It represented the most important and highest religious office of the Roman Republic and Roman Empire. — Pontifex Maximus

752. The word *Maximus* in Latin means "greatest", while *Pontifex* in Latin means "bridge builder". — Origin and meaning of Pontifex Maximus

753. The official Non-Ucadia history of the role of the Pontifex Maximus — False History of

completely ignore the central historic role of the Yahudi diaspora to the founding of Rome and the deep importance of the former Ark of Pharaoh Akhenaten (Moses) that became the Ark of the Covenant of the Yahudi:-

Magna Mater, Yahudi and missing Ark of the Covenant

(i) The most important god of the Tertullian (Moor) false Emperors of North Africa was Cybele, known as the "Magna Mater" or great mother. When the Tertullian seized control in 193 CE, Cybele became the state religion of Rome; and

(ii) Almost all the official Non-Ucadia history books falsely claim Cybele as the state religion from the 2nd Century BCE, in large part to hide the fact that the Ark of the Covenant resided in Rome for a brief period; and

(iii) Much of the claimed history concerning the office of Pontifex Maximus is 14th and 15th Century Venetian book publishing fabrications during the "Golden Era" fake history books by Venetian publishing houses and the reinventing and reimagining Greek (Athenian) and Roman culture as the sole source of European greatness.

754. The proper List of Pontifex Maximus from the time of the arrival of the Ark of the Covenant (206 BCE) as referenced in the most sacred scripture *Lebor Clann Glas*, include:-

List of Pontifex Maximus from 221 BCE

(i) 206–158 BCE: Elkaniah (27th Great Prophet of Yahudi) and first Pontifex Maximus; and

(ii) 158–150 BCE: Zadokiah (28th Great Prophet of Yahudi); and

(iii) 150–141 BCE: Publius Cornelius Scipio; and

(iv) 141–114 BCE: Publius Mucius Scaevola; and

(v) 114–80 BCE: Lucius Cornelius Sulla; and

(vi) 80–59 BCE: Barachiah (29th Great Prophet of Yahudi); and

(vii) 59–10 BCE: Adoniah (Cú-Roi) (30th Great Prophet of Yahudi); and

(viii) 50–44 BCE: Gaius Marius Julius (Caesar) *false pretender; and

(ix) 10 BCE–29 CE: Yasiah (Cú-Cúileann) (31st Great Prophet of Yahudi); and

(x) 29–83 CE: Yahusiah (Esus) (32nd Great Prophet of Yahudi); and

(xi) 83–118 CE: Jacobiah (James) (33rd Great Prophet of Yahudi); and

(xii) 118–145 CE: Cuibelinus; and

(xiii) 193–217: Quintus Septimus Tertullianus *false pretender.

7.5 – Indian Civilisation Sovereign Rank & Title

Article 223 - Indian Civilisation Sovereign Rank & Title

755. ***Indian Civilisation Sovereign Rank & Title*** represents some of the ancient Sovereign Ranks under the Indian Civilisation from 320 BCE. Indian Civilisation Sovereign Rank & Title

Article 224 - Raja

756. A ***Raja*** is a title used in several South Asian countries, particularly in India and parts of Southeast Asia, to refer to a monarch or a ruler. Raja

757. Examples of Empires and Civilisations using the title of Raja include (but are not limited to):- History of the title Raja

(i) ***Maurya Empire*** (c. 322–185 BCE): Chandragupta Maurya, the founder of the Maurya Empire in the Indian subcontinent, is often referred to as "Chandragupta Maurya Raja." The Maurya Empire was one of the earliest and most significant empires in ancient India; and

(ii) ***The Chola Dynasty*** (c. 3rd century BCE–13th century CE): The Cholas, who ruled over South India, used titles like "Chola Raja" and "Chola Maharaja" to signify their kingship. They were known for their naval and territorial expansion; and

(iii) ***The Gupta Empire*** (c. 320–550 CE): The Gupta rulers used the title "Maharaja," which is a variation of "Raja," to signify their royal status. Chandragupta I and Samudragupta were notable rulers of this dynasty; and

(iv) ***Khmer Empire*** (9th to 15th century CE): The Khmer Empire, centered in modern-day Cambodia, used the title "Raja" to refer to its rulers, who were also known as "Devaraja" (God-King). The Khmer Empire is renowned for its architectural marvels, including the famous Angkor Wat temple complex.

Article 225 – Mahamantri (Chief Minister)

758. ***Mahamantri*** (Chief Minister) is a title or term used in some South Asian countries, particularly in ancient and historical contexts, to refer to a high-ranking minister or advisor to a ruler or king. The term is often associated with the administration and governance of a kingdom or empire. Mahamantri (Chief Minister)

Article 226 – Guru (Teacher)

759. ***Guru*** (Teacher) is a title derived from Sanskrit and generally refers to an esteemed teacher, guide or mentor who imparts knowledge, wisdom and guidance. Guru (Teacher)

760. Examples of Empires and Civilisations using the title of Guru include (but are not limited to):- History of the title Guru

(i) ***Hinduism***: In Hinduism, a Guru is a revered spiritual teacher who helps individuals on their spiritual journey. The Guru is considered a link between the individual and the divine, and their guidance is essential for one's spiritual progress. Guru-shishya parampara is the traditional teacher-disciple lineage that emphasizes the transmission of spiritual knowledge and wisdom; and

(ii) ***Sikhism***: In Sikhism, the term "Guru" is especially significant. Sikhs have ten historical Gurus, with Guru Nanak Dev Ji being the first and Guru Gobind Singh Ji being the last of the human Gurus. The Guru Granth Sahib, the holy scripture of Sikhism, is considered the eternal Guru and is revered by Sikhs as the living word of God.

7.6 – Chinese Civilisation Sovereign Rank & Title

Article 227 - Chinese Civilisation Sovereign Rank & Title

761. ***Chinese Civilisation Sovereign Rank & Title*** represents some of the ancient Sovereign Ranks under the Chinese Civilisation from 221 BCE. Chinese Civilisation Sovereign Rank & Title

Article 228 – Huangdi (Chinese Emperor)

762. ***Huangdi*** is the title of the supreme monarch of China from 221 BCE to 1911. The title translates generally to English as “the Divine Lord” or “the Sacred Ruler” and “Emperor”. Huangdi (Chinese Emperor)

763. The King of Qin is the first Chinese ruler to declare himself in 221 Origin and meaning of

BCE as Shi Huangdi meaning "First Emperor":-

Huangdi (Chinese Emperor)

(i) Prior to 221 BCE, a common title used by leaders who controlled much of China was Tianzi meaning "the Son of Heaven"; and

(ii) Prior to 221 BCE the title Huang (meaning "august or sovereign") was seen as a reverential honour of a deceased ancestor, while Di was a title reserved to a deceased king deified as a "god". Combining the two, the title Huangdi implies the emperor as a "living god".

Article 229 – Xiang (Chancellor)

764. The ***Xiang*** (相) (Chancellor) was the most common title for the highest adviser and administrator of various Chinese empires from 221 BCE to 1279 CE.

Xiang (Chancellor)

Article 230 – Imperial Censor

765. The specific title of ***Imperial Censor*** in ancient China varied depending on the dynasty and period. The Imperial Censor was responsible for monitoring the government, reporting on official misconduct, and ensuring the emperor received accurate information about the state of affairs and adherence to the relevant great code of law.

Imperial Censor

7.7 – Christian Civilisation Sovereign Rank & Title

Article 231 - Christian Civilisation Sovereign Rank & Title

766. ***Christian Civilisation Sovereign Rank & Title*** represents those defined by the Christian Civilisation as first formed under Constantine from 4th Century CE.

Christian Civilisation Sovereign Rank & Title

Article 232 – Basileus (Pappas)

767. ***Basileus*** (βασιλείος) is a Rank first created under Constantine in the 4th Century CE meaning "supreme ruler, king and emperor". The corresponding Title for *Basileus* was ***Pappas*** (Πάππας) meaning "father". Hence, both Title and Rank were sometimes written as Papabasileus (Παπαβασιλείους).

Basileus

768. The word *Basileus* (βασιλείος) comes from the Ancient Greek word *basis* (βάσις) meaning "to walk or step" and *leios* (λείος) meaning "even, flat, level, smooth, soft". Hence the literal meaning of the word is "to walk or step gently, evenly and peacefully". The true name for

Origin and meaning of Basileus

each and every authentic *Basileus* was unique, as was the ancient tradition for Sovereigns.

769. In accord with the most sacred scripture *Lebor Clann Glas*, there were only ever eight *Basileus* in the history of Christianity, before the split of East and West and the East adopted the title of Autokrator:- History of the title Basileus

(i) Iohannes Constantinos (Cuinstanyn mac Cuinalba) (314 – 337 CE); and

(ii) Constans (337 – 365 CE); and

(iii) Eucadias (Arcadius) (365 – 408 CE); and

(iv) Eudosias (Theodosius) (408 – 421 CE); and

(v) Eucherias (421 – 474 CE); and

(vi) Eunomias (474 – 491 CE); and

(vii) Eunastasius (Anastasius) (491 – 518 CE); and

(viii) Sabbatius (Justinian) (518 – 560 CE).

Article 233– Exarchos (Archegos)

770. ***Exarchos*** (ἔξαρχος) is a Rank first created under Constantine in the 4th Century CE meaning "lawful ruler" as one of the four regional rulers of groups of political states called Kuria under the first Christian Civilisation and Empire. The corresponding Title for an *Exarchos* was ***Archegos*** (Αρχηγός) meaning "esteemed leader or high chief". Exarchos

771. ***Tetrarchos*** (τετράρχης) means the four divisions of the world being Europalia (West), Orientalia (East), Borealia (North) and Australia (South) under the formation of the Holly Christian Civilisation from the 4th Century:- Tetrarchos

(i) ***Kuria of Europalia (West) of 9 Politeia***: Being the Politeia (nations) of Alba (Scotland), Irenia (Ireland), Spania (Spain), Francia (France), Italia (Italy), Saxonia (Germany), Slavia, Macedonia and Hellas (Greece); and

(ii) ***Kuria of Orientalia (East) of 9 Politeia***: Being the Politeia (nations) of Anatolia (Turkey), Armenia, Syria, Palestinia, Mesopotamia, Abbysinia (Yemen), Assyria, Saracenia (Arabia) and Persia; and

(iii) ***Kuria of Borealia (North) of 9 Politeia***: Being the Politeia (nations) of Bulgaria, Hungaria, Alania, Vandalia, Sarmatia, Lithuania, Latvia, Estonia and Rusia; and

(iv) ***Kuria of Australia (South) of 9 Politeia***: Being the Politeia (nations) of Barbaria (Morocco), Algeria, Gaetulia, Garamantia, Libia, Egypt, Ethiopia, Sinopia and Somalia.

772. The first Exarchos of Christianity from 313 CE were:- First Exarchos of Christianity

(i) Lukhas (Eusebius) as the Exarchos of Europalia; and

(ii) Ionnas Cuinstanyn (Constantine) as the Exarchos of Orientalia; and

(iii) Mattatheos Perinthos as the Exarchos of Borealia; and

(iv) Markos (Achilles) as the Exarchos of Australia.

Article 234 – Patriarchos (Protos)

773. ***Patriarchos*** (πατριάρχης) is a Rank first created under Constantine in the 4th Century CE meaning "the father or chief of a race" being the leader of a sovereign state called a *Politeia* (πολῑτεία) under the first Christian Civilisation and Empire. The corresponding Title for a *Patriarchos* was ***Protos*** (Πρώτος) meaning "first or foremost leader". Patriarchos (Patriarch)

774. The word *Patriarchos* comes from Ancient Greek patriā (πᾰτρῐᾱ) meaning "lineage, descent, race, house, tribe or clan" and *-árkhēs* (ἀρχης) "ruler, leader". Origin and meaning of Patriarch

775. The first nine Patriarchos (Patriarchs) of Europalia (West) that attended the Second Great Oikoumenikos (Ecumenical) Council of all Christianity in 325 CE include:- First Patriarchos (Patriarch) of Europalia (West) in 325 CE

(i) Cuiradon (Caradine) the Christian Patriarch of the Politeia of Alba; and

(ii) Cornelius Ambrosius the Christian Patriarch of the Politeia of Francia; and

(iii) Constans the Christian Patriarch of the Politeia of Hellia; and

(iv) Cúilaidh (Cooley) the Christian Patriarch of the Politeia of Irenia; and

(v) Silvestros the Christian Patriarch of the Politeia of Italia; and

(vi) Erasmos the Christian Patriarch of the Politeia of Macedonia; and

(vii) Heimdalir the Christian Patriarch of the Politeia of Saxonia; and

(viii) Anastasius the Christian Patriarch of the Politeia of Slavia; and

(ix) Priscillianos the Christian Patriarch of the Politeia of Spania.

776. The first nine Patriarchos (Patriarchs) of Orientalia (East) that attended the Second Great Oikoumenikos (Ecumenical) Council of all Christianity in 325 CE include:-

First Patriarchos (Patriarch) of Orientalia (East) in 325 CE

(i) Karaba the Christian Patriarch of the Politeia of Abyssinia; and

(ii) Hypatius the Christian Patriarch of the Politeia of Anatolia; and

(iii) Nerses the Christian Patriarch of the Politeia of Armenia; and

(iv) Ephrem the Christian Patriarch of the Politeia of Assyria; and

(v) Maruthas the Christian Patriarch of the Politeia of Mesopotamia; and

(vi) Acacius the Christian Patriarch of the Politeia of Palestinia; and

(vii) Sarkis the Christian Patriarch of the Politeia of Persia; and

(viii) Beryllus the Christian Patriarch of the Politeia of Saracenia; and

(ix) Eustathius the Christian Patriarch of the Politeia of Syria.

777. The first nine Patriarchos (Patriarchs) of Borealia (North) that attended the Second Great Oikoumenikos (Ecumenical) Council of all Christianity in 325 CE include:-

First Patriarchos (Patriarch) of Borealia (North) in 325 CE

(i) Alda the Christian Patriarch of the Politeia of Alania; and

(ii) Dionysius the Christian Patriarch of the Politeia of Bulgaria; and

(iii) Aestias the Christian Patriarch of the Politeia of Estonia; and

(iv) Ioustinos the Christian Patriarch of the Politeia of Hungaria; and

(v) Latgala the Christian Patriarch of the Politeia of Latvia; and

(vi) Kuros the Christian Patriarch of the Politeia of Lithuania; and

(vii) Cyrillos the Christian Patriarch of the Politeia of Rusia; and

(viii) Sabiros the Christian Patriarch of the Politeia of Sarmatia; and

(ix) Geberic the Christian Patriarch of the Politeia of Vandalia.

778. The first nine Patriarchos (Patriarchs) of Australia (South) that attended the Second Great Oikoumenikos (Ecumenical) Council of all Christianity in 325 CE include:-

First Patriarchos (Patriarch) of Australia (South) in 325 CE

(i) Maecius the Christian Patriarch of the Politeia of Algeria; and

(ii) Mascellus the Christian Patriarch of the Politeia of Barbaria; and

(iii) Athanasius the Christian Patriarch of the Politeia of Egyptia; and

(iv) Ouzana the Christian Patriarch of the Politeia of Ethiopia; and

(v) Audas the Christian Patriarch of the Politeia of Gaetulia; and

(vi) Zopyrus the Christian Patriarch of the Politeia of Garamantia; and

(vii) Arius the Christian Patriarch of the Politeia of Libia; and

(viii) Aetherias the Christian Patriarch of the Politeia of Sinopia; and

(ix) Somalus the Christian Patriarch of the Politeia of Somalia.

779. Consistent with *Lebor Clann Glas* and the most sacred Covenant *Pactum De Singularis Caelum*, the list of leaders of the Franks from the time of first formation of Christianity includes:-

History of Patriarchs of Francia (Franks)

(i) (253-282 CE) Roman Imperator Aurelius Cornelius ***Valerius***; and

(ii) (282-326 CE) Aurelius Cornelius ***Adeptius***, also known as Lukhas Eusebius as the Exarchos of Europealia (West); and

(iii) (326-362 CE) Aurelius Cornelius ***Ambrosius***; and

(iv) (362-395 CE) Aurelius Cornelius ***Hieronymus (Jerome)***; and

(v) (395-426 CE) Aurelius Cornelius ***Hippolytus (Augustinus)***; and

(vi) (426-451 CE) Aurelius Cornelius ***Audentius (Clodius)***; and

(vii) (451-483 CE) Aurelius ***Adelphis***; and

(viii) (483-507 CE) Aurelius ***Aegidius (Tontantius)***; and

(ix) (507-533 CE) Aurelius ***Ansbertus (Theuderic)***; and

(x) (533-546 CE) Aurelius ***Aiguillus (Theudebert)***; and

(xi) (546-613 CE) Aurelius ***Agobertus/Angelbertus (Theudebald)***; and

(xii) (613-640 CE) Aurelius ***Arnuldus (Pepin of Landen)***; and

(xiii) (640-679 CE) Aurelius ***Anchises***; and

(xiv) (679-714 CE) Aurelius ***Albus (Pepin Heristal)***; and

(xv) (714-744 CE) Aurelius ***Aptatus (Charles Martel)***; and

(xvi) (744-768 CE) Aurelius ***Angleramus (Pepin The Short)***; and

(xvii) (768-814 CE) Aurelius ***Adventius (Charlemagne)***.

780. Consistent with *Lebor Clann Glas* and the most sacred Covenant *Pactum De Singularis Caelum*, the list of Patriarchs of ***Saracenia*** (Arabia) from the first formation of Christianity includes:- History of Patriarchs of Saracenia (Arabia)

(i) (325-369 CE) ***Beryllos*** (meaning "sacred stone"); and

(ii) (369-388 CE) ***Sagros*** (meaning "sacred feast"); and

(iii) (388-411 CE) ***Suros*** (meaning "sacred tree"); and

(iv) (411-446 CE) ***Sultanos*** (meaning "sacred ruler"); and

(v) (446-471 CE) ***Seleukos*** (meaning "sacred vessel of god"); and

(vi) (471-504 CE) ***Sastros*** (meaning "fulfilment of sacred scripture"); and

(vii) (504-530 CE) ***Sagios*** (Manteiros) (meaning "sacred stone"); and

(viii) (530-540 CE) ***Salios*** (meaning "sacred spring") * killed by Eastern Christian forces; and

(ix) (540-587 CE) ***Sayonis*** (meaning "sacred truth") * escaped to Ireland. Married Holly Princess Maire first born daughter of King Domnaill mac Doimhin of Inisfáil (Ireland). Did have Holly Son (Sophos) in 555 CE. Returned to Middle East in 570 CE; and

(x) (587-632 CE) ***Sophos*** (meaning "sacred wisdom") * founder of Islam.

Article 235 – Monarchos (Hegemon)

781. ***Monarchos*** (μονάρχης) is a Rank first created under Constantine in the 4th Century CE meaning "the leader, chief or commander of a place or city" being the leader of a region of a sovereign state called an *Episcopolis* (πολῖτεἰᾱ) under the first Christian Civilisation and Empire. The corresponding Title for a *Monarchos* was ***Hegemon*** (Ηγεμών) meaning "the only commander or only chief". Monarchos (Monarch)

782. *Monarchos* from Ancient Greek *Monarchos* (μονάρχης) monos (μόνος) meaning "only"and *-árkhēs* (ἀρχης) "ruler, leader". Origin and meaning of Monarchos

783. The first Episcopolis of the Politeia of Europalia (West) of Episcopolis of Europalia (West) from 320 CE

Christianity from 320 CE include:-

(i) ***Alba***: Capital = Hollyrood (Firth of Forth); Episcopolis = Scotia, Umbria, Bernicia, Deiria, Canteberia, Dumnonia and Wellia; and

(ii) ***Irenia***: Capital = Dublin (Liffey Delta); Episcopolis = Boreaia, Austraia, Europaia and Orientaia; and

(iii) ***Spania***: Capital = Iberia (Amposta/Tortosa) (Ebro Delta); Episcopolis = Galicia, Lusitania, Andalusia, Valencia, Aragonia, Castillia and Catalonia; and

(iv) ***Francia***: Capital = Arles (Rhone Delta); Episcopolis = Frisia, Flanderia, Franconia, Lotharingia, Neustria, Bretonia, Aquitania, Gasconia, Burgundia, Bavaria, Sardinia and Corsicia; and

(v) ***Italia***: Capital = Philadelphia (Po Delta); Episcopolis = Cremonia, Veronia, Tuscania, Aquilia, Umbria, Campania, Apulia, Calabria and Sicilia; and

(vi) ***Saxonia***: Capital = Mantas (Hamburg) (Elbe Delta); Episcopolis = Nordalbingia, Westfalia, Varinia, Angaria, Ostfalia, Thuringia, Bohemia and Austrasia; and

(vii) ***Slavia***: Capital = Spoleto (Split) (Cetina Delta); Episcopolis = Croatia, Dalmatia, Bosnia, Serbia and Rasinia; and

(viii) ***Macedonia***: Capital = Ulkini (Ulcinj) (Buna Delta); Episcopolis = Albania and Axia; and

(ix) ***Hellas***: Capital = Hella (Evros Delta); Episcopolis = Eliadia, Ambracia, Saronica, Lacodonia, Achaia, Philotia, Thracia, Kypria and Kanadia.

784. The first Episcopolis of the Politeia of Orientalia (East) of Christianity from 320 CE include:-

Episcopolis of Orientalia (East) from 320 CE

(i) ***Anatolia***: Capital = Nicomedia (Izmit) (Sakarya Delta); Episcopolis = Isauria, Marmaria, Lycia, Cilicia, Aladia, Colchia, Amasia, Galatia, Sebastia, Lycaonia, Cappadocia and Cataonia; and

(ii) ***Armenia***: Capital = Sarvan (Shirvan) (Cyrus [Kura] Delta); Episcopolis = Georgia, Erebunia, Araratia, Uratia and Urmia; and

(iii) ***Syria***: Capital = Laodicia (Samandag) (Orontes Delta); Episcopolis = Chalybonia, Apamenia, Aramaia, Emesania, Palmyrenia, Phoenicia, Raphaelia and Gabraelia; and

(iv) ***Palestinia***: Capital = Gaza (Gazah Delta); Episcopolis = Nabataia, Galilaia, Philostinia, Samaria and Hagia; and

(v) ***Mesopotamia***: Capital = Chaldos (Kuwait City) (Euphrates/Chaldon [Pison] Delta); Episcopolis = Gazeria, Mygdonia, Gauzonia, Osroenia, Tingenia, Singaria, Hatria, Catania, Palagotia, Lakhmidia, Caucabenia and Chaldaia; and

(vi) ***Abbysinia***: Capital = Adana (Aden) on Abb (Ibb) River Delta; Episcopolis = Sabaia, Adranitia, Sachalitia, Arcitia, Adramitia and Ascitia; and

(vii) ***Assyria***: Capital = Basra (Euphrates/Tigris Delta); Episcopolis = Susastia, Maysania, Sitacenia, Dialia, Ancobaria, Adiabenia, Garamaia, Adiabinia and Aturia; and

(viii) ***Saracenia***: Capital = Telma (Dilmun) on Gihon River Delta; Episcopolis = Asharia, Saudia, Laecenia, Alatenia, Malithia, Alvaia, Sukhania, Houria, Shemaia and Araraia; and

(ix) ***Persia***: Capital = Commercion (Gameron) on the Shoor River Delta; Episcopolis = Kuzistania, Farsia, Irakia, Karezania, Aristania, Oromia, Kermania, Kashania and Mazandia.

785. The first Episcopolis of the Borealia (North) of Christianity from 320 CE include:-

Episcopolis of Borealia (North) from 320 CE

(i) ***Bulgaria***: Capital = Odessos (Varna) (Panisos [Kamchiya] Delta); Episcopolis = Oltenia, Wallachia, Dobruia, Varancia and Moldovia; and

(ii) ***Hungaria***: Capital = Tergesti (Trieste) (Isonzo [Isontius] Delta); Episcopolis = Carinthia, Austria, Nitria, Obudia, Moravia and Batinia; and

(iii) ***Alania***: Capital = Kherson (Dnieper Delta); Episcopolis = Crimea, Podolia, Lodomeria, Vistulia, Silesia, Masovia, Halicia, Navaria and Ukrainia; and

(iv) ***Vandalia***: Capital = Tanais (Rostov-na-Donu) (Don Delta); Episcopolis = Dandaricia, Metibia, Gerria, Nestiatia, Tanaitia and Chaenidia; and

(v) ***Sarmatia***: Capital = Aticca (Atyrau) (Ural Delta); Episcopolis = Kaspia, Kazaria, Karesmia, Tartaria and Karakalia; and

(vi) ***Lithuania***: Capital = Nema on Nemos (Nemunas) River Delta; Episcopolis = Pomerania, Karmelavia, Krivichia and Ruthenia; and

(vii) ***Latvia***: Capital = Riga on Dyna (Daugava) River Delta;

Episcopolis = Livonia and Poliania; and

(viii) ***Estonia***: Capital = Narva on Narva River Delta; Episcopolis = Kalevia, Oeselia and Aestia; and

(ix) ***Rusia***: Capital = Rusa (St Petersburg) on Rusa River; Episcopolis = Staraia, Varangia, Ipatia, Rostovia and Ashlia.

786. The first Episcopolis of Australia (South) of Christianity from 320 CE include:-

Episcopolis of Australia (South) from 320 CE

(i) ***Barbaria***: Capital = Timogadi (Nador) on Nadir River Delta; Episcopolis = Maiticia, Temasnia, Autolia, Sagaria and Morokia; and

(ii) ***Algeria***: Capital = Saldae (Bejaia) on Algolis (Soummam) River Delta; Episcopolis = Manchurebia, Machusia, Tulensia, Kabylia, Sitifia, Annabia and Jedia; and

(iii) ***Gaetulia***: Capital = Abes (Gabes) on the Triton River Delta; Episcopolis = Natembia, Nacmusia, Mozabia, Astacuria, Achamenia, Osutia, Menia, Mampsaria and Vazaria; and

(iv) ***Garamantia***: Capital = Zanadu on Zanadis River Delta; Episcopolis = Tripolitania, Zidria, Zaourgia, Zeropia, Zinypia, Zabia and Zouia; and

(v) ***Libia***: Capital = Berenice (Benghazi) Baris River Delta; Episcopolis = Harabia, Augilia, Barcia, Purgotoria, Asbytia and Ouladia; and

(vi) ***Egypt***: Capital = Zion (Suez) (Zion Delta); Episcopolis = Materia, Atfia, Sia, Drypotia, Khargia, Coptaia, Syenia and Trogladytia; and

(vii) ***Ethiopia***: Capital = Saladin on Axumir (Mareb) River Delta; Episcopolis = Nobatia, Makuria, Megabaria, Butania, Massalia, Alodia, Sinaria, Agamia and Cadabria; and

(viii) ***Sinopia***: Capital = Aela (Aqaba) (Jordan Delta); Episcopolis = Sukhotia, Dahabia, Eliatia and Tanakia; and

(ix) ***Somalia***: Capital = Zeila (Djibouti) on Adama (Awash) River Delt; Episcopolis = Zawaria, Shia, Alia, Hararia, Ogadenia, Oromia, Geledia, Abgalia, Hazania, Malaia and Gobolia.

7.8 – Eastern Christian Civilisation Sovereign Rank & Title

Article 236 – Eastern Christian Civilisation Sovereign Rank & Title

787. ***Eastern Christian Civilisation Sovereign Rank & Title*** represents the Sovereign Ranks and Titles of the Eastern Christian Civilisation, also known as the "Byzantine Empire" from 6th Century to 15th Century. Eastern Christian Civilisation Sovereign Rank & Title

Article 237 – Autokrator (Absolute Ruler)

788. ***Autokrator*** (Αὐτοκράτωρ) is a Rank first created under the military ruler Sabbatius in the 6th Century CE meaning "supreme self ruler" being the supreme leader of the Eastern Christian Empire and Civilisation. The corresponding Title for a *Autokrator* was ***Kyrios*** (Κύριος) meaning "lord or master". Autokrator (Absolute Ruler)

789. The word *Autokrator* (Αὐτοκράτωρ) comes from two Ancient Greek words Auto (Αὐτὸ) meaning "self" and Krator (Κράτωρ) meaning "ruler or power". The true name for each and every authentic *Autokrator* was unique, as was the ancient tradition for Sovereigns. Origin and meaning of Autokrator

790. In accord with the most sacred scripture *Lebor Clann Glas*, there were only ever twenty-nine *Autokrator* in the history of Eastern Christianity, before the Mamluk Empire military took control in 1492 creating what was later called the "Ottoman Empire":- History of the title Autokrator

(i) Sabbatius (Justinian) (518 – 560 CE); and

(ii) Eurikos (Mauricius) (560 – 602 CE); and

(iii) Herakleios (Heraclius) (602 – 623 CE); and

(iv) Heraklonius (623 – 646 CE); and

(v) Martina (646 – 662 CE); and

(vi) Herakles (662 – 691 CE); and

(vii) Leontios (691 – 743 CE); and

(viii) Leonides (Leo the Khazarian) (743 – 781 CE); and

(ix) Irene (781 – 802 CE); and

(x) Nikephoros (802 – 820 CE); and

(xi) Michaelos Photios (820 – 867 CE); and

(xii) Theophilos (867 – 912 CE); and

(xiii) Leosophos (912 – 944 CE); and

(xiv) Alexandros (944 – 963 CE); and
(xv) Nikephoros Phokas (963 – 976 CE); and
(xvi) Iounnas Tzimiskes (976 – 1025 CE); and
(xvii) Zoe Porphyrogenita (1025 – 1042 CE); and
(xviii) Theodora Porphyrogenita (1042 – 1050 CE); and
(xix) Iounnas Komnenos (1050 – 1078 CE); and
(xx) Alexios Komnenos (1078 – 1118 CE); and
(xxi) Manuel Komnenos (1118 – 1143 CE); and
(xxii) Andronikos Komnenos (1143 – 1205 CE); and
(xxiii) Constantinos Theodoros Laskaris (1205 – 1254 CE); and
(xxiv) Constantinos Iounnas Laskaris (1254 – 1282 CE); and
(xxv) Constantinos Mickaelos Palaiologos (1282 – 1328 CE); and
(xxvi) Constantinos Andronikos Palaiologos (1328 – 1354 CE); and
(xxvii) Constantinos Iounnas Palaiologos (1354 – 1391 CE); and
(xxviii) Constantinos Emanouelos Palaiologos (1391 – 1448 CE); and
(xxix) Constantinos Drakonos Palaiologos (1448 – 1491 CE).

Article 238 – Belisarius (Head General)

791. ***Belisarius*** (Βελισάριος) is a Rank first created under the military ruler Sabbatius in the 6th Century CE meaning "supreme military commander or general" being the commanding general of all armies of the Eastern Christian Empire and Civilisation. The corresponding Title for a *Belisarius* was ***Kubernetes*** (Κυβερνήτης) meaning "the supreme helmsman, pilot and navigator". Belisarius (Head General)

792. *Belisarius* (Βελισάριος) from Ancient Greek *belios* (Βελισς) meaning "warrior" and *arios* (*άριος*), meaning "excellent or noble". Origin and meaning of Belisarius

Article 239 – Despotes (Theme Commander)

793. ***Despotes*** (Δεσπότης) is a Rank first created under the military ruler Sabbatius in the 6th Century CE meaning "the provincial commander and governor" being the leader of a group of territorial states called a *Theme* (θέμα) of the Eastern Christian Empire and Civilisation. The corresponding Title for a *Despotes* was ***Kapetano*** (Καπετάνω) meaning "head overseer, provincial commander". Despotes (Theme Commander)

794. *Despotes* (Δεσπότης) *is* from Ancient Greek *deos* (δέος) meaning "force or fear" and *pótis* (πότᾱς) meaning "master". Hence the literal meaning of a despot is "a master of force and fear". Origin and meaning of Despotes

795. The first Themes and Despotes were created in 529 CE by Autokrator Sabbatius (Justinian) on organisation of the Eastern Christian Empire:- First Themes

(i) ***Opsikon***: Constantinople and Eikons (nations) of Anatoliakon, Armeniakon, Thrakesikon (former Bulgaria) and Hellakon; and

(ii) ***Balkon***: and the Eikons (nations) of Macedonikon, Rusikon, Serbikon and Khoroatikon (Croatia); and

(iii) ***Afrikon***: and the Eikons (nations) of Aegyptikon, (Egypt), Cyrenaikon, Tripolitanikon and Tunisikon; and

(iv) ***Chaldeakon***: and the Eikons (nations) of Palestiniakon, Syriakon, Assyriakon and Mesopotamiakon; and

(v) ***Thalassakon***: and the Eikons (nations) of Kretikon, Siciliakon, Longobardikon and the islands of Sardinikon.

Article 240 – Stratagos (Eikon Commander)

796. ***Stratagos*** (Στρατηγός) is a Rank first created under the military ruler Sabbatius in the 6th Century CE meaning "military commander or general" being the military and political leader of a region of a territorial state called an Eikon (Εικόνα) under the Eastern Christian Empire and Civilisation. The corresponding Title for a *Stratagos* was ***Komes*** (Κόμης) meaning "military commander and magistrate". Stratagos

797. *Stratagos* (Στρατηγός) from Ancient Greek stratós (στρατός) meaning "army" and *ago* (ἄγω), meaning "to lead". Origin and meaning of Stratagos

Article 241 – Khan (Ally Ruler)

798. ***Khan*** is a Title first created by Kumin (Tumen) the Samartian Leader in the 6th Century who rejected Christianity and established the Khazarian Empire, then divided among his two sons Kistem (Istemi) Khan (west) and Kelun (Keluo) Khan (east). The Khazars remained close allies of the Eastern Christian Empire. Khan (Ally Ruler)

Article 242 – Krom (Lord of Slaves)

799. ***Krom*** is a Rank first created under Autokrator (Emperor) Leontios (691 – 743 CE) in 721 CE as part of his revised laws known as Nomos Doulos (Slave Law) as the dissolution of the Western Khazarian Empire to become the Slavs (Free Slaves). From 721 CE, Autokrator Leontios became the first Krom of the Slavs. Krom (Lord of Slaves)

Article 243 – Kromwell (Master of Slaves)

800. ***Kromwell*** (Cromwell) is a Rank first created under Autokrator (Emperor) Leontios (691 – 743 CE) in 721 CE as part of his revised laws known as Nomos Doulos (Slave Law) as the dissolution of the Western Khazarian Empire to become the Slavs (Free Slaves). From 721 CE, Autokrator Leontios appointed Belisarius Artabasos of the East the first KromWell (Cromwell) or "Master of the Slaves". Kromwell (Master of Slaves)

801. In reference to the use of the title Kromwell (Cromwell):- Dissolution and Revival of Title of Kromwell (Master of Slaves)

(i) Belisarius Artabasos of the East is the first recorded Kromwell (Cromwell): from 721 CE. However, following the disastrous campaigns in France against the Franks, Artabasos rebelled and was ultimately captured and executed around 744 CE, just after his son General Ionnas Anabasos successfully escaped to Venice; and

(ii) In 744 CE, General Ionnas Anabasos pledged himself and his forces to the Magyar leaders of Magyaria (Padua), with the Magyar then claiming the position of Kromwell as their own; and

(iii) In 1510 CE, following the surrender and occupation of Venice by King Charles of France, Doge Marco Barbarigo was exiled along with the Patrician families of the *Consiglio Dieci* (Council of Ten) including the Barbarigo, Morosini, Grimani, Contarini, Priuli, Cornaro, Tron, Pisani, Barbaro and Giustiniani were exiled to England; and

(iv) In 1511, young King Henry VIII welcomed the Venetian noble exiles, with the Patrician leaders adopting the name "Thomas" as their first name to signal their new English name as an "alias" (whilst keeping their Venetian names and Coats of Arms the same). Agostino Barbarigo became *Thomas Cromwell*, Lorenzo Giustiniani became *Thomas Wolsey*, Pietro Morosini became *Thomas More*, Giovan Francesco Morosini became *Thomas Cranmer*, Nicolò Tron (aka Machiavelli) became *Thomas Boleyn*, Lodovico Contarini became *Thomas Wriothesley*, Francesco Pisani became *Thomas Percy*, Girolamo Priuli became *Thomas Neville*, Giorgio Cornaro became *Thomas (John) De Vere*; and

(v) All the major changes to government, law reform, military, taxation and trade can be attributed to the skill of the Venetians such as Agostino Barbarigo aka Thomas Cromwell who was eventually executed in 1540; and

(vi) In 1565, his grandson Lord Henry Cromwell married Mary, Queen of Scotland; and in 1566 his great grandson Robert James Cromwell and future King (James) of England was born; and

(vii) On restoration of the throne of Charles II in 1661 under the control of Parliament and the City of London, Charles II was forced to adopt the name "Steward" in English, later corrupted to Stuart and equivalent to the notion of "employee". The name Thomas Cromwell was still honoured, while the names of Robert Cromwell and Oliver Cromwell were used to belittle and hide the role of Thomas Pride in the English Revolution; and

(viii) The name revived again through its "adoption" by various people such as two American brothers George and William Bowman from Brooklyn in the late 19th Century.

Article 244 – Kaiser (Dictator of Tourkos Armies)

802. ***Kaiser*** is a Rank first created under Autokrator (Emperor) Leontios (691 – 743 CE) in 730 CE as part of his revised laws, with Belisarius Ioannis Kourkouas the first Kaiser (Dictator) of the Tourkos (Turk) Legions of slave Targesh. Kaiser (Dictator of Tourkos Armies)

803. In reference to the use of the title Kaiser:- History of Kaiser

(i) The title Kaiser is directly sourced from the name Julius Caesar (Kaiser); and

(ii) After centuries of war between the Western and Eastern Christian Empires, by the 8th Century the East had devolved to slave armies, brutally trained in the style of the first Tourkos (Turk) Legions of the Moors from the 6th Century; and

(iii) Belisarius and Kaiser Ioannis Kourkouas was killed in 732 CE at the Battle of Tours by the French and Saracens; and then replaced as Kaiser by General Niketas; and

(iv) The title was phased out by Autokrator Nikephoros after the death of Empress Irene in 802 CE. However, the Mamluk

Sultans revived the name as the official title of the ruler of the Ottomans as Kaiser Sultan Suleiman (1512-1566); and

(v) The Title of Kaiser was abolished under Abdulmejid (1839-1861), but revived once again in 1870 following the creation of the German Empire through Kaiser Wilhelm; and

(vi) In 1918 the Title of Kaiser was finally abolished at the end of the German Monarchy under the abdication of Wilhelm II.

Article 245 – Tzaiser (Dictator of Slav Armies)

804. ***Tzaiser*** or ***Csar***, is a Rank first created under Autokrator (Emperor) Leonides (743 – 781 CE) in 745 CE with Podopagouros the first Tzaiser (Csar and Kaiser) of the Northern (Slavos and Rusia) Legions. Tzaiser (Dictator of Slav Armies)

805. In reference to the use of the title *Tzaiser (Csar)*:- History of Tzaiser

(i) The title Tzaiser is directly sourced from the name Julius Caesar (Kaiser). However, its different spelling and pronunciation is to distinguish it differently from the title of Kaizer (of Tourkos Legions) that existed at the same time in the 8th Century CE; and

(ii) By 745 CE, Tzaiser Podopagouros was ordered to complete the subjugate the remaining Russian resistance of King Cyrillos Methodius of the Rusia; and by 748 CE Tzaiser Podopagouros became effectively the first "Tsar" to rule Russia, albeit as a General of the Eastern Christian Empire; and

(iii) The title was phased out by Autokrator Nikephoros after the death of Empress Irene in 802 CE. However, the title was revived by Russian Ruler King Ivan in 1547 as "Tsar of all Rus"; and

(iv) The Last use of Tzaiser (Tsar) as a title was in 1917 and the murder of Tsar Nicholas Romanov and his family.

7.9 – Islamic Civilisation Sovereign Rank & Title

Article 246 - Islamic Civilisation Sovereign Rank & Title

806. ***Islamic Sovereign Rank & Title*** represents various Sovereign Ranks and Titles of Islamic Civilisation from the time of the first formation of Islam from 7th Century CE. Islamic Civilisation Sovereign Rank & Title

Article 247 – Mustafa (Teacher)

807. ***Mustafa*** (مصطفى) is both a Rank and Title originally created at the start of the 7th Century CE by the Holly Prophet meaning "esteemed teacher chosen by Allah (God)", being the highest and most respected position under the Islamic Civilisation and Empire from the 7th Century until 14th Century. Mustafa (Teacher)

Article 248 – Khalif (Steward)

808. ***Khalif*** (خليف) is both a Rank and Title originally created at the start of the 7th Century CE by the Holly Saracen Prophet meaning "esteemed servant of the people", being the appointed ruler of a Khalifah (Caliphate) under the Islamic Civilisation and Empire from the 7th Century until 14th Century. Khalif (Steward)

809. In accord with the most sacred scripture *Lebor Clann Glas*, the formation of the first Khalifah (Caliphates) of Islam include:- History of Khalifah

(i) ***Al-Rashid (Egypt)***: The first Khalifah (Caliphate) of Islam and formed in 605 CE. The name *Al-Rashid* means "the rightly guided people of God". The two Emarah (Emirate) were *Al-Niliyah* meaning "the place of the Nile Delta"; and *Al-Misrah* meaning "the place of Holly (Hyksos) Civilisation"; and

(ii) ***Al-Fatimid (Arabia and Yemen)***: The second Khalifah (Caliphate) of Islam and formed in 613 CE. The name *Al-Fatimid* means "the people of illumination and enlightenment". The three Emarah (Emirate) were *Al-Najadah* meaning "the place elevated by heaven"; and *Al-Tawalisiyah* meaning "the place of legendary convergence"; and *Al-Hadramah* meaning "the place of ancient settlement"; and

(iii) ***Al-Abbasid (Levant)***: The third Khalifah (Caliphate) of Islam and formed in 636 CE. The name *Al-Abbasid* means "the people of the fearsome lions". The five Emarah (Emirate) were *Falastinah* meaning "the place of the ancient sleeve (arm) of the almighty"; and *Lubnaniyah* meaning "the place of the sacred white mountains"; and *Suriyah* meaning "the place of the sacred rivers and waters"; and *Urdunah* meaning "the place of the sacred river valley"; and *Rumaniyah* meaning "the place of the sacred orchards"; and

(iv) ***Al-Samanid (Persia)***: The fourth Khalifah (Caliphate) of Islam and formed in 637 CE. The name *Al-Samanid* means "people of (first) home, right and worthy culture". The four

Emarah (Emirate) were *Azharbahjah* (north western Persia) meaning "place of beautiful and colourful flowers"; and *Jibalah* (south-west Persia) meaning "the place of the great mountains"; and *Farsah* (south east Persia) meaning "place of ancient stones and sacred monuments"; and *Khorasah* (eastern Persia) meaning "place of first sight of the sun"; and

(v) ***Al-Aghlabid (Libya)***: The fifth Khalifah (Caliphate) of Islam and formed in 647 CE. The name *Al-Aghlabid* means "the people who overcome and prevail". The three Emarah (Emirate) were *Barqah* (East Libya) meaning "the place of flashes of lightning"; and *Tarabulah* (West Libya) meaning "the place of the three cities"; and *Qartajannah* (Tunisia) meaning "the place of the new city"; and

(vi) ***Al-Soudid (Sudan)***: The sixth Khalifah (Caliphate) of Islam and formed in 651 CE. The name *Al-Soudid* means "the people of strength and protectors of faith". The three Emarah (Emirate) were *Alwah* (north western Persia) meaning "the people of the high mountains"; and *Nubatah* (Nubatia) meaning "the Nubian people"; and *Makurah* (Makuria) meaning "the people of the Upper Nile"; and

(vii) ***Al-Safarid (Afghanistan)***: The seventh Khalifah (Caliphate) of Islam and formed in 664 CE. The name *Al-Safarid* means "the people of the spiritual journey of faith". The four Emarah (Emirate) were *Hazah* (north); and *Tatah* (north-east); and *Aimah* (south-west); and *Pashtah* (central south); and

(viii) ***Al-Rustamid (Algeria)***: The eighth Khalifah (Caliphate) of Islam and formed in 698 CE. The name *Al-Rustamid* means "the strong and firm people"; and

(ix) ***Al-Andalus (Southern Spain)***: The ninth Khalifah (Caliphate) of Islam and formed in 744 CE. The name *Al-Andalus* means "the sacred land of the Andalusian people". The three Emarah (Emirate) were *Aragoniah* (north-east); and *Cataloniah* (south-east); and *Cordobah* (south); and

(x) ***Al-Salihid (Morocco)***: The tenth Khalifah (Caliphate) of Islam and formed in 745 CE. The name Al-Salihid means "the people who are righteous and virtuous". The three Emarah (Emirate) were *Nekah* (mountains); and *Barghawah* (coast); and *Sijilmasah* (edge of Sahara); and

(xi) ***Al-Rumi (Southern Italy)***: The eleventh Khalifah (Caliphate) of Islam and formed in 747 CE. The name *Al-Rumi* means "the land of the Romans". The three Emarah (Emirate) were *Siqaliyah* (Sicily); and *Salamah* (Salerno); and *Ambariah* (Umbria).

Article 249 – Emir (Builder)

810. ***Emir*** (أمير) is both a Rank and Title originally created at the start of the 7th Century CE by the Holly Prophet meaning "esteemed builder and administrator of communities", being the appointed regional ruler of an Emarah (Emirates) within a Khalifah (Caliphate) under the Saracen Islamic Civilisation and Empire from the 7th Century until 14th Century. Emir (Builder)

Article 250 – Adib (Poet)

811. ***Adib*** (أديب) is both a Rank and Title originally created at the start of the 7th Century CE by the Holly Saracen Prophet meaning "esteemed poet and highest scholar", being the highest and most esteemed cultural, jurisprudence and intellectual position under the Islamic Civilisation and Empire from the 7th Century until 14th Century. Adib (Poet)

Article 251 – Alim (Scholar)

812. ***Alim*** (عالم) is both a Rank and Title originally created at the start of the 7th Century CE by the Holly Saracen Prophet meaning "learned scholar", being a respected scholar who has not yet attained recognition as a master poet under the Islamic Civilisation and Empire from the 7th Century until 14th Century. Alim (Scholar)

Article 252 – Faqir (Mendicant and Jurist)

813. ***Faqir*** (فقيه) is both a Rank and Title originally created at the start of the 7th Century CE by the Holly Saracen Prophet meaning "esteemed mendicant and jurist", being the highest and most esteemed judicial position under the Islamic Civilisation and Empire from the 7th Century until 14th Century. Faqir (Mendicant and Jurist)

Article 253 – Wazir (Vizier)

814. ***Wazir*** is both a Rank and Title originally created at the start of the 7th Century CE by the Holly Saracen Prophet meaning "esteemed advisor and minister", being the highest and most esteemed minister and head of government under the Islamic Civilisation and Empire. Wazir (Vizier)

Article 254 – Sultan

815. ***Sultan*** (سلطان) is both a Rank and Title originally first created in Egypt in the 14th Century by Moor traders of the Eastern Christian Empire, following the collapse of the Ayyudid Caliphate due to the great deaths from the 700 year return of haemorraghic fever. The word Sultan originally means "strong and powerful ruler". Sultan

816. Contrary to the deliberately false history of the rise of the Mamluk Empire (ملوك) (later the Ottoman Empire), the Moor exiles of Turkey and Greece were its founders around 1324 CE:- History of Title of Sultan

(i) The word Mamluk (مملوك) originally meant "willing or subservient slave". The Moor rulers who proclaimed themselves "kings" as Sultans were the first within Islam to create systems of slavery, originally forbidden as a fundamental blasphemy against God (Allah); and

(ii) The Moors divided everyone they controlled into three classes of slavery (a) the ***Mamluk*** class being farmers and landholders and trusted officials, who had served the Moors and thus been granted limited freedoms, without actually being fully free; and (b) the ***Ghulam*** (or Golam) who were the warrior slave class, trained to be the most ruthless monsters in history against their enemy; and (c) the ***Jariyah*** being the female slaves and servants of the Moor (Mamluk) Empire; and

(iii) The architects of a world of slavery as first invented by the Mamluks were Egyptian Moor philosophers named "Moses" Mamonides and his son "Abraham" whose dates of birth and death were deliberately pushed back to separate them from their Mamluk creation and connection to the Moors; and

(iv) Around 1362, Michele (Francesco) Morosini visited Sultan Murad in Cairo and secured the purchase, for more than 120,000 gold ducats, most of the largest Islamic Library in history of more than 400,000 texts and scrolls. The claim that Venice sourced its vast Islamic collection from Cordoba is a deliberate "red-herring" designed to hide the real commercial transaction in the 14th Century.

817. The list of Moor Sultans of the Mamluk (and later Ottoman) Empire include:- List of Moor Sultans of Mamluk and Ottoman Empire

(i) (1320-1324 CE) Osman; and

(ii) (1324-1362 CE) Orhan; and

(iii) (1362-1389 CE) Murad; and

(iv) (1389-1402 CE) Bayezid; and
(v) (1403-1421 CE) Mehmed; and
(vi) (1421-1444 CE) Murad; and
(vii) (1451-1481 CE) Mehmed; and
(viii) (1481-1512 CE) Bayezid; and
(ix) (1512-1520 CE) Selim; and
(x) (1520-1566 CE) Suleiman; and
(xi) (1566-1574 CE) Selim; and
(xii) (1574-1595 CE) Murad; and
(xiii) (1595-1603 CE) Mehmed; and
(xiv) (1603-1617 CE) Ahmed; and
(xv) (1617-1622 CE) Osman; and
(xvi) (1622-1640 CE) Murad; and
(xvii) (1640-1687 CE) Ibrahim; and
(xviii) (1687-1691 CE) Suleiman; and
(xix) (1691-1695 CE) Ahmed; and
(xx) (1695-1703 CE) Mustafa; and
(xxi) (1703-1730 CE) Ahmed; and
(xxii) (1730-1754 CE) Mahmud; and
(xxiii) (1754-1757 CE) Osman; and
(xxiv) (1757-1774 CE) Mustafa; and
(xxv) (1774-1789 CE) Abdul Hamid; and
(xxvi) (1789-1807 CE) Selim; and
(xxvii) (1807-1808 CE) Mustafa; and
(xxviii) (1808-1839 CE) Mahmud; and
(xxix) (1839-1861 CE) Abdulmejid; and
(xxx) (1861-1876 CE) Abdulaziz; and
(xxxi) (1876-1909 CE) Abdul Hamid; and
(xxxii) (1909-1918 CE) Mehmed.

7.10 – Western Civilisation Sovereign Rank & Title

Article 255 – Western Civilisation Sovereign Rank & Title

818. ***Western Civilisation Sovereign Rank & Title*** represents the Sovereign Ranks and Titles of the Western Christian Civilisation, also known as the "Anglo-Saxon Empire" from 8th Century to 14th Century. Western Civilisation Sovereign Rank & Title

Article 256 – Emperor (Father)

819. ***Emperor*** is a Rank first created under the three main Holly Bloodlines known as the *Fleur-de-lif* (flower of life) in the 8th Century CE meaning "Supreme Christian Sovereign" of the Western Christian Civilisation and Empire. The corresponding Title for an *Emperor* was ***Father***. Emperor

820. The Sacred Law defining both the Holy Roman Emperor and the function of the Roman Pontiff, was first defined no later than 741 CE as immutable and unchangeable before all Heaven and Earth:- Sacred Law of Holly Roman Emperors

(i) Only a suitable male of Holly Blood of one of the three primary lines called the *Fleur-de-lif* (flower of life) and known in history as the *Sangreal* and *Holy Grail*, could be Holy Roman Emperor. No person, not of Holly Blood has ever been a legitimate or valid Holy Roman Emperor; and

(ii) The three stems of the *Fleur-de-lif* (flower of life) were the (1) Holly Cornelius Lines, dating back to the original Holly Roman Emperors; and then (2) Holly Saxon Lines, as the protectors of Civilised Law and the Holly; and (3) Holly Irish Lines as the central and original stem; and

(iii) Under Sacred Law of Western Civilisation and the founding of the Roman Catholic Church, one stem could only produce seven Emperors and Popes, before the next stem would receive its right. Thus under such a law, it was conceived that the world could not possibly be without valid Divine Representation. This is the birth of the saying "seven times seven times seven"; and

(iv) The first emperors were to be the Franks, followed by the Saxons and then the Irish, before returning to the Franks; and

(v) The first Holy Roman Emperor was Charles Martel in 741 CE and not his son Charlemagne in 800 CE; and

(vi) None of the Holly Bloodlines have ever died out, as falsely misrepresented in the corruption of Sacred Law and the function of the *Fleur-de-lif* (flower of life) and "seven times seven times seven".

821. The Franks, Saxons and Irish all adopted standard regnal names for positions of Holly Roman Emperors:- Standard Regnal Names of Holly Roman Emperors

(i) ***Charles*** (Franks): In Latin *Carolus* meaning "great; one who sings the praises of God"; and

(ii) ***Henry*** (Saxons): In Old Saxon Heinrick means "benevolent ruler of the home"; and

(iii) ***Bórá*** (Boru) (Irish): In Ancient Irish means "fair and gracious ruler".

822. The following is the proper list of Holly Roman Emperors of the *Fleur-de-lif* (flower of life) as referenced in the most sacred scripture *Lebor Clann Glas*, from the first foundation of the Western Christian Empire and the Roman Catholic Church:- History of Holly Roman Emperors

Carolingian Emperors

(i) (744-768 CE) ***Charles*** (Aurelius Angleramus also known as "Pepin The Short"); and

(ii) (768-814 CE) ***Charles II*** (Aurelius Adventius also known as "Charlemagne"); and

(iii) (814-845 CE) ***Charles III*** (Aurelius Adalbertus); and

(iv) (845-857 CE) ***Charles IV*** (Aurelius Artaldus); and

(v) (857-861 CE) ***Charles V*** (Aurelius Adeldus); and

(vi) (861-886 CE) ***Charles VI*** (Aurelius Angelvin); and

(vii) (886-936 CE) ***Charles VII*** (Aurelius Anscharus); and

Saxon Emperors

(viii) (936-973 CE) ***Otto*** (Hatto Hedwig); and

(ix) (973-983 CE) ***Henry I*** (Hatto Heinrik); and

(x) (983-1024 CE) ***Henry II*** (Hatto Heinrik II); and

(xi) (1024-1065 CE) ***Henry III*** (Heinrik III); and

(xii) (1065-1106 CE) ***Henry IV*** (Heinrik IV); and

(xiii) (1106-1125 CE) ***Henry V*** (Heinrik V); and

(xiv) (1125-1166 CE) ***Henry VI*** (Heinrik VI); and

Irish Emperors

(xv) (1166-1171 CE) ***Bórá (Boru) I*** (Diarmaida (Dermod) Mór); and

(xvi) (1171-1194 CE) ***Bórá (Boru) II*** (Domnall Mór (mac Diarmaida)); and

(xvii) (1194-1215 CE) ***Bórá (Boru) III*** (Donal Mór na Corra); and

(xviii) (1215-1240 CE) ***Bórá (Boru) IV*** (Donnchadh Mór Cairbreach); and

(xix) (1240-1271 CE) ***Bórá (Boru) V*** (Domnall Mór Ruad); and

(xx) (1271-1307 CE) ***Bórá (Boru) VI*** (Domchadh Mór Ruadh); and

French Emperors

(xxi) (1307-1328 CE) ***Charles VIII*** (King Charles VI); and

(xxii) (1328-1380 CE) ***Charles IX*** (King Louis X); and

(xxiii) (1380-1422 CE) ***Charles X*** (King Charles VII); and

(xxiv) (1422-1461 CE) ***Charles XI*** (King Louis XI); and

(xxv) (1461-1483 CE) ***Charles XII*** (King Charles VIII); and

(xxvi) (1483-1515 CE) ***Charles VIII*** (King Louis XII).

823. The creation of false Holy Roman Emperors was first orchestrated in 1166 by the Morosini in Venice as the House of Welf (the Wolves) and Kings of Italy (since 1061) and "Holly" by marriage through Beatrice the first born child and daughter of Holly Roman Emperor Henry III:- Creation of False Holy Roman Emperors

(i) The marriage of Domenico Morosini (as King Konrad of Italy 1051-1099) and Holly Princess Beatrice, first born daughter of Saxon Holly Roman Emperor Henry III, created the famous House of Welf and elevated for the first time a Moor bloodline to "Holly". The Morosini then saw themselves as the rightful heir to the third leaf of the *Fleu-de-Lif*, in direct competition to the Holly Irish Emperors and Popes at Avignon in France. Thus when Henry VI died in 1166, Pietro Domenico Morosini as King Konrad of Italy, was "coronated" by his first cousin "Holly" Antipope Lucius (Pietro III Leoni Orsini) in Rome; and

(ii) The Morosini continued to maintain their war and dispute against the Irish and French as legitimate Holly Popes and Emperors until Pisa was defeated and destroyed in 1184, then Giovanni Gaetano Orsini as Pope Lucius IV was captured and executed in 1303 and finally Pietro Marino Morosini as Emperor Frederick II was finally captured and executed in 1307. If not for the sudden return of Haemorrhagic Fever, Laguna (Venice) itself would have been destroyed; and

(iii) The function of Anti Holy Roman Emperor did not then return until Frederick the Habsburg, crowned by Antipope Gabriele Corraro aka "Pope Alexander" around 1452; and

(iv) The name ***Habsburg*** is a title and rank created by Venetian Antipope Angelo Corraro meaning "custodian of (all) cities" from *habs, haben* meaning "to have, hold or own" and *burg* meaning "city, cities"; and

(v) The false Holy Roman Emperor line was abolished in 1806 by Napoleon, with Francis, son of Leopold the Last.

Article 257 – Roman Pontiff (Pope)

824. ***Roman Pontiff*** is a Rank first created under the three main Holly Bloodlines known as the *Fleur-de-lif* (flower of life) in the 8th Century CE meaning "Supreme Spiritual Leader" of the Western Christian Civilisation and Empire. The corresponding Title for *Roman Pontiff* was ***Pope*** (Ηγεμών) meaning "the only commander or only chief". Roman Pontiff

825. The following is the proper list of Holly Popes of the *Fleur-de-lif* (flower of life) as referenced in the most sacred scripture *Lebor Clann Glas*, from the first foundation of the Western Christian Empire and the Roman Catholic Church from 741 to 1515:- History of Holly Roman Pontiffs

Carolingian Popes

(i) (741-772 CE) ***Petrus*** (Aurelius Abellus); and

(ii) (772-813 CE) ***Stephen*** (Aurelius Animosus); and

(iii) (814-845 CE) ***Pius*** (Aurelius Adalbertus as Charles II); and

(iv) (845-857 CE) ***Paschal*** (Aurelius Artaldus as Charles III); and

(v) (857-861 CE) ***Boniface*** (Aurelius Adeldus as Charles IV); and

(vi) (861-886 CE) ***Eugenius*** (Aurelius Angelvin as Charles V); and

(vii) (886-936 CE) ***Formosus*** (Aurelius Anscharus as Charles VI); and

Saxon Popes

(viii) (936-973 CE) ***Benedict*** (Hatto Hedwig); and

(ix) (973-983 CE) ***Benedict*** (Hatto Heinrik); and

(x) (983-1024 CE) ***Benedict*** (Hatto Heinrik II); and

(xi) (1024-1065 CE) ***Benedict*** (Heinrik III); and

(xii) (1065-1106 CE) ***Benedict*** (Heinrik IV); and

(xiii) (1106-1125 CE) ***Benedict*** (Heinrik V); and

(xiv) (1125-1144 CE) ***Benedict*** (Heinrik VI); and

Irish Popes

(xv) (1166-1171 CE) ***Celestine*** (Diarmaida (Dermod) Mór); and

(xvi) (1171-1194 CE) ***Nicholas*** (Domnall Mór (mac Diarmaida)); and

(xvii) (1194-1215 CE) ***Vigilis*** (Donal Mór na Corra); and

(xviii) (1215-1240 CE) ***Adrianus*** (Donnchadh Mór Cairbreach); and

(xix) (1240-1271 CE) ***Honorius*** (Domnall Mór Ruad); and

(xx) (1271-1307 CE) ***Martinus*** (Domchadh Mór Ruadh); and

(xxi) (1307-1316 CE) **Vitalis** (Diarmuid Cléirech); and

French Popes

(xxii) (1316-1328 CE) ***Clemens I*** (King Charles VI); and

(xxiii) (1328-1380 CE) ***Clemens II*** (King Louis X); and

(xxiv) (1380-1422 CE) ***Clemens III*** (King Charles VII); and

(xxv) (1422-1461 CE) ***Clemens IV*** (King Louis XI); and

(xxvi) (1461-1483 CE) ***Clemens V*** (King Charles VIII); and

(xxvii) (1483-1515 CE) ***Clemens VI*** (King Louis XII).

826. The following is the list of Anti-Popes as referenced in the most sacred scripture *Lebor Clann Glas*, that ruled until the introduction of the College of Cardinals:- List of Anti-Popes

(i) (1166-1198) ***Lucius*** (Pietro III Leoni Orsini, Rome); and

(ii) (1198-1227) ***Lucius II*** (Pietro IV Orsini, Rome); and

(iii) (1127-1261) ***Lucius III*** (Giacinto Bobone Orsini, Rome); and

(iv) (1261-1303) ***Lucius IV*** (Giovanni Gaetano Orsini, Rome)* captured and killed by King Charles VI (1285-1328) of France; and

(v) (1328-1362) ***Alexander*** (Niccolò Orsini, Venice); and

(vi) (1362-1378) ***Innocens*** (Pietro Condulmer, Venice); and

(vii) (1378-1406) ***Urbanus*** (Pietro Barbo, Venice); and

(viii) (1406-1447) ***Gregory*** (Angelo Corraro, Venice); and

(ix) (1447-1464) ***Callixtus*** (Gabriele Condulmer-Corraro, Venice); and

(x) (1464-1494) ***Sixtus*** (Pietro Barbo-Corraro, Venice) * captured and killed by Charles VIII (1461-1483) of France; and

(xi) (1494-1513) ***Julius*** (Giuliano della Rovere, Genoa) * killed by Cosimo de Medici; and

(xii) (1513-1534) ***Leo*** (Giovanni di Lorenzo de Medici, Florence) * killed by Charles V Habsburg after siege and conquest of Florence; and

(xiii) (1534-1559) ***Paul*** (Alessandro Farnese (Orsini), Venice).

827. The following is the list of Roman Pontiffs as referenced in the most sacred scripture *Lebor Clann Glas*, elected under the College of Cardinals model:- List of Roman Pontiffs

(i) (1559-1565) ***Pius*** (IV) (Giovanni Angelo de Medici, Florence); and

(ii) (1566-1572) **Pius** (V) (Antonio Ghislieri, Genoa); and

(iii) (1572-1585) ***Gregory*** (XIII) (Ugo Boncompagni, Venice); and

(iv) (1585-1590) ***Sixtus*** (V) (Felice Peretti di Montalto, Venice); and

(v) (1590-1590) **Urban** (VII) (Giovanni Battista Castagna, Genoa); and

(vi) (1590-1591) **Gregory** (XIV) (Niccolò Sfondrati, Genoa); and

(vii) (1591-1591) **Innocent** (IX) (Giovanni Antonio Facchinetti, Bologna); and

(viii) (1592-1605) **Clement** (VIII) (Ippolito Aldobrandini, Florence); and

(ix) (1605-1605) ***Leo*** (XI) (Alessandro Ottaviano de Medici, Florence); and

(x) (1605-1621) ***Paul*** (V) (Camillo Borghese, Siena); and

(xi) (1621-1623) ***Gregory*** (XV) (Alessandro Ludovisi, Bologna); and

(xii) (1623-1644) ***Urban*** (VIII) (Maffeo Barberini, Florence); and

(xiii) (1644-1655) ***Innocent*** (X) (Giovanni Battista Pamphili, Genoa); and

(xiv) (1655-1667) **Alexander** (VII) (Fabio Chigi, Siena); and

(xv) (1667-1669) ***Clement*** (IX) (Giulio Rospigliosi, Pisa); and

(xvi) (1670-1676) ***Clement*** (X) (Emilio Bonaventura Altieri,

Venice); and

(xvii) (1676-1689) ***Innocent*** (XI) (Benedetto Odescalchi, Genoa); and

(xviii) (1689-1691) ***Alexander*** (VIII) (Pietro Vito Ottoboni, Venice); and

(xix) (1691-1700) ***Innocent*** (XII) (Antonio Pignatelli, Naples); and

(xx) (1700-1721) ***Clement*** (XI) (Giovanni Francesco Albani, Urbino); and

(xxi) (1721-1724) ***Innocent*** (XIII) (Michelangelo Conti, Lazio); and

(xxii) (1724-1730) ***Benedict*** (XIII) (Pietro Francesco Orsini, Venice); and

(xxiii) (1730-1740) ***Clement*** (XII) (Lorenzo Corsini, Florence); and

(xxiv) (1740-1758) ***Benedict*** (XIV) (Prospero Lorenzo Lambertini, Bologna); and

(xxv) (1758-1769) ***Clement*** (XIII) (Carlo della Torre di Rezzonico, Venice); and

(xxvi) (1769-1774) ***Clement*** (XIV) (Giovanni Vincenzo Ganganelli, Venice); and

(xxvii) (1775-1799) ***Pius*** (VI) (Count Giovanni Angelo Braschi, Venice); and

(xxviii) (1800-1823) ***Pius*** (VII) (Barnaba Niccolò Chiaramonti, Venice); and

(xxix) (1823-1829) ***Leo*** (XII) (Count Annibala della Genga, Genga); and

(xxx) (1829-1830) ***Pius*** (VIII) (Francesco Saverio Castiglioni, Marche); and

(xxxi) (1831-1846) ***Gregory*** (XVI) (Bartolomeo Alberto Cappellari, Venice); and

(xxxii) (1846-1878) ***Pius*** (IX) (Count Giovanni Mastai-Ferretti, Ancona); and

(xxxiii) (1878-1903) ***Leo*** (XIII) (Gioacchino Luigi Pecci, Rome); and

(xxxiv) (1903-1914) ***Pius*** (X) (Giuseppe Melchiorre Sarto, Venice); and

(xxxv) (1914-1922) ***Benedict*** (XV) (Giacomo Della Chiesa, Genoa); and

(xxxvi) (1922-1939) ***Pius*** (XI) (Achille Ambrogio Ratti, Venice); and

(xxxvii) (1939-1958) ***Pius*** (XII) (Eugenio Pacelli, Rome); and

(xxxviii) (1958-1963) ***John*** (XXIII) (Angelo Roncalli, Bergamo); and

(xxxix) (1963-1978) ***Paul*** (VI) (Giovanni Montini , Venice); and

(xl) (1978-1978) ***John Paul*** (I) (Albino Luciani, Belluno); and

(xli) (1978-2005) ***John Paul*** (II) (Karol Józef Wojtyła, Poland); and

(xlii) (2005-2013 ***Benedict*** (XVI) (Joseph Ratzinger, Germany); and

(xliii) (2013- ***Francis*** (Jorge Bergoglio, Argentina) * Recognised as first of Supreme Patriarchs under most sacred Covenant *Pactum De Singularis Caelum.*

Article 258 – King/Queen

828. ***King or Queen*** are a Rank and Title first created under the three main Holly Bloodlines known as the *Fleur-de-lif* (flower of life) in the 8th Century CE meaning "Holly Christian Sovereign" of the Western Christian Civilisation and Empire. The corresponding Title for a King or Queen was "majesty". King

829. Contrary to deliberately false etymology and absurd claims, the word King (and Queen) originate from the Irish term ***Cuíng*** from the Irish root words *cuí* meaning "fitting, proper" and *ung* meaning "anoint, anointed". The original true seven meanings of *Cuíng* (King) are:- Origin of Word for King

(i) Leader and guide; and

(ii) Bond, obligation; and

(iii) Ruler, tie, beam; and

(iv) Humility, strength; and

(v) Support, assistance; and

(vi) Defensive armour, protection; and

(vii) Champion.

830. From the 8th Century, the fundamental requirements to be a King (or Queen) has always been:- Requirements of being King (or Queen)

(i) One born from a legitimate and recognised Holly Bloodline;

and

(ii) One demonstrating the necessary character and traits to be a Christian Sovereign, as defined by the word King itself; and

(iii) One who has been duly and properly anointed through Coronation into the person of Sovereign.

831. So strong is the history of the title King to requirement of Holly Blood and service, there is no credible evidence of the title being used by Non-Holly or merchant pirate clans until the 18th Century at the earliest:- Strength of history of Holly origin of King (and Queen)

(i) It appears the title "Prince" was used extensively as the Non-Holly alternative to a Ruler from the 13th Century to the present; and

(ii) Even when Non-Holly administrations finally began falsely claiming to be Kings (or Queens) from 18th Century, the titles frequently defaulted back to Prince and "Majesty".

832. Given there is clear evidence that Holly lines reconnected through Sovereign Monarch lines in Europe by the 19th and 20th Centuries, the present Maxims recognise that most reigning European Sovereign Monarchs are true and legitimate Kings and Queens, subject to the following:- Recognition of Sovereign Monarchs as true Kings and Queens

(i) A Sovereign family that denies the present maxims or the most sacred Covenant *Pactum De Singularis Caelum* therefore denies their own legitimacy, heritage and authority and is equivalent to abdication of any spiritual, moral or legal authority; and

(ii) A Sovereign family by definition is solemnly obligated to support, defend and protect Ucadia and its laws and precepts. A Sovereign family that does not support, defend or protect Ucadia, disavows their own rights of authority and power.

Article 259 – Statholder

833. A ***Statholder*** is an 8th Century CE rank and title created under Holly Western Civilisation in recognition of Non-Holly leaders elected by a Noble Class of a State to represent the people. The title of Statholder is equivalent to "steward". Statholder

834. The title of Statholder represented a significant number of States within the Western Christian Empire from the 8th Century until its collapse in the 1300s due to the Great Death of over 100 million people:- History and background of Statholder

(i) The Statholder as steward, was equivalent to a Holly bloodline King, except such a position required election by the Noble class of Marque and Barons; and

(ii) The role of Statholder had a profound influence across Europe and the world and was the primary model adopted by Pisa, Venice and other merchant city states and empires as they rose to power; and

(iii) The title of Statholder ceased to be used after 1300s until being revised in the 16th Century as Stadholder under the Dutch Republic of United Provinces; and

(iv) Unlike the original function of the Statholder, the House of Orange-Nassau functioned more as monarchs than stewards, culminating with the family being recognised as the first monarchs of Netherlands in the 19th Century.

Article 260 - Marque/Marquess

835. ***Marque*** or ***Marquess*** is a Rank first created under the three main Holly Bloodlines known as the *Fleur-de-lif* (flower of life) in the 8th Century CE meaning "Regional Christian Ruler" of the Western Christian Civilisation and Empire. The corresponding Title for *Marque* was ***Lord or Lady***. Marque

Article 261 - Baron/Baroness

836. ***Baron*** or ***Baroness*** is a Rank first created under the three main Holly Bloodlines known as the *Fleur-de-lif* (flower of life) in the 8th Century CE meaning "Local Ruler" of the Western Christian Civilisation and Empire. The corresponding Title for a *Baron* was ***Sir or Madam***. Baron

Article 262 - Bishop

837. ***Bishop*** is a Title and Rank first created under the three main Holly Bloodlines known as the *Fleur-de-lif* (flower of life) in the 8th Century CE meaning "the leaders of the church" of the Western Christian Civilisation and Empire. The word comes from the ancient Irish word *biscóip* meaning "pivotal support and hinge". Bishop

838. The concept of Bishop (*Biscóip*) originates from the famous twelve priories (*Prióireacht*) and Primate (*Primáit*) of Ireland as the reconstituted Tree of Life in 527CE and then the design of the Roman Catholic Church by 722 CE:- History of Title of Bishop

(i) The *Tree of Life* were twelve world famous centres of learning in Ireland, positioned as a great Irish Cross including Canoin, Cuilde (Armagh), Cliathré (Central Dublin), Cairbre (Inishmurray), Chuirche, Carrickmacross, Carrick, Cill (Kells), Cúill, Cuilinn Airdhe (Clonard), Creevelea and Cluain (Clonmacnoise). The Primates were known as the "Twelve Apostles"; and

(ii) Irish Primáit (Primate) Béocáin of Prióireacht (Priory) Cuilinn Airdhe (Clonard) was the main architect of creating the Roman Catholic Church in oppositions to the corruptions of the Eastern Christian Empire, with the highest position being the Roman Pontiff as Pope, then Biscóips (Bishops), Preíosts (Priests), Móinks (Monks) and then Nóins (Nuns); and

(iii) In 722 CE, the first office of Biscóip (Bishop) created in history was the Holly Primáit Biscóip King (Primate Bishop) of true Christianity and the Roman Catholic Church being Holly King Domnall Ua Breá (Mac Carthair Breá) of Inisfáil (Ireland). The position did not end until the murder of the last Holly Bishop King Domhnal na Druimanam by the Venetian English mercenaries at Black Castle, near Glin, Co. Limerick in 1589; and

(iv) In 734 CE, the second Biscóip (Bishop) appointed in history was Irish Apostle Ailerán (Alcuin) of Cuilinn Airdhe (Clonard) the first Primate Biscóip (Bishop) of Angland (France) of the Royal Household of the Franks and Head Tutor of the Royal Household; and

(v) In 734/735CE, the next Biscóip (Bishop) appointed in history were Irish Apostle Donnán (Dallán Forgaill) of Cuilde (Armagh) as the first Primate Biscóip (Bishop) of Wealand (Wales) in history; and Irish Apostle Cillín (Killian) of Carrickmacross as the first Primate Biscóip (Bishop) of Deutschland (Germany) in history; and and Irish Apostle Colúnbó (Columba) of Cill (Kells) as the first Primate Biscóip (Bishop) of Scotland in history; and and Irish Apostle Gahl (Gall) of Cliathré (Central Dublin) as the first Primate Biscóip (Bishop) of Burgenland (Austria and Switzerland) in history; and Irish Apostle Breandán of Carrick as the first Primate Biscóip (Bishop) of Friesland (Netherands) in history; and Irish Apostle Áedan (Máedóc) of Chuirche as the first Primate Biscóip (Bishop) of Daneland (Central and South West England), and the first Archbishop of Canterbury in history; and

(vi) For the first one hundred years in the formation of the Roman

Catholic Church until the 9th Century, almost all Catholic Bishops were Irish; and from the 9th Century to the 13th Century CE, almost all Catholic Bishops were expected to be educated first in one of the great Christian Priories of Ireland.

Article 263 – Seneschal

839. ***Seneschal*** is an 8th Century Rank and Title of the primary head of government administration of the Holly Roman Emperor. The word comes from Irish *Seanascal* meaning "great person of the council". Seneschal

Article 264 – Mayor (Mayer)

840. ***Mayor*** or ***Mayer*** is an 8th Century Rank and Title as head official of a city. The word from the Irish word *méara* meaning "key digit, finger, toe, arm or leg". From the 1300s following the Black Death, the function and power of a Mayor increased significantly as city states became the centre of civilisation and the rebuilding of society. Mayor (Mayer)

Article 265 – Marschal (Marshal)

841. ***Marshal*** is an 8th Century Rank and Title as head of armed forces. The word comes from the Irish word and title *Marascal* meaning "Great person of the sea". Marschal (Marshal)

Article 266 – Steward

842. ***Steward*** is a 14th Century Rank and Title denoting the protector of people, livestock and property of a city or estate. The word originally comes from the word *sty* meaning "enclosure, hall, compound" and *ward* meaning "keeper, guard, protector". Steward

Article 267 – Chancellor

843. ***Chancellor*** is an 8th Century Rank and Title of the chief administrative officer of a chancery under the Holly Western Christian Empire. The position was revived to mean "chief administrative officer" from 1660 under the reforms of parliament and the City of London appointing Charles II as monarch of England. Chancellor

Article 268 – Chamberlain

844. **Chamberlain** is an 8th Century Rank and Title of the vaults and chambers of money and valuables under the Holly Western Christian Empire. The position was revived to mean "chief of the royal household" from 1660 under the reforms of parliament and the City Chamberlain

of London appointing Charles II as monarch of England.

Article 269 - Duke/Duchess

845. ***Duke*** is a Title and Rank first created in England in 1511 as the highest ranking minister and head of government under the young King Henry VIII (1509-1547) upon the arrival of the exiled Venetian Patrician families. Duke/Duchess

846. The word Duke comes from the adaption in 1511/1512 of the Old Gaelic word *dúchan/dúch* meaning "nightfall, to plunge (into) darkness, to lower the head (and body) to prevent being struck":- Origin of Title of Duke

(i) The claim that the word Duke comes from Latin is an absurdity, as the Latin words *dux* and *duco* are late medieval constructs with no root language provenance. The Roman Empire never used the word *dux* and any claims to the contrary are patently false and deliberately misleading; and

(ii) It is far more likely that the word Duke was chosen by the Venetian exiles from Gaelic because of its phonetic similarities to the word "Doge", and its similarity of subservience to a higher power.

847. The Rank and Title of *Duke* and not Chancellor or Lord Chancellor is the first creation of a prime minister and head of government title in England by 1512, as the title of Chancellor was not introduced until the Commonwealth Government of Great Britain (1642-1660):- Duke not Lord Chancellor as first minister

(i) The seven Great Officers of the Commonwealth of Great Britain (1641-1660) was a creation under Venetian descended officers and officials under the court of Charles I, who sought to create new model based upon the Republic of Venice being Thomas Pride, Thomas Grei, Thomas Roth, Thomas Ire, Thomas Lusty, Thomas Monck and Thomas Constable; and

(ii) Under the seven Lords of the Commonwealth of Great Britain, Thomas Pride (Pryde) was appointed the first *Lord Steward*, Thomas Grei was appointed the first *Lord Chancellor*, Thomas Roth was appointed the first *Lord Chamberlain (Treasurer)*, Thomas Ire was appointed the first *Lord Proctor (Judge)*, Thomas Lusty was appointed the first *Lord Keeper* of the Seal, Thomas Constable was appointed the first *Lord Marshal,* Thomas Monck was appointed the first *Lord Reeve* (Sheriff); and

(iii) After the City of London Guilds funded mercenary forces to defeat the Commonwealth of Great Britain and appoint

Charles II as an "agent" of Parliament by 1660, the title of Lord Chancellor was made the supreme minister of government until the 19th Century when the position of Prime Minister was introduced under the United Kingdom; and

(iv) From 1660, the position of Duke was converted into five sub-kingdoms of England and Wales being Cornwall, Norfolk, Somerset, Richmond and Grafton.

848. Contrary to false and misleading history, the prime minister and head of government of England as Duke was held by Venetian nobility under English names from its first creation in 1512, to its dissolution in 1641:- History of Title of Duke/Duchess

(i) (1515-1529) Thomas Wolsey (Lorenzo Giustiniani, son of Bernardo); and

(ii) (1529-1532) Thomas More (Morosini); and

(iii) (1532-1544) Thomas Audley; and

(iv) (1544-1551) Thomas Wriothesley; and

(v) (1551-1579) Thomas Goodrich; and

(vi) (1579-1587) Thomas Bromley; and

(vii) (1596-1625) Thomas Egerton; and

(viii) (1625-1640) Thomas Coventry.

Article 270 - Earl

849. ***Earl*** is a Title and Rank first created around 1514 under Henry VIII specifically for key exiled Venetian nobility as they created English names and settled. Any claim that the title has an earlier provenance than the 16th Century is a falsity. Earl

850. The original Title and Ranks of Earl as created from 1514 to 1618 include:- History of Title of Earl

(i) The Earl of Shrewsbury; and

(ii) The Earl of Derby; and

(iii) The Earl of Huntingdon; and

(iv) The Earl of Pembroke (1551) and

(v) The Earl of Devon (1553); and

(vi) The Earl of Lincoln (1572); and

(vii) The Earl of Suffolk (1603); and

(viii) The Earl of Exeter (1605); and

(ix) The Earl of Salisbury (1605); and

(x) The Earl of Montgomery (1605); and

(xi) The Earl of Northampton (1618).

Article 271 - Cardinal

851. ***Cardinal*** is a Rank and Title first created in 1534 under AntiPope Paul (1534-1559) (Alessandro Farnese (Orsini), Venice) to end the bloodshed between the Italian banking families of Venice, Genoa and Florence through the creation of the College of Cardinals. The meaning of Cardinal is a direct copy of the original meaning of Bishop meaning "hinge". Cardinal

852. The claims that the position of Cardinal and the College of Cardinals was created in 9th Century is an absurdity and falsity, designed to hide the true origin of the Roman Catholic Church:- History of Title of Cardinal

(i) Prior to the arrival of AntiPope Paul (1534-1559) (Alessandro Farnese (Orsini), Venice), the Italian Banking States in opposition to the true Roman Catholic Church had not established any effective administrative hierarchy of their religion; and

(ii) AntiPope Paul was instrumental in introducing the position of Cardinal to appease the Patrician families of Florence, Genoa and Venice by granting them ecclesiastical and voting rights of Bishops without necessarily having to profess or live as consecrated clergy. Consequently, all of the heads of major Patrician families in Italian states suddenly became Cardinals in the 16th Century, without any previous genuine history of ecclesiastical calling; and

(iii) The creation of the College of Cardinals had the immediate effect of quelling (for a time) the wars for Rome and the papacy between the Italian states by using force.

Article 272 – Prince/Princess

853. A ***Prince*** is a Rank and Title that arose in the mid to late 1200s to describe a *warlord* or "one who rules by force and terror (war)". The word comes from the Latin *prae* meaning "first, before" and *incipio* meaning "I seize upon, I take, I lay hold of". Prince/Princess

854. There appears no attempt to imply any form of "royalty" associated with the concept of a Prince (as warlord) until the 16th Century:- Changing nature of Prince

(i) The publication of the text "The Prince" by Venice marks the first time a publication was specifically addressed to such powerful warlords (princes) scattered across Europe and how they might rise up to become leaders of "states" as princedoms, in contrast to the ancient Holly concept of Kingdoms; and

(ii) The text essentially carried the offer to powerful warlords across Europe to unify under a new structure controlled by the Italian city state controlled Vatican as a "New World Order".

Article 273 – Plantagentis

855. ***Plantagentis*** is a Rank and Title first formed by the Holly French Bloodlines in the 10th Century for Vasconia (Gascony) leaders as the head of the French Foreign Legion. The title comes from two Latin words *planta* meaning "heal of the foot" and *agentis* meaning "authorised representative, agent". Plantagentis

856. Throughout the history of the first formation of the French Foreign Legion from 10th Century to 16th Century, the Plantagentis (Basque leaders) of Vasconia (Gascony) remained steadfast and loyal to the Holly throughout their campaigns:- Plantagentis and Vasconia (Gascony)

(i) It was Carolingian Leader Charles Martel who first recognised the Basque as their own state and people from the 8th Century as Vasconia (Gascony); and

(ii) In 1099, Plantagentis Guillermo of Vasconia (Gascony), also known as "William the Conqueror" crushed the Amorican pirates once and for all on the Island of Aestings (Battle of Hastings), also known as the Isle of White; and

(iii) In the 14th Century, Plantagentis Eduardo of Vasconia (Gascony) was instrumental in bringing the French coastal cities back under control including Bordeaux, Bayonne, Rochelle, Nantes and Calais, before restoring order in London by 1355; and

(iv) The last Plantagentis Lord Marshal of England was Ricardo of Angoumois who died in battle in 1485 against the Venetian funded Welsh mercenary warlord Henry Tudor of Chester; and

(v) By the 17th Century, the Venetian exiles in England, began using the line of "Plantagenet" in support of the Tudor claim to be Plantagenet and blood descendants of the Holly Carolingians and thus the Holly Family.

Article 274 – President

857. A ***President*** is an 18th Century commercial Rank and Title first used in the creation of the Constitution of the United States of America by 1782, representing the "chief executive officer of a republic" as a corporation operating as a nation. President

Article 275 – Prime Minister

858. A ***Prime Minister*** is a Rank and Title first formalised in the United Kingdom under Benjamin Disraeli in 1868 to 1869 and then from 1874 to 1880. Prior to this time, it was a title of ridicule as opposed to a recognised position. The office of Prime Minister of the United Kingdom was not officially mentioned in statute until the 20th century and the Ministers of the Crown Act 1937. Prime Minister

7.11 – Ucadia Civilisation Sovereign Rank & Title

Article 276 – Ucadia Civilisation Sovereign Rank & Title

859. ***Ucadia Civilisation Sovereign Rank & Title*** represents the Sovereign Ranks and Titles of Ucadia Civilisation for the next three thousand two hundred and ten years. It incorporates recognition and acknowledgment of all enlightened Civilisations from the time of the Holly Hyksos of Egypt to the present day, with particular attention to the need for competent, efficient yet flexible government at every level of society. Ucadia Civilisation Sovereign Rank & Title

860. Within Ucadia Civilisation, there exists three primary categories of Sovereign Rank and Title being Executive, Administrative and Agency:- Three categories of Sovereign Rank and Title

(i) ***Executive Offices***: Are supreme positions of office appointed by mandate and defined by constitutional charter; and

(ii) ***Administrative Offices***: Are key administrative positions of office appointed by mandate and defined not only by constitutional charter, but the operation of the Ucadia Codes of Law; and

(iii) ***Executive Agents***: Are key administrative positions derived from the authority of Administrative Offices and appointed by mandate with powers derived from the Administrative Office as Principal.

Article 277 – Ucadia Globe Union Rank & Title

861. The ***Ucadia Globe Union*** is the Highest Sovereign Body within Ucadia Civilisation, representing all regional unions and nations (or "Universities" under Ucadia law). Ucadia Globe Union Rank & Title

862. The following is the list of Executive Offices of the Ucadia Globe Union:- Executive Offices of Ucadia Globe Union

(i) ***General Secretary***: Head of the Globe Secretariat and ex-officio member (Globe Councillor) of the Supreme (Globe) Council; and

(ii) ***Prefect of Globe Senate***: Head of the Globe Senate of Justice and ex-officio member (Globe Councillor) of the Supreme (Globe) Council; and

(iii) ***General Justice***: Head of the Globe Court of Justice and ex-officio member (Globe Councillor) of the Supreme (Globe) Council; and

(iv) ***General Treasurer***: Head of the Globe Treasury and ex-officio member (Globe Councillor) of the Supreme (Globe) Council; and

(v) ***General Marshal***: Head of the Globe Guard and ex-officio member (Globe Councillor) of the Supreme (Globe) Council; and

(vi) ***General Architect***: Head of the Globe Economic Council and ex-officio member (Globe Councillor) of the Supreme (Globe) Council; and

(vii) ***General Ecologist***: Head of the Globe Ecological Council and ex-officio member (Globe Councillor) of the Supreme (Globe) Council; and

(viii) ***General Conservator***: Head of the Globe Cultural Council and ex-officio member (Globe Councillor) of the Supreme (Globe) Council; and

(ix) ***General Surveyor***: Head of the Global Space Council and ex-officio member (Globe Councillor) of the Supreme (Globe) Council; and

(x) ***Globe Councillor***: One Elected Member (Globe Councillor) of the Supreme (Globe) Council from each of the Union Free Societies and Permanent Space Colonies; and

(xi) ***Globe Senator***: Member of the Globe Senate as supreme legislative body of the Ucadia Globe Union.

863. The following is the list of Administrative Offices of the Ucadia Globe Union:-

Administrative Offices of Ucadia Globe Union

(i) ***Executor-General***: Head of one of the twenty two permanent and standard systems and agencies of the Ucadia Globe Union; and

(ii) ***International-Secretary***: Permanent head of Systems Secretariat for one of the twenty two permanent and standard systems and agencies of the Ucadia Globe Union.

864. The following is the list of Executive Agents of the Ucadia Globe Union:-

Executive Agents of Ucadia Globe Union

(i) ***Chief of Staff Globe Councillor***.

Article 278 – Faith of One-Christ Rank & Title

865. The Universal Ecclesia of One Christ, also known as the One Holy Apostolic Universal Ecclesia is the first, highest and supreme association, aggregate, fraternity, body, entity and society of One Heaven sharing spiritual heritage associated with all forms of Christian and Jewish faiths.

Faith of One Christ Rank & Title

866. The following is the list of Ecclesiastical Offices of One Christ:-

Ecclesiastical Offices of Faith of One Christ

(i) ***Supreme Patriarch***: Supreme head of the body of One Christ; and

(ii) ***Patriarch***: Pastoral see of a University or a Customary and Traditional Rite; and

(iii) ***Bishop***: Pastoral custodian of a Diocese or Community of a Customary and Traditional Rite; and

(iv) ***Deacon***: Senior cleric as Deacon-Abbot, Deacon-Diocesan, Deacon-Dean, Deacon-Canon, Deacon-Vicar, Deacon-Prelate or Deacon-Chief of One Christ; and

(v) ***Presbyter***: Ordained and registered cleric of One Christ.

867. The following is the list of Administrative Offices of One Christ:-

Administrative Offices of Faith of One Christ

(i) ***Minister-Secretary***: Patriarch or Bishop as head of one of the supreme organs of One-Christ; and

(ii) ***Minister-General***: Bishop or Deacon as head of university organs of One-Christ; and

(iii) ***Minister***: Deacon or Presbyter as head of diocese organs of One-Christ.

Article 279 – Faith of One-Islam Rank & Title

868. The most sacred and Holy Society of One Islam, also known as the One True Way of Allah is the first, highest and supreme association, aggregate, fraternity, body, entity and society of One Heaven sharing spiritual heritage associated with all forms of Islam. Faith of One Islam Rank & Title

869. The following is the list of Ecclesiastical Offices of One Islam:- Ecclesiastical Offices of Faith of One Islam

(i) ***Supreme Caliph***: Supreme head of the body of One Islam; and

(ii) ***Caliph***: Pastoral steward of a University or a Customary and Traditional Rite; and

(iii) ***Mufti***: Pastoral custodian of a Community or Community of a Customary and Traditional Rite; and

(iv) ***Ulama***: Senior cleric as Ulama-Spiritual, Ulama-Instructional, or Ulama-Chief of One Islam; and

(v) ***Imam***: Ordained and registered cleric of One Islam being: Imam-Fraternal, Imam-Communal, Imam-Militaral, Imam-Instructional, Imam-Secularal or Imam-Missionaral.

870. The following is the list of Administrative Offices of One Islam:- Administrative Offices of Faith of One Islam

(i) ***Wazir-Amanah***: Caliph or Mufti as head of one of the supreme organs of One-Islam; and

(ii) ***Wazir-Aam***: Mufti or Ulama as head of university organs of One-Islam; and

(iii) ***Wazir***: Ulama or Imam as head of community organs of One-Islam.

Article 280 – Faith of One-Spirit Rank & Title

871. The most Sacred Society of One Spirit, also known as the One Holy Apostolic Spirit, also known as One Spirit Tribe and also known simply as One Spirit is the first, highest and supreme association, aggregate, fraternity body, entity and society of One Heaven sharing spiritual heritage associated with traditional, indigenous, Earth based, meditative and eastern customary faiths. Faith of One Spirit Rank & Title

872. The following is the list of Ecclesiastical Offices of One Spirit:- Ecclesiastical Offices of Faith of One Spirit

(i) ***Supreme Recurrence***: Supreme head of the body of One Spirit; and

(ii) ***Elder***: Pastoral steward of a University or a Customary and Traditional Rite; and

(iii) ***Senior***: Pastoral custodian of a Community or Community of a Customary and Traditional Rite; and

(iv) ***Master***: Senior cleric as Master-Spiritual, Master-Instructional, or Master-Chief of One Spirit; and

(v) ***Cleric***: Ordained and registered cleric of One Spirit being: Cleric-Fraternal, Cleric-Communal, Cleric-Militaral, Cleric-Instructional, Cleric-Secularal or Cleric-Missionaral.

873. The following is the list of Administrative Offices of One Spirit:-

Administrative Offices of Faith of One Spirit

(i) ***Mantri-Ayojak***: Elder or Supervisor as head of one of the supreme organs of One-Spirit; and

(ii) ***Mantri-Sardar***: Supervisor or Master as head of university organs of One-Spirit; and

(iii) ***Mantri***: Master or Cleric as head of diocese organs of One-Spirit.

Article 281 – Original Nations Rank & Title

874. The ***Original Nations Rank & Title*** is an Original Sovereign Body of first peoples as native inhabitants as recognised within Ucadia Civilisation.

Original Nations Rank & Title

875. The following is the list of Executive Offices of an Original Nation:-

Executive Offices of Original Nations

(i) ***Elder***: Member of the Council of Elders of an Original Nation as oversight, guidance and wisdom; and

(ii) ***Rà***: Head of the government; and

(iii) ***Seniors***: Representatives of the Members, who elect the Elders.

876. The following is the list of Administrative Offices of the Original Nation:-

Administrative Offices of Original Nations

(i) ***Chief***: Head of a system of government and member of the Council of Chiefs headed by the Rà.

877. The following is the list of Executive Agents of an Original Nation:-

Executive Agents of Original Nations

(i) ***Chief of Staff of Rà***.

Article 282 – Ucadia Regional Union Rank & Title

878. The ***Ucadia Regional Union*** is the second highest Sovereign Body within Ucadia Civilisation. Ucadia Regional Union Rank & Title

879. The following is the list of Executive Offices of a Ucadia Regional Union:- Executive Offices of Ucadia Regional Union

(i) ***Mediator***: Head of the Synod (supreme legislative body of the Union) and ex-officio member (Exarch) of the Sunedrion; and

(ii) ***Alexander***: Head of the Academy (supreme administrative body of the Union) and ex-officio member (Exarch) of the Sunedrion; and

(iii) ***Basileus***: Head of the Basilica (supreme juridical, plenary and appellate forum of law of the Union) and ex-officio member (Exarch) of the Sunedrion; and

(iv) ***Economos***: Head of the Econos (supreme treasury for all revenue, banking and finances concerning the Union) and ex-officio member (Exarch) of the Sunedrion; and

(v) ***Stratagos***: Head of the Stratos (supreme military command resources concerning the Union) and ex-officio member (Exarch) of the Sunedrion; and

(vi) ***Kephalos***: Head of the Energeia (supreme business and trade body of the Union) and ex-officio member (Exarch) of the Sunedrion; and

(vii) ***Mentor***: Head of the Psyches (supreme spiritual and ecclesial body of the Union) and ex-officio member (Exarch) of the Sunedrion; and

(viii) ***Archon***: Member of the Synod as supreme legislative body of the Ucadia Regional Union.

880. The following is the list of Administrative Offices of the Ucadia Regional Union:- Administrative Offices of Ucadia Regional Union

(i) ***Regional-General***: Head of one of the twenty two permanent and standard systems and agencies of the Ucadia Regional Union; and

(ii) ***Regional-Secretary***: Permanent head of Systems Secretariat for one of the twenty two permanent and standard systems and agencies of the Ucadia Regional Union.

881. The following is the list of Executive Agents of the Ucadia Regional Executive Agents of Ucadia

Union:- Regional Union

(i) ***Chief of Staff of Archon***.

Article 283 – Ucadia University Rank & Title

882. The ***Ucadia University*** is a national or state sovereign body within Ucadia Civilisation. Ucadia University Rank & Title

883. The following is the list of Executive Offices of a Ucadia University:- Executive Offices of Ucadia University

(i) ***President***: Head of the Executive Government, Chair of Cabinet, Administration, Military and Law Enforcement; and

(ii) ***Vice-President (Domestic)***: Also known as "Chancellor" as Chair of Domestic Affairs Committee and head of University Court of Chancery; and

(iii) ***Vice-President (International)***: Also known as "Plenipotentiary" as Chair of International Affairs Committee and head of University Sacristy; and

(iv) ***Prefect***: Head of the Parliament (primary legislative Organ of the University); and

(v) ***Justiciar***: Head of the Supreme Court (primary judicial Organ of the University); and

(vi) ***Chamberlain***: Head of the University Secretariat and ex-officio member of the Cabinet; and

(vii) ***Dean***: Head of the University College and ex-officio member of the Cabinet; and

(viii) ***Exchequer***: Head of the University Court of the Exchequer (Treasury) and ex-officio member of the Cabinet; and

(ix) ***Marshal***: Head of the Military and ex-officio member of the Cabinet; and

(x) ***Narrator***: Head of the Library and ex-officio member of the Cabinet; and

(xi) ***Custodian***: Head of the Vestry and ex-officio member of the Cabinet; and

(xii) ***Censor***: Head of the Archives and ex-officio member of the Cabinet; and

(xiii) ***Representative***: Member of the Parliament as supreme legislative body of the Ucadia University.

884. The following is the list of Administrative Offices of a Ucadia Administrative Offices of Ucadia

University:- University

(i) ***Director-General***: Head of one of the twenty two permanent and standard systems and agencies of the Ucadia University; and

(ii) ***Systems-Secretary***: Permanent head of Systems Secretariat for one of the twenty two permanent and standard systems and agencies of the Ucadia University.

885. The following is the list of Executive Agents of a Ucadia University:- Executive Agents of Ucadia University

(i) ***Chief of Staff of President***.

Article 284 – Ucadia Province Rank & Title

886. The ***Ucadia Province*** is the second smallest sovereign administrative body within Ucadia Civilisation. Ucadia Province Rank & Title

887. The following is the list of Executive Offices of a Ucadia Province:- Executive Offices of Ucadia Province

(i) ***Governor***: Head of the government and Chair of the executive Council; and

(ii) ***Speaker***: Head of the Assembly; and

(iii) ***Province Court Justice***: Head of the Province Judiciary; and

(iv) ***Deputy Governor***: Ex-officio member of Provincial Council; and

(v) ***Province Comptroller***: Ex-officio member of Provincial Council; and

(vi) ***Province Procurator***: Ex-officio member of Provincial Council; and

(vii) ***Province Counsel***: Ex-officio member of Provincial Council; and

(viii) ***Province Law Commissioner***: Ex-officio member of Provincial Council.

888. The following is the list of Administrative Offices of a Ucadia Province:- Administrative Offices of Ucadia Province

(i) ***Provincial-General***: Head of one of the twenty two permanent and standard systems and agencies of the Ucadia Province; and

(ii) ***Provincial-Secretary***: Permanent head of Systems Secretariat for one of the twenty two permanent and standard systems and agencies of the Ucadia Province.

889. The following is the list of Executive Agents of a Ucadia Province:- Executive Agents of Ucadia Province

(i) ***Chief of Staff of Governor***.

Article 285 – Ucadia Campus Rank & Title

890. The ***Ucadia Campus*** is the smallest sovereign administrative body within Ucadia Civilisation. Ucadia Campus Rank & Title

891. The following is the list of Executive Offices of a Ucadia Campus:- Executive Offices of Ucadia Campus

(i) ***Campus Commissioner***: Supreme leader of the Campus, and Chair of the executive Campus Convention (Chairman of the Board of Directors); and

(ii) ***Campus Treasurer***: Ex-officio member of Campus Convention (Director); and

(iii) ***Campus Magistrate***: As judicial official of Local Court; and

(iv) ***Campus Superintendent***: Ex-officio member of Campus Convention (Director); and

(v) **Campus Sheriff**: As highest authority of law enforcement within the bounds of the Campus.

Article 286 – Ucadia Foundation Rank & Title

892. The ***Ucadia Foundation*** is a Ucadia entity established by mandate for the formation of a key Ucadia Organ or structure. Ucadia Foundation Rank & Title

893. The following is the list of Executive Offices of the Ucadia Foundation:- Executive Offices of Ucadia Foundation

(i) ***Chairperson***: Chair of the Board; and

(ii) ***Director***: Director of the Board; and

(iii) ***Secretary***: Foundation Secretary; and

(iv) ***Treasurer***: Board Director as Treasurer; and

(v) ***Minister-General***: Chief Executive Officer; and

(vi) ***Executive Officer***.

894. The following is the list of Administrative Offices of the Ucadia Foundation:- Administrative Offices of Ucadia Foundation

(i) ***Manager***: Non-Executive Manager.

Title VIII - Saviour Rank & Title

8.1 – Saviour Rank & Title

Article 287 - Saviour Rank & Title

895. ***Saviour Rank & Title*** is the identification of the office of a particular Divine Saviour of a faith, culture or civilisation by their Rank, Title, Qualifications, Attributes and Works. Saviour Rank & Title

896. A ***Divine Saviour*** is a *Sovereign Claim* or *Sovereign Mandate* via *Sovereign Rule by Revelation* whereby a "flesh and blood" person is proclaimed through self-evident signs, attributes and qualifications that they are a Divine Saviour sent from Heaven to Earth:- Saviour as a Sovereign Claim or Mandate

(i) The Claim of Divine Saviour is one of the oldest methods of claiming supreme sovereign authority and power from the beginning of Human Civilisation; and

(ii) Almost every civilisation and culture has had a Divine Saviour such as the Akkadians who worshipped Adad, the Sumerians who worshipped Ishkur, the early Babylonians who worshipped Hadad, the ancient Egyptians who worshipped Horus, the early Greeks had Adonis, the Phrygians (Turkey and Syria) who worshipped Attis, the Persians and colonies who worshipped Mithra and the Celts who worshipped Esus (later listed as Jesus); and

(iii) Within the faiths of Christianity, Islam, Judaism, Buddhism, Hinduism and many other faiths, the Rank and Title of *Divine Saviour* (or by some other specific cultural Title), is unquestionably accepted as the highest of all sovereign authority and power; and

(iv) Many of these same cultures have recognised in the oldest forms of law the fact that the legitimate appearance of a Divine Saviour matching the specific cultural context requires all followers of a particular faith to acknowledge and obey the authority and direction of the Divine Saviour; and

(v) The primary meaning and nature of "Saviour" is literally one who saves, as the architect of a new civilisation restoring the rule of law, as opposed to a tyrant or despot or impostor.

897. ***Criteria for Qualification of a Divine Saviour*** refers to a set of specific requirements or standards that must be met in order for an individual to be considered eligible or suitable to be identified as a Divine Saviour:- Criteria for Qualification of a Divine Saviour

(i) Each and every major faith, culture and civilisation that refers to a Divine Saviour has specific and established requirements and standards that must be met; and

(ii) The most important and primary source of requirements and standards that any candidate as Divine Saviour must meet is usually found within one or more sacred texts where the necessary qualifications of a Divine Saviour are expressed or implied; and

(iii) As authentic sacred scripture is frequently written using some level of "allegory", many scriptural passages use symbols and metaphors to represent deeper or profound ideas. This can sometimes give rise to confusion and conflict when used as a requirement or standard associated with a Divine Saviour. Some adherents may accept and understand its allegorical nature, while others may insist on its literal truth i.e. "the saviour will come in the clouds from heaven" meaning some human being will have supernatural powers of flight; and

(iv) Many faiths, cultures and civilisations mix the array of requirements and standards for a Divine Saviour together as a "master list", where some standards are highly highly technical but relatively minor, while others represent universal prophecies of the global collapse of civilisation itself; and

(v) Consequently, the requirements and standards for a Divine Saviour in each faith, culture and civilisation can be observed and classified according to "external signs", "major qualifications" and "minor qualifications"; and

(vi) *External Signs* refers to the analysis or description of the state of societies and civilisation or climactic events that may (or may not) signify a prophetic time. These are separated as such analysis and description is notoriously subjective throughout history and has nothing to do with the specific qualifications and actions of a Divine Saviour themselves.

Major Qualification of a Divine Saviour

898. ***Major Qualifications of a Divine Saviour*** refers to fundamental requirements and standards for a Divine Saviour that necessitate overwhelming proof and delivery of substantive, verifiable and detailed actions:-

(i) A candidate must have produced a detailed global solution, not a placeholder document or more scripture, but real, practical and implementable solutions to either save civilisation or in most cases herald the birth of a new better civilisation. This is virtually a universal requirement of all faiths of any authentic Divine Saviour; and one of the key requirements that have allowed the dismissal of the claims of so many who falsely assert themselves as some Divine Saviour; and

(ii) Many faiths and cultures require an authentic candidate to demonstrate a truly global and effective solution to existing or new civilisation that encompasses not only the faith or culture, but other faiths and cultures. Representing yet a further profound paradox, the authentic Divine Saviour is somehow supposed to deliver the answer that genuinely unites all people, without squashing or minimising differences of faith and culture; and

(iii) A candidate usually must possess unprecedented powers of knowledge and wisdom equal to (or in some cases greater than) the first Divine Saviour that founded the particular faith, culture or civilisation. This is especially the case in Christianity, Islam and Judaism; and

(iv) A candidate often must possess specific blood heritage back to a line of prophets or the first Divine Saviour that founded the particular faith, culture or civilisation; and in many cases such a bloodline must be the authentic line not simply the one listed in scripture, yet must somehow reconcile the differences. This is especially the case in Christianity, Islam and Judaism; and

(v) A candidate frequently cannot be an "establishment choice", or from a currently wealthy family, or live and enjoy a life of luxury. Instead many faiths and cultures require a candidate to suffer and endure great hardship and trials of the spirit to fulfil their purpose as Divine Saviour; and

(vi) Many faiths and cultures require an authentic candidate as a Divine Saviour not to act, or claim to be the Divine Saviour – a kind of paradox. In Christianity, Christ himself was claimed to have stated this as a fundamental criteria; and yet there remains dozens of people alive at any given time who falsely claim to be Jesus Christ returned.

899. The generally "universal" major qualification of any authentic Divine Saviour to represent the Architect of a New Civilisation deserves particular attention as it is arguably the most difficult sign to "fake":-

Architect of New Civilisation

(i) All functioning and major civilisations were built from complex and detailed models requiring many tens of thousands of integrated concepts, models and systems across many hundreds or thousands of texts; and

(ii) A single document, even if a thousand pages in length, is still a "placeholder" for a model of civilisation and not the detailed blueprint any authentic Divine Saviour is supposed to deliver;

and

(iii) Because such a major qualification is technically the most difficult, time consuming and complex qualification of any authentic Divine Saviour, it also happens to be the sign argued as least important or "promised will be delivered in the future" by impostors and false Divine Saviours.

900. ***Minor Qualifications of a Divine Saviour*** refers to requirements and standards for a Divine Saviour that are more subjective and open to interpretation:-

Minor Qualifications of a Divine Saviour

(i) The manner and place of birth, the dress and behaviour of the candidate and the claims of piety and miracles are all potentially highly subjective areas that have been blatantly exploited by impostors in the past; and

(ii) Many faiths and cultures require an authenticate candidate to demonstrate extraordinary miracles as demonstration of the endorsement from Heaven of their claim. Rather than being the most difficult, the claim of "miracles" has most frequently been the method that false claimants have asserted themselves to their beguiled followers.

901. The list of key Saviours of various civilisations, empires and cultures over the past 2,500 years include (but is not limited to):-

List of Key Saviours over past 2,500 years

(i) ***Mithra***: Being the Divine Saviour of the Persian Empire and its colonies, including Rome and Athens until 69 CE; and

(ii) ***Lucifer***: Being the Divine Saviour of the Romans from 70-114 CE and then revived from 1660s as "the Holy One" and "Christ" for some groups and institutions; and

(iii) ***Sabaoth (Moloch)***: Being the Divine Saviour of some Yahudi prior to 1st Century BCE and then revived as "the Hidden One" in the 17th Century under the Ashkenazi cult and then again in the 18th Century through the Hasidic cults; and

(iv) ***Risen Christ (Second Coming)***: Being the Divine Saviour of Christians under Roman Catholicism from 8th Century and then all Christians from 17th Century; and

(v) ***Messiah of the Yahudi (Jews)***: Being the Divine Saviour of the Old Testament and "Torah" from 17th Century creation of the Holy Bible; and

(vi) ***Mahdi of Islam***: Being the Divine Saviour of Islam initially from the 14th Century and then updated from the 17th Century with the changes made within Islam following the Holy Bible;

and

(vii) ***Kulkulkan of Maya (Sth America)***: Being the Divine Saviour of the Maya; and

(viii) ***Maitreya of Buddhism***: Being the Divine Saviour and fifth and future Buddha of this world era; and

(ix) ***Kalki of Hinduism***: Being the Divine Saviour and future avatar of Lord Vishnu.

902. In accord with Article 43 (*Sacred Offices and Officers*) of the most sacred Covenant *Pactum De Singularis Caelum*, the nine (9) Forbidden Offices in Heaven and throughout the Solar System are Christ, Cuilliaéan, Emperor, God King, God Queen, Lucifer, Messiah, Anti-Christ and Prophet. This means in practice that other than Ucadia itself, no person, group or entity may claim to hold sovereign authority or power by virtue of one or more of these traditional Sacred Offices. Forbidden Offices in Ucadia

903. Whilst any and all Ucadia members, officers, entities, bodies and associations are forbidden from recognising the active occupation or holding of one or more Forbidden Offices or related office of Divine Saviour, nothing prevents any member, officer, entity, body or association from recognising the fulfilment of one or more criteria, attributes and qualifications in relation to one of more Divine Saviours of different faiths, cultures and civilisations and the formation of Ucadia. Divine Saviour Characteristics and Ucadia

Article 288 – Mithra

904. ***Mithra*** is a Divine Saviour from 5th Century BCE Persian Civilisation representing light, justice, oaths, prosperity and fraternity. Mithra

905. In reference to the origin and context of the Divine Saviour known as *Mithra*:- Origin of Title Mithra

(i) First appears in the Avesta sacred scriptures of Persia and Zoroastrianism; and

(ii) Mithra is the progeny of Ahura Mazda (Sky, Heaven) as father and Anahita (Earth, Life) as mother; and

(iii) Mithra is said to have been born from sacred "holy" rock hill known as (Peta) in the centre of Jerusalem on 14 Nisan (14th March); and

(iv) Mithra was also said to have sacrificed himself for the good of all Humanity, to save Humanity on the same day of his Birth on 14 Nisan (14th March). This day was the most sacred day of all Persia and Roman Calendar known as Dies Sanguinus or "Day of Blood". The night before was called the Paschal, the Passion or "Passover"; and

(v) The Most sacred Prophecy Text of Mithra was the Book of Daniel (from around 5 BCE). No unaltered copy still exists and the version within the Holy Bible from the 17th Century has been heavily altered in terms of key words.

Prophetic Signs & Qualifications of Mithra

906. Within surviving sacred prophetic Mithraic texts of the Book of Daniel, there exists several passages concerning the circumstances and timing of the return of Mithra to Earth at some future date, including:-

(i) Christ Mithra shall come again to Earth (Daniel 7:13-14); and

(ii) Christ Mithra shall return as a flesh and blood man (Daniel 7:13-14); and

(iii) Christ Mithra shall be born again in Jerusalem (Daniel 9:1-19); and

(iv) There shall be those who falsely claim to be Mithra and shall deceive others (Daniel 7:8; 7:20-25); and

(v) One of the key signs of the return of Christ Mithra shall be when the Holly Bloodlines (Holly People) have no power and the world no longer has knowledge of their true history (Daniel 12:7); and

(vi) One of the key signs of the return of Christ Mithra shall be when most of the world shall be desolate of morality (Daniel 11:31,12:11); and

(vii) A sign often attributed to the return of Christ Mithra is the belief in law that all the "dead in law" shall rise and be freed by some miraculous singular act of judgment (Daniel 12:2-3); and

(viii) The greatest sign that Christ has already returned shall be the arrival of the greatest of all climactic tribulations (such as a major once in several million year pole displacement coming to a climax in the next short period of time) being something human civilisation has never in history had to face before (Daniel 12:1); and

(ix) Christ Mithra on his return shall forbid all forms of blood sacrifice (Daniel 12:11); and

(x) Christ Mithra made flesh shall appear overwhelmingly to be a failure and weak, even poor (Daniel 8:24); and

(xi) The works of the true Christ Mithra shall save humanity (Daniel 12:1).

907. There is significant evidence to support that the birth of Holly Irish Prince Cú-Laoch (Yahusiah) the son of Cú-Cúileann (Yasiah and Joseph), also known as Esus Christos (Jesus Christ) was a planned birth to fulfil the Book of Daniel and the prophecies of the Return of Mithra as well as the undisputed king of the Yahudi diaspora:-

Birth of Esus (Cú-Laoch) in 6CE and Mithra

(i) There is strong evidence that Cú-Laoch (Yahusiah), also known as Jesus Christ was born on Dies Sanguinus (Day of Blood), the most important day for Mithra on Nisan (March) 14th and that he was born at the Holly Bethesda Estate at the Mount of Olives in Jerusalem to fulfil the prophecies; and

(ii) As a Holly blood descendent of the old lines of Messiah Kings of the Yahudi, there would have been no dispute as to the claim of Cú-Laoch as Esus being the legitimate Yahudi Messiah. By fulfilling Mithraic prophecy at the same time, his legitimacy would have been universally acknowledged across the ancient world; and

(iii) The proposed arranged marriage of Cú-Laoch as Esus to Princess Mariamne the daughter of Herod Agripiah (Agrippa) demonstrates the acceptance of the legitimacy of Esus as the ultimate Yahudi Messiah to the new line of Yahudi Kings. The offspring of Esus (Jesus Christ) and Mariamne would then be the first bloodline in history to reunify the two opposite and historically opposed Yahudi sects, with one worshipping the one true Divine Creator and the other traditionally worshipping Baal Moloch under different names; and

(iv) The deliberate and clumsy corruptions within the 17th Century English Bibles of Douay-Rheims and King James did not in anyway reinforce or support the historic evidence of Esus as Christ, but introduced contradictions, confusions and inconsistencies that fatally weakened the previous indisputable trust in Esus as Christ under Western Civilisation. This was done in part to create the false story of the Jewish faith that had never existed at the time; and to allow its new religious leaders to claim Esus was never the Yahudi (Jewish) Messiah.

908. There is strong and compelling evidence that Albert Einstein (born March 14, 1879) was groomed from a young age to become the prophetised "Lightbringer" (Mithra returned, Lucifer returned and the Jewish Messiah) and to be promoted as the greatest mind in modern human history:-

Albert Einstein as claimed return of Mithra and Jewish Messiah

(i) Born into a comfortable middle class secular Ashkenazi Jewish German family, the family was strangely offered and granted Swiss Citizenship, with the family moving by 1895. From the earliest age, Albert Einstein was granted exclusive education at some of the most prestigious, expensive and best schools in all of Europe (and the world) at the time, including Petersschule Catholic Elementary School in Munich, then the Luitpold Gymnasium in Munich and then Alte Kanti at Aarau in Switzerland. Despite being an average student and failing entry examination, Albert Einstein was somehow accepted by the world famous Federal Polytechnic School system of Zurich. This is where he met the enigmatic and brilliant young Serbian physics student Mileva Marić. They married by 1903 and it was Mileva Marić who should have been honoured at least as co-author for most of his early famous scientific papers, including his PhD doctoral dissertation; and

(ii) Despite his average academic abilities, Einstein was somehow granted a plum position in the Swiss Patent Office for a few years until it was deemed he was ready to continue his grooming as the "greatest scientist the world has ever known", starting as a junior professor at University of Bern by 1908, before being welcomed in 1913 to Berlin. By 1922 has was awarded the Nobel Prize for Physics; and

(iii) A life long pacifist and notorious womanizer, Einstein is reputed to have had more than three dozen affairs – a scandal for the early 20th Century. Yet despite all the problems that Einstein caused the American custodians of his image, by the time he was convinced to emigrate to the United States, his reputation as the "Lightbringer" was forever etched in US folklore.

Article 289 – Lucifer

909. ***Lucifer*** is a Divine Saviour from 70 CE within the Roman Empire and Persian Civilisation representing light, justice, oaths, prosperity and fraternity. The Luciferian Cult was primarily formed in response to the collapse of Mithraism. Lucifer

910. In reference to the origin and context of the Divine Saviour known as *Lucifer*:- Origin of Lucifer

(i) The word was first introduced as part of the Nomen of the Emperor (Imperator) of the Roman Empire under the official imperial state religion of Iudaeism (Judaism) from 70 CE to 117 CE, upon the collapse of the official state religion of

Mithraism; and

(ii) Lucifer itself means "light bringer", "the illuminator", "saviour", "messiah" and "bringer of good fortune"; and

(iii) The word *Lucifer* was constructed from two (2) Latin words *iucio* meaning "good fortune, good skill, gold work" and *fero* meaning "to carry, to bring forth, produce, to provide"; and

(iv) Both Latin words used to form "Lucifer" are directly taken from ancient Holly Irish being Luci (pronounced 'lucky'), the patron of skills, good fortune, gifts, goldsmiths and craftsman who celebrated his feast day upon the Ides (full moon) of August and is the god of the planet Venus; and feara meaning "men; the best of".

911. The three Lucifer Imperators under Iudaism (Judaism) following the collapse of Mithraism were:- Luciferian Imperators

(i) (69-79 CE) ***Vespasian*** (Luciferus Vespasianus Augustus); and

(ii) (79-81 CE) ***Titus*** (Luciferus Titus Vespasianus Augustus); and

(iii) (81-97 CE) ***Domitian*** (Luciferus Domitianus Augustus).

912. In 70 CE, a new symbol was promulgated across the Roman Empire, adopted from ancient Egyptian symbology to Horus to signify the messianic and all-powerful abilities of the Roman Emperor as Lucifer called "Oculus Omni" meaning "All Seeing Eye" referring to "All Seeing Eye of Lucifer" or simply "All Seeing Eye of Lord God" which represented the modified eye of Horus surrounded by a representation of the rays of Venus. All Seeing Eye (Oculus Omni)

913. The word "Occult" originates as a core element of the faith of Iudaeism (Judaism) and refers in its original sense as Occultus from 70 CE onwards as literally "the knowledge of/from the eye of Lucifer". After 117 CE, this direct association with the highest level of "occult" was itself largely hidden to all but the very elite initiates. Occult

914. Any claim that the "Oculus Omni" or "All Seeing Eye of Lucifer" wholly originates from ancient Egypt prior to 70 CE is patently absurd, as the Egyptians used a stylized symbol of the eye, while the Romans used an actual eye in their design. Oculus Omni and Eye of Horus

915. As the title Lucifer was directly sourced from the ancient beliefs of the Holly (Cuilliaéan) God known as *Luci*, also known as Loki, the Roman Emperor as "Lucifer" also became associated with the Sun and the most important saviour celebration of Rome changed from the Ides of March, also known as the "Day of Blood" on the 14th Lucifer and Holly

March, to the feast of Lucifer upon the Ides (full moon) of August, originally 14th August, but later considered the 15th August under the Roman Cult "Gregorian" Calendar.

916. The "Oculus Omni" was returned upon the resurrection of the title and position of Lucifer upon a new feast day to Lucifer on August 15th 1534. The symbol became an exclusively associated symbol with the occult lodges known as the "Freemasons" of England following the reconstitution of England and the Island of Britain as the "New Jerusalem". Return of Oculus Omni

917. The use of the "Oculus Omni" within the artwork and symbology of the Freemasons founded in the 16th Century has always meant "The All Seeing Eye of Lucifer" and signifies the ultimate position and force to whom the Masons serve. Only a handful of the most senior Masons in history have ever known the true meaning of "Oculus Omni". Freemasons and Symbol

918. Controversially, it is the Book of Revelation (revised and updated in 17th Century) that provides the core of prophecies concerning the return of Lucifer:- Prophetic Signs & Qualifications of Lucifer

(i) Made flesh around the time of the fulfilment of the End of Days (Revelations 9:1-2; 9:11); and

(ii) Made flesh upon the Earth as a common person (Revelations 13:1); and

(iii) Born in March/April at the most prominent positioning of Ursa Major and Ursa Minor in the Northern Hemisphere, specifically coinciding with the ancient Ides of Mars, also known as Dies Sanguinis on March 14th (reference to Draco) (Revelations 13:2); and

(iv) Suffers a traumatic life event, pivotal to the actions and events that are to follow (Revelations 13:3); and

(v) Born into the "Golden Age of Luciferianism" (Revelations 13:8); and

(vi) Some distinct group of Luciferians with true knowledge as to the identity of Lucifer and the provenance of his birth, whilst others are not convinced and search out for other candidates (Revelations 13:4); and

(vii) Lucifer made flesh being born to suffer for a period in "perdition" on Earth. One who proclaims himself (or herself) to be Lucifer is therefore, by definition *not*, whereas the one who "they" have always known is Lucifer, who rejects the notion of being "Christ" (hence Anti-Christ), *is* (Revelations

17:8); and

(viii) Lucifer made flesh as being the worst blasphemer against himself and various Luciferian networks in a world "controlled" by Luciferians (Revelations 13:5-6); and

(ix) Must suffer a period of life of "living hell" and torment as a "trial", (Revelations 19:20,20:10); and

(x) Lucifer made flesh, as a Philosopher-Priest shall form a new global and religious model comprising in one part a group of seven political structures of a similar nature (e.g. seven unions) and then three that are separate but also part of the complete structure (e.g. three new religious covenants). It is also clear by the prophecy that this model is in complete blasphemy to the existing models of Western-Roman Law (Revelation 13:1).

919. There exist additional key prophecies associated with Lucifer, most significantly from the works of Dante Alighieri (1265-1321) "*Divine Comedy*":-

Additional Prophecies of Lucifer

(i) In all of the history of western literature, only two books (The Bible and Divine Comedy) speak of two separate characters travelling to Hell, then Purgatory and then Heaven. One is Jesus Christ, the other is Dante himself – his name being pseudonym for "Lucifer"; and

(ii) In Divine Comedy, Lucifer returns to Earth via "Purgatory" upon a great rocky outcrop in the South (Southern Hemisphere); and

(iii) There is strong evidence that the British colonisation Expedition of Australia by 1788, when no expense nor resources were spared to send hundreds of healthy convicts to New South Wales, was an attempt to seed the conditions for the fulfilment of this prophecy and not one of the most expensive penal reform projects in modern history.

920. In reference to the prophetised works of Lucifer returned:-

Prophetised Works of Lucifer

(i) A Philosopher-Priest shall form a new global and religious model comprising in one part a group of seven political structures of a similar nature (e.g. seven unions) and then three that are separate but also part of the complete structure (e.g. three new religious covenants). It is also clear by the prophecy that this model is in complete blasphemy to the existing models of Western-Roman Law and structures (Revelation 13:1); and

(ii) Shall prepare and promulgate a new covenant of One Heaven, having the power and authority to overcome all spiritual resistance as a Treaty to unite Heaven and end the duality of Heaven and Hell (Revelations 13:6-7); and

(iii) Lucifer made flesh shall bring forth a number or mark of some description, consistent with other philosophies of restoring the Golden Rule of Law, ending slavery arranged as three sets of six numbers as a symbol of the new covenant (Revelation 13:16-18).

921. There is overwhelming evidence that Dutch German and American influences in the late 19th Century and 20th Century sought to completely ignore and circumvent their own 400 years of prophecy and make up their own in order to claim that Lucifer had returned and blessed America forever as the land of "Imperial Exceptionalism" by the mid 20th Century:- Dutch German-American Attempt to Circumvent Prophecy

(i) The events of World War II, the grooming of Albert Einstein and the countless other activities all point to the systematic, deliberate and false claims of American elite to have fulfilled the prophecies of Lucifer; and

(ii) The endemic corruption of corporate America and the perpetual war against the rest of the human population, including the collapse of the American Consumerism model by the start of the 21st Century all point to a complete failure of the arrogant and heretical assertions made in the mid 20th Century; and

(iii) In contrast, there is significant evidence that European and British powers, as well as a growing number in the United States have successfully recognised the fulfilment of such prophecies from the arrival of a figure, with Holly and ancient Venetian blood heritage as well as Jewish ancestry on both sides of his parents, born on Emerald Hill, Melbourne on March 14, 1965.

Article 290 – Sabaoth (Moloch)

922. ***Sabaoth (Moloch)***, also known as the "Hidden One" is a Divine Saviour originally from 800 BCE Yahudi and Judaic culture, but revived from the 15th Century as G-d of the Jewish people and then by 17th Century as the G-d of the Israelites. "Sabaoth" is literally the hidden name of one aspect of the Jewish G-d. Sabaoth (Moloch)

923. In reference to the origin and context of the Divine Saviour known as *Sabaoth, Yaldabaoth and Moloch*:- Origin of Sabaoth (Moloch)

(i) Sabaoth, also known as Yaldabaoth and Moloch is a relative modern 15th to 17th Century revival of Yahudi history, without necessarily the precision or understanding of the god Baal Hamon or Moloch of the Yahudi more than 2,500 years ago; and

(ii) More than 2,500 years ago, the Yahudi were split between two opposing priest lines, with one being the Holly continuing to follow Yahu (YHWH) and the others working Baal Hamon or Moloch, with their supreme temple at Baalbek in Lebanon; and

(iii) Given the significance of Jerusalem as the claimed birthplace of Mithra under Persian civilisation, the Priests of Baal-Hamon aligned themselves with the cult of Mithra and Baalbek became a central religious site for the worship of Mithra and for a time the Baal Hamon priests controlled the Great Temple of Mithra at Jerusalem; and

(iv) Controversially, the god Baal Hamon, also known as Sabaoth or "G-d" to the Ashkenazi and Hasidic sects has always been associated with sacrifice, with burnt offerings to Moloch known by the religious term "Holocaust"; and

(v) For the first time in history, the priestly lines of Moloch (Sabaoth) were united with the priestly lines of Yahu in the birth of the children of Cú-Laoch (Yahusiah), also known in history as Jesus Christ and Mariamne, daughter of Herod Agrippa; and

(vi) Only descendents of this priestly line can rightly claim to possess the authority of Baal Hamon, or Sabaoth or Moloch and no other.

Prophetic Signs & Qualifications of Sabaoth

924. The Hasidic Sect funded and invented by Lithuanian-Polish noble Prince Kazimierz Czartoryski (b.1674- d.1741) through the creation of the false messiah Israel Baal Shem Tov (b. 1688 – d. 1780) is responsible for creating a string of modern prophecies associated with Sabaoth (Moloch), with little historic competence or respect to the bloodline history of the original priest lines and context. However, given the extraordinary influence of these "modern" prophecies to modern world politics since the 19th Century, these "prophecies" need to be considered:-

(i) (476) "*The children of Israel shall be redeemed from exile by the Vav*". The sixth letter of the Hebrew Alphabet is vav. In Hasidic Kabbalah mysticism, the Vav as number six represents a form of God through the Messiah, a sign of "sacrifice and redemption" and the binding connection of heaven and earth. In English it is the letter F; and

(ii) (481) "*When the century is completed. the vav will join the hei. And they shall bring all your brethren out of all the nations for an offering to Hashem*". This is a Hasidic Kabbalist reference to an offering of "6" to Sabaoth in order to fulfil the prophecy of the birth of Israel. The ancient and only proper name of an offering to Sabaoth, also known as The Hidden One or "Hashem" is a Holocaust; and

(iii) Jesus is "sacrificed" on the cross in order to achieve redemption on the sixth day of Passover according to the 17th Century corruption of ancient scripture and history. (John 19:31).

Article 291 – Risen Christ (Second Coming)

925. ***Risen Christ*** (Second Coming) is a Divine Saviour originally promised under the Holly Carolingians in the 8th Century CE and the creation of the Roman Catholic Church, against the "Anti-Christs" of the Eastern Christian Empire at the time.

Risen Christ (Second Coming)

926. Within the New Testament, there exists several passages claimed to have been spoken by Christ himself concerning the circumstances and timing of his return to Earth at some future date, including:-

Gospel Quotes from Christ himself on Signs & Qualifications of his return

(i) Christ shall come again to Earth (John 14:28); and

(ii) Christ shall return as a flesh and blood man (Mark 13:34); and

(iii) Christ on his return in flesh shall not immediately be recognised or honoured as a king, but (once again) shall be discarded and ignored by many as a criminal (thief) (Matt 24:43-44); and

(iv) There shall be many who falsely claim to be Christ and shall deceive many followers (Matt 24:5, Mark 13:6, Luke 21:8); and

(v) There shall be many who falsely claim to be a prophet (messenger of God) and shall deceive many (Matt 24:5); and

(vi) False claimants as Divine Saviours (Christ) and as prophets will go to such incredible lengths to trick the world, that many – including the very highest authorities of religions – will be deceived by their "great signs and wonders" (Matt 24:23, Mark 13:22); and

(vii) The ultimate "fail-safe" in discerning the true Christ from "impostors" is that by his works, the true Christ (returned) shall be revealed and self evident without any need to claim or act in such manner. Thus anyone who ever says (or claims or acts in such manner) to be Christ automatically exposes themselves as a fraud and must not be believed (Matt 24:23 Mark 13:21); and

(viii) One of the key signs of the return of Christ shall be when most of the world shall be so immoral and selfish that many shall have cold hearts and show no love nor empathy towards the plight of others (Matt 24:5); and

(ix) One of the key signs of the return of Christ shall be when morality and decency of the people of the world has degraded to the same as the days of "Sodom and Gomorrah" during the times of Noah (Matt 24:37-42); and

(x) A sign often attributed to the return of Christ is the belief in law that all the "dead in law" shall rise and be freed by some miraculous singular act of judgment (John 5:28-29); and

(xi) The greatest sign that Christ has already returned shall be the arrival of the greatest of all climactic tribulations (such as a major once in several million year pole displacement coming to a climax in the next short period of time) being something human civilisation has never in history had to face before (Matt 24:21 Mark 13:19, Luke 21:25); and

(xii) The greatest of all climactic tribulations shall collapse human civilisation and cause devastation to much of humanity (Matt 24:29 Mark 13:24-25 Luke 21:26); and

(xiii) After the greatest of all tribulations, all of humanity will finally understand that Christ has already returned in the form of some extraordinary signs concerning the coming of Heaven to Earth demonstrating "power and great glory" (Matt 24:30 Mark 13:26 Luke 21:27); and

(xiv) The works of the true Christ concerning the coming of Heaven to Earth, shall finally unify all of Heaven and all of Earth (Mark 13:27); and

(xv) The works of the true Christ shall save humanity (Luke 21:28).

Article 292 – Messiah of the Yahudi (Jews)

927. ***Messiah of the Yahudi (Jews)*** is a Divine Saviour originally promised under the Yahudi faith from end of fall of the Messiah Kings in 6th Century BCE, then revived again after the expulsion of all Yahudi and followers of Iudeasim from Roman controlled Palestine and the renaming of Jerusalem to Aelia Capitolina in 122 CE by Emperor Hadrian as an annex of the Capitolinium of Rome. Messiah of the Yahudi (Jews)

928. In reference to the origin and context of the Divine Saviour known as *Messiah and Messiah of the Jews*:- Origin of Messiah of the Yahudi (Jews)

(i) The sacred texts and supporting texts are all creations starting from the 17th Century and the complete conversion of the Yahudi to "Jews" and the corruption of the ancient kingdom of Judah to being a competitor to a fictitious state called "Israel"; and

(ii) The term "Israel" is a 16th Century occult word created by English Alchemist John Dee (1527-1609) from Isis, Ra and El and not an accurate historic term; and

(iii) The lack of knowledge of Baal Hamon and the subsequent use of the name of Sabaoth as the hidden name of "G-d" of the Jews is partly caused by the age of the grimoires and black magic in England, France and Italy at the end of the 16th Century.

929. In reference to the qualities and signs of the Jewish Messiah:- Prophetic Signs & Qualifications of Jewish Messiah

(i) He Must be a member of the tribe of Yahudi (Judah) (Genesis 49:10); and

(ii) He must be a direct male descendant of King David and King Solomon (2 Samuel 7:12 - 13); and

(iii) (Deut. 30:3; Isaiah 11:11-12; Jeremiah 30:3, 32:37; Ezekiel 11:17, 36:24) When the Messiah returns the Yahudi (including Jews) will return to their homeland; and

(iv) (Isaiah 2:2-3, 56:6-7, 60:7, 66:20; Ezekiel 37:26–27; Malachi 3:4; Zech. 14:20-21) The Temple in Jerusalem will be rebuilt through the Messiah; and

(v) (Micah 4:1-4; Hoseah 2:20; Isaiah 2:1-4, 60:18) There will be universal disarmament and worldwide peace with a complete end to war; and

(vi) (Ezekiel 37:24; Deut. 30:8,10; Jeremiah 31:32; Ezekiel 11:19-20, 36:26-27) The Messiah will reign at a time when all the

Yahudi will observe Divine Law; and

(vii) (Zechariah 3:9, 8:23,14:9,16; Isaiah 45:23, 66:23; Jeremiah 31:33; Ezekiel 38:23; Psalm 86:9; Zeph. 3:9) The Messiah will rule at a time when all the people of the world will come to acknowledge and serve the one true Divine Creator.

930. In reference to the requirement for the Jewish Messiah to be a blood descendant of both King David and King Solomon:-

The Bloodlines of King David and King Solomon

(i) Yahudi descendant King Solomon, properly known as King Sulmanu of the Assyrians (859-824 BCE) is a famous historical king that built the Great Temple of Baalbek. He worshipped Baal Hamon and later his priests and descendants worshipped Mithra; and

(ii) Yahudi King U'vid (Da'vid) (999-931 BCE) son of Great Prophet Zadokiah is a famous historical king and for hundreds of years the mortal enemies of the Baal Hamon (Moloch) Yahudi Priests; and

(iii) Mariamne, the daughter of King Agripiah (Agrippa) and wife of Cú-Laoch (Yahusiah), also known in history as Jesus Christ, is a blood descendent of the High Priests of Baal Hamon. Thus all Holly descendents of Jesus and Mariamne are the only ones that carry the united bloodlines of the Yahudi priests of David and Solomon; and

(iv) Cú-Cúileann (Yasiah), also known in history as Joseph, is the main Holly blood descendant of the first Messiah Priest Kings of Yahu and the Great Prophets of Yeb; and

(v) Only descendents of this priestly line can rightly claim to be descended from both King Solomon and King David; and

(vi) Absolutely no one of Sephardi, Mizrahi or Ashkenazi heritage can be claimed, or claim themselves as a Jewish Messiah, unless they also carry the bloodline of the Holly descendents of Jesus and Mariamne; and

(vii) Apart from Jesus, there has only been one example in the past two thousand years of any potential candidate meeting such criteria, including the contemporary criteria of modern Jewish faith, being one born with Jewish ancestry on both sides of his parents, born on Emerald Hill, Melbourne on March 14, 1965.

Article 293 – Mahdi of Islam

931. ***Mahdi of Islam*** is a Divine Saviour and major figure in Islamic eschatology originally promised under the oppressions of the Mamluk and then Ottoman Sultans from the 14th and 15th Centuries, to free all Muslims from such anti-messiahs or "Dajjal" and restore the sacred scriptures and wisdom of Islam to its original Holly roots. Mahdi of Islam

932. In reference to the origin and context of the Divine Saviour known as *Mahdi*:- Origin of Mahdi of Islam

(i) The Mahdi is believed to be a prophesied messianic figure who will appear during a time of great turmoil and injustice in the world. Muslims expect him to be a descendant of the Holy through his daughter Fatimah; and

(ii) The Mahdi is expected to appear in the end times, preceding the Day of Judgment (Qiyamah). His arrival is often associated with various signs and events, including widespread chaos, social upheaval, and moral decay; and

(iii) According to Islamic tradition, the Mahdi will lead a global Islamic community and unite Muslims from various sects and backgrounds. He will then guide humanity towards a period of prosperity and peace; and

(iv) Whilst there is general consensus among Muslims concerning key signs of what the Mahdi will achieve, there are significant contradictions in some of the claimed detail and amount of detail generated by various scholars of Islam concerning the Mahdi since the founding of Islam; and

(v) The concept of the Mahdi is a source of hope and anticipation for many Muslims, who believe that his arrival will mark a new era of peace and prosperity. Believers are encouraged to lead righteous lives and prepare for his coming by upholding moral and ethical values.

933. Within Islamic Sacred Hadith Texts (claimed sayings and actions of the Holy Prophet), there exists numerous passages and quotes concerning the circumstances and timing of the arrival of Mahdi to Earth at some future date. Listed below are the primary signs generally agreed by all Muslims including:- Prophetic Signs & Qualifications of Mahdi

(i) The Mahdi will come as a flesh and blood man; and

(ii) The Mahdi shall be a flesh and blood descendent of the Holly Prophet through his daughter Fatima. Because the Holly Prophet is descended from both the Saracen (Arabic) and

Holly (Irish) bloodlines and his daughter married her first cousin Diarmait Ua Bláthaigh also known as Ali ibn Abbas Talib meaning "the exulted son of the great lions of knowledge", it means the Mahdi can only be descended from this particular Holly Bloodline and no other; and

(iii) The Mahdi on his return in flesh shall not immediately be recognised or honoured, except by a few with deep spiritual insight and faith who will realise his true status; and

(iv) There shall be many who falsely claim to be the Mahdi and shall deceive many followers; and

(v) False claimants as the Mahdi will go to such incredible lengths to trick the world, that many – including the very highest authorities – will be deceived by their "great signs and wonders"; and

(vi) The ultimate "fail-safe" in discerning the true Mahdi from "impostors" is that by his works, the true Mahdi (returned) shall be revealed and self evident without any need to claim or act in such manner. Thus anyone who ever says (or claims or acts in such manner) to be the Mahdi automatically exposes themselves as a fraud and must not be believed; and

(vii) One of the key signs of the return of the Mahdi shall be the prevalence of injustice and oppression in the world, with corruption and tyranny becoming widespread; and

(viii) The period preceding the Mahdi's arrival will be characterized by widespread deceit, falsehood, and moral decay. Immorality and ignorance will be commonplace and the true Qur'an will be forgotten and religion will be abandoned by many; and

(ix) The greatest sign that the Mahdi has already returned shall be the arrival of the greatest of all climactic tribulations (such as a major once in several million year pole displacement coming to a climax in the next short period of time) being something human civilisation has never in history had to face before; and

(x) After the greatest of all tribulations, all of humanity will finally understand that the Mahdi has already returned in the form of some extraordinary signs concerning the coming of Heaven to Earth; and

(xi) The works of the true Mahdi concerning the coming of Heaven to Earth and restoring the true Qur'an and ending wilful ignorance and corruption, shall finally unify all of Heaven and all of Earth and all the Muslim Ummah (community) under a new great civilisation; and

(xii) The works of the true Mahdi shall save humanity. The Mahdi will establish justice, equity, and peace on Earth, and the world will experience an era of righteousness and tranquillity; and

(xiii) Since the founding of Islam, there has only been one example of any potential candidate meeting such criteria, being a direct blood descendent of the Holly Prophet of Islam, born on Emerald Hill, Melbourne on March 14, 1965.

Article 294 – Kulkulkan of Maya (Sth America)

934. ***Kulkulkan*** of Maya (Sth America) or Quetzalcoatl in Aztec culture, is a Divine Saviour of the South American civilisations. Kulkulkan of Maya (Sth America)

935. In reference to the origin and context of the Divine Saviour known as *Kulkulkan of Maya*:- Origin of Kulkulkan of Maya (Sth America)

(i) Kukulkan is a deity often depicted as a feathered serpent, combining the characteristics of a serpent and a bird, specifically a quetzal bird. This fusion symbolizes the union of the earth (serpent) and the sky (bird) and represents Kukulkan's role as a bridge between the two realms; and

(ii) Kukulkan is considered a creator god and a bringer of knowledge and civilization. He is associated with various aspects of life, including agriculture, fertility, wind and rain. Kukulkan's significance extends to rulership, as he was also seen as a patron deity of rulers and nobility; and

(iii) In Maya mythology, Kukulkan is often associated with creation myths and is sometimes credited with helping create the world and humanity. His actions in these stories are often linked to the introduction of important cultural elements and knowledge, such as agriculture and calendar systems; and

(iv) Kukulkan's importance is notably reflected in Maya architecture, particularly at the archaeological site of Chichen Itza in Mexico. The Pyramid of Kukulkan, also known as El Castillo, is a prominent temple that serves as a physical representation of the deity's significance. During the two equinoxes, the angle of the sunlight creates the illusion of a serpent returning and descending the pyramid's staircase, emphasizing the god's role as a celestial being and prophecy of return.

936. Given the deliberate and intentional wholesale destruction of Prophetic Signs priceless Maya sacred texts and materials, and limitations on decoding any surviving stone glyphs, there is little evidence surviving as to the prophetic signs of the return of Kukulkan and Quetzalcoatl. However, given the historic record of a few dozen Spanish mercenaries led by Cortez being given effective full control of a sophisticated culture and civilisation of millions, with Cortez being seen as "Quetzalcoatl returned", some prophetic signs and qualifications can be made:-

& Qualifications of Kulkulkan

(i) Kukulkan shall return as a "white skinned" flesh and blood man; and

(ii) Kukulkan shall perform certain "miracles" to establish his authenticity; and

(iii) Kukulkan shall reveal new knowledge and future, possibly even a new civilisation.

Article 295 – Maitreya of Buddhism

937. ***Maitreya*** is a Divine Saviour of Buddhism and prophesied to be the next Buddha to appear in our world, following the historical Buddha, Siddhartha Gautama (Shakyamuni Buddha).

Maitreya of Buddhism

938. In reference to the origin and context of the Divine Saviour known as *Maitreya*:-

Origin of Maitreya of Buddhism

(i) The name *Maitreya* is derived from the Sanskrit word *maitrī* meaning "divine friendship and mercy", that is in turn derived from the noun *mitra*, signifying "divine friend and saviour"; and

(ii) The Maitreya is regarded as the fifth and final Buddha of the current kalpa (long epoch of time); and

(iii) Despite many religious figures and spiritual leaders claiming to be Maitreya throughout history, diverse Buddhist sects insist that these are false claims, while underscoring that Maitreya has yet to appear, and that he is the Buddha of the future.

939. Within the Buddhist Sacred Texts, there exists several passages concerning the circumstances and timing of the arrival of the Maitreya to Earth at some future date, including:-

Prophetic Signs & Qualifications of Maitreya

(i) Maitreya shall return as a flesh and blood man (Lalitavistara Sutra); and

(ii) Maitreya will be marked by his great compassion (karuna) and wisdom (prajna) (Lotus Sutra and Avatamsaka Sutra); and

(iii) Maitreya shall appear, after the teaching of the current Buddha, Gautama, has declined to a fraction of what it once was; and a time when the dharma will have been forgotten by most (Maitreya Vyakarana); and

(iv) The Maitreya will teach the dharma, providing a path to enlightenment for all beings (Lotus Sutra and Avatamsaka Sutra); and

(v) The coming of Maitreya is sometimes seen as a time when all beings will be able to achieve enlightenment (Mahayana texts); and

(vi) Maitreya is expected to establish a society based on righteousness and truth (Mahayana texts); and

(vii) Maitreya will create a pure land, or an ideal realm (civilisation) for the practice and realization of the dharma (Pure Land Sutras); and

(viii) Maitreya's teachings are expected to gain global recognition and acceptance. This idea is more prominent in Mahayana Buddhism.

Article 296 – Kalki of Hinduism

Kalki of Hinduism

940. ***Kalki*** is a Divine Saviour of Hinduism that refers to the tenth and final avatar (incarnation) of the god Vishnu, who is believed to appear in the future. The concept of *Kalki* is part of Hindu eschatology, which deals with the end of the current cosmic cycle and the eventual renewal of the universe.

Origin of Kalki of Hinduism

941. In reference to the origin and context of the Divine Saviour known as *Kalki*:-

(i) *Kalki* is the future and final avatar of the god Vishnu in Hinduism, expected to appear at the end of the current age to restore righteousness and bring about a new era of virtue and truth; and

(ii) The concept of Kalki is mentioned in various Hindu scriptures, including the Puranas (ancient texts), where prophecies about his coming are described in detail; and

(iii) Kalki is an important figure in Hindu mythology and has influenced various aspects of Indian culture, including art, literature and religious rituals. The belief in Kalki's eventual arrival is a source of hope and inspiration for many Hindus.

Prophetic Signs & Qualifications

942. Within the Hindu Sacred Texts (such as the Puranas), there exists several key passages concerning the circumstances and timing of the arrival of Kalki to Earth at some future date, including:- of Kalki

(i) Kalki shall be born as a flesh and blood man (Bhagavata Purana); and

(ii) Kalki shall be born at a sacred place that is part of, or connected to a sacred kingdom known for its well known spiritual significance. The Hindu and Buddhist word "Shambhala" is usually used to describe such a place (Kalki Purana); and

(iii) Kalki shall be born into a family with ancient sacred (holy) priestly lineage (Kalki Purana); and

(iv) One of the key signs of the arrival of Kalki shall be when most of the world is in a state of chaos, with humanity facing immense suffering and adversity (Bhagavata Purana); and

(v) One of the key signs of the arrival of Kalki shall be a time of moral and spiritual decline (Vishnu Purana); and

(vi) Kalki is believed to possess divine attributes and qualities, such as supreme knowledge, wisdom, and spiritual prowess. These attributes equip him to fulfil his role as the savior of humanity (Bhagavata Purana); and

(vii) Kalki is prophesied to overthrow oppressive and unrighteous rulers who exploit and tyrannize their subjects (Bhagavata Purana); and

(viii) Kalki is also seen as a world teacher who imparts spiritual wisdom and guidance to humanity, leading them towards enlightenment and righteousness (Bhagavata Purana); and

(ix) Kalki's primary purpose is to restore righteousness (dharma) and establish an era of truth and virtue (Satya Yuga), (Vishnu Purana); and

(x) Kalki's arrival is expected to bring about a state of universal harmony and balance, where all beings live in peace and coexistence (Bhagavata Purana); and

(xi) Kalki's advent marks the beginning of the Satya Yuga, a period characterized by truth, righteousness, and spiritual enlightenment (Vishnu Purana).

8.2 – Anti-Saviour Rank & Title

Article 297 – Anti-Saviour Rank & Title

943. ***Anti-Saviour Rank & Title*** refers to figures regarded as the "opposites" to the foretold Divine Saviour. Anti-Saviour Rank & Title

Article 298 – Anti-Christ

944. The ***Anti-Christ*** is a figure associated with the end times and the second coming of Jesus Christ. The concept of the *Anti-Christ* is primarily derived from biblical passages, especially from the New Testament, particularly the books of 2 Thessalonians and the Book of Revelation. Anti-Christ

945. In reference to the origin and context of the *Anti-Saviour* known as the *Anti-Christ*:- Origin of Anti-Christ

(i) The Antichrist is commonly believed to be a person or entity who will oppose and work against the teachings and purposes of Jesus Christ; and

(ii) This figure is often associated with deception, great worldly power, and a false claim to divinity. The specific characteristics and identity of the Antichrist can vary among different Christian denominations and interpretations.

946. Within the Christian Sacred Texts, there exists several key passages concerning the circumstances and timing of the arrival of the *Anti-Christ* to Earth at some future date, including:- Prophetic Signs & Qualifications of Anti-Christ

(i) The False Prophet is said to perform great signs and wonders, deceiving many (Revelation 13:13-14); and

(ii) A beast rises from the sea and is described as having multiple heads and horns. This beast is often associated with a symbol of political power and authority that opposes God. (Revelation 13:1-10); and

(iii) Another beast rises from the earth, often referred to as the False Prophet. This figure is associated with religious deception and promotes worship of the first beast (13:11-18); and

(iv) The beast from the sea is said to have "a mouth speaking great things and blasphemies (Revelation 13:5); and

(v) Revelation 13:16-18 mentions the infamous "mark of the beast," which is often associated with the Antichrist's system of control. Those who receive this mark are seen as followers of the beast; and

(vi) The Book of Revelation speaks of persecution and tribulation for believers who refuse to worship the beast or receive his mark (Revelation 13:7, 15-17).

Article 299 – Al-Masih ad-Dajjal of Islam

947. ***Al-Masih ad-Dajjal of Islam*** is a major eschatological figure, often described as a false messiah or a great deceiver. *Ad-Dajjal* is believed to be a human-like figure who will emerge in the end times as a sign of the Day of Judgment. Al-Masih ad-Dajjal of Islam

948. In reference to the origin and context of the *Anti-Saviour* known as *Ad-Dajjal*:- Origin of ad-Dajjal

(i) Dajjāl (دجّال) comes from the word dajl meaning "lie" or "deception". The word Dajjāl literally means "deceiver". Thus, al-Masīḥ ad-Dajjāl means "the deceiving Messiah"; and

(ii) In Islamic eschatology *Ad-Dajjal* will pretend to be the promised Messiah, appearing before the Day of Judgment; and

(iii) The word Dajjal is not mentioned in the Quran; and

(iv) Corresponding to the Antichrist in Christian tradition, the Dajjal will imitate the miracles performed by Jesus Christ, such as healing the sick and raising the dead; and

(v) A large body of conflicting claims exist between different schools and sects of Islam concerning the expected characteristics, timings and actions of the claimed Dajjal.

949. Within Islamic sacred Hadith, there exists several commonly agreed signs and qualifications concerning the circumstances and timing of the arrival of *Ad-Dajjal* to Earth at some future date, including:- Prophetic Signs & Qualifications of ad-Dajjal

(i) He will be a flesh and blood man; and

(ii) He will claim to be a Divine figure, even though he is a flesh and blood man. He will assert himself as God on earth and demand worship from people; and

(iii) He is expected to possess such extraordinary supernatural powers that he will be able to heal the sick and raise the dead back to life; and

(iv) He will use his supernatural powers to spread deception; and

(v) He will wander the earth, spreading chaos and destruction. His emergence will be accompanied by widespread confusion and turmoil; and

(vi) His ultimate defeat is prophesied to occur with the return of Jesus (Isa) in Islamic eschatology.

8.3 – False, Absurd & Prohibited Saviour Rank & Title

Article 300 - False, Absurd & Prohibited Saviour Rank & Title

950. ***False, Absurd & Prohibited Saviour Rank & Title*** are any claims of Saviour Rank & Title that are absurd, false or prohibited under Ucadia Law.

False, Absurd & Prohibited Saviour Rank & Title

951. In accord with the most sacred Covenant *Pactum De Singularis Caelum*, all offices of Saviour Rank & Title have been fully vested and absorbed into the authority and power of Ucadia upon the fulfilment of sacred scripture, signs, standards and qualifications. Therefore, no Ucadia Person or Non-Ucadia Person may logically, morally, reasonably, lawfully, legally or ethically claim one or more offices of Sovereign Saviour.

All offices of Saviour Rank & Title Prohibited under Ucadia

Title IX - Sovereign Realm

9.1 – Realm

Article 301 - Realm

952. A ***Realm*** is an 8th Century CE word first defined by Sacré Loi ("Sacred Law") to describe a political region and hereditaments (estate) over which a Sovereign is granted to rule. Realm

953. The word *Realm* is derived from the combination of two (2) Latin words *res/rei* meaning "matter, business, transactions, possessions, wealth, money, interest" and *alma* meaning "kind, nourishing". Origin of the word Realm

954. By definition, the original true meaning of Realm implies an obligation of the Sovereign to tend, nurture and develop kindly and fairly those territories for which they have authority. Original Meaning of Realm

Article 302 – Land

955. ***Land*** is a term first invented by the Carolingians in the 8th Century CE under Sacré Loi (Sacred Law) to define a new concept whereby all the earth was absolutely owned by the Divine Creator and then bestowed to the Roman Catholic Church (as created by the Carolingians by 741 CE) as perpetual trustee of the "land", except for the sacred Island of Ireland under the Holly (Cuilliaéan). Everyone else then only had "right of use" as tenants from the church. Land

956. The word *Land* is originally derived from ancient 1st Millennium BCE Irish term *lann* meaning "an enclosed piece of ground; a place". The term "*lann*" was introduced as part of the historic 3rd Century CE law reforms of Holly (Cuilliaéan) Irish Leader Cormac Mac Art which also saw the invention of such concepts as "lease", "terrain", "acre" and "survey". Origin of the word and concept of Land

957. In terms of a brief history of the Sovereign nature of Land:- Sovereign history of Land

(i) Prior to the conquest of territory by the Roman Empire, the Celtic Empire was based on the concept that all earth was "owned" by the Cuilliaéan (Holly) as the Divine Messengers, or "Living Gods" with authority then passed to leaders and chiefs; and

(ii) In contrast, the Romans adopted a "socialist" model of ownership whereby all territory was claimed "in commune" for Rome; and

(iii) The Carolingian model of the 8th Century introduced a new notion by claiming a "Church" or entity, association or company of people held absolute "ownership"; and

(iv) Laws concerning Land were corrupted by the Venetians in England by the mid 16th Century to claim that only the crown held absolute dominion over the land and not the church or some other historical body. The Venetian mercenaries then completely disavowed the sacred history of Ireland by attempting several invasions; and

(v) The ancient rights of the Cuilliaéan (Holly) were partially recognised by the 20th Century in the British Crown acknowledging the Irish Free State. However, the City of London, the Banks and the Crown Corporation continue to defy the fundamental civilised laws of Western Civilisation and Christianity by continuing to obstruct the unification of Ireland.

958. In terms of tenancy of land (lend), the Carolingians in the 8th Century CE introduced the concepts of Tenant and the Tenancy Agreement (from Latin tenere meaning to 'hold/keep') which meant literally "one who holds land by tenure" – with tenure meaning "an agreement for holding immovable property (tenement), equivalent to lease":- Tenancy of Land

(i) The one who granted the tenancy was known as the "lord" or "landlord" of the tenancy; and

(ii) The one who received the tenancy was known as the "valet" or simply the tenant; and

(iii) The valet (tenant) as well as the landlord were required to formally pledge themselves to each other in accordance with the true and original sacraments of the Catholic Church through a solemn ceremony known as *committo* meaning literally "to join, bring together, bestow or assign"; and

(iv) The landlord was then bound as *patronus* and senior or "father" to the tenant to act honorably and with kindness; and

(v) The tenant was then bound as *iunior* or "younger" to the landlord as their "father" and patron under *fidelitas* or "faithfulness".

959. From the beginning of the laws of Land and Western Civilisation in the 8th Century, there were three (3) types of Tenancy:- First types of tenancy

(i) ***Tenens ad Vitam (Tenant for Life)*** was one of the type of tenancies granted by Barons to valet (tenants) whereby one held lands or tenements for the term of their own life; and

(ii) ***Tenens ad Annum (Tenant for years)*** was one type of tenancy whereby one had temporary use and possession of lands of tenements not his own by virtue of a lease or demise granted to him by the landlord for a determined period of time, as for a year or a fixed number of years; and

(iii) ***Tenens ad Voluntate (Tenant at will)*** was one type of tenancy whereby lands or tenements were let by one man to another, to have and to hold to him at the will of the lessor (landlord). These Tenants at Will were later known as "ward tenants" and then "copyhold tenants" by the start of the 18th Century CE.

960. In terms of maxims of law, the Carolingians in the 8th Century CE set in place a series of thirteen (13) key maxims by which all tenancies and land were to be honoured:-

Maxims of Law and Land

(i) *Tenere sequitur legem* meaning "tenancy follows the law"; and

(ii) *Aqua comitatur solo* meaning "the water accompanies the soil"; and

(iii) *Fructus pendentes pars fundi videntur* meaning "Hanging fruits make part of the land"; and

(iv) *Ius descendit et non terra* meaning "A right descends, not the land"; and

(v) *Domus sua cuique est tutissimum refugium* meaning "every man's domicile (home) is his castle"; and

(vi) *Nullus tenetur cogendum domo* meaning "No man is bound to be forced from his home"; and

(vii) *Concessit sessionem non maius a quo derivata* meaning "the session (estate) granted cannot be larger than that from which it is derived"; and

(viii) *Sessionem concessit potest non iterum concessum* meaning "the session (estate) granted cannot again be granted (at the same time)"; and

(ix) *Non potest tenere eadem session statim de duo plures dominus* meaning "No man can hold the same session (estate) immediately of two or several landlords"; and

(x) *Nemo potest esse tenes et dominus* meaning "no man can be at the same time tenant and landlord of the same tenement"; and

(xi) *Dominus potest exigere bis tributa tenet idem* meaning "a landlord cannot demand twice payment from a tenant for the same thing"; and

(xii) *Iunior tenet ius equitatis* meaning "(the) junior (tenant) holds the right of equity"; and

(xiii) *Ius redemptionis non extinguetur praeter delictum* meaning "the right of redemption cannot be extinguished except by delinquency".

961. To ensure uniformity of leases and rights of use of land, the Carolingians in the 8th Century CE introduced the first hierarchy of tenancies and leases in history being:- Hierarchy of Tenancies

(i) The Lords held tenancies under Carta (Charter) known as a *Tenens in Capite* (Tenant in Chief); and

(ii) Barons held tenancies under Lords under Carta (Charter) or Convenia (Covenant) called *Tenens in Manor* (Tenant in (the) Manor); and

(iii) Villages held common land (Culturae) in tenancy known as *Tenens in Communis* (Tenancy in Common) under Barons, while individual families may also have held land as *Tenens ad vitam* (Tenant for Life), *Tenens ad annum* (Tenant for Years) or *Tenens ad voluntate* (Tenant at Will).

962. From the beginning of Western Civilisation and the Roman Catholic Church, it was strictly forbidden to ever treat human beings as animals and part of the land. Thus all forms of Allodial Title and Crown Land since the 17th Century is illegitimate, immoral, reprobate and contrary to all forms of civilised law because it permitted poor people to be considered "animals" and part of Land. Persons and Human Beings never Land

963. Any attempted defense of Allodial Title or Crown Land, or refutation of the facts that all modern Non-Ucadian Land law includes persons as part of Land, is itself an immoral and indecent act against Civilised Law. Denials against Allodial Title and Crown Land

964. In accord with the most sacred Covenant *Pactum De Singularis Caelum*, Ucadia societies hold the absolute dominion as custodians of all forms of Land above any and all Non-Ucadian societies and entities. Ucadia as absolute Landlord

Article 303 – Hollyland

965. ***Hollyland*** also known as ***Holyland***, is a sovereign state under the complete control of Holly Western Christian Civilisation from the 8th Century CE until the 14th Century CE, with boundaries equivalent to the ancient Roman region of Palestine and Jerusalem as its capital. The modern state of Israel is in part a revival of this ancient state given the Holly Bloodlines of the elite families of the world via the Moor House of Welf (Este). Hollyland

966. In terms of a brief history of the Hollyland:-

Sovereign history of Hollyland

(i) The state known as *Hollyland* was first ceded by the Holly Saracen Islamic Empire to the full control of the Holly Franks in the middle of the 8th Century as part of the estate for Holly Emperors in recognition of the ancient Holly Irish estates held by the famous historic figures of Yasiah (Cú-Cúileann/Joseph) and his son Yahusiah (Cú-Laoch/Jesus); and

(ii) The Hollyland became the primary pilgrimage destination for Western Catholic Christians from as early as the 9th Century. Due to the protection of Saracen forces throughout the Middle East, the site was never attacked until the Mamluk/Ottoman Sultans out of Egypt by the 14th Century; and

(iii) The history of the crusades is a complete fabrication to mask the fact that a Catholic state held Palestine and Jerusalem in complete peace and agreement with the successive administrations of the Saracen and Islamic Empire for more than 700 years; and

(iv) By the late 17th Century, there is strong evidence to suggest the attempted revival of the "Holyland" by the Holly House of Welf Venetian and European lines, first as a plan for England and then second in the creation of "Holland". The third attempt to revive the "Holyland" was by the late 19th Century in the planning of events that could lead to the formation of the state of Israel.

Article 304 - Dominion

967. ***Dominion*** is both the supreme sovereign authority to rule and the extent of such authority and jurisdiction over a particular kingdom, state or territory.

Dominion

968. By Divine Right and innate nature of true law, only Ucadia societies properly possess Dominion. No Non-Ucadia society, nation, kingdom, state or body corporate and politic may possess higher Dominion than Ucadia.

Dominion and Ucadia

Article 305 – Kingdom

969. A ***Kingdom*** is an 8th Century CE word first defined by *Sacré Loi* ("Sacred Law") to specifically define a Realm ruled by a Bloodline (House) with Holly Blood. The word Kingdom literally means "Holly (king) Dominion (dom)".

Kingdom

970. By Divine Right and innate nature of true law, only Ucadia societies

Kingdom and Ucadia

ruled by a coronated sovereign monarch may be recognised and called a Kingdom. This is because a proper Ucadia sovereign monarch is recognised as possessing the necessary Holly nature to be called a King or Queen. In contrast, no Non-Ucadia society, state or nation possessing a person claiming to be a monarch may be properly classed as a Kingdom.

Article 306 – State

971. A ***State*** is an 8th Century political term meaning the formal recognition of a Territory as a legitimate independent sovereign entity by virtue of an act of recognition by the laws of other Kingdoms and States. State

972. A State is one of two types of political organisations at a "nation" level under Holly Western Christian Civilisation from the 8th Century. The other is a Kingdom, ruled by a Holly (bloodline) Sovereign Monarch. Origin of concept of State

973. Unlike a proper Kingdom, the Sovereign Authority of a State has always rested in a body politic such as a council of nobles that then elects a Statholder (Steward) to administer and oversee the functions of government. Sovereign Authority of a State

Article 307 – Nation

974. A ***Nation*** is a late 17th Century political term describing a new method of classification of societies as either: (a) A sovereign body politic and corporate; or (b) a people without full sovereign authority. The first "nation" as a sovereign body politic and corporate was the Kingdom of England and Wales by 1661. Nation

975. The qualifications of what constitutes a Nation and its type is derived from the philosophical works written to establish new international laws from the late 17th Century into the 18th Century:- Qualifications of Nation

(i) To qualify to be called a "Nation" an indigenous people must first share a common cultural identity and system of law, demonstrating a historic continuity of habitation within a distinct place with defined boundaries; and

(ii) To qualify to be called a "Sovereign Nation" such a people sharing a common cultural identity and system of law must then be represented by a Body Politic and Corporate formally recognised politically through one or more treaties.

976. The Non-Ucadian Law of Nations was developed over a period from the 16th Century to 18th Century around the following major works:- Development of Law of Nations

(i) "**Relectiones Theologicae**" (Theological Reflections)

Francisco de Vitoria (1483–1546): In the early 16th century, Vitoria, a Spanish theologian and jurist, gave a series of lectures that laid the groundwork for modern international law. His work addressed the rights of indigenous peoples and the legality of conquest, which was highly relevant during the age of European exploration and colonization; and

(ii) **"De Jure Belli ac Pacis"** (On the Law of War and Peace) Hugo Grotius (1583–1645): Published in 1625, this work by the Dutch scholar Hugo Grotius is often regarded as the foundational text of international law. It laid out a system of principles of natural law, which are applicable to the conduct of states and international relations; and

(iii) **"De Jure Naturae et Gentium"** (On the Law of Nature and of Nations) Samuel von Pufendorf (1632–1694): Published in 1672, this work by Pufendorf further developed the ideas of natural law and its application to the law of nations. His work emphasized the importance of state sovereignty and international morality; and

(iv) **"Le Droit des gens"** (The Law of Nations) Emer de Vattel (1714–1767): Published in 1758, Vattel's work is a significant contribution to the development of international law. He expanded on the ideas of Grotius and others, focusing on the rights and duties of states.

977. Ucadia recognises traditional States and Nations that choose to confirm their sovereign status through Ucadia, or choose to treaty with Ucadia. Within Ucadia Law, the highest form of Nations are called "**Original Nations**" being the innate rights that cannot be surrendered, waived, seized, forfeited, sold or impeded in relation to Indigenous Peoples. Ucadia and Nations

978. The key elements by original definition of what constitutes an *Original Nation* under Ucadia Law are Indigenous People, Common Cultural Identity, System of Law, Historic Continuity of Habitation, Body Politic and Political Recognition:- Ucadia and Original Nations

(i) An ***Indigenous People*** means literally a body of people born to a land or region, especially sharing ancestry before any settlement or claims before territories or countries; and

(ii) ***Common Cultural Identity*** means a distinct and unique cultural identity in the form of stories, history, conflict and resolution, language and phrases, arts and music, sacred sites and texts compared to other people within the larger region; and

(iii) ***Historic Continuity of Habitation*** means permanent settlement of the land beyond three (3) generations whereby claimed ownership and possession of land exceeds one hundred (100) years; and

(iv) A ***Body Politic*** of a Nation is the existence of a form of government or collective representation by which the people agree at some level to be governed; and

(v) ***Political Recognition*** in the form of one or more treaties between Ucadia Bodies, whether or not any Non-Ucadia bodies recognise their own laws concerning original persons or not.

Article 308 - Territory

979. A ***Territory*** is an 8th Century term meaning part of a society separated from the rest having a unique geographic and topographical position, possessing one or more permanent settlements united by a distinct body politic and demography and formally recognised through one or more treaties. Territory

980. The word *Territory* is derived from the combination of two (2) Latin words *Terra* meaning "land" and *Torus* meaning "bind by (strong) knot". Hence the literal meaning of Territory is "to bind (the use of) the land by some strong knot (treaty)". Origin of the word Territory

981. The key elements by original definition of what constitutes a Territory are Geography, Topography, Settlements, Body Politic, Demography, Parent Country, Nation and Political Recognition: Territorial Definition

(i) ***Geography*** of a Territory is the survey and measurement of the physical characteristics of a particular place including its boundaries that it may be described uniquely; and

(ii) ***Topography*** of a Territory is the application of certain names and language of cultural meaning to landmarks, maps, charts and surveys of the Geography including the physical evidence of these points of topography including but not limited to posts, monuments and markers; and

(iii) ***Settlements*** within a Territory is the existence of at least one permanent settlement upon declared and claimed sovereign soil, also representing a topographical post; and

(iv) A ***Body Politic*** of a Territory is the existence of a form of government and sovereignty by which the permanent settlements agree to be governed; and

(v) The ***Demography*** of a Territory is the unique survey and characteristics of the people, the political and administrative divisions of the place according to the Topography of the Territory; and

(vi) A ***Parent Country*** of a Territory is that Country claiming ultimate sovereignty over the boundaries of the Territory and whose citizens or subjects primarily founded one or more of the Settlements granted partial legislative autonomy; and

(vii) A ***Nation*** being a homogenous race of traditional land owners, usually called "Natives", "Aborigines" or "Indians" possessing a distinct documented culture and leadership formally recognized as a "Nation" and capable of entering into a formal binding agreement or "treaty"; and

(viii) ***Political Recognition*** of a Territory being the signing and enacting of a Treaty between the Body Politic of Settlers and the Nation of Traditional and Indigenous Land Owners involving some transfer of rights of recognition of the sovereignty of land claimed by the Settlers.

Article 309 – Country

982. A ***Country*** is a 17th Century term meaning a State as defined by its demography and political status. Country

983. The word "Country" is derived from the combination of two (2) Latin words *Conti* meaning "poles (posts)" and *Tres* meaning "three". Hence the literal meaning of Country is "three posts or poles on conquered /claimed land". Origin of the word Country

984. The key elements by original definition of what constitutes a Country are Geography, Topography, Settlements, Body Politic, Demography and Political Recognition:- Elements of Country

(i) Geography of a Country is the survey and measurement of the physical characteristics of a particular place including its boundaries that it may be described uniquely; and

(ii) Topography of a Country is the application of certain names and language of cultural meaning to landmarks, maps, charts and surveys of the Geography including the physical evidence of these points of topography including but not limited to posts, monuments and markers; and

(iii) Settlements within a Country is the existence of a minimum of three (3) permanent settlements upon declared and claimed sovereign soil, also representing topographical posts, distinct and separate from one another; and

(iv) A Body Politic of a Country is the existence of a form of government and sovereignty by which the permanent settlements agree to be governed; and

(v) The Demography of a Country is the unique survey and characteristics of the people, the political and administrative divisions of the place according to the Topography of the Country; and

(vi) Political Recognition of a Country is any formal act by the government or legislature of another Country whereby the existence and status of the Country is publicly acknowledged by decree, deed, statute, gazette, treaty or some other means.

985. The different types of Countries may be defined by any of the variations in the key elements of what constitutes a Country, especially by type of Body Politic or by Independent Sovereign Jurisdiction of its boundaries:- Types of Countries

(i) A Country may be capable of exercising exclusive and full independent Sovereign Jurisdiction within its boundaries; or

(ii) A Country may be partially annexed whereby some of its claimed territory is occupied by forces of a different Country; or

(iii) A Country may be fully occupied by forces of a different Country; or

(iv) A Country may itself also represent a Territory of another "higher" Country. Alternatively, a Country may possess one or more Territories itself, that may also qualify as being defined as a Country; and

(v) The non-recognition of a Country by an external body or other Countries does not diminish or abrogate the validity of a Country that is capable of demonstrating all other key elements of what constitutes a Country.

Article 310 – Plantation

986. A ***Plantation*** is a term invented in the mid 17th Century to describe the disenfranchised and privatised English Colonies, particular those in the Americas, that had their rights and self governance disbanded by Charles II (1660-1685) after siding with Parliament against the Crown during the English Civil War. Plantation

987. The term Plantation as a 17th Century invented legal term derived from two (2) Latin words *planta* meaning "plant, growth, fruits, the sole of the foot" and *atio* meaning "state of; condition of". Hence the Origin of Plantation literal etymological meaning of Plantation is "a state of a planter" or simply "a planters' estate". The first reference in statute in the Western-Roman Law is 15 Car. 2. c.7. (1663) and then extensively in 25 Car. 2. c.7. (1670).

9.2 – Sovereign Terrain

Article 311 – Sovereign Terrain

988. ***Sovereign Terrain*** is a term used to define a fundamental system by which a sovereign makes claim over the earth, water and air of a place on the planet and how such a claim is then justified and maintained. Sovereign Terrain

989. The word Terrain is derived from the Latin *terra* meaning "land, earth, ground, soil, country and the world". The Latin word *terra* itself is derived from the 1st Millenium BCE ancient Irish word tàra, also spelt in many ancient texts as Torá(h) meaning "land, earth, ground, rule of law". Origin of the word Terrain

990. All systems of claim of Sovereign Terrain are predicated on the truth that no man or woman can "own" the physical earth, water or air, except the Divine Creator. Instead, fictional elements created by men and women may be "added" within, below or on top of the earth, water or air and therefore claimed as private property. Thus Sovereign Terrain depends on claims of fictions. Principle of Sovereign Terrain

991. There are essentially three (3) systems and layers used to create the fabric of Sovereign Terrain being geography, topography and demography: Creation of Sovereign Terrain

(i) ***Geography*** is the use of fictional standards of measurement to survey the physical structures of a particular region; and

(ii) ***Topography*** is the use of fictional language and culture to name a place defined by certain Geography; and

(iii) ***Demography*** is the use of fictional measures, registers and numbering to count and label people, political and administrative divisions and their activities according to particular Topography of a place.

992. Whilst each layer of the system of Sovereign Terrain may be viewed independently, Demography depends on the existence of Topography and Topography depends on the existence of Geography. Interdependence of Elements

Article 312 - Geography

993. ***Geography*** is the use of fictional standards of measurement to survey the physical structures of a particular region. Geography is also sometimes used to describe all three (3) layers of defining sovereign terrain as one (1) (geography, topography and demography). Geography

994. The word Geography comes from Ancient Greek γεωγραφία (geographia) from γεω (gēo) meaning "earth" and γράφω (grapho) meaning "carve, draw, sketch or write". Origin of the word Geography

995. Geography is the root fictional system of any claim of sovereign terrain layered over the physical earth, air and water of a place and presumes the existence of some uniquely owned fictional system of measurement of distance, height, position and time through survey. Geography as root of claim of Terrain

996. It is the presence of some uniquely owned fictional system of measurement of distance, height, position and time, the physical process of survey and then reflection of such survey on maps that produces a Geography. Systems of Measurement and Geography

997. By ancient custom and tradition since the 1st Millennium BCE in accordance with Holly (Tará) Law, the physical process of survey required to derive a valid Geography requires the official visitation of a place by an agent or representative of a sovereign under seal, such that the act of visitation and definition of Geography is undertaken as if the sovereign did perform the act themselves. Origin of Geography and Terrain

998. By ancient custom and tradition since the 1st Millennium BCE in accordance with Holly (Tará) Law, the commencement of a Geographic survey by an official agent or representative of the Sovereign requires a "point of beginning", usually a historic marker, flag or monument representing the first and primary claim of the Sovereign. Permanent markers, posts or monuments are then placed at certain distances and locations around the point of beginning to both validate the claim the land has been surveyed and to enable accurate measurement. Tradition of Process of Geography

999. A Geographic survey is not invalidated should the permanent markers, posts or monuments be destroyed. Only when a completely new geographic survey is undertaken with physical evidence of its occurrence, including new maps and descriptions may the original Geographic survey and claim be invalidated. Validation of Survey

1000. By ancient custom and tradition since the 1st Millennium BCE in accordance with Holly (Tará) Law, a Geographic survey must be undertaken by an agent or representative of the sovereign and new Mandate of Surveyor maps produced every seven (7) years to be a claim without legal or lawful challenge.

Article 313 - Topography

1001. ***Topography*** is the use of fictional language and culture to name a place defined by certain Geography. Topography

1002. The word Topography comes from Ancient Greek τοπογραφία (topographia) from τόπος (topos) meaning "place" and γράφω (grapho) meaning "carve, draw, sketch or write". Origin of word Topography

1003. In reference to Topography:- Key elements of Topography

(i) Similar to Geography, Topography requires the physical visitation to the place by an agent or official of the sovereign, or sovereign themselves and the honouring of key place names and associated cultural history to validate claim of sovereign terrain; and

(ii) Topography depends on the pre-existence of a Geographic survey first. In the absence of a Geographic survey, Topography has no context; and

(iii) Unlike Geographic Surveying which requires the physical walking of the "metes and bounds" of a place, the surveying of Topography is accomplished by the creation and dedication of permanent memorials and the recording of certain historically significant events of a place; and

(iv) If Topography boundaries are Non-Linear then they may be in deference to ancient rights, habitation and ancient custom. Where Topography boundaries are linear (straight line) then it is wholly an artificial and political and military imposition.

1004. Topographical surveying is the ability to walk a geographically defined area and recount names for geographically significant land marks as well as stories of historic significance as to previous events that account for those named land marks. Topological Survey

1005. A Topographical survey cannot be extinguished by the deliberate destruction of monuments and associated history of the Geography by a conquering force. Even if false history and false monuments are inserted as an attempt by a sovereign power to an earlier claim than is entitled, once the true history is revealed, all such claims are rendered null and void. Topological Survey and Geography

1006. A new culture may perform its own Topographical survey upon the ruins of a conquered culture. However, such survey only holds true so long as the previous culture remains vanquished and does not re- New Civilisation and Topography assert its rights.

1007. Similar to Geographic surveys, Topographic surveys by ancient custom and tradition since the 3rd Century CE in accordance with Holly (Tará) Law must be undertaken by an agent or representative of the sovereign every seven (7) years to be a claim without legal or lawful challenge. Lawful Rights of Topography

Article 314 - Demography

1008. ***Demography*** is the use of fictional measures, registers, numbering, people characteristics and infrastructure to define political and administrative divisions and their activities according to particular Topography of a place. Demography

1009. The word Demography comes from Ancient Greek δημογραφία (demographia) from δημος (dēmos) meaning "people" and γράφω (grapho) meaning "carve,draw, sketch or write". Origin of word Demography

1010. Similar to Geography and Topography, Demography involves the act of survey by an agent or representative of the sovereign. However, unlike Geography and Topography, Demographic surveying is usually centred on the collection of information into a ledger which then "encloses" those items from being re-surveyed by original claim of title. Demography and Survey

1011. The concept of collecting information into a ledger as being equivalent to physical survey was first invented by the Romans through the concept of "census" whereby it was the property owners that had to prove their claim of right over property, not the Roman officials who had to visit every farm and village to check facilities and infrastructure. Census and Demography

9.3 – False, Absurd & Prohibited Realms

Article 315 - False, Absurd & Prohibited Realms

1012. False, Absurd and Prohibited Realms are any realms that seek to usurp or contradict Ucadia Law and the present Maxims. False, Absurd & Prohibited Realms

Title X – Civilisation Models of Sovereign Law

10.1 – Civilisation Models of Sovereign Law

Article 316 – Civilisation Models of Sovereign Law

1013. ***Civilisation*** refers to one or more complex human societies that have developed extensive systems of law, urban development, division of labour, trade, governance, cultural development, and unifying cultural identity. Civilisations are typically characterised by their advancements in various fields such as language, technology, arts, institutions and administration, compared to contemporary or previous societies. Civilisation

1014. A *Civilisation* differs from an *Empire* in that a "civilisation" usually defines homogeneous advances in cultural and societal development, technology, language and knowledge, whereas an "empire" primarily concerns military, political and economic dominance. Confusion can sometimes arise given Civilisations can exist without forming empires, and empires can take control of civilisations. Differences between Civilisations and Empires

1015. ***Civilisation Model of Sovereign Law*** refers to a conceptual framework and system of laws that governs the authority and conduct of a sovereign body within the particular *Civilisation*. Sovereignty in law means that a state has supreme authority within its territory and is the ultimate source of all its laws. Civilisation Models of Sovereign Law

1016. Common elements of a *Civilisation Model of Sovereign Law* that distinguish a new Civilisation from an Empire include (but are not limited to):- Common Elements of Civilisation Models of Sovereign Law

(i) ***Religion and Belief Systems***: Civilisations can be distinguished by the introduction of profound and significant new religious or belief systems and thought, that provide a new perspective and framework for understanding the world, ethics and spirituality; and

(ii) ***Language and Knowledge Systems***: Civilisations typically engineer new languages for expressing knowledge, science, law, culture and information; and

(iii) ***Sacred Texts and Primary Law Forms***: Civilisations usually showcase the application of new language and knowledge systems with the introduction of primary sacred texts and primary law forms that form the "foundation stone" for new cultures and function of societies; and

(iv) ***Legal Systems***: Civilisations have legal systems that define rights, responsibilities, and consequences for violations of societal norms and laws; and

(v) ***Political Structure***: Civilisations have organized political systems with rulers or governments that establish and enforce laws, maintain order, and make decisions for the society; and

(vi) ***Social Organization***: Civilisations typically have complex social hierarchies with various social classes, offices, positions and functions. Social roles and norms are well-defined; and

(vii) ***Writing and Record-Keeping***: Writing systems are crucial for preserving knowledge, history, laws, and cultural achievements. The development of records and registers was a significant milestone in human civilisation; and

(viii) ***Education and Knowledge Transfer***: Systems for education and knowledge transfer, such as schools, libraries, and mentorship, are integral to civilisations' intellectual growth; and

(ix) ***Technology and Tools***: Civilisations advance technologically, developing tools, machinery and techniques that improve quality of life, production, and infrastructure; and

(x) ***Economy and Trade***: Civilisations engage in economic activities such as trade, barter and currency exchange, allowing for the specialization of labour and the exchange of goods and services.

1017. Consistent with the definition and qualification of what constitutes a Civilisation (versus an Empire), the Twelve Greatest Civilisations over the past four thousand years include:- Twelve Greatest Civilisations

(i) Egyptian (Hyksos) Civilisation (1670 BCE – 314 CE); and

(ii) Keltoi (Tará) Civilisation (590 BCE – 314 CE); and

(iii) Persian Civilisation (550 BCE - present); and

(iv) Indian Civilisation (320 BCE – present); and

(v) Chinese Civilisation (221 BCE – present); and

(vi) Khmer Civilisation (160 CE – 1767); and

(vii) Maya Civilisation (1400 BCE – 1533 CE); and

(viii) Christian Civilisation (314 CE – 740 CE); and

(ix) Eastern Christian Civilisation (518 CE – present); and

(x) Islamic Civilisation (600 CE – present); and

(xi) Western (Christian) Civilisation (740 CE – present); and

(xii) Ucadia Civilisation (2001 CE – present).

1018. So while all of the twelve Greatest Civilisations over the past four thousand years were influenced in part by the Holly, only six (or half) of them were purpose built by the Holly (Cuilliaéan) Bloodlines, including:-

Six Greatest Civilisations created by Holly (Cuilliaéan) Bloodlines

(i) Egyptian (Hyksos) Civilisation (1670 BCE – 314 CE); and

(ii) Keltoi (Tará) Civilisation (590 BCE – 314 CE); and

(iii) Christian Civilisation (314 CE – 740 CE); and

(iv) Islamic Civilisation (600 CE – present); and

(v) Western (Christian) Civilisation (740 CE – present); and

(vi) Ucadia Civilisation (2001 CE – present).

10.2 – Egyptian (Hyksos) Civilisation (1670 BCE – 314 CE)

Article 317 - Egyptian (Hyksos) Civilisation (1670 BCE – 314 CE)

1019. The ***Egyptian (Hyksos) Civilisation*** (from 1670 BCE – 314 CE) is the first of the twelve Greatest Civilisations formed over the past four thousand years, that at its height stretched across an area from Ireland and the whole of the Mediterranean to North Africa, Middle East and Asia Minor. It is the first of the six Great Civilisations created by the Holly (Cuilliaéan) Bloodlines.

Egyptian (Hyksos) Civilisation

1020. Great Empires within the Egyptian Civilisation since 3100 BCE include:-

Great Empires within the Egyptian Civilisation

(i) ***Pre-Hyksos*** (3100 – 1670 BCE); and

(ii) ***Hyksos Holly Pharaohs*** (1670 – 1324 BCE); and

(iii) ***False Pharaohs*** (1324 – 525 BCE); and

(iv) ***Persian Empire*** (525 – 323 BCE); and

(v) ***Greek (Ptolemaic) Empire*** (332 – 30 BCE); and

(vi) ***Roman Empire*** (30 BCE – 310 CE); and

(vii) ***Christian Empire*** (310 – 521 CE); and

(viii) ***Eastern Christian Empire*** (521 – 620 CE); and

(ix) ***Islamic Caliphate*** (620 – 1330 CE); and

(x) ***Mamluk (Ottoman) Empire*** (1330 – 1798 CE).

1021. Egyptian (Hyksos) Civilisation Religion and Belief Systems:-

Egyptian (Hyksos)

Civilisation Religion and Belief Systems

(i) ***Ultimate Oneness of Reality (Nun)***: The primeval abyss that exists and existed before the creation of the ordered Universe. Nun is the personification of this unmanifest, formless, and undifferentiated state, often represented as a vast cosmic ocean or a chaotic, swirling mass of waters. It represents the very beginning of existence and was the source whereby all creation emerged; and

(ii) ***Ma'at (Mut)***: A central concept in Egyptian religion, representing the principles of balance, harmony, and order. It was personified as a goddess and was believed to be essential for maintaining cosmic and social order; and

(iii) ***Polytheism***: Ancient Egyptians believed in a pantheon of gods and goddesses, each with their own attributes, responsibilities, and importance. Some of the most prominent deities included Ra (the sun god), Osiris (god of the afterlife), Isis (goddess of magic and motherhood), and Horus (god of kingship and the sky); and

(iv) ***Pharaoh as a Divine Ruler***: The pharaoh was seen as a god on Earth and a mediator between the mortal world and the divine. Pharaohs were believed to be the offspring of the god Ra, and their rule was legitimized by their divine connection.

1022. Egyptian (Hyksos) Civilisation Language and Knowledge Systems:-

Egyptian (Hyksos) Civilisation Language and Knowledge Systems

(i) ***Type of Language***: *Logographic* and *Alphabetic:* ***Egyptian Hieroglyphs*** are a combination of logographic and alphabetic elements, while ***Egyptian Demotic*** is a simplified and cursive script. They include logograms (symbols representing words or concepts) and phonetic signs (symbols representing sounds or syllables). This combination allowed for the representation of both words and sounds in the script; and

(ii) ***Number of Symbols/Characters***: 700-800 graphemes for both Egyptian Hieroglyphs and Egyptian Demotic Language; and

(iii) ***Number of Common Nouns***: 85,000+ Main Common Noun Categories: Animals (27.15%), Plants (14.76%), People(14.17%), Objects(13.93%), Religion(9.92%), Science(7.50%), Law(1.65%) and Trade(1.32%); and

(iv) ***Language Rules Complexity***: *Simple*: Written to be read right-to-left, left-to-right, and top-to-bottom. Verbs conjugated to indicate tense, mood, aspect, person and number. Nouns declined to indicate nominative, accusative and genitive cases. Adjectives can come before or after the noun they modify and must agree with the noun in gender, number and case. Word order is typically Verb-Subject-Object (VSO); and

(v) ***Noble Class Vocabulary***: 30,000 – 40,000; and

(vi) ***Professional Class Vocabulary***: 15,000 – 25,000; and

(vii) ***Worker Class Vocabulary***: 7,500 – 15,000.

1023. Egyptian (Hyksos) Civilisation Sacred Texts and Primary Law Forms include (but not limited to):-

Egyptian (Hyksos) Civilisation Sacred Texts and Primary Law Forms

(i) ***Instructions of Amenhotep*** (1541 BCE); and

(ii) ***Book of Emerging into the Light*** (Book of the Dead) (1600 BCE); and

(iii) ***Book of the Two Ways (of the blessed Dead)*** (1660 BCE); and

(iv) ***Kabalaah of Akhenaten*** (Moses) (1320 BCE): As recognised and restored in accord with the most sacred Covenant *Pactum De Singularis Caelum*; and

(v) ***Lebor Clann Glas of the Holly Diaspora***: As recognised and restored in accord with the most sacred Covenant *Pactum De Singularis Caelum*.

1024. Egyptian (Hyksos) Civilisation Legal Systems:-

Egyptian (Hyksos) Civilisation Legal Systems

(i) ***Religious Influence***: The highest law was considered Divine Law; and many laws were influenced by religious beliefs and the concept of Ma'at; and

(ii) ***Pharaoh's Authority***: The pharaoh was the ultimate authority and lawgiver, believed to be a divine messenger who upheld Ma'at (cosmic balance and order); and

(iii) ***Hierarchical Structure***: A complex hierarchy of officials, judges and scribes administered justice; and

(iv) ***Local Courts***: Justice was dispensed at local and regional levels, addressing various civil and criminal matters; and

(v) ***Codified Laws***: Some periods saw the development of legal codes, like the famous *Code of Ur-Nammu*; and

(vi) ***Family Law***: Matters like marriage, divorce, inheritance and adoption had specific legal regulations; and

(vii) ***Property Rights***: Property ownership, boundaries and disputes were addressed through legal means; and

(viii) ***Statutes of Limitations***: Some laws had statutes of limitations, limiting the time for pursuing legal claims; and

(ix) ***Formal Legal Procedures***: Courts followed formal procedures, and witnesses and documentation were important; and

(x) ***Case-by-Case Basis***: Decisions were made on a case-by-case basis, considering circumstances and evidence; and

(xi) ***Papyrus Records***: Legal documents and contracts were often recorded on papyrus; and

(xii) ***Oaths and Ordeals***: Making oaths and undergoing ordeals were methods to determine guilt or innocence; and

(xiii) ***Compensation***: Victims often received compensation, and restitution was a common form of punishment; and

(xiv) ***Punishments***: Punishments included fines, labor, exile, mutilation and in severe cases, execution.

1025. Egyptian (Hyksos) Civilisation Key Positions:-

Egyptian (Hyksos) Civilisation Key Positions

(i) **Pharaoh**: The highest title, denoting the king or ruler of Egypt, often considered a god in human form; and

(ii) **Hery-Akht-Nswt (Chief Vizier)**: The pharaoh's chief advisor and the highest-ranking government official, responsible for administration and justice; and

(iii) **Hery-Hem-Netjer (Chief Prophet)**: The top religious leader in a temple, responsible for rituals, ceremonies, and managing temple properties and personnel; and

(iv) **Khet-Per-Nesu (Treasurer)**: Responsible for managing the wealth and economic resources of Egypt, including collecting taxes and overseeing granaries; and

(v) **Khet-Abu-Nesu (Royal Seal Bearer)**: A trusted official who held the royal seal, a symbol of the pharaoh's authority, used to stamp official documents; and

(vi) **Khet-Hemu-Nesu (Overseer of Works)**: In charge of public works and construction projects, including temples, tombs, and other significant buildings; and

(vii) **Khet-Wuhem-Nesu (Overseer of Granaries)**: In charge of the storage and distribution of grain, a vital role in a society where agriculture was the backbone of the economy; and

(viii) **Khet-Wat-Nesu (Head General)**: Military leader responsible for the pharaoh's army, defense strategies and military campaigns; and

(ix) **Wab-Nesut** (Provincial Governor): A governor or ruler of a nome (district), responsible for local administration, taxation, and justice.

1026. Egyptian (Hyksos) Civilisation Social Organization:-

Egyptian (Hyksos) Civilisation Social Organization

(i) ***Priest Class*** (< 1%): The priesthood was the most powerful and respected class in ancient Egypt. They played a significant role in religious rituals and ceremonies, including the maintenance of temples and tombs. Temples were also centres of economic and political power; and

(ii) ***Noble Service Class*** (< 1%): The noble service class represented high ranking officials and their families and the second most powerful and respected class in ancient Egypt. This class included individuals like viziers (chief advisors) and generals. They were responsible for governing the various regions of Egypt and managing its resources; and

(iii) ***Public Servant Class*** (2-5%): The public service class represented members of skilled professions, such as scribes, artisans, craftspeople, engineers and project managers as the third class; and

(iv) ***Agricultural Class*** (20-30%): The agricultural class represented the majority of the population in ancient Egypt. Their labour was crucial for producing food for the entire society. Farmers were organized into villages and worked the land collectively; and

(v) ***Merchant Class*** (5-10%): The merchant class represented a small but influential class of Egyptian society in the provision of objects, materials and items; and

(vi) ***Worker Class*** (30-40%): The worker class were predominantly associated with massive building projects as contractors; and

(vii) ***Slave and Bonded Service Class*** (1-2%): Slaves were typically prisoners of war or individuals who had fallen into debt. They were at the bottom of the social hierarchy and had few rights.

10.3 – Keltoi (Tará) Civilisation (590 BCE – 314 CE)

Article 318 - Keltoi (Tará) Civilisation (590 BCE – 314 CE)

1027. The ***Keltoi (Tará) Civilisation*** (from 590 BCE – 314 CE) is the second of the twelve Greatest Civilisations formed over the past four thousand years, that at its height stretched across an area from Ireland and the whole of Europe to Asia Minor and North Africa. It is the second of the six Great Civilisations created by the Holly (Cuilliaéan) Bloodlines. Keltoi (Tará) Civilisation

1028. Great Empires that began or arose within the framework and context of Keltoi Civilisation include (but are not limited to):- Great Empires within the Keltoi (Tará) Civilisation

(i) Early Keltoi (Celt) Empire (590 – 40 BCE); and

(ii) Late Keltoi (Celt) Empire (70 – 180 CE).

1029. Keltoi (Tará) Civilisation Religion and Belief Systems include (but are not limited to):- Keltoi (Tará) Civilisation Religion and Belief Systems

(i) ***Ultimate Oneness of Reality (Día)***: The ultimate divine reality and presence that is the source of all nature and the cosmos. Día is both the personification of this ultimate unmanifest, formless, and undifferentiated oneness of reality and the presence or "animism" in every living and non living thing including (but not limited to) trees, rivers, rocks, animals, and celestial bodies; and

(ii) ***Nature Worship***: The Celts held a deep reverence for nature. They believed that spirits or deities resided in natural features such as trees, rivers, and mountains. Sacred groves and natural sites were important for religious rituals; and

(iii) ***Cuilliaéan (Holly)***: Holly were the religious leaders and scholars of Celtic society, later corrupted as "Druids". They played a central role in Celtic religious practices, conducting rituals, offering sacrifices, and providing guidance on matters of spirituality and the natural world; and

(iv) ***Ancestor Worship***: Ancestor worship was an integral part of Celtic spirituality. Ancestors were believed to have a continued presence and influence on the living, and they were honoured through rituals and offerings; and

(v) ***Sacred Symbols***: Celtic art and symbolism featured intricate designs, including spirals, knots, and animal motifs. These symbols were often associated with spiritual significance and protection; and

(vi) ***Seasonal Festivals***: The Celts celebrated a variety of seasonal festivals that marked agricultural and astronomical events.

1030. Keltoi (Tará) Civilisation Language and Knowledge Systems:- Keltoi (Tará) Civilisation Language and Knowledge Systems

(i) ***Type of Language***: *Alphabetic*: Alphabetic symbols whereby individual characters (letters) represent consonants and vowels; and

(ii) ***Number of Characters***: 18 graphemes. There is no equivalent symbols for the letter J, K, Q, V, W, X, Y and Z; and

(iii) ***Number of Common Nouns***: 66,000+ Main Common Noun Categories: Animals(26.90%), Plants(15.69%), People(14.95%), Objects(14.20%), Science(7.51%), Religion(6.40%), Law(2.24%) and Trade(1.79%); and

(iv) ***Language Rules Complexity***: *Simple*: Written to be read left-to-right. Verbs conjugated to indicate tense, mood, person, and number. Nouns declined based on number, and case with five grammatical cases: nominative, vocative, genitive, dative, and accusative. Adjectives must agree in gender, number, and case with the nouns they describe. Ancient Gaelic typically follows a Verb-Subject-Object (VSO) word order. No personal pronouns, possessive pronouns, and reflexive pronouns or nouns categorised as masculine or feminine until language was deliberately and intentionally targetted to be corrupted from 18th to 19th Century to create "modern Irish"; and

(v) ***Noble Class Vocabulary***: 20,000 – 30,000; and

(vi) ***Professional Class Vocabulary***: 12,000 – 20,000; and

(vii) ***Worker Class Vocabulary***: 6,500 – 12,000.

1031. Keltoi (Tará) Civilisation Sacred Texts and Primary Law Forms:- Keltoi (Tará) Civilisation Sacred Texts and Primary Law Forms

(i) ***Tara of Jeremiah and the Celts***: As recognised and restored in accord with the most sacred Covenant *Pactum De Singularis Caelum*; and

(ii) ***Lebor Clann Glas of the Holly Diaspora***: As recognised and restored in accord with the most sacred Covenant *Pactum De Singularis Caelum*.

1032. Keltoi (Tará) Civilisation Legal Systems:- Keltoi (Tará) Civilisation Legal Systems

(i) **Religious Influence**: The highest law was considered Divine Law; and

(ii) **Celtic Law Codes**: Codes were used to standardise laws across key areas including property, family and trade; and

(iii) **Property Rights**: Laws governed land ownership, inheritance and property disputes; and

(iv) **Women's Rights**: Celtic societies recognized the legal rights of women, including property ownership and inheritance; and

(v) **Hospitality**: The concept of hospitality was highly regarded, and laws protected guests and hosts; and

(vi) **Oaths**: Oaths were taken seriously and often used as evidence in legal proceedings; and

(vii) **Role of the Holly**: The Holly held influence in legal matters, along with religious and cultural roles; and

(viii) **Brehons**: Were legal experts or judges who played a crucial role in interpreting and applying the law; and

(ix) **Conflict Resolution**: Mediation and negotiation were common methods for resolving disputes; and

(x) **Compensation**: The system emphasized restitution and compensation for harm or wrongdoing, rather than strict punishment; and

(xi) **Fines (Eric)**: The payment of fines, known as "eric," was a common form of compensation for injuries or offences; and

(xii) **Exile**: Exile was a form of punishment for serious offences, removing the offender from the community.

1033. Keltoi (Tará) Civilisation Key Positions:-

Keltoi (Tará) Civilisation Key Positions

(i) **Ard Rà** (High King): The emperor or supreme ruler of the Celts; and

(ii) **Rui Rà** (Overrule King): The leader and ruler, responsible for several Truatha called a "banda"; and

(iii) **Tigarna Rà** (Lord King): The leader and responsible for responsible for a clan or a Truatha ("tuatha"); and

(iv) **Ollamh Érenn** (Chief Judge of Ireland): Head of the High Druid Council of (Holly) Cuilliaéan. Abolished around 368 CE; and

(v) **Brehon** (Holly): Cuilliaéan Judge.

1034. Keltoi (Tará) Civilisation Social Organization:-

Keltoi (Tará) Civilisation Social Organization

(i) ***Aos Dé*** (< 1%) "people of the divine": The Celtic priesthood was the most powerful and respected class in ancient Keltoi

Civilisation; and

(ii) ***Aos Rátha*** (< 1%) "people of protection, prosperity and good fortune": The noble service class represented high ranking officials and their families and the second most powerful and respected class in ancient Keltoi Civilisation, who owed their position not by wealth but by trusted service. This class included individuals like viziers (chief advisors), generals and managers. They were responsible for governing the various regions of Celtic society and managing its resources; and

(iii) ***Aos Dána*** (15-20%) "people of knowledge, skill and artistry": Keltoi (Celtic) Civilisation had one of the highest proportions of skilled class. This class included all manner of scribes, artisans, masons, craftspeople, engineers and project managers; and

(iv) ***Aos Feara*** (40-50%) "people of the land": The largest class of agricultural and general labourers; and

(v) ***Aos Fianna*** (10-15%) "people of heroic warrior skills": The warrior class of professional soldiers were considered their own class; and something that was adopted by many other civilisations such as the Romans; and

(vi) ***Aos Gnóa*** (5-10%) "people of knowledge of trade and calculation": The merchant class represented a small but influential class of Celtic society in the provision of objects, materials and items; and

(vii) ***Aos Mála*** (2-5%) "people condemned as notorious, ill tempered and untrustworthy": Condemned criminals called the *ui nial* (O'Niell) meaning "people without honour"; and *ui brien* (O'Brien) meaning "bonded service" as debtors. Celtic law, similar to all Holly law forbid slavery in all its forms.

10.4 – Persian Civilisation (550 BCE - present)

Article 319 – Persian Civilisation (550 BCE - present)

1035. The ***Persian Civilisation*** (from 550 BCE - present) is the third of the twelve Greatest Civilisations formed over the past four thousand years, that at its height stretched across an area from Greece, North Africa, Asia Minor and Persia to Afghanistan and Northern India. Persian Civilisation

1036. The following is a brief summary of the historical context in relation to the rise of the Persian Civilisation:- Historical Context of Persian Civilisation

(i) Persian Civilisation is not the product of a single Empire, but a history of multiple Empires that technically can be traced (in part) back to the Golden Age of Babylon (2012 BCE – 1670 BCE); and

(ii) Beginning around 1245 BCE, Ancient Western Civilisation went through a dark and oppressive period that saw the rise and fall of a number of brutal empires including the Kananites of Syria and the Phoenician states of Palestine and North Africa, culminating in catastrophic meteorite showers, earthquakes and tsunami around 1159 BCE that destroyed the functionality of all major empires at the time; and

(iii) After 500 years of warring city states, one of the first functional empires to return was under King Cambyses, also known as Nebuchadnezzar of Babylon by 610 CE. Yet it was Cyrus the Great (600-530 BCE) that established the new state religion of Mithraism, created a new language and new law forms that heralded the proper "birth" of the first Persian Empire, variously known as the "Achaemenid Empire" (560 – 330 BCE); and

(iv) Contrary to false history, the city of Rome was founded no earlier than 540 BCE as a Persian colony called Setyan-Ur meaning "city of Satan" by Chaldean Yahudi diaspora from šumur (Chaldis) šulumur (Erétria) from the Island of Euboea. In 481 BCE, the city was renamed Roma by its Patron Shah Xerxes I (486-465 BCE). The Praetorian were always first a Royal Persian Garrison charged with ensuring the loyalty of the colony, as well as protection of the government of Rome. The official state religion of Rome was always Mithraism until 70 CE and the Roman Emperors were honoured with burial at the sacred Mithraic City of the Dead at Petra. Hence, Rome was technically always part of the Greater Persian Civilisation until 313 CE; and

(v) Contrary to false history, by 480 BCE, Xerxes I of Persia conquered all of Greece and was largely the architect and builder of Athens, including the Parthenon and the Acropolis. Thus, Athens was similar to Rome in being a Persian colony, with Mithraism being the official state religion until 70 CE.

1037. Great Empires that began or arose within the framework and context of Persian Civilisation include (but are not limited to):- Great Empires within the Persian Civilisation

(i) ***Achaemenid Empire*** (550 – 330 BCE): Founded by Cyrus the Great, it encompassed a vast territory and was known for its administrative innovations, including the use of a standardized currency and a network of roads known as the Royal Roads; and

(ii) ***Parthian Empire*** (247 BCE - 320 CE): Known for its skilled cavalry and its conflicts with the Roman Empire. The Parthians blended Hellenistic and Persian culture and played a crucial role in Silk Road trade before the advent of Christianity; and

(iii) ***Christian Empire*** (320 – 527 CE): Persia was a key Politea (Nation) within the structure of Christianity until the split of East and West. There were several Neo-Zoroastrian rebellions throughout this period, deliberately misrepresented in the fictitious history of the "Sassanids" to hide the fact that Persia was Christian for two centuries; and

(iv) ***Islamic Caliphates*** (637-1219): Peacefully converted to Islam as the Caliphate of Al-Samanid meaning "people of the first home of humanity and a righteous and worthy culture". Absorbed into a large Caliphate with Syria and Middle East known as Al Abbasid 658 CE. Caliphate was dissolved upon the conquests of the Mongols by 1219; and

(v) ***Mongol Empire*** (1219-1335): The Mongol Empire, under Genghis Khan and his successors, conquered Persia in the 13th century. The Mongols ruled Persia through the Ilkhanate, adopting some Persian administrative practices, until the empire fragmented, leading to the rise of regional dynasties in the region; and

(vi) ***Safavid Empire*** (1530-1736): Creation of Shia Islam and the founding of Tehran as "Eden". It saw a flourishing of Persian culture, art and architecture, notably under Shah Abbas the Great; and

(vii) ***Qajar Dynasty***: The Qajar Dynasty ruled Persia (modern-day Iran) from the late 18th to early 20th century culminating in the Persian Constitutional Revolution of 1905-1911.

1038. The foundational Religious and Belief System established under Cyrus the Great that spread across the world under Persian Civilisation was Mithraism:- Persian Civilisation Religion and Belief Systems

(i) ***Ultimate Duality of Reality (Ahura Mazda vs Angra Mainyu)***: The Universe is ruled by two opposing forces Order and Chaos. *Ahura Mazda* is the supreme and benevolent deity who represents the ultimate reality of goodness, order and truth. The opposite or adversary of Ahura Mazda is *Angra Mainyu* as the embodiment of evil, chaos, and falsehood; and

(ii) **Mithraism**: Was a blending of the religion of the Yahudi followers of rebel Hyksos Egyptian Pharaoh Akhenaten (Moses) and the former state religion of Zoroastrianism of Babylon; and

(iii) ***Polytheism***: The main pantheon and trinity of Gods were Yahu (or Ahura) the ultimate Creator Being; and Setyan the hidden god of the void and sky, power and chaos; and Kybele the virgin mother god of the earth; and Mithra, the saviour god of light, knowledge and trust; and

(iv) **Setyan**: The god Setyan was a derivation of the ancient Hyksos god Set as god of the desert, storms and power. Under the religious tolerance laws of the Persian Civilization, the gods were permitted to be named locally. Thus the Greeks called Setyan "Zeus", while the Romans called Setyan "Saturn". The most important religious festival of Ancient Rome was "Saturnalia" in honour of the founding city god "Setyan"; and

(v) **Mithra**: Born from sacred rock by virgin on the 14 Nisan (14 Mars) by Persian Calendar. He was called the "lightbringer", the "saviour god" and hero, who sacrificed his own life on his birthday 14 Nisan (14 Mars) so that humanity would be saved. The night before the birthday of Mithra famously became known as the Passion or "Pascha" or the Passover, while the birthday of Mithra famously became the Day of Blood or "Dies Sanguinus" to the Romans; and

(vi) **Sacred Symbols**: To the Persian and Roman armies, Mithra was their most sacred god; and many of the symbols and ceremonies concerning Roman Legions revolved around the beliefs and important symbols of Mithra.

1039. The Persian Civilisation Language and Knowledge System of ***Pahlavi*** as introduced from 550 BCE includes:- Persian Civilisation Language and Knowledge Systems

(i) ***Type of Language***: *Abjad*: Meaning the symbols represent only consonant sounds and typically omit vowel sounds that are indicated through diacritics or context; and

(ii) ***Number of Characters***: 23 to 29 graphemes for consonants; and

(iii) ***Number of Common Nouns***: 53,000+ Main Common Noun Categories: Animals(20.86%), Objects(19.91%), People(15.17%), Plants(12.33%), Science(9.05%), Law(4.55%), Religion(4.36%) and Trade(3.64%); and

(iv) ***Language Rules Complexity***: *Simple*: Written to be read right-to-left. Suffixes and prefixes added to root words to convey grammatical information. Verbs conjugated to indicate tense, mood, voice and person. Nouns declined based on gender, number and case. Postpositions, rather than prepositions, to indicate relationships between words. Verbs usually comes at the end of a sentence or clause; and

(v) ***Noble Class Vocabulary***: 15,000 – 24,000; and

(vi) ***Professional Class Vocabulary***: 10,000 – 18,000; and

(vii) ***Worker Class Vocabulary***: 2,500 –4,500.

1040. Persian Civilisation Sacred Texts and Primary Law Forms:- Persian Civilisation Sacred Texts and Primary Law Forms

(i) ***Missal of Baal Mithra***: As recognised and restored in accord with the most sacred Covenant *Pactum De Singularis Caelum*; and

(i) ***Acadia of Xerxes***: As recognised and restored in accord with the most sacred Covenant *Pactum De Singularis Caelum*; and

(ii) ***Lebor Clann Glas of the Holly Diaspora***: As recognised and restored in accord with the most sacred Covenant *Pactum De Singularis Caelum.*

1041. Persian Civilisation Legal Systems:- Persian Civilisation Legal Systems

(i) ***Religious Influence***: The highest law was considered Divine Law; and Zoroastrianism and then Mithraism as the state religion, that played a significant role in shaping Persian legal principles, emphasizing truth, justice and morality; and

(ii) ***Royal Authority***: The Persian king, or Shah, held supreme authority and was often seen as the living embodiment of the law; and

(iii) ***Codified Laws***: The most famous Persian legal code was the "Codex of Hammurabi" as one of the earliest known legal codes that covered a wide range of civil and criminal matters; and

(iv) ***Courts and Judges***: Persian courts and judges were responsible for interpreting and applying the law, and they had authority to settle disputes; and

(v) ***Infrastructure***: The Persian Empire had an advanced infrastructure for communication and record-keeping, facilitating the administration of justice; and

(vi) ***Fair Treatment***: Persian law aimed at fairness and justice, and judges were expected to make impartial decisions; and

(vii) ***Property Rights***: Laws protected property rights, including land ownership, inheritance and contracts; and

(viii) ***Tort Law***: Persian law addressed issues of personal injury and property damage, allowing victims to seek compensation; and

(ix) ***Contract Law***: Contracts were legally binding, and breaches were subject to penalties; and

(x) ***Family Law***: Laws governed matters such as marriage, divorce and inheritance, often influenced by Zoroastrian customs; and

(xi) ***Taxation***: Taxation laws were well-defined, specifying who was responsible for paying taxes and in what form; and

(xii) ***Witnesses and Evidence***: Witnesses and evidence played a crucial role in legal proceedings, and false testimony was punished; and

(xiii) ***Punishments***: Punishment for crimes included fines, imprisonment, and physical punishments. The severity of punishment varied with the nature of the offence; and

(xiv) ***Exile***: Exile was used as a punishment for certain crimes, removing the offender from the community.

1042. Persian Civilisation Key Positions:- Persian Civilisation Key Positions

(i) ***Shahanshah*** (King of Kings): The emperor or supreme ruler of the Persian Empire; and

(ii) ***Vizier***: A high-ranking advisor to the king, often involved in policy making and administration; and

(iii) ***Magi***: Priests of Zoroastrianism, responsible for religious ceremonies, rituals, and advising the king on spiritual matters; and

(iv) ***Daricbearer***: Treasurer or financial administrator, responsible for managing the empire's treasury and finances; and

(v) ***Spahbed***: A high-ranking general in the Persian military, commanding large army divisions; and

(vi) ***Satrap***: Governor of a satrapy (province), responsible for administration, tax collection and military recruitment within their province; and

(vii) ***Frataraka***: Regional or local governors or rulers, often in charge of smaller territories within a satrapy.

1043. Persian Civilisation Social Organization:- Persian Civilisation Social Organization

(i) ***Aryān*** "noble class" (< 1%): The "Aryan" class were the highest class in Persian society, gaining trust through loyal and effective service, then over time gaining enormous personal wealth and power through the ownership of people as slaves as well as valuable resources; and

(ii) ***Magān*** "priest class" (< 1%): The priesthood was less significant under Persian society than many other civilisations. However, the Priest class was the source of political power and vital to holding any form of "legitimacy" through the other classes ; and

(iii) ***Rāzīgān*** "military class" (10-15%): The professional military class of ancient Persia and its colonies (such as Rome and Greece) were a major class and the ultimate source of gaining power; and

(iv) ***Rāyānagān*** "public service class" (2-5%): The public service class represented members of skilled professions, such as scribes, artisans, craftspeople, engineers and project managers; and

(v) ***Pādagān*** "merchant class" (5-10%): The merchant class represented a significant class of Persian society in the provision of objects, materials and items; and

(vi) ***Kārdārgān*** "labourer class" (20-30%): The agricultural class represented the majority of the "free" population in ancient Persia. Their labour was crucial for producing food for the entire society; and

(vii) ***Bandagān*** "slave class" (20-30%): Slaves were typically prisoners of war or individuals convicted of crimes. Slaves were owned as private property and one of the major "assets" for the noble classes.

10.5 – Indian Civilisation (320 BCE - present)

Article 320 – Indian Civilisation (320 BCE - present)

1044. The ***Indian Civilisation*** (from 320 BCE - present) is the fourth of the twelve Greatest Civilisations formed over the past four thousand years, that at its height stretched across an area from eastern Persia, Afghanistan and India to South-East Asia. Indian Civilisation

1045. Great Empires that began or arose within the framework and context of Indian Civilisation include (but are not limited to):- Great Empires within the Indian Civilisation

(i) ***Maurya Empire*** 322 BCE - 185 BCE founded by Chandragupta Maurya and expanded by Ashoka the Great, was one of the earliest empires to unify a large part of the Indian subcontinent. Ashoka is known for his conversion to Buddhism and his efforts to spread the teachings of Buddhism; and

(ii) ***Gupta Empire*** 320 CE - 550 CE often referred to as the "Golden Age of India". It was a time of great cultural and scientific achievements, including advancements in mathematics, astronomy and the arts. The Gupta rulers supported Hinduism; and

(iii) ***Mughal Empire*** 1526 CE - 1857 CE founded by Babur, was known for its cultural and architectural achievements. It was a period of relative religious tolerance, with emperors like Akbar promoting a policy of religious inclusivity. The Taj Mahal is one of the most famous Mughal architectural wonders.

1046. Indian Civilisation Religion and Belief Systems:- Indian Civilisation Religion and Belief Systems

(i) ***Ultimate Oneness of Reality (Brahman, Siddha)***: The the ultimate reality or supreme cosmic power, from which everything emanates. An eternal, transcendent reality; and

(ii) **Polytheism**: Many Indian religions, such as Hinduism and some forms of Buddhism, are polytheistic, meaning they involve the worship of multiple gods and goddesses. Each deity represents various aspects of the divine or natural world; and

(iii) **Dharma**: Dharma is the moral and ethical duty or responsibility that individuals have in life. It varies depending on one's age, caste, gender and social role. Fulfilling one's dharma is essential for spiritual progress; and

(iv) **Karma**: Reincarnation is a central belief in Indian religions, wherein the soul is reborn into a new body after death. The concept of karma, the principle of cause and effect, is closely linked to reincarnation. Good actions lead to positive outcomes in future lives, while bad actions lead to suffering; and

(v) **Caste System**: The caste system has been a prominent social and religious institution in India, particularly in Hinduism. It categorizes society into hierarchical groups (castes) with defined roles and duties.

Indian Civilisation Language and Knowledge Systems

1047. The Indian Civilisation Language and Knowledge System of ***Sanskrit*** as first introduced around 320 BCE, (but claimed to have a much older provenance by thousands of years), includes:-

(i) ***Type of Language***: *Abugida*: Meaning each character represents a consonant with an inherent vowel sound that can be modified with diacritical marks to represent different vowel sounds; and

(ii) ***Number of Characters***: 33 distinct graphemes for consonants and around 12 distinct graphemes for vowels, resulting in a total of approximately 45 basic graphemes; and

(iii) ***Number of Common Nouns***: 56,000+ Main Common Noun Categories: Animals(22.87%), Religion(21.29%), Objects(13.20%), Plants(11.44%), People(10.56%), Science(7.61%), Law(2.64%) and Trade(2.11%); and

(iv) ***Language Rules Complexity***: *Simple*: Written to be read left-to-right. Verbs conjugated to indicate tense, mood, voice, and person. Nouns declined based on gender, number, and case. Adjectives must agree in gender, number, and case with the nouns they describe. Verbs usually comes at the end of a sentence or clause. Subject-Object-Verb (SOV); and

(v) ***Noble Class Vocabulary***: 14,000 – 26,000; and

(vi) ***Professional Class Vocabulary***: 4,000 – 16,000; and

(vii) ***Worker Class Vocabulary***: 2,500 – 4,000.

Indian Civilisation Sacred Texts and Primary Law Forms

1048. Indian Civilisation Sacred Texts and Primary Law Forms:-

(i) ***Vedas (Shruti)***: The four Vedas: Rigveda, Yajurveda, Samaveda and Atharvaveda; and

(ii) ***Mahabharata (Smriti)***: The Mahabharata is one of the longest epic poems in the world and includes the Bhagavad Gita as one of its chapters; and

(iii) ***Tripitaka (Pali Canon)***: Vinaya Pitaka, Sutta Pitaka and Abhidhamma Pitaka; and

(iv) ***Agamas***: Digambara Agamas, Svetambara Agamas; and

(v) ***Sanatana Dharma of Supreme Creator (Brahman)***: As recognised and restored in accord with the most sacred Covenant *Pactum De Singularis Caelum*; and

(vi) ***Lebor Clann Glas of the Holly Diaspora***: As recognised and restored in accord with the most sacred Covenant *Pactum De Singularis Caelum*.

1049. Indian Civilisation Legal Systems:- Indian Civilisation Legal Systems

(i) ***Religious Influence***: The highest law was considered Divine Law; and Central to Indian law was the concept of dharma, which encompassed moral and ethical duties and principles that guided individuals and society; and

(ii) **Varna System**: The Indian social hierarchy, based on varna (caste), affected legal rights and responsibilities; and

(iii) **Customary Laws**: Customary practices and traditions played a crucial role in legal matters, often varying by region, caste and community; and

(iv) **Legal Texts**: Ancient Indian legal principles were documented in texts like Manusmriti, Arthashastra, and others, serving as guidelines for legal matters; and

(v) **Courts and Judges**: Legal disputes were resolved through the court system, with appointed judges making judgments based on dharma and local customs; and

(vi) **Panchayats**: Village councils, or panchayats, played a significant role in resolving disputes at the local level, following customary laws; and

(vii) **Property Rights**: Legal principles protected property ownership and land rights, with specific rules for land distribution and use; and

(viii) **Women's Rights**: Women had legal rights, though these rights often varied depending on the region and time period; and

(ix) **Family Law**: Laws regulated marriage, divorce, inheritance and adoption, often following religious and community customs; and

(x) **Contract Law**: Ancient India had well-developed contract laws, with agreements being legally binding and enforceable; and

(xi) **Witnesses and Evidence**: Witnesses and evidence were crucial in legal proceedings, with oaths and testimonies playing a role; and

(xii) **Public Justice**: Legal proceedings and judgments were often conducted openly, involving the community in the process; and

(xiii) **Justice and Mercy**: Ancient Indian legal systems balanced justice with compassion, emphasizing the importance of forgiveness and reconciliation; and

(xiv) **Appeals System**: An appeals process allowed parties dissatisfied with a lower court's decision to seek recourse in higher courts or authorities.

1050. Indian Civilisation Key Positions:- Indian Civilisation Key Positions

(i) **Raja** (King): The ruler of the Empire; and

(ii) **Mahamantri** (Chief Minister): A high-ranking advisor to the king, often involved in policy making and administration; and

(iii) **Guru** (Teacher): Esteemed teacher, guide or mentor who imparts knowledge, wisdom and guidance.

1051. Indian Civilisation Social Organization:- Indian Civilisation Social Organization

(i) ***Brahmanas*** "enlightened caste" (1-2%): The highest class of Indian society of priests and nobles. Originally and always based on intellect, skill and self discipline, this class has continued to corrupt and devolve over centuries into tyrannical family and dynastic birthrights, with less and less attention or care to the once strict standards of intellect and spiritual training of India to be known as a "Brahman"; and

(ii) ***Kshatriyas*** "warrior and ruler caste" (5-10%): The warrior and ruler class both protected the interests of the Brahman caste as well as the kingdoms; and

(iii) ***Vaishyas*** "merchant and artisan caste" (10-20%): India Civilisation has always possessed a thriving and wealthy merchant and artisan class, mainly supported by the fact that this is the class that "owned" (and still owns) huge numbers of slaves, rather than the noble class (Brahmans) who were technically "forbidden" to even touch food or materials prepared by Daasyas ("slaves"); and

(iv) ***Shudras*** "labourer and worker caste" (20-30%): Much smaller by tradition to the slave class and mainly engaged as servants and workers for noble class; and

(v) ***Daasyas*** "slaves and bonded servants" (30-40%) : The largest class of permanent slaves, denied rights or any form of cmancipation, as well as condemned even in modern society as being known as the "untouchables".

10.6 – Chinese Civilisation (221 BCE - present)

Article 321 – Chinese Civilisation (221 BCE - present)

1052. The ***Chinese Civilisation*** (from 221 BCE - present) is the fifth of the twelve Greatest Civilisations formed over the past four thousand years, that at its height stretched across an area from Mongolia and Tibet to the whole of China and the Islands of Hainan and Taiwan. Chinese Civilisation

1053. Great Empires that began or arose within the framework and context of Chinese Civilisation include (but are not limited to):- Great Empires within the Chinese Civilisation

(i) ***Zhou Dynasty*** (1046 BCE - 256 BCE): One of the longest-reigning dynasties in Chinese history. It was marked by the development of Confucianism and Daoism, as well as the fragmentation of power during the later Eastern Zhou period; and

(ii) ***Qin Dynasty*** (221 BCE - 206 BCE): Under the rule of Qin Shi Huang, unified China and standardized various aspects of governance, including the written script and currency. It is known for the construction of the Great Wall and the Terracotta Army; and

(iii) ***Han Dynasty*** (206 BCE - 220 CE): Considered a golden age in Chinese history. It saw significant advancements in agriculture, technology and culture. The Silk Road trade route was established during this time; and

(iv) ***Three Kingdoms Period*** (220 CE - 280 CE): The Three Kingdoms Period followed the collapse of the Eastern Han Dynasty and was marked by the rivalry of three major states: Wei, Shu and Wu. It is a popular subject in Chinese literature and history; and

(v) ***Sui Dynasty*** (581 CE - 618 CE): The Sui Dynasty reunified China after centuries of division. It is known for completing the construction of the Grand Canal, which facilitated transportation and trade; and

(vi) ***Tang Dynasty*** (618 CE - 907 CE): The Tang Dynasty is often regarded as a high point in Chinese civilization. It saw great achievements in poetry, art, science and trade. The Tang Empire extended its influence along the Silk Road; and

(vii) ***Song Dynasty*** (960 CE - 1279 CE): Known for its economic prosperity, technological innovations, and the invention of movable-type printing. It saw advancements in philosophy and

Confucian thought; and

(viii) ***Yuan Dynasty*** (1271 CE - 1368 CE): The Yuan Dynasty was established by the Mongol Empire under Kublai Khan. It marked a period of Mongol rule in China; and

(ix) ***Ming Dynasty*** (1368 CE - 1644 CE): Known for its cultural renaissance and the construction of the Forbidden City in Beijing. It was a time of exploration and maritime expansion under Admiral Zheng He; and

(x) ***Qing Dynasty*** (1644 CE - 1912 CE): The Qing Dynasty was established by the Manchu people. It was the last imperial dynasty in China and saw territorial expansion and engagement with Western powers.

1054. Chinese Civilisation Religion and Belief Systems:-

Chinese Civilisation Religion and Belief Systems

(i) ***Ultimate Oneness of Reality (Tao)***: The ultimate oneness of all reality; and underlying, unifying principle or source of all existence. The Tao is formless, ineffable and transcendent, and it encompasses the interconnectedness and unity of all things in the universe; and

(ii) ***Confucianism****:* Confucianism centers on the importance of *li* (rituals, propriety, and moral conduct) and *ren* (benevolence, humanity, and compassion) in shaping an individual's character and society; and Confucianism emphasizes the importance of harmonious relationships, particularly those between ruler and subject, father and son, husband and wife, elder and younger sibling, and friend and friend; and

(iii) ***Buddhism****:* Buddhism's foundational principles include the Four Noble Truths, which address suffering (dukkha), its causes, and the path to liberation from suffering; and The Eightfold Path provides guidelines for ethical and mental development, including right understanding, intention, speech, action, livelihood, effort, mindfulness and concentration; and like Indian Buddhism, Chinese Buddhism incorporates beliefs in reincarnation and karma, with the aim of achieving enlightenment (nirvana).

1055. The Chinese Civilisation Language and Knowledge Systems of Classical Chinese or Guwen (古文):-

Chinese Civilisation Language and Knowledge Systems

(i) ***Type of Language***: *Logographic*: Using Chinese Characters or Hanzi; and *Phonetics*: In tonal pronunciation of syllables to convey meaning; and

(ii) ***Number of Characters***: 45,000 – 50,000 Hanzi (Chinese

Logographic symbols); and around 25 to 30 consonants and a smaller number of vowels; and

(iii) ***Number of Common Nouns***: 48,000+ Main Common Noun Categories: Animals(26.96%), Objects(16.59%), Plants(13.48%), People(12.44%), Science(9.20%), Religion(6.51%), Law(3.11%) and Trade(2.49%); and

(iv) ***Language Rules Complexity***: *Simple*: Written to be read right-to-left. Verbs usually come in the middle of a sentence or clause. Subject (S) - Verb (V) - Object (O); and

(v) ***Noble Class Vocabulary***: 14,000 – 26,000; and

(vi) ***Professional Class Vocabulary***: 4,000 – 16,000; and

(vii) ***Worker Class Vocabulary***: 2,500 – 4,000.

1056. Chinese Civilisation Sacred Texts and Primary Law Forms:- Chinese Civilisation Sacred Texts and Primary Law Forms

(i) **I Ching (Yijing or Book of Changes)**: (551-479 BCE); and

(ii) **The Analects (Lunyu)**: (551-479 BCE); and

(iii) **The Great Learning (Daxue)**: (551-479 BCE); and

(iv) **Tao Te Ching (Dao De Jing)**: 6th Century BCE; and

(v) **Qin (Legal) Code**: (221-206 BCE); and

(vi) **Tang (Legal) Code**: (618-907 CE); and

(vii) **Ming (Legal) Code**: (1368-1644 CE); and

(viii) ***Tiandi of Qin Shi Huang***: As recognised and restored in accord with the most sacred Covenant *Pactum De Singularis Caelum*; and

(ix) ***Zhongdao of Kong Qiu (Confucius)***: As recognised and restored in accord with the most sacred Covenant *Pactum De Singularis Caelum*; and

(x) ***Lebor Clann Glas of the Holly Diaspora***: As recognised and restored in accord with the most sacred Covenant *Pactum De Singularis Caelum*.

1057. Chinese Civilisation Legal Systems:- Chinese Civilisation Legal Systems

(i) ***Religious Influence***: The highest law was considered Divine Law; and Confucian principles, emphasizing social order, hierarchy and moral behaviour, greatly influenced Chinese law; and

(ii) ***Imperial Authority***: The emperor was the highest authority and the ultimate lawgiver, often considered the "Son of

Heaven."; and

(iii) ***Legal Codes***: Different dynasties implemented legal codes, such as the "Laws of the Tang" and the "Great Qing Legal Code," to regulate various aspects of society; and

(iv) ***Bureaucratic Structure***: A complex bureaucracy was responsible for administering and enforcing the law, with officials at various levels; and

(v) ***Magistrates***: Local magistrates played a key role in adjudicating disputes and enforcing laws at the provincial and local levels; and

(vi) ***Property Rights***: Legal principles protected property ownership and land rights, though land distribution often reflected social hierarchy; and

(vii) ***Family Law***: Laws governed matters like marriage, divorce, and inheritance, often following Confucian principles; and

(viii) ***Contract Law***: Contracts were recognized and enforced by the legal system; and

(ix) ***Legal Records***: Records were kept to document legal proceedings and judgments; and

(x) ***Judicial Procedures***: The legal system had established procedures for trials, including the presentation of evidence and the role of witnesses; and

(xi) ***Examinations***: The civil service examination system aimed to select qualified officials based on merit and knowledge of Confucian classics, ensuring competence in legal matters; and

(xii) ***Punishments***: A range of punishments existed, including fines, exile, labour, corporal punishment and, in some cases, execution; and

(xiii) ***Banishment and Exile***: Banishment and exile were used as punishments, removing offenders from their communities; and

(xiv) ***Reconciliation***: Mediation and reconciliation were encouraged to resolve disputes without formal legal proceedings.

1058. Chinese Civilisation Key Positions:-

Chinese Civilisation Key Positions

(i) ***Huangdi*** (Chinese Emperor): The supreme monarch of China; and

(ii) **Xiang** (Chancellor): The chief advisor to the emperor, responsible for overseeing the administration of the empire; and

(iii) **Yushi Dianzhong** (Imperial Censor): Officials responsible for monitoring the conduct of other officials and reporting any wrongdoing to the emperor; and

(iv) ***Taiwei or Taishi*** (Grand Commandant): High-ranking military and administrative officials who assisted the emperor in governing and military matters; and

(v) ***Da Sinong or Da Sifu*** (Minister of Finance): In charge of fiscal policy, taxation and financial matters.

1059. Chinese Civilisation Social Organization:- Chinese Civilisation Social Organization

(i) ***Noble and Aristocratic Class*** (< 1%): This class included noble by birth and other hereditary titles. They often served in high-ranking government positions and were responsible for managing regional territories; and

(ii) ***Scholars and Officials Class*** (1-2%): This class consisted of educated individuals who passed the imperial examinations based on Confucian principles. They were responsible for governing the country, serving as administrators, judges and advisors to the emperor; and

(iii) ***Military Class*** (2-5%): This class consisted of professional soldiers who were responsible for the highest security as well as training armies during mandatory service or forced conscription; and

(iv) ***Artisans and Craftsmen*** (2-5%): Artisans and craftsmen were skilled workers who produced goods such as pottery, textiles, and metalwork. They played a vital role in supporting the economy and trade; and

(v) ***Merchants and Traders*** (2-3%): Merchants and traders were often viewed with suspicion and ranked lower in social status because their wealth was seen as acquired through profit-making rather than productive labour. However, their role in facilitating trade and commerce was essential; and

(vi) ***Peasant Class*** (70-80%): The majority of the Chinese population belonged to the peasant class. They were responsible for agricultural labour and provided the essential food supply for the empire. Peasants were heavily taxed and had limited social mobility; and

(vii) ***Slave and Bonded Service Class*** (5-10%): Slavery was not as prevalent in China as it was in some other ancient societies, but it did exist, especially among the wealthy and powerful.

10.7 – Khmer Civilisation (160 CE – 1767)

Article 322 – Khmer Civilisation (160 CE – 1767)

1060. The Khmer ***Civilisation*** (from 160 CE - 1767) is the sixth of the twelve Greatest Civilisations formed over the past four thousand years, that at its height stretched across an area from the whole of South-East Asia, south to the Islands of Sumatra, Java and Bali and east to the Islands of the Philippines. — Khmer Civilisation

1061. Great Empires that began or arose within the framework and context of Khmer Civilisation include (but are not limited to):- — Great Empires within the Khmer Civilisation

(i) ***Khmer Empire*** (Angkor Empire) (340 CE - 1431 CE): The Khmer Empire, centered around the city of Angkor, was a powerful and influential empire in Southeast Asia. It is renowned for its monumental temple complexes, particularly Angkor Wat, and its vast irrigation and architectural achievements. The empire reached its zenith during the reign of King Jayavarman VII; and

(ii) ***Ayutthaya Kingdom*** (1451 CE - 1767 CE): The Ayutthaya Kingdom, centered around the city of Ayutthaya, became one of the most powerful kingdoms in Southeast Asia. It traded with various foreign powers and was known for its rich cultural heritage. The kingdom was eventually sacked by the Burmese in 1767.

1062. Khmer Civilisation Religion and Belief Systems:- — Khmer Civilisation Religion and Belief Systems

(i) ***Ultimate Duality of Reality (Shiva vs Vishnu)***: Brahma (the Universe) is neither good nor bad. Instead, the Universe is ruled by two opposing forces Shiva (Transformation) versus Vishnu (Preservation). *Shiva* is the supreme (female) deity of transformation, destruction and creation. The opposite is Vishnu the supreme (male) deity of preservation, protection and order; and

(ii) ***Trimurti***: The concept of the Trimurti, representing the three major Hindu deities—Brahma (the creator), Vishnu (the preserver), and Shiva (the destroyer)—was central to Khmer Hinduism; and

(iii) ***Devaraja Cult****:* The Devaraja, or "god-king" cult was a unique aspect of Khmer religion. It elevated the Khmer monarch to a divine status, emphasizing the king's role as the link between heaven and earth; and

(iv) ***Ancestor Worship and Animism***: Ancestor worship and indigenous animistic beliefs were practised alongside Hinduism and Buddhism. These beliefs involved the veneration of deceased ancestors and spirits associated with natural elements.

1063. Khmer Civilisation Language and Knowledge Systems known as Khmer (Old Khmer) includes:-

Khmer Civilisation Language and Knowledge Systems

(i) ***Type of Language***: *Abugida*: Whereby each character represents a consonant with an inherent vowel sound, and additional diacritics or modifications are used to indicate different vowel sounds or tone marks; and

(ii) ***Number of Characters***: 72 to 76 basic graphemes for consonants in the Khmer script. These consonantal graphemes can be modified with various diacritics to indicate different vowels, vowel lengths, and other phonetic features; and

(iii) ***Number of Common Nouns***: 54,000+ Main Common Noun Categories: Animals(22.17%), Religion(19.96%), Objects(14.78%), Plants(12.01%), People(11.09%), Science(7.70%), Law(2.22%) and Trade(1.77%); and

(iv) ***Language Rules Complexity***: *Simple*: Written to be read left-to-right, and top-to-bottom. Verbs conjugated to indicate tense, mood, voice and person. Nouns declined based on gender, number and case. Adjectives must agree in gender, number and case with the nouns they describe. Flexible word order. However the most common was Subject-Object-Verb (SOV); and

(v) ***Noble Class Vocabulary***: 14,000 – 26,000; and

(vi) ***Professional Class Vocabulary***: 4,000 – 16,000; and

(vii) ***Worker Class Vocabulary***: 2,500 – 4,000.

1064. Khmer Civilisation Sacred Texts and Primary Law Forms:-

Khmer Civilisation Sacred Texts and Primary Law Forms

(i) **Vedas (Shruti)**: The four Vedas: Rigveda, Yajurveda, Samaveda, and Atharvaveda; and

(ii) **Mahabharata (Smriti)**: The Mahabharata is one of the longest epic poems in the world and includes the Bhagavad Gita as one of its chapters; and

(iii) ***Tripitaka (Pali Canon)***: Vinaya Pitaka, Sutta Pitaka and Abhidhamma Pitaka; and

(iv) ***Sanatana Dharma of Supreme Creator***: As recognised and restored in accord with the most sacred Covenant *Pactum De Singularis Caelum*; and

(v) ***Lebor Clann Glas of the Holly Diaspora***: As recognised and restored in accord with the most sacred Covenant *Pactum De Singularis Caelum*.

1065. Khmer Civilisation Legal Systems:-

Khmer Civilisation Legal Systems

(i) ***Religious Influence***: The highest law was considered Divine Law; and Hindu and Buddhist principles influenced Khmer law, with an emphasis on dharma, karma and moral conduct; and

(ii) ***Royal Authority***: The king held supreme authority and was considered the divine ruler responsible for upholding and enforcing the law; and

(iii) ***Legal Codes***: Some Khmer rulers, like King Jayavarman VII, promulgated legal codes, inscriptions, and stelae to codify laws and regulations; and

(iv) ***Bureaucracy***: A hierarchical administrative system included officials responsible for enforcing laws and collecting taxes; and

(v) ***Family Law***: Laws governed matters like marriage, divorce, inheritance and adoption, often influenced by Hindu and Buddhist customs; and

(vi) ***Land Tenure***: Land ownership and distribution were governed by specific regulations, with a focus on maintaining agricultural productivity; and

(vii) ***Contract Law***: Contracts were recognized and enforced, particularly in trade and commerce; and

(viii) ***Corvée Labour***: Labour obligations were imposed on certain individuals, primarily for public works and construction projects; and

(ix) ***Taxation***: The legal system regulated taxation, often based on land ownership and agricultural production; and

(x) ***Cultural Preservation***: Khmer law and edicts often emphasized the preservation of cultural and religious heritage, including temple construction and maintenance; and

(xi) ***Legal Records***: Written records, inscriptions, and stone carvings served to document legal proceedings, land grants, and royal edicts; and

(xii) ***Justice and Punishment***: Punishments for crimes included fines, forced labour, imprisonment, mutilation and, in severe cases, execution.

1066. Khmer Civilisation Social Organization:- Khmer Civilisation Social Organization

(i) ***Elite Nobility (Amatya)*** (< 1%): Beneath the king were the nobility, including high-ranking officials, ministers, and members of the royal family. These elites held significant political power and often served as advisors to the king; and

(ii) ***Priestly Class (Brahmins)*** (< 1%): Brahmins were Hindu priests who played a crucial role in the Khmer Empire's religious and social life. They performed religious ceremonies, maintained temple complexes, and provided spiritual guidance to the people. Hinduism was a prominent religion in the early Khmer Empire; and

(iii) ***Warrior Class (Kshatriyas)*** (2-5%): The military class, or Kshatriyas, served as the defenders of the empire and played important roles in maintaining law and order. They were responsible for protecting the realm and expanding its territories through military campaigns; and

(iv) ***Merchants & Artisans Class (Vaishyas)*** (5-10%): The merchant and artisan class were below the warrior class; and

(v) ***Labourers & Worker Class (Shudras)*** (55-65%): Commoners made up the majority of the population. They were primarily engaged in agriculture, trade, and various crafts. Commoners could include farmers, merchants, artisans and labourers. Some commoners also served as soldiers when needed; and

(vi) ***Slave and Bonded Service Class (Daasyas)*** (10-15%): At the lowest rung of the social hierarchy were slaves and servants, who had limited rights and were often bound to the land or their masters. They were responsible for performing menial tasks and providing labour to the upper classes.

10.8 – Maya Civilisation (1400 BCE – 1533 CE)

Article 323 – Maya Civilisation (1400 CE – 1533 CE)

1067. The ***Maya Civilisation*** (from 1400 CE - 1533) is the seventh of the twelve Greatest Civilisations formed over the past four thousand years, that at its height stretched across an area from Central to South America.

Maya Civilisation

1068. Great Empires that began or arose within the framework and context of Maya Civilisation include (but are not limited to):-

Great Empires within the Maya Civilisation

(i) ***Olmec Civilization*** (1400 BCE - 400 BCE): Considered one of the earliest Mesoamerican cultures. They are known for their monumental stone heads and jade artifacts and had a significant influence on later Mesoamerican civilizations; and

(ii) ***Maya Civilization*** (400 BCE - 1430 CE): Known for its advanced mathematics, astronomy and hieroglyphic writing system, flourished in present-day Mexico, Guatemala, Belize, Honduras and El Salvador. It had a complex social and political structure; and

(iii) ***Inca Empire*** (1438 CE - 1533 CE): Located in the Andes Mountains of South America, was the largest pre-Columbian empire in the Americas. It had advanced engineering, road networks and a centralized government. It fell to the Spanish conquistadors, led by Francisco Pizarro; and

(iv) ***Aztec Empire*** (1428 CE - 1521 CE): Centered in Tenochtitlan (present-day Mexico City), was a powerful Mesoamerican state known for its advanced agriculture, military prowess and tribute system. It was conquered by the Spanish led by Hernán Cortés in 1521.

1069. Maya Civilisation Religion and Belief Systems:-

Maya Civilisation Religion and Belief Systems

(i) ***Ultimate Oneness of Reality (K'uh)***: The ultimate divine reality and source of all nature and the cosmos. K'uh is both the personification of this ultimate oneness of reality and the belief that that all things, even inanimate objects, have a soul or K'uh; and

(ii) ***Cosmic Beliefs***: The Maya had a deep connection to the cosmos and believed that celestial events, such as the movement of planets and stars, were tied to earthly events and the fate of individuals and the community. They were skilled astronomers and mathematicians who developed complex calendars to track celestial events; and

(iii) ***Polytheism***: The Maya believed in a pantheon of gods and goddesses who represented various aspects of the natural world, celestial bodies, and human experiences. Some prominent deities included Itzamna (the supreme creator god), Kukulkan (the feathered serpent god) and Ixchel (the moon and fertility goddess); and

(iv) ***Sacred Places and Temples***: Mayan religious rituals were often conducted at temples and pyramids, which were built to align with astronomical events. The temples were considered portals to the spirit world and places of communication with the gods; and

(v) ***Bloodletting Rituals***: Bloodletting ceremonies were a significant aspect of Mayan religious practices. Mayan rulers and priests would perform self-inflicted bloodletting as an offering to the gods. Blood was believed to carry life force and connect the human realm to the divine; and

(vi) ***Divination and Oracles***: Divination, such as the casting of lots or reading the entrails of animals, was used to seek guidance from the gods and make important decisions. Priests and shamans played a crucial role in these practices; and

(vii) ***Human Sacrifice***: The Maya practised human sacrifice in certain religious ceremonies, particularly during times of crisis or major calendrical events. Captives from warfare were often used as sacrificial victims.

1070. Maya Civilisation Language and Knowledge Systems known simple as Mayan, includes:- Maya Civilisation Language and Knowledge Systems

(i) ***Type of Language***: *Logographic* and *Syllabic*: Meaning it combines logograms (symbols that represent words or concepts) with syllabic elements; and

(ii) ***Number of Characters***: 72 to 76 basic graphemes for consonants in the Maya script. These consonantal graphemes can be modified with various diacritics to indicate different vowels, vowel lengths, and other phonetic features; and

(iii) ***Number of Common Nouns***: 63,000+ Main Common Noun Categories: Animals(28.43%), Plants(16.59%), Objects(15.01%), Religion(12.48%), People(9.48%), Science(7.33%), Law(1.74%) and Trade(1.39%); and

(iv) ***Language Rules Complexity***: *Simple*: Written to be read right-to-left, left-to-right, and top-to-bottom. Verbs conjugated to indicate tense, mood, voice and person. Nouns declined based on gender, number and case. Adjectives must agree in gender, number and case with the nouns they describe; and

(v) ***Noble Class Vocabulary***: 30,000 – 40,000; and

(vi) ***Professional Class Vocabulary***: 15,000 – 25,000; and

(vii) ***Worker Class Vocabulary***: 7,500 – 15,000.

1071. Maya Civilisation Sacred Texts and Primary Law Forms:-

Maya Civilisation Sacred Texts and Primary Law Forms

(i) ***Kikilil Yuum Witzil***: As recognised and restored in accord with the most sacred Covenant *Pactum De Singularis Caelum*; and

(ii) ***Lebor Clann Glas of the Holly Diaspora***: As recognised and restored in accord with the most sacred Covenant *Pactum De Singularis Caelum*.

1072. Maya Civilisation Legal Systems:-

Maya Civilisation Legal Systems

(i) **Religious Influence**: The highest law was considered Divine Law; and Maya religion played a significant role in legal matters, with laws often reflecting religious beliefs and rituals; and

(ii) **Kings and Rulers**: Rulers, often seen as divine intermediaries, were responsible for upholding and enforcing the law. They had the authority to issue decrees and judgments; and

(iii) **Hierarchical Structure**: The Maya legal system operated within a hierarchical society, with rulers and nobles having distinct legal privileges and responsibilities; and

(iv) **Ceremonial Centres**: Maya ceremonial centres and temples served as focal points for legal proceedings and religious rituals; and

(v) **Glyphic Records**: Inscriptions and glyphs on monuments and stelae sometimes documented legal events, including royal decrees and land grants; and

(vi) **Legal Specialists**: Some individuals within Maya society specialized in legal matters, providing advice and expertise in legal proceedings; and

(vii) **Territorial Rights**: Maya city-states had territorial boundaries and legal claims to specific regions and resources; and

(viii) **Water Rights**: Water management and access to water sources were regulated by law, given their importance for agriculture; and

(ix) **Laws of Kinship**: Family and kinship were central to Maya society, and laws often governed marriage, inheritance, and social roles within the family; and

(x) **Tribute and Taxation**: The legal system regulated tribute payments and taxation, with nobles and commoners having distinct obligations; and

(xi) **Community Participation**: The community often played a role in legal proceedings, with public forums for dispute resolution; and

(xii) **Mediation**: Mediation and negotiation were common methods for resolving disputes, emphasizing reconciliation over punishment; and

(xiii) **Trial by Ordeal**: Maya law sometimes relied on trial by ordeal, where the outcome was determined by a physical test or supernatural intervention; and

(xiv) **Punishments**: Punishments for crimes could include fines, forced labour, exile, and in some cases, human sacrifice.

1073. Maya Civilisation Key Positions:- Maya Civilisation Key Positions

(i) ***Ahauh*** (King): The Ahauh had both political and religious authority and was seen as a divine figure, responsible for maintaining cosmic order and the well-being of their people; and

(ii) ***Ah Halauh Uinic*** (Chief Minister): A high-ranking advisor to the king, often involved in policy making and administration; and

(iii) ***Ah Cacauh*** (Chief Military Leader): The war chief or military leader responsible for leading armies into battle and defending the city-state from external threats; and

(iv) ***Ah Kin*** (High Priest): The high priest who played a crucial role in religious ceremonies and rituals, often overseeing offerings and communicating with the gods on behalf of the ruler and the people; and

(v) ***Ah Tz'ihb*** (Royal Treasurer): The royal treasurer responsible for managing the city's wealth, including tribute from subordinate communities and trade with other city-states.

1074. Maya Civilisation Social Organization:- Maya

Civilisation Social Organization

(i) ***Priest Class*** (< 1%): The priesthood was the most powerful and respected class in ancient Maya. They played a significant role in religious rituals and ceremonies, including the maintenance of temples and tombs. Temples were also centres of economic and political power; and

(ii) ***Noble Service Class*** (< 1%): The noble service class represented high ranking officials and their families and the second most powerful and respected class in ancient Maya. This class included individuals like viziers (chief advisors), generals, and high priests. They were responsible for governing the various regions of Maya Civilisation and managing its resources; and

(iii) ***Public Servant Class*** (2-5%): The public service class represented members of skilled professions, such as scribes, artisans, craftspeople, engineers and project managers as the third class; and

(iv) ***Agricultural Class*** (20-30%): The agricultural class represented the majority of the population in ancient Maya. Their labour was crucial for producing food for the entire society. Farmers were organized into villages and worked the land collectively; and

(v) ***Merchant Class*** (5-10%): The merchant class represented a small but influential class of Maya society in the provision of objects, materials and items; and

(vi) ***Worker Class*** (30-40%): The worker class were predominantly associated with massive building projects as contractors; and

(vii) ***Slave and Bonded Service Class*** (1-2%): Slaves were typically prisoners of war or individuals who had fallen into debt. They were at the bottom of the social hierarchy and had few rights.

10.9 – Christian Civilisation (314 CE – 740 CE)

Article 324 – Christian Civilisation (314 CE – 740 CE)

Christian Civilisation

1075. The ***Christian Civilisation*** (from 314 CE – 740 CE) is the eighth of the twelve Greatest Civilisations formed over the past four thousand years, that at its height stretched across the whole of western, northern and eastern Europe, north and east Africa, Middle East, Asia Minor, Persia and as far east as the edge of Mongolia. It is the third of the six Great Civilisations created by the Holly (Cuilliaéan) Bloodlines.

1076. Great Empires that began or arose within the framework and context of Christian Civilisation include (but are not limited to):- Great Empires within the Christian Civilisation

(i) ***Christian Empire*** (314 – 518 CE): Founded by Iohannes Constantinos (Cuinstanyn mac Cuinalba) (314 – 337 CE) as the largest Empire the world has ever known to date; and

(ii) ***Eastern Christian Empire*** (518 – 1492 CE): Founded by Sabbatius (Justinian) upon the death of Eunastasius (Anastasius) (491 – 518 CE) and his refusal to hand authority to Frank Emperor Aurelius Ansbertus (Theuderic) as the natural Holly Successor; and

(iii) ***Western Christian Empire*** (740 CE – present): Founded by Frank leader Aurelius Aptatus also known as "Charles Martel" by 740 CE. Technically the most successful Civilisation since the Ancient Egyptians. The Holly finally lost control of Roman Catholic Church and Civilisation in early 16th Century; and

(iv) ***Venetian Empire*** (1200 – present): The Republic of Venice reached a high point in terms of trading ports and colonies across eastern and western Mediterranean, including thriving coastal and inland river based merchant cities; and

(v) ***Spanish-Portuguese Empire*** (1400s – 1800): Early rivals to the Venetian City States, its vast wealth and power was built upon some of the worst crimes against humanity in deliberate genocide, theft, knowledge destruction, slavery and barbarity across the world, particularly South America, South East Asia and parts of Africa; and

(vi) ***English (Venetian) Empire*** (1511 - present): The exiled Patrician families took control of the government and finances of England by 1511 and then the crown of England itself upon the death of Elizabeth I (1558-1603). Manufactured the "Reformation", crippling many of its rivals in Germany, Belgium, Netherlands and Switzerland. Formed the British Empire as the Kingdom of Great Britain; and

(vii) ***American (Dutch-English) Empire*** (1796 - present): The exiled Dutch Patrician families having been granted control and restoration of ownership of the land of the former Dutch colonies of eastern North America, soon became the largest banking nation in the world, causing the annual GDP of the United States to explode to $200 million in 1800 compared to the total GDP of the British Empire in the same year at £220 million. By no later than 1815, the United States was the largest economy in the world at around an annual GDP of $700 million. These facts are deliberately hidden, or corrupted to hide the fact that an apparent "fledgling" nation could in less than 50 years become the largest modern economy in the world.

1077. Christian Civilisation Religion and Belief Systems:-

Christian Civilisation Religion and Belief Systems

(i) ***Ultimate Oneness of Reality (Monad)***: The ultimate reality or supreme, totally transcendent, containing no division, multiplicity, or distinction; beyond all categories of being and non-being; and

(ii) ***Divine Mind (Nous)***: The One emanates the "Nous" (Intellect or Divine Mind) as the second hypostasis, which contains the divine archetypes or Forms; and

(iii) ***The World Soul***: The third emanation from the One is the "World Soul," which is responsible for the unity and order of the material world. It connects the higher realms of reality with the material realm; and

(iv) ***The Material World***: The material world is the lowest level of existence and represents the realm of the least reality. It is a mere reflection of the higher spiritual realities. The imperfections and limitations of the material world arise from its distance from the One.

1078. Christian Civilisation Language and Knowledge System of Ancient Greek includes:-

Christian Civilisation Language and Knowledge Systems

(i) ***Type of Language***: *Alphabetic*: Meaning characters represent individual sounds or phonemes. Each character typically corresponds to a specific letter or combination of letters; and

(ii) ***Number of Characters***: 24 basic graphemes for consonants and vowels; and

(iii) ***Number of Common Nouns***: 54,000+ Main Common Noun Categories: Animals(18.65%), Objects(20.51%), People(18.65%), Science(9.19%), Plants(8.39%), Religion(6.41%), Law(3.36%) and Trade(2.69%); and

(iv) ***Language Rules Complexity***: *Medium Complexity*: Written to be read left to right. Verbs conjugated to indicate tense, mood, voice, and person. Nouns declined based on gender, number, and case. Nouns are categorized as masculine or feminine, and adjectives and verbs must agree in gender. Verbs usually comes at the end (after the subject) of a sentence or clause; and

(v) ***Noble Class Vocabulary***: 14,000 – 26,000; and

(vi) ***Professional Class Vocabulary***: 4,000 – 16,000; and

(vii) ***Worker Class Vocabulary***: 2,500 – 4,000.

1079. Christian Civilisation Sacred Texts and Primary Law Forms:-

Christian Civilisation Sacred Texts and Primary Law Forms

(i) ***Bibliographe of Christianity of Constantine***: As recognised and restored in accord with the most sacred Covenant *Pactum De Singularis Caelum*; and

(ii) ***Lebor Clann Glas of the Holly Diaspora***: As recognised and restored in accord with the most sacred Covenant *Pactum De Singularis Caelum*.

1080. Christian Civilisation Legal Systems:-

Christian Civilisation Legal Systems

(i) **Religious Influence**: The highest law was considered Divine Law; and laws were influenced by Christian moral values, including concepts of justice, charity and forgiveness; and

(ii) **Church-State Relations**: Legal systems defined the relationship between the Church and the state, addressing issues of authority and jurisdiction; and

(iii) **Religious Tolerance**: Some emperors, such as Constantine, issued decrees that promoted religious tolerance, allowing freedom of worship for Christians and others; and

(iv) **Family Law**: Laws governed issues related to marriage, divorce and inheritance, often influenced by Christian teachings on the sanctity of marriage and family; and

(v) **Property Rights**: Laws addressed property ownership, often influenced by Christian teachings on stewardship and just distribution of resources; and

(vi) **Oaths and Swearing**: Legal proceedings frequently involved religious oaths and swearing on religious texts.

1081. Christian Civilisation Key Positions:-

Christian Civilisation Key Positions

(i) ***Basileus*** (Pappas): Supreme ruler, king and emperor; and

(ii) ***Exarchos*** (Archegos): Lawful ruler as one of the four regional rulers of groups of political states called Kuria under the first Christian Civilisation and Empire; and

(iii) ***Patriarchos*** (Protos): Leader of a sovereign state called a

Politeia (πολῑτείᾱ) under the first Christian Civilisation and Empire; and

(iv) ***Monarchos*** (Hegemon): The leader of a region of a sovereign state called an Episcopolis (πολῑτείᾱ) under the first first Christian Civilisation and Empire.

1082. Christian Civilisation Social Organization:-

Christian Civilisation Social Organization

(i) ***Priest Class*** (< 1%): The priesthood was the most powerful and respected class in Christian Civilisation. They played a significant role in religious rituals and ceremonies, including the maintenance of temples and tombs. Temples were also centres of economic and political power; and

(ii) ***Noble Service Class*** (< 1%): The noble service class represented high ranking officials and their families and the second most powerful and respected class in Christian Civilisation. This class included individuals like viziers (chief advisors) and generals. They were responsible for governing the various regions of Christian Civilisation and managing its resources; and

(iii) ***Public Servant Class*** (2-5%): The public service class represented members of skilled professions, such as scribes, artisans, craftspeople, engineers and project managers as the third class; and

(iv) ***Agricultural Class*** (20-30%): The agricultural class represented the majority of the population in Christian Civilisation. Their labour was crucial for producing food for the entire society. Farmers were organized into villages and worked the land collectively; and

(v) ***Merchant Class*** (5-10%): The merchant class represented a small but influential class of Christian society in the provision of objects, materials and items; and

(vi) ***Worker Class*** (30-40%): The worker class were predominantly associated with massive building projects as contractors; and

(vii) ***Slave and Bonded Service Class*** (1-2%): Slaves were typically prisoners of war or individuals who had fallen into debt. They were at the bottom of the social hierarchy and had few rights.

10.10 – Eastern Christian Civilisation (518 CE - present)

Article 325 – Eastern Christian Civilisation (518 CE - present)

1083. The ***Eastern Christian Civilisation*** (from 518 CE - present) is the ninth of the twelve Greatest Civilisations formed over the past four thousand years, that at its height stretched across an area from Spain, North Africa, Italy, Greece, Middle East, Asia Minor and parts of Persia.

Eastern Christian Civilisation

1084. Eastern Christian Civilisation Religion and Belief Systems:-

Eastern Christian Civilisation Religion and Belief Systems

(i) ***Ultimate Duality of Reality (Good vs Evil)***: The Universe is ruled by the forces of Agathos (Good and Beauty) versus Ponēros (Evil and Suffering); and

(ii) ***Emperor as Defender of Orthodoxy***: The Autokrator is the earthly representative and protector of the Christian faith. This concept of the "Emperor as God's Vicegerent" (Christos Pantokrator) was crucial to Eastern Christian political and religious ideology; and

(iii) ***Primacy of Humanism, Reason and Law***: True Christian values not based on history or birthright, but on the primacy of humanism, intellect and reason as embodied within the law; and

(iv) ***Secular Ethics and Law***: The laws of the state are the embodiment of ethics and Christian morality and rather than morality being derived from old religious texts, the foundation of ethics is to obey the laws of the state without question or dispute; and

(v) ***State as Central Christian Religious Body***: The state and its organisation is the central religious body, not old temples or churches. The officials of government represent the Autokrator and so possess both ecclesiastical and administrative authority, greater than priests.

1085. Eastern Christian Civilisation Language and Knowledge Systems:-

Eastern Christian Civilisation Language and Knowledge Systems

(i) ***Type of Language***: *Alphabetic*: Meaning characters represent individual sounds or phonemes. Each character typically corresponds to a specific letter or combination of letters; and

(ii) ***Number of Characters***: 24 basic graphemes for consonants and vowels; and

(iii) ***Number of Common Nouns***: 57,000+ Main Common Noun Categories: Objects(22.86%), People(21.11%), Animals(17.59%), Science(9.57%), Plants(6.16%), Religion(3.73%), Law(3.69%) and Trade(2.95%); and

(iv) ***Language Rules Complexity***: *Medium Complexity*: Written to be read left-to-right. Verbs conjugated to indicate tense, mood, voice and person. Nouns declined based on gender, number and case. Nouns are categorized as masculine or feminine, and adjectives and verbs must agree in gender. Verbs usually comes at the end (after the subject) of a sentence or clause; and

(v) ***Noble Class Vocabulary***: 14,000 – 26,000; and

(vi) ***Professional Class Vocabulary***: 4,000 – 16,000; and

(vii) ***Worker Class Vocabulary***: 2,500 – 4,000.

Eastern Christian Civilisation Sacred Texts and Primary Law Forms

1086. Eastern Christian Civilisation Sacred Texts and Primary Law Forms:-

(i) ***Pandektes*** (Pandects): Meaning all encompassing knowledge; and

(ii) ***Sunaptikos Kodikas*** (Codex Sinaiticus): Meaning the Book of Christian Unity, divided into two sections called Diathiki or testaments with the first or Palaia Diathiki (Old Testament) containing fourteen books including: Genesis, Chronicles, Ezra, Esther, Tobit, Judith, Joel, Nehemiah, Isaiah, Jeremiah, Ecclesiastes, Psalms, Lamentations and Maccabees; and the second or Kaini Diathiki (New Testament) containing seven books including: Mattatheos (Matthew), Markos (Mark), Lukhas (Luke), Iohannes (John), Epistles (Acts) of the Exarchs, Epistles (Acts) of the Autokrators (Emperors) and Apokalypsis (Revelations) of Iohannes (John); and

(iii) ***Pege Gnoseos*** (Πηγὴ Γνώσεως): Meaning the Source of all Knowledge, divided into three sections being Theologia (θεολογία), Hairesis (Αἵρεσις) and Orthodoxia (Ὀρθοδοξία); and

(iv) ***Ecloga Basilei*** (Ἐκλογή βασιλεία): Meaning the collection of laws of the empire and containing modified laws of Sabbatius in the form of the Pandektes (Πανδέκτης), and beginning section called Archai (Ἀρχαί) also known as the Institutes, containing alleged legal jurist opinions and statements from Rome that supported the east as the legitimate new capital; and

(v) ***Lebor Clann Glas of the true Holly Diaspora***: As recognised and restored in accord with the most sacred Covenant *Pactum De Singularis Caelum*.

1087. Eastern Christian Civilisation Legal Systems:- Eastern Christian Civilisation Legal Systems

(i) **Religious Influence**: The highest law was considered Divine Law; and laws were influenced by Christian moral values, including concepts of justice, charity and forgiveness; and

(ii) **Judicial Structure**: The Eastern Christian legal system had a hierarchical judicial structure with officials responsible for administering justice, including the praetorian prefects and magistrates; and

(iii) **Property Rights**: Property ownership and distribution were regulated by law, often influenced by Christian teachings on stewardship and just distribution of resources; and

(iv) **Family Law**: Laws governed matters related to marriage, divorce and inheritance, often influenced by Christian teachings on the sanctity of marriage and family; and

(v) **Oaths**: Legal proceedings frequently involved religious oaths made on religious texts.

1088. Eastern Christian Key Positions:- Eastern Christian Civilisation Key Positions

(i) ***Autokrator***: Supreme self ruler; and

(ii) **Belisarius** (Head General): The commanding general of all armies of the Eastern Christian Empire; and

(iii) ***Despotes*** (Theme Commander): The leader of a group of territorial states called a Theme (θέμα) of the Eastern Christian Empire; and

(iv) ***Stratagos*** (Eikon Commander): The military and political leader of a region of a territorial state called an Eikon (Εικόνα) under the Eastern Christian Empire; and

(v) ***Kromwell*** (Master of Slaves); and

(vi) ***Kaiser*** (Dictator of Tourkos Armies); and

(vii) ***Tzaiser*** (Dictator of Slav Armies).

1089. Eastern Christian Civilisation Social Organization:- Eastern Christian Civilisation Social Organization

(i) ***Aristocracy*** "upper class" (2-5%): The noble service class represented high ranking officials and their families and the most powerful and respected class in Eastern Christianity. This class included individuals like viziers (chief advisors), generals, and high priests. They were responsible for governing the various regions of Eastern Christianity and managing its resources; and

(ii) ***Taxis*** "middle class" (15-20%): The public service class represented members of skilled professions, such as scribes, artisans, craftspeople, engineers and project managers as the second class; and

(iii) ***Douloi*** "working (slave) class" (75-85%): The working class represented the majority of the population. Their labour was crucial for producing food for the entire society. Everyone of the working class were bound to the state, with the only difference whether one had more or less rights as a "slave of the state".

10.11 – Islamic Civilisation (600 CE - present)

Article 326 – Islamic Civilisation (600 CE - present)

1090. The ***Islamic Civilisation*** (from 600 CE – present) is the tenth of the twelve Greatest Civilisations formed over the past four thousand years, that at its previous height stretched across all of North Africa, Southern Spain, Southern Italy, Middle East, Asia Minor to Afghanistan and India. It is the fourth of the six Great Civilisations created by the Holly (Cuilliaéan) Bloodlines.

Islamic Civilisation

1091. Great Empires that began or arose within the framework and context of Islamic Civilisation include (but are not limited to):-

Great Empires within the Islamic Civilisation

(i) ***First Holly Caliphates*** (605 – 800s): Creation of first sacred Caliphates under the descendents of the Holly Prophet as Mustafa. First Caliphates include: Al-Rashid (Egypt) in 605 CE, Al-Fatimid (Arabia and Yemen) 613 CE, Al-Abbasid (Levant) in 636 CE, Al-Samanid (Persia) in 637 CE, Al-Aghlabid (Libya) in 647 CE, Al-Soudid (Sudan) in 651 CE, Al-Safarid (Afghanistan) in 664 CE, Al-Rustamid (Algeria) in 698 CE, Al-Andalus (Southern Spain) in 744 CE, Al-Salihid (Morocco) in 745 CE and Al-Rumi (Southern Italy) in 747 CE; and

(ii) ***Consolidated Caliphates*** (1170s – 1300s): From the late 12th Century, there was a rapid consolidation of previous Caliphates under Saladin in the formation of Al-Ayyubid of North Africa, Egypt, Saudi Arabia, Yemen, Middle East, Syria and parts of Persia (1171 – 1324); and

(iii) ***Mamluk/Ottoman Empire*** (1324 – 1918): A Moor merchant empire constructed by the Maimoides Moor School in partnership with the Venetians. Completely corrupted Islamic history, creating contradictory, conflicting and fanatical practices contrary to the foundations of Islam. Introduced a complete "slave empire" in complete contradiction to the teachings of Islam; and

(iv) ***Safavid Empire*** (1530 – 1736): Creation of Shia Islam and the founding of Tehran as "Eden". It saw a flourishing of Persian culture, art and architecture, notably under Shah Abbas the Great.

1092. Islamic Civilisation Religion and Belief Systems:- Islamic Civilisation Religion and Belief Systems

(i) ***Monotheism*** (Tawhid): Central to Islam is the belief in the absolute oneness of God (Allah). Muslims believe in the singularity, uniqueness and omnipotence of God, rejecting any form of polytheism; and

(ii) ***Sufism***: Sufism is a mystical and spiritual dimension of Islam that focuses on achieving a closer connection with God through practices like *dhikr* (remembrance of God), meditation and seeking spiritual insight; and

(iii) ***Word of God Spoken never Written***: A fundamental principle of Islam was inherited from the Holly (Cuilliaéan) of Ireland that the sacred word of God (Allah) was to be recited (spoken) and never written, because truth has its own resonance and the faithful must have the knowledge and discernment of heart to know the difference; and

(iv) ***Holly Quran*** (Recitations): The Holly Recitations (the literal meaning of Quran) are the most sacred verses of Islam, believed to be the literal word of God as revealed to the Holly Prophet. It serves as the primary source of guidance for Muslims in matters of faith, ethics and practice; and

(v) ***Pillars of Islam***: The Pillars are the core acts of worship and practice for Muslims in declaring their faith, in bearing witness and in demonstrating their devotion through daily acts of prayer, charity and virtue.

1093. Islamic Civilisation Language and Knowledge System of Arabic includes:- Islamic Civilisation Language and Knowledge Systems

(i) ***Type of Language***: *Abjad*: Meaning the symbols represent only consonant sounds and typically omit vowel sounds that are indicated through diacritics or context; and

(ii) ***Number of Characters***: 28 distinct graphemes for consonants. In addition to these consonantal graphemes, Arabic uses diacritics and vowel marks to indicate vowel sounds. These diacritics can be used to specify short vowels, long vowels and other phonetic features. The use of diacritics can significantly expand the number of characters in Arabic script when fully represented; and

(iii) ***Number of Common Nouns***: 39,000+ Main Common Noun Categories: Animals(22.84%), Objects(19.03%), People(15.22%), Religion(10.81%), Science(9.06%), Plants(6.34%), Law(3.55%) and Trade(2.84%); and

(iv) ***Language Rules Complexity***: *Medium Complexity*: Written to be read right-to-left. Verbs conjugated to indicate tense, mood, aspect, person and number. Nouns declined in three grammatical cases (nominative, accusative, genitive) to show their relationship in a sentence. Nouns are categorized as masculine or feminine, and adjectives and verbs must agree in gender. Agreement in gender, number and case is fundamental. The typical word order in Arabic sentences is Verb-Subject-Object, though this can vary based on emphasis and context. No complex verb inflections, complex verb conjugations or complex pronoun rules until language was deliberately and intentionally targetted by Mamluk/Ottomans to be corrupted from 14th to 16th Century to create "modern Arabic"; and

(v) ***Noble Class Vocabulary***: 14,000 – 26,000; and

(vi) ***Professional Class Vocabulary***: 4,000 – 16,000; and

(vii) ***Worker Class Vocabulary***: 2,500 – 4,000.

1094. Islamic Civilisation Sacred Texts and Primary Law Forms:- Islamic Civilisation Sacred Texts and Primary Law Forms

(i) ***Quran Al Sufian (Recitations of The Way) of The Holly Prophet and Islam*** or simply as the"***Holy Quran***": As recognised and restored in accord with the most sacred Covenant *Pactum De Singularis Caelum*; and

(ii) ***Lebor Clann Glas of the true Holly Diaspora***: As recognised and restored in accord with the most sacred Covenant *Pactum De Singularis Caelum.*

1095. Islamic Civilisation Legal Systems:- Islamic Civilisation Legal Systems

(i) **Religious Influence**: The highest law was considered Divine Law; and laws were influenced by Islamic moral values, including concepts of justice, charity and forgiveness; and

(ii) **Judicial Structure**: The Islamic legal system had a hierarchical judicial structure with officials responsible for administering justice, including prefects and magistrates; and

(iii) **Property Rights**: Property ownership and distribution were regulated by law, often influenced by Islamic teachings on stewardship and just distribution of resources; and

(iv) **Family Law**: Laws governed matters related to marriage, divorce, and inheritance, often influenced by Islamic teachings on the sanctity of marriage and family; and

(v) ***Slavery Forbidden***: Similar to all Holly Civilisations, Islam until 1324 CE expressly forbid slavery in all its forms, until the Moors created the Mamluk Empire; and

(vi) **Oaths**: Legal proceedings frequently involved religious oaths on religious texts.

1096. Islamic Civilisation Key Positions:-

Islamic Civilisation Key Positions

(i) ***Mustafa*** (Teacher): Esteemed teacher chosen by Allah (God) being the highest and most respected position under the Islamic Civilisation; and

(ii) ***Khalif*** (Steward): Esteemed servant of the people being the appointed ruler of a Khalifah (Caliphate) under the Islamic Civilisation; and

(iii) ***Emir*** (Builder): Esteemed builder and administrator of communities being the appointed regional ruler of an Emarah (Emirates) within a Khalifah (Caliphate) under Islamic Civilisation; and

(iv) ***Adib*** (Poet): Esteemed poet and highest scholar being the highest and most esteemed cultural, jurisprudence and intellectual position under the Islamic Civilisation; and

(v) ***Faqir*** (Mendicant and Jurist): Esteemed mendicant and jurist being the highest and most esteemed judicial position under the Islamic Civilisation; and

(vi) ***Wazir*** (Vizier): Advisor and minister.

1097. Islamic Civilisation Social Organization:-

Islamic Civilisation Social Organization

(i) ***Intellectual Class*** (3-6%): The most esteemed members of society were the intellectual class, rather than personal wealth or property; and

(ii) ***Professional Class*** (5-10%): The professional class were the next largest segment of original Islamic Civilisation; and

(iii) ***Warrior Class*** (10-15%): The Warrior Class was the third largest segment of society as a professional military; and

(iv) ***Worker Class*** (60-70%): The worker class were the largest segment of society.

10.12 – Western (Christian) Civilisation (740 CE - present)

Article 327 – Western (Christian) Civilisation (740 CE - present)

1098. The ***Western (Christian) Civilisation*** (from 740 CE – present), also known as simply ***Western Civilisation***, is the eleventh of the twelve Greatest Civilisations formed over the past four thousand years, that at its present height stretches across planet Earth. It is the fifth of the six Great Civilisations created by the Holly (Cuilliaéan) Bloodlines.

Western (Christian) Civilisation

1099. Great Empires that began or arose within the framework and context of Western Christian Civilisation include (but are not limited to):-

Great Empires within the Western (Christian) Civilisation

(i) ***Western Christian Empire*** (740 CE – present): Founded by Frank leader Aurelius Aptatus also known as "Charles Martel" by 740 CE. Technically the most successful Civilisation since the Ancient Egyptians. The Holly finally lost control of Roman Catholic Church and Civilisation in early 16th Century; and

(ii) ***Venetian Empire*** (1200 – present): The Republic of Venice reached a high point in terms of trading ports and colonies across eastern and western Mediterranean, including thriving coastal and inland river based merchant cities; and

(iii) ***Spanish-Portuguese Empire*** (1400s – 1800): Early rivals to the Venetian City States, its vast wealth and power was built upon some of the worst crimes against humanity in deliberate genocide, theft, knowledge destruction, slavery and barbarity across the world, particularly South America, South East Asia and parts of Africa; and

(iv) ***English (Venetian) Empire*** (1511 - present): The exiled Patrician families took control of the government and finances of England by 1511 and then the crown of England itself upon the death of Elizabeth I (1558-1603). Manufactured the "Reformation", crippling many of its rivals in Germany, Belgium, Netherlands and Switzerland. Formed the British Empire as the Kingdom of Great Britain; and

(v) ***American (Dutch-English) Empire*** (1796 - present): The exiled Dutch Patrician families having been granted control and restoration of ownership of the land of the former Dutch colonies of eastern North America, soon became the largest banking nation in the world, causing the annual GDP of the United States to explode to $200 million in 1800 compared to the total GDP of the British Empire in the same year at £220 million. By no later than 1815, the United States was the largest economy in the world at around an annual GDP of $700 million. These facts are deliberately hidden, or corrupted to hide the fact that an apparent "fledgling" nation could in less than 50 years become the largest modern economy in the world.

1100. Western (Christian) Civilisation Religion and Belief Systems:-

Western (Christian) Civilisation Religion and Belief Systems

(i) ***Ultimate Duality of Reality (God vs Satan)***: The Universe is ultimately a duality between Good and Evil personified by God versus Satan; and

(ii) ***Belief in Jesus Christ***: Central to Christianity is the belief in Jesus Christ as the Son of God and the Messiah (Christ) prophesied. Jesus' life, teachings, crucifixion and resurrection are foundational events in Christian faith; and

(iii) ***New Testament***: Early Christians regarded the New Testament as sacred scripture, comprising the Gospels (Matthew, Mark, Luke, and John), letters (Epistles) written by apostles like Paul, and the Book of Revelation. These texts provide guidance, teachings and accounts of Jesus' life; and

(iv) ***Christian Ethics***: Early Christians followed ethical teachings attributed to Jesus, emphasizing love for one's neighbour, forgiveness, humility and a commitment to moral living; and

(v) ***Resurrection and Salvation***: Christians believe in the resurrection of Jesus, which signifies victory over sin and death. The promise of salvation through faith in Jesus and his sacrifice is a fundamental aspect of Christian belief; and

(vi) ***Eschatology***: Western Christians held beliefs about the imminent return of Jesus Christ, known as eschatology. They anticipated a final judgment and the establishment of God's kingdom on Earth.

1101. Western (Christian) Civilisation Language and Knowledge System of Anglais (Old French):-

Western (Christian) Civilisation Language and Knowledge

(i) ***Type of Language***: *Alphabetic*: Meaning characters represent individual sounds or phonemes. Each character typically corresponds to a specific letter or combination of letters; and Systems

(ii) ***Number of Characters***: 24 basic graphemes for consonants and vowels. Did not have letter for X or Z; and

(iii) ***Number of Common Nouns***: 47,000+ Main Common Noun Categories: Animals(21.31%), Objects(21.31%), People(17.05%), Science(9.51%), Plants(7.46%), Religion(5.93%), Law(3.41%) and Trade(2.73%); and

(iv) ***Language Rules Complexity***: *Simple*: Written to be read left-to-right. Verbs conjugated to indicate tense, mood and person. Nouns declined based on gender, number, and case. Adjectives must agree in gender, number and case with the nouns they describe. Verbs usually comes at the end (after the subject) of a sentence or clause. No subject pronouns, object pronouns, possessive pronouns or nouns categorised as masculine or feminine until language was deliberately and intentionally targetted to be corrupted from 16th to 18th Century to create "modern French"; and

(v) ***Noble Class Vocabulary***: 14,000 – 26,000; and

(vi) ***Professional Class Vocabulary***: 5,000 – 16,000; and

(vii) ***Worker Class Vocabulary***: 3,500 – 5,500.

1102. Western (Christian) Civilisation Sacred Texts and Primary Law Forms:- Western (Christian) Civilisation Sacred Texts and Primary Law Forms

(i) ***Holy Bible of Catholicism of the Franks***: As recognised and restored in accord with the most sacred Covenant *Pactum De Singularis Caelum*; and

(ii) ***Lebor Clann Glas of the Holly Diaspora***: As recognised and restored in accord with the most sacred Covenant *Pactum De Singularis Caelum*.

1103. Western (Christian) Civilisation Legal Systems:- Western (Christian) Civilisation Legal Systems

(i) **Religious Influence**: The highest law has always been considered Divine Law; and laws were influenced by Christian moral values, including concepts of justice, charity, and forgiveness; and

(ii) **Judicial Structure**: The Western Christian legal system introduced the concept of Courts and local and central courts for administering justice, including the concepts of justices, major and petty sessions and major courts or placitum; and

(iii) **Property Rights**: Property ownership and distribution were regulated by law, often influenced by Christian teachings on stewardship and just distribution of resources; and

(iv) **Family Law**: Laws governed matters related to marriage, divorce and inheritance, often influenced by Christian teachings on the sanctity of marriage and family; and

(v) ***Slavery Forbidden***: Similar to all Holly Civilisations, Western Christianity expressly forbid slavery in all its forms, until the Moors through the Venetian Empire corrupted Western Christianity; and

(vi) **Oaths**: Legal proceedings frequently involved religious oaths made on religious texts.

1104. Western (Christian) Civilisation Political Structure:-

Western (Christian) Civilisation Political Structure

(i) ***Parlomentum*** (Parliament): First started in 748 CE in Paris and attended by Kings and Marquees. Every four years; and

(ii) ***Nation States***: Including Angland (France), Deutschland (Germany), Ireland, Scotland, Wealand (Wales), Friesland (Netherlands), Daneland (south east England), Burgenland (Austria) and Holyland (Palestine).

1105. Western (Christian) Civilisation Key Positions:-

Western (Christian) Civilisation Key Positions

(i) ***Emperor (Father)***: Supreme Christian Sovereign; and

(ii) ***Roman Pontiff (Pope)***: A high-ranking advisor to the king, often involved in policy making and administration; and

(iii) ***King/Queen***: Leader of a Nation; and

(iv) ***Bishop***: Spiritual Leader; and

(v) ***Marque/Marquess***: Leader of a province; and

(vi) ***Baron/Baroness***: Leader of community.

1106. Western (Christian) Civilisation Social Organization:-

Western (Christian) Civilisation Social Organization

(i) ***Priest Class*** (< 1%): The priesthood was the most powerful and respected class. They played a significant role in religious rituals and ceremonies; and

(ii) ***Noble Service Class*** (< 1%): The noble service class represented high ranking officials and their families and the second most powerful and respected class; and

(iii) ***Public Servant Class*** (2-5%): The public service class represented members of skilled professions, such as scribes, artisans, craftspeople, engineers and project managers as the third class; and

(iv) ***Military Class*** (5-10%): Professional military given the necessity to defend against the Eastern Christian Empire; and

(v) ***Guild (Merchant) Class*** (5-10%): The guild merchant class represented a small but influential class of society in the provision of objects, materials and items; and

(vi) ***Worker Class*** (60-70%): The worker class was the largest class.

10.13 – Ucadia Civilisation (2001 CE - present)

Article 328 – Ucadia Civilisation (2001 CE - present)

1107. The ***Ucadia Civilisation*** (from 2001 CE – present): Also simply known as ***New Civilisation***, is the twelfth of the twelve Greatest Civilisations formed over the past four thousand years, that from the beginning stretches across the whole of Planet Earth and the entire Solar (Sol) System, including such planets as Mars and moons such as Titan and Io. It is the sixth of the six Great Civilisations created by the Holly (Cuilliaéan) Bloodlines.

Ucadia Civilisation

1108. Ucadia Civilisation Religion and Belief Systems:-

Ucadia Civilisation Religion and Belief Systems

(i) ***Ultimate Oneness of Reality (UCA)***: The ultimate divine reality and presence that is the source of all nature and the cosmos. Unique Collective Awareness (UCA) is both the personification of this ultimate unmanifest, formless, and undifferentiated oneness of reality and the presence or "animism" in every living and non living thing including (but not limited to) trees, rivers, rocks, animals and celestial bodies; and

(ii) ***Synergism***: Synergism is a central concept representing the principles of balance, harmony and order.

1109. Ucadia Civilisation Language and Knowledge Systems of ***Psygos*** and ***Logos***:-

Ucadia Civilisation Language and Knowledge Systems

(i) ***Type of Language***: *Logographic (Psygos)* and *Syllabic (Logos)*: ***Ucadia Psygos Glyphs*** are logographic, while ***Logos Characters*** are syllabic. However, both languages can be merged as the same essential grammar rules apply to both languages; and

(ii) ***Number of Symbols/Characters (Psygos)***: 64 basic outer shapes, 1024 recurring internal elements, 400 core sets,

2 million+ graphemes; and

(iii) ***Number of Symbols/Characters (Logos)***: 700-800 graphemes; and

(iv) ***Number of Common Nouns***: 2,275,000+ Main Common Noun Categories: Animals (27.25%), Objects(11.43%), People(10.99%), Science(8.89%), Religion(8.13%), Plants (7.03%), Trade(2.37%) and Law(1.05%); and

(v) ***Language Rules Complexity***: *Simple*: Written to be read right-to-left, left-to-right, and top-to-bottom. Tensors not Verbs conjugated to indicate tense, mood, aspect, person and number. Adjectives can come before or after the noun they modify. Word order is typically Tensor-Verb-Subject-Object (TVSO); and

(vi) ***Intellectual Class Vocabulary***: 60,000 – 120,000; and

(vii) ***Professional Class Vocabulary***: 30,000 – 70,000; and

(viii) ***Worker Class Vocabulary***: 8,500 – 25,000.

1110. Ucadia Civilisation Sacred Texts and Primary Law Forms:-

Ucadia Civilisation Sacred Texts and Primary Law Forms

(i) ***Pactum De Singularis Caelum*** (Covenant of One Heaven); and

(ii) ***Pactum De Singularis Christus*** (Covenant of One Christ); and

(iii) ***Pactum De Singularis Islam*** (Covenant of One Islam); and

(iv) ***Pactum De Singularis Spiritus*** (Covenant of One Spirit); and

(v) ***Authentic Sacred Deposit of Trust*** (Thirty-Three (33) Sacred Covenants between Authentic, Apostolic and Anointed Divine Messengers of the Divine Creator of all Existence and all the Heavens and Earth and the peoples of the Earth); and

(vi) ***Divine Collection of Maxims of Law*** (22 books of Maxims and Canons of Law); and

(vii) ***Voluntatem Et Testamentum*** (Will and Testament); and

(viii) ***Testamentum Lucis*** (Testament of Light); and

(ix) ***Testamentum Noctis*** (Testament of Darkness); and

(x) ***Carta Sacrum De Congregationis Globus*** (Ucadia Globe Union Constitutional Charter); and

(xi) ***Carta Sacrum De Congregationis Africans*** (Ucadia

Africa Union Constitutional Charter); and

(xii) ***Carta Sacrum De Congregationis Americas*** (Ucadia Americas Union Constitutional Charter); and

(xiii) ***Carta Sacrum De Congregationis Arabia*** (Ucadia Arabia Union Constitutional Charter); and

(xiv) ***Carta Sacrum De Congregationis Asia*** (Ucadia Asia Union Constitutional Charter); and

(xv) ***Carta Sacrum De Congregationis Oriens*** (Ucadia Levant Union Constitutional Charter); and

(xvi) ***Carta Sacrum De Congregationis Europa*** (Ucadia Euro Union Constitutional Charter); and

(xvii) ***Carta Sacrum De Congregationis Oceania*** (Ucadia Oceanic Union Constitutional Charter); and

(xviii) ***Carta Economia De Congregationis Globus*** (Ucadia Globe Union Economic Charter); and

(xix) ***Carta Economia De Congregationis Africans*** (Ucadia Africa Union Economic Charter); and

(xx) ***Carta Economia De Congregationis Americas*** (Ucadia Americas Union Economic Charter); and

(xxi) ***Carta Economia De Congregationis Arabia*** (Ucadia Arabia Union Economic Charter); and

(xxii) ***Carta Economia De Congregationis Asia*** (Ucadia Asia Union Economic Charter); and

(xxiii) ***Carta Economia De Congregationis Oriens*** (Ucadia Levant Union Economic Charter); and

(xxiv) ***Carta Economia De Congregationis Europa*** (Ucadia Euro Union Economic Charter); and

(xxv) ***Carta Economia De Congregationis Oceania*** (Ucadia Oceanic Union Economic Charter); and

(xxvi) ***Carta Iudicialis De Congregationis Globus*** (Ucadia Globe Union Judicial Charter); and

(xxvii) ***Carta Iudicialis De Congregationis Africans*** (Ucadia Africa Union Judicial Charter); and

(xxviii) ***Carta Iudicialis De Congregationis Americas*** (Ucadia Americas Union Judicial Charter); and

(xxix) ***Carta Iudicialis De Congregationis Arabia*** (Ucadia

Arabia Union Judicial Charter); and

(xxx) ***Carta Iudicialis De Congregationis Asia*** (Ucadia Asia Union Judicial Charter); and

(xxxi) ***Carta Iudicialis De Congregationis Oriens*** (Ucadia Levant Union Judicial Charter); and

(xxxii) ***Carta Iudicialis De Congregationis Europa*** (Ucadia Euro Union Judicial Charter); and

(xxxiii) ***Carta Iudicialis De Congregationis Oceania*** (Ucadia Oceanic Union Judicial Charter).

1111. Ucadia Civilisation Legal Systems:- Ucadia Civilisation Legal Systems

(i) **Religious Influence**: The highest law is considered Divine Law; and laws influenced by spiritual moral values, including concepts of justice, charity and forgiveness; and

(ii) **Comprehensive Rights Structure**: A comprehensive rights structure for all levels of society so that no law is expressed without a properly associated right; and

(iii) **Complete Maxims and Arguments of Law**: A complete system of maxims and arguments of law, covering the full spectrum of systems, issues and categories of society; and

(iv) **Full System of Codes of Law**: A full and complete system of codes of law, including forms and procedures able to be automated and streamlined; and

(v) **Judicial Structure**: A hierarchical and complete judicial structure with officials responsible for administering justice; and

(vi) **Comprehensive Property Rights**: Comprehensive Property ownership and rights system capable of ensuring effective management of all property rights issues; and

(vii) **Intelligent Digital Low-cost Arbitration and Enforcement**: Intelligent and low cost services and systems to support arbitration and automatic enforcement support – especially in relation to the guarantee and enforcement of agreements.

1112. Ucadia Civilisation Key Positions:- Ucadia Civilisation Key Positions

(i) ***Supreme Patriarch***: Supreme head of the body of One Christ; and

(ii) ***Supreme Caliph***: Supreme head of the body of One Islam;

and

(iii) ***Supreme Recurrence***: Supreme head of the body of One Spirit; and

(iv) ***General Secretary***: Head of the Globe Secretariat and ex-officio member (Globe Councillor) of the Supreme (Globe) Council; and

(v) ***Prefect of Globe Senate***: Head of the Globe Senate of Justice and ex-officio member (Globe Councillor) of the Supreme (Globe) Council; and

(vi) ***General Justice***: Head of the Globe Court of Justice and ex-officio member (Globe Councillor) of the Supreme (Globe) Council; and

(vii) ***General Treasurer***: Head of the Globe Treasury and ex-officio member (Globe Councillor) of the Supreme (Globe) Council; and

(viii) ***General Marshal***: Head of the Globe Guard and ex-officio member (Globe Councillor) of the Supreme (Globe) Council; and

(ix) ***General Architect***: Head of the Globe Economic Council and ex-officio member (Globe Councillor) of the Supreme (Globe) Council; and

(x) ***General Ecologist***: Head of the Globe Ecological Council and ex-officio member (Globe Councillor) of the Supreme (Globe) Council; and

(xi) ***General Conservator***: Head of the Globe Cultural Council and ex-officio member (Globe Councillor) of the Supreme (Globe) Council; and

(xii) ***General Surveyor***: Head of the Global Space Council and and ex-officio member (Globe Councillor) of the Supreme (Globe) Council; and

(xiii) ***Elder***: Member of the Council of Elders of an Original Nation as oversight, guidance and wisdom; and

(xiv) ***President***: Head of the Nation (University) Executive Government, Chair of Cabinet, Administration, Military and Law Enforcement; and

(xv) ***Vice-President (Domestic)***: Also known as "Chancellor" as Chair of Domestic Affairs Committee and head of University Court of Chancery; and

(xvi) ***Vice-President (International)***: Also known as "Plenipotentiary" as Chair of International Affairs Committee and head of University Sacristy.

1113. Ucadia Civilisation Social Organization:-

Ucadia Civilisation Social Organization

(i) ***Community Vocation Class*** (2-5%): Those dedicated to a religious or secular service of community in positions of trust and authority; and

(ii) ***Community Wellness Class*** (5-10%): Those dedicated to the wellness, health and care of others in the community; and

(iii) ***Community Knowledge Class*** (5-10%): Those dedicated to the knowledge and technology applications and services of the community; and

(iv) ***Community Systems Class*** (5-10%): Those dedicated to the infrastructure and systems of the community; and

(v) ***Community Security Class*** (5-10%): Those dedicated to the local and national security and defence of the community; and

(vi) ***Entrepreneurs Class*** (5-10%): Those invested in developing innovation and opportunities in creating and marketing of products and services; and

(vii) ***Operators Class*** (10-20%): Those who operate computers, robots and other elements; and

(viii) ***Services Class*** (20-30%): Those who support in service positions.

Title XI – Empire Models of Sovereign Law

11.1 – Empire Models of Sovereign Law

Article 329 – Empire Models of Sovereign Law

1114. An ***Empire*** refers to a political construct of several states or countries ruled over by a single monarch, or oligarchy, or a sovereign state. Empires are typically characterised by their forced military, political or economic conquest, control and assimilation of other peoples, rather than the unifying cultural identity of a civilisation. Empire

1115. An *Empire* differs from a *Civilisation* in that an "empire" primarily concerns military, political and economic dominance, whereas a "civilisation" usually defines homogeneous advances in cultural and societal development, technology and knowledge. Civilisations can exist without forming empires, and empires can take control of civilisations. Differences between Empires and Civilisations

1116. ***Empire Model of Sovereign Law*** refers to a conceptual framework and system of laws that governs the authority and conduct of states or territories within the *Empire*. Sovereignty in law means that a state has supreme authority within its territory and is the ultimate source of all its laws. Empire Models of Sovereign Law

1117. Common elements of an *Empire Model of Sovereign Law* include (but is not limited to):- Common Elements of Empire Models of Sovereign Law

(i) **Central Authority**: A strong central government that exercises authority over the empire's affairs, often embodied by a monarch, emperor, or central administration; and

(ii) **Unified Legal System**: While local laws may vary, empires typically have overarching legal frameworks that integrate different legal traditions and apply to the entire empire; and

(iii) **Legal Pluralism**: The coexistence and application of various legal traditions and systems within the empire, allowing some degree of autonomy for local laws under the imperial framework; and

(iv) **Imperial Citizenship or Subject Status**: Determinations of the rights and privileges of individuals within the empire, which may vary greatly depending on one's status as a citizen, subject, or slave; and

(v) **Conflict and Conquest Laws**: Regulations on how the empire expands its territory, including laws of war, treatment of conquered peoples, and integration of new territories; and

(vi) **Taxation and Revenue Laws**: Systems for collecting taxes and revenues from various regions to fund the central government and military.

Examples of Influential Empires

1118. While there have been many significant Empires of human civilisation, a select number of Empires that have fundamentally influenced the development of world history, civilisation and society include (but are not limited to):-

(i) ***Imperial Roman Empire (31 BCE – 313 CE)***: Founded by Gaius Julius Caesar Augustus (Octavian), the Empire rose to its height under Trajan in the 2nd Century CE; and

(ii) ***Imperial Holly Christian Empire (314 – present)***: Founded by Iohannes Constantinos (Cuinstanyn mac Cuinalba) (314 – 337 CE) as the largest Empire the world has even known to date; and

(iii) ***Western Holly Christian Empire (740 – present)***: Founded by Frank leader Aurelius Aptatus also known as "Charles Martel" by 740 CE. Technically one of the most successful Civilisation since the Ancient Egyptians. The Holly finally lost control of Roman Catholic Church and the Empire by the early 16th Century; and

(iv) ***Venetian Roman Empire (1200 – present)***: The Republic of Venice reached a high point in terms of trading ports and colonies across eastern and western Mediterranean, including thriving coastal and inland river based merchant cities; and

(v) ***Venetian British Empire (1511 – present)***: The exiled Patrician families took control of the government and finances of England by 1511 and then the crown of England itself upon the death of Elizabeth I (1558-1603). Manufactured the "Reformation", crippling many of its rivals in Germany, Belgium, Netherlands and Switzerland. Formed the British Empire as the Kingdom of Great Britain; and

(vi) ***American Dutch-English Empire (1796 – present)***: The exiled Dutch Patrician families having been granted control and restoration of ownership of the land of the former Dutch colonies of eastern North America, soon became the largest banking and then military nation in the world.

11.2 – Imperial Roman Empire

Article 330 – Imperial Roman Empire

1119. ***Imperial Roman Empire***: The Roman Empire was a vast and influential ancient civilization that existed from 27 BC to 313 CE. It originated from the Roman Republic and expanded across Europe, Asia, and Africa, reaching its zenith in the 2nd century AD under emperors like Trajan. The empire's decline resulted from internal strife, external pressures, and economic challenges until 313 CE when the city of Rome was utterly destroyed and burnt to the ground, including the destruction and condemnation of all its laws, standards, edicts and rituals by Constantine prior to the formation of Christianity in 314 CE. Imperial Roman Empire

1120. In reference to the Imperial Roman Empire, there exist some notable inventions and elements that still impact Sovereign Law today, including (but not limited to):- Significant Elements of Imperial Roman Empire and Sovereign Law

(i) Latin (Language); and
(ii) Rome; and
(iii) Twelve Tables; and
(iv) Fascism; and
(v) Gens (Race); and
(vi) Nomen (Name); and
(vii) Rex (Sacred Law); and
(viii) Lex (Social Law); and
(ix) Possessio (Possession); and
(x) Occupatio (Occupation); and
(xi) Usus (Use); and
(xii) Custos (Slavery); and
(xiii) Mancipatio (Transfer of Ownership); and
(xiv) Province; and
(xv) Civitas (City); and
(xvi) Municipium (Municipality); and
(xvii) District.

Article 331 – Latin (Language)

1121. ***Latin*** is a language that originated in the region of Italy around the city of Rome. It was the language of the Roman Republic and the Roman Empire and played a significant role in the development of Western civilization. Latin is a member of the Italic branch of the Indo-European language family. In reference to the key elements of Latin:- Latin (Language)

(i) ***Alphabe***t: Latin uses the Latin alphabet, which is the same as the modern English alphabet, with some minor variations in letter pronunciation and spelling; and

(ii) ***Inflected***: Latin is an inflected language, which means that the endings of words change to convey grammatical information such as case, gender, number, and tense. This feature allows for flexibility in word order; and

(iii) ***Classical and Ecclesiastical Latin***: Latin has two major forms: Classical Latin and Ecclesiastical Latin. Classical Latin is the form of the language used in ancient Rome and is associated with classical literature and historical texts. Ecclesiastical Latin, on the other hand, is the form of Latin used in the Roman Catholic Church and is still used in religious contexts today.

1122. The *Ancient Latin Language* is one of more than two dozen major ancient and contemporary languages around the world that were targetted for major corruption, obfuscation and sabotage from the 16th Century by the Venetians in order to promote the power and influence of the "new" language of English and preserve the effectiveness of Italian, proper Ancient Greek as some ciphers of Ecclesiastical Greek and Latin as some ciphers of Ecclesiastical Latin:- Deliberate corruption, obfuscation and sabotage of Ancient Latin

(i) ***Hide Inherit Agglutinative Construction***: Words in Latin, like Ancient Greek and most other ancient languages were generally formed by combining some simple root with various affixes (prefixes, suffixes etc) to denote tense, case, number, person or common noun category. The understanding of natural common noun categories using prefixes and suffixes was removed and instead replaced with the nonsensical idea that nouns themselves have to grammatically agree in tense, case, number, mood and person. This had the effect of stripping much of the knowledge embedded in common nouns in Latin as to their deeper and true meaning; and

(ii) ***Remove, Switch and Corrupt Meanings***: With the inherit "Semantic Agglutinative Nature" of common nouns obscured, meanings of words were then switched, corrupted and inverted; and

(iii) ***Degrade Proper Declension of Verbs and Adjectives***: To emphasize greater focus and complexity on the grammatical rules of common nouns by hiding the real purpose for declension of affixes in the first place (to denote its context as a category of belonging), the emphasis on properly declaring the tense, mood, number, case and person of verbs and adjectives was corrupted, leading to the absolute absurdity that many supposedly "grammatically correct" sentences could no longer be immediately and perfectly translated without wider context; and

(iv) ***Focus effort on the declension and case of nouns***: Having destroyed the common sense of the language, corrupted many of its meanings, the focus of "proper grammar" then became the obsession of a complex time wasting in grammatically requiring nouns to behave like verbs in other languages.

1123. The intentional corruption of Latin and the deliberate inclusion of useless complexity had a profound number of intentional and unintentional consequences, including (but not limited to):-

Consequences of deliberately corrupted rules of Latin

(i) The general and continued death of the Latin language as a living spoken language, given how almost impossible the corrupt rules had made the language to be effectively and spontaneously created; and

(ii) The creation of nonsensical Latin, called "Dog Latin" or "Vulgar Latin" whereby sentences using such corrupted rules of grammar were unwittingly declared into meaningless "gibberish" from a proper ecclesiastical and true legal sense; and

(iii) The creation of an almost impenetrable "barrier" to be able to investigate the past, challenge the status quo, or discover information beyond the official "propaganda" of the government and its agencies, using such an ancient language; and

(iv) The use of corrupted Latin in the creation of libraries full of blatant fakes, forgeries and meaningless documents, in support of false history, false law and false sacred texts; and

(v) The greatest unintentional consequence of the use of corrupted Latin, corresponding to the corruption of so many other languages is that any document or artefact claimed from an earlier period than the 16th Century that written in corrupted Latin is therefore a fake, corruption and fraud.

Article 332 – Rome

1124. ***Rome*** is located on an ancient flood marsh plain, near the midpoint on the western side of the Italian peninsula, approximately 15 miles (25 kilometres) upstream along the Tiber River from the coastline (Tyrrhenian Sea). The first Etruscan settlement was probably originally founded on Tiber Island approx 890 ft (270m) long and 220 ft (67m) wide as the largest naturally occurring island on the river.

Rome

1125. In reference to the Origins, History and Nature of Rome-

Brief Summary of Origins, History and Nature of Rome

(i) Built only 43 ft (13m) above sea level on a relatively flat ancient flood marsh plain, the location of Rome has a long history of high and uncomfortable humidity, with four to five months (May-Oct) of the year being especially hot and above 80°F (26.7°C); and

(ii) Contrary to false and absurd histories, Rome was founded by Darius the Great as both the primary location for the central garrison of Persian forces in Italy and as a neutral meeting place between the Etruscan cities from the North and the Graecian cities. Hence the mythological formation of Rome between "two brothers" represents the actual history of the Northern Yahudi as Levites and "Remus" (Sumer) finding peace with the Southern Yahudi as Simonites and "Remulus" (Sulumer); and

(iii) The original meaning of the name Rome from 509 BCE was Rama meaning literally "sacred and neutral field". However, within just eight years the Etruscans broke their word and attacked Rome and the Persian garrison in 501 BCE. Rather than destroying all the Etruscan cities, the Persians forced the northern Italian tribes to provide 10 years service to the Persian army, creating the first "Roman Legions"; and

(iv) In 398 BCE, the city of Rome was destroyed and its inhabitants slaughtered by the Carthaginians. In 397 BCE, the bravery of the Persian garrison caused Artaxerxes II to dedicate a new garrison of ten thousand for Rome as "Immortals" – the first and only time in the history of Persia that any force outside of Persia was ever given such a title. When Alexander dissolved the "Immortals" by 330 BCE, the Romans changed the name of their garrison to the *Praeternae* (Praetorian) meaning *prae* as "in the form of" and *aeternae* as "immortals"; and

(v) From 397 to 360 BCE under Artaxerxes II, the city of Rome underwent a historic infrastructure period, with the creation of the most advanced drainage and sewer system of any city in ancient history (later called the Cloaca Maxima); and a massive aqueduct and clean water system (later called Aqua Appia), bringing quality water from the Alban Hills more than 10 miles (16 km) away; and the first of three large public baths called the *Thermae*; and the Roman Forum; and the circus (Circus Maximus); and the creation of a defensive wall with nine gates for the city; and the formation of state of the art roads to the south (Via Appia), the west to the coast (Via Aurelia) and to the north (Via Flamina). As a consequence, the population of the city grew from less than 15,000 prior to 400 BCE to over 150,000 by 300 BCE, making it at the time the 6th largest city in the world behind Athens (250,000), Alexandria (200,000), Babylon (200,000), Carthage (175,000) and Thebes (175,000); and

(vi) By around 30 BCE, the population of Rome reached at least 1 million people, the first city in ancient history to reach such a number (and only matched again by Baghdad under the Abbasid Caliphate by 800 CE and only then again by London by 1801 CE). A major set of infrastructure works were commissioned to cope with the enormous growth in population, including expanding the Cloaca Maxima (drainage and sewage system); and new aqueducts (Aqua Novus, Aqua Virgo); and

(vii) After the Great Fire of 65 CE that destroyed over a third of Rome, major works were envisaged, including the Great Coliseum (finished by 80 CE); and

(viii) Rome was finally emptied of people under the Edict of Rome 313 CE by Constantine, that saw the whole city condemned. It remained in ruins until the 8th Century when the first reconstruction work began under the Carolingians. The city did not return to around 50,000 residence again until the 17th Century.

Article 333 – Twelve Tables

1126. The ***Twelve Tables***, also known as the "Law of the Twelve Tables" (Latin: *Lex Duodecim Tabularum*), were a set of laws in ancient Rome that formed the foundation of Roman legal and social institutions. These tables were displayed in the Roman Forum from the 4th Century CE and represented a significant development in the history of Roman law. Twelve Tables

1127. Based on historic analysis and comparisons to other "table" law forms introduced around the same period, the main subjects of the twelve tables appears to have been:- Twelve Tables Contents

(i) Table I: Judicial; and

(ii) Table II: Property; and

(iii) Table III: Creditor; and

(iv) Table IV: Paternal [Father] ; and

(v) Table V: Inheritance; and

(vi) Table VI: Ownership and Possession; and

(vii) Table VII: Compensation; and

(viii) Table VIII: Land; and

(ix) Table IX: Public; and

(x) Table X: Funeral; and

(xi) Table XI: Matrimonial; and

(xii) Table XII: Slave.

1128. In reference to the origin and background of the Twelve Tables:- Origin and background of twelve tables

(i) The Twelve Tables were created no earlier than 380 BCE during the reign of Persian Ruler Artaxerxes II as a gift to the new city he had helped construct. They applied to all people in Italy not just the people of Rome; and are modelled on the concept of the public laws of Athens; and

(ii) The primary purpose of the Twelve Tables was to provide a written legal framework that governed various aspects of Roman society, including property rights, family law, debt, and civil procedure; and

(iii) The laws were inscribed on twelve bronze tablets or tables (hence the name) and were publicly displayed in the Roman Forum for all citizens to see. This transparency was important to ensure that citizens were aware of their legal rights and obligations; and

(iv) The Twelve Tables covered a wide range of legal matters, including rules for inheritance, marriage, property ownership, debt, and criminal offences. They also included provisions related to legal procedures and the role of magistrates; and

(v) The false laws created in the 16th Century under Venetian Empire and claimed to be derived from Rome had no real provenance or relation to the Twelve Tables.

Article 334 – Fascism

1129. ***Fascism*** is a term used to describe any authoritarian nationalistic political model (or its symbols) that prioritises the state over the individual; and that ultimately claims its power and authority from Rome or as a claim of being "New Rome". Fascism

1130. The most common, historical and blatantly obvious symbols of *Fascism* and any "fascist state" since the time of the Imperial Roman Empire to the 18th Century revival include, but are not limited to:- Symbols of Fascism

(i) ***The Golden Eagle (Aquila Aurea)***: The personification of imperial power and authority. It has always been used prominently across all standards of a fascist state. Under Imperial Rome, it was carried by an *Aquilifer*, the standard-bearer who carried the eagle standard. The eagle has always symbolised victory, valour, and the military strength of the fascist state. The eagle has always served as a symbol of the absolute authority of the executive branch of a fascist state over the military and the state itself. The eagle was also associated with the Roman gods, particularly Saturn (Saytan), the chief deity of the Roman pantheon legions and the Roman state itself in providing "supernatural" protection against all enemies of the state. The claim that Jupiter was the "king of the gods" is a deliberate falsity to hide the provenance and position of Saturn – the god who was celebrated via "Saturnalia" being the most important week long feast of Imperial Rome every year around 23rd to 29th December; and

(ii) ***The Golden Sign (Signa Aurea)***: A distinctive golden sign and pole of an emblem or standard. It has always represented the jurisdiction and power of imperial law as a weapon against the enemy. It was carried by an *Signifer*, the standard-bearer who carried the sign standard, as notice of the authority and identity of a military unit; and when the generic fascist abbreviation of "SPQR", such a sign denoted the claimed absolute authority and jurisdiction of Roman Law; and

(iii) ***The Golden Flag (Vexilla Aurea)***: A distinctive gold trimmed flag on a pole, paraded on ceremonial occasions, but usually placed next to or behind officials as the personification and presence of the living spirit (animus) of the state, especially in matters of law. It was carried by an *Vexiller*, during ceremonial processions and during the ritual of *Vexilla Procreatio* (Mating of the Flags) when such ceremonial flags would touch one another from a "mother flag" signifying a claimed transfer of power. With fascist states, the gold trimming has always represented the "supernatural" claims of rays of light emanating from the object and never simply ornamental. In more recent centuries and since the revival of fascism, the Golden Flag has come to symbolise both Admiralty Law and the claimed power of "Rome" and then "New Rome" as the supreme fascist state. Any claim to the contrary regarding Gold Flags is simply absurd and deliberately false; and

(iv) ***Fasces (bundle of bound wooden rods and an axe)***: Literally the source and original meaning of fascism as the symbol of fascist rule. Carried by Roman Legions with their other symbols, it has never meant equality or mercy or civilised rule of law, but brutal rule by cruelty, deception and military force. Its presence in public buildings and monuments (such as Lincoln Memorial, Capitol Building) is public notice to any competent person of the true fascist nature of a state or empire; and

(v) ***Cratis (bundle of spears or arrows)***: Closely aligned to Fasces (a bundle of sticks), a Cratis represented two states – war (as spears or arrows) or peace as (as cages, subjugation and trade). The symbol of Cratis has always and only meant "rule by conquest and rule by force" either in war as *Autocratis* (military law) or subjugation (in peace) of the people as slaves as *Democratis* (democracy). Any claim that "democracy" has ever meant rule by all of the people is both an absurd fantasy and cruel falsity. Under Fascist rule, Democracy has only ever meant "rule of the slaves by an elite few"; and

(vi) ***Roman Salute (Full or half salute)***: The Roman Salute either as Full (arm and hand outstretched at 45 degrees) or Half (45 degrees from the elbow and hand outstretched to the brow) has always been a sign of respect to loyal subjects and military of a fascist state from the time of Imperial Rome to its revival in the 19th Century. While the Full Roman Salute has been outlawed, the Half Roman Salute continues to be used by fascist states. Any claims to the contrary are false and deceptive.

1131. The term ***Fasces*** (as the source of the words "fascism and fascist") is the formal name for the ancient symbol of Roman judicial and military authority being a bundle of wooden rods/sticks and an axe, with its blade pointing outwards, bound together by leather straps:- Origin and meaning of Fasces

(i) The wooden rods or *vis/vires* symbolized power, force, strength, quantity, standards and corporal punishment; and

(ii) The axe or *securis* symbolized authority and supreme power to inflict capital punishment; and

(iii) The leather straps or *lorum* symbolized binding duty and reigns of power, whip and lash of enforcement; and

(iv) The largest symbols of Fasces of any Fascist State in human history, including Nazi Germany, is the Lincoln Memorial in Washington DC.

1132. Claims and definitions that paint *Fascism* as an ultra right wing nationalistic philosophy are deliberately false, misleading and absurd, as the history of fascist states have overwhelmingly been socialist such as World War II States of Germany, Italy and Spain:- Fascism and Forms of Government

(i) ***Imperial Rome*** was overwhelmingly a socialist state, with most property owned by the state; and the use of "bread and circuses" to keep the populace entertained and dulled in mind; and

(ii) The *Nationalsozialistische Deutsche Arbeiterpartei* (German for 'National Socialist German Workers' Party') otherwise known as the ***Nazi Party***, were completely socialist in their corrupted outlook; and continued the "bread and circuses" approach with new cars, roads, transport, employment, supermarkets and the birth of urban consumerism; and

(iii) The foundations of the United States of America as the Fourth Reich of Fascism was created by the Democrats and President Roosevelt from 1933 and the birth of Social Welfare; and has continued with endless "bread and circuses" to entertain, feed, support and dull the minds of most Americans to what has always been in front of their faces.

1133. Claims and definitions that claim *Fascism* has always been an anti-Jewish and anti-Semitic philosophy are deliberately false, misleading and absurd:- Fascism and Forms of Government

(i) ***The name "Jews" or "Israel" did not exist at time of Imperial Rome***: The area now called "Israel" was once a Yahudi state called Judea and then later under Imperial Roman occupation called Palestine. There was no such thing as "Jews" or even a "Jewish Religion". Nor had there ever been an ancient state called "Israel". Any claimed history from this time is either complete fabrication or the blatant and immoral cultural appropriation of the true Yahudi history from the time of Akhenaten (Moses) to the states of Judea and Nabatea and the Nazarene uprisings; and

(ii) ***Nazi forced deportations of Jews to Palestine enabled Israel to be formed***: Without the forced deportation by Adolf Hitler and the Nazi Fascist State of more than 390,000 Jews from all parts of Europe to Palestine from 1933-1939, the Jewish State of Israel could not possibly have been formed, as even in 1922 (contrary to the false British Census of Palestine) more than 98% of the population were Muslim and Christian; and less than 1% of the population of Palestine were Jewish. In 1935 alone, Adolf Hitler deported more than 62,000 Jews to Palestinian prison camps operated by the British Government; and

(iii) ***The Holocaust forever created the unquestioned moral authority and justification to create Israel and shield Jewish organisations and elite leaders from normal scrutiny***: Without the 300 mile wide Pentagram perfectly formed by sacrifice sites operated as "concentration camps" to Sabaoth (G-d or Moloch in occult Hasidism) around the Czartoryski Palace at Pulawy as the 18th Century "spiritual home" and the "Pious Ones" חסידים (chasidim) movement at its centre; and then the horrendous murder of millions of Protestants, Ethnic Minorities and Jews at these sites, there would never have been the overwhelming global support to create the state of Israel. The Pentagram of death camps only became operational the day after September 11, 1941 (9/11) and the founding of the second "invisible Pentagram" of the Pentagon in Washington DC. Both Pentagrams of Fascist states form a right Angle in alignment to the north star above the Arctic; and

(iv) ***America has been vital to the survival of Israel***: Without the constant and continued financial, military and political support of the United States of America since 1948, the State of Israel would not have continued to survive and thrive and successfully annex upwards of 90% of remaining

Palestinian land within its outer borders, in open defiance to international law and the rules of Civilised Societies.

1134. Since the revival of *Fascism* in the mid 19th Century and subsequent foundation of the purpose built fascist capital of Washinton DC starting in 1864, Hasidic (Chabad) and Christian Fascist Leaders have claimed a false history of "four reichs". German for "four ages or epochs":- Fascism and the Four Reichs

(i) ***First Reich (Erstes Reich)***: The term "First Reich" was used by the American and European Fascists to refer to the Holy Roman Empire (Heiliges Römisches Reich), which existed from the Middle Ages until 1806. The Holy Roman Empire was a complex political entity in Central Europe that included parts of what is now modern-day Germany. The American and European Fascists invoked this term to create a sense of continuity with European history; and

(ii) ***Second Reich (Zweites Reich)***: The term "Second Reich" was used by the American and European Fascists to refer to the German Empire (Deutsches Kaiserreich), which was established in 1871 when Germany unified under the leadership of Prussia. This period lasted until the end of World War I in 1918 when the German monarchy was abolished, and the Weimar Republic was established. The Nazis employed this term to emphasize the supposed greatness of Imperial Germany and to downplay the intervening Weimar period; and

(iii) ***Third Reich (Drittes Reich)***: The term "Third Reich" was used by the German Nazis to describe their own regime, which they believed would last for a thousand years and be the culmination of German history. The Third Reich refers to Nazi Germany, which was in power from 1933 until 1945 under the leadership of Adolf Hitler; and

(iv) ***Fourth Reich (Viertes Reich)***: The term "Fourth Reich" is not officially used by American Fascists or officials of Government, as it exposes and reinforces the connection between the European Fascists and American Fascists. Instead, the term "New World Order" is generally used in terms of describing the post war belief of a "thousand years" of the American Empire.

1135. Any Imbalanced Model of Government leads to fragmentation or Autocratic rule and Fascism. Therefore, the Imbalanced Models of Republicanism are synonymous with Fascism and Fascist symbols:- Fascism and Republic Model

(i) The word "republic" comes from the Latin words *res* meaning "property, form and things" and *publico* meaning "confiscation (of property) to the custody of mature and adult men (custodians)". The word public itself is derived from *pubes* meaning "adult men, manhood, manly maturity and fraternity of men" as "the people"; and

(ii) The first Fascist Model and Fascist State and Republic was in 203 BCE under Publius Sulpicius Galba as Caesar and the creation of a two-tier male dominated legal system, confiscating certain property and rights of "second class" citizens or "plebians" to be managed by the Senate as the "public" in trust (or fundus). Hence the creation of "public property" meaning literally property held in trust for another; and

(iii) An Imbalanced Republican and Fascist Model form of government is historically prone to deviancy, corruption, nepotism, misogyny, cruelty, stupidity and insanity as demonstrated throughout history, particularly in the 20th and 21st Centuries.

1136. As a Fascist form of Government is fundamentally in opposition to the Golden Rule of Law, there is nothing lawful, or just or reasonable about such a system, except to maintain power in the hands of a few men. However, all Fascist models have depended on similar concepts to maintain control of power:-

Fascism against Civilised Law

(i) Complete and total domination of all forms of media, education and communication to ensure constant propaganda, re-writing of history, conditioning and control; and

(ii) Total male domination and absolute enslavement, corruption, objectification, abuse and weakening of the feminine to ensure at least half of the population is mentally and physically incapable of overcoming propaganda and the misogynists (women haters) within power; and

(iii) Conversion of all rights into mere privileges and liberties, while ensuring the vast majority of the poor have as little as possible, or periodically stripping from the poor via depression, war or other artificially created external threat any little wealth they have gained over a few generations; and

(iv) Confected Consent through deliberate falsity, deception, trickery, intimidation and threat so that the poor people believe they live in a democracy when they live under tyranny; and believe they have rights when they have none; and believe there is no alternative when there are many better ways of government than Fascism; and

(v) Organized terror, opposition, wars and violence to keep the people in a constant state of unrest, preventing reasoned thinking and using the children of people as a threat and bargaining chip not to rebel against such evil.

1137. Given any Imbalanced Model of Government such as Fascism ferments unbalance, tyranny, injustice, misogyny (women hating), crime, poverty, corruption, famine, war, violence, environmental disaster, stupidity and insanity, such models of thinking are a clear and present threat to the sustainable future of human civilization. Therefore, all such models and systems are reprobate, suppressed, forbidden and not permitted to be revived. Fascism Forbidden

Article 335 – Gens (Race)

1138. ***Gens (Race)*** refers to a family tribe consisting of all those individuals who share the same nomen and claimed descent from a common ancestor. A group of gens was then referred to as *gentes.* Gens (Race)

1139. The Latin word *gens* is sourced and shortened from *genus* meaning "birth, descent, race, kind, class, species". Hence, *Gens* literally means "a family race, class or species". Origin of Word Gens

1140. Unlike a generalized tribe which traditionally incorporated a variety of roles and functions within a family group, a Roman gens more closely represented the ancient Hyksos social structure of Egypt whereby families and larger family groups tended to specialize into certain fields such as military service, arts, priests or particular types of commerce. Function of Gens

1141. Roman society divided itself essentially into three (3) main Gens being *Patrician, Plebian* and *Proletari*:- Patricians, Plebians and Proletari

(i) ***Patrician***: The term patrician originally referred to the "highest class" of elite priest and noble families or "gentes" that influenced the foundation of ancient Rome and by default the early Roman Empire. The word patrician is sourced from ancient Greek word πατρικός (patrikós) meaning "fatherly, paternal" and refers to the original members and their families of the Roman Senate who were known as "patres" or "fathers of Rome"; and

(ii) ***Plebian***: The term plebian, also sometimes referred to as "equestrian" class originally referred to the "middle class" families or "gentes" of free and land-owning Roman citizens known as "civis". The word plebeian is sourced from ancient

Latin word *plebeius* meaning “low or common”. The word equestrian is derived from equis meaning "horse"; and

(iii) ***Proletari (Proletarian)***: The term proletarian, also known as the “capite censi”, originally referred to the “lowest class” of Roman citizens being free and land - owning Roman citizens known as “municeps” of Roman provinces. The word proletarian is sourced from ancient Latin word *proles* meaning “lowest offspring or lowest race”.

1142. In terms of the origins of the three (3) main Gens being *Patrician, Plebian* and *Proletari*:- Origins of the Gens of Rome

(i) The Patrician gens by default were those original Yahudi colonists from Cumae and Reggio and earlier from šumur (Chaldis) and šulumur (Erétria) in Greece. Later, Patrician status was granted to the priestly classes of Yahudi descendents and diaspora around the world such as Ireland, Tarsus, Syria, Baalbek, Persia and Jerusalem; and

(ii) The Plebians were originally those Persian militia who came under Darius in the 6th Century and later in the 5th Century BCE under Xerxes who were granted citizenship if they remained and fought for Rome. Later Plebian status was granted to noble and military leaders of conquered lands that pledged absolute loyalty to Rome; and

(iii) The Proletari gens did not emerge as the third class until the 2nd Century BCE when people in conquered territories were able to “purchase” citizenship through service in the Legion or a straight out financial purchase if a trader. Thus, the creation of the Proletari that could be earned through military service to Rome was one of the key reasons the Romans were able to recruit such numbers to serve in their armies.

Article 336 – Nomen (Name)

1143. ***Nomen (Name)*** is a formal system of individual identification created by the Romans from corrupting the ancient Celt naming traditions whereby one immediately declares their social standing within Roman law through the construction of their “name” as a form of title. Nomen (Name)

1144. The word nomen is derived from *nomina* which itself is sourced from two (2) ancient Latin roots *nos* meaning “we us, I or me” and *mina* meaning “value”. Hence the original etymological meaning of nomen is “my value” in reference to the system denoting both social standing Origin of word Nomen and identity.

1145. The Nomen System comprised of several key components then assembled under certain naming (nomenclature) conventions being:- Nomen System of Rome

(i) Full Citizen status, usually denoting one of the ancient Patrician families as "Civilus"; and

(ii) Auctoritas being the highest authority attained by the individual; and

(iii) Officium being the highest office attained by the individual; and

(iv) Praenomen being the given name; and

(v) Nomen or Gentilicium being the name of their gens of clan; and

(vi) Patrimonicus being the filial relation to a great Roman; and

(vii) Cognomen being name of the family lines within the gens; and

(viii) Agnomen being a popular nickname, identity or word of honour applied to the individual.

1146. Under Roman society, Nomen or Gentilicium, and later Cognomen and Agnomen were virtually always hereditary. Hereditary Nomen

1147. Auctoritas as part of nomen was usually reserved for the highest and greatest of officials and included such examples as "Divi Filius" meaning literally divine authority reserved for the nomen of emperors such as Civilis Divi Filius Caesar Octavianus and Imperator Caesar Divi Filius Augustus. Auctoritas

1148. Officium as part of nomen was usually reserved for the highest and greatest of officials and included such examples as:- Officium

(i) Imperator being the highest administrative official from which "emperor" is derived; and

(ii) Executor being a senior administrative official and precursor to senators; and

(iii) Rector being the governor of a province; and

(iv) Censor being an official visitor and overseer of the Senate; and

(v) Senator being a member of the senate and head advisory body to the Pontificum Collegium (College of Pontiffs) that controlled Rome.

1149. Praenomen as the first part of nomen distinguished a Roman Citizen by their order of birth, omen of birth, or negative social condition at time of birth and included such examples as:- Praenomen

(i) Order of son being Primus (P.) “first”, Secundus "second", Tertius "third", Quartus “fourth”, Quintus (Q.) "fifth", Sextus (Sex.) "sixth", Septimus (Sept.) "seventh", Octavianus (O.) "eight", Nonus “ninth”, Decimus (D.) "tenth"; and

(ii) Omen of birth being Faustus “auspicious”, Lucius (from Lucifer) (L.) “the best of luck, good fortune”, Flavus “golden”, Gallus “confident, cocksure”, Canus “wise”; and

(iii) Peculiarity of birth being Agrippa “born feet first”, Caeso “cut from the womb”, Spurius (Sp.) “illegitimate birth” ; and

(iv) Station at birth being Miser (M. or Mr.) “debt or bond slave”, Servius (S. or Ser.) “indentured or contracted slave”.

1150. Gentilicium or Gens (Clan) name traditionally identified whether one was borne of the highest class (Patrician), or lower class (Plebian). For example, famous Patrician families included (but were not limited to): Antonius, Aquillia, Atilia, Claudius, Cornelius, Curtia, Didius, Domitius, Fabia, Furia, Julius, Marcia, Pompeius, Romilia, Sestia, Siccia, Sulpicia, Valeria, Vitellia, Tarpeia and Valerius. Gentilicium (Gens)

1151. Agnomen or “nicknames” were a key feature of the nomen of famous Romans, especially leaders and included such key examples as:- Agnomen

(i) Augustus meaning “majestic or venerable”; and

(ii) Caesar meaning “one who sacrifices the enemy (of Rome) in a bloody ritual”.

1152. Agnomen Females were usually known by the feminine form of their father's nomen gentile, followed by the genitive case of their father's or husband's cognomen and an indication of order among sisters through praenomen. Female Agnomen

Article 337 – Rex (Sacred Law)

1153. ***Rex (Sacred Law)***, also known as “Rex Sacrorum” also known as “Sacred Rites”, also known as “Sacred Law” was a form of law developed by the Yahudi founders of Rome from the 6th Century BCE onwards exclusively for the benefit and protection of the most elite families of all known as Patricians. Rex (Sacred Law)

1154. The claim that Rex Sacrorum is derived from some earlier history of Kings of Rome is patently false and absurd history designed to hide the fact that the previous Etruscan city that originally occupied the site of Rome was conquered by the Chaldeans Yahudi diaspora from šumur (Chaldis) and šulumur (Erétria) with a sizeable military support from Darius the Great of Persia until 509 BCE. Furthermore, the name “Rome” was not consecrated until the reign of Xerxes I of Changing nature of Rex Sacrorum

Persia at around 481 BCE.

1155. The claim that Rex Sacrorum is derived from some earlier history of Kings of Rome, or that it remained largely consistent throughout the history of Rome is patently false and absurd:- False claims of Rex Sacrorum

(i) ***Rex Sacrorum dramatically changed at least five times during Rome History***: Roman Sacred Law underwent at least five dramatic ages of change, beginning with (1) the consecration of Rome until the reign of Xerxes I of Persia at around 481 BCE until around (2) 206 BCE and then (3) 69 CE and the destruction of the Great Temple of Mithra in Jerusalem and the formation of Iudaism until (4) 98 CE and the reign of Emperor Trajan; and then (5) the formation of the dark occult religions of the Tertullian Emperors of North Africa from 193 CE until 257 CE; and

(ii) ***The positions, titles, buildings and structures of Rex Sacrorum changed with the Law***: Not only did the Sacred Laws of Rome undergo major periods of change, but the positions, titles, buildings and rituals underwent similar significant changes so that none may credibly claim any form of continuity for such structure as the "College of Pontiffs" or the celebration of Saturnalia, or the function of the Vaticanus; and

(iii) ***The Collegium Pontificum (College of Pontiffs)***: Was always the highest body and the one and only college with the Senate subordinate to the College. Under the reign of Augustus leaders, in most cases the Imperator was firstly Pontifex Maximus and therefore supreme administrative and spiritual leader of Rome.

1156. From 204 BCE to 69 CE, and the brief period the Ark of the Covenant was held at Rome, Sacred Roman Law (Rex Sacrorum) underwent a major transformation in the formation of the office of Pontifex Maximus or "Primary Prophet":- Pontifex Maximus and Sacred Law

(i) Contrary to deliberately false and absurd history, the function of Pontifex Maximus was "custom created title" as a high honour to the Great Prophet of the Yahudi, also known as the Great Prophets of Yeb (Elephantine Island). The first Pontifex Maximus was therefore Elkaniah (206–158 BCE); and

(ii) The Collegium Pontificum (College of Pontiffs) was created no earlier than 114 BCE, as a means of keeping greater control and peace among the Roman Patrician families by Lucius Cornelius Sulla, who held the title until it returned to the Great prophets of the Yahudi by 80 BCE and Barachiah (80–59 BCE).

1157. While the official state religion of Rome was Mithraism since the 5th Century BCE, the primary god worshipped by the Patricians privately was Satan (Saturn), in honour of the Yahudi ancient connection to the Celtic God Satandi followed by the god of good fortune and luck they named Lucifer (lucifear) after 69 CE. Mithraism and Saturn

Article 338 – Lex (Social Law)

1158. ***Lex (Social Law)*** also known as "Legis" was a form of law developed over centuries exclusively for the benefit and protection of the highest classes of citizens in Roman society known as "civilis" incorporating Patricians and Plebians. Lex (Social Law)

1159. Lex was defined largely by several bodies of law expressed as "rights" or *ius* in Latin being:- Structures of Lex

(i) ***Ius Civile***, also known as "citizen law" was the body of rights of citizens (civilis) within Roman society; and

(ii) ***Ius Gentium***, also known as "law of peoples" was the body of rights of citizens versus foreigners; and

(iii) ***Ius Forum***, also known as common or public spaces law included a wide variety of laws and customs such as the Twelve (12) Tablets within the forum of obligations and expectations of Roman citizens, administrative functions and duties; and

(iv) ***Ius Domus***, also known as law of the home was essentially the law of the household; and

(v) ***Ius Commune***, rights of common property, equality and use (of the lowest class); and

(vi) ***Ius Municeps***, also known as the law of non Roman citizens and slaves.

1160. The most notable features of Lex compared to other systems of ancient law and subsequent law are: Inequality, Complexity, Corruption, and Injustice:- Inherit Injustice of True Roman Law

(i) Inequality is the first feature of Lex in that the Roman System did not allow claims from those of lower class to prevail against a higher class, even if the claim was justified; and

(ii) Complexity is the second feature of Lex in that the Roman System of law permitted the writing of customized laws and rulings in favour of one person against another, creating an ever growing complex system of statutes; and

(iii) Corruption is the third feature of Lex whereby money, greed and avarice were all able to be accommodated under Roman Law against legitimate concerns, for the benefit of an elite few; and

(iv) Injustice is the fourth feature whereby Roman Law was never intended to be just and equal, but a tool to exploit power and advantage.

Article 339 – Occupatio

1161. ***Occupatio*** is the act and process of registering possession and/ or claim by which legal and lawful possession is then established. Occupatio

1162. Occupatio does not, nor has it ever challenged the sacred principle of possession. Instead, occupation only applies to conquered land and states that a citizen of Rome may make a claim of "ownership" on a first claim, best claim basis reflected in a register. Thus occupation is the record or title of the register, not physical possession. Occupatio and Possessio

1163. A principle of occupation from the earliest times is that it is forbidden for a claim of ownership to be valid on conquered land if the land itself is deemed sacred. So seriously did the Romans take this rule that any breach was considered the very gravest of transgressions against the empire. Occupatio and Sacred Land

Article 340 – Usus (Use)

1164. ***Usus (Use)*** refers to one of only two rights to property under the Roman Empire. The other being Dominium, being absolute ownership of the land to the republic (or empire). The highest right any individual could have in property under Roman Law was through *Usus* (Use). Usus (Use)

1165. In reference to the ancient Roman Property Law system of *Usus* (Use):- General Concepts of Usus (Use)

(i) ***Usucapio and Usufructus***: There were only two types of *Usus* being *Usucapio* and *Usufructus*. *Usucapio* is the Roman term defining and referred to ownership; and *Usufructus*, is when one person enjoys certain rights in property owned by another; and

(ii) **Public and Non-Transferability**: In many cases, *Usus* could not be freely transferred or sold to another person. It was often tied to the specific individual or purpose for which it was granted; and

(iii) **Use and Enjoyment**: The holder of *Usus* had the right to use and enjoy the property for personal or specific purposes. This might include using a piece of land for agriculture, living in a house, or using tools or equipment for a particular trade; and

(iv) **Maintenance and Care**: The person holding *Usus* typically had a responsibility to maintain and care for the property during the period of *Usus*. This included ensuring that the property did not fall into disrepair; and

(v) **Limited Duration**: *Usus* was typically a temporary or limited right to use property. It was not an absolute or perpetual ownership right. The duration of *Usus* could be specified in a legal agreement or could be based on customary practices.

1166. Usucapio (Ownership of Use) had its own specific conditions that needed to be met:- Additional Conditions of Usucapio

(i) To maintain the argument of lawfulness, the Romans invented even further legal fictions concerning Usucapio whereby certain land could be claimed as "ownerless" and therefore could be "lawfully occupied" (occupation) as private ownership – excluding temples – by the first person to take possession; and

(ii) Thus, these extraordinary claims opened up a ready made motive for legions and their leaders to conquer their enemies as the only permitted private land was conquered land.

1167. Usufructus (Fruits of Use) had its own specific conditions that needed to be met:- Additional Conditions of Usufructus

(i) Contrary to the mythical history created that Roman law honoured justice and fairness, the ordinary leaseholder had no protection beyond a contractual right against a landlord and could not assign tenancy; and

(ii) Fields and arable land were called fundus by the Romans, (from which the word and meaning of "fund" is directly derived). Thus even if a Roman citizen, if one did not possess sufficient "fundus" (funds), then one could be forced into servitude to another, even conscripted into the army.

1168. In contradiction to most historical claims, this Roman legal invention of usufruct was not some enlightened legal concept, but a means of making the arbitrary and unilateral seizure of any and all possessions, land, tenements of a population at any time completely lawful, while at the same time enabling the poorest to manage the Cruelty of usufruct land and make a living while denying them lawful land rights and ownership of the land.

1169. The Roman concept of usufruct was reintroduced in the 16th Century, whereby all conquered land by the "Crown" is considered in allodium (absolute ownership), with all tenancy in usufruct. Reintroduction of usufruct

Article 341 – Custos (Slavery)

1170. ***Custos*** is the correct and original legal term for Slavery under Roman Law. Slavery was so fundamental to Roman Law that it had its own set of laws of property separate to Dominium and Usus. Custos (Slavery)

1171. Claims that the word *Servus* was the proper name for Slavery is an absurd and deliberate falsity. Servus not used to describe Slaves

1172. The word *Custos* for slavery originates from the Latin root *cuso* meaning "to mark or to impress as property or money". It relates to the ancient principle of "impressing" an image to create coins as well as to brand or mark slaves. Origin of Word Custos

1173. Under the Imperial Roman Empire there were four essential types of legal slavery, each with its own unique property rights, conditions and laws:- Custos and Types of Slavery

(i) ***Classicus***: This was the term given to military slaves, such as galley slaves and those attached to legions; and

(ii) ***Spartacus***: This was the term given to slaves attached to various entertainment groups that provided the gruesome entertainment to the public through arena such as the Colosseum; and

(iii) ***Articus***: This was the term given to business and industry slaves, bound to a business such as bread making, or tannery, or pottery etc.; and

(iv) ***Rusticus***: This was the term given to estate slaves, such as those indentured to powerful villa within Roman and major urban centres, as well as those connected to larger rural estates.

1174. Unlike other forms of "chattel" such as horses, cows and livestock, the hot iron branding of slaves was forbidden, in preference to permanent ink tattoo:- Marking of Custos (Slaves)

(i) ***Classicus Ink Tattoos***: As a slave attached to the Military remained public property of the Empire forever, a simple and generic tattoo was usually applied such as SPQR. Unlike other categories of slavery, a Classicus through bravery and battle could be promoted in rank and even earn certain privileges. However, a Classicus was always bound to the military for life; and

(ii) ***Spartacus Ink Tattoos***: Similar to Military Slaves, those bound to entertainment groups for public entertainment were usually generically and simply branded, given the short life expectancy; and

(iii) ***Articus Ink Tattoos***: Business and Industry Slaves were considered valuable property on account of their skills and ability to make money for the owner. Similar to Estate (Rusticus) Slaves, Business (Articus) Slaves were usually uniquely marked with a number rather than a business or industry, to maintain market value for the trade of such slaves and enable any new purchaser to uniquely identify the individual slave as property. A good example of a similar type of slave serial system is the American serial number system created and maintained by one of the first and most famous American computing companies for the Nazis and the concentration camps in World War II. It is well established on the historic public record that most of the industry and advanced technology companies supporting the Nazis from 1933 to the very end of 1945 were American owned subsidiaries; and

(iv) ***Rusticus Slave Tattoos***: Often were a simplified version of the gens insignia of the famous or powerful family, but could also be uniquely identified by a serial number tattoo.

1175. All Custos (Slaves) were required to be registered as property on the *Custos Rotalorum* meaning "Slave Rolls":- Custos Rotalorum

(i) Both Military and Entertainment Slaves tended to be listed in batches, rather than individual slaves given the high turnover rate and that such slaves were never "re-sold"; and

(ii) Business Slaves, particularly as property of skilled businesses were often individually listed; and

(iii) Slavery and Slave Rolls were prohibited under the Holly Imperial Christian Empire and again under the Holly Western Christian Empire by the 8th Century. However, the Anglo-Dutch banking families succeeded in having *Custos Rotalorum* returned by the 17th Century and such slave rolls have remained in place ever since under different names and functions such as "Electoral Rolls" and "Birth and Death Rolls".

Article 342 – Mancipatio (Transfer of Ownership)

1176. ***Mancipatio*** is system and ritual of lawful conveyance of property under Roman law. Mancipatio (Transfer of Ownership)

1177. *Mancipatio* is a classic example of how the Romans considered ritual and procedure greater than oath and consent without duress:- Ritual of Mancipatio

(i) The ceremony of mancipatio was typically conducted in the presence of the transferor, transferee, five (5) male Roman citizens as witnesses, an usher holding a pair of scales representing fair law and an ingot of copper or bronze (later gold) or some consideration for the transferee; and

(ii) If the land owner did not speak Latin – which most did not, then a "person" would be put in their place; and

(iii) The transferee then grasped the object being transferred and is alleged to have said in Latin, "I assert that this thing is mine by Quiritarian (Roman) law; and let it have been bought by me with this piece of copper and these copper scales."; and

(iv) He then struck the scales with the ingot, which he handed to the transferor "by way of price".

Article 343 – Province

1178. ***Province*** comes from the Latin word *provincia* originally meaning "sphere of military action" of the Roman legions in their conquest and subjugation of other Italian civilisations. Province

1179. In relation to the origin and concept of Province:- General Origin of concept of Province

(i) Prior to the capture of Sicily in 241 BCE, each province was managed by a magistrate, elected from the elite of Rome; and

(ii) Upon the capture of Sicily in 241 BCE, the first permanent province separate to Italy was secured and a new position called Rector Provinciae or "Rector of the Province" as governor of the province – rector meaning "teacher, ruler, director and master". The head of a Roman Province was always called Rector even though the individual would already hold some other esteemed rank such as consul, praetor or tribune; and

(iii) In 241 BCE, a second in command was also created for the Rector called the Curator (from Latin cura meaning care) meaning "manager, keeper, overseer and custodian". The Curator held an essential responsibility within the command

and control structure of Roman Fascism as the "Keeper of the (Slave) Rolls" called Custos Rotulorum compiled through a forced "census" being a survey of the conquered people where a handful of the former nobles of the conquered culture were made Roman Citizens and excluded from the rolls and the rest of the population were entered onto the rolls or tabluae as property or "res" also known as "re"; and

(iv) By 29 BCE, Rome had succeeded in subjugating and creating no less than seventeen (17) Provinces. By this time, a new honorary position was created greater than the Rector – called the Censor. The Censor being an emissary appointed directly by the Emperor or Senate was tasked with visiting each province and "surveying" the property registered on the rolls through a "census" meaning literally a survey of the wealth and property of Rome. The role of the Censor was immense and they were terribly feared, even by Rectors as the Censor carried the Imperium of both the Emperor and Senate with their powers to judge and to strip any powers, rights or lands that were not in order; and

(v) By 117 CE, the pagan Roman Empire held no less than forty six (46) Provinces, including: Achaea • Aegyptus • Africa • Alpes Cottiae • Alpes Maritimae • Alpes Poeninae • Arabia Petraea • Armenia • Asia • Assyria • Bithynia et Pontus • Britannia • Cappadocia • Cilicia • Corsica et Sardinia • Creta et Cyrenaica • Cyprus • Dacia • Dalmatia • Epirus • Galatia • Gallia Aquitania • Gallia Belgica • Gallia Lugdunensis • Gallia Narbonensis • Germania Inferior • Germania Superior • Hispania Baetica • Hispania Tarraconensis • Italia • Iudaea • Lusitania • Lycia et Pamphylia • Macedonia • Mauretania Caesariensis • Mauretania Tingitana • Mesopotamia • Moesia Inferior • Moesia Superior • Noricum • Pannonia Inferior • Pannonia Superior • Raetia • Sicilia • Syria • Thracia; and

(vi) The whole system collapsed in the West by the 5th Century, yet continued in the East until the end of the 6th Century when the Byzantine Empire introduced the concept of the Exarchates and Themes; and

(vii) However, in 1540 CE the Roman Provincial System was resurrected as the model of command and control of the Jesuits, including the role of Rector, Curator also called the "Superior" and Censor also called the "Visitor" (from Latin visito meaning literally 'to go with strength, authority, power and force').

Article 344 – Civitas (city)

1180. ***Civitas*** is the name given under Roman Law to a city or city - state recognized as possessing a civil agreement (concilium) and a social body of administration (cives) and free from tribute to Rome. Civitas (city)

1181. Within a Civitas (city), there were usually one or more neighbourhoods known as vicus (or vici plural). The city of Rome possessed no fewer than two hundred and sixty five (265) Vici aggregated into fourteen (14) regions (regiones) by the 1st Century BCE. Civitas Neighbourhood

1182. The primary Civitas under Roman Law was Rome itself. The other Civitas, also known as "civitates foederatae" were limited and included but not limited to Neapolis (Naples), Messina and Reggio (Sicily), Persepolis and Babylon (Persia), Tarsus in Turkey and Jerusalem in Palestine. Rome as Civitas

Article 345 – Municipium (Municipality)

1183. ***Municipium*** is a city or town of a Roman province that was obligated to pay tribute to Rome and did not possess the same self - determination as a Civitas. Municipium (Municipality)

1184. A citizen of a recognized *Municipium* was called a *municeps* being the lowest form of Roman citizen and as such as obligated to perform their duties called munera. Municep

1185. An important distinction with *Municipium* was the fact that municeps (lowest citizens) were considered citizens of the city/town they were born, regardless of their location since birth. Therefore, whenever a census was called for the purpose of collecting taxes (tribute), municeps were required to return to their birth town. Citizen of Town of Birth

11.3 – Imperial Holly Christian Empire

Article 346 – Imperial Holly Christian Empire

1186. ***Christian Law Form***, also known as "Christian Law", also known as "Divine Christian Law" and simply "Divine Law", is the Form of sovereign territorial law, sovereign law, noble law, land law, property law and society law first formed by British borne Holly descended Constantine (Custennyn/ Custennin) in 314 CE onwards upon the creation of a new religion and model of civilised society called Christianity and Empire known as "Theke". Christian Law Form

1187. The word "byzantine" is a 16th Century invention by Venetian funded German historical fraud known as Hieronymus Wolf who was tasked Byzantine with creating a counterfeit history of the Christian Empire called Corpus Historiae Byzantinae published in 1557 CE. The claim that the word was the original name of the city that became the capital of Βασιλείαπόλις (Basileiapólis) is completely absurd and false.

1188. In reference to the Imperial Holly Christian Empire, there exist some significant inventions and elements that still impact Sovereign Law today, including (but not limited to):- Significant Elements of Imperial Holly Christian Empire and Sovereign Law

(i) Ancient Greek (Language); and

(ii) Antioch (Constantinople); and

(iii) Kuklos (Wheel); and

(iv) Sunedrion (Council); and

(v) Kuria (Curia); and

(vi) Politia; and

(vii) Diokesia (Diocese); and

(viii) Paroikia (Parochial/Parish); and

(ix) Epistole (Epistle); and

(x) Edict of Rome (313 CE); and

(xi) Epistole of Nicomedia (325 CE); and

(xii) Bibliographe (Original Bible); and

(xiii) Pandektes (Pandect).

1189. In 313 CE, Constantine introduced a new series of law that represented a watershed in the restoration of equity and justice being the existence of one law for all, abolition of slavery, abolition of human sacrifice and Mithraism, prohibition of compound interest called Ανατοκοισμός (anatokoismos) meaning literally "the state of high or excessive interest throughout the year" and the abolition of special privileges of clergy:- New Laws of Constantine

(i) The new official motto (INRI) of the Empire signalled the end to the three (3) level pagan Roman system of one law for the rich and their loyal servants and one law for everyone else as slaves; and

(ii) The abolition of slavery meant the freedom of tens of millions of people and the end to deliberate systems of perpetual slavery through economic control; and

(iii) The abolition of compound interest anatokoismos and excessive simple interest (simus) being unreasonable interest and setting interest fixed at three (3) percent, heralded the end to hyperinflation and deliberate manipulation of the economy by bankers and merchants; and

(iv) The abolition of human sacrifice and Mithraism heralded a brief end to state sponsored terrorism; and

(v) The abolition of special privileges of clergy ended the claims of immunity of pagan clergy for being held to account for unspeakable crimes, abuse and corruption.

1190. In 325 CE, the new official laws and scriptures of the Christian Empire were distributed across the Empire through a sacred historic text called βιβλιογράφη (Bibiliographe) meaning "library; store of knowledge; official records (of law)", derived from the Ancient Greek words βίβλος (biblos) meaning "official book or text" and γράφω (graphe) originally meaning “sacred scripture, symbols of great meaning/importance, written law, indictment or command”. This is the first official and true name of the Christian Bible.

Bibiliographe (first Christian Bible)

1191. Contrary to the revisionist claims that the concept of “Christians” existed since the time of Nero (1st Century), there is no credible independent evidence of the word “Christian” being used prior to the Epistole of Antioch in 314 CE by Constantine.

Origin of word Christian

1192. As Imperial Christian Law was introduced in part to destroy the legacy of Rome and end the age of Mithraism, from 326 CE onwards, all previous Constitutiones Imperium (pronouncements by pagan Roman Emperors) were rendered null and void and the official archives ordered to be destroyed. Therefore, all claimed Constitutiones Imperium included in the false documents by the Roman Cult from the 12th Century onwards are false.

False Latin Judicial Texts

Imperial Christian Law from 326 CE not only ordered all previous edits of Roman Emperors to be destroyed, but all previous works by Latin Jurists banned and to be replaced by the works of Gnostic Jurists aligned to the ancient teachings of the Holly and Celts. Therefore, even if the alleged Jurists of Uplianus and Paulus did actually exist in the 3rd Century CE, all such works were forbidden to be used. Therefore, any claim that Roman Jurist works were incorporated into the founding fabric of the Holly Roman Empire is a clumsy and untenable falsity.

1193. In accord with these Maxims and the most sacred Covenant *Pactum De Singularis Caelum*, the Society of One Heaven and all valid associated entities are the one, true and only legitimate successors to the Holly Christian Empire and no other.

Successor to Holly Christian Empire

All authority, tradition, power and custom of the Holly Christian Empire is solely and completely vested to the Society of One Heaven and Ucadia through the most sacred Covenant *Pactum De Singularis Caelum* as the one and only true apostolic successor of Christ, Christianity, the Apostles and Prophets and no other.

Article 347 – Ancient Greek Language

1194. ***Ancient Greek Language*** is the historical predecessor of the modern Greek language and is one of the most significant and influential languages in the history of Western civilisation. Ancient Greek Language

1195. As Ancient Greek became the official language of the Christian Empire following the banning of Latin as an official administrative language from 325 CE, any text claiming to be officially issued by the Christian Empire written in Latin between 326 CE and 700 CE are absurd and pathetic frauds. False Latin Texts

Article 348 – Antioch (Constantinople)

1196. ***Antioch*** (Constantinople), from the Ancient Greek "αντεοχος" is a title first commissioned and used by Constantine to describe the new capital of the Holly Christian Empire also known as Βασιλείαπόλις (Basileiapólis) from 325 CE. The city was never called "Constantinople" until the 7th Century. Antioch (Constantinople)

1197. The word Antioch from the Ancient Greek "αντεοχος" comes from two (2) words Αντε (ante-) meaning "first, before, beginning" and οχος (okhos) meaning "hub of wheel, axle, carriage or foundation". Hence, the literal meaning of Antioch as the name of the new capital of the Christian Empire from 325 CE was "the first hub of the wheels (Kuklos); the first foundation". Origin of word Antioch

1198. The claim that Heliopolis on the Orentes River in Syria or that Baalbek in Lebanon as Heliopolis was called Antioch is one of the greatest frauds and deliberate sacrileges in history:- False history of Antioch

(i) Heliopolis was the ancient headquarters of the eastern Roman provinces and was considered one of the four (4) most sacred cities, with the city dedicated to the Phyrgian goddess as depicted by Lucian in the text *De Dea Syria*. In 115 CE, the city was totally destroyed to its foundations, killing more than two hundred thousand (200,000) people and nearly killed Trajan and his administration. The ruins were largely abandoned on account of superstition and all across the empire, it was said that the land was "cursed" by the gods; and

(ii) Until the 15th Century, no other location than the former capital of the Christian Empire was known as Antioch.

1199. In accordance with the most sacred Covenant *Pactum De Singularis Caelum*, all power and authority of Antioch and the Patriarch of Antioch is hereby vested within the Societies of Ucadia and its authorized officials. Antioch and Ucadia

Article 349 – Kuklos (Wheel)

1200. ***Kuklos***, from the Ancent Greek "κύκλος" was the term introduced by Constantine in 313 CE to the new regional administrative structures replacing "districts" and "prefectures" of the former pagan Roman Empire. Kuklos (Wheel)

1201. The term Kuklos (κύκλος) in Ancient Greek meant "wheel, rotation; self contained process or cycle". Origin of Kuklos

Article 350 – Sunedrion (Council)

1202. ***Sunedrion*** (Council), also known as συνέδριον in Ancient Greek, was a term used to describe the highest appellate judicial body and the highest legislative body of the Holly Christian Empire first formed in 313 CE. Sunedrion (Council)

1203. The term *Sunedrion*, also known as συνέδριον in Ancient Greek meant "council" and was constructed from two (2) Ancient Greek terms σύν meaning "with" and εδρα meaning "seat". Hence, the original and literal meaning of Sunedrion was "sitting together as equals". Origin of word Sunedrion

1204. The Sunedrion Oikoumenikos (Ecumenical), also known as συνέδριον οἰκουμενικός in Ancient Greek, was the official title first granted to the legislative body that replaced the dissolution of the Roman Senate:- Christian Ecumenical Councils (Sunedrion)

(i) The Sunedrion Oikoumenikos constituted representatives (Patriarchos and Momnarchos) from all the Politea and Dioceses of the Holly Christian Empire who then met every ten years to debate and discuss matters of law for the Empire; and

(ii) The first session of the Sunedrion Oikoumenikos was the Sunedrion Oikoumenikos in 314 CE, followed by the Sunedrion Oikoumenikos in 325 CE that approved the new laws of the Empire embedded within the most sacred text and original Bible known as the Bibiliographe, or βιβλιογράφη; and

(iii) The Sunedrion Oikoumenikos (Ecumenical Councils) ceased being every ten years by the end of the 4th Century CE and then ceased entirely with the split between Western Christian nations and the East on the regime of Sabbatius (Justinian) from 518 CE.

1205. The false claims of a supreme Jewish clerical council called the "Sanhedrin" is a deliberate and clumsy 17th Century corruption of the true history of the Sunedrion:- False claims of Sanhedrin

(i) There was no such thing as a "Sanhedrin" back at the time of Holly Prince Esus in Jerusalem in the 1st Century CE, as there was no such thing then as a "Jewish People" or a "Jewish Religion"; and

(ii) All claims of a continuity of "Sanhedrin" to the present day is false and revisionist history, with no credible historic provenance; and

(iii) In the 19th Century, Napoleon I permitted the formation of the "Grand Sanhedrin" in 1806 CE. However, all claims of earlier history are false.

Article 351 – Kuria (Curia)

1206. ***Kuria*** (Curia) was the largest ecclesiastical and administrative division of an official Christian body since the first formation of Christianity in 314 CE by Constantine. A Curia is comprised of several subdivisions called Politia (Politea):- Kuria (Curia)

(i) The Supreme See or Sacred See or "sacropolis sedos" in Ancient Greek was the nominated capital city of a Kuria (Curia) and the home of the leading spiritual, legal and administrative head known as an Exharchos (ἔξαρχος) or "Exarch"; and

(ii) The primary building symbolizing the seat of power or "sacropolis sedos" was known as a Kathedra (καθέδρα) or "Cathedral" as the seat of "supreme authority"; and

(iii) The first Kuria (Curia) in history (from 314 CE) were Borealia (North See), Australia (South See), Europalia (West See) and Orientalia (East Sea) corresponding to the four cardinal directions emanating from Antioch (Constantinople); and

(iv) The first Exharchos or Exarchs in history (from 314 CE) were Mattatheos (Perinthos) Exarchos of Borealia (North), Markos Achilles (Marcus Aurelius Cornelius Achilleus) Exarchos of Australia (South), Lukhas Eusebius (Lucius Aurelius Cornelius Adeptius) Exarchos of Europealia (West) and Iohannes (Constantinos) Exarchos of Orientalia (East). Until the 16th Century and introduction of false, deceptive and misleading curses or "god spells" by the Roman Cult, the original four Exarchs were simply known as Matthew, Mark, Luke and John; and

(v) The Supreme See or Sacred See or "sacropolis sedos" as the capitals of the Kuria (Curia) in history (from 314 CE) were the Supreme See of Borealia (North See) named Galatia on the north bank of the Danube River Delta and Black Sea, the Supreme See of Australia (South See) named Alexandria on the Nile River Delta and the Mediterranean Sea, the Supreme See of Europalia (West See) named Philippi (Thessalonika) on the Axios River Delta and the Mediterranean Sea and the Supreme See of Orientalia (East Sea) named Samson (Samsun) at the deltas of the Mert and Halys rivers and the Black Sea in northern Anatolia.

1207. The word Curia or Kuria (κυρία) originates from Ancient Greek and means literally "supreme authority". Hence a Kurios (κυριος) means literally "highest lord; or greatest master". All claims and assertions that the term originates from Latin and was used in ancient Roman affairs are absurd, blatantly false, deceptive and misleading as the fundamental units of tribe for Rome were gens/gentes and the business, assembly and affairs of Rome were conducted in the forum and via the Senate.

Origin of the word Curia (Kuria)

Article 352 – Politia (Politea)

1208. ***Politia*** (Politic, or Body Politic), is the second largest ecclesiastical and administrative division of an official Christian body since the first formation of Christianity in 314 CE by Constantine. A Politia is comprised of several subdivisions known as Diokesia (Diocese):-

Politia (Politea)

(i) The Metropolitan See or "metropolis sedos" in Ancient Greek was the nominated capital city of a particular political city-state or "Politia" and the home of the spiritual, legal and administrative head known as a Patriarchos (πατριάρχος) or "Patriarch". The term Patriarchos meaning literally "the ruler, leader and father of the Christian tribe or people"; and

(ii) The primary building symbolizing the seat of power or "metropolis sedos" was known as a Basilikos (βασιλικος) or "Basilica" as the seat of "regional authority"; and

(iii) The first Politia (Body Politic) in history (from 314 CE) were nine (9) Politia of Borealia (North See), nine (9) Politia of Australia (South See), nine (9) Politia of Europalia (West See) and nine (9) Politia of Orientalia (East See) corresponding to the four cardinal directions emanating from Antioch (Constantinople); and

(iv) The first Politia (Body Politic) of Borealia (North See) were Bulgaria, Hungaria, Alania, Vandalia, Sarmatia, Lithuania, Latvia, Estonia and Rusia; and

(v) The first Politia (Body Politic) of Australia (South See) were Barbaria (Morocco), Algeria, Gaetulia, Garamantia, Libia, Egyptia, Ethiopia, Sinopia and Somalia; and

(vi) The first Politia (Body Politic) of Europalia (West See) were Alba, Irenia (Ireland), Spania, Francia, Italia, Saxonia, Slavia, Macedonia and Hellas; and

(vii) The first Politia (Body Politic) of Orientalia (East Sea) were Anatolia, Armenia, Syria, Palestinia, Mesopotamia, Abbysinia (Yemen), Assyria, Saracenia (Arabia) and Persia; and

(viii) The first Metropolitan Sees of Borealia (North See) were Odessos (Varna) at the Panisos [Kamchiya] Delta on the Black Sea as the Metropolis of Bulgaria, Tergesti (Trieste) at the Isonzo Delta on the Adriatic Sea as the Metropolis of Hungaria, Kherson at the Dnieper Delta on the Black Sea as the Metropolis of Alania, Tanais (Rostov-na-Donu) at the Don Delta on the Black Sea as the Metropolis of Vandalia, Aticca (Atyrau) at the Ural Delta on the Caspian Sea as the Metropolis of Sarmatia, Nema at the Nemos (Nemunas) River Delta on the Baltic Sea as the Metropolis of Lithuania, Riga at the Dyna (Daugava) River Delta on the Baltic Sea as the Metropolis of Latvia, Narva at the Narva River Delta on the Baltic Sea as the Metropolis of Estonia and Rusa (St Petersburg) at the Rusa River Delta on the Baltic Sea as the Metropolis of Rusia; and

(ix) The first Metropolitan Sees of Australia (South See) were Timogadi (Nador) at the Nadir River Delta on the Meditteranean Sea as the Metropolis of Barbaria, Saldae (Bejaia) at the Algolis (Soummam) River Delta on the Mediterranean Sea as the Metropolis of Algeria, Abes (Gabes) at the Triton River Delta on the Mediterranean Sea as the Metropolis of Gaetulia, Zanadu at the Zanadis River Delta on the Mediterranean Sea as the Metropolis of Garamantia, Berenice (Benghazi) at the Baris River Delta on the Mediterranean Sea as the Metropolis of Libia, Zion (Suez) at the Zion Delta on the Red Sea as the Metropolis of Egyptia, Saladin on Axumir at the Axumir (Mareb) River Delta on the Red Sea as the Metropolis of Ethiopia, Aela (Aqaba) at the

Jordan Delta on the Red Sea as the Metropolis of Sinopia, and Zeila (Djibouti) at the Adama (Awash) River Delta on the Red Sea as the Metropolis of Somalia; and

(x) The first Metropolitan Sees of Europalia (West See) were Hollyrood at the Firth of Forth on the North Sea as the Metropolis of Alba, Dublin at the Liffey Delta on the Irish Sea as the Metropolis of Irenia, Iberia (Amposta/Tortosa) at the Ebro Delta on the Mediterranean Sea as the Metropolis of Spania, Arles at the Rhone Delta on the Mediterranean Sea as the Metropolis of Francia, Philadelphia at the Po Delta on the Adriatic Sea as the Metropolis of Italia, Mantas (Hamburg) at the Elbe Delta on the North Sea as the Metropolis of Saxonia (Germany), Spoleto (Split) at the Cetina Delta on the Adriatic Sea as the Metropolis of Slavia, Ulkini (Ulcinj) at the Buna Delta on the Adriatic Sea as the Metropolis of Macedonia and Hella at the Evros Delta on the Aegean Sea as the Metropolis of Hellas; and

(xi) The first Metropolitan Sees of Orientalia (East See) were Nicomedia (Izmit) at the Sakarya Delta on the Black Sea as the Metropolis of Anatolia, Sarvan (Shirvan) at the Cyrus Delta on the Caspian Sea as the Metropolis of Armenia, Laodicia (Samandag) at the Orontes Delta on the Mediterranean Sea as the Metropolis of Syria, Gaza at the Gazah Delta on the Mediterranean Sea as the Metropolis of Palestinia, Chaldos (Kuwait City) at the Euphrates/Chaldon [Pishon] Delta on the Persian Gulf as the Metropolis of Mesopotamia, Adana (Aden) at the Abb (Ibb) River Delta on the Persian Gulf as the Metropolis of Abbysinia (Yemen), Basra at the Euphrates/Tigris Delta on the Gulf of Aden as the Metropolis of Assyria, Telma (Dilmun) at the Ashar (Aftan) River Delta on the Persian Gulf as the Metropolis of Saracenia and Commercion (Gameron) at the Shoor River on the Persian Gulf as the Metropolis of Persia.

1209. The word Politia (πολιτια) originates from Ancient Greek and means literally "constituted city; or constituted people; or the public". Hence Politics, from politikos (πολιτικος) means literally "constitutional affairs; or civic affairs; or public affairs (of law)". Origin of word Politia

1210. A valid Politia, or Body Politic is any such association or body or aggregate recognized as formed under the authority, rights and powers of the most sacred Covenant *Pactum De Singularis Caelum* and the present Maxims. Valid Politia

1211. Only a valid Ucadia University possesses, owns and occupies the Right of Politia

absolute true apostolic authority, rights and powers of a Politia (Body Politic) as first constituted in 314 CE upon the formation of true Christianity under Constantine. Therefore, when anyone speaks, or writes, or claims authority of a Politia (Body Politic), it shall mean one or all of the valid Ucadia bodies and no other.

Article 353 – Diokesia (Diocese)

1212. A ***Diokesia*** (Diocese) is the second smallest ecclesiastical and administrative division of an official Christian body since the first formation of Christianity in 314 CE by Constantine. A Diokesia (Diocese) is comprised of several subdivisions known as Paroikia (Parish or Parochial):- Diokesia (Diocese)

(i) The Episcopal See or "episcopolis sedos" in Ancient Greek was the nominated city of a particular region or state within the boundaries of a "Diakesia" and the home of the spiritual, legal and administrative head known as a Monarkhos (μόναρχος) or "Monarch". The term Monarkhos meaning literally "sole ruler"; and

(ii) The primary building symbolizing the seat of power or Episcopal See (episcopolis sedos) was known as a Sunagoga (συναγωγή) or "Synagogue" as the seat of "local state or city authority".

1213. The word Diocese comes from the Ancient Greek διοίκησις (dioikēsis) meaning "internal administration". The word does not originate from Ancient Latin. Origin of word Diokesia (Diocese)

The claim that Emperor Diocletian first introduced the term "diocese" is deliberately false and designed to diminish clarity as the administrative design and structure of the Holly Christian Empire.

1214. Only a valid Ucadia Province possesses, owns and occupies the absolute true apostolic authority, rights and powers of a Diokesia (Diocese) as first constituted in 314 CE upon the formation of true Christianity under Constantine. Therefore, when anyone speaks, or writes, or claims authority of a Diocese (Diokesia), it shall mean one or all of the valid Ucadia Provinces and Ecclesiastical Bodies and no other. Ucadia Provinces and Diokesia (Diocese)

Article 354 – Paroikia (Parochial/Parish)

1215. A ***Paroikia*** (Parish or Parochial) is the smallest ecclesiastical and administrative division of an official Christian body since the first formation of Christianity in 314 CE by Constantine. Paroikia (Parochial/ Parish)

1216. The word Paroikia (παροικία) originates from Ancient Greek and the first formation of Christianity in 314 CE under Constantine and literally means "constituted (Christian) communities/ neighbourhoods". The word comes from the combination of the Ancient Greek words para (παρὰ) meaning "beside; or equal" and oikos (οικος) meaning "house, or dwelling". Origin of word Paroika

1217. Only a valid Ucadia Campus possesses, owns and occupies the absolute true apostolic authority, rights and powers of a Paroikia (Parish or Parochial) as first constituted in 314 CE upon the formation of true Christianity under Constantine. Therefore, when anyone speaks, or writes, or claims authority of a Parish or Parochial (Paroikia), it shall mean one or all of the valid Ucadia Campuses or Ecclesiastical Parishes and none other. Ucadia and Paroika

Article 355 – Epistole (Epistle)

1218. ***Epistole***, also known as ***Epistle*** is a term first invented and used under Constantine in 313 CE onwards for all official edicts, decrees and messages issued by a supreme ruler or "Exarch" or the Tetrachy (four Exarchs) of the Christian Empire. Epistole (Epistle)

1219. From 313 CE onwards, the official term Epistole (Epistle) or επιστολή in Ancient Greek replaced the former pronouncements and legal powers of pagan Roman Emperors known as Constitutiones Imperium, Decretum and Rescriptum in Latin. Official Function of Epistole (Epistle)

1220. The term Epistole or επιστολή in Ancient Greek comes from two (2) words επί (epi) meaning "upon, on, over, above" and στέλλω (stellō) meaning "I prepare, send". Hence, the literal etymological meaning of Epistole (Epistle) "I send an official message from above". Origin of word Epistole (Epistle)

1221. The first *Epistole* (Epistle) in civilized history was the Epistole of Milan, the former Capital of the Western Roman Empire by Constantine in 313 CE which introduced Christianity for the first time as the official religion of the new Holly Christian Empire. First Epistle (Epistole)

1222. While the first Christian Bible in history known as Bibiliographe, or βιβλιογράφη was being assembled between 313 to 325 CE as well as the construction of the new capital at Antioch (Constantinople), Constantine issued several more Epistole (epistle) while travelling to each of the new capitals of the Empire twice before 325 CE. These Historic Epistle (Epistole)

Epistles were known by the name of the capital from which they were issued, being:-

(i) Two (2) Epistole (Epistles) known as the First and Second Epistole of Galatia (Arles); and

(ii) Two (2) Epistole (Epistles) known as the First and Second Epistole of Philadelphia (Ravenna); and

(iii) Two (2) Epistole (Epistles) known as the First and Second Epistole of Alexandria; and

(iv) Two (2) Epistole (Epistles) known as the First and Second Epistole of Philippi (Thessalonica); and

(v) Two (2) Epistole (Epistles) known as the First and Second Epistole of Ephesus; and

(vi) Two (2) Epistole (Epistles) known as the First and Second Epistole of Jerusalem.

1223. All claims of any Christian Epistole (Epistle) having been written prior to 313 CE is completely absurd, false and designed to curse and corrupt the true founders of Christianity including the Nazarene leader known as Esus Christos. False claims of Epistle (Epistole)

1224. The Edict of Rome on the 14th March, 313 CE, also known as the Edictum Perpetuum, is the most famous, important and significant Edict in the history of the Roman Empire as the Edict issued by Constantine as the last valid Emperor of Rome to dissolve the Roman Empire and ultimately destroy the city of Rome itself. The claim of the existence of an Edict known as the Edict of Milan is a clumsy and absurd 16th Century Fraud. Edict of Rome

1225. On the 14th March (Martis) in 313 CE, Constantine did pronounce the Edict of Rome, also known as the *Edictum Perpetuum* at the main Forum before departing the city:- Effect of Edict of Rome

(i) The Edict made clear the undisputed and absolute authority possessed by Constantine as Imperator Caesar Augustus ("Commander in Chief") Iohannus Conablus Constaninius; and Vaticanus Divinitus ("Divinely inspired Prophet"); and Pontifex Maximus ("Supreme Pontiff"); and Dominus ("Head of State"); and Pater Patriae Fiscus ("Father of the Public Funds"); and Imperium Proconsulare Maius ("Highest Elected Official"); and Princeps Senatus ("Leader of the Senate"); and Potestas Tribunicia ("Chief Judge and Magistrate"); and Great Victor over the Goti, Aryans and Suebi; and

(ii) The Edict did then systematically dissolve each and every official position, body and authority of Rome from the bottom up, before condemning Rome to be evacuated and then destroyed.

Article 356 – Edict of Rome (313)

1226. The Edict of Rome or Edictum Perpetuum of 313 CE is the only legitimate surviving law of Rome. All other laws, letters, edicts, prescripts, orders, instruments and records were rendered absolutely revoked, dissolved, annulled and made void by the Edict of Rome itself:-

Edict of Rome (313 CE)

(i) The Domus Vaticanae, known (then) as the House of the Prophet and simply as the Vatican was condemned three times as a place barren of any spiritual power or connection to spirit or demon and closed and ordered to be destroyed to its foundations and never revived or rebuilt; and

(ii) The Office of Vaticanus Divinitus ("Divinely inspired Prophet") was abjured three times, abolished and Damnatia Memoriae (damned forever in memory), to be removed from all records and never be revived; and

(iii) The Office of Pontifex Maximus ("Supreme Pontiff") and the College Of Pontiffs and all colleges of celibate priests and nuns and virgins and attendants were abjured three times, abolished and Damnatia Memoriae (damned forever in memory), to be removed from all records and never be revived; and

(iv) The city of Rome was forbidden by the edict ever to be known as Christian, or to be visited by a Christian leader and was to be perpetually condemned and cursed as the AntiChrist as representing everything against Christianity; and

(v) The Senate was dissolved and Damnatia Memoriae (damned forever in memory), to be removed from all records and never be revived and all its previous records destroyed; and

(vi) Every Roman Court was shut and Damnatia Memoriae (damned forever in memory), including the office of Potestas Tribunicia (Chief Judge) and no forum associated with the AntiChrist or an agent of the AntiChrist ever permitted thereafter to claim itself a forum of law ; and

(vii) All Roman coins were to be surrendered or seized and destroyed as Rome was forbidden thereafter to have any power, or authority whatsoever to claim ownership, occupation, possession or use of any rights or property or wealth or assets. Furthermore, the office of Pater Patriae Fiscus and all Roman money and funds were Damnatio Memoriae (damned forever in memory); and

(viii) All Roman offices were dissolved and Damnatio Memoriae (damned forever in memory) with no one claiming authority from the AntiChrist or an agent of the AntiChrist capable or permitted or able to hold or form any office whatsoever.

1227. The *Edict of Rome* was finally, conclusively and completely dissolved through the authority of the most sacred Covenant *Pactum De Singularis Caelum* on March 14, 2009, on the strict and irrevocable condition that all legitimate, civilised and proper authority claimed and located in Rome or "New Rome" is solely derived through the most sacred Covenant and Ucadia and no other. Dissolution of Edict of Rome

Article 357 – Epistole of Nicomedia (325)

1228. The ***Epistole (Epistle) of Nicomedia*** now known as the Epistle of Jude followed by the last ten (10) Chapters of the Book of Revelation has been horrendously corrupted, with the false Mithraic and Satanic beliefs inserted into the text in direct contradiction to its original message. Epistole of Nicomedia (325 CE)

1229. Prior to the deliberate corruption and sacrilege of the first act of true international law by an ecumenical representative body, the Epistole (Epistle) of Nicomedia heralded the introduction of the 1st Bible in civilized history, also known as the Bibiliographe, or βιβλιογράφη. The Epistle also completed the Divinely inspired prophecy of Constantine as to the future of the world and a time of complete redemption. Epistole of Nicomedia and Bibliographe

Article 358 – Bibliographe (Original Bible)

1230. ***Bibiliographe***, or βιβλιογράφη is the name of the first official text of the Christian Church issued by Constantine in 326 CE throughout the Holly Christian Empire. The text was also known simply as "The Bible" or βίβλος (biblos) for short. Bibliographe (Original Bible)

1231. The official name "Bibiliographe" for the first Christian Bible is derived from two (2) Ancient Greek words βιβλίον (biblion) meaning "book") and γράφω (graphe) originally meaning "sacred scripture, symbols of great meaning/importance, written law, indictment or command". Origin of name Bibliographe

1232. The main features of the first, true and official Christian Bible "Bibiliographe" are:- Features of Bibliographe

(i) The Book opened with the Epistole of Milan; and

(ii) The Book was then divided into two (2) main sections defining two (2) covenants with the Divine called "themes" (θέμα) which is the Ancient Greek word for a sacred oath or pledge before the word itself was deliberately corrupted; and

(iii) The first "theme" was the old covenant re-establishing the sacred scriptures of the Tará (Torá(h)) of Jeremiah and foundation law of the Holly Celt Empire. The first theme then included the writings of the Great prophets of Yeb (Elephantine Island) including but not limited to Ezekiel, Isaiah, Enoch and Jeremiah himself; and

(iv) The second "theme" was the new covenant of Gnostic and Nazarene teaching of the Holly Irish Prince known as "esus" who establish Nazarene teachings in Palestine to end Mithraism such as the Wisdom of Iesus (Proverbs), the Song of Iesus and the Gospel of Truth and the Origin of the World; and

(v) In the first "theme", there was no reference or inclusion of Persian and Mithraic scripture in the form of Judges, Kings or Chronicles. Nor was the writings of the founding priests of Mithraism included such as Ezra or Nehemiah; and

(vi) In the second "theme", there was no Gospel of Luke, nor reference to any writings of Menesheh High Priest Saul (Paul), or Acts of the Apostles, nor reference to "Virgin Birth" and other Mithraic symbology; and

(vii) The book ended with the collection of Epistole of Constantine and the Epistole of Nicomedia at the end.

1233. The official books of the old "theme" of the first and true official Christian Bible were:- Old Theme

(i) Genesis (γένεσις) meaning "origin, source, beginning, nativity"; and

(ii) Deuteros (δεύτερος) meaning "second, second coming"; and

(iii) Exodos (εξοδος) meaning "expedition, ritual, procession, departure"; and

(iv) Anakineos (ανάκινές) meaning "summons, call, (pray), invoke the divine, from above"; and

(v) Nemos (νέμος) meaning "distribute fairly, dispense the law, promised pasture".

1234. During the 8th Century, the βίβλος (biblos) was updated by the Carlonginians in the creation of the Catholic Church to be Biblos Sacrorum, or "Holly Bible", with inclusions of the Acts of the Apostles and other references to support the claim of the Christian Church originating in Rome. Holy Bible

1235. During the 17th Century, the βίβλος (biblos) was wholly corrupted through the publication of the Douis Rheims and King James Bible, later translated back into Latin as the Vulgate:- King James Bible

(i) The most sacred Nazarene texts written by Esus Christos such as the "Wisdom of Iesus" was corrupted into the proverbs, the "Song of Iesus" was corrupted to be something wholly different as Solomon's Song and the Psalms of Iesus became the Psalms of Saul in reference to both the mythical founder of the Menesheh High Priests of Tarsus and Paulus Piso the founder of Iudaism philosophy in Londonium in the 1st Century CE; and

(ii) The King James Bible and its revisions to include a wholly false history and massive fraud of scriptures and law that resulted in a text that bears little resemblance to the true and original Christian Bible.

Article 359 – Pandektes (Pandect)

1236. The ***Pandektes*** (πανδέκτης), also known as Pandect, is the unique and formal name of the first encyclopedia, the first concordance and dictionary of law in civilised history written in Ancient Greek in late 529 CE and promulgated by Sabbatius, also known as Justinian the Great. Pandektes (Pandect)

1237. The term Pandektēs (πανδέκτης) in Ancient Greek meant "all encompassing, encyclopedia" as a reflection of the text incorporating not only the original Christian Bible known as Bibiliographe, or βιβλιογράφη, but all the Epistole (Epistle) of rulers of the Holly Roman Empires since Constantine, arranged by both subject and the original text. Meaning of Pandektes

1238. In reference to the Pandektes:- Contents of Pandektes

(i) The Pandektēs (πανδέκτης) did not include the Constitutiones Imperium, Decretum or Rescriptum of any pagan Roman Emperor as all such documents and laws were rendered null and void by Constantine in 313CE and ordered to be destroyed. Therefore, any claim that the Pandektēs (Pandect) included pagan Mithraic law in direct contradiction to the intentions of Justinian and every Holly Roman Ruler for the past two hundred years is a clumsy and absurd fraud; and

(ii) The Pandektēs (πανδέκτης) did not include the works or references of any pagan Roman Jurist such as Uplianus and Paulus as the double standard laws of the previous pagan Roman Empire had been ordered to be destroyed two hundred (200) years prior; and

(iii) At the end of the 16th Century, Denis Godefroy, a star student from Latin Collège de Navarre in Paris published a completely fraudulent text called Corpus Iuris Civilis or C.I.C. claiming that it had been sourced from codes of law written by Justinian including the Pandektēs (Pandect). Despite the horrendous fraud, the Corpus Iuris Civilis was used to corrupt much of modern Western (Roman) Law including but not limited to Maritime Law, Admiralty Law, Civil Law and Administrative Law.

1239. In the historically clumsy and fraudulent text known as Corpus Iuris Civilis or C.I.C. formed by Denis Godefroy, a number of the core foundations of Christianity at the heart of the Pandektēs (πανδέκτης) of Sabbatius (Justinian) were deliberately reversed as the very worst heresies including but not limited to:-

Major false claims within Corpus Iuris Civilis

(i) Falsely claiming that the Holly Roman Empire not only permitted slavery, but refined the notion of slavery to perpetual slavery by virtue of birth, or "serfdom" a concept even the pagan Romans considered unlawful fifteen hundred (1500) years prior; and

(ii) Falsely claiming that not only did the Holly Roman Empire permit one set of laws for the rich and the poor in contradiction to the Holly Tetragrammaton, but expanded injustice by making all Christian clergy exempt and "above" the law; and

(iii) Falsely claiming that rather than the whole purpose of Christianity and the Holly Roman Empire was to end Mithraism and the rule of Rome, that Justinian actually pledged allegiance to a mythical "Christian" pope in Rome as had all previous "emperors" from the time of Constantine; and

(iv) Falsely claiming that far from the abolition of torture and human sacrifice, that Justinian and his predecessors mandated the penalty for heresy was to be burnt alive, a form of torture even the pagan Satanic worshipping Roman Emperors considered too barbaric.

11.4 – Western Holly Christian Empire

Article 360 – Western Holly Christian Empire

1240. The Western Holly Christian Empire is the Empire first formed by the Holly Franks, Saxons, Irish, Scottish and Welsh in the 8th Century in opposition to Eastern Christianity. So well designed were the components of this new civilisation, that many of its core infrastructure remains active to the present day. Western Holly Christian Empire

1241. Anglo-Saxon Form, also known as "Anglaise Law Form", "Catholic Law Form", also known as "Sacre Loi" (Sacred Law) and "Carolingian Law" is the Form of sovereign territorial law, sovereign law, noble law, land law, property law and society law first introduced by Charles Martel of the Franks in the 8th Century in the new language of "Anglaise". Anglo-Saxon Law Form

1242. In reference to the Western Holly Christian Empire, there exist some significant inventions and elements that still impact Sovereign Law today, including (but not limited to):- Significant Elements of Western Holly Christian Empire and Sovereign Law

(i) Anglaise; and

(ii) Paris; and

(iii) Holy Bible; and

(iv) Sacré Loi (Sacred Law); and

(v) Scriptura (Official Text); and

(vi) Instatuti (Institutions of Law); and

(vii) Capitulum (Statute of Law); and

(viii) Sacré Rit (Holy Writ); and

(ix) Convenia (Covenant); and

(x) Carta (Charter); and

(xi) Gilds (Guilds); and

(xii) Almanac (Dates & Times); and

(xiii) Parlomentum (Parliament); and

(xiv) Consistorium (Consistory); and

(xv) Coronatum (Coronation); and

(xvi) Rex Romanum (King of the Romans); and

(xvii) Concilium (Council); and

(xviii) Courts (Curia & Placitum); and

(xix) Nobilitum (Nobility); and

(xx) Orders & Fraternities.

Article 361 – Anglaise

1243. ***Anglaise***, also known as "Old French", is a language invented in the 8th Century as the official language of Western Civilisation and the Roman Catholic Church by Primáit (Primate) Béocáin of Prióireacht (Priory) Cuilinn Airdhe (Clonard) and the other *Twelve Irish Apostles* of the Great Tree of Life being Seannán of Canoin, Donnán (Dallán Forgaill) of Cuilde (Armagh), Gahl (Gall) of Cliathré (Central Dublin), Senán of Cairbre (Inishmurray), Áedan (Máedóc) of Cavan, Cillín (Killian) of Clones, Colúnbó (Columba) of Cill (Kells), Caillín of Cúill (Fenagh), Ailerán (Alcuin) of Cuilinn Airdhe (Clonard), Féilim of Creevelea, Ciarán of Cluain (Clonmacnoise) and Breandán of Carrick. Prior to the 8th Century, neither Anglaise nor any form of Old French existed.

Anglaise

1244. It is because the language of Anglaise was invented by Primáit (Primate) Béocáin (falsely listed in history as Venerable Bede) and the Twelve Apostles of Ireland, that virtually all key foundational concepts of Western Civilisation and the Roman Catholic Church owe their heritage to Ireland. It is also why the Venetian English Empire spent so many centuries and effort hiding this true etymology by creating entire libraries full of false histories, texts, languages and false trails so that as few as possible could trace back the true history of Civilised Law of the West and true faith of Roman Catholic Church:-

Irish as true etymology of key concepts of Western Civilisation Law

(i) Whilst fake histories and fake sacred scripture may be believed, the etymological nature of words has always presented a clear and present threat to those who corrupted and weaponised the law for their own ends; and

(ii) In deciphering the true origins and etymology of key concepts of Western Civilisation and the Roman Catholic Church from the 8th Century beyond twenty words to fifty words or even several hundred words of true Irish origin, it presents a stark binary choice that either the whole edifice of modern merchant slavery and perpetual warfare is either false or it is not.

Article 362 – Paris

1245. ***Paris*** is located on an ancient marsh flood plain intersected by the river Seine in northern France, approximately 100 miles (160 km) south east from the English Channel coastline. North-west from the city, the Seine meets the coast at La Havre about 233 miles (375 km) downstream. The first Celtic settlements of the Remi and Parisi tribes were founded on the two large natural river islands of Île Saint-Louis being 1,800 ft (550 metres) from west to east and 500 ft (150 metres) from north to south; and Île de la Cité being 3,400 ft (1,036 metres) from west to east and 800 ft (244 metres) from north to south. Paris

1246. In reference to the origins, history and natural history of Paris:- Brief Summary of Origins, History and Nature of Paris

(i) Built around 40 ft (12m) above sea level on a flat plain, the highest point in Paris is Montmartre at 130 m (427 ft). The city has a history of mild and pleasant climate of around 15 to 25 °C (59 to 77 °F) from May to September and cool to cold daily temperatures in the winter months of November to February of around 3 to 8 °C (37 to 46 °F); and

(ii) It was Julius Caesar who conquered the original Celtic settlements in the Paris region in 52 BCE, with his legions Legio X Equestris and Legio XII Victrix, Legio XIII Gemina and Legio XIV Gemina. Julius Caesar then built the first Roman fortress on the island of Île de la Cité, initially held as a garrison of Legio XIII Gemina; and then founded the Roman trading settlement of Lutetia on the left bank of the Seine. In a rare honour, the city was known as early as 49 BCE as *Lutetia Parisiorum* and the original home city of the *Legio III Gallica* with veterans from the Alpine Gaul legions of Julius Caesar and recruits from the local Remi and Parisi tribes themselves; and

(iii) By as early as 40 BCE, the Romans began using the natural springs located around *Lutetia Parisiorum* (Paris) for drinking, bathing and industry with the first sources via natural gravity sloping pipes being from the Belleville Springs, 2 miles (3.5km) north east of the island of Île de la Cité; and The Montmartre Springs 2.3 miles (3.7 km) north of the island of Île de la Cité. As the population of the city continued to grow, the Romans added the Belleville Springs 2.3 miles (3.7 km) north east of the island of Île de la Cité and Ourcq Springs 2.9 miles (4.6 km) north east of the island of Île de la Cité. Most of this infrastructure remained an integral system of Paris until the deliberate decline of city maintenance and competence from the 18th Century; and

(iv) By as early as 10 BCE, the city was already the largest in Gaul with a population over 15,000; and simply came to be known as "*Parisius*"; and the *Legio III Gallica* became legendary fighters and one of only a handful of Legions to serve with honour across the Empire and throughout the entire history of the Imperial Roman Empire; and

(v) Contrary to deliberately false, absurd and ignorant claims, it was the Romans who first solved the engineering problems of Paris concerning frequent flooding and handling of sewerage, by creating a network of vaulted catacombs under the present site of the Louvre. A network of drains would then funnel excess water into these caverns during flooding and then would be released gradually after the deluge had passed. This infrastructure was not dismantled intentionally until the 18th Century; and

(vi) Around 59 CE, the Roman Empire experienced multiple uprisings among the Celtic legions on the actions of Gaius Suetonius Paulus and Arrius Calpernius Piso in the murder of Holly leaders. Many of the Celtic tribes in Gaul (France) then united under Gaius Cornelius Tacticus (also known as Reichmor) of the famous Cornelius Gens (Family) and the son in law to Jesus (Yahusiah), as the first King of the Franks. Paris remained thereafter the spiritual home of the Holly Frank bloodlines until their final extinction in the 16th Century; and

(vii) By 742 CE and the time of Charles Martel (Aurelius Aptatus) as King of the Franks and founder of the Roman Catholic Church, Paris had grown to a population of over 250,000 making it the third largest city in the world behind Baghdad (950,000) and Constantinople (650,000). The foundation stone for Notre Dome (meaning "Our House of Worship") was set down on Holly Island (Ile de la Cite). It would take another 90 years for the first home of the Roman Catholic Church to be completed; and

(viii) In the 8th Century CE, the Carolingians commissioned a network of vaulted catacombs and sewerage system more than fifty times the size of the original infrastructure to be built 1.6 miles (2.5 km) south west of the island of Île de la Cité. Flood water and waste would then be pumped from the catacombs west and back into the river when the flood risk had subsided. Most of this infrastructure remained an integral system of

Paris until the deliberate decline of city maintenance and competence from the 18th Century by destroying pipes, blocking tunnels and repurposing the space as an underground cemetery; and

(ix) In the 8th Century CE, the Carolingians dramatically increased the natural water resources of Paris by building the famous Bièvre River Springs aqueduct and pipe network from the south of over 16.2 miles (26 km) and the Vaujours Springs natural gravity pipe network 11.8 miles (18.9 km) east of the island of Île de la Cité. Contrary to deliberately ignorant and false history, the water infrastructure and quality of Paris from the 9th Century to the 18th Century was arguably the best in the world until it was intentionally, secretly and systematically sabotaged and dismantled over 80 years, to create the miserable conditions for revolution; and

(x) By the 14th Century and the Black Death, the quality of Paris infrastructure greatly assisted in minimising the awful effects of the return of haemorrhagic fever; and assisted in the city quickly recovering to become for a time the largest city in Europe with a population of over 350,000; and

(xi) After a major victory against the Catholics on March 14, 1590, Henry of Navarre and a combined English and Huguenot force of over 25,000 lay siege to Paris by May of the same year - not to capture it, but to exact revenge and destroy the city and all its inhabitants. At the time, the highest noble leading the 30,000 to 50,000 defenders was the Duke of Nemours. There is strong evidence that following the defenders refusal to surrender (and almost certainly die) the Duke escaped, only to resurface in Lyon. During the siege, it was Irish and Holly crown prince Domhain na Searrach (1566-1603), also known as Blessed Dominic Cuileann (O'Collins), who led the defenders and saved Paris from complete annihilation. Dominic Cuileann (O'Collins) was ultimately betrayed by the Spanish on his return to Ireland and executed by the English in 1603; and

(xii) The horrendous and inhuman conditions of Paris in the prior decades of the French Revolution was intentionally and deliberately brought against the people of Paris in order to create the conditions for Revolution; and

(xiii) The revitalization of Paris after the French Revolution was primarily spearheaded by Georges-Eugene Haussmann in the mid-19th century during the reign of Napoleon III.

Haussmann's urban planning and renovation efforts transformed the city with wide boulevards, parks, and modern infrastructure, reshaping its landscape and character to the Paris that is known today.

Article 363 – Holy Bible

1247. ***Biblia Sacra***, also known as the "Holy Bible" is the first official Christian translation and edict promulgated in Latin from 738 CE of the Bibliographe or βιβλιογράφη first officially published by Constantine in 326 CE.

Biblia Sacra (Holy Bible)

1248. The name of the Divine Creator listed by the Carolingians in the Old Covenant and first *Biblia Sacra* (Holy Bible) in Latin in the 8th Century was Yehovah (Yahovah, or Jehovah) in honor of the Yahudi being the original and true name of those who followed the religion of Akhenaten (Moses). In the New Covenant, the name God was used.

Yehovah and God

1249. The main features of the first, true and official Catholic *Biblia Sacra* (Holy Bible) are:-

Main elements of original Holy Bible

(i) The name of the the two (2) main sections by which the Book was divided were re-named vetus testamentum (old covenant) and novum testamentum (new covenant); and

(ii) The Gospel of Peter was introduced to make him into the anointed leader. The old gospels were modified so Peter was made the leader not James, brother of Jesus; and

(iii) The Acts of the Apostles were introduced in order to describe the mission to Rome; and

(iv) There remained none of the Persian or mithraic symbolism corrupting the text, nor of the crucifixion or resurrection, nor description of "sin".

1250. In the 17th Century, the most sacred Nazarene texts written by Esus Christos such as the "Wisdom of Iesus" was corrupted into the proverbs, the "Song of Iesus" was corrupted to be something wholly different as Solomon's Song; and the Psalms of Iesus became the Psalms of Saul.

Corruption of Wisdom of Jesus

Article 364 – Scriptura (Official Text)

1251. ***Scriptura*** (Official Text) official style of writing, composition and structure of documents.

Scriptura (Official Text)

1252. ***Scriptura Manualis*** ("Scripture Manual"), also known simply as "Scriptura" and also as simply the "Manual" is the name of the first and most detailed set of document style standards ever published in history by which all official texts were to be composed including but not limited to: type of paper, color of ink, format, language, type style, topic, grammar, content, folding and binding. The first Scriptura was published in 738 CE under the reign of Charles Martel.

Scriptura Manualis ("Scripture Manual")

1253. The word *scriptura* comes from the Latin word *scriptio* and means "official style of writing, composition and structure of documents". The word *manualis* comes from Latin meaning "by one's own hand; by hand". The meaning of the word "scripture" as text exclusively of a sacred and ecclesiastical nature only appears by the 16th Century.

Origin of word Scripture

1254. Not only did the Carolingians under Charles Martel introduce a new uniform and secular language for their empire called Anglaise, in the 8th Century, but Charles Martel is also the first major leader in history to introduce a standard form of "lower case" writing both in Anglaise and Latin known as "miniscule". Thus by being the first to create an easy to read, standard of lower case letters and writing in Latin and Anglaise, Charles Martel may accurately be called the Father of modern bicameral (upper and lower case) written language scripts.

Majuscule and Miniscule

1255. The miniscule characters of European languages, including Latin are almost entirely based on the standards of character and grammar defined under the reign of Charles Martel in the 8th Century, including the lower case "s" and "f" being the same character.

Miniscule Characters

1256. Any claim that the miniscule of Latin is derived from half uncial, or that the original and first characters of miniscule are derived from a source other than the Carolingians in the 8th Century is a deliberate fraud and designed to belittle the historic competence and abilities of this European dynasty.

False claims of Miniscule

1257. The Sacré Loi (Sacred Law) of Scriptura is historic under the Carolingians of the 8th Century as the first leaders in history to forbid the use of writing material created from the skin or intestines of animals or human beings. Instead, the courts of Charles Martel created new standards for writing material in the form of high quality linen made from the hemp plant which they called velum, in honour of the Latin words original meaning of "sails, curtains and awnings"

Linen and Forbidden use of animal skins for writing

made of linen.

1258. The claim that *vellum*, comes from the word *velin* and represents authorized texts written on calf or sheep skin under the Carolingians is a terrible fraud and affront to the Sacré Loi (Sacred Law) of Scriptura of the Carolingians that forbid any writing on the skin of animals. False claims of Vellum

1259. To promote competence in the historic invention of grammar, in the 8th Century, the Carolingians introduced a completely new system and syllabus of education called *Trivium, Quadrivium* and *Universum*:- New Education System

(i) ***Trivium*** meaning in Latin "the three ways" was the "primary" and essential study required of all officials and nobles of the Carolingian Empire in Grammatica, Logica and Rhetorica; and

(ii) ***Quadrivium*** meaning in Latin "the four ways" was the "secondary" and essential study of all senior nobles, merchants and artists being Arithmetic, Geometry, Music and Astronomy; and

(iii) ***Universum*** meaning in Latin "universe (of knowledge) or philosophy" was the tertiary and final studies required of all senior clergy and members of the royal family.

1260. In terms of the medium for writing, the Scriptura of the 8th Century CE established clear rules for the forms of writing material, the creation of originals, copies and their safe keeping which have remained the foundation of Sacré Loi (Sacred Law):- Rules of Writing

(i) Completed original texts were to be written on one continuous scroll of the finest white linen called "velum" to then be stored at an official Cancellocum (Chancery Archive); and

(ii) Individual pages of reports were to be bound into folios, or liber (books); and

(iii) Copies of original texts would then be issued on either bound or separate sheets of linen or paper under official seal by the scribes of the scriptorium within the Cancellocum (Chancery Archive).

1261. The effect of the 8th Century Carolingian ban under Sacré Loi (Sacred Law) of Scriptura in the use of animal or human skin as a writing material, replaced by the finest manufactured linen ("velum") or paper was an explosion in the production of manuscripts on account of the abundance and cheapness of linen and paper as the new official writing medium of Europe. Effect of Linen

1262. In terms of grammar of writing, the Sacré Loi (Sacred Law) of Scriptura of the 8th Century Carolingian Empire established clear standards which remain the foundational rules of valid Grammar for all European Languages, namely:- Rules of Grammar

(i) All valid writing under Sacred Law and Scripture is from left to right and from the top of a page to its bottom; and

(ii) Letters are to be separated from one another, written in the same size to each other and generally in a straight line from left to right across the page; and

(iii) Excluding the first majuscule letter of a page, letters are to be functional to a word and phrase, not ornamental; and

(iv) Abbreviations are generally not permitted as each word must be properly expressed; and

(v) Words are generally to be separated from one another; and

(vi) Words are to contain the same letter characters as is considered its standard spelling; and

(vii) All texts or books must begin with its incipit (beginning phrase) in majuscule; and

(viii) Sentences begin with a majuscule and are separated by either an interpunctus (full stop) or punctus elevates (semi-colon).

1263. In terms of the publication of formal texts and instruments of authority, the Sacré Loi (Sacred Law) of Scriptura of the 8th Century Carolingian Empire established clear standards which remain the foundational rules of what constitutes a valid legal and lawful instrument today, namely:- Validation of Publications

(i) The *insignio* of the inventor or scriptor of the text meaning their distinguishing mark, seal, badge, decoration or name; and

(ii) The *obsignio* of the official authorizing the instrument being their sign, or official seal; and

(iii) The *testabus* of the obsignio meaning a sentence or phrase as a testification or attestation, usually at the bottom of a document that it has been duly authorized; and

(iv) The *imprimo* being the distinguishing mark, seal, decoration or watermark of the cancellocum (publishing location) from which the instrument was issued.

Article 365 – Instatuti (Institutions)

1264. The ***Instatuti***, also known as the Institutions, is the compendium of Sacré Loi (Sacred Law) promulgated to the first Parlomentum (Parliament) in 738 CE and the first text written in the new language of Anglaise. Thereafter, the word became synonymous with the master compendium of capitulum (ordinances) passed by parlomentum and the campus de marches until the collapse of the Carolingian Empire.

Instatuti (Institutions)

1265. The word *Instatuti* (institutions) comes from the Latin in+statutum meaning literally "the collection of statutes (laws)". Thus the promulgation of the Instatuti in 738 CE also represents the first official statutes issued under Catholic Law, Sacred Law and Western Law as it is known today.

Origin of word Instatuti

Article 366 – Capitulum (Statute of Law)

1266. **Capitulum**, or **capitula**, or **cap.** for short is a Latin term first used in law in the 8th Century by the Carolingians to describe Statutes that were debated and passed by a parliamentary body possessing ecclesiastical authority.

Capitulum

1267. The word *capitulum* and *capitula* in Latin means literally "article, important section or chapter"; and its use in reference to laws under the Carolingian Empire from the 8th Century was the practice of binding various capitulum to other ordinances as additional chapters to the body of law known as the *Instatutum* (Institutions) simply meaning "the statutes of law".

Origin of the word Capitulum

1268. The earliest rules concerning Capitulum as Statutes include:-

Earliest Laws of Statutes (Capitulum)

(i) A Capitulum is a valid law created by a Precept, or Rescript, or Order or Deed approved by a Legislative Act of a valid parliamentary body possessing ecclesiastical authority; and

(ii) A Capitulum is always constrained by the established ecclesiastical authority of the parliamentary body that issued it. A rule issued by a body with no authority has no effect morally or legally; and

(iii) A Capitulum is only valid if it is written clearly so all may comprehend. There is no such thing as a valid secret law or a law that is written that few may comprehend; and

(iv) A Capitulum only ever addresses one subject matter of law and thus only remedies and penalties in relation to that specific subject of law; and

(v) A Capitulum benefits all of a particular class and jurisdiction, or it benefits no one. No law is valid that is written for the benefit of one or a few; and

(vi) A Capitulum can only be enforced at some future date when enacted. No law is valid that seeks to alter what was permitted or not permitted in the past; and

(vii) A Capitulum can only ever be moral, virtuous and benevolent. There is no such thing as a valid immoral, wicked or repugnant law; and any such claim is a profound injury to the law itself.

1269. In terms of the earliest authentic Capitulum of Western Civilisation and first Parliaments, the following is an accurate assembly of known laws passed including (but not limited to):- List of earliest Capitulum of Western Civilisation

748 CE 1st Parlomentum at Paris

(i) *Lex Legum*: Legislative Law; and

(ii) *Lex Mensurarum*: Standards and Measure Law; and

(iii) *Lex Regia*: Sovereign Law; and

(iv) *Capitula Principis Capitulare*: The first Capitularies; and

(v) *Capitula Divinum Regum*: The Capitularies of the Divine Rights of Kings; and

(vi) *Capitula Regis Cartum*: The Capitularies of the Kings Charter; and

752 CE 2nd Parlomentum at Paris

(vii) *Lex Ecclesiastica*: Ecclesiastical Law; and

(viii) *Lex Militaris*: Military Law; and

(ix) *Lex Fidei*: Fiduciary (Noble) Law; and

(x) *Capitula Ecclesiastica*: The Capitularies of Ecclesiastical and Spiritual Authority; and

(xi) *Capitula Magisterium*: The Capitularies of Legal and Moral Authority; and

(xii) *Capitula Servus*: The Capitularies of Service and Noble Authority; and

756 CE 3rd Parlomentum at Paris

(xiii) *Lex Civis*: Civil Law; and

(xiv) *Lex Criminalis*: Criminal Law; and

(xv) *Lex Administratum*: Administrative Law; and

(xvi) *Capitula Aequalitum*: The Capitularies of Egalite (Equality); and

(xvii) *Capitula Libertum*: The Capitularies of Freedom; and

(xviii) *Capitula Fraternitum*: The Capitularies of Fraternity; and

760 CE 4th Parlomentum at Paris

(xix) *Lex Communis*: Property (Common) Law; and

(xx) *Lex Mercatorum*: Trade Law; and

(xxi) *Lex Collegiorum*: Guilds Law; and

(xxii) *Capitula Dominium Communium*: The Capitularies of Property Rights; and

(xxiii) *Capitula Praemium Honoris*: The Capitularies of Honouring Price; and

(xxiv) *Capitula Laborum*: The Capitularies of Work; and

764 CE 5th Parlomentum at Paris

(xxv) *Lex Successionis*: Succession Law; and

(xxvi) *Lex Missorum*: Diplomatic Law; and

(xxvii) *Lex Gentis*: International Law; and

(xxviii) *Capitula Successio Apostolica*: The Capitularies of Apostolic Succession; and

(xxix) *Capitula Missorum*: The Capitularies of the Envoys; and

(xxx) *Capitula Parens Patriae*: The Capitularies of the Parent of the Nations; and

768 CE 6th Parlomentum at Paris

(xxxi) *Lex Scholasticus*: Education Law; and

(xxxii) *Lex Litteraturae*: Literature and Language Law; and

(xxxiii) *Lex Scientiae*: Science Laws; and

(xxxiv) *Capitula Litteras Colendis*: The Capitularies of nurturing of learning.

1270. All claimed capitulum or capitula from the Carolingian era that are not in accord with these Maxims are hereby declared as deliberately fraudulent and designed to hide the origin of both Sacred Law and the original laws of the Roman Catholic Church as first created in the 8th Century CE. Fraudulent claims of Capitulum

1271. All claimed Capitulum or "Cap." allegedly issued prior to Henry VIII (1509-1547) are deliberate frauds designed to hide the fact that the Fraudulent claims of English

use of the system for identifying ordinances in line with the sacred law system of the Carolingians did not start until after 1536. Capitulum prior to 16th Century

1272. All claimed public ordinances debated and passed by a "parliament" of England, Great Britain or the United Kingdom since the 16th Century that contradicts the most ancient rules and principles of Capitulum and Statutes, must therefore be rendered null and void (from the beginning). Invalid and illegitimate Ordinances

Article 367 – Sacré Rit (Holy Writ)

1273. ***Sacré Rit*** or ***Holy Writ*** are two names for a type of peremptory precept adhering to "Scriptura" first invented in the 8th Century under the Carolingians, issued under authority of the Sovereign from a Cancellocum (Chancery Publishing Scriptorium) to an officer, agent or subject to perform or cease some act or attend some place and answer some claim or controversy. All writs are ultimately derived from the original form, purpose and structure of "Sacre rits". Sacré Rit (Holy Writ)

1274. The word *rit* comes from the Latin word *rite* meaning "proper formality, ritual, ceremony or manner". Therefore, the first and original meaning of Sacre rit, or "Holy Writ" is "a form of action consistent with proper formality, ritual, ceremony or the manner of the law". Origin of Rit

1275. As an ecclesiastical instrument always issued from the cancellocum, a writ by its very name and nature from its origin is an absolute and precise instrument that must conform to the strictest standards to be considered valid. Therefore, from its inception under the Carolingians in the 8th Century, a writ is only valid if it possesses the following attributes:- Ancient Rules of Writs

(i) An associated ***memorandum*** of petition or simply "memorandum" signed and witnessed by at least three other parties; and

(ii) The ***insignio*** of the inventor or ***scriptor*** issuing the writ meaning their distinguishing mark, seal, badge, decoration or name; and

(iii) The ***obsignio*** of the official authorizing the writ being their official seal; and

(iv) The ***testabus*** of the obsignio meaning a sentence or phrase as a testification or attestation, usually at the bottom of a document that it has been duly authorized; and

(v) The ***imprimo*** being the distinguishing mark, seal, decoration or watermark of the cancellocum (publishing location) from which the writ was issued.

Article 368 – Convenia (Covenant)

Convenia (Covenant)

1276. ***Convenia (Covenant)*** or ***Venia*** for short, is a formal instrument and style of agreement or "pact" first formed under the Carolingians from the 8th Century CE as the primary means by which all legal and lawful property transactions and conveyances were to be made.

Origin of word Convenia (Covenant)

1277. The word convenia (covenant) created by the Carolingians in the 8th Century CE is derived from the Latin *con* meaning "with" and *venia* meaning "favor, permission, kindness, grace, esteem or forgiveness".

Original intention of Convenia (Covenant)

1278. In accordance with the standards of Scriptura invented by the Carolingians in the 8th Century, the original version of the Convenia (Covenant) was to be given to the immediate cancellocum of the region or manor as the official archives with the parties then each receiving an authorized copy or "certificate" of the original. A Covenant not recorded in this manner, was not considered valid.

Rules of Convenia (Covenant)

1279. Since its invention in the 8th Century CE, all valid Convenia (Covenant or Venia) have been required to possess the nine (9) essential elements Incipio (Beginning), Oratio (Prayer), Exordio (Introduction), Condicio (Conditions), Decretio (Decree), Obsignio and Insignio, Testificatio (Attestation) and Acceptio (Acceptance):-

(i) ***Incipio (Beginning)*** at the very top of the instrument, usually in majuscule (capitals) being Omnibus Christi fidelibus ad quos presents littere peruenerint <> salutem sempiternam meaning "To all the faithful of Christ to whom these present letters shall come <> everlasting greeting; and

(ii) ***Oratio (Prayer)*** as the opening words before any actual gift, grant or permission being Graciam quam a deo gracis accepimus libenter fidelibus populis dispensare cupientes omnibus uere confessis contritis meaning "By the Grace of God, from whom all favors are gladly accepted by the faithful, desiring then to dispense (them) to (those/one) who confess true contrition"; and

(iii) ***Exordio (Introduction)*** being the introductory sentence or words indicating a summary of the grant or conveyance, or simply the word grant is made; and

(iv) ***Condicio (Conditions)*** being the listing of any conditions, obligations and terms of performance, by Roman numeral (if any) to the grant or conveyance outlined by the first three (3) elements; and

(v) ***Decretio (Decree)*** being the decree that the instrument had been handed (delivered) to become public notice also known as "patenting" being In cuius rei testimonium has litteras nostras fieri fecimus patentes meaning "In Witness whereof we have caused these our Letters to be made patents (public notice)"; and

(vi) ***Obsignio*** of the official authorizing the instrument being their sign, or official seal; and

(vii) ***Insignio*** of the inventor or scriptor, also known as the "signati recordis" being usually a wax seal of their distinguishing mark, seal, badge, decoration or name connected by red and/or gold cord to the linen; and

(viii) ***Testificatio (Attestation)*** being the testification of the maker that it is their wish reflected in the covenant being Teste me ipso apud <> then date in Latin meaning "Witness myself at the place <> date"; and

(ix) ***Acceptio (Endorsement)*** of the party receiving the gift, usually on the back of the instrument with the Latin word acciputur meaning "it is accepted" handwritten and then their insignio and any obsignio if they possess a seal or symbol. This is the source of the modern concept of endorsement.

1280. In accordance with the standards of Scriptura invented by the Carolingians in the 8th Century, if the fundamental form of a Convenia (Covenant) was defective, the instrument itself would be defective legally and lawfully. Defective Convenia (Covenant)

1281. In accordance with the standards of law defined by Instatutum (Institutions) by the Carolingians from the 8th Century, all forms of agreement such as Convenia (Covenant), Carta (Charter) or other Pacts were subject to fifteen (15) principles (maxims) of law:- Rules of enforcement of Convenia (Covenant)

(i) *In bona fide* meaning "(all agreements are made) in good faith"; and

(ii) *Forma legalis forma essentialis* meaning "Legal form is essential form"; and

(iii) *Dictum meum pactum* meaning "my spoken word [is] my covenant"; and

(iv) *Pacta sunt servanda* meaning meaning "agreements are to be kept"; and

(v) *Conventio non vincit legem* meaning "an agreement can not overcome the law"; and

(vi) *Nemo contra factum suum venire potest* meaning "no man may contradict his own agreement"; and

(vii) *Cujus est dare ejus est disponere* meaning "he who has a right to give, has the right to dispose of the gift"; and

(viii) *Locum pactum regit actum* meaning "The place of the agreement governs the act"; and

(ix) *Pactum nulla res est non valet* meaning "An agreement of a non-existent thing is not valid"; and

(x) *Nihil oritur in consensu sine conditiones* meaning "No action arises on an agreement without conditions"; and

(xi) *Mala grammatica non vitiat pactum* meaning "Bad grammar does not vitiate an agreement"; and

(xii) *Consensus facit pactum* meaning "Consent makes the agreement (valid)"; and

(xiii) *Nemo tenetur ad impossibile* meaning "No one is bound to an impossibility"; and

(xiv) *Nemo est, nisi sciat cum quod convenit* meaning "no one is present unless he knows with what he agrees"; and

(xv) *Nemo potest sibi devere* meaning "No one can owe to himself".

1282. From their inception in the 8th Century CE, Convenia (Covenant) and associated rules of form were almost wholly restricted to the noble classes. Agreements between a noble and their tenants in turn were managed through a detailed entry in the Maner Role as to the purpose of the record, any special terms of the lease and some kind of mark as agreement of the tenant. Restricted use of Convenia (Covenant)

1283. As the original of all valid Convenia (Covenant) were supposed to be stored safely at a cancellocum (archive), one who claimed possession (right of use) of land or property by convenia (covenant) was required to produce their copy of the convenia (covenant) in any legal dispute. Failure to produce a copy and the failure to find the original rendered such claim to the property null and void. Requirement to produce Convenia (Covenant)

Article 369 – Carta (Charter)

1284. A ***Carta*** (Charta or Charter) is a form of Convenia (Covenant or Venia) first issued as “sovereign grants” under the Carolingians from the 8th Century CE onwards that combines some form of map, survey or inventory of land or rights granted as part of the Convenia (Covenant). The word Carta (Charta) in Latin means “map or inventory (list)”. Carta (Charter)

Criteria of Carta (Charter)

1285. Since its invention in the 8th Century CE, all valid Carta (Charta or Charter) have been required to possess eight (8) essential elements Incipio (Beginning), Oratio (Prayer), Exordio (Introduction), Condicio (Conditions), Decretio (Decree), Obsignio, Insignio and Testificatio (Attestation):-

(i) ***Incipio (Beginning)*** at the very top of the instrument, usually in majuscule (capitals) being <> Dei Gratia Rex Romanorum meaning "<> by the Grace of God, King of the Romans"; and

(ii) ***Oratio (Prayer)*** as the opening words before any actual gift, grant or permission was usually customized and intertwined in the Exordio (Introduction)"; and

(iii) ***Exordio (Introduction)*** being the introductory sentence or words indicating a summary of the grant or conveyance, or simply a grant is made; and

(iv) ***Condicio (Conditions)*** being the listing of any conditions, by Roman numeral (if any) to the grant or conveyance outlined by the first three (3) elements; and

(v) ***Decretio (Decree)*** being the decree that the instrument had been handed (delivered) to become public notice also known as "patenting" being In cuius rei testimonium has litteras nostras fieri fecimus patentes meaning "In Witness of what we have caused these our Letters to be made Patent"; and

(vi) ***Obsignio*** of the Sovereign authorizing the instrument being their sign, or official seal; and

(vii) ***Insignio*** of the Sovereign, also known as the "signati recordis" being usually a wax seal of their distinguishing mark, seal, badge, decoration or name connected by red and/or gold cord to the linen; and

(viii) ***Testificatio (Attestation)*** being the testification of the maker that it is their wishes reflected in the covenant being Teste me ipso apud <> then date in Latin meaning "Witness myself at the place <> date".

1286. As a Carta (Charter) under Iuris Canonum (Canon Law) from the 8th Century CE represented the primary instrument of authority granting the right of rule to a particular family by the highest sovereign and the church, the Carta (Charter) has traditionally remained the cornerstone of law upon which the law of a particular realm is based, with subsequent laws or ordinances (capitulum or cap.) added to it.

1287. Similar to Convenia (Covenant), Carta (Charters) were supposed to be stored safely at a cancellocum (archive). Therefore (in theory) if the right of rule of one (1) family or leader was challenged, or the borders of their land were challenged then a copy of the original charter was required to be produced. Failure to produce a copy and the failure to find the original rendered such claim to the property null and void.

Charters and Chancery

1288. The most famous historic examples of Carta (Charter) were the Great Charters (Magna Carta) of the Holly Roman Emperors:-

Examples of Historic Carta (Charter)

(i) 744 CE ***Magna Carta*** (Great Charter) of ***Charles*** (Aurelius Angleramus also known as "Pepin The Short"); and

(ii) 768 CE ***Magna Carta*** (Great Charter) of ***Charles II*** (Aurelius Adventius also known as "Charlemagne"); and

(iii) 814 CE ***Magna Carta*** (Great Charter) of ***Charles III*** (Aurelius Adalbertus); and

(iv) 845 CE ***Magna Carta*** (Great Charter) of ***Charles IV*** (Aurelius Artaldus); and

(v) 857 CE ***Magna Carta*** (Great Charter) of ***Charles V*** (Aurelius Adeldus); and

(vi) 861 CE ***Magna Carta*** (Great Charter) of ***Charles VI*** (Aurelius Angelvin); and

(vii) 886 CE ***Magna Carta*** (Great Charter) of ***Charles VII*** (Aurelius Anscharus); and

(viii) 936 CE ***Magna Carta*** (Great Charter) of ***Otto*** (Hatto Hedwig); and

(ix) 973 CE ***Magna Carta*** (Great Charter) of ***Henry I*** (Hatto Heinrik); and

(x) 983 CE ***Magna Carta*** (Great Charter) of ***Henry II*** (Hatto Heinrik II); and

(xi) 1024 CE ***Magna Carta*** (Great Charter) of ***Henry III*** (Heinrik III); and

(xii) 1056 CE ***Magna Carta*** (Great Charter) of ***Henry IV*** (Heinrik IV); and

(xiii) 1106 CE ***Magna Carta*** (Great Charter) of ***Henry V*** (Heinrik V); and

(xiv) 1125 CE ***Magna Carta*** (Great Charter) of ***Henry VI*** (Heinrik VI); and

(xv) 1144 CE ***Magna Carta*** (Great Charter) of ***Bórá (Boru) I*** (Diarmaida (Dermod) Mór); and

(xvi) 1166 CE ***Bórá (Boru) II*** (Domnall Mór (mac Diarmaida)); and

(xvii) 1191 CE ***Bórá (Boru) III*** (Donal Mór na Corra); and

(xviii) 1215 CE ***Bórá (Boru) IV*** (Donnchadh Mór Cairbreach); and

(xix) 1240 CE ***Bórá (Boru) V*** (Domnall Mór Ruad); and

(xx) 1272 CE ***Bórá (Boru) VI*** (Domchadh Mór Ruadh).

1289. The claimed "Magna Carta" of 1215 of "King John of England" is an absurd fraud written no earlier than the 16th Century, in order to help cement the framework of a false mythology concerning the legal history of England:- False English Magna Carta

(i) Southern England, including London at the time of 1215 was still in control of the Dane Kings as Daneland. Prior to this date there had never been a country or state called "England". The first time the word "England" was used was in the 16th Century on the arrival of the exiled Venetian patricians; and

(ii) The claim that Plantagenet meant an English and Normandy House and not a title of the foreign Basque (Gascony) forces of the French Kingdom is a clumsy historic falsity that exposes the lie of the claimed figure of "John Lackland" as "King John"; and

(iii) The claimed rights within the Magna Carta are in fact both a watering down and corruption of pre-existing rights under the Holly Western Christian Civilisation, meaning the Magna Carta corrupts the historic rule of law, rather than supports it.

Article 370 – Gilde (Guilds)

1290. A ***Gilde (Guild)*** is a formal association of individuals sharing a common profession or trade. Gilds (Guilds)

1291. The word *Gilde* originates from the Irish word *Gildé* meaning "an authentic vocation; an intelligent (bright) and cheerful character". The Irish word itself is an abbreviation of two Irish root words *gil* originally meaning the seven qualities of "intellect (brightness), purity, gratitude, cheerfulness, diligence, esteem and care" and *dé* meaning "smoke, breath or spirit". The false and misleading claims that the etymology of the word Gilde means itself (gilde means gilde), or payment or feast are absurd. Origin of the word Gilde (Guild)

1292. The original structure of Gilds (Guilds) in history by the 8th Century under the Holly Western Christian Empire was divided into a logical structure of a "three tier" economy, mirroring the functioning of modern economies:-

Original Structure of Gilds (Guilds)

(i) Major Gilds (Guilds): These associations of trades represented the fundamental services of cities, town and villages and mirror the modern concept of the "retail and services sector"; and

(ii) Minor Gilds (Guilds): These associations of trades represented the heavier industries of the day and are equivalent to the modern economic concept of the "manufacturing sector"; and

(iii) Auxiliary Gilds (Guilds): These associations of trade represent the export and import of goods across the broader regions of the Holly Western Christian Empire and is equivalent to the modern concept of the "wholesale and commercial services sector" of economies.

1293. The following were the twelve *Major Gilds* (Guilds) as first formed by law in the 8th Century:-

Major Gilds (Guilds)

(i) Honourable Guild of Stonemasons; and

(ii) Honourable Guild of Shoemakers; and

(iii) Honourable Guild of Metalsmiths; and

(iv) Honourable Guild of Potters; and

(v) Honourable Guild of Candlemakers; and

(vi) Honourable Guild of Bakers; and

(vii) Honourable Guild of Butchers; and

(viii) Honourable Guild of Fishmongers; and

(ix) Honourable Guild of Greengrocers; and

(x) Honourable Guild of Tavernkeepers; and

(xi) Honourable Guild of Cheesemongers; and

(xii) Honourable Guild of Apothecaries.

1294. The following were the twelve *Minor Gilds* (Guilds) as first formed by law in the 8th Century:-

Minor Gilds (Guilds)

(i) Honourable Guild of Carpenters and Woodcarvers; and

(ii) Honourable Guild of Brewers and Winemakers; and

(iii) Honourable Guild of Weavers and Spinners; and

(iv) Honourable Guild of Ropemakers and Cordwainers; and

(v) Honourable Guild of Curriers and Tanners; and

(vi) Honourable Guild of Furriers and Skinners; and

(vii) Honourable Guild of Millers and Distillers; and

(viii) Honourable Guild of Glassblowers and Glaziers; and

(ix) Honourable Guild of Brickmakers and Tilers; and

(x) Honourable Guild of Coopers and Hoopers; and

(xi) Honourable Guild of Cartwrights and Wheelwrights; and

(xii) Honourable Guild of Locksmiths and Toolmakers.

1295. The following were the twelve *Auxiliary Gilds* (Guilds) as first formed by law in the 8th Century:- Auxiliary Gilds (Guilds)

(i) Honourable Guild of Grain Merchants; and

(ii) Honourable Guild of Timber Merchants; and

(iii) Honourable Guild of Stone Merchants; and

(iv) Honourable Guild of Wool and Cloth Merchants; and

(v) Honourable Guild of Dye and Pigment Merchants; and

(vi) Honourable Guild of Spice Merchants; and

(vii) Honourable Guild of Salt Merchants; and

(viii) Honourable Guild of Sugar Merchants; and

(ix) Honourable Guild of Jewel and Ivory Merchants; and

(x) Honourable Guild of Gold and Silver Merchants; and

(xi) Honourable Guild of Foreign Cloth and Silk Merchants; and

(xii) Honourable Guild of Mercers and Traders.

1296. The Italian trading states such as Venice, Florence and Genoa did not invent the notion of Gilds (Guilds). However, by the 13th and 14th Century they deliberately corrupted the economic model of guilds by inverting all authority to merchants and not those that make goods or possess skilled trades:- Corruption of Gilds (Guilds) under Italian States

(i) It was the Pisans who first introduced gunpowder to Europe and immediately began exploiting the notion of merchant-piracy, also known as "gunboat diplomacy" as later used by the British Empire and American Empire through its corporations. This lessened the need for certain trades of raw materials and manufacturing, as such resources were illegally, unlawfully and immorally seized through merchant-piracy; and

(ii) It was the Italian city states in the 13th and 14th Centuries that conceived of the notion of both controlling the rules of trade as well as the flow of money and goods via guilds as their "unique market position" to the rest of the world. Thus for the first time in human history, law and information was both weaponised and commercialised through the creation of the Arte de Guidici e Notai known as the Guild of Judges and Notaries; and the Arte del Cambio known as the Guild of the Money Changers; and the Arte de Libre known as the Guild of Book Publishers; and

(iii) Under the Italian city states of Venice and Genoa, it was the Cloth and Silk merchants that were initially the most senior and powerful. However, by the start of the 16th Century, it was the Guild of Book Publishers that were the wealthiest and most powerful guild in Venice; and

(iv) This "inverted model" of merchant piracy has remained in place within Western Civilisation ever since the 16th Century to the present day.

Corruption of Gilds (Guilds) under City of London

1297. Under the City of London, the notion of Guilds were corrupted further by the 17th Century to not only merchants being the most powerful, but in falsely and wickedly claiming occult and ecclesiastical rights to inflict damage, torture and oppression against all others in the course of day to day trade:-

(i) The bizarre and highly occult word "Livery" was introduced to describe the guilds of the City of London, the word itself being an adjective of Liver, with the organ historically believed to be the seat of the soul, life and intelligence. Thus in corrupted Greek Mythology, Prometheus was punished by Zeus because he stole fire to give back to mankind. He was chained to a rock in the Caucasus Mountains, and every day an eagle came and ate part of his liver. In the Prometheus myth, the liver was chosen as the focus of torture because the ancient Greeks regarded the liver as the seat of life, soul, and intelligence; and

(ii) The City of London guilds are also called "worshipful companies", clearly denoting ecclesiastical authority, contrary to the true origins of civilised law, Christian law and Western Civilisation law; and

(iii) Under the terribly twisted and corrupted model of merchant piracy of the City of London, it is the Mercers and Traders that are the most powerful guild.

Article 371 – Almanac

1298. ***Almanac*** is a yearly publication containing a wide range of information, such as calendars, weather forecasts, astronomical data, historical events, and practical advice. It serves as a reference guide for various topics, helping people plan their activities and stay informed about significant events and trends for the upcoming year

Almanac

1299. The word *Almanac* originates from the ancient Irish word *Almainis* originally meaning "charts of birth of the seasons (climate); charts for prognostication of the weather". The word Almainis itself from two Irish root words *al* meaning "birth, brood" and *mainis* originally meaning "climate, weather". Almainis (Almanacs) in ancient Irish history date back more than 3,500 years and were considered priceless to the famous ancient Irish navigators. Contrary to deliberately false etymology, the Arabic word Al-munak (الْمُنَاخ) originates from the Irish word Almainis.

Origin of word Almanac

1300. The key concepts of the original Almanac include (but are not limited to):-

Key Concepts of the Original Almanac

(i) Anne (year); and

(ii) Anniversus (leap year); and

(iii) Iubhaile (Jubilee of 100 years); and

(iv) Teirme (month); and

(v) Dei (day); and

(vi) Maindei (week of seven days).

1301. In reference to a year or Anno/Anne within the original Almanac:-

Almanac of Year

(i) An Anne (Year) contains three hundred and sixty five (365) Dei (Days); and

(ii) An Anniversus (Leap Year) contains three hundred and sixty six 366 Dei (Days); and

(iii) An Iubhaile (Jubilee) is an Anniversus (Leap Year) every one hundred years that may be 365 or 366 Dei (Days); and

(iv) Every year that is exactly divisible by four is an Anniversus (Leap Year), except for years that are exactly divisible by 100, but these centurial years are leap years if they are exactly divisible by 400.

1302. The Holly Irish Scholars introduced the word ***Teirme (Term)*** to replace the Eastern Christian definition of thirteen Aemetos (months) and the ancient Roman definition of twelve Mensis (months). Under

Term (Month)

the new Roman Catholic Church and Western Civilisation, a *Year (Anne)* is divided into twelve Terms (Months), with Odd numbered Terms (Months) having thirty one (31) days and Even numbered Terms (Months) having thirty (30) days, except the last Term having thirty-one (31) days in a *Leap Year*. The proper names of the Terms (Months) are:-

(i) ***Unus*** (first Term equivalent to Venetian month of January); and

(ii) ***Dous*** (second Term equivalent to Venetian month of February); and

(iii) ***Trinitus*** (third Term equivalent to Venetian month of March); and

(iv) ***Martius*** (forth Term equivalent to Venetian month of April); and

(v) ***Quintus*** (fifth Term equivalent to Venetian month of May); and

(vi) ***Sextus*** (sixth Term equivalent to Venetian month of June); and

(vii) ***Septimus*** (seventh Term equivalent to Venetian month of July); and

(viii) ***Octobus*** (eighth Term equivalent to Venetian month of August); and

(ix) ***Novembus*** (ninth Term equivalent to Venetian month of September); and

(x) ***Decembus*** (tenth Term equivalent to Venetian month of October); and

(xi) ***Hilarius*** (eleventh Term equivalent to Venetian month of November); and

(xii) ***Michaelmus*** (twelfth Term equivalent to Venetian month of December).

1303. The Maindei (week of seven days) of the original Western Christian Civilisation and Roman Catholic Church are:-

Maindei (week of seven days)

(i) ***Humilus Dei (Monday)*** – Day of Humility; and

(ii) ***Tempus Dei (Tuesday)*** – Day of Self Control and Moderation; and

(iii) ***Caritus Dei (Wednesday)*** – Day of Respect and Regard (for others); and

(iv) ***Fortus Dei (Thursday)*** – Day of Courage and Strength; and

(v) ***Fidus Dei (Friday)*** - Day of Faith, Trust and Loyalty; and

(vi) ***Servus Dei (Saturday)*** – Day of Service; and

(vii) ***Dominus Dei (Sunday)*** – Day of Rest in the Lord.

1304. In order to corrupt Christianity and weaken the bonds between heaven and earth, the Roman Catholic Church in the late 16th Century deliberately introduced heretical pagan month names. Contrary to false claims, this collection of anti-Christian names had never been used prior to the 16th Century to describe the months by any empire, including Rome:-

16th Century Pagan Month Names applied to Christian Time System

(i) ***January***: Means the month of the god ***Janus***, a 15th Century CE invented god falsely claimed back to ancient Rome; and that symbolises duality, duplicity, hypocrisy, perfidy, mendacity and obscurity; and

(ii) ***February***: Means the month of rituals dedicated to the goddess (she-wolf) ***Lupa***, the creator of Rome and a manifestation of Juno. The word *februum* in Latin means "belonging to a burnt offering; a purification" and a Roman wolf festival called *Lupercalia*; and

(iii) ***March***: Means the month of the god ***Mars***, the Roman god of War, equivalent to the Greek god Ares; and

(iv) ***April***: Means the month of the Greek goddess ***Aphros***, also known as Aphrodite, the goddess of lust, desire, beauty, pleasure, passion, procreation and underage virgins; and

(v) ***May***: Means the month of the Greek goddess ***Maia Hecate*** or the "pregnant goddess of dark magic, witchcraft and the moon"; and the mother of Hermes; and

(vi) ***June***: Means the month of the goddess ***Juno*** as Roman Queen of Heaven; and

(vii) ***July***: Means the month of the god ***Julius Caesar*** as "Mithra returned", who committed suicide in an elaborate ritual involving multiple leaders of Rome on 14 Mars (14th March) on Dies Sanguinis (Day of Blood) the most sacred feast day to Mithra; and

(viii) ***August***: Means the month of the god ***Augustus*** being Gaius Octavius Augustus (27 BCE – 14 CE) and the first Emperor of Rome; and

(ix) ***September***: Means the month of the god ***Lucifer*** in the enslavement of the members of the Body of Christ into an enclosure as if cattle, with the Latin words *saeptum* meaning enclosure or fold for cattle or pond for fish; and *membrum* meaning "member of state, member of body of Christ"; and

(x) ***October***: Means the first month of the god ***Hermes Logios***, as Roman god of merchants, orators, travellers and thieves. In 16th Century Kabbalist thinking, the number *eight* (octo in Latin) represents transcendence and spiritual transformation, while the abbreviation *ber* or *berus* means "truth, real and actual reality" as allegory to the mysteries of Hermeneutics; and

(xi) ***November***: Means the second month of the god ***Hermes Psychopompos***. In 16th Century Kabbalist thinking, the number nine (novem in Latin) represents the foundation of the soul, the real of the subconscious and the bridge between the spiritual and material worlds; and

(xii) ***December***: Means the third month of the god ***Hermes Aretos***. In 16th Century Kabbalist thinking, the number ten (*decem* in Latin) represents a state of completion, divine perfection, and the manifestation of spiritual principles in the material world.

1305. In order to corrupt Christianity and weaken the bonds between heaven and earth, the Roman Catholic Church in the late 16th Century deliberately introduced heretical pagan day names. Contrary to false claims, this collection of anti-Christian names had never been used prior to the 16th Century to describe the months by any empire, including Rome:-

16th Century Pagan Day Names applied to Christian Time System

(i) ***Monday***: Means the day of ***Mona (Morrigon)*** the pagan goddess of mystery, occlusion, fate, conflict, doom and death; and

(ii) ***Tuesday***: Means the day of ***Tur (Tyr),*** as the pagan god of battle and sacrifice; and

(iii) ***Wednesday***: Means the day of ***Weden (Odin)***, as the pagan god of death, hanging, warfare, sorcery, spells, occult knowledge and victory of enemies; and

(iv) ***Thursday***: Means the day of ***Thur (Thor)***, as the pagan god of strength, power, lightning and thunder and storms; and

(v) ***Friday***: Means the day of the goddess ***Fria,*** as the pagan goddess of prophecy, clairvoyance and motherhood; and

(vi) ***Saturday***: Means the day of ***Saturn (Satan)***, as the pagan god of time, wealth, abundance, prosperity and periodic renewal; and

(vii) ***Sunday***: Means the day of the pagan god of ***Syn (Sin)***, as the pagan god of depravity, iniquity, blasphemy, betrayal and deception.

1306. The day, time and names of the week were all deliberately corrupted for Western Christian Civilisation and the Roman Catholic Church under Pope Gregory XIII (1572-1585) through the papal bull *Inter gravissimas (1582)*:- Corrupted Gregorian Calendar

(i) The persistent claims that Pope Gregory introduced a new calendar and time system to "improve accuracy" is patently false, absurd and deliberately misleading. The original Almanac of Western Christian Civilisation and the Roman Catholic Church has always been more accurate than the Gregorian Calendar; and

(ii) The original calendar and time system of Western Christian Civilisation and the Roman Catholic Church from the 8th Century to the 16th Century was wholly Christian and respectful. Yet the Church under Pope Gregory in 1582 replaced a Christian Calendar with a wholly demonic, sacrilegious and pagan system honouring the opposite of Christ and deliberately weakening Christianity.

Article 372 – Parlomentum (Parliament)

1307. ***Parlomentum*** from which the word "Parliament" originates, is an official term first created under Charles Martel (737-741 CE) in March 738 CE to uniquely describe a mandated assembly of all nobles and clergy summonsed each year from across the Western Christian Empire to hear, discuss, debate and approve matters of legal importance. Parlomentum (Parliament)

1308. The word *Parlomentum* is derived from the Latin words *parla* meaning "equal speech" and *mentum* "by like agreement, character, chin". Hence the original literal meaning of "parliament" is a "meeting of equal speech and character by like agreement". Origin of the word Parlomentum

1309. A "parliament" by definition and the original legal and ecclesiastical meaning of the term, is a legislature whose power and function are in accordance with Sacré Loi (Sacred Law) as first instituted by the Franks from the 8th Century. A body that is not in accord with the precepts of Sacré Loi (Sacred Law) cannot therefore be properly called a "parliament" but some lesser body. Nature of a Parlomentum

Article 373 – Consistorium (Consistory)

1310. ***Consistorium***, also known as "Consistory", is a term first used by the Carolingians in the 8th Century to describe the official legislative ecclesiastical body responsible for debating and approving the rules and standards or "canons" of the newly created Catholicus Ecclesia (Catholic Church). Consistorium (Consistory)

1311. The term Consistorium comes from the earlier Latin word consist meaning "to standard form, to solidify, to take up position or duty". Meaning of Consistorium

1312. The first Consistorium was held in late 742 CE in Paris at which a number of the first rules and regulations of the newly formed Catholicus Ecclesia (Catholic Church) called *Iuris Canonum*, or "Canon Laws" were approved, including (but not limited to):- First Consitorium

(i) The new rule that a "thing not named in Latin, has no ecclesiastical authority" under Sacré Loi (Sacred Law) was approved; and

(ii) The doctrine of the Latin Rite and supremacy of the Catholicus Ecclesia (Catholic Church) as the one (1), true and only universal apostolic church above all other Christian faiths was approved; and

(iii) The positions of Primates equivalent to Lords of the Church, Bishops equivalent to Barons of the Church and Priests equivalent to Aldermen of the Church were approved; and

(iv) The doctrine of the Church as supreme tenants and stewards of the land and secular leaders (Lords, Barons and Aldermen) as their "vassals" was approved; and

(v) The Primates for the Metropolitans of Britannia, Scotia, Aquitania, Austrasia, Frisia, Burgundia and Alamannia were elected; and

(vi) The candidate Carloman, son of Charles Martel was unanimously elected Vicarius Christi Zacharias and Primate of Regnum Italiae.

Article 374 – Coronatum (Coronation)

1313. ***Coronatum***, also known as "Coronation", being the formal investiture of a sovereign through a series of formal rituals including the placement of a crown upon their head, was first invented and introduced as a key Sacrament of Sacré Loi (Sacred Law) by the Carolingians in the 8th Century CE. Coronatum (Coronation)

1314. The word *Coronatum* is Latin for "placement (on the head) of a crown or garland; encirclement (circumscription) as a ritual of sanctification". Origin of word Coronatum (Coronation)

1315. The significant differences with the Carolingian ceremony of Coronation to any previous formal ritual or ceremony of investiture of a ruler or leader are:- Requirements of Coronatum (Coronation)

(i) The candidate must first be declared of suitable character and exemplification of the true sacraments of the Catholic Church as "notorious" candidates were automatically ineligible; and

(ii) The candidate must secondly have been elected either by unanimous acclamation or ballot from "elector" nobles; and

(iii) The candidate must thirdly profess a sacred oath before the electors, the church and members of the public, to serve as a true Christian sovereign; and

(iv) A legitimate bishop holding apostolic authority then anoints the candidate as having the authority of heaven as well as earth, followed by a call for any contrary view; and

(v) The candidate was then crowned as sovereign.

Article 375 – Rex Romanum (King of the Romans)

1316. ***Rex Romanum***, also known as King of the Romans, is the sovereign title first created by Charles Martel in the 8th Century CE as the "supreme Christian Sovereign" and to support a series of false claims that the Carolingian Empire was a direct continuation of the "first and true" founders of Christianity through Jesus Christ in Rome and not Antioch (Constantinople) under Constantine. Rex Romanum (King of the Romans)

1317. Unlike hereditary monarchies, the Carolingians determined a "true sovereign" must first be elected by unanimous acclamation or ballot by authorized electors and then accept such high office under sacred oath memorialized by a written and sealed covenant in order to be legitimate in accordance with Sacre Loi (Sacred Law). Therefore, succession to the position of Romanorum Rex ("King of the Romans") from its inception was by election. Election of Rex Romanum (King of the Romans)

1318. In accordance with Sacre Loi (Sacred Law), only persons of title and property were permitted to be known as "electors" for the purpose of an election. The first electors were called "Elector Palatine" meaning the Electors of Palatine Hill (Rome), being the former location for the palace of the pagan Roman Emperor prior to loss of power of the city in the 3rd Century CE. Electors Palatine

Article 376 – Concilium (Council)

1319. A ***Concilium (Council)*** is a political body, defined by proper law, holding certain sovereign and administrative authority as first created in the 8th Century under under the Holly Western Christian Empire. Concilium (Council)

1320. Under the foundation laws of Western Civilisation since the 8th Century, Concilium (Councils) have played an essential element of the function of sovereign states and governments:- Key background and elements of Concilium (Councils)

(i) Sovereign States not ruled by Holly Bloodline, were instead ruled by a Concilium (Council) of noble families, who then elected a steward known as a Statholder. The first sovereign states of this kind were Friesland (later Netherlands), Burgenland (Austria and Switzerland) and Daneland (Central and South West England); and

(ii) Every Sovereign State was administered by a Concilium (Council) of competent ministers as the government. Across the Holly Roman Empire, this government was called the Curia Romanum. For Holly Kingdoms, this government (council) was called the Curia Regis; and for sovereign states administered by a Concilium and Statholder, the government was called the Minor Concilium (Council); and

(iii) So successful was this structure of government and authority, that the Italian Merchant City States themselves copied and adopted the same structures in their own administration, modifying the role of the steward to the "Doge"; and

(iv) Lesser courts were themselves identified as forms of legitimate Concilium (Councils) being Concilium Quatro Sessionis (Court of Major Sessions) and Concilium Peto Sessionis (Court of Minor Sessions).

Article 377 – Courts (Curia & Sessions)

1321. A ***Court*** is a formal institution and forum and first created in history in the 8th Century under Holly Western Christian Empire whereby disputes and cases may be resolved through a structured and formal process. Courts (Curia & Sessions)

1322. The word *Court* originates from the Holly Irish word ***Coirt*** meaning "a place where disputes are formally heard and judged in accord with Sacré Loi (Sacred Law)":- Origin of the word Court

(i) The word *Coirt* is a compound of the ancient Irish word ***cos*** meaning (but not limited to) "measurement, agreements, underlings, barriers, previous judgments, small estates, illness (or injury), shining light on wickedness"; and ***oir*** meaning "suit, pleas, prayers"; and ***te*** meaning "dispute"; and

(ii) Contemporary definitions in Irish of *Coirt* (as bark of tree or skin, fur etc.) is a deliberate falsity and corruption of the origin of western civilisation law; and

(iii) The claim that *Court* originates from *cohors* in Latin is neither plausible, nor sensible and is a deliberate and intentional distraction to hide the true origin of courts, court formality, process, rules, the true origin of trial by jury and the very foundations of western civilised law.

1323. From the first formation of Courts and Western Civilised Justice under the Holly Western Christian Empire there existed only three legitimate and valid forms of Locations for Court:- Locations of Court

(i) ***Paradias (Paradise)***: First formed from Holly Irish meaning "the location where sanctified souls live together with the Divine Creator after death"; and

(ii) ***Pálás (Palace)***: First formed from Holly Irish meaning "a location dedicated as a seat of sovereign authority"; and

(iii) ***Plás (Place)***: First formed from Holly Irish meaning "a location of equality, fairness and just actions".

1324. From the first formation of Courts and Western Civilised Justice under the Holly Western Christian Empire there existed only two legitimate and valid forms of Formation for Courts:- Formation of Court

(i) ***Curia***: From Ancient Greek Kuria (κυρία) meaning "supreme authority". The Holly Irish and French resurrected the word after it ceased being used by the Eastern Christian Empire 300 years earlier; and

(ii) ***Concilium***: From Latin meaning "a solemn pronouncement; a summons to meet; a council".

1325. From the original inception of Courts under the Holly Western Christian Empire, there has always been a valid hierarchy of Courts:- Types and Jurisdiction of Court

(i) ***Curia Divina (Divine Court)***: There is no higher authority, or forum of law, or court than the Court of Heaven; and

(ii) ***Curia Romanum (Court of Rome)***: The Court of Rome, also simply known as the Curia, that serves the King of Rome (Rex Romanum) was the highest earthly court of law, representing the Curia Divina; and

(iii) ***Curia Regis (Court of the Holly King)***: Was the second highest form of earthly court, under the Court of Rome. Only a valid monarch may form and hold a Court of the King; and

(iv) ***Concilium Quatro Sessionis (Court of Major Sessions)***: Was the third highest form of court, hearing matters every 3 months in front of a Jury of Peers and before a Marquee, or a tribunal of Barons; and

(v) ***Concilium Peto Sessionis* (Court of Minor Sessions)**: Was the lowest forms of courts, run by a Justice, tasked with travelling from town to town and city to city ensuring the law is upheld and disputes are resolved.

Article 378 – Nobilitum (Nobility)

1326. ***Nobilitum (Nobility)*** first introduced in history by Charles Martel with the introduction of uniform titles and ranks and associated criteria in accordance with the promulgation of the *Instatutum* ("Institutions") in 738 CE. Nobilitum (Nobility)

1327. The Latin word *nobilis* is a corruption of the ancient Gaelic and Greek term *gnosis* meaning "wisdom, worthy or enlightened". It is consistent with the Sacré Loi (Sacred Law) of the Carolingians whereby the claim of right to nobility was no longer simply by birthright, but by demonstration of worthiness through knowledge, education and character. Origin of word Nobility

1328. The word ***Knight*** comes from the ancient Holly Irish word *Cniocht* meaning a "good, kind, brave and honourable man devoted to upholding the Sacré Loi (Sacred Law) of true Christianity". The word Cniocht itself is a compound word of Irish *cnis* meaning "good character or appearance"; and *iocht* meaning "kindness, clemency, trust, confidence". Origin of word Knight

Article 379 – Orders & Fraternities

1329. ***Sacred Christian Vocation and Military Orders & Fraternities*** were first introduced in the 8th Century under the formation of the Holly Western Christian Empire and not before. Orders & Fraternities

1330. Four Holy Orders were first formed under the formation of the Roman Catholic Church by 742 CE:- First Holy Orders

(i) ***Ordo Sancti Rosae Crucis (Order of the Rose Cross)***: Founded by the leading priories and its leaders (the Twelve Apostles of Ireland). Its sacred mission throughout its history was to protect the integrity of scripture, of true knowledge and wisdom. Destroyed by the 16th Century but secretly revived as the Rosicrucians; and

(ii) ***Ordo Sancti Aquae Vitae (Order of the Holy Waters of Life)***: Founded at mount Fonteveoir (Fontevraud), the famous site of the battle of Tours that helped define the creation of Western Civilisation and arguably one of the most sacred sites in all Christian history. Destroyed by the 16th Century; and

(iii) ***Ordo Sangréal (Order of the Holy Blood)***: Founded at Cashel Ireland around a famous re-creation of the round table of Tara. Known in history as the Knights of the Holy Grail (corruption of Holy Blood and Sangreal). The order successfully protected the lineage of Holly Bloodlines for centuries. Disbanded by the 14th Century, with evidence that like the Rosicrucians and Templars, the Knights of the Holy Grail were either revived or survived in some form; and

(iv) ***Ordo Temporeal (Order of the Sacred Temple)***: Founded upon the top of Montmarte in Paris. Known throughout history as the Knights Templar. The order successfully protected nobility and the movement of treasuries, pilgrims and goods for centuries. Disbanded by the 14th Century, but secretly revived by the Venetians by 16th Century as one of their claims over goods and wealth as "temporal" a corruption of temporeal.

1331. Upon the Saxons taking authority for the Holly Roman Empire by the 10th Century, the German Emperors and Popes added two more Orders:- Saxon (Germanic) Orders

(i) ***Ordo Sancti Benedicti (Order of Saint Benedict)***: Named in honour of the name of all Holly Saxon Emperors as Popes (as they were all named Benedict). Better known in history as the Benedictines. The strength of organisation, defense and adaption saw the order survive and continue to the present day; and

(ii) ***Ordo Tutoreal (Order of the Sacred Guardians)***: Falsely known in modern history as the Teutonic Order after some non existent tribe, whilst defaming their honourable history. The knights were the first to build hospitals and schools in many European cities and towns. Whilst surviving the 14th Century, their true history has been unfortunately deeply corrupted.

11.5 – Venetian Roman Empire

Article 380 – Venetian Roman Empire

1332. The ***Venetian Roman Empire*** is the merchant military empire of Pisa and then Venice and its merchant colonies that arose from the growing power and good fortune of these merchant city states and the central strategic religious and political importance of Rome and the Italian Peninsula from the 8th Century CE. Venetian Roman Empire

1333. In reference to the Venetian Roman Empire, there exist some significant inventions and elements that still impact Sovereign Law today, including (but not limited to):- Significant Elements of Venetian Roman Empire and Sovereign Law

(i) Three Sacred Oaths (of Moors); and

(ii) Pisa; and

(iii) Venice; and

(iv) Consiglio (Council); and

(v) Lira (Paper Money).

Article 381 – Three Sacred Oaths (of Moors)

1334. The ***Three Sacred Oaths of the Moors*** (Original Moor: *Ksen Tavawsa*), represented the most sacred and solemn bound oaths of all Moors to the Holly Bloodlines and Western Christianity that held from 812 CE to the end of the 13th Century. The Hebrew *Keser Elohim* (כֶּתֶר אֱלֹהִים) is a modern revival and corruption of the *Ksen Tavawsa*. Three Sacred Oaths (of Moors)

1335. The original three Sacred Oaths of the Moors (*Ksen Tavawsa*) were:- Ksen Tavawsa (Three Sacred Oaths of Moors)

(i) A Moor is bound by blood to never to set foot upon any Holly Land in arms; and

(ii) A Moor is bound by blood to protect and defend the Holly

Bloodlines (Holy Grail and Sangreal) against any and all enemies; and

(iii) The Holly (Holy Grail and Sangreal) are bound by their oaths not to curse or oppress the Moors.

1336. In terms of the historic context of the Three Oaths of the Moors (*Ksen Tavawsa*):- Historic Context of the Three Oaths of the Moors

(i) The Moors lost their independent kingdom of Morokon (North Africa) and their hold on southern Spain by 744 CE, through a combined conquest of Holly Christian Armies and Holly Saracen (Islamic) forces. The same union of forces saw the conquest of the Italian peninsula a few years later. Rather than eliminate the former royal lines of the Moors, the Carolingian Holly Kings exiled them as prisoners to Lucca in Italy; and

(ii) By 812 CE, Holly Emperor Charlemagne granted the Moors limited freedoms under the famous law *Capitula Mauri: The Capitularies of the Moors* (falsely written as the Jews), providing the Moors pledged a sacred blood oath to the Holly and to Western Christianity; and

(iii) If the Three Oaths and Capitula Mauri (Law of the Moors) had not occurred, then Pisa would not have been reconstructed and risen; and Venice, Genoa, Bruges, Amsterdam and all the subsequent history could not have happened; and

(iv) In 1057, at Este 35 miles (57 km) south west of Laguna (Venice), Holly Roman Emperor Henry III presided over the matrimony of his first born child and daughter Beatrice to Domenico Morosini, the first born son of important ally Giovanni Morosini, the new leader of all northern Italy. This Union created the House of Welf (Wolf), also known as the House of Este (after the city) and represented the first time in history that Moor and Holly blood united. From this point, the Moors properly regarded themselves as Holly. However, under the sacred Fleur-de-Lif, they regarded themselves as the natural successors of the Saxons when the seventh Saxon Emperor died and not the Irish; and

(v) When Holly Roman Emperor Henry VI died in 1166, Pietro Domenico Morosini as Holly King Konrad II of Italy (1154-1186) demanded that Holly King Diarmaida (Dermod) Mór of Ireland and Emperor Bórá (Boru) abdicate. When Diarmaida (Dermod) Mór as Holly Emperor and Pope at Avignon (France) refused, the Moors attacked Ireland destroying over thirty buildings and precious artefacts as the first attacks against Ireland in over a thousand years. When Diarmaida (Dermod) Mór died in 1171, the Moors sent a mercenary force to destroy Ireland. However, the French had already positioned an army they called the FitzGerald (New Shield) against the Moor mercenaries and the attack failed; and

(vi) Hostilities against the Moors claiming to be the rightful Holly against the Irish and French culminated in 1284 that saw land and sea invasions from the Genoese, Basque (Gascon) Mercenaries, French and Irish forces, completely destroying Pisa and leaving it an uninhabited ruin for more than 50 years; and

(vii) The Moors never forgave the Irish for the destruction of Pisa, even though it was on account of their blatant disregard to their own oaths. In particular, the Pisans blamed the last Irish Bórá (Boru) Holy Roman Emperor (1272-1312 CE) Bórá (Boru) VI (Domchadh Mór Ruadh). There is strong evidence that this visceral hatred against the Irish drove the complete and systematic destruction of Ireland from the 17th Century and beyond; and

(viii) The memory of the Three Oaths and the Moors were revived when creating the new religion of Judaism in the 17th Century with the three oaths relating to the authority granted to the Jews by God to reclaim their "homeland" of Israel under certain conditions; and

(ix) In the 20th Century, Jewish leaders, as descendents of the Moors once again broke these new 17th Century oaths by creating the conditions to force the formation of the state of Israel; and

(x) Modern Jewish thought treats the three oaths as a legend and not a condition to be met. This is despite of the contradictory claim that the modern state of Israel was granted by G-d. No account of this open and serious contradiction is ever properly explained; and

(xi) Popularised since the early 20th Century and falsely and absurdly claimed as ancient rite, is the *Kol Nidre Recitation* spoken by Jewish congregations at the evening service of Yom Kippur. The *Kol Nidre* disavows and breaks all oaths, vows and promises made by Jewish people and all bonds, prohibitions or judgements made against any Jewish people. The *Kol Nidre* further makes the blasphemous and outrageously false claim that G-d "by the authority of the Heavenly Court" gives the Jewish people this exclusive right to break the Rule of Law of Civilised people.

1337. In accord with the present Maxims and the most sacred Covenant *Pactum De Singularis Caelum*, the practice of Kol Nidre is repudiated as a blasphemous, false and wickedly evil act against Heaven and Earth and all united spirits and beings. Repudiation of Kol Nidre and breaking of oaths

Article 382 – Pisa

1338. ***Pisa (Piso)*** is located on an ancient plain of alluvial marshes and lagoons formed by the Serchio River (to the north) and the Arno River (to the south). After centuries of silt build-up and land reclamation, the city is now about 6 miles (10 km) from the Ligurian Sea and 50 miles (80 km) west of Florence. The city is unique in retaining its name from first Etruscan settlements and tribe of the area that became one of the most famous (and infamous) Gens (Houses) of Roman History as the Gens Calpernia of Piso. Pisa

1339. In reference to the origins and history of Pisa:- Brief Summary of Origins and History of Pisa

(i) At just between 6ft (2m) and 13 ft (4m) above sea level, the regional climate is known for hot summers with moderate rainfall and cool, damp winters; and

(ii) By 20 CE, Pisa (Piso) was firmly the largest and most political and economically influential coastal city in north-western Italy, with an estimated population of over 40,000; and making it the fifth largest Roman city in Italy behind Rome (1 million), Milan (Mediolanum (120,000)), Capua (60,000) and Aquileia (50,000); and

(iii) The Piso Gens (Family) were infamous in their campaigns of political intrigue and betrayal among the Patrician class, culminating in their complicity with an attempted coup against Emperor Nero around 64 CE; and later in 65 CE in the events that led to the disastrous fires that destroyed more than one third of Rome and caused the deaths of at least 200,000 people. For such crimes, the Piso were among the first Patricians ever to be crucified in Roman History and the first to be executed in more than 50 years. The city of Pisa (Piso) was then condemned and utterly destroyed as cursed ground, with anyone calling themselves “Pisan” a capital crime under Roman Law; and

(iv) In 747 CE, Holly King Aurelius Angleramus (Pepin the Short) of the Franks conquered the Northern half of the Italian Peninsula, aided by Saracen Khalifah (Caliph) Safwan Abd Al-Khalbi of Al-Rashid (Egypt) who conquered the southern half of the Italian Peninsula, naming it the Caliphate of Rumi. The northern city of Luca (Lucca) near the abandoned ruins of Pisa became the new Marche (State) of Lucia (north west Italy) and the new home of exile for the Moors led by Zaida; and

(v) By 830 CE, the Moors as the Morosini (meaning "High Moors") had gained permission to rebuild a port and trading settlement on the ruins of old Pisa, reconstituting it as a "floating city" of buildings and canals. By 845 CE, the Pisans were granted permission to build a second port and colony they called *Genoa* (from Latin *Ianua* meaning "entrance, access, doorway"). By 855 CE, the Pisans founded a settlement on the tidal marsh islands in the Lagoon of the Po River, they called *Laguna* (later called Venice); and

(vi) In 961 CE, Otto I (936 - 973) of Germany made Marco Morosini, also known as Marco di Piso (Marco the Pisan), the new Margrave of Tuscia (961 - 1001) with Pisa the new capital of Tuscia for the first time; and beginning in 962 CE, Marco Morosini (Marco di Piso) commenced the establishment of a network of fortified, trading posts across Tuscany, leading from the Alps south to Rome including: *Florence*, *Perugia* and *Assisi*; and

(vii) In 963 CE, Harald II (961 - 970) of Daneland granted Marco Morosini (Marco di Piso) and the Pisans perpetual ownership of the land at the mouth of the River Zwin. The Pisans then founded their second sovereign community called Brygga (Bruges); and

(viii) From 973 CE, Marco Morosini (961 - 1001) (Marco di Piso), began the expansion of Genoa as a second major port city to the north; And at the same time began massive expansion of building a second man-made Island of Laguna (later Venice) called Marco Island next to Rialto Island. The fortified trading posts established by the Pisans allowed trade to flow along the Po River from Turin and Milan to Laguna (Venice) and then the Adriatic Sea; by-passing any Saracen blockades of the Tyrrhenian Sea and west of Italy; and

(ix) In 1001 CE, Marco Morosini died and was succeeded by his son Giovanni Morosini as hereditary ruler of Pisa. In 1022 CE, following the death of Kalifah Al-Hakim (996-1021), a rare eruption of civil war in Saracen North Africa was quickly exploited by Autokrator Iounnas Tzimiskes (976 – 1025 CE) of the Eastern Christian Empire in retaking the islands of Cyprus and Crete; and in retaking parts of the southern Italian emirate of Al-Rumi, including control of part of Sicily and the Calabria region in southern Italy. At the same time, the effective government of southern Spanish Caliphate of Al-Andalus collapsed. In the western Mediterranean, the Pisans under Doge Giovanni Morosini quickly took advantage in seizing control of Corsica, Sardinia and the island of Mallorca, while establishing colonial control of Barcelona, Valencia, Malaga and Gibilterra (Gibraltar); and North African colonies of Algeri, Orano, Tangeri, Sale and Safi; and

(x) In 1042 CE, Theodora Porphyrogenita took over as Empress of Eastern Christian Empire and demanded that Belisarius Theophylactus complete the reconquest of Sicily against the Saracens and northern Italy against the Western Christian Empire. The Eastern Christians then secured a treaty with Magioria (Magyar) Leader Alphan (St Stephen) and the Swabian Leader Conrad, to aid in his defeat of Holy Roman Emperor Henry III (1038 – 1056); and

(xi) In 1043 CE, Doge Giovanni Morosini of Pisa died and was replaced by his son Marco II Morosini (1043 – 1060). Fearing a combined attack from Eastern Christian Belisarius Theophylactus and Magioria (Magyar) Leader Alphan (St Stephen), Marco II Morosini secured the services of over 30,000 Catalonian mercenaries under the command of Rogelio Borja and Roberto Borja. By 1044 CE, Doge Marco II Morosini of Pisa (1043 – 1060) moved half his mercenary forces with Roberto Borja east to the Po River and then to Laguna to link up with Pisan ambassador Pietro III Orso (Orsini) Leoni. The Pisans defeated Magyar Leader and Eastern Christian ally Alphan (St Stephen), destroying the city of Magyara (Padua) to its foundations. When in the same year Belisarius Theophylactus moved north in Italy, he was confronted by two mercenary armies and the risk of being outflanked. Marco II Morosini then appointed Pietro III Orso (Orsini) Leoni as protector of Rome with one army, while the remainder protected Pisa and Tuscany against any counter attack from the Swabians or Eastern Christians. When Holy Roman Emperor Henry III finally arrived with his forces in 1047, the Morosini were rewarded with the creation of the new title Margrave of Pisa, an area that absorbed not only Tuscia but Ivrea (Turin) and effectively the whole of Northern Italy; and

(xii) Despite the successes of the Morosini, Pisa and its colonies and patrician families by 1050 CE were effectively insolvent, given the enormous costs of funding such a huge Catalonian mercenary army as well as the building project tripling the size of the settlement of Laguna. In order to quell further instability across the remaining Pisan colonies, Pisa declared itself a commune of cities and a Republic, forming for the first time a *Consiglio Undici* also known as the Council of Eleven being the patrician families of Caetani, Crivelli, Colonna, Dori, Gusmini, Morosini, Orlando, Orso (Orsini), Sforza, Simonetti and Visconti; Which pronounced the election of Marco II Morosini as the first Doge (from Latin meaning "in the service of the Gens") in history. At the same time, the patrician families of Laguna (Venice) were granted the same privilege, electing Domenico Contarini (1051 - 1057) as technically the first Doge of Laguna (Venice); and

(xiii) By 1052 CE, Holy Roman Emperor Henry III agreed to help with the cost of keeping the Catalonian mercenaries in Italy on the condition that they attack and defeat Belisarius Theophylactus and the Eastern Christian forces in Southern Italy and Sicily. Yet when Doge Marco II Morosini died in 1056, the noble families of Pisa revolted against the hereditary rule of the Morosini, forcing the election of Giovani Orlando (1056 - 1057) as the new Doge. Giovanni Morosini and and the Morosini family were forced to flee to Venice. On news of the rebellion, Holy Roman Emperor Henry III returned to Italy by 1057 and to the fortified city of Este, 35 miles (57 km) south west of Laguna (Venice). At Este, Henry offered his first born daughter Beatrice in marriage to the young unmarried first born son of Giovanni Morosini named Domenico. Upon the marriage at Este, Henry declared Domenico be Holly as King Konrad of Italy. King Konrad then ordered the arrest and execution of Giovani Orlando, while his father Doge Giovanni Morosini of Laguna (Venice), ordered the rebel Pisan families into exile including the Cavanna, Riario, Aleramici, Orlando, Amidei, Grimaldo and Pallavicini; and

(xiv) Under the new Holly Morosini King (Konrad) of Italy, both Roberto and Rogelio Borja and their mercenaries captured Messina by 1061 and by 1072 Palermo in Sicily. King Konrad then elevated Rogelio to Count of Sicily with Roberto Borja as Count of Naples; and

(xv) In 1062 CE Doge Giovanni Morosini of Pisa and Laguna (Venice) permanently dissolved the Great Council of Pisa, appointing his second son Michele as the first Governor (Podesta). The Morosini then appointed governors for all of its other colonies. By 1072, promulgated the first comprehensive modern international law and "law of the sea" called Consuetudini di mare (translates literally as 'customs of the sea') produced by the Academia Pisa (University of Pisa) declaring Pisa the Stato de Mari or the "State of the Sea(s)"; and

(xvi) By 1185 CE, the Pisan - Venetian forces aided by Sicilian, Catalonian and English mercenaries succeed in capturing significant Ionian Islands (Greece) including Kefalonica and Zakynthos. Agios Georgios (Zorzi) also known as Kastro becomes a major strategic port and fortress and the brief capital of Matthew I, an Orsini (1185 – 1238) later known as "di Zorzi" and founder of the House of Zorzi; and

(xvii) In 1204 CE, the Pisan-Venetian forces aided by Sicilian, Catalonian and English mercenaries complete the capture of Greece, Crete and Constantinople and the establishment of the "Latin Empire" (1204 - 1261), massively increasing their influence and importance in Europe. Pisa established its fifth university (University of Chalcis) by 1204, the sixth university as University of Athens by 1209 and the seventh as the University of Candia (Crete) by 1212 CE; and

(xviii) In 1209 CE, the Pisans commenced a thirty year campaign using English and Catalonian mercenaries to attack the Irish forces and Emperor at Avignon in the south of France. This became known as the infamous "Cathair Crusade" or campaign against the olive skinned (Cathair or Mac Cathair) Holly Irish Emperors and Popes; and

(xix) In 1216 CE, the Pisan-Venetian forces founded a university, which was granted fifty miles (80km) north on the River Cam, being the University and Trading post of Cambria (Cambridge); and Around 1223 CE, Pisa claimed exclusive right over the ruins of Padua as its tenth University, rebuilding Padua as a university town and trading post; and

(xx) In August 1284 CE, a combined Genoese, Spanish and French fleet under the command of Benedetto Zaccaria and Obert Doria destroyed the entire Pisan fleet through the use of fire ships and blockade. By 1290 CE, French, Saxon and Irish forces as well as Gascon and Genovese mercenaries destroyed Pisa, including filling in its port and forever ending Pisa as a major physical power; and

(xxi) By 1290 CE, as reward for their support in destroying Pisa, Genoa was granted full control of the former trading colonies of Pisa to the west, including (but not limited to) Islands of Corsica, Sardinia and Mallorca; and the Mediterranean colonies of Marsiglia (Marsailles), Barcelona, Valencia, Malaga and Gibilterra (Gibraltar); and North African colonies of Algeri, Orano, Tangeri, Sale and Safi.

Article 383 – Venice

1340. ***Venice*** is located within the marshes of the river Po and at the top of the Adriatic Sea, approximately 100 miles (160 km) south east from the English Channel coastline. North-west from the city, the Seine meets the coast at La Havre about 233 mi (375 km) downstream. The first Celtic settlements were probably founded on the two large natural river islands of Île Saint-Louis being 1,800 ft (550 metres) from west to east and 500 ft (150 metres) from north to south; and Île de la Cité being 3,400 ft (1,036 metres) from west to east and 800 ft (244 metres) from north to south. Venice

1341. The name *Venice* (Venezia in Italian) originates from the 13th Century word *Veniteo* from the Latin *ve* meaning "to" and *eniteo* meaning "shine forth (out of darkness); distinguished, exceptional or eminent":- Origin of the name Venice

(i) The claim by some scholars since the mid 19th Century 20th Century that the word Venice comes from an ancient tribe called the "Veneti" that supposedly inhabited the region for thousands of years is a laughable and absurd hoax, with no credible evidence; and

(ii) Until most of the Pisan Patrician families finally re-settled in lagoon settlements by the end of the 13th Century after the destruction of their own city (Pisa), there is strong historical evidence that the inhabitants of the man-made islands in the lagoon were collectively known simply as the *Lagunari* or "people of the lagoon"; and

(iii) The choice of the name Venice (from Latin Veniteo) meaning literally "to shine forth from the darkness; to be exceptional, distinguished and eminent" appears to be the rallying cry and new mission of the Pisans who firmly took control of the lagoon Islands upon their migration from their destroyed city on the other side of Italy.

1342. In reference to the origins and history of the place now known as Venice:- Brief Summary of Origins and History of Venice

(i) In 717 CE, after Khazar mercenaries slaughtered Goth King Arvila (Tervel) and much of his army in an Eastern Christian

Empire orchestrated ambush, his son Avarica (Avarik) fled west to the ancient Roman and fortified Goth city of Medovium (Padua) built on the Medoacus (Brenta) River around 36 miles (58 km) from the Adriatic coastline and natural lagoons. Avarica (Avarik) then renamed this city *Magyaria* meaning "place of the Magioria" and thus the birth of the term Magyar; and

(ii) In 744 CE, rebel Eastern Christian General and Kromwell (Cromwell) Anabasos and 6,000 of his men and ships were granted sanctuary in the city of Magyaria (Padua) by Magioria (Magyar) leader Avarica (Avarik), boosting the population of the city to over 30,000; and

(iii) By 855 CE, the Pisans secured an agreement from Magioria (Magyar) leader Almos to purchase outright control of the uninhabited tidal marsh islands of Rialto, Guidecca, Cannaregio and smaller islands and waters around them in the natural lagoons 25 miles (40 km) east of Magyaria (Padua). The Pisans then appointed Pietro Orso (Orsini) Tradonico to oversee the creation of the first "tidal proof" buildings, starting on Rialto Island, using the same techniques used to build Pisa. The name of the trading settlement was then simply called *Laguna*; and

(iv) By 1000 CE, the Magioria (Magyar) had created their new summer capital on the Danube at Eszter (Budapest) of over 10,000 inhabitants. However, the city of Magyaria (Padua) was by far their largest and most important city, with a population of over 55,000; and

(v) In 1045 CE, Doge Marco II Morosini of Pisa (1043 – 1056) moved his forces east to the Po River and then to Laguna to link up with Pisan ambassador Pietro III Orso (Orsini) Leoni. The Pisan army led by Pietro III Orso (Orsini) Leoni then defeated Magyar Leader and Eastern Christian ally Alphan (St Stephen), destroying the city of Magyaria (Padua) to its foundations and enslaving the surviving Magyar population to greatly expand the building of "Marco (Venezia) Island" of the city of Laguna (Venice); and

(vi) By 1056 CE, Laguna became the permanent home of the Morosini and consequently (for a time) the Holly Kings of Italy. By 1057, Giovanni Morosini became the new Doge. By 1061, Laguna (Venice) became the only city for a time under a Doge, as the Council and Office was dissolved in Pisa. Upon his death by 1090, the position of Doge of Laguna (Venice) became a perpetual hereditary title of the head of the Morosini family as Holly Kings of Italy; and

(vii) By 1307, Pietro Marino Morosini as Emperor Frederick II was finally captured and executed in 1307. Within a year after, the first cases of Haemorrhagic Fever (beginning of the Black Death) began spreading, causing the collapse of the blockade against Laguna (Venice) and saving the city. Pietro Marco Morosini then declared the new name for the city for the first time as Venice; and

(viii) During 1509, after the defeat of Venice at the battle of Agnadello, by the League of Cambrai of Spain, Germany, Naples, France and Genoa led by the French, the Venetian Patrician families were forced into exile to England and subsequent adoption and integration into the court of King Henry VIII (1509-1547).

Article 384 – Consiglio (Council)

1343. ***Consiglio*** (Council) is a term first introduced in the 11th Century CE Pisa and afterwards Venice to describe a new form of aristocratic rule by a few elite families. The in word Consilium in the 13th Century CE was later extended to temporarily constituted bodies, formed with the authority to discuss and pass laws, but having limited life span.

Consiglio (Council)

1344. In terms of the brief history of Consiglio:-

Brief history of Consiglio (Council)

(i) In 1006 CE in order to quell further instability across the remaining Pisan lands, Pisa declared itself a commune of cities and a "State" known as Stato de Mari or the "State of the Sea(s)", forming for the first time a permanent government known as the Consiglio Dodici, also known as the Council of Twelve and the Gran Consiglio ("Great Council"), being the families: Caetani, Crivelli, Dori, Fieschi, Grimo, Gusmini, Morosini, Orlando, Sforza, Simonetti, Verchionesi and Visconti that pronounced the election of Giovanni Morosini (1006 - 1043) as the first Doge (from Italian meaning "staff") in history; and

(ii) In 1045 CE, the Morosini of Pisa formed a new government of the colony through a Council of twelve (12) noble families called the Consiglio Dodici or "Council of Twelve" being the families of Barbaro, Contarini, Cornaro, Dandelo, Faliero, Gradenigo, Micheli, Morosini (Pisani), Priuli, Tiepolo, Valiero and Ziani. The Consiglio Dodici then promptly pronounced the election of Domenico Contarini (1041 - 1084) as the second

Doge in history; and

(iii) In 1172 CE a new series of councils (consiglio) were formed and the existing Consiglio Undici was reformed to the Consiglio Dieci (Council of Ten) after the House of Micheli was banished from the council; and the Maggior Consiglio or (Great Council of Venice) was then formed from all families that had name and property prior in Venice to 1000 CE, known as the longhi. The Maggior Consiglio was then granted the power to elect the Doge from a Consiglio Dieci (Council of Ten) as well as the membership of the Minor Consiglio (Minor Council) of forty (40); and

(iv) The Minor Consiglio (Minor Council) of forty (40) also known as the "Quarantia" was first formed with the power to veto the decisions of the Doge, prepare and review legislation of Venice and conduct court investigations; and

(v) In 1223, the Minori Consiglio (Minor Council) of Venice was converted to a religious fraternity (brotherhood) known as Ordo Fraternum Minori or "Fraternal Order of Frugality" later known by the late 13th Century as the "Franciscans" headed by a Minister-General; and

(vi) While the Minori Consiglio (Minor Council) as the Ordo Fraternum Minori was stripped of its legislative powers by 1229, the Ordo Fraternum Minori reserved the supreme Judicial, Chancery and Financial functions now performed as a religious brotherhood; and

(vii) In 1229 CE, the Consiglio dei Pregadi or "Senate" of Venice was formed whereby sixty (60) members were to be elected from the Maggior Consiglio or (Great Council of Venice) as the supreme legislative body.

Article 385 – Lira (Paper Money)

1345. ***Lira*** is a form of paper money, historically symbolised by a stylised capital "***L***", first introduced in 1374 by Venetian Doge Michele Morosini (1367-1382) through the formation of the first Venetian central bank known as *Banco della Rialto (Bank of Rialto Island).* Lira (Paper Money)

1346. The term *Lira* originates from the Venetian word equivalent to the ancient Latin term of *Libra* meaning "a pound (measure), a weighted scales, level, trade and transaction of exchange". A Roman Pound was equivalent to about 329g (10.58 troy ounces) of high purity silver. Origin of the word Lira

1347. In terms of the brief history of the Venetian *Lira*:- Brief history of the Venetian

(i) By the late 14th Century, Rialto Island (Isola di Rialto) was arguably the banking, financial and market trading capital of the world. However, around 1373-74, the collapse of two of the largest private banks of Venice (Piovego Bank and Dandolo Bank) threatened the economic stability of Venice. Doge Michele Morosini (1367-1382) then formed the first Venetian central bank known as *Banco della Rialto*, ultimately reporting to the Venetian Senate. This bank then offered merchants and other private banks the Lira as a stable medium of exchange and unit of value to settle debts and obligations; and

Lira

(ii) The Banco della Rialto was dissolved along with several other institutions by 1510, when the Venetian patrician families were finally exiled by the French to England and the court of King Henry VIII (1509-1547). At the same time, the Lira as paper money was banned in Venice and the Spanish Gold Ducado (later Ducat) and Silver Escudo (later Scudo) were imposed as the standard currencies of Venice; and

(iii) By 1544, the Venetians forced Henry VIII to hand over control of the monetary system to a new institution called the "Exchequer", falsely claimed of much older provenance and the Venetian Lira returned as the "Pound", still using the "L" symbol; and

(iv) By the late 17th Century and the formation of the Bank of England, the Venetian Lira as the "Pound" was given the added name of "Sterling" from stere meaning "steer a vessel or ship" and linge meaning "fishes" a historic slang word among slave traders for a cargo of "slaves"; and

(v) By the late 1970's the symbol for the Venetian Lira as the "Pound Sterling" was given an extra line across it.

11.6 – Venetian British Empire

Article 386 – Venetian British Empire

1348. The ***Venetian British Empire*** is the Empire first formed by the exiled Venetian patrician families settling in England under Henry VIII. The core strength of the Venetian British Empire has been its revival of Western Holly Christian Civilisation and Infrastructure and then usurping the role of the Holly as impostors for more than 450 years.

Venetian British Empire

1349. Unlike other merchant pirate empires, the Venetian British Empire

Core Strengths

has (until the present decades) been built upon a core set of strengths that have enabled its longevity:-

of the Venetian British Empire

(i) ***The supremacy of parliament***: Similar to the original model of the Venetian Senate, the forced equality under common rules for the patrician merchant families of England, has ensured a stability of power among the elite not seen in other countries with powerful monarchs or dominant ruling families. It has effectively ensured a single despotic ruler cannot effectively take control of Britain; and

(ii) ***The strength and power of the City of London***: Unlike many other former empires and regimes, the political strength of the merchant and professional class through the City of London has ensured (until now) the protection, growth and continued wealth and influence of the merchant and professional classes of England and Great Britain, providing a solid, stable second layer and class structure; and

(iii) ***The legal and commercial power of English Language***: The English Language since its first creation in the 16th Century has been a powerful weapon and tool in prosecuting the law and pursuit of commercial dominance. In contrast, many other European languages are substantially weaker in their applicability in law, commerce and the occult; and

(iv) ***The power and mythology of English Speaking Media and Academia***: No other empire has created more myths, forgeries, stories and fakes than the British Empire, until Pax Americana (Anglo-Dutch American Empire) and more recently the modern state of Israel. Such documents, stories and continued distractions have played a fundamental part in maintaining power and authority; and

(v) ***Voluntary Servitude***: No empire has succeeded more in converting slavery (involuntary servitude) to "voluntary enslavement". Through the revival as impostors of Western Holly Christian Civilisation value of Law and Infrastructure, the elite and the merchant and professional classes are arguably the greatest promoters of voluntary servitude in civilised history. By constant manipulation of the truth, history and important mythology, the Venetian British Empire has built huge military forces under voluntary servitude; and industrial workforces willingly under voluntary servitude; and the whole middle class experiment of the 20th Century whereby a new layer of society jealously guard their "right" to voluntary servitude as "slaves".

1350. In reference to the Venetian British Empire, there exist some significant inventions and elements that still impact Sovereign Law today, including (but not limited to):- Significant Elements of Venetian British Empire and Sovereign Law

(i) English (Language); and

(ii) London; and

(iii) New Jerusalem; and

(iv) King James Bible (KJB); and

(v) New Rome.

Article 387 – English (Language)

1351. ***English*** is a late 15th Century CE artificially formed phonological language created by Dutch and Venetian language and printing experts at the Palace of Westminster with the authority of King Henry VII Tudor of England (1457-1509) for commercial and political purposes in introducing a unified language for the Island of Britain and reduce the long term influence of Gaelic, Norse and Anglaise (falsely listed as Old French). English (Language)

1352. While the first Lexicons of English coincided with the invention of the language itself from the end of the 15th Century, the invention of Dictionaries providing rich information on definition, etymology, phonetics and pronunciation did not emerge until the end of the 16th Century:- Dictionaries

(i) In 1592, the Company of Mercers and Adventurers of London authorized the first English Dictionary of eight thousand (8000) English words called *Elementarie* created by Richard Mulcaster. The reference text did not attempt to be a medium for creating new words, only to collect and aggregate existing words; and

(ii) The first monolingual and alphabetical Dictionary of English was in 1604 by Robert Cawdrey called "*A Table Alphabeticall*" containing just two thousand five hundred forty three (2,543) words in one hundred twenty (120) pages; and

(iii) By 1656 Thomas Blount published a work called *Glossopgraphia* containing eleven thousand (11,000) word entries and was the first to include etymologies and the first to cite sources for the words defined. It was also the last dictionary of substantial note that maintained a strict objectivity in avoiding crossing the line as a collection of fact, versus a means of propagating new words and new meanings; and

(iv) In 1658, Edward Philips, the nephew of John Milton published a far more popular dictionary known as *The New World of Words* containing some eleven thousand (11,000) new words, of which at least one hundred percent (100%) were simply plagiarised from the work of Thomas Blount. However, by the fifth (5th) edition the number had grown to seventeen thousand (17,000) new words largely through the creative license of the editor and his uncle. By 1706, the work had grown to over thirty eight thousand (38,000) under the editing of John Kersey. This work therefore heralds the dictionary as the primary means for officially introducing new words and new meanings into the English language as much a writer of fiction or playwright; and

(v) The influence of dictionaries as a purely fictional and creative medium to invent the English language was highlighted with the publication by Nathan Bailey in 1721 of the work entitled *An Universal Etymological English Dictionary* containing more than forty two thousand (42,000+) word forms, largely plagiarized from the work of John Kersey with yet new fictitious words and etymologies. The dictionary was so popular, it went through at least thirty (30) editions until 1802; and

(vi) At the end of the 19th Century, the *Oxford English Dictionary* (OED) project attempting to be the "most objective", and detailed dictionary of the English language commenced. The full volume set was issued in 1895. As at the end of the 20th Century over six hundred thousand (600,000) words in the English language are recognized; and

(vii) A project originally inspired by the Oxford English Dictionary commenced in the United States by Henry Campbell Black who by 1891 published the first (1st) edition of the *Black's Law Dictionary*, the second (2nd) edition in 1910. The ninth (9th) edition of Black's Law Edition was published in 2009. Most significantly, Black's Law Dictionary is one (1) of the most infamous publications for demonstrating complete and utter disregard to the etymological preservation of legal words from edition to edition in preference to the flexibility to define the same word differently in light of creative, political and commercial interests. As a result, most courts and official bodies in the United States refuse to acknowledge definitions that are sourced from editions older than the most recent edition.

1353. Due to false claims regarding the etymology of certain English words, the infusion of occult and cryptic meanings from the 16th Century, as well as the flagrant creative license of dictionary creators prior to the 18th Century and still exhibited currently, in specialist dictionaries such as law, the reliability of meaning, etymology, usage and purpose of English words as stated in "official texts" can only be substantiated as claims, rather than as facts. Therefore, Lexical works that seek to objectively identify true etymology since the foundation of the language such as UCADIA have every right to be regarded as a credible source.

Ucadia Official Texts and English

Article 388 – London

1354. ***London*** is located on ancient flood marshes approximately 50 miles (80 km) miles upstream along the tidal Thames River from the North Sea at Tilbury. The first major settlement was a Roman fort founded in 43 CE by Roman Emperor Claudius on the former largest natural island on the river (now site of Westminster, Victoria, Millbank and Pimlico) that was approximately 1.4 miles (2.29km) long and 1 mile (1.6km) wide at the time, with the Thames River roughly twice as wide as it is today.

London

1355. In reference to the origins, history and natural history of London:-

Brief Summary of Origins, History and Nature of London

(i) Built on a relatively flat ancient flood marsh plain, the location of London has a long history of flooding and disease. The site of the original Island city of Londinium (now site of Westminster, Victoria, Millbank and Pimlico) was presumably chosen by Emperor Claudius given the island gave the Romans enough room to build a strong defensive position, as well as complete control of all trade along the second longest river in England. Roman Londinium was badly damaged around 70 CE and ultimately abandoned no later than the 4th Century CE. The site was not revived with any building until the 16th Century; and

(ii) Contrary to false and absurd histories and maps of claimed Roman Londinium on the north bank of the River Thames, this settlement, (including the ancient tidal flood walls and forts) was founded by the Danes no earlier than the late 8th Century as their new capital of Daneland (southern eastern England). The Dane wall was about 3 kilometres (1.9 miles) long, 6 metres (20 ft) high, and 2.5 metres (8.2 ft) thick; and designed to protect the city against floods and tidal surges. The

Danes then were the first to build the original Tower of London from the 900s, that gave them control of all traffic and defence against attack; and

(iii) Unlike other locations, the Romans did not create aqueducts for Londinium, instead taking advantage of the natural fresh spring streams flowing down from the ridge of hills from North Hill and back north west to Elstree on the north side of the River Thames. When New London was built by the Danes from the late 8th Century, the new walled city relied for water upon a series of public wells and a pump system drawing water from the large natural aquifer system underneath the greater Thames basin. By the 16th Century, it was the Venetians that first introduced major infrastructure and the Great Conduit from the springs at Tyrburn, Middlesex to supply London. By the late 17th Century, London was home to a growing number of private "waterworks" companies drawing water from the Thames and then "filtering it" for commercial and domestic use; and

(iv) Unlike other cities in England and Europe, the Romans did not create a permanent sewer system for Londinium, indicating (along with lack of robust fresh water infrastructure) that the original fort and settlement on the island was never intended to be a permanent city. Consequently, when the Danes built New London a mile away (falsely claimed to be the first Roman settlement), there was no effective sewerage system and the Thames remained the "open sewer of London" until the 19th Century, when major works finally were taken to build a comprehensive sewerage system for the city; and

(v) Contrary to false and absurd histories and maps of claimed Roman Londinium on the north bank of the River Thames, this settlement, (including the ancient walls and forts) was founded by the Danes no earlier than the late 8th Century as their new capital of Daneland (southern eastern England); and

(vi) The city of London remained largely defined by the boundary of the Danish flood and tidal wall for at least 750 years until the permanent arrival of the Venetian exiles in the early 16th Century. By 1530, the population of London was still less than 25,000, compared to a generally stable population of around 15,000 over the past centuries, excluding the Great Haemorrhagic Fever plagues of the 14th Century; and

(vii) By the 16th Century, the exiled Venetian patriarchs and their merchants refused to live within the filthy and stinking walls of ancient London; and preferred to build their new homes sufficiently far enough upstream to avoid the stench and pollution, starting with estates at Kew, Richmond, Ham, Hampton, Windsor, Marlow, Reading and as far upstream as Oxford. The Venetians even built Henry VIII extravagant new palace called Hampton Court so that court business could be conducted well away from London; and

(viii) The era of Venetian English nobility saw a rapid expansion of the population of London from around 50,000 by 1530 to over 225,000 by 1605. However, much of this population growth was connected to industry and exploitation of the poor, with living conditions in London said to be the worst in Europe and some of the worst of any city in human history; and

(ix) The expansion of London beyond the boundaries first set by the Danes in the late 8th Century did not occur until the planned rebuilding after hundreds of thousands of poor souls were sacrificed in the Great Fire of London in 1666. The new "hub and spoke" model of major roads and landmarks such as the first proper "London Bridge", including the first rudimentary sewerage systems, plus the building of a grand palace at Whitehall and new aristocratic residences at Westminster, saw the population of London rise to 500,000 by 1675 and wealthy nobles and merchants having a residence within the city of London for the first time. As the city continued to grow, these effective "gated communities" of the elite continued to grow in the building of other elite and aristocratic enclaves in the expanding city at Belgravia, Knightsbridge, Mayfair, Kensington and Chelsea; and

(x) By 1801, the population of London reached more than 1.1 million, making London only the second city (apart from Baghdad) to reach the heights of ancient Rome in terms of a million soul city.

Article 389 – New Jerusalem

1356. ***New Jerusalem*** is the effective name given to the intentionaly rebuilt parts of London from the early 18th Century, including the various mythology associated with the prophecies within the contemporary King James Bible of the "Rebuilding of the Third Temple". New Jerusalem

1357. ***The Temple***, also known as the Inner, Middle and Outer Temple, also known as the Inner and Middle Temple is a historic and secret The Temple ecclesiastical, legal and financial structure established from no earlier than 1714, but claimed from much older provenance whereby a "guild" of lawyers trained lawyers as members of four (4) Inns being the Lincoln Inn, Grays Inn, Inner Temple and Middle Temple; and effectively were granted control of a new court system as well as the purchase and control of the Court of Chancery:-

(i) Since the 10th Century, the Danish lords of Daneland (south and east England) granted the "Knights Templar" former grounds and surrounds west from Arundel St and the boundaries of the Thames and Fleet St east to the boundary of Bouverie St and Temple Ave; and

(ii) Similar to all banking compounds, the Knights Templar commissioned significant and imposing stone defences and walls to be erected around its London land holding, completed by 1194, with two (2) minor entrances to the east and west, one (1) major entrance from the docks and area onto the Thames (now known as the Middle Temple Gatehouse) and the primary land gate located at the beginning of Fleet St near St Clement Danes known as Bar Gate, or simply the Bar; and

(iii) Within the walled compound known collectively as "The Temple", the Knights Templar created a massive wall following the path of Essex St dividing the western compound and the "Bar Gate" from the eastern remainder of the compound. This became known as the Outer Temple and was the walled compound in which banking, money changing, conveyances, loans and credit were conducted via entrance from the north or "Bar Gate". By tradition, a merchant or trader had to be "admitted to the Bar" in order to engage in commerce within the walled compound known as the "Outer Temple"; and

(iv) A second internal wall was also constructed dividing the Outer Temple to the west from the north eastern part of the Temple compound following the Middle Temple Lane. This internal divide separated the Outer Temple from the Middle Temple area and the "Inner Temple" to the north east corner. The Middle Temple area then housed warehouses, markets were erected connected from the south gate (Middle Temple Gate) and the warehouses and docks for merchants. The Middle Temple was therefore for wholesale trade and business between merchants of the sea and the bank; and

(v) The Inner Temple to the North East corner was only accessible by an internal gate from the Middle Temple and the East Gate and was the main treasure vaults, chancery of documents and accommodation for banking staff, mercenaries and visiting nobles. This is the site of what is known as the Temple Church; and

(vi) It is claimed that in 1608 James I Stuart (1603-1625) granted the Temple lands jointly to the Lincoln's Inn and Gray's Inn as a Royal Peculiar. However, the bizarre concept of beer taverns (inns) becoming common courts was not invented until the start of the 18th Century to quell civil unrest. Similarly, the claim that in 1673, the Inner and Middle Temple as well as the Lincoln's Inn and Gray's Inn successfully purchased the Temple property as well as the property upon which both the Lincoln's Inn and Gray's Inn reside from Charles II Stuart (1660-1685) as a non-Royal Peculiar owned as absolute Allodium in perpetuity, free from any rent, taxes or claims for £666 including the purchase of the Court of Chancery seems equally far fetched and absurd.

Article 390 – King James Bible (KJB)

1358. The ***Authorized Version***, commonly known as the King James Bible (KJB) first published in 1611 – then subsequently significantly modified and reedited in later editions – is a pseudo Christian Bible wholly plagiarised from the Douay–Rheims Bible first created by the Jesuit English College based at Douai, France and the Jesuits at Reims. The Jesuits based the Douay–Rheims Bible on fusing three (3) wholly disparate sets of sacred texts into one (1) being: (1) the wholesale corruption of the Bibliographe or βιβλιογράφη first officially published by Constantine in 326 CE; and (2) the infamous and unholy Septuaginta of Iudaeism (Judaism) by Emperor Vespasian as "Lucifer" from 71 CE; and (3) elements of the Jewish Talmud, first invented in Venice by the 14th Century.

King James Bible (KJB)

1359. The major features of the King James Bible, as reflected in other coordinated publications by the Venetian "Protestant" movement were:-

Key Elements of King James Bible

(i) The insertion of the Septuaginta as part of the "Old Testament", corrupting the original Christian teachings considering the Septuaginta to be the most unholy of works; and

(ii) The Creation of the Gospels, including the "Gospel of the Wolf (Luke)" as key; and

(iii) The wholesale re-writing of the Epistles of the Christian Church to become the writings of the head Satanist of Tarsus

(Ancient Greek for Hell) known as Paul as the "anti-Christ" to the Gospel teachings of Christ; and

(iv) The return of Mithraic symbols of crucifixion, blood sacrifice in the story of Jesus, including the return of the Osiris mythology of rising from the dead; and

(v) The creation of a new "elite" class called the Jews, being the deliberate corruption of the true history of the Yahudi; and

(vi) The creation of a purely fictional place called Israel and a fictional people called the Israelites from the work of John Dee and the gods of Isis, Ra and El; and

(vii) The conversion of the sacred name for the Divine in Christianity known as Yahovah (YHVH) to "God", the Persian public name for Sabaoth, also known as Satan, so that the whole King James Bible became a worship of Satan as Lord of Mundi (Underworld) by the ignorant.

Article 391 – New Rome

1360. ***New Rome*** is the fundamental purpose, design and function of the artificial city known as Washington DC from the beginning of its construction from 1864, following the decisive victory of Gettysburg by July 4, 1863, through the intentional massacre of up to 9,000 Confederate soldiers and 10,000 Union soldiers at Cemetery Ridge through the deployment of up to 150 Gatling Machine Guns mounted on the back of wagons along the ridge, firing for several hours. New Rome

1361. Under the model of Washington as New Rome and the birthplace of the religion of Secularism from 1863 until its rapid decline at the end of the 20th Century:- Washington as the New Rome of a New Religion of Secularism

(i) The State is the New Religion as Father/Mother, with Politicians, Judges and Academics as the High Priests and various Orders; and

(ii) Secularism has historically been seen by its acolytes as the "only enlightened form of governance". Thus, everything is justified in its permeation around the world, including historic levels of propaganda, wars, assassinations, corruption, nepotism and every other form of evil, given "the end justifies the means"; and

(iii) The Government of each nation is "free" to choose one of the several "denominations" of Secularism from Capitalism, Fascism, to Socialism and Communism. Some of these may require substantial funding and assistance to grow and thrive, such as the billions in United States financial aid in funding the creation of the Soviet Union from 1922 to 1933, or the many billions in Wall Street investment in creating, building and helping arm Nazi Germany from 1926 until the end of World War II; and

(iv) To ensure compliance, every country was coerced into bankruptcy, to comply with the American model of global finance. Any country or government choosing to rebel was to be crushed and destroyed, until some (such as China and now Russia) have managed to escape. Only America is able to print as much money as it wants, draining the collective value of all other countries, bound to its global financial controls. The only two levers limiting an every growing "orgy" of US spending being (1) the debt ceiling and (2) the budget bills; and

(v) Most importantly, Secularism requires the world be in constant turmoil, war, terror and fear, so that only governments run by Secular Acolytes and High Priests are seen as the solution. Given, most people and states tend towards peaceful resolution of disputes, this means the United States since 1863 has had to constantly design, train, fund, maintain and then destroy many dozens of "enemy regimes" and many hundreds of dictators – all created by the United States Governments over the decades to justify an insane, unsustainable and wickedly evil false claim of sovereign power and authority.

1362. Ucadia has instituted societies, bodies and entities in support of seeing the peaceful transition of the United States to a sustainable model of governance, consistent with what it claims to be through the Declaration of Independence and Constitution:- Washington DC and Ucadia

(i) Ucadia seeks peaceful, amicable and harmonious relations with the United States and its institutions to assist in the reconciliation of a history of crimes against humanity, blasphemy and wicked evil against its own people and the people of the world; and

(ii) Through proper treaties and agreements with Ucadia, the United States of America shall be recognised as possessing the full authority and power it claims through its "founding documents" for the betterment of the world. However, until such treaties and peaceful arrangements are fully realised, the United States of America is wholly without any legitimate moral, legal or spiritual authority.

Title XII – Original Nations (Tribes)

12.1 – Original Nations, Civilisations & Empires

Article 392 – Original Nations (Tribes)

1363. An ***Original Nation (Tribe)*** is a significant community of people originating from a traditional bounded area of land, having long standing continuous human habitation, and association to one or more ancient covenants of law, culture and rights recognised under Civilised Ucadia and Non-Ucadia Law. An Original Nation (Tribe) has no legitimacy or validity in law, unless it is duly registered and possesses a proper mandate under Ucadia Law. Original Nations (Tribes)

1364. In reference to the use of the word *nation* and *tribe* in respect of Original Nations (Tribes):- Nation and Tribe

(i) *Nation* originates from Latin *natio* meaning "a group of people bound together by common characteristics, including birth, language, customs, and culture"; and

(ii) *Tribe* originates from ancient Irish *tríbe* meaning literally "three (or more) be united" and "a group of people with common characteristics, cultures, or affiliations"; and

(iii) As both words share common characteristics, they are united in the description of Original Nations, with the word tribe placed in brackets, to indicate groups smaller than claimed international states and countries.

1365. A properly registered body claiming to be an Original Nation (Tribe), possessing a current mandate under Ucadia Law, is a valid Sovereign Body and Community, superior in all and every aspect to an Uncivilised regime, or body or corporation claiming authority through oppression, occupation, and morally repugnant behaviour. Sovereignty of properly registered Original Nation (Tribe)

1366. In respect of administrative divisions of government and authority within Ucadia Societies such as Unions, Universities, Provinces, Campuses and Foundations:- Original Nation (Tribe) and Ucadia Administrative Divisions

(i) ***Original Nation (Tribe) always smaller than University***: A valid Original Nation (Tribe) under Ucadia Law is always smaller than the second largest administrative division of government and authority known as a Ucadia University; and

(ii) ***Original Nation (Tribe) usually smaller than Province***: A valid Original Nation (Tribe) under Ucadia Law is usually smaller than the third largest administrative division of government and authority known as a Ucadia Province; and

(iii) ***Original Nation (Tribe) usually equal to Campus***: A valid Original Nation (Tribe) under Ucadia Law is usually equal to the smallest administrative division of government and authority known as a Ucadia Campus.

1367. Common elements of a valid Sovereign Original Nation (Tribe) include (but are not limited to):- Key elements of a Sovereign Original Nation (Tribe)

(i) ***Significant community of people***: Means a community of more than a few thousand and less than a few million; and

(ii) ***Long standing continuous human habitation***: Means a location where humans have lived for a long period of time, usually for several thousands of years; and

(iii) ***Traditional bounded area of land***: Means a defined boundary for the area of land that is recognised as having some tradition and historic context, even if it also associated with some Non-Ucadia body politic or corporate; and

(iv) ***Association to one or more ancient covenants of law***: Means that one or more ancient covenants of law, as defined in accord with Ucadia Law have been associated with the location for an extended period of time, even if such forms of law and culture are no longer recognised by Non-Ucadian societies and governments; and

(v) ***Registration under Ucadia***: Means a provisional, probational or permanent government of an Original Nation (Tribe) has no authority, rights nor legitimacy unless duly registered under Ucadia Law as a complete and perfected new Civilisation; and

(vi) ***Current Mandate under Ucadia Law***: Means that even if an Original Nation (Tribe) was originally registered under Ucadia, a current mandate is still required to validate that the government and administration of the Original Nation (Tribe) to be in good standing.

1368. An individual Person born within the bounds of a valid Original Nation (Tribe), or whose direct blood ancestor was born within those same bounds, shall by innate right be entitled to be a member of that same Original Nation (Tribe) in accord with the following essential criteria, including (but not limited to):- Right as Member of Original Nation

(i) ***Born of Land is connected to Land***: Ucadia Law recognises that a person born to a certain location is forever connected in a meaningful way to the place of their birth. This birthright can never be extinguished, waived, sold or abrogated; and

(ii) ***Family from Land is connection to Land***: Means that when an individual Persons blood related mother, or father (or in some circumstances grandfather or grandmother etc.) is from a particular Land, then a family is connected in a meaningful way to such a location, even if they have never visited, or even are ignorant of their own family history and culture; and

(iii) ***Full Member is directly born of land***: Means a full member of an Original Nation is an individual person directly born within the bounds of the particular location, regardless of family ethnicity, race, religion, gender, sexuality or political ideology. An individual can only be a full member of only one Original Nation (Tribe); and

(iv) ***Associate Member is when a parent or ancestor born of land***: Means an individual person whose blood parent (or direct blood ancestor) was born within the bounds of the particular location. An individual can be an associate member of one or more Original Nations (Tribes); and

(v) ***Original Nation has right to limit number of generations to qualify as associate member***: Means that an Original Nation (Tribe) has the right to limit the number of generations to qualify as associate member from a minimum of one (blood parents) to a maximum of four (great great grandparents).

1369. An individual Person born within the bounds of a valid Original Nation (Tribe) may qualify as an officer and representative of the government of the Original Nation (Tribe) in accord with the following essential criteria, including (but not limited to):- Qualification as Officer and Representative of Original Nation

(i) ***Mental and Intellectual Competence***: Means the individual has clearly demonstrated their mental and intellectual competence, especially in knowledge of Ucadia and Ucadia Law; and

(ii) ***Emotional and Empathetic Capacity***: Means the individual has the emotional maturity and empathetic capacity to function in such a position of trust; and

(iii) ***Financial Stability***: Means the individual is financially stable and not otherwise insolvent or an undischarged bankrupt; and

(iv) ***Not Otherwise Disqualified or Ineligible***: Means an individual is not otherwise disqualified or ineligible from applying to fulfil an office or representation of an Original Nation due to a previous disqualification, or minimum age, or ongoing serious criminal matters within Ucadia or Non-Ucadia jurisdiction.

Article 393 – Original Law & Original Nations

1370. ***Original Law & Original Nations*** refers to the fact that only a properly formed Original Nation (Tribe) has right and access to *Original Law*, being the first "law of the land" above and ahead of any other lesser claim from a Non-Ucadia society, body, government, military or agency. Original Law & Original Nations

1371. ***Original Law*** is a recognised Sacred Covenant between an Authentic, Apostolic and Anointed Divine Messenger of the Divine Creator of all Existence and all the Heavens and Earth and the peoples of the Earth, that provides some form of moral direction, teaching and rules. Thus, as all proper law is ultimately derived from Divine Law, valid *Original Law* is first in order, bearing its own authority; and not deriving authority from an outside or lesser Non-Ucadian source. Original Law

1372. Contrary to deliberately false, invalid and absurd arguments, *Original Law* does not mean the first laws of any given claimed sovereign body, or body politic or corporate, or those laws passed by such a body or corporation:- Invalid and absurd claims of Original Law

(i) ***Governing Law and Instruments not Original Law***: Means the first laws of any claimed sovereign body, or body politic or corporate are its governing laws or governing instruments in an original form. Whilst technically the "first laws" of such a body or corporation, it does not come anywhere close to the Divine, Revelatory and Historic Civilised Nature of valid Original Law; and

(ii) ***Original Form of Law not Original Law***: Means that a law as originally passed or made or reprinted or published is an "original form of law" of that given claimed sovereign body, or body politic or corporate. To then misrepresent "original form" as *Original Law* is an absurdity or deliberately dishonest, deceitful and false.

Article 394 - Original Authority & Original Nations

Original Authority & Original Nations

1373. ***Original Authority & Original Nations*** refers to the fact that only a properly formed Original Nation (Tribe) has the rights of *Original Authority*, being the first "authority of office" and "authority, rights and powers" above and ahead of any other lesser claim from a Non-Ucadia society, body, government, military or agency.

Original Authority

1374. ***Original Authority*** is the recognised rights, positions and powers given by a valid Divine Mandate through a recognised Sacred Covenant to one or more persons concerning the right to direct, teach, demand or control someone or something. Thus, as all proper authority and office is ultimately derived from Divine Law, valid *Original Authority* is first in rights, positions and power; and not deriving authority, rights or powers from an outside or lesser Non-Ucadian source.

Invalid and absurd claims of Original Law

1375. Contrary to deliberately false, invalid and absurd arguments, *Original Authority* does not mean the first claimed rights or powers or positions of any given claimed sovereign body, or body politic or corporate through its governing instruments, or those laws passed by such a body or corporation:-

(i) ***First Claims of Rights and Powers not Original Authority***: Means the first claims of rights and powers of any claimed sovereign body, or body politic or corporate are defined by its governing laws or governing instruments. Whilst technically the "first authority" of such a body or corporation, it does not come anywhere near to a Divine Mandate as granted through a valid Sacred Covenant that is clearly self evident and connected to Divine Revelation and valid Original Law; and

(ii) ***Original Delegated Authority not Original Authority***: Means that an authority or power as originally delegated is an "original delegated authority" and not an Original Authority. To then misrepresent "original delegated authority" as *Original Authority* is an absurdity or deliberately dishonest, deceitful and false. Any police officer or police service or courts culpable of such fraud and perfidy may be prosecuted under Ucadia Criminal Laws.

Article 395 - Original Registers & Original Nations

1376. ***Original Registers & Original Nations*** refers to the fact that only a properly formed Original Nation (Tribe) has the right to manage *Original Registers*, being the first jurisdiction, claim, title, property and dominion above and ahead of any other less claim from a Non-Ucadia society, body, government, military or agency. Original Registers & Original Nations

1377. ***Original Register*** is a recognised book, table or roll authorised by a valid Divine Mandate through a recognised Sacred Covenant, for the original recording of events, rights, dominion, property, persons, title or claims then relied upon in the administration of rights, powers, property, obligations, agreements, assets or disputes. Thus, as all money, property and rights are ultimately derived from Divine Law, valid *Original Registers* are the first recordings of events, rights, dominions, property, title, persons, positions and power; and not derived from an outside or lesser Non-Ucadian register. Original Registers

1378. Contrary to deliberately false, invalid and absurd arguments, *Original Registers* does not mean the registers of any given claimed sovereign body, or body politic or corporate through its governing instruments, or those laws passed by such a body or corporation:- Invalid and absurd claims of Original Registers

(i) ***Primary Register not Original Register***: Means the primary registers of any claimed sovereign body, or body politic or corporate are defined by its governing laws or governing instruments. Whilst technically the "first registers" of such a body or corporation, it does not mean that such a register possesses any Divine Mandate as granted through a valid Sacred Covenant to record such events, rights, property, agreements or persons; and

(ii) ***First Registration not Original Registration***: Means that a first or earliest claimed registration or "first in time" does not mean an Original Registration or superior registration. To then misrepresent "first registration" as *Original Registration* is an absurdity or deliberately dishonest, deceitful and false. Any such misrepresentation has no force or effect in law.

Article 396 – Original Administration & Original Nations

1379. ***Original Administration & Original Nations*** refers to the fact that only a properly formed Original Nation (Tribe) has the first right of *Original Administration* and *Original Jurisdiction;* and to assign, or withdraw such powers and authorities to qualified and competent Original Administration & Original Nations officers and elected officials within the framework of Ucadia Societies or Non-Ucadia Civilised Societies that recognise the immutable authority of original law, original authority, original registers and original administration.

1380. ***Original Administration*** is cumulative powers and authority of first or primary government of any given sovereign state or authority. Properly constituted and mandated Original Nations (Tribes) are unique in having undisputed *Original Administration* in both Ucadia and Non-Ucadia civilisations. Original Administration

1381. ***Original Jurisdiction*** is the scope and limit of authority of a political or judicial body, or judicial or law enforcement officer to pursue or decide matters of law. By innate right, Ucadia possesses *Original Jurisdiction* over all its persons, events and matters of Law. Original Jurisdiction

1382. Within Ucadia Law and properly constituted Original Nations (Tribes), the political administration of a collective sovereign state occurs through the temporary vesting and assigning of powers and authority to a central body as "executive government" to function in accord with their mandate for the benefit of the nation and its citizens:- Key elements of Original Administration

(i) The primary function of Original Nations (Tribes) is to support and strengthen competent government for the benefit of a given nation, by strengthening the foundations and mandate of such authority; and

(ii) It is never the role of individual or collective Original Nations (Tribes) to usurp the function of executive government of a given nation. Rather, the Original Administration Powers and Authorities of the Original Nations (Tribes) of a given country or sovereign state are temporarily vested to the new executive government at the conclusion of a valid and proper election; and

(iii) It is only in those instances where the integrity of a sovereign state or country are threatened by incompetent or corrupt government or administrative behaviour where the collective Original Nations (Tribes) may censure a government or official, or suspend the authority and powers of the government, forcing a new election.

1383. Contrary to deliberately false, invalid and absurd arguments, *Original Jurisdiction* does not mean the control of a matter first filed in a given jurisdiction or the right of a court in that jurisdiction to be the first to hear a legal case:- Invalid and absurd claims of Original Jurisdiction

(i) ***Claim of Authority not Original Jurisdiction***: Means that the claim of a court that it has the power or authority to hear a matter, simply means "first claim" not Original Jurisdiction. Unless such a claim is properly heard and adjudicated in a public and competent forum of law, then such a claim, even if upheld is an injury against proper justice; and

(ii) ***First Registration not Original Jurisdiction***: Means that a first or earliest claimed registration or "first in time" does not mean an Original Jurisdiction or superior position under valid law. Regardless of whether a matter concerning a person or property or matter under the custody or authority of Ucadia is registered in a Non-Ucadia jurisdiction first, Ucadia and its courts shall have Original Jurisdiction.

12.2 – Original Nations & Sacred Covenants of Original Law

Article 397 - Sacred Covenants of Original Law

1384. ***Sacred Covenant of Original Law*** is a recognised Sacred Covenant between an Authentic, Apostolic and Anointed Divine Messenger of the Divine Creator of all Existence and all the Heavens and Earth and the peoples of the Earth; and acknowledged as having merit, authority, power and jurisdiction above other lesser claims of law by custom and tradition. Sacred Covenants of Original Law

1385. Authentic living transmission, accomplished under the authority and power of the Divine Creator is called ***Tradition*** since it is distinct from Sacred Scripture itself, whilst closely connected to it. Through Tradition, each generation in life and reverence for the Golden Rule of Law, may then perpetuate and transmit to every other generation all that is trusted as the most valuable and important of knowledge. Tradition

1386. Ucadia recognises thirty-three (33) Sacred Covenants between Authentic, Apostolic and Anointed Divine Messengers of the Divine Creator of all Existence and all the Heavens and Earth, namely: Tradition of the Thirty-Three Sacred Covenants of Heaven

(i) "**De Dea Magisterium**" of the Serpens (Creators); and

(ii) "**Yapa**" of the Pacific Saltwater People; and

(iii) "**Mandi**" of the African Plains People; and

(iv) "**Tia**" of the Asiatic Mountain People; and

(v) "**Waiata**" of the Pacific Sea People; and

(vi) "**Adamus**" of Prometheus and the Cuilliaéan; and

(vii) "**Nana**" of the Mother Goddess of Heaven and Earth; and

(viii) "**Alma**" of South Arabia, East Africa and India; and

(ix) "**Elohim**" of Abraham and Patriarchs of Ebla; and

(x) "**Kabalaah**" of Akhenaten (Moses) and the Yahudi; and

(xi) "**Revelations**" of the thirty-three Great Prophets of Yeb; and

(xii) "**Tara**" of Jeremiah and the Celts; and

(xiii) "**Five Worlds**" of North-Central America; and

(xiv) "**Missal**" of Baal Mithra; and

(xv) "**Acadia**" of Xerxes; and

(xvi) "**Eliada**" of Alexander; and

(xvii) "**Tabiti**" of Great Asiatic Plains People; and

(xviii) "**Tiandi**" (Heaven and Earth) of Qin Shi Huang; and

(xix) "**Nazara (Truth)**" of Yahusiah (Jesus Christ); and

(xx) "**Nirvana**" (Freedom & Awakening) of Gautama (Buddha); and

(xxi) "**Zhongdao**" (The Middle Way) of Kong Qiu (Confucius); and

(xxii) "**Septuaginta**" of Iudaism (Josephus); and

(xxiii) "**Eucadia**" of Heracles; and

(xxiv) "**Kikilil Yuum Witzil**" (Great Cycle of Celestial Realm and Earth) of South-Central America; and

(xxv) "**Digesta**" of Marcus Aurelius; and

(xxvi) "**Sanatana Dharma**" (Eternal Truth) of Brahman (Hinduism); and

(xxvii) "**Bibliographe**" of Christianity of Constantine; and

(xxviii) "**Dao**" (the Way); and

(xxix) "**Kami Yoso Seimei**" (Spirits of Elements and Life) of the way of Shinto (Japan); and

(xxx) "**Quran Al Sufian**" (Recitations of Wisdom of the Way)" of The Great Prophet (Islam); and

(xxxi) "**Holy Bible**" of Catholicism of the Franks; and

(xxxii) "**Eternal Truth**" of Gurmat (Sikhism); and

(xxxiii)"**Lebor Clann Glas**" of the true Holly Diaspora.

1387. In accord with the most sacred Covenant *Pactum De Singularis Caelum*, the thirty-three (33) Covenants between Authentic, Apostolic and Anointed Divine Messengers of the Divine Creator of all Existence and all the Heavens and Earth and the peoples of the Earth are entrusted as the "**Authentic Sacred Deposit of Trust**", contained in Sacred Canonical Scripture and Tradition, to the embodiment of Ucadia and no other.

Authentic Sacred Deposit of Trust

Article 398 - De Dea Magisterium Covenant of the Serpens (Creators)

1388. The Covenant of ***De Dea Magisterium*** of the Serpens (Creators) embodies in sacred trust the complete consciousness, culture, languages, rules, symbols, rituals, laws and rights of the Serpens as the creators of Homo Prometheus, the "horned ones", that chose to integrate within the Homo Sapien species in the form of the Cuilliaéan, to help free the Homo Sapien species of its programming and condemnation by the Griseo Morbidus (Standard Grey) and Griseo Altus (Tall Grey) as architects of the Homo Robustus, the Homo Habilis and Homo Sapiens.

Covenant of De Dea Magisterium of the Serpens (Creators)

1389. *De Dea Magisterium* represents the uninterrupted and unextinguished Original Law and Original Rights of the Original Nations (Tribes) that have always been present upon the lands now known as Ireland. The complete consciousness, culture, languages, rules, symbols, rituals, laws and rights of the first cultures and traditional owners of hominid species of Ireland embodied within the Covenant of De Dea Magisterium of the Serpens is irrevocably entrusted through the Authentic Sacred Deposit of Trust, to the embodiment and organs of the most sacred Covenant *Pactum De Singularis Caelum* and no other.

De Dea Magisterium as Original Law and Rights of Original Nations (Tribes)

Article 399 - Yapa Covenant of the Saltwater People

1390. The Covenant of ***Yapa*** of the Saltwater People embodies in sacred trust the complete consciousness, culture, languages, rules, symbols, rituals, laws and rights of the first cultures and traditional owners of hominid species of South-East Asia, Australia and parts of the Pacific.

Covenant of Yapa of the Saltwater People

The *Saltwater People* are the aggregate of the first cultures and traditional owners of hominid species of South-East Asia, Australia and parts of the Pacific beginning in the mid-Palaeolithic period and rising to a high culture of law, language and knowledge during the Mesolithic period.

1391. *Yapa* represents the uninterrupted and unextinguished Original Law and Original Rights of the Original Nations (Tribes) that have always been present upon the lands now known as Australia, West Papua, Papua New Guinea, Solomon Islands, Vanuatu, New Caledonia and Fiji. The complete consciousness, culture, languages, rules, symbols, rituals, laws and rights of the first cultures and traditional owners of hominid species of South-East Asia, Australia and parts of the Pacific embodied within the Covenant of Yapa of the Saltwater People is irrevocably entrusted through the Authentic Sacred Deposit of Trust, to the embodiment and organs of the most sacred Covenant *Pactum De Singularis Caelum* and no other.

Yapa as Original Law and Rights of Original Nations (Tribes)

Article 400 – Mandi Covenant of the Africa Plains People

1392. The Covenant of ***Mandi*** of the Africa Plains People embodies in sacred trust the complete consciousness, culture, languages, rules, symbols, rituals, laws and rights of the first cultures and traditional owners of hominid species of the ancient African Lakes, Great River and Fertile Plains of Northern Africa and the whole of Africa.

Covenant of Mandi of the Africa Plains People

The *Africa Plains People* of planet Earth are the aggregate of the first cultures and traditional owners of hominid species of Africa beginning in the mid-Palaeolithic period and rising to a high culture of law, language and knowledge during the Mesolithic period.

1393. *Mandi* represents the uninterrupted and unextinguished Original Law and Original Rights of the Original Nations (Tribes) that have always been present upon the lands now known as Algeria, Angola, Benin, Botswana, Burkina Faso, Burundi, Cameroon, Cape Verde, Central African Republic, Chad, Comoros, Democratic Republic of the Congo (Kinshasa), Djibouti, Equatorial Guinea, Eritrea, Ethiopia, Gabon, Gambia, Ghana, Guinea, Guinea-Bissau, Ivory Coast, Kenya, Lesotho, Liberia, Libya, Madagascar, Malawi, Mali, Mauritania, Morocco, Mozambique, Namibia, Niger, Nigeria, Republic of the Congo (Brazzaville), Réunion, Rwanda, São Tomé and Príncipe, Senegal, Seychelles, Sierra Leone, Somalia, South Africa, South Sudan, Sudan, Swaziland, Tanzania, Togo, Tunisia, Uganda, Western Sahara, Zambia and Zimbabwe. The complete consciousness, culture, languages, rules, symbols, rituals, laws and rights of the first cultures and traditional owners of hominid species of Africa embodied within the Covenant of *Mandi* of the Africa Plains People is entrusted

Mandi as Original Law and Rights of Original Nations (Tribes)

through the Authentic Sacred Deposit of Trust, to the embodiment and organs of the most sacred Covenant *Pactum De Singularis Caelum* and no other.

Article 401 – Tia
Covenant of the Asiatic Mountain People

1394. The Covenant of ***Tia*** of the Asiatic Mountain People embodies in sacred trust the complete consciousness, culture, languages, rules, symbols, rituals, laws and rights of the first cultures and traditional owners of hominid species of mountainous Asia and the Indian sub continent. Covenant of Tia of the Asiatic Mountain People

The *Asiatic Mountain People* are the aggregate of the first cultures and traditional owners of hominid species of mountainous Asia and the Indian sub continent beginning in the mid-Paleolithic period and rising to a high culture of law, language and knowledge during the Mesolithic period.

1395. *Tia* represents the uninterrupted and unextinguished Original Law and Original Rights of the Original Nations (Tribes) that have always been present upon the lands now known as Iran, Afghanistan, Pakistan, Tajikistan, Kyrgyzstan, Tibet, Kashmir (India), Mongolia, Qinchai (China), Sichuan (China), Yunnan (China), Nepal and Bhutan. The complete consciousness, culture, languages, rules, symbols, rituals, laws and rights of the first cultures and traditional owners of hominid species of mountainous Asia and the Indian sub continent embodied within the Covenant of Tia of the Asiatic Mountain People is entrusted through the Authentic Sacred Deposit of Trust, to the embodiment and organs of the most sacred Covenant *Pactum De Singularis Caelum* and no other. Tia as Original Law and Rights of Original Nations (Tribes)

Article 402 – Waiata
Covenant of the Sea People

1396. The Covenant of ***Waiata*** of the Sea People embodies in sacred trust the complete consciousness, culture, languages, rules, symbols, rituals, laws and rights of the cultures and traditional owners of hominid species of the Pacific and Asia. Covenant of Waiata of the Sea People of Asia and Pacific

The *Sea People of Asia and Pacific* are the aggregate of the cultures and traditional owners of hominid species of the Pacific and Asia beginning in the Mesolithic period and rising to a high culture of law, language and knowledge during the Neolithic period.

1397. *Waiata* represents the uninterrupted and unextinguished Original Law and Original Rights of the Original Nations (Tribes) that have Waiata as Original Law always been present upon the lands now known as Aotearoa (New Zealand), Hawaii, Samoa, Tonga, Tuvalu, Polynesia (France), Cook Islands (New Zealand), Tokelau (New Zealand) and Hawaiki (Easter Island). The complete consciousness, culture, languages, rules, symbols, rituals, laws and rights of the cultures and traditional owners of hominid species of the Pacific and Asia embodied within the Covenant of *Waiata* of the Sea People is entrusted through the Authentic Sacred Deposit of Trust, to the embodiment and organs of the most sacred Covenant *Pactum De Singularis Caelum* and no other.

and Rights of Original Nations (Tribes)

Article 403 – Adamus Covenant of the Prometheus & Cuilliaéan

1398. The Covenant of ***Adamus*** of Homo Prometheus and the Cuilliaéan embodies in sacred trust the complete consciousness, culture, languages, rules, symbols, rituals, laws and rights of the Cuilliaéan as the first sons and daughters of men; and the founders of the first empires; and the historic emissaries and representatives of the Griseo Morbidus (Standard Grey), the Cerastis Sapiens (Horned Reptoids), the Serpens Sophos (Smooth Skinned Reptoids), the Griseo Altus (Tall Grey) and the Serpens Alatus (Winged Reptoids).

Covenant of Adamus of Prometheus and the Cuilliaéan

The Cuilliaéan of planet Earth are the strongest blood aggregate and personification within the form of Homo Sapiens of the ancient hominid Homo Prometheus, itself the perfected union of the hominids of planet Earth and the Serpens species of other worlds, emerging at the beginning of the Neolithic period and rising to a high culture of law, religion, language and knowledge during the late Neolithic period.

1399. *Adamus* represents the uninterrupted and unextinguished Original Law and Original Rights of the Original Nations (Tribes) that have always been present upon the lands now known as Ireland (Eire). The complete consciousness, culture, languages, rules, symbols, rituals, laws and rights of the first cultures and traditional owners of hominid species of Homo Sapiens of the ancient hominid Homo Prometheus embodied within the Covenant of *Adamus* of the Cuilliaéan are entrusted through the Authentic Sacred Deposit of Trust, to the embodiment and organs of the most sacred Covenant *Pactum De Singularis Caelum* and no other.

Adamus as Original Law and Rights of Original Nations (Tribes)

Article 404 – Nana Covenant of the Mother Goddess of Heaven & Earth

1400. The Covenant of ***Nana*** of the Mother Goddess of Heaven and Earth embodies in sacred trust the complete consciousness, culture, languages, rules, symbols, rituals, laws and rights of the worship of the feminine as goddess and Queen and Mother of Heaven of ancient Mesopotamian and Near-East Cultures.

Covenant of Nana of the Mother Goddess of Heaven and Earth

The most ancient reverence of the feminine personification of planet Earth, or Life and Spirit in the form of Queen and Mother of Heaven exists through many cultures, peoples and religions from the earliest city-states of Sumeria and Syria, even to the present day.

1401. *Nana* represents the uninterrupted and unextinguished Original Law and Original Rights of the Original Nations (Tribes) that have always been present upon the lands now known as Turkey, Georgia, Azerbaijan, Syria, Lebanon, Iraq, Iran, Kuwait, Oman, Yemen, UAE, Qatar, Bahrain, Saudi Arabia, Jordan and Palestine. The complete consciousness, culture, languages, rules, symbols, rituals, laws and rights of the cultures and peoples embodied within the Covenant of *Nana* as Queen and Mother of Heaven are entrusted through the Authentic Sacred Deposit of Trust, to the embodiment and organs of the most sacred Covenant *Pactum De Singularis Caelum* and no other.

Nana as Original Law and Rights of Original Nations (Tribes)

Article 405 – Alma
Covenant of the Gardens of Eden (Southern Arabia)

1402. The Covenant of ***Alma*** of the Mother Goddess embodies in sacred trust the complete consciousness, culture, languages, rules, symbols, rituals, laws and rights of the worship of the feminine as goddess and Queen of ancient southern Arabia, East Africa and Indus Valley (India).

Covenant of Alma of South Arabia, East Africa and India

1403. *Alma* represents the uninterrupted and unextinguished Original Law and Original Rights of the Original Nations (Tribes) that have always been present upon the lands now known as Yemen, Western India, Bangladesh and Ethiopia. The complete consciousness, culture, languages, rules, symbols, rituals, laws and rights of the cultures and peoples embodied within the Covenant of *Alma* as Queen are entrusted through the Authentic Sacred Deposit of Trust, to the embodiment and organs of the most sacred Covenant *Pactum De Singularis Caelum* and no other.

Alma as Original Law and Rights of Original Nations (Tribes)

Article 406 – Elohim
Covenant of Abraham and Patriarchs of Ebla

1404. The Covenant of ***Elohim*** of Abraham and the Patriarchs embodies in sacred trust the complete consciousness, culture, languages, rules, symbols, rituals, laws and rights of the first cultures and traditional owners of Ebla and the regions of Syria, the Levant and Mesopotamia.

Covenant of Elohim of Abraham and Patriarchs of Ebla

The city of Ebla in northern Syria represented one of the greatest cities of human civilisation and the cradle of high culture, knowledge and religion more than four and a half thousand years ago. It is by tradition, the birthplace of some of the greatest Patriarchs of antiquity including, but not limited to Ab-ra-mu (Abraham), E-sa-um (Esau), Ish-ma-ilu (Ishmael), Da-'u'dum (David) and Sa-'u-lum (Saul), later to be overshadowed by the city of Urgarit.

1405. *Elohim* represents the uninterrupted and unextinguished Original Law and Original Rights of the Original Nations (Tribes) that have always been present upon the lands now known as Syria, Jordan, Lebanon and Palestine. The complete consciousness, culture, languages, rules, symbols, rituals, laws and rights of the first cultures and traditional owners of Ebla and the regions of Syria, the Levant and Mesopotamia embodied within the Covenant of *Elohim* of Abraham and the Patriarchs is entrusted through the Authentic Sacred Deposit of Trust, to the embodiment and organs of the most

Elohim as Original Law and Rights of Original Nations (Tribes)

sacred Covenant *Pactum De Singularis Caelum* and no other.

Article 407 – Kabalaah
Covenant of Akhenaten (Moses) and the Hyksos

1406. The Covenant of ***KaBaLaAh*** of Akhenaten (Moses) and the Yahudi embodies in sacred trust the complete consciousness, culture, languages, rules, symbols, rituals, laws and rights of the Hyksos in honouring supremacy of the Divine Creator of all existence; and the spirits of the Earth; and in acknowledging the positive influence and wisdom of the Serpens and the repudiation of the Griseo Morbidus (Standard Grey) and Griseo Altus (Tall Grey).

Covenant of Kabalaah of Akhenaten (Moses) and the Hyksos

The Hyksos culture of planet Earth is a successor of the Cuilliaéan culture as the strongest blood aggregate and personification within the form of Homo Sapiens of the ancient hominid Homo Prometheus, itself the perfected union of the hominids of planet Earth and the serpens species of other worlds, emerging in Egypt from around 1800 BCE and rising to a high culture of law, religion, language and knowledge by the beginning of the reign of Akhenaten around 1350 BCE.

It is Akhenaten that is Moses and did pledge his symbols of power and authority of Egypt as signs of a new covenant, such as his Ark of the Spirit of Re, to signify the new Ark of the Covenant. Thus all cultures and religions since that place the Ark of the Covenant at the forefront of their claims of authenticity and origin are therefore derived from the Covenant and powers of Akhenaten.

1407. *KaBaLaAh* represents the uninterrupted and unextinguished Original Law and Original Rights of the Original Nations (Tribes) that have always been present upon the lands now known as Egypt, Libya, Sudan, Eritrea, Palestine, Jordan, Arabia, Lebanon and Syria. The complete consciousness, culture, languages, rules, symbols, rituals, laws and rights of the Yahudi embodied within the Covenant of KaBaLaAh of Akhenaten (Moses) and the Yahudi are entrusted through the Authentic Sacred Deposit of Trust, to the embodiment and organs of the most sacred Covenant *Pactum De Singularis Caelum* and no other.

Kabalaah as Original Law and Rights of Original Nations (Tribes)

Article 408 – Revelations
Covenant of the thirty-three Great Prophets of Yeb

1408. The Covenant of ***Revelations*** of the Great Prophets of Yeb embodies in sacred trust the complete consciousness, culture, languages, rules, symbols, rituals, laws and rights of the Great

Covenant of Revelations of the thirty-three Great Prophets

Prophets and Divine Messengers of the ancient world. of Yeb

The Great Prophets of Yeb (Elephantine Island) at Yei-Hu (Yahu) on the Nile River in Upper Egypt, are the oldest and most famous continuous hereditary and apostolic lineage of Divine Messengers of Cuilliaéan blood in the history of the ancient world. As the site of Yei-Hu was the base of the Kabalaah and the Tree of Life between Heaven and Earth, in honour of the primordial mother (Mut) of all Heaven and Earth, the writings of the thirty-three (33) Great prophets of Yeb remains some of the most important scripture of humanity.

The thirty-three (33) Great Prophets of Yeb were Aaroniah, Enociah, Zedekiah, Obadiah, Uvidiah (David), Elijiah, Ahijiah, Azariah, Ananiah, Amoziah, Isaiah, Ezekiah, Amariah, Edaliah, Zephaniah, Ilkiah (Michaiah), Jeremiah, Barukiah, Osiah (Hosea), Osanniah (Hosanna), Eliah, Oadiah, Oananiah, Adiah, Oniah, Eleziah, Elkaniah, Zadokiah, Barachiah, Adoniah (Cu-Roi), Yasiah (Joseph, Cu-Cuileann), Yahusiah (Jesus, Cu-Laoch) and Yahobiah (Jacob).

1409. *Revelations* represents the uninterrupted and unextinguished Original Law and Original Rights of the Original Nations (Tribes) that have always been present upon the lands now known as Egypt, Libya, Sudan, Eritrea, Palestine, Jordan, Arabia, Lebanon and Syria. The complete consciousness, culture, languages, rules, symbols, rituals, laws and rights of the Great Prophets and Divine Messengers of the ancient world embodied within the Covenant of Revelations of the Great Prophets of Yeb is entrusted through the Authentic Sacred Deposit of Trust, to the embodiment and organs of the most sacred Covenant *Pactum De Singularis Caelum* and no other.

Revelations as Original Law and Rights of Original Nations (Tribes)

Article 409 – Tara
Covenant of Jeremiah and the Celts

1410. The Covenant of ***Tara*** of Jeremiah and the Celts embodies in sacred trust the complete consciousness, culture, languages, rules, symbols, rituals, laws and rights of the Celts cultures of Europe and the Middle East.

Covenant of Tara of Jeremiah and the Celts

The Celtic culture of planet Earth is a successor of the Cuilliaéan culture as the embodiment of the oldest priest-king bloodlines of Syria, Mesopotamia, Egypt and Europe and the personification of the greatest messengers of Heaven in the form of the Great Prophets of Yeb as the Sons of Man, the Holly Spirit made flesh and ones anointed (Christs) by Divine Commission to teach, to guide and to admonish the people of planet Earth.

1411. *Tara* represents the uninterrupted and unextinguished Original Law

Tara as Original

and Original Rights of the Original Nations (Tribes) that have always been present upon the lands now known as Ireland (Eire), Great Britain, Spain, Portugal, France, Belgium, Netherlands, Germany, Finland, Sweden, Norway, Iceland and Greenland. The complete consciousness, culture, languages, rules, symbols, rituals, laws and rights embodied within the Covenant of Tara of Jeremiah and the Celts are entrusted through the Authentic Sacred Deposit of Trust, to the embodiment and organs of the most sacred Covenant *Pactum De Singularis Caelum* and no other. Law and Rights of Original Nations (Tribes)

Article 410 - Five Worlds Covenant of North-Central America

1412. The Covenant of ***Five Worlds*** of the People of North-Central America embodies in sacred trust the complete consciousness, culture, languages, rules, symbols, rituals, laws and rights of the cultures and traditional owners of hominid species of North and Central America. Covenant of Five Worlds of North-Central America

The *Five Worlds* of the People of North-Central America are the aggregate of the cultures and traditional owners of hominid species of North America and Central America beginning in the late Mesolithic period and rising to a high culture of law, language and knowledge during the end of the Neolithic period.

1413. *Five Worlds* represents the uninterrupted and unextinguished Original Law and Original Rights of the Original Nations (Tribes) that have always been present upon the lands now known as Canada, St. Pierre and Miquelon, United States of America and Mexico. The complete consciousness, culture, languages, rules, symbols, rituals, laws and rights of the cultures and traditional owners of hominid species of North America and Central America embodied within the Covenant of the Five Worlds of the First Nations is entrusted through the Authentic Sacred Deposit of Trust, to the embodiment and organs of the most sacred Covenant *Pactum De Singularis Caelum* and no other. Five Worlds as Original Law and Rights of Original Nations (Tribes)

Article 411 – Missal Covenant of Baal Mithra

1414. The Covenant of ***Missal*** of Baal Mithra embodies in sacred trust the complete consciousness, culture, languages, rules, symbols, rituals, laws and rights of all sects and versions of Baal and Mithra of the ancient world. Covenant of Missal of Baal Mithra

The ancient worship of Baal as saviour was personified under the

Persian kings and later under Roma in the form of Mithra, borne upon the Ides of Mars (14 Nisan, 14th March) as the lamb of god, the saviour king and bringer of balance and return to harmony of the planet of the ancient world. By the 1st Century CE, the worship and respect of Mithra dominated all other religions as the symbol of all oaths, vows and agreements.

1415. *Missal* represents the uninterrupted and unextinguished Original Law and Original Rights of the Original Nations (Tribes) that have always been present upon the lands now known as Iran, Afghanistan, Turkmenistan, Kuwait, Iraq, Azerbaijan, Armenia, Georgia, Turkey, Syria, Lebanon, Jordan, Palestine, Egypt, Cyprus, Libya, Tunisia, Algeria, Greece, North Macedonia, Albania, Kosovo, Bulgaria, Serbia, Croatia, Slovenia, Austria, Switzerland, Italy, France and Spain. The complete consciousness, culture, languages, rules, symbols, rituals, laws and rights of all sects and versions of Baal and Mithra of the ancient world embodied within the Covenant of Missal of Baal Mithra is entrusted through the Authentic Sacred Deposit of Trust, to the embodiment and organs of the most sacred Covenant *Pactum De Singularis Caelum* and no other.

Missal as Original Law and Rights of Original Nations (Tribes)

Article 412 – Acadia Covenant of Xerxes

1416. The Covenant of ***Acadia*** of Xerxes embodies in sacred trust the complete consciousness, culture, languages, rules, symbols, rituals, laws and rights of the cultures of higher learning and respect through the blending of Zoroastrian philosophies and Cuilliaéan wisdom.

Covenant of Acadia of Xerxes

The Acadian Empire of Asia and Europe is the embodiment of the most ancient knowledge of Asia, Europe, Africa and the Middle East beginning around 500 BCE as to the emancipation of all men and women through knowledge, self discipline and virtue to be equals with the most ancient priest-kings of the Cuilliaéan, not by blood right, but by the Golden Rule of Law and recognition of Sacred Rights bestowed to all.

1417. *Acadia* represents the uninterrupted and unextinguished Original Law and Original Rights of the Original Nations (Tribes) that have always been present upon the lands now known as Greece, Albania, North Macedonia, Kosovo, Bulgaria, Turkey, Cyprus, Syria, Lebanon, Jordan, Palestine, Egypt, Libya, Iran and Italy. The complete consciousness, culture, languages, rules, symbols, rituals, laws and rights embodied within the Covenant of Acadia of Xerxes are entrusted through the Authentic Sacred Deposit of Trust, to the embodiment and organs of the most sacred Covenant *Pactum De*

Acadia as Original Law and Rights of Original Nations (Tribes)

Singularis Caelum and no other.

Article 413 – Eliada
Covenant of Alexander

1418. The Covenant of ***Eliada*** of Alexander embodies in sacred trust the complete consciousness, culture, languages, rules, symbols, rituals, laws and rights of the cultures and traditions of enlightenment throughout Asia.

Covenant of Eliada of Alexander

The Eliada Empire of planet Earth is a successor of reformed Cuilliaéan culture as the embodiment of the oldest priest-king bloodlines of Syria, Mesopotamia, Egypt, Europe and Asia and the personification of the greatest messengers of Heaven in the form of the Great Prophets of Yeb as the Sons of Man, the Holly Spirit made flesh and ones anointed (Christs) by Divine Commission no longer to rule as Gods, but to serve and free humanity from false teachings and errors of doctrine as saviours.

1419. *Eliada* represents the uninterrupted and unextinguished Original Law and Original Rights of the Original Nations (Tribes) that have always been present upon the lands now known as Iran, Afghanistan, Turkmenistan, Kuwait, Iraq, Azerbaijan, Armenia, Georgia, Turkey, Syria, Lebanon, Jordan, Palestine, Egypt, Cyprus, Libya, Tunisia, Algeria, Greece, North Macedonia, Albania, Kosovo, Bulgaria, Serbia, Croatia, Slovenia, Austria, Switzerland and Italy. The complete consciousness, culture, languages, rules, symbols, rituals, laws and rights as embodied within the Covenant of *Eliada* of Alexander are entrusted through the Authentic Sacred Deposit of Trust, to the embodiment and organs of the most sacred Covenant *Pactum De Singularis Caelum* and no other.

Eliada as Original Law and Rights of Original Nations (Tribes)

Article 414 – Tabiti
Covenant of Great Asiatic Plains People

1420. The Covenant of ***Tabiti*** (Sacred Fire) of the Great Asiatic Plains People embodies in sacred trust the complete consciousness, culture, languages, rules, symbols, rituals, laws and rights of the cultures and traditions of enlightenment of the Great Asiatic Plains People that lived from the steppes of Russia and Ukraine to Mongolia across to China.

Covenant of Tabiti of Great Asiatic Plains People

1421. *Tabiti* represents the uninterrupted and unextinguished Original Law and Original Rights of the Original Nations (Tribes) that have always been present upon the lands now known as Russia, Belarus, Ukraine, Kazakhstan, Uzbekistan, Turkmenistan, Kyrgyzstan, Xinjiang (China)

Tabiti as Original Law and Rights of Original Nations (Tribes)

and Mongolia. The complete consciousness, culture, languages, rules, symbols, rituals, laws and rights as embodied within the Covenant of *Tabiti* (Sacred Fire) of the Great Asiatic Plains are entrusted through the Authentic Sacred Deposit of Trust, to the embodiment and organs of the most sacred Covenant *Pactum De Singularis Caelum* and no other.

Article 415 – Tiandi (Heaven and Earth) Covenant of Qin Shi Huang

1422. The Covenant of ***Tiandi*** (Heaven and Earth) of Qin Shi Huang embodies in sacred trust the complete consciousness, culture, languages, rules, symbols, rituals, laws and rights of unified China.

Covenant of Tiandi (Heaven and Earth) of Qin Shi Huang

Qin Shi Huang, also known as Ying Zheng, is the King of the State of Qin that around 235BCE commissioned his finest scholars to travel West to obtain the knowledge of Aristotle and the Empire of Alexander and then help form a philosophy to unite China and end the war between the kingdoms. It is Qin Shi Huang that history should rightly recognise as the architect of the Covenant of Heaven and Earth that united China for the first time as the Qin Dynasty.

1423. *Tiandi* represents the uninterrupted and unextinguished Original Law and Original Rights of the Original Nations (Tribes) that have always been present upon the lands now known as China. The complete consciousness, culture, languages, rules, symbols, rituals, laws and rights of unified China embodied within the Covenant of *Tiandi* of Qin Shi Huang is entrusted through the Authentic Sacred Deposit of Trust, to the embodiment and organs of the most sacred Covenant *Pactum De Singularis Caelum* and no other.

Tiandi as Original Law and Rights of Original Nations (Tribes)

Article 416 – Nazara (Truth) Covenant of Yahusiah (Jesus Christ)

1424. The Covenant of ***Nazara*** (Truth) of Yahusiah (Jesus Christ) embodies in sacred trust the complete consciousness, culture, languages, rules, symbols, rituals, laws and rights of the cultures and traditions of enlightenment of the Holly.

Covenant of Nazara of Yahusiah (Jesus Christ)

The Nazarenes, as seekers and followers of Divine Truth, are the apostolic successors of reformed Cuilliaéan culture through the teachings of the thirty second and last Great Prophet of Yeb, also known as Yahusiah, also known as Jesus Christ, as to the equality and freedom and rights of all men and women; the redemption and forgiveness of all debts through the symbol and knowledge of the resurrection; and the absolute right of all men and women to knowledge of heaven; and the sacred mission of Holly Messengers to be teachers and saviours and not as rulers of humanity.

1425. *Nazara* represents the uninterrupted and unextinguished Original Law and Original Rights of the Original Nations (Tribes) that have always been present upon the lands now known as Palestine, Great Britain, Ireland (Eire) and France. The complete consciousness, culture, languages, rules, symbols, rituals, laws and rights of the Nazarenes embodied within the Covenant of *Nazara* of Yahusiah are entrusted through the Authentic Sacred Deposit of Trust, to the embodiment and organs of the most sacred Covenant *Pactum De Singularis Caelum* and no other.

Nazara as Original Law and Rights of Original Nations (Tribes)

Article 417 - Nirvana (Freedom & Awakening) Covenant of Gautama (Buddha)

1426. The Covenant of ***Nirvana*** (Freedom & Awakening) of Gautama (Buddha) embodies in sacred trust the complete consciousness, culture, languages, rules, symbols, rituals, laws and rights of the cultures and traditions of enlightenment throughout Asia, including but not limited to the teachings of Prince Gautama as Buddha.

Covenant of Nirvana (Freedom & Awakening) of Gautama (Buddha)

1427. *Nirvana* represents the uninterrupted and unextinguished Original Law and Original Rights of the Original Nations (Tribes) that have always been present upon the lands now known as Northern and North East India, Nepal, Tibet, Bhutan, Bangladesh, Sichuan (China), Yunnan (China), Taiwan (China), Hong Kong, Burma, Laos, Thailand, Vietnam, Cambodia, Malaysia, Singapore, Philippines and Indonesia. The complete consciousness, culture, languages, rules, symbols, rituals, laws and rights of the cultures and traditions of Buddhism throughout Asia, including but not limited to the teachings of Prince Gautama as Buddha embodied within the Covenant of *Nirvana* are entrusted through the Authentic Sacred Deposit of Trust, to the embodiment and organs of the most sacred Covenant *Pactum De Singularis Caelum* and no other.

Nirvana as Original Law and Rights of Original Nations (Tribes)

Article 418 - Zhongdao (The Middle Way) Covenant of Kong Qiu (Confucius)

1428. The Covenant of ***Zhongdao*** (The Middle Way) of Kong Qiu (Confucius) embodies in sacred trust the complete consciousness, culture, languages, rules, symbols, rituals, laws and rights of the cultures and traditions of enlightenment throughout Asia, including but not limited to the teachings of Kong Qiu (Confucius).

Covenant of Zhongdao (The Middle Way) of Kong Qiu (Confucius)

1429. *Zhongdao* represents the uninterrupted and unextinguished Original

Zhongdao as

Law and Original Rights of the Original Nations (Tribes) that have always been present upon the lands now known as China, Taiwan (China), Korea, Japan, Vietnam, Singapore, and Malaysia. The complete consciousness, culture, languages, rules, symbols, rituals, laws and rights embodied within the Covenant of *Zhongdao* (The Middle Way) is entrusted through the Authentic Sacred Deposit of Trust, to the embodiment and organs of the most sacred Covenant *Pactum De Singularis Caelum* and no other.

Original Law and Rights of Original Nations (Tribes)

Article 419 – Septuaginta Covenant of Iudaism (Josephus)

1430. The Covenant of ***Septuaginta*** of Iudaism embodies in sacred trust the complete consciousness, culture, languages, rules, symbols, rituals, laws and rights of founding of Iudaism (Judaism) from 70 CE to 120 CE as the Cult of Lucifer across the Roman Empire.

Covenant of Septuaginta of Iudaism (Josephus)

The formation of the official cult of *Iudaism* upon the complete collapse of the religion of Mithra in 69 CE upon the destruction of the Great Temple Mint to Mithra, six hundred and sixty-six (666) years to the day since the destruction of the Temple of Setien (Satan) in Jerusalem, heralded an unprecedented change in the ancient world, when Emperor Vespasian proclaimed himself Lucifer and saviour of Rome under the symbol of the blazing sun and the Trigram IHS or *Invictus Hoc Signum* meaning "By this sign (we are) unconquerable". Furthermore, new scriptures were commissioned by blending and re-writing other ancient texts, especially the prophecies of the Great Prophets of Yeb so that the foretelling of Vespasian as Lucifer would be fulfilled. The scholars of Qumran near the Dead Sea, along with Josephus were commissioned to re-write many of the ancient texts to fulfil this task.

The complete consciousness, culture, languages, rules, symbols, rituals, laws and rights embodied within the Covenant of *Septuaginta* of Iudaism is entrusted through the Authentic Sacred Deposit of Trust, to the embodiment and organs of the most sacred Covenant *Pactum De Singularis Caelum* and no other.

Article 420 – Eucadia Covenant of Heracles

1431. The Covenant of ***Eucadia*** of Heracles of Eliada and Larissa embodies in sacred trust the complete consciousness, culture, languages, rules, symbols, rituals, laws and rights of Illuminated Men and Women at the height of self-knowledge and as exemplars of the

Covenant of Eucadia of Heracles

noblest of virtues.

The Eliada and Larissa cultures of ancient Greece at the time of Heracles in the 1st and 2nd centuries CE, signify the highest point of cultural and spiritual advancement of the region in the conscious and deliberate formation of a Utopia as a Kingdom of Heaven upon the Earth known as Eucadia (Ucadia) as the manifestation of the highest ideals of truth, the Golden Rule of law, justice and human dignity.

1432. *Eucadia* represents the uninterrupted and unextinguished Original Law and Original Rights of the Original Nations (Tribes) that have always been present upon the lands now known as Greece. The complete consciousness, culture, languages, rules, symbols, rituals, laws and rights of Eucadia (Ucadia) of ancient Greece embodied within the Covenant of Eucadia (Ucadia) of Heracles of Eliada and Larissa as Heaven on Earth are entrusted through the Authentic Sacred Deposit of Trust, to the embodiment and organs of the most sacred Covenant *Pactum De Singularis Caelum* and no other.

Eucadia as Original Law and Rights of Original Nations (Tribes)

Article 421 - Kikilil Yuum Witzil Covenant of Great Cycle of Celestial Realm and Earth

1433. The Covenant of ***Kikilil Yuum Witzil*** (Great Cycle of Celestial Realm and Earth) of South and Central America civilisations embodies in sacred trust the formation of advanced civilisation, knowledge and culture, resting upon social discipline and authority.

Covenant of Kikilil Yuum Witzil of South-Central America

1434. *Kikilil Yuum Witzil* represents the uninterrupted and unextinguished Original Law and Original Rights of the Original Nations (Tribes) that have always been present upon the lands now known as Mexico, Guatemala, Belize, Honduras, El Salvador, Nicaragua, Cuba, Costa Rica, Panama, Colombia, Venezuela, Curacao, Trinidad and Tobago, Guyana, Ecuador, Peru, Brazil, Suriname, Guiana (French), Bolivia, Paraguay, Uruguay, Chile and Argentina. The complete consciousness, culture, languages, rules, symbols, rituals, laws and rights of ancient Central and South American Civilisations embodied within the Covenant of *Kikilil Yuum Witzil* (Great Cycle of Celestial Realm and Earth) are entrusted through the Authentic Sacred Deposit of Trust, to the embodiment and organs of the most sacred Covenant *Pactum De Singularis Caelum* and no other.

Kikilil Yuum Witzil as Original Law and Rights of Original Nations (Tribes)

Article 422 – Digesta Covenant of Marcus Aurelius

1435. The Covenant of ***Digesta*** of Marcus Aurelius embodies in sacred trust the formation of the dignity of the enlightened soul, capable of

Covenant of Digesta of Marcus Aurelius

rising beyond their weaknesses to a firm command of self-discipline, truth and virtue, whilst championing the freedoms and rights of all men and women.

Marcus Aurelius as the undisputed Emperor of Rome, King of the Franks, blood descendant of Yahusiah (Jesus Christ) and the Cuilliaéan, is the founder and architect of Rome Redeemed in the form of self-disciplines, virtues and knowledge adopting a truly democratic and benevolent Roman Empire ending slavery and acknowledging the equality of all men and women upon planet Earth.

1436. *Digesta* represents the uninterrupted and unextinguished Original Law and Original Rights of the Original Nations (Tribes) that have always been present upon the lands now known as France, Spain, Portugal, Switzerland, Austria, Belgium, Netherlands, Italy, Germany, Poland, Slovenia, Croatia, Czech Republic, Slovakia, Hungary, Serbia, North Macedonia, Albania, Greece, Romania, Bulgaria, Turkey, Cyprus, Syria, Lebanon, Jordan, Palestine, Egypt, Libya, Tunisia and Algeria. The complete consciousness, culture, languages, rules, symbols, rituals, laws, authorities and rights of Rome Redeemed as first formed by Marcus Aurelius embodied within the Covenant of *Digesta* of Marcus Aurelius are entrusted through the Authentic Sacred Deposit of Trust, to the embodiment and organs of the most sacred Covenant *Pactum De Singularis Caelum* and no other.

Digesta as Original Law and Rights of Original Nations (Tribes)

Article 423 – Bibliographe Covenant of Christianity of Constantine

1437. The Covenant of ***Bibliographe*** of Christianity embodies in sacred trust the formation of a global model of democracy, law, rights and dignity for planet Earth known as "Theke" (pronounced the key) as the authentic and original body of Christian authority, church and community.

Covenant of Bibliographe of Christianity of Constantine

Constantine as the last Emperor of Rome and the Emperor of the Celts and the Priest-King of Eukadia (Ucadia) as Heaven on Earth, as a blood descendent of Yahusiah (Jesus Christ) and the Cuilliaéan, is the founder and architect of Christianity and its highest ideals, knowledge and operation as the first truly democratic and representative model of the equality of all men and women upon planet Earth.

1438. *Bibliographe* represents the uninterrupted and unextinguished Original Law and Original Rights of the Original Nations (Tribes) that have always been present upon the lands now known as ***(1)***

Bibliographe as Original Law and Rights of Original Nations (Tribes)

Borealia (North See): being Bulgaria, Romania, Moldova, Hungary, Slovakia, Poland, Lithuania, Latvia, Estonia, Ukraine, Belarus, Russia, Kazakhstan, Uzbekistan, Turkmenistan; and ***(2) Australia (South See)***: being Morocco, Algeria, Tunisia, Libya, Egypt, Ethiopia, Somalia and Sinai; and ***(3) Europalia (West See)***: being Ireland, Great Britain, Spain, Portugal, France, Belgium, Netherlands, Germany, Italy, Slovakia, Croatia, North Macedonia and Greece; and ***(4) Orientalia (East See)***: being: Turkey, Albania, Armenia, Syria, Palestine, Jordan, Iraq, Iran, Yemen and Saudi Arabia. The complete consciousness, culture, languages, rules, symbols, rituals, laws, authorities and rights of the Christian Body as first formed by Constantine to the four corners of the Earth embodied within the Covenant of Bibliographe of Christianity are entrusted through the Authentic Sacred Deposit of Trust, to the embodiment and organs of the most sacred Covenant *Pactum De Singularis Caelum* and no other.

Article 424 – Dao (the Way)
Covenant of Taoism

1439. The Covenant of ***Dao*** (the Way) the Supreme Creator embodies in sacred trust the complete consciousness, culture, languages, rules, symbols, rituals, laws and rights of the first cultures and traditions of Taoism since its creation. Dao (the Way) Covenant of Taoism

1440. *Dao* represents the uninterrupted and unextinguished Original Law and Original Rights of the Original Nations (Tribes) that have always been present upon the lands now known as Korea, Japan and China. The complete consciousness, culture, languages, rules, symbols, rituals, laws and rights of Taoism since its creation embodied within the Covenant of *Dao* is entrusted through the Authentic Sacred Deposit of Trust, to the embodiment and organs of the most sacred Covenant *Pactum De Singularis Caelum* and no other. Dao as Original Law and Rights of Original Nations (Tribes)

Article 425 – Kami Yoso Seimei
Covenant of Spirits of Elements and Life

1441. The Covenant of ***Kami Yoso Seimei*** (Spirits of Elements and Life) of the way of Shinto (Japan) embodies in sacred trust the complete consciousness, culture, languages, rules, symbols, rituals, laws and rights of the first cultures and traditions of Shintoism since its creation. Covenant of Kami Yoso Seimei (Spirits of Elements and Life) of the way of Shinto (Japan)

1442. *Kami Yoso Seimei* represents the uninterrupted and unextinguished Original Law and Original Rights of the Original Nations (Tribes) that Kami Yoso Seimei as Original Law have always been present upon the lands now known as Japan. The complete consciousness, culture, languages, rules, symbols, rituals, laws and rights of Shintoism since its creation embodied within the Covenant of *Kami Yoso Seimei* is entrusted through the Authentic Sacred Deposit of Trust, to the embodiment and organs of the most sacred Covenant *Pactum De Singularis Caelum* and no other.

and Rights of Original Nations (Tribes)

Article 426 – Sanatana Dharma (Eternal Truth) Covenant of Brahman (Hinduism)

1443. The Covenant of ***Sanatana Dharma*** (Eternal Truth) of Brahman (Hinduism) embodies in sacred trust the complete consciousness, culture, languages, rules, symbols, rituals, laws and rights of the first cultures and traditions of Hinduism since its creation.

Covenant of Sanatana Dharma (Eternal Truth) of Brahman (Hinduism)

The refugees of the Aryan Empire in the 4th Century CE that fled eastward as a result of Christianity, formed the basis of the Gupta Empire in India and the founding of the Hindu version of Aryanism as Brahmanism. This is the true era of birth of Hindu and caste literature, including the introduction of numerous Aryan symbols such as the Swastika.

1444. *Sanatana Dharma* represents the uninterrupted and unextinguished Original Law and Original Rights of the Original Nations (Tribes) that have always been present upon the lands now known as India, Sri Lanka and Cambodia. The complete consciousness, culture, languages, rules, symbols, rituals, laws and rights of Hinduism since its creation embodied within the Covenant of Sanatana Dharma of the Supreme Creator is entrusted through the Authentic Sacred Deposit of Trust, to the embodiment and organs of the most sacred Covenant *Pactum De Singularis Caelum* and no other.

Sanatana Dharma as Original Law and Rights of Original Nations (Tribes)

Article 427 – Quran Al Sufian Covenant of Recitations of Wisdom of the Way of Islam

1445. The Covenant of ***Quran Al Sufian*** (Recitations of Wisdom of the Way) of The Great Prophet (Islam) embodies in sacred trust the complete consciousness, culture, languages, rules, symbols, rituals, laws and rights of Islam as first given to the Great Prophet by the Creator of All Existence and of Heaven and Earth through the miracle of the text and covenant known as *Quran Al Sufian*.

Covenant of Quran Al Sufian (Recitations of Wisdom of the Way) of The Great Prophet (Islam)

The Leader of the Saracenia Empire, also known as the Great Prophet, being an educated and compassionate man, having both the blood of the ancient Keepers of Time and Space of Saracenia (Arabia) in his veins as well as descended of the Cuilliaéan, was the architect in Ancient Greek of a philosophy and Divine Revelation honouring the Divine Creator of all existence and heaven and earth, calling for all men and women to cease such wilful ignorance, blasphemy and profanity in living without virtue, killing in the name of religion and serving the interests of slave traders and merchants of doom.

1446. *Quran Al Sufian* represents the uninterrupted and unextinguished Original Law and Original Rights of the Original Nations (Tribes) that have always been present upon the lands now known as Saudi Arabia, Egypt, Lebanon, Palestine, Syria, Jordan, Iraq, Iran, Turkey, Libya, Tunisia, Algeria, Morocco, Azerbaijan, Afghanistan, Kuwait, Qatar, Oman, Bahrain, United Arab Emirates, Yemen, Sudan and Pakistan. The complete consciousness, culture, languages, rules, symbols, rituals, laws and rights of Islam embodied within the Covenant of *Al Sufian* of the Great Prophet and Islam are entrusted through the Authentic Sacred Deposit of Trust, to the embodiment and organs of the most sacred Covenant *Pactum De Singularis Caelum* and no other.

Quran Al Sufian as Original Law and Rights of Original Nations (Tribes)

Article 428 – Holy Bible
Covenant of Catholicism of the Holly

1447. The Covenant of ***Holy Bible*** of Catholicism of the Franks embodies in sacred trust the complete consciousness, culture, languages, rules, symbols, rituals, laws and rights of the cultures of the true and original Catholic Church as first formed in 741 CE, particularly the formation of the Four (4) Gospels.

Covenant of Holy Bible of Catholicism of the Holly

The Kings of the Franks, also known as the Carolingians, as true descendants of Constantine; and blood descendants of Yahusia (Jesus Christ) and the Cuilliaéan, are the true founders and original architects of the Catholic Church in 741 CE and its highest ideals, knowledge and operation as the restoration of the Rule of Law and the ideals of Christianity upon planet Earth.

1448. *Holy Bible* represents the uninterrupted and unextinguished Original Law and Original Rights of the Original Nations (Tribes) that have always been present upon the lands now known as Western Civilisation. The complete consciousness, culture, languages, rules, symbols, rituals, laws and rights of the Catholic Church embodied within the Covenant of *Nova Testamentum* of Catholicism of the Franks is entrusted through the Authentic Sacred Deposit of Trust, to the embodiment and organs of the most sacred Covenant *Pactum De Singularis Caelum* and no other.

Holy Bible as Original Law and Rights of Original Nations (Tribes)

Article 429 – Gurmat
Covenant of Eternal Truth

1449. The Covenant of ***Gurmat*** (Eternal Truth) of Sikhism embodies in sacred trust the teachings, knowledge, discipline and wisdom of Guru Nanak and the Gurma of the founding Gurus of Sikhism, including the consciousness, complete culture, languages, rules, symbols, rituals, laws and rights of Sikhism.

Covenant of Eternal Truth of Gurmat (Sikhism)

The Sikh culture and philosophy, as first revealed through Guru Nanak in the 15th Century in Northern India, is testament to an extraordinary covenant of heroism, self-discipline and aesthetic learning. The term Gurma honours the teachings of Guru Nanak as the "self-evident" truths of a teacher and divine messenger.

1450. *Gurmat* represents the uninterrupted and unextinguished Original Law and Original Rights of the Original Nations (Tribes) that have always been present upon the lands now known as Northern and Central India. The complete consciousness, culture, languages, rules, symbols, rituals, laws and rights of the first cultures of Sikhism embodied within the Covenant of Eternal Truth of Gurma is entrusted through the Authentic Sacred Deposit of Trust, to the embodiment and organs of the most sacred Covenant *Pactum De Singularis Caelum* and no other.

Gurmat as Original Law and Rights of Original Nations (Tribes)

Article 430 – Lebor Clann Glas
Covenant of the Holly Diaspora

1451. The Covenant of ***Lebor Clann Glas*** of the Diaspora of the Holly, also known as the Sangreal (Holy Grail), also known as the Cuilliaéan and by many other names embodies in sacred trust the complete consciousness, history, culture, languages, rules, symbols, rituals, laws and rights of the one, true and only Diaspora throughout the ages.

Covenant of Lebor Clann Glas of the Holly Diaspora

The complete consciousness, history, culture, languages, rules, symbols, rituals, laws and rights of the Cuilliaéan as the Diaspora embodied within the Covenant of *Lebor Clann Glas* is entrusted through the Authentic Sacred Deposit of Trust, to the embodiment and organs of the most sacred Covenant *Pactum De Singularis Caelum* and no other.

www.ingramcontent.com/pod-product-compliance
Lightning Source LLC
Chambersburg PA
CBHW051427290326
41932CB00049B/3260
9781644190296